Lecture Notes in Artificial Intelligence 1342

Subseries of Lecture Notes in Computer Science
Edited by J. G. Carbonell and J. Siekmann

Lecture Notes in Computer Science

Edited by G. Goos, J. Hartmanis and J. van Leeuwen

Springer

Berlin
Heidelberg
New York
Barcelona
Budapest
Hong Kong
London
Milan
Paris
Santa Clara
Singapore
Tokyo

Abdul Sattar (Ed.)

Advanced Topics in Artificial Intelligence

10th Australian Joint Conference
on Artificial Intelligence, AI'97
Perth, Australia
November 30 - December 4, 1997
Proceedings

Springer

Series Editors
Jaime G. Carbonell, Carnegie Mellon University, Pittsburgh, PA, USA
Jörg Siekmann, University of Saarland, Saarbrücken, Germany

Volume Editor

Abdul Sattar
Griffith University, School of Computing and InformationTechnology
Faculty of Information and CommunicationTechnology
Nathan, Brisbane, Australia, 4111
E-mail: sattar@cit.gu.edu.au

Cataloging-in-Publication Data applied for

Die Deutsche Bibliothek - CIP-Einheitsaufnahme

Advanced topics in artificial intelligence : proceedings / 10th
**Australian Joint Conference on Artificial Intelligence, AI '97, Perth,
Australia, November 30 - December 4, 1997 / Abdul Sattar (ed.). -
Berlin ; Heidelberg ; New York ; Barcelona ; Budapest ; Hong Kong
; London ; Milan ; Paris ; Santa Clara ; Singapore ; Tokyo : Springer,
1997**
  (Lecture notes in computer science ; Vol. 1342 : Lectures notes in
  artificial intelligence)
  ISBN 3-540-63797-4

CR Subject Classification (1991): I.2, I.5.4

ISBN 3-540-63797-4 Springer-Verlag Berlin Heidelberg New York

© Springer-Verlag Berlin Heidelberg 1997
Printed in Germany

Typesetting: Camera ready by author
SPIN 10652728   06/3142 – 5 4 3 2 1 0   Printed on acid-free paper

Preface

The Australian Joint Conference on Artificial Intelligence series is steered by the Australian Computer Society's (ACS) National Committee on Artificial Intelligence and Expert Systems. It aims at stimulating research by promoting exchange and cross-fertilisation of ideas among different branches of Artificial Intelligence. It also provides a common forum for researchers and practitioners of AI to exchange new ideas and share their experience.

This volume contains the proceedings of the Tenth Australian Joint Conference on Artificial Intelligence (AI'97) held in Perth, Australia. AI'97 received 143 submissions, of which 46 came from 18 overseas countries. From these, 48 papers (33.5%) were accepted for presentation and included in this volume. Over 30 papers were accepted for poster presentations and are published separately. Most of the papers were refereed by three reviewers (at least one from overseas) selected by the Program Committee members.

The papers in this volume give an indication of recent advances in Artificial Intelligence. The topics covered include Knowledge Representation and Reasoning, Machine Learning, Knowledge-Based Systems, Constraint Satisfaction and Scheduling, Distributed Artificial Intelligence, Neural Networks, Robotics and Machine Perception, Image Analysis and Vision, Evolutionary Computation, Natural Language and User Interfaces, and Temporal/Qualitative Reasoning.

The technical program comprised two days of workshops and tutorials, followed by paper sessions, keynote talks, and special sessions. The keynote speakers — Hector Levesque, Ruud Bolle, and Leon Sterling — are internationally distinguished researchers and need no introduction. I must thank them for preparing full papers on their talks. These papers are included in these proceedings. The special session on Robotics and Machine Perception was chaired by Ray Jarvis and that on Learning and Machine Vision was chaired by Terry Caelli.

The success of a conference depends on the support and cooperation from many individuals and organisations; AI'97 is no exception. The Conference Committee gratefully acknowledges financial support from the ACS National Committee on AI & ES, the Australian Artificial Intelligence Institute, Curtin University and IBM Australia.

I would like to take this opportunity to thank the authors, Program Committee members, reviewers and fellow members of the Conference Committee for their time and effort spent on making AI'97 a successful and enjoyable conference. Among all these people, I must single out Terry Caelli who has been a cheerful guide throughout this process.

Finally, I thank Springer-Verlag and its Computer Science Editor Alfred Hofmann, and Anna Kramer for efficient assistance in publishing these proceedings of AI'97 as a volume in its Lecture Notes in Artificial Intelligence series.

December 1997   Abdul Sattar
                                                               Program Chair

Sponsors

AI'97 gratefully acknowledges financial support from the following sponsors:

The ACS National Committee on Artificial Intelligence and Expert Systems
The Australian Artificial Intelligence Institute
Curtin University
IBM Australia

The ACS National Committee on AI & Expert Systems

Honarary Members:

Robin Stanton (Chair)	The Australian National University
Michael Georgeff	Australian Artificial Intelligence Institute
Stephen Hood	DSTO
Ray Jarvis	Monash University
Ross Quinlan	Sydney University

Executive Members:

John Debenham (Chair)	University of Technology, Sydney
Phil Collier	University of Tasmania
Dickson Lukose	University of New England
Bob McKay	Australian Defence Force Academy
Abdul Sattar	Griffith University
Xin Yao	Australian Defence Force Academy
Chengqi Zhang	University of New England

Conference Committee

General Chair:

Terry Caelli	Curtin University

Program Chair:

Abdul Sattar	Griffith University

Local Arrangements Chair:

Geoff West	Curtin University

Treasurer:

C. P. Tsang	University of Western Australia

Workshops/Tutorial Chair:

Kym MacNish	University of Western Australia

Conference Secretariat:

	Australis Promotions and Technologies Pty Ltd

Program Committee

Grigoris Antoniu	Griffith University
John Debenham	University of Technology, Sydney
Joachim Diederich	Queensland University Technology
Simon Dixon	Flinders University
David Dowe	Monash University
Peter Eklund	University of Adelaide
D. Fearley-Sanders	University of Tasmania
Norman Foo	University of Sydney
John Gero	University of Sydney
Aditya Ghose	University of Wollongong
Greg Gibbon	University of Tasmania
Roderic Girle	University of Auckland
Randy Goebel	University of Alberta
Scott Goodwin	University of Regina
Lee Hing-Yan	Japan-Singapore AI Centre, Singapore
Joxan Jaffar	National University Singapore, Singapore
R.A.Jarvis	Monash University
Nikola Kasabov	University of Otago, New Zealand
Zhi-Qiang Liu	University of Melbourne
Dickson Lukose	University of New England
Michael Maher	Griffith University
Hiroshi Motoda	ISIR, Osaka University, Japan
Mehmet Orgun	Macquarie University
Pavlos Peppas	Macquarie University
Anand Rao	Australian Artificial Intelligence Institute
R. Sadananda	Asian Institute of Technology, Bangkok
Claude Sammut	University of New South Wales
R. K. Shyamasundar	Tata Institute of Fundamental Research, India
John Slaney	The Australian National University
Liz Sonenberg	University of Melbourne
John Staples	University of Queensland
Leon Sterling	University of Melbourne
C. P. Tsang	University of Western Australia
Eric Tsui	Continuum Australia
Olivier de Vel	James Cook University
Geoff Webb	Deakin University
Geoff West	Curtin University
Mary-Anne Williams	University of Newcastle
Wayne Wobcke	University of Sydney
Xin Yao	Australian Defence Force Academy
Wai-Kiang Yeap	University of Otago
Chengqi Zhang	University of New England
Yan Zhang	Western-Sydney University

Administrative Support

Zhiyi Huang	Griffith University
Wan-Ju Lei	Griffith University
M. R. K. Krishna-Rao	Griffith University
Mary Mulligan	Curtin University
Abhaya Nayak	University of New South Wales
Maurice Pagnucco	University of New South Wales
Rattana Wetprasit	Griffith University

AI'97 Reviewers

AI'97 is indebted to the following reviewers:

Nizam Ahmed	Adnan Amin	Ayusni Amran
Grigoris Antoniou	Nick Barnes	Peter Bartlett
Anup Basu	David Billington	Anthony Bloesch
Mark Bofinger	Sarah Boyd	Ariel Bud
Andrew Burrow	Terry Caelli	Jinhai Cai
Paul Calder	V. Chandrasekaran	Chuah Yeow Chong
Jo Coldwell	Richard Cole	Joe Culberson
Robert Dale	Terry Dartnall	John Debenham
Peter Deer	Wenxuan Ding	Simon Dixon
David Dowe	Tom Drummond	John Eklund
Peter Eklund	Renee Elio	Jon Lau Khee Erng
Dominique Estival	Joshua Poh-Onn Fan	D. Fearnley-Sander
Gerard D. Finn	Norman Foo	Marilyn Ford
Simon Fox	Brian Garner	S. Geva
Aditya K. Ghose	Greg Gibbon	Tim Gill
Rod Girle	Randy Goebel	Farshid Golchin
Scott Goodwin	Dmitry O. Gorodnichy	Richard Hagen
Howard J. Hamilton	David Heckerman	J. M. Hogan
Suresh Hungenahally	Joxan Jaffar	Ray Jarvis
Shyam Kapur	Nikola Kasabov	Stephen Kirkby
Les Kitchen	M. R. K. Krishna-Rao	Swamy Kutti
C. Peng Lam	Brendon Lilly	Yit Li Ling
Bing Liu	Zhi-Qiang Liu	Seng Wai Loke
Dickson Lukose	Michael Maher	Frederic Maire
Cindy Marling	Andrew McCabe	Brendan McCane
Bob McKay	Phillip McKerrow	Tim Menzies
Ron van der Meyden	Bernd Meyer	David Morley
Hiroshi Motoda	Santhi Muthiah	Sivakumar Nagarajan
Abhaya Nayak	Richi Nayak	Chris Nowak
Mehmet A. Orgun	Maurice Pagnucco	Wanlin Pang
Malti Patel	Adrian Pearce	Robert Pearson
Jeff Pelletier	Mark Pendrith	Pavlos Peppas
Richard Price	Glen Pringle	Paul Pritchard
Rafael Ramirez	Anand Rao	Greg Restal
Bill Roberts	Joseph Ryan	R. Sadananda
Claude Sammut	Arun Sharma	Prakash P. Shenoy
R. K. Shyamasundar	Pavan Sikka	Simeon J. Simoff
John Slaney	Harald Søndergaard	Liz Sonenberg
R. Soodamani	Wee Hock Soon	Leon Sterling
Linda Stern	Paul Strooper	Geoff Sutcliffe
Masahiro Takatsuka	Chong Thiam Teck	John Thornton
Gil Tidhar	Rodney Topor	C. P. Tsang

Contents

Evolutionary Computation

Knowledge-Based Systems

Knowledge Representation and Reasoning

Learning and Machine Vision
(Special Session)

Machine Learning

NLP and User Modelling

Neural Networks

Robotics and Machine Recognition
(Special Session)

Temporal Qualitative Reasoning

Author Index

Controlling Autonomous Robots with GOLOG

K. Tam[1], J. Lloyd[2], Y. Lespérance[1], H. Levesque[2], F. Lin[2], D. Marcu[2], R. Reiter[2], M. Jenkin[1]

[1]Department of Computer Science, York University,
North York, Ontario, Canada, M3J 1P3

[2]Department of Computer Science, University of Toronto,
Toronto, Ontario, Canada, M5S 1A4

kenneth@cs.yorku.ca, jlloyd@cs.toronto.edu, lesperan@cs.yorku.ca,
hector@cs.toronto.edu,
lin@cs.toronto.edu, marcu@cs.toronto.edu, reiter@cs.toronto.edu,
jenkin@cs.yorku.ca

Abstract. The vast majority of mobile robotic systems have been designed to solve "one off", unique problems, with specialized sensors, robot hardware and computation; and porting robotics software from one platform to another has always been a thorny problem. In this paper, we show how by choosing an appropriate level of abstraction, one can write hardware-independent controllers for robots that perform complex navigation and reasoning tasks. We describe the steps that we have taken towards specifying a general interface through which our high-level programs can interact with a variety of robotic platforms. As an example, we discuss a mail delivery program that runs on both an RWI B21 and a Nomad200 system.

1 Introduction

Although autonomous robots have been built to follow roads, survey industrial environments, deliver material in hospitals, etc., most of them are still "one off" systems: they are good only for the task for which they were designed. Changing the platform on which these systems are implemented or the task that they perform requires major effort. The position that we advocate here is that in order to move autonomous robotics from the arena of task- and platform-dependency, one needs tools and techniques that support the specification and implementation of more general forms of behavior.

In this paper, we describe our efforts towards developing a *cognitive robotics* approach, whose ultimate goal is a theory that supports the implementation of general agents that reason, act and perceive in changing, incompletely known, unpredictable environments. Such agents must have higher level cognitive functions that involve reasoning about goals, actions, about when to perceive and what to look for, about the cognitive states of other agents, collaborative task execution, etc. In short, cognitive robotics deals with integrating reasoning, perception and action within a uniform theoretical and implementation framework.

Because the best proof in robotics is a system that works, in this paper we concentrate primarily on showing what cognitive robotics can bring to the world in which "the rubber meets the road". To support our claims, we describe how *the same high-level program* was used successfully to control two robots that not only run on different hardware platforms, but that also use totally different mechanisms for point-to-point navigation, map construction, etc. We believe that the action-based programming languages that we propose constitute a first step in a trend that will take robot system designers more and more away from the details of the platforms that they use, in very much the same way high-level programming languages enabled computer programmers to move away from the hardware and assembly-language details.

We describe first the theoretical foundations of our work and give details on GOLOG, our action-based language. We then show how a "mail delivery" program can be written in GOLOG and describe the architectures and modules of the robots on which the program has been ported. We also discuss interface issues and ways to extend this work.

2 Logical Foundations

Our framework is based on a theory of action expressed in the situation calculus, a first-order language for representing dynamically changing worlds in which all of the changes are the result of named *actions* performed by some agent. Terms are used to represent states of the world, i.e., *situations*. If α is an action and s a situation, the result of performing α in s is represented by $do(\alpha, s)$. The constant S_0 is used to denote the initial situation. Relations whose truth values vary from situation to situation, called *fluents*, are denoted by predicate symbols taking a situation term as the last argument. For example, ROBOT_CARRYING(p, s) means that the robot is carrying package p in situation s. Functions whose denotations vary from situation to situation are called *functional fluents*. They are denoted by function symbols with an extra argument taking a situation term, as in POS(ROBOT, s), i.e., the robot's position in situation s. The actions in a given domain can be specified in a straightforward way in the situation calculus. We show how this works in section 4, where we axiomatize a simple robotics application domain.

In our framework, we distinguish between two types of actions: actions such as GO_TO$(position)$ and PICK_UP$(package)$ that have effects on the world in which the robot acts, and actions such as SENSE_WHETHER_DOOR_IS_OPEN that affect the robot's knowledge of the world. To model the effects of perceptual actions, we followed the approach of Moore [4] and adapted the standard possible-world model of knowledge to the situation calculus. Informally, we think of there being a binary accessibility relation over situations, where a situation s' is understood as being accessible from a situation s if as far as the agent knows in situation s, he might be in situation s'. So something is known in s if it is true in every s' accessible from s, and conversely something is not known if it is false in some accessible situation. For the rest of the paper, we will use KNOWS(P, s)

to denote that fluent P is known in situation s (the formal details concerning the way knowledge is treated in our framework are discussed by Scherl and Levesque [7]).

3   Complex Actions and GOLOG

GOLOG [3] is a situation calculus-based logic programming language for defining complex actions using a repertoire of user specified primitive actions. GOLOG provides the usual kinds of imperative programming language control structures as well as three flavors of nondeterministic choice. Briefly, these are:

1. *Sequence:* α ; β. Do action α, followed by action β.

2. *Test actions: p?* Test the truth value of expression p in the current situation.

3. *While loops:* **while** p **do** α.

4. *Conditionals:* **if** p **then** α **else** β.

5. *Nondeterministic action choice:* $\alpha \mid \beta$. Do α or β.

6. *Nondeterministic choice of arguments:* $(\pi\ x)\alpha$. Nondeterministically pick a value for x, and for that value of x, do the action α.

7. *Nondeterministic repetition:* α^*. Do α a nondeterministic number of times.

8. *Procedures*, including recursion.

The semantics of GOLOG programs is defined by macro-expansion, using a ternary relation Do (see [3] for a full description). Do is defined inductively on the structure of its first argument as follows:

Primitive actions:

$$Do(a, s, s') \stackrel{\text{def}}{=} Poss(a, s) \wedge s' = do(a, s). \tag{1}$$

Test actions:

$$Do(\phi?, s, s') \stackrel{\text{def}}{=} \phi[s] \wedge s = s'.$$

Here, ϕ is a test expression of our programming language; it stands for a situation calculus formula, but with all situation arguments suppressed. $\phi[s]$ denotes the situation calculus formula obtained by restoring situation variable s to all fluent names mentioned in ϕ.

Sequence:

$$Do(\delta_1; \delta_2, s, s') \stackrel{\text{def}}{=} (\exists s^*).Do(\delta_1, s, s^*) \wedge Do(\delta_2, s^*, s').$$

Similar definitions are given for nondeterministic choice, iteration, conditionals and procedures.

$Do(program, s, s')$ is an *abbreviation* for a situation calculus formula whose intuitive reading is that s' is one of the situations reached from s by executing *program*. This means that to execute *program*, one must *prove*, using the situation calculus axiomatization of some background domain, the situation calculus formula $(\exists s)Do(program, S_0, s)$. Any binding for s obtained by a constructive proof of this sentence is an execution trace, in terms of the primitive actions, of *program*.

GOLOG is designed as a compromise between classical planning and detailed programming. It is a high-level nondeterministic language in which one can express schematic plans. These schemas give advice to a robot about how to achieve certain effects without necessarily specifying in detail how to perform this action. The details are to be figured out by the theorem prover when the program is executed.

Besides GOLOG, we have also defined a concurrent version of the language called CONGOLOG, which is particularly useful for programming reactive behaviors. For both languages, we have implemented interpreters in Prolog. We use GOLOG in the rest of the paper.

4 Specifying hardware-independent programs in GOLOG

Suppose that we are given the task to write a hardware-independent program that will instruct a robot how to do mail delivery in a department. Obviously, the robot will need to be able not only to navigate, but also to pick and drop packages, to reason about when and how to get to a specific location, to recover from failures, etc. In order to use GOLOG to program the robot to accomplish this task, we first need to come up with a specification of the application domain at some appropriate level of abstraction. In GOLOG, this means that we have to specify the primitive actions, the fluents that describe the states of the robot, the preconditions that need to be satisfied in order to execute the primitive actions, and the effect of the actions on the fluents. On the basis of the primitive actions, we can then define complex behaviors.

For the mail delivery application, suppose we take the following as primitives actions:

$$\text{GO\_TO}(position),$$
$$\text{PICK\_UP}(package),$$
$$\text{DROP\_OFF}(package), \text{ and}$$
$$\text{SENSE\_REQUESTS}.$$

The GOLOG system will essentially treat these as external procedures. Obviously, one should choose actions that can be implemented on the robot's architecture. We model states of the robot and environment using the following fluents:

$$\text{ORDERED\_SHIPMENT}(package, s),$$
$$\text{ROBOT\_CARRYING}(package, s), \text{ and}$$
$$\text{POS}(object, s).$$

We specify the preconditions of the PICK_UP action with the following axiom:

$$Poss(\text{PICK\_UP}(package), s) \equiv$$
$$\text{ORDERED\_SHIPMENT}(package, s) \land \tag{2}$$
$$\text{POS}(\text{ROBOT}, s) =$$
$$\text{POS}(\text{OUT\_BOX}(\text{SHIPPER}(package)), s)$$

Thus, PICK_UP is possible when someone has ordered the package to be shipped and the robot is positioned at the shipper's out-box. Similarly, we define a precondition axiom for DROP_OFF. The actions GO_TO and SENSE_REQUESTS are assumed to be always possible.

Once the primitive actions and the fluents that characterize a domain have been chosen, we need to specify how the truth values of fluents are affected by the execution of the actions. A classic hurdle for theories of actions is "frame problem": how can the effects of actions be specified without requiring one to stipulate explicitly the numerous conditions not affected by the action? Our framework incorporates a solution to the "frame problem" due to Reiter [5]. This involves specifying a *successor state axiom* for each fluent. For example, the successor state axiom for the functional fluent POS specifies that objects' positions are unaffected by all actions other than GO_TO(**pos**), which results in the robot's being at **pos** with everything it is carrying.

$$Poss(a, s) \rightarrow [\text{POS}(x, do(a, s)) = \mathbf{pos} \equiv$$
$$(x = \text{ROBOT} \lor \text{ROBOT\_CARRYING}(x, s))$$
$$\land a = \text{GO\_TO}(\mathbf{pos})$$
$$\lor \text{POS}(x, s) = \mathbf{pos} \land \tag{3}$$
$$((x \neq \text{ROBOT} \land \neg\text{ROBOT\_CARRYING}(x, s))$$
$$\lor \forall \mathbf{pos}' a \neq \text{GO\_TO}(\mathbf{pos}'))]$$

This avoids the need for "frame axioms". The solution was extended to deal with knowledge-producing actions by Scherl and Levesque [7].

The successor state axiom for ROBOT_CARRYING (4) specifies that the robot is carrying a package if he has just picked it up or if he was carrying it and did not drop it off.

$$Poss(a, s) \rightarrow$$
$$[\text{ROBOT\_CARRYING}(package, do(a, s)) \equiv$$
$$a = \text{PICK\_UP}(package) \lor \tag{4}$$
$$\text{ROBOT\_CARRYING}(package, s) \land$$
$$a \neq \text{DROP\_OFF}(package)]$$

Now note for example that if ROBOT_CARRYING(P_1, S_0), then it also follows (assuming that $\text{P}_1 \neq \text{P}_2$) that ROBOT_CARRYING($\text{P}_1, do(\text{DROP\_OFF}(\text{P}_2, S_0))$).

The successor state axiom for ORDERED_SHIPMENT specifies that a shipment has been ordered in state $do(a, s)$ iff action a is a request to that effect or it had already been ordered in s and a is not the action of picking up the shipment.

$$
\begin{aligned}
Poss(a,s) \rightarrow & \\
[\text{ORDERED\_SHIPMENT}&(shipper, package, \\
& recipient, do(a,s)) \equiv \\
a = \text{REQUEST\_SHIPMENT}&(shipper, package, \\
& recipient) \vee \\
\text{ORDERED\_SHIPMENT}&(shipper, package, \\
& recipient, s) \wedge \\
a \neq \text{PICK\_UP}&(package, shipper, recipient)]
\end{aligned}
\tag{5}
$$

In a similar way, we have defined a successor state axiom for the knowledge fluent: it specifies that the action SENSE_REQUESTS results in the robot knowing what shipments have been ordered and the other actions have no effects on the robot's knowledge other than its knowing that they have been performed.

Which shipments are on order in a situation depends not only on the robot's actions but on what shipment requests have been made (by other agents). The robot will find out about shipment orders by sensing rather than reasoning, so we do not need to provide a successor state axiom for the fluent OR-DERED_SHIPMENT. Nevertheless, we include the following axiom:

$$
\begin{aligned}
Poss(a,s) \rightarrow & \\
[\text{ORDERED\_SHIPMENT}&(package, s) \wedge \\
a \neq \text{PICK\_UP}&(package) \rightarrow \\
\text{ORDERED\_SHIPMENT}&(package, do(a,s))]
\end{aligned}
\tag{6}
$$

This allows the robot to avoid resensing whether a shipment that has not been picked up is still on order.

Now that we have an axiomatization of the domain, we can write GOLOG programs to control the robot in terms of the primitives specified above. The first two procedures defined below, GRAB_ALL_LETTERS_FOR and SERVE, are used by CONTROL_1 and CONTROL_2, which are simple examples of top-level procedures one might use to control this event-driven robot.

```
proc GRAB_ALL_LETTERS_FOR(r)
    SENSE_REQUESTS;
    for p : ORDERED_SHIPMENT(p) ∧ RECIPIENT(p) = r do
        GO_TO(POS(OUT_BOX(SHIPPER(p)))); PICK_UP(p)
end

proc SERVE(r)
    GRAB_ALL_LETTERS_FOR(r);
    if ∃p(ROBOT_CARRYING(p) ∧ RECIPIENT(p) = r) then
        GO_TO(POS(IN_BOX(r)));
        for p : ROBOT_CARRYING(p) ∧ RECIPIENT(p) = r
            do DROP_OFF(p)
end
```

```
proc CONTROL_1
   SENSE_REQUESTS;
   while ∃p ORDERED_SHIPMENT(p) do
      Π r [∃p(ORDERED_SHIPMENT(p) ∧
             RECIPIENT(p) = r)?; SERVE(r)];
      SENSE_REQUESTS
end

proc CONTROL_2
   SENSE_REQUESTS;
   while ∃p ORDERED_SHIPMENT(p) do
      Π p [ORDERED_SHIPMENT(p)?;
         GO_TO(POS(OUT_BOX(SHIPPER(p))));
         PICK_UP(p);
         GO_TO(POS(IN_BOX(RECIPIENT(p))));
         DROP_OFF(p)];
      SENSE_REQUESTS
end
```

One of the main advantages of GOLOG is that it enables the programmer to ignore completely the concerns pertaining to the way the world changes as the robot goes from one state to another: the Golog interpreter updates automatically the state of the robot (using the successor state axioms), decides whether actions can be taken or not (using the precondition axioms), and chooses nondeterministically actions when more than one is appropriate. Moreover, once an axiomatization of a domain has been completed, GOLOG enables the development of hardware-independent libraries of programs that can be used for navigation and reasoning.

5   Embedding GOLOG control programs in mobile robots

Once the domain of interest has been properly axiomatized and GOLOG programs have been developed and thoroughly tested, one can work on porting these programs to a wide range of robotics platforms. The main job that needs to be done at this point is to provide an implementation for each primitive action in the GOLOG program in terms of the actual operations available on the target robotics platform. In other words, one needs give implementations of primitive actions such as GO_TO and PICKUP in terms of the routines that drive a specific robot.

We have used GOLOG to control a Nomad200 and an RWI B21 mobile robot (see Figure 1). Both robots are synchronous drive vehicles equipped with on-board sensors and computation. In spite of these physical similarities, the two robots have very different computational and interaction models. We describe the port to each each robot, in turn.

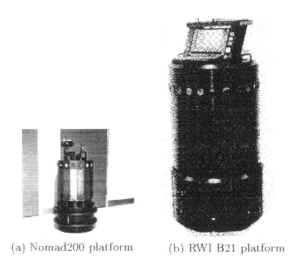

(a) Nomad200 platform   (b) RWI B21 platform

Fig. 1. The two robots controlled with GOLOG.

5.1 Nomad200

The Nomad200 platform (Floyd) was built as an experimental vehicle to conduct survey/inspection tasks in an industrial environment (see [2] for details on the project). Floyd is capable of performing point to point navigation in a previously mapped environment and uses pre-positioned visual landmarks to correct odometry errors. It relies on touch, infrared and sonar sensors to sense unmodeled obstacles.

Floyd has two levels of control. An onboard *reactive system*[6] performs all time-critical tasks such as collision avoidance and straight line path execution. The reactive system assumes that the robot is always in motion and communicates with an offboard global path planner and user interface module known as the *Navigator*. The Navigator takes as inputs a metric/topological map of the environment in which the robot is located and the coordinate (as defined in the map) of the two end points, i.e., the source and the destination of a path. By making use of some predefined path-finding algorithms such as breadth first search (BFS) or A^* the Navigator identifies a feasible path between the source and the destination. To follow the path, the Navigator decomposes it into segments (a segment is a straight line between two adjacent way-points) and then forwards the segments to the reactive system for execution. The Navigator supervises the reactive system and identifies failures in the reactive system's ability to execute a path segment.

Figure 2 shows the general structure of the original robot software (the right hand side of the figure) and the interaction between the original robot software and the GOLOG system. Implementations have been defined for a number of primitive actions including point to point motion, and simulated pickup mail/putdown mail operations for the mail delivery task. For example, the GOLOG primitive action GO_TO(*position*) is defined as [plan_path(*position*);

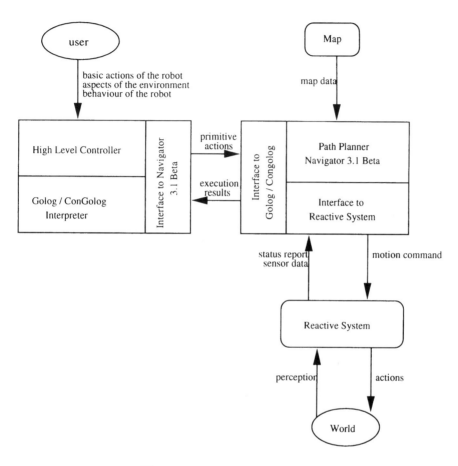

Fig. 2. Nomad200 System Overview

follow_path(*position*)], where plan_path(*position*) and follow_path(*position*) are functions within the Nomad robot controlling software. GOLOG, the Navigator and the Reactive system are all asynchronous tasks, possibly operating on different hosts. As in the case in the communication between the Reactive System and the Navigator, the GOLOG level communicates with the Navigator through a socket interface.

5.2   RWI B21

Most of the software components of our RWI B21 platform (Golem) were developed by the Rhino project [1]. The software components are independent modules that communicate via Ethernet. Some of these modules are shown in Figure 3: a) the BASE performs translations, rotations, and sensing; it transmits position information to the MAP and the PATH PLANNER and sonar information to the SONAR INTEGRATOR; b) the SONAR INTEGRATOR collects periodically sonar readings and builds partial maps of the immediate environment; c)

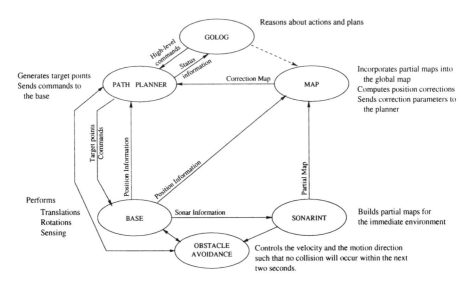

Fig. 3. RWI B21 System Overview

the MAP module compares the local maps generated by the SONAR INTEGRA-
TOR, computes position corrections and sends correction parameters to the PATH
PLANNER; d) the PATH PLANNER generates target points and sends commands
to the BASE; and e) the OBSTACLE AVOIDANCE module controls both the velocity and motion direction of the robot such that no collision will occur within
the next two seconds. In the implementation that we discuss here, the GOLOG
program is integrated within the general architecture as an independent module
that communicates with the PATH PLANNER.

For the mail-delivery task, we initially let Golem explore the environment
autonomously. During this stage, the learning algorithms associated with the
MAP module built an occupancy map of the floor on which the robot operates. After the map had been built, we specified in GOLOG the grid cells that
correspond to the locations of the offices and mailboxes of the people in the
team. We mapped the primitive action GO_TO(*position*) to an analogous procedure that was already available in the PATH PLANNING module and the actions
PICK_UP(*package*) and DROP_OFF(*package*) to speech synthesizer actions: since
the robot is not equipped with arms, it simply asks the users to put or take packages from its bail. The SENSE_REQUESTS action was implemented as a process
that monitors incoming messages from users.

5.3 Interface issues

In both systems that we described here, defining the primitive actions of the
GOLOG program in terms of the procedures that were already implemented was
trivial: for the Nomad platform, the GO_TO(POSITION) was defined in terms of
the PLAN_PATH and FOLLOW_PATH procedures, while for the RWI platform there

already existed a GO_TO procedure. We believe that in scaling up the behavioral complexity of autonomous systems, the mapping of high-level primitive actions to robotic procedures will not always be that easy. To address this issue, we have started working on a general interface that supports more elaborate forms of navigation and recovery from failures. This interface defines a taxonomy of primitive actions that a GOLOG programmer can assume to be linked to appropriate low-level procedures. For example, if the robot programmer knows that the robot will be used in an environment where the robot can always get from one point to another, then it will be appropriate for her to use a GO_TO action similar to the one described above. However, if the robot is to act in an environment where it cannot achieve certain goals, a different level of abstraction will be needed. In such a case, it will be more appropriate for the robot to be able to ask questions such as "is this door open?" and "for how long did I try to achieve this goal?". The interface that we have built so far contains actions such as TRY_GO_TO(*position*), POLL_ROBOT(*status*), SET_MAXIMUM_SPEED(*v*), etc.

6 Conclusion

The vast majority of existing autonomous robotic systems are designed as 'one off' platforms for specific tasks. For autonomous robots to find more general application it is necessary to provide programming support at a somewhat higher level than is currently the norm. GOLOG provides a high-level, *cognitive robotics* environment for robot programming.

This paper describes the process of connecting GOLOG to two different mobile platforms; a Nomad200 and a RWI B21. Although physically quite similar, these robots have remarkably different software environments. Although they both provide mechanisms for pose correction and point to point locomotion through their environment, they use drastically different models, sensors, and sensing mechanisms in order to accomplish this task. In spite of these differences, GOLOG has proven sufficiently robust in order to act as a high-level control module for these two robots.

Current research is investigating enhancements to the GOLOG specification, as well as the development of more sophisticated behaviors for the robots.

References

1. J. Buhmann, W. Burgard, A.B. Cremers, D. Fox, T. Hofmann, F. Schneider, J. Strikos, and S. Thrun. The mobile robot Rhino. Technical Report IAI-TR-95-2, Intitut für Informatik III, University of Bonn, January 1995.
2. M. Jenkin, N. Bains, J. Bruce, T. Campbell, B. Down, P. Jasiobedzki, A. Jepson, B. Majarais, E. Milios, B. Nickerson, J. Service, D. Terzopoulos, J. Tsotsos, and D. Wilkes. ARK: Autonomous mobile robot for an industrial environment. In *Proc. IEEE/RSJ IROS*, Munich, 1994.
3. Hector J. Levesque, Raymond Reiter, Yves Lesperance, Fangzhen Lin, and Richard B. Scherl. Golog: A logic programming language for dynamic domains. *To appear*

in Journal of Logic Programming. Special issue on Reasoning about Action and Change, 1997.

4. R. C. Moore. Reasoning about knowledge and action. Technical report, AI Center, SRI International, Menlo Park, CA, 1980. Technical Report 191.

5. R. Reiter. The frame problem in the situation calculus: A simple solution (sometimes) and a completeness result for goal regression. In V. Lifschitz, editor, *Artificial Intelligence and Mathematical Theory of Computation: Papers in Honor of John McCarthy*, pages 359–380. Academic Press, San Diego, CA, 1991.

6. M. Robinson and M. Jenkin. Reactive low level control for the ARK. In *Proc. VI '94*, pages 41–47, 1994.

7. Richard B. Scherl and Hector J. Levesque. The frame problem and knowledge producing actions. In *Proceedings of the Eleventh National Conference on Artificial Intelligence*, pages 689–695, Washington, DC, July 1993.

Video Query and Retrieval

Ruud M. Bolle, Boon-Lock Yeo and Minerva M. Yeung
{bolle,yeo,yeung}@watson.ibm.com

IBM Thomas J. Watson Research Center

Abstract. All video will eventually become fully digital – there seems to be no way around it. Consequently, digital video databases will become more and more pervasive and finding video in large digital video databases will become a problem just like it is a problem today to find video in analog video databases. The digital form of the video, however, opens up tremendous possibilities. Just like it is possible today to retrieve text documents from large text document databases by querying document content represented by indices, it will become possible to index digital video databases based (semi-)automatically derived indices.

In this paper, we address the problem of automatic video annotation — associating semantic meaning with video segments to aid in content-based video retrieval. We present a novel framework of structural video analysis which focuses on the processing of low-level visual data cues to obtain high-level (structural and semantic) video interpretations. Additionally, we propose a flexible framework for video query formulation to aid rapid retrieval of video. This framework is meant to accommodate the "depth-first searcher" – i.e., the power user, the "breath-first searcher," and the casual browser.

1 Introduction

Digital video is the ultimate multi-media document. It contains both deterministic data, like text in the form of closed-caption or the script, and stochastic data – data that is obtained by measuring the world such as imagery sensed by a camera and sound sensed by a microphone.

Eventually all video storage and video transport mechanisms to television receivers and computer displays will be dominated by digital technology [1]. With the advent of fully digital television, many things will become possible. Many of these things can be envisioned today while others will only be imagined during the years to come. Digital televisions will become powerful desktop computers, allowing for tremendous interactivity. Viewers will be able to search on-line TV guides and schedule their viewing according to their needs and interests [3]. Moreover, the digital form of the video stream allows for performing direct computations on the video without the analog to digital conversion, the common practice today.

One possibility opening up is *rapid content-based video retrieval:* The digital form allows processing of the video data to generate appropriate, possibly semantic, data abstractions that enable content-based archival and retrieval of video. That is, very much like today's large text databases can be searched with text queries, video databases will be able to be searched with combined text and visual queries.

It is *this* topic that we would like to discuss. Till now, most of the video in large existing legacy video databases has been annotated solely by hand by meticulously previewing the video, if it has been annotated at all. Semantic labels are extracted visually by the annotator and added manually, often with the assistance of user interfaces. Ideally, the digital video would be automatically annotated through full machine semantic interpretation. In practice, given the state of the art in computer vision and speech recognition, such sophisticated semantic video interpretation is not feasible. Rather, the computer may offer intelligent assistance for manual annotation, or the computer performs automatic limited semantic annotation. Video-on-demand is an area that has concerned itself with the above issues for quite a while. The consensus is that, to scale to larger video databases, automatic extraction of video content information is desired [10].

This paper proposes a model of video retrieval and a novel framework of structural video analysis for video annotation. In particular, the paper is about the process of video query, and about the automatic recognition and generation of syntactic and semantic video annotations. In Section 2, we formulate and discuss a flexible interactive framework for video retrieval. In Section 3, we specifically focus on the analysis of visual content. We briefly survey the state-of-the-art in automatic video annotation and introduce a processing paradigm called "between-shot" processing illustrated with some examples.

This research is part of the NIST/ATP funded research consortium[1] to develop a video query station for the High Definition Television (HDTV) studio of the future. This consortium is charged with performing the breakthrough research and development needed to have the necessary components ready for a fully integrated HDTV studio.

2 Interactive Query

Associated with video are parametric data (date of shooting, type of footage), textual data (bibliographic data, closed-captions, annotated keywords), but also audio and visual data. The former is deterministic data while the latter is stochastic data in the sense that acquisition of this data is inherently a noisy process. Digital video should ideally be retrievable by querying on all these information modalities in a seamless fashion. The user interface of the query system should assists in a user-friendly way and the search results should be presented clearly while this presentation may depend on the query that is posed and the type of user that has posed the query. Video databases should be searchable so that intermediate candidate lists are brought down to a manageable size and duration as quickly as possible.

---

[1] Prog. Mgr.: D.K. Hermreck, david.hermreck@nist.gov

Different types of queries and users can be expected: (1) A query for a particular piece of video; (2) A query for a specific video, but the user has not seen it; and, (3) A query where the user only has some vague idea of the content. The query formulation process should ideally accommodate these types of queries plus the queries of a user who just wants to browse video. In other words, ideal video query systems should accommodate a wide range of users: the *power user* who is used to retrieval of video from legacy databases (such user can be called "depth-first searchers"), the journalist or professional editor who is searching for video based on its documentary value or artistic content (such users can be called "breath-first searchers"), and the casual browser. Especially casual browser access to video databases would open up tremendous opportunities for re-purposing video. Video clips can be (remotely) viewed for a one-time viewing fee or (remotely) purchased for multiple use.

We model the formulation of a video inquiry as a sequence of steps – each step is itself an active filtering of information, sought to reduce the size of the candidate data pools. The sequence of steps is as follows: query on the category and class of video (*navigating*), query on the text, and/or audio and visual feature descriptions of video (*searching*), query on the semantic summary of the content (*browsing*), and query on the full-motion audio-visual content (*viewing*).

Navigating: This is the stage at which the user decides which category of video is to be searched. It is the capability of the user to navigate based on metadata, for example, direct the search to a specific interval of time, or direct the search to a topic, or direct the search to a specific type of footage (sitcoms, documentaries, raw footage), or even direct the search to a specific video server. Almost all video has some text associated with it, though it may be little – say, a few keywords. And the initial navigating through video databases will most certainly be based on textual queries. In theory, techniques from the text retrieval area called *source selection* (i.e., deduce from the query which body of data should be searched) can be used to reduce the search space.

Searching: Search is the center stage of query in video database systems. The result of the search is a list of candidate videos that satisfy in some sense the constraints of the query. The ultimate goal of the search is to make this list as short as possible without missing the video of interest.

Much work has been done in the area of text document retrieval [14], and the technology that has been developed should be brought to bear in the video retrieval area as is described in [2]. However, the amount of text associated with the individual video clips in the video database is potentially unbalanced. Some video may have only two or three keywords associated with it stemming from traditional alpha-numeric databases and annotation technology, while other video may have the script, closed-caption, or speech transcript available. Hence, at some point in the search it will help to look at the other (visual and audio) attributes, annotated or computed. The difficult question is to define the appropriate audio-visual properties that can be extracted from video and that will bring down this candidate list to manageable size.

One would like to interactively constrain visual and/or audio attributes of the candidates and narrow down the candidate list. Static visual attributes may be in the form of color, object shape and texture. There is also active ongoing research in audio indexing to extract special audio features (e.g., [4]). The dynamic nature of the audio-visual content, opens up visual search beyond keyframes. We will address the attributes of video based on visual content in Section 3.

Browsing: The search result is a series of video clips with a total duration that could be quite long. In the browsing phase, representations of the video should be displayed which are good high-level overviews of the visual content of the candidate videos (*visual summaries*). Just as with textual summaries of text documents, a user will be able to get a quick understanding of the candidate content. In addition, the user gets a quick idea whether she or he is asking the "right" question and how to redefine or refine query. Ideally, the user should also have random access to *any* point of *any* video.

Visual summaries are an important facet of the video query process – both for the problem of search query result representation, interpretation and refinement; and for low-bandwidth video and transmission. The problem is to derive mappings of the video data to a plane for screen presentation.

Viewing: After a video clip (or a few video clips) is (are) selected as the most likely candidate(s), the user may decide to view the search results. In such cases, the traditional functionality of today's VCRs should be available. Further, capabilities like *semantic fast-forward* should be available in the viewing phase. Such semantic random access is the ability to truly skip through video based on semantic content, rather than using timecodes.

3 Video Analysis

We survey some of the results in automatic video analysis that have been achieved to date and we indicate the research that needs to be done to arrive at flexible video retrieval systems as described above. We concentrate on edited video documents – as opposed to raw footage. These documents are *structured* in nature conveying stories and messages. That is, the shots are combined in specific ways and according to special orders, to form the *montage* in telling the story.

We first look at the most fundamental unit of video production – the shot. Techniques for detection of shots and current work on processing individual shots are briefly discussed. We then concentrate on a new video analysis paradigm, called *between-shot processing*.

3.1 The Video Shot

The importance of the shot is widely realized and computational detection of video shot boundaries has gotten much attention. The act of segmenting a video into shots is commonly called *scene-change detection*, which should be more properly called *shot discontinuity detection*. (This avoids confusion with the cinematographic term *scene* which is a collection of shots.)

Many types of shot transitions are used, among these are abrupt and gradual (*dissolves*). In Figure 1, we show these two types. The difficulty of shot transition

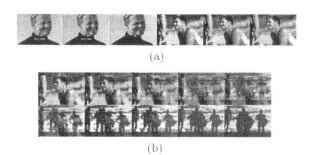

(a)

(b)

Fig. 1. Example shot boundaries from an IBM commercial: (a) abrupt boundary — three frames before and after the boundary (b) gradual transition — ten frames showing the transition of one shot into the next.

detection can be seen from, for example, Figure 1b.

Major efforts have focused on algorithms that operate on the full frames of the video (see references in [2]). There are also recent efforts in performing the segmentation on compressed video. Most works study shot boundary detection on MPEG compressed video (for example, [15] and references herein). These schemes are sufficiently accurate in segmentation of most videos and they save both auxiliary storage and computation costs.

Various researchers have made the observation that representing a video shot as a single still image could be a significant step toward the video indexing problem. A simple way to obtain a single image to represent a shot is the selection of a keyframe or, if there is much motion and action in the shot, the selection of a multiple keyframes (for example, [16]). Alternatively, subsequent frames can be "computed together" into a larger image (this is *within-shot processing*). Techniques such as salient stills (also known under other names) are proposed to obtain such still images ([6] and references). One of the rationales is that if shots are represented by images, image search techniques such as [5] can be applied.

Besides the fact that the dynamic video information is lost, an hour of video is typically composed of a few hundred shots. Thus, searching large video databases amounts to searching very large image databases and searching a small number of hours of video may already push the limits of image search engines in terms of computational requirements.

3.2 Beyond Shots

In video and film, a story is told by the presentation of the *images of time*. Actions have to develop sequentially, simultaneous or parallel processes have to be shown one after the other in a concatenation of shots. As observed by Miller [7], video has a continuity of meaning that overwhelms the inherent discontinuity of presentation. There is something that ensures that the continuity of meaning is preserved when viewing the program. The continuity that obtains from shot to shot – from wide shot to close-up, from one speaker's face to another and so on – is achieved by the viewer overlooking the interruption by using the more or less conscious knowledge or understanding of the fact that the situation is identifiable from one shot to the next and that what is shown is nothing more than various aspects of the same scene, as noted by [7].

A video is built up from shots to form a story. Groups of shots are concatenated in sequences to form a depiction of this story which may be continuous in time – such a concatenation of shots is called a *scene* or a *story segment.* A video, usually, consists of multiple segments where beyond the segment discontinuity there may or may not be continuity of time. Either way, the continuity of time is not what is really important, what is important is if there is continuity of meaning. This is perhaps the most challenging aspect of automatic video annotation, *finding the underlying discontinuities of meaning.* Once video segmentation based on meaning or subject has been achieved, one is left with video data that deals with a particular subject and is uninterrupted by video segments about different subjects such as commercials. The task of automatic video analysis, and the subsequent annotation, then is one of finding high-level interpretations, *not* of the individual shots but of collections of shots and possibly of the video as a whole. It seems that to find these higher-level interpretations, between-shot analyses are at least as important as within-shot analyses via image computations.

The goals of between-shot processing are to derive high-level video structure for automatic annotation of video segments and for visual presentation of the segment. Some research efforts in exploiting between-shot relationships are surveyed in the following sections to further explain the ideas presented in this section.

3.3   News story indexing

Closed-caption is textual information which essentially comes for free and conventional text search engines can be used to index into video. It should be noted, however, that closed-caption does not always contain information about discontinuities in meaning. Processing of the visual data may have to be done to find these discontinuities.

We mention two approaches to closed-caption indexing. Mohan [8] uses a unique combination of sources of information to segment news items. Typically, for the closed-captioning, the beginning of a new news item is indicated by the symbols >>>. Because of the real-time nature of captioning, the closed-caption may be lagging behind the actual spoken words. A shot-boundary detection algorithm in combination with the detection of audio silences plus the new-item indicator of the closed-captioning is used to segment and synchronize the individual news items. A different approach is found in [11]: The Pictorial Transcript system transcribes news programs into HTML-based summaries. Each HTML page has several news stories and each story is represented by a few keyframes with detailed text derived from closed-captions. Furthermore, linguistic processing and closed-caption control information are used to align sentences to keyframes and to capitalize the text.

More domain specific *a priori* models to recover news segments are used in [21, 12]. The video can be in different states, such as, "anchor," "reporter," "weather forecast," etc and model-based parsing recovers the basic news story or episode guided by domain knowledge of spatial frame layouts. Knowledge of station logos is used to identify the return from commercial breaks. News segment retrieval is achieved through an interface which offers a high-level of random access into different news items. Thus, if a user is only interested in the weather forecast, content-based fast-forward allows for this.

3.4 Hierarchical decomposition

The above techniques find news stories by labeling the video shots with relatively high-level semantic interpretations. The labeling is based on the spatial layout of keyframes and uses very domain-specific models.

More generic models can be used to parse video that tells a dramatic story. Typically, such video, like sitcoms, is composed as a sequence of story units and each of these story units, in turn, is a sequence of shots. *Time-constrained clustering* [17] uses symbolic labels based on the data content (e.g., color distribution of keyframes) to compute this hierarchical structure. Typically, the story takes place in a small number of locales and in each locale, a small number of cameras is used. The labels that are associated with shots taken in the same locale tend to cluster together while labels of shots from different locales tend to be dissimilar. The clustering also takes into account the temporal location of shots within the video, i.e., it prevents two shots that are far apart in time but similar in data content to be clustered together. Hence, a high-level syntactic model of video editing is defined. Time-constrained clustering computes video structure by fitting this model to the data derived from shots.

The data content of a shot that is used for clustering is a color histogram of a representative frame in the shot. The metric used is is a distance between color histograms, hence shots that are filmed in the same locale cluster together. The result is that one can group the shots into several clusters and these clusters correspond to the different story units. Other features (than color) extracted from the shots, of course, can also be used. Such features include shot duration, color distribution of the shots, dominant motion characteristics, dominant texture patterns, spatial moments, audio features, etc. The same approach can be taken by clustering these features derived from the shots and different groupings of the shots will be found.

It is reported in [17] that there is one order magnitude of reduction from the number of shots to the number of story units For example, for a typical sitcom, there are about 300 shots in a half-hour of program and about 20 story units identified. This implies that for each half-hour program, a user needs to examine 20 units instead of 300 shots to get a first glance of the program. Furthermore, it means that a user can index into one of 20 units, instead of into one of 300 shots.

Different algorithms that also operate in time-complexity which depends only on the number of shots in a video are reported in [17]. Moreover, these algorithms can be applied to partially decoded MPEG streams similar to the shot discontinuity detection described in [15].

3.5   Label sequence semantics

In the above section, a symbolic label sequence is used to compute the hierarchical structure of dramatic video. Label sequences can be used to recognize concatenations of shots that correspond to dialogues and action event [20]. By looking at the degree of repetition or the lack of repetition in a subsequence of (shot) labels, subsequences can be classified into one of three categories: "dialogues," "actions," and "other."

A dialogue refers to actual conversation or a conversation-like montage presentation of two or more concurrent processes, which have to be shown sequentially, one after the other. The parallel events are possibly interspersed by so-called establishing shots or shots of other parties ("noise" shots or labels). A model of such repetition can be constructed and parsed to the shot labels. Consider the following example, it is a video sequence of 16 shots, with the following label sequence:

$$A, B, A, X, Y, Z, \overbrace{A, B, A, B, A, B}, C,$$
$$\underbrace{D, E, F, E, D, E}, G, H, I$$

Again, here the labels are derived from visual data content of the shots and hence equally labeled shots are likely to be of the same object and background – for a dialogue, the object is a person. The label subsequence A, B, A at the start of the sequence is not considered a valid label sequence of a dialogue event. The label subsequence A, B, A, B, A, B characterizes a dialogue. Here, there is no "noise" label. In addition, the subsequence D, E, F, E, D, E also characterizes a dialogue; here label F is a "noise" label.

An action sequence, on the other hand, in motion pictures or video, is characterized by a progressive presentation of shots with contrasting visual data content to express the sense of fast movement and achieve strong emotional impact. In such a sequence, there is typically little or no recurring of shots taken from the same camera, of the same person or background locale. Such a sequence of shots constitutes an *action event*. A model that captures lack of repetition can be constructed and parsed to label sequences. In addition, further classifications can consider shot durations. For example, one could characterize an action sequence with many shots of short durations as a "fast action" sequence.

In [20] it is reported that dialogue and action events constitute an average of about 50 to 70% of each video program. In programs such as sitcoms and talk shows, there is a high percentage of dialogue. On the other hand, the percentage of action events are significantly higher in action movies.

In speech processing, Hidden Markov Models [9] have been successfully used for word recognition and speaker identification, both of which are classification problems. Such techniques could also be applied to video classification. Here, the challenges are in the use of appropriate features, the judicial choice of model and the assignment of probability distribution. An example of such work can be found in [13]. Here Hidden Markov Models on the one-dimensional sequence of shot durations are used to detect inserted commercial material and action-like sequences within long video sequences.

3.6   Visual summaries

A simple form of visual summary is a storyboard of depictive keyframes – though automatic determination of "depictive" frames is a non-trivial task. Visual summaries give the end-user the ability to quickly get an idea of the content of a hit and the ability to flexibly refine the query. They should also allow for non-linear viewing of the video. It is important that such summaries are compact so that minimal real estate is taken up on the user interface.

A compact representation of *both* video content and structure called the *Scene Transition Graph* [18] can be built by clustering the data content of video shots. It maps a sequence of video shots into a two-dimensional graph. The graph has nodes which display individual shot content and directed edges which depict time. Clusters of nodes (shots) represent the progression of the story, with each story unit being represented by a connected subgraph and connected to the next. A simple example would be a video clip of a conversation between two persons where the camera alternates between shots of each person. Here, the graph consists of two nodes – "establishing shots" or other types of interspersed shots would result in additional clusters, possibly with only one member shot. Graphs depicting the story units and flow of the story for a half-hour video story can displayed on a single computer screen.

Figure 2 shows a four-node graph of the IBM Commercial "France." The bottom-window shows the linear view of the commercial, where each image represents a shot. The content of a node consisting of four different shots of the two characters in the cast is also shown.

Another form of visual summary called the *pictorial summary* is introduced in [19]. A pictorial summary is a sequence of representative images, arranged in temporal order. Each representative image is called a *video poster* and is comprised of at least one-subimage, each of which represents a unique dramatic element of the underlying story, and such that the layout of the sub-images differentiates the dominance of individual elements.

4   Discussion

We have proposed a framework for video retrieval and inquiry formulation which is based on an iterated sequence of *navigating, searching, browsing,* and *viewing.*

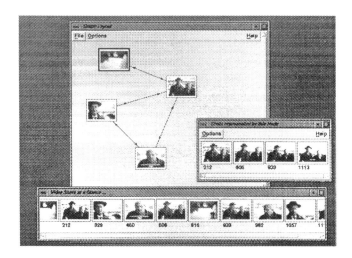

Fig. 2. The Scene Transition Graph for Commercial "France"

This framework calls for certain capabilities of video query systems, in particular, search on dynamic visual properties of video and the ability for rapid non-linear viewing of video. To achieve these capabilities, algorithms have to be developed for automatic extraction of dynamic visual video properties and for processing of video to extract visual features for compact presentation of the video content. Such representations, provide nonlinear access into video and give quick views of the visual content of video. The algorithms need to involve a type of processing which we have called between-shot video analysis.

As noted, video is a multi-media document that contains both deterministic and stochastic data. The essence of video query is that a user-formulated query represents a combined textual and visual pattern. The retrieval process is then concerned with matching this pattern to patterns that are derived from video and finding the "closest" matches. The challenges we face in video retrieval are plenty, just to name a few: (1) the definition of visual patters that both can be computed from video and that are interesting patterns that users want to search for; (2) the definition of what constitutes a match for a combined textual and visual pattern (query); and, (3) determining the relative importance of combined deterministic matches and stochastic matches.

Acknowledgments

The work reported is funded in part by NIST/ATP under Contract Number 70NANB5H1174. The support of the NIST program and the NIST Technical Program Manager David Hermreck and Barbara Cuthil is greatly acknowledged.

References

1. D. Anastassiou. Digital television. *Proc. IEEE*, 82(4):510–519, April 1994.
2. R.M. Bolle, M.M. Yeung, and B.L. Yeo. Video query: Beyond the keyframes. Technical Report RC 20586, IBM T.J. Watson Research Center, October 1996.
3. J. Brinkley. *Defining Vision*. Harcourt Brace & Company, New York, NY, 1997.
4. E. Chan, S. Garcia, and S. Roukos. KNN nearest neighbor information retrieval, 1997.
5. W. Niblack et al. The QBIC project: Querying images by content using color, texture and shape. In *Storage and Retrieval for Image and Video Databases*, volume SPIE 1908, pages 13–25, 1993.
6. S. Mann and R.W. Picard. Virtual bellows: Constructing high quality stills from video. In *Int. Conf. Image Processing*, volume 1, pages 363–367, 1994.
7. J. Miller. Moving pictures. In H. Arlow, C. Blakemore, and M. Weston-Smith, editors, *Images and Understanding*, pages 180–194. Cambridge University Press, October 1986.
8. R. Mohan. Text based indexing of TV news stories. In *Proceedings, SPIE Multimedia Storage and Archiving Systems*, volume SPIE 2916, pages 2–13, November 1996.
9. L. R. Rabiner. A tutorial on hidden markov models and selected applications in speech recognition. *Proceedings of the IEEE*, 77(2):257–286, February 1989.
10. L.A. Rowe, J.S. Boreczky, and C.A. Eads. Indices for user access to large video database. In *Storage and Retrieval for Image and Video Database II, IS&T/SPIE, Symposium on Elec. Imaging Sci. & Tech.*, pages 150–161, February 1994.
11. B. Shahraray and D. Gibbon. Automatic generation of pictorial transcripts of video programs. In *Multimedia Computing and Networking 1995*, volume SPIE 2417, pages 512–528, February 1995.
12. D. Swanberg, C. F. Shu, and R. Jain. Knowledge guided parsing in video databases. In *Storage and Retrieval for Image and Video Databases*, volume SPIE 1908, pages 13–25, 1993.
13. Y-P Tan and R.M. Bolle. Binary video classification. Technical Report TBD, IBM T.J. Watson Research Center, 1997.
14. I. Witten, A. Moffat, and T. Bell. *Managing gigabytes: Compressing and indexing documents and images*. Van Nostrand Reinhold, New York, NY, 1994.
15. B. L. Yeo and B. Liu. Rapid scene analysis on compressed videos. *IEEE Trans. on Circuits and Sys. For Video Techn.*, 5(6):533–544, December 1995.
16. M. M. Yeung and B. Liu. Efficient matching and clustering of video shots. In *International Conference on Image Processing*, volume I, pages 338–341, 1995.
17. M. M. Yeung and B. L. Yeo. Time-constrained clustering for segmentation of video into story units. In *Int. Conf. on Pattern Recog.*, pages 375–380, August 1996.
18. M. M. Yeung, B. L. Yeo, W. Wolf, and B. Liu. Video browsing using clustering and scene transitions on compressed sequences. In *Multimedia Computing and Networking 1995*, volume SPIE 2417, pages 399–413, February 1995.
19. M.M. Yeung and B. L. Yeo. Video visualization for compact presentation and fast browsing of pictorial content. to appear in *IEEE Transactions on Circuits and Systems For Video Technology*, August 1997 (also IBM Research Report RC 20615, 1996).

20. M.M. Yeung and B.L. Yeo. Video content characterization and compaction for digital library applications. In *SPIE Storage and Retrieval for Image & Video Databases*, volume SPIE 3022, pages 45–58, February 1997.
21. H. J. Zhang, Y. H. Gong, S. W. Smoliar, and S. Y. Yan. Automatic parsing of news video. In *Int. Conf. Multimedia Computing and Sys.*, pages 45–54, 1994.

On Finding Needles in WWW Haystacks

Leon Sterling

Intelligent Agents Laboratory
Department of Computer Science
University of Melbourne
leon@cs.mu.oz.au

Abstract. This paper discusses experience in retrieving specific items from the WWW. The Intelligent Agents Laboratory at the University of Melbourne has spent the last two years building programs to autonomously retrieve items such as sports scores, university subject descriptions, and paper citations. A wide variety of Web resources have been used. The approach is knowledge-based in the spirit of expert systems, where domain and task specific knowledge is crafted into general purpose shells. The key insights are the value of designing conceptual models that can mesh with physical models of the WWW, and the value of classifying domain and task knowledge. Licence is taken to place the research in the context of wide-ranging issues such as the information revolution, styles of computer science research, and the metaphor of software agents.

1 The Information Revolution and the WWW

It will be up to historians to decide the eventual impact of the digital computer and the changing role of information within society that its manipulations allow. For the moment, it is breathtaking to watch the rapid evolution of technology and the changes being wrought, and tempting to herald the coming of an Information Revolution. The possibilities enabled by the new technologies emerging around the computer are exciting to contemplate and implement.

New terminology and metaphors have appeared in rapid succession. Cyberspace, the information superhighway, flames, softbots, new typography :-) are but a few. At Melbourne University, academics are being exhorted to 'mainstream the digital revolution' to transform teaching and learning. This paper will not make profound judgments on the changes or the forces that drive them, but asks the reader to share in the wonder of all the hype, activity, and excitement going on around us, and participate in a modest way.

A major part of the information revolution, at least in current popular perception, is the Internet. The Internet has made a huge difference in what is easily accessible. The world is suddenly at your fingertips. Messages can go to all sorts of people at breakneck speed. There is suddenly so much information that is potentially visible through the computer screen.

The World Wide Web (WWW) is the primary public face of the Internet, and is the environment for our research. There are any number of indicators that could be flagged or stories that could be told about the significance of the WWW. Phone books are on-line. Schools are insisting that students have laptops. Classes are being organised around using the WWW. My friends rush to get connected so their children will not be left behind. Dale Spender wrote in a column in *The Australian* (August 30, 1997) of throwing away 2000 books of nonfiction because they were no longer necessary.

There are also negative indicators. In a recent *Campus Review*, Burbules (1997) [2] explores the "misinformation, messed-up information, and mostly useless information on the Internet." In an article in the *Communications of the ACM* earlier this year, Soloway and Wallace [14] question the value of the Internet for dominating children's learning. In an invited talk at the 1997 Australian Conference on Computer Science Education, the keynote speaker reported abandoning a project where students wrote papers based solely on information obtained from the WWW. The problem there was no way to objectively determine what was true and what was false and some students reported on worthless topics.

There is certainly both good and bad in the WWW (and Internet more generally). It is both entertaining and instructive to read of the successes and failures that educators have in using the WWW. What is the relevance for Artificial Intelligence?

In my opinion, there is immense scope for mutual influence. The AI researcher should, in my opinion, be more than an interested observer in the WWW. The WWW is a wonderful experimental testbed for investigating intelligent search, knowledge representation, discovery, and synthesis. Conversely, effective utilisation of the WWW will require intelligence. This paper concerns one collection of AI-influenced 'experiments' on how to use the WWW effectively.

2 The Problem: Search for specific information on the WWW

The problem I have focussed on in the Intelligent Agents Laboratory is how to find specific information on the WWW. The WWW provides an infrastructure for browsing for information, but provides limited facilities for systematically locating specific information.

People's experience is widely variable. Sometimes the desired information is readily located, while at other times, much time can be wasted with nothing useful found.

The prime resource for finding information are search engines. The engine developers build indexing systems which traverse the WWW automatically, creating large indices off-line. these indices are used to respond in real-time to user queries. The user of the search engine types in keywords that are matched against the indices, and a list of URLs is returned, purportedly ranked as to relevance.

As an example of a query we have investigated, consider finding out about classes in Artificial Intelligence at the University of Melbourne. Using a search engine with the input "Artificial Intelligence University Melbourne" is not particularly successful. Here is a sample of what is returned. AltaVista reports over 250,000 documents matching the query, the first 50 of which do not contain the correct information nor pointers to it. The three most highly ranked URLs returned are of pages showing FTP sites for weather information, hosted at Allentown and Dodge City in the U.S. The same query made to Yahoo! reported one match, the home page of the Department of Computer Science at Monash. Electric Library returned 30 choices, all of which were irrelevant. The top choice of the Excite search engine (and AOL Netfind) was a pointer to the University of Durham in the UK. The second choice returned by Excite did point to the Vision Lab at the University of Melbourne, though navigation was still needed to find the page with the Artificial Intelligence subject description.

Yet a person can find out about classes in Artificial Intelligence at the University of Melbourne by straightforward browsing. Go to the home page of the University of Melbourne, which is easy enough to find. From there, click on links to the home pages of the Faculty of Engineering and Department of Computer Science and undergraduate course information.

Not all information is easy to find. Most people using the WWW to search for specific information report some frustrating experiences, though individual tolerance of the frustration varies. From the user's perspective, two problems frequently arise when using the search engine. First, the words might not match exactly and hence nothing is returned by the search engine. Second, and much more common, is that too many URLs are returned by the search engine, often hundreds, thousands, or even tens of thousands. Ranking schemes, intended to alleviate the overload, are at best opaque and often unhelpful. The advanced searching features made available in some search engines are advanced Boolean operations and allow the specification of proximity of words, recognition of strings, etc. They have an Information Retrieval flavour and deliberately do not try to address the (very difficult) semantic issues.

A thesis of the research in the Intelligent Agents Laboratory is that a limited amount of common sense knowledge can be usefully brought to bear when searching on the WWW. What I mean by common sense knowledge are the things that people know which are taken for granted. We know a lot more than we articulate. The common sense knowledge is used in a similar style to how expert knowledge is used in expert systems.

Incorporating common sense knowledge into AI systems has been a major bottleneck in the progress of AI systems. The largest project to focus on common sense knowledge is CYC [10], which has had limited success. Even restricting common sense knowledge to a limited, though open-ended, domain as food and nutrition is difficult [15]. On the other hand, limited common sense knowledge can be very useful in solving a narrow class of problems, as has happened in some expert systems.

To summarize, the problem being addressed in our lab is:

"How can we build software to find specific items of information on the WWW, that can use limited common sense knowledge to guide search, and can interact with the range and diversity of the WWW?"

The range and diversity of the WWW are what makes the research significant and interesting. Coping with the characteristics of openness and frequent change marks a change for AI systems. Key characteristics of the WWW are

- there are simple, common, universal protocols for communication such as http;
- it is based on hypermedia, where navigation of links is essential and a variety of media must eventually be taken into account;
- it is dynamic - pages are constantly being added, deleted and modified;
- it is open - the complete knowledge present cannot be charaterised.

Having posed information search on the WWW as a problem, how do we go about solving it. Two differing approaches can be immediately identified, which can loosely be cast as the neat and scruffy approaches. The neat approach is to concentrate on building a model before extensive system development. There are advantages to formalism in the ability to prove theorems about properties of models, for example. There are dangers in that the models won't adequately reflect the reality.

The scruffy approach eschews formalism and models in favour of building systems. Examples built with insight should lead to identification of key difficulties, useful abstractions and a general method for solving the problem and revelation of the issues. The difficulty of the experimental approach, shared with all experimental Computer Science, is evaluating the systems and reproducibility of experiments.

In general, at an early stage of research as we are currently at with the WWW, I favour a scruffy approach. It is necessary to have real examples of systems to think about. This paper reports largely on the experimental research from our lab. We recognise the difficulties of evaluation and reproducibility, but don't offer a solution. We have developed a model for describing WWW knowledge as will be alluded to later.

3 The Metaphor: Autonomous agents

A convenient metaphor for building software to interact with the range and diversity of the WWW is that of a agent. An agent is a person that performs some task on your behalf. We would like to have a program that navigates the WWW to find the specific information that you strongly suspect is out there. You care about the result, and are happy to delegate the process to an assistant.

It is worth commenting on some associations that come with the agent metaphor of a software agent. You expect an agent to act even if all the details are not specified, or the situation changes. You expect an agent to communicate effectively with other agents.

Having a program working on your behalf for finding WWW information is an idea that has occurred to many (AI) researchers. The area of (intelligent) software agents is booming. Like many fields that suddenly grow very quickly, definitions are not consistent. I could spend the bulk of this paper quibbling over definitions. Let me instead refer you to Franklin and Graesser (1997) [5] which discusses eleven definitions of agents and lays out the landscape well.

Are agents practical? Are agents truly revolutionary as some of the hype claims? It is useful in a classroom setting to take specific programs and try and decide if they are an agent or not. Two I do want to claim as agents are Eudora as a mail agent and a virus as a malevolent agent.

One distinction that is worth making is useful agents versus intelligent agents. This issue is argued in [4]. Intelligent agents involve planning and reasoning about beliefs and intentions. Useful agents such as the shopping agent ShopBot just perform a specific task. The bulk of the work on agents for the WWW performed in our lab fits better under the category of useful agents.

Let me conclude with two more general observations. Agents can be viewed as a new model for developing software to interact over a network. This view has emerged because of the predominance of networks in the world. Information, knowledge, and electronic resources in general, are distributed across a network and programs and methods are needed to access them. Using agents adds a layer of abstraction that localises decisions about dealing with local peculiarities of format, knowledge conventions, etc. Discussing that is beyond my current scope.

Studying how software reacts to the environment in which it operates may shed light on how we interact intelligently to our environment. The Internet is arguably an ideal testbed to gauge the intelligence of a software agent. It is a complex, dynamic environment. There are other software entities, such as automatic mail handlers, with which software agents must interact. Persistence of agents in the network and their mobility will be important for their effective performance and may lead us to label some agents as more intelligent than others.

4   Experiences: Good Domains for Retrieving Information

Having decided on a research direction, the following question emerges. What constitutes a good domain and problem? The bulk of this section describes domains which have proven to be interesting for the Intelligent Agents Laboratory. The key characteristic of an interesting domain is that there is a variety of pages in differing formats but there is some common overall structure. Too much structure reduces the problem to known methods. Too little structure reduces the problem to natural language understanding which is difficult. Having structure is useful to guide the search.

4.1   Navigating University sites

The first (pen-and-paper) exercise on whether an agent could find information from the WWW concerns universities and their courses. We wrote down a list of fourteen questions about Computer Science courses, and hired a summer student to document how he went about finding the answers. The hope, in the spirit of expert systems development, was that he would develop specific heuristics that could be encoded in an agent. The question about Artificial Intelligence at the University of Melbourne used before as a motivating example came from this study..

The summer research, reported in [13], was of limited success. No set method that an agent could follow was identified. There was too much variability among the University sites. There were two positive conclusions:

1. the domain was worth further investigation;
2. bounded search using limited key word matching could be effective from a good starting URL.

That immediately suggested identifying two separate problems for finding information. One is locating a good starting URL. The second is searching from the known URL. Note that search engines do not make such a distinction. Most of our research is concerned with the latter, searching from a known URL.

University information was chosen as the application domain for Stewart Baillie's M.Cog. Sci. thesis [1]. Baillie did a detailed study of two problems:

- navigating from the University home page to the home page of the Computer Science home page, and
- navigating from a Departmental home page to the subjects of a Computer Science degree course.

The study was instructive. Note that locating the starting URLs for a University is not a problem. Addresses for the University home pages were readily available, and published in many places. The address can often be guessed. Certainly there was sufficient diversity among the thirty eight Australian universities to make the problem interesting.

For the first problem, the agent was able to navigate from the University home page to the Computer Science home page in 31 out of 35 pages. The second problem was more resource intensive, and seven Computer Science departments were chosen. Of these, the agent found the desired information in four out of the seven cases.

Some of the difficulties are:

- graphical pages caused problems for an agent. It wasn't obvious how to get to the Computer Science page from one University map.
- There is a variety of University structures. Some have more emphasis on faculties, others on schools.
- Computer science is in different faculties in different universities.
- Some universities have multiple computer science departments. Which should be returned?
- One university had two home pages for Computer Science. Which should be returned?

The strategies and heuristics that were developed were expressed in human terms such as departmental home pages, and lists of faculties. The Web pages themselves are syntactic structures. What is needed is a way to link the human terms to the physical hyperlinks of the WWW. Much of Baillie's thesis is discussing a 'duallist' model linking a conceptual model to the physical WWW.

A fragment of the knowledge used to guide the search is contained in Figure 1. The knowledge is easily modelled with a form of conceptual graph. The terms contain knowledge about universities (common sense knowledge for academics and students). These terms are related to the search.

```
A university usually contains faculties.
A university may contain Boards of study.
A faculty usually contains departments.

Computer science may be in the engineering faculty.
Computer science may be in the sciencefaculty.
```

Fig. 1. A knowledge fragment for guiding University search.

4.2 Citation Finding

The first 'agent' constructed in the lab was CiFi, a *citation finder*. What is the purpose of a citation finder? Consider the situation of a journal editor trying to improve the image of their journal. One issue taken into account when assessing the quality of a journal is the quality of the references cited in papers published in the journal. Citations of refereed journal and conference proceedings are more highly rated than departmental technical reports, for example. Yet often, the technical reports are what have been actually available and used by the author in preparing the paper. By the time that the paper has passed through the reviewing process and is ready for the final version, the technical report may have appeared in a more widely accessible publication. It would be helpful to be able to update the reference to the technical report.

How can the best citation for a particular paper be found? There is a reasonable chance that the information may be posted on the WWW. Posting papers on the WWW is increasingly common, especially in Computer Science. Tracking down a particular paper on the WWW can be boring and time-consuming, and is an ideal task to give to a research assistant. The intent is to give author(s) and (part of a) title to CiFi, and have it return a citation for that paper.

The Artificial Intelligence method for developing programs is to imitate how an intelligent person solves the problem. Here are two possible heuristics for searching for the citation.

1. check out the author(s)' home page and look from there.

2. check out the author(s)' department's home page and look for its publications page.

Using those terms immediately points out what an issue is (which is also true for browsing University pages.) Terms such as author's home pages are conceptual ones. There is no universal syntactic methods for determining a home page. The agent needs to search physical pages, whereas author methods are on conceptual terms. This is analogous to the University methods. Conceptual graphs were used as in Figure 1.

We have built a preliminary prototype called CiFi, reported in [11] and [8], which incorporates these two heuristics, among others. Inferring addresses and home pages requires common sense knowledge about the Internet which has been incorporated in CiFi.

We did some experiments using existing Internet search typing in the title and authors as keywords. The results were not all that successful. What happened was that sometimes a page corresponding to the paper was found, perhaps as a postscript file, but usually the citation wasn't given. CiFi works significantly better than direct indexing by incorporating the two heuristics given above plus several others.

What ways can the citation finder be extended? Here is one idea. If a proper citation is not found after a reasonable search effort, email could be sent. Most authors would be happy to answer a simple question about their papers from an agent interested in citing their research. Sending a message to the author automatically is technically straightforward - there are many automatic mailers. Specifying issues, such as when email is to be sent and what to do on receipt, will require some procedural component most likely in the form of scripting capability. Receiving the mail in reply is much trickier and raises questions about robustness and persistence. How long should an agent wait for an answer? What should be done with a reply from a vacation program?

4.3 Sports Results

We briefly describe three projects for retrieving scores in baseball, cricket, and soccer respectively. Each of the projects had slightly different motivation, but they were all useful in identifying issues in retrieving WWW information. Note that the request was narrow in scope for each of the sports - 'tell me the latest score of my team'. Tracking a favourite batsman, or soccer star, would require a different approach to what was developed.

The baseball 'agent' was called IndiansWatcher [3]. It sent a daily email message with the result of the Cleveland Indians baseball team for most of the 1996 season. IndiansWatcher visited the WWW site of the Cleveland Indians, checked if there was a new Web page corresponding to a new game result, and if so, extracted the score and sent a mail message. The project was written in Perl [16] and gave us experience in managing Web documents. It also highlighted issues of knowing what a baseball score was, what rules were for washed out games, and other baseball miscellany.

Cricket scores were investigated in the context of the experimental agent shell ARIS [9] which will be mentioned in more detail in the section on Observations. The starting URL was idea was the well-known CricInfo site. This was done successfully, though admittedly in an ad-hoc manner.

There was interest in the cricket score retrieval from a small company providing cricket scores on the WWW. A summer student adapted the program to do some checks on the cricket scores returned, that the totals summed correctly, for example, which apparently is not always the case. It was straightforward to do the programming, but the work was not obviously generalisable from cricket to another sport.

A more elaborate example we have investigated is retrieving soccer scores. It is a good example to study because it highlights the contrast in the WWW between uniformity and diversity. The wide interest in the game, multi-lingual issues, and the relative simplicity of the scores (in contrast for example to cricket), all contribute to make this an intriguing project. I have posed retrieving soccer scores as a project for my agents class and it is an appropriate level of difficulty, being enjoyed by the students.

In his 1997 Honours project, Alex Wyatt (1997) [18] has investigated several strategies for finding soccer scores from a variety of international leagues. Here are some useful heuristics.

- Exploit table structures where possible. Free text versions of scores are harder in general to process.
- Exploit typography, for example semi-colons instead of commas can delimit games, and HTML typography is very useful.
- Have expert handlers of date formats.
- Have dictionary support to identify words as opposed to team names, though words like united can be confusing.
- Use common sense knowledge for checking sensibility of scores. One version of the heuristic produced a score of 69 to 23 which turned out to be the minutes in which the goals were scored.

The complexity of building a general program to recognize scores can easily be appreciated by looking at the sports results in a daily newspaper. Score formats differ, the significance of numbers are different, the order of two teams sometimes reflects winners and losers, and sometimes where the game was played. Using capitals for names can reflect home teams (in U.S. Football for example) while it reflects Australian nationality (for tennis). A lot of terminology and style of reporting is cultural as anyone who has lived in a different country can attest to. Capturing that knowledge for a specific sport is essential for effective retrieval of scores.

4.4 Classified Ads

The final domain we consider is classified ads. Here the value of a personal assistant can be easily seen. A newcomer to a city must find a car, accommodation, etc. Wouldn't it be wonderful if a personal assistant just took the person's preferences and found something suitable. Here the metaphor of an agent is already in practice in the form of real estate agents and car salesmen.

To investigate whether common sense knowledge can be suitably circumscribed and readily plugged in for new applications, e.g. from looking for flats to looking for cars to looking for furniture, we have built a prototype agent for searching real estate ads, called CASA [6].

Some of the knowledge needed that has been identified in the construction of CASA is:

- A real estate ad contains a location, price and size at bare minimum.
- The price is per week or per month.
- Bigger flats and houses will usually cost more.
- Car Parking is a feature for some.

It remains to be tested how easily the framework of CASA can be adapted to cars and other domains appearing in classified ads.

5 Discussion

We have identified three broad types of knowledge which have been useful for effective information gathering, and essential to incorporate in agents. We examine each in turn and comment on the ease that each of the three types of knowledge can be made available for agents.

- WWW authoring conventions
- Domain specific common sense knowledge
- Domain specific browsing knowledge for a given task

WWW conventions that we have used fall loosely into three categories.

- Knowledge of Web protocols such as http and ftp.
- Technical information about HTML markup conventions, format of headers, paragraphs, links, and anchors, etc.
- Knowledge of page structures, home pages, which pages are just lists of links, etc.
- Knowledge of Web addresses, and starting URLs. We will use existing tools such as Ahoy! to help find starting URLs, and will not focus on the issue of guessing starting URLs.

Knowledge of WWW protocols can be incorporated in agents in standard packages existing in a variety of languages. We have found useful classes in Perl (http://www.perl.com/perl/), Java (http://java.sun.com), and Eclipse Prolog (http://www.ecrc.de/research/projects/eclipse/). Knowledge of HTML conventions is also straightforward to incorporate and we have used, modified, and developed classes to strip out tags, for examples. Knowledge of page structures will be built into the agents, as will the knowledge about Web addresses.

Technical WWW knowledge is probably the easiest of the three types of knowledge to incorporate.

Domain specific common sense knowledge is recognised as a product that is needed. Indeed the CYC project evolved from a single encyclopedic source of common sense knowledge into pieces that agents might use. [7]. Standard AI techniques can be used to represent some of this knowledge. For example, university hierarchies are easily represented, as in Figure 1. More general knowledge that can be useful is beginning to become available. For example, the on-line dictionary WordNet [12] is a useful resource.

Task specific domain knowledge is by its nature more specific and in general must be specified by an end user. We have begun experimenting with a language and interface that would be user friendly for a computer-literate but agent-naive user. A prototype shell, ARIS, was built [9] wherein we were able to reconstruct CiFi and a simple subject finder for university classes. ARIS represented conceptual graphs as information about types of pages and likely links between pages. The user had to specify both the page types and the words that might suggest the page types. ARIS was manipulated to find cricket scores, but it certainly wasn't intuitive for a naive user. The shell will be redesigned in light ofw our accumulated experience.

The deeper issue of modelling human conceptual knowledge and mapping it to actual WWW pages has also progressed through the experiences so far. Viewing the WWW as a communication medium and relating hypertext structure to domain organisation, web pages to discourse structure, and the multimedia objects as having semantic content seems promising.

6   Conclusions

It is exciting times for exploring with the WWW. Web pages are a moving target and programs that visit them must be easy to adapt. While it is promising that digital assistants will find more and more information and knowledge for us, the methods are by no means standard or universally agreed. We are still learning what specific items are easy to retrieve and which require more involved text processing. A good conceptual model is essential for expressing human intelligible knowledge on how to find information. The classification of knowledge into three types, Web conventions, common sense knowledge about the domain and task specific knowledge, is helpful.

To take a philosophical perspective, 'Computer Science is the applied mathematics of our generation'. Applied mathematics of the previous century investigated heat and energy. In our generation, the challenge is to understand the essence of data, information, knowledge, learning and experience, so they can be used effectively for the betterment of society. Investigating agents on the WWW is tackling information and knowledge head on.

Acknowledgments. Support for this research came from the University of Melbourne through a small ARC grant and through start-up funds to help the

Intelligent Agents Laboratory. My thinking has been strongly influenced by discussions with the members of the Intelligent Agents Laboratory, especially Liz Sonenberg.

References

1. Baillie, S. Pragmatic Information Discovery in the World-Wide Web, M.Cog. Sci. thesis, University of Melbourne, 1996
2. Burbules, N. Struggling with the Internet, *Campus Review*, p.. 19-20, August, 1997
3. Cassin, A. and Sterling, L. IndiansWatcher: A Single Purpose Software Agent, Proc. Practical Applications of Agent Methodology, p. 529, Practical Application Co. 1997 (Longer version available as Tech. Report, CS Dept., University of Melbourne, 1996)
4. Etzioni, O. Moving up the Information Food Chain: Deploying Softbots on the World-Wide Web, *AI Magazine*, 18(2), pp. 11-18, 1997
5. Franklin, S. and Graesser, A. Is it an Agent, or just a Program?: A Taxonomy for Autonomous Agents, Proc. 3rd Intl. Workshop on Agent Theories, Architectures, and Languages, published as Intelligent Agents III, Springer-Verlag, pp. 21-35, 1997
6. Gao and Sterling, Using Limited Common Sense Knowledge to Guide Knowledge Acquisition for Information Agents, Tech. Report, CS Dept., University of Melbourne, 1997
7. Guha, R. Lenat, D. Enabling Agents to Work Together, *Comm. ACM*, **37**(7), pp. 33-38, 1995
8. Han, Y, Loke, S.W. and Sterling, L.S. Agents for Citation Finding on the World Wide Web, Proc. Practical Applications of Agent Methodology, pp. 303-317, Practical Application Co. 1997
9. Kim, H. ARIS: An Agent Shell, Honours thesis, University of Melbourne, 1996
10. Lenat, D. CYC: A Large-Scale Investment in Knowledge Infrastructure, *Comm. ACM*, **38**(11), pp. 33-38, 1995
11. Loke, S.W., Davison, A., and Sterling, L.S. CiFi: An Intelligent Agent for Citation Finding on the World-Wide Web, Proc. 4th Pacific Rim Intl. Conf. on AI, (PRICAI-96), Springer Lecture Notes in AI, Vol. 1114, pp. 580-591, 1996
12. Miller, G.A. WordNet: A Lexical Database for English. *Comm. ACM*, **38**(11), pp. 39-41, 1995.
13. Rive, Nicholas Summer Student project, CS Dept., University of Melbourne, February, 1996
14. Soloway, E and Wallace, R. Does the Internet Support Student Inquiries? Don't Ask, *Comm. ACM*, **40**(5), pp. 11-16, 1997
15. Sterling, L.S., Petot, G., Marling, C., Kovacic, K., and Ernst, G. The Role of Common Sense Knowledge in Menu Planning, Expert Systems with Applications, **11**(3), pp. 301-308, 1996
16. Wall, L., Christiansen, T., and Schwartz, R. Programming Perl, 2nd Ed., O'Reilly & Associates, 1996
17. Wooldridge, M. and Jennings, N. Intelligent Agents: Theory and Practice, Knowledge Engineering Review, **10**(2), 1995
18. Wyatt, A. SportsFinder: An Information Gathering Agent to Return Sports Results, Honours thesis, University of Melbourne, 1997

Extending Dynamic Backtracking
for
Distributed Constraint Satisfaction Problems

William S. Havens

Intelligent Systems Laboratory
School of Computing Science
Simon Fraser University
Burnaby, B.C., Canada   V5A 1S6
email: havens@cs.sfu.ca
phone: 604.291.4973
fax: 604.291.3045

Keywords: multiagent systems, cooperative problem solving, intelligent backtracking, distributed constraint satisfaction

Abstract

A recent constructive search technique called dynamic backtracking (DB) achieves a systematic and complete search while allowing significant movement in the search space. The algorithm constructs tuples of inconsistent variable assignments called nogoods. An important issue is managing the number of nogoods constructed and remembered (cached) during the search. The nogood caching scheme for DB limits the size of the cache as the search proceeds through the space. Recently a new constructive search algorithm for the distributed constraint satisfaction problem (DCSP) was described called asynchronous backtracking (AB). In this method, agents construct nogoods and convey them to other agents to effect the backtrack search. A obvious question to ask if whether the nogood caching scheme employed by DB can be extended for the DCSP. In this paper, we briefly analyse the existing DB caching scheme from this perspective and suggest two new improved caching algorithms. Finally we provide some preliminary experimental evidence that our new caching algorithms outperform dynamic backtracking in the multiagent context.

1. Introduction

We are concerned with finding effective search algorithms for the *distributed constraint satisfaction problem* (DCSP). Recently, [Yokoo *et al.* 92] showed how *intelligent backtracking* (IB) methods could be applied to the DCSP. His algorithm, called *asynchronous backtracking* (AB), constructs inconsistent sets of variable bindings (nogoods) and communicates them among multiple agents to effect an IB search. The method has also been extended to incorporate heuristic search [Yokoo 93]. The key idea is that agents can make local autonomous decisions yet effect a global systematic search. Since AB is claimed to be complete, an obvious question to ask is: How space efficient is the algorithm? In particular, how many nogoods are derived and then communicated among agents during the search?. The reports cited above do not indicate the size of the nogood store but its size is certainly crucial to practical application.

Recent advances have also been made in sequential IB algorithms. A technique called *dynamic backtracking* (DB) [Ginsberg 93] provides considerable flexibility in the search direction while maintaining completeness. Furthermore, the algorithm exhibits a polynomial space bound on the number of nogoods stored at any time [Ginsberg& McAllester 94]. Can this nogood caching scheme be extended for the DCSP and algorithms such as AB? We seek to understand these issues.

This paper is a sequel to another report [Havens97] which analysed the nogood caching behaviour of DB from the perspective of its application to the DCSP. We report here on our preliminary experimental results on these new caching algorithms. In the next section, we review the DCSP and the basic method of intelligent backtracking. From this framework, the nogood caching rule given by Ginsberg and McAllester [94] is examined. A DCSP example is given which is problematic for the DB caching rule. Next we consider two alternative caching algorithms which removes this difficulty. Preliminary experimental results are given comparing all three algorithms.

2. Distributed CSPs and Backtrack Search

Definition 1:   A *constraint satisfaction problem*, CSP = (X_N, C), where X_N is a set of discrete variables and C is a set of k-ary constraints on these variables.

We will refer to subsets of the variables in X_N using index set notation. The set of all subscripts is N={1...n}. The complete set of n variables in the CSP is then X_N. A particular subset of variables $X_J \subseteq X_N$ refers to the variables { X_j }$_{j \in J}$ such that $J \subseteq N$. Each variable $X_i \in X_N$ has a domain D_i of discrete values. Likewise any constraint $C_J \in C$ is a relation on variables $X_J \subseteq X_N$.

Definition 2:   A *distributed constraint satisfaction problem* (DCSP) is a CSP where the variables X_N and the constraints C are distributed among a finite set of agents.

There are many possible mappings of variables and constraints to agents. For simplicity, we assume (like AB) that each agent has exactly one variable and knows every constraint on that variable. Unlike AB, constraints are not binary directed arcs in the constraint graph but general k-ary predicates C_J for k = |J|. We will informally substitute variables for agents and *vice versa* when the distinction is not important.

Definition 3:   The *binding* of a variable X_i to some element $\alpha \in D_i$ is the assignment $X_i = \alpha$.

We can abbreviate the notation by referring simply to α_i as the binding since the subscript "i" identifies which variable X_i it is assigned. A set of bindings (a tuple) is denoted also using index set notation. Hence $\alpha_J = \{\alpha_j\}_{j \in J}$ represents the set of bindings for variables X_j, $j \in J$. A constraint C_J holds on this tuple iff $\alpha_J \in C_J$.

Definition 4:   A *solution* to the DCSP is a tuple α_N for all variables X_N such that $\alpha_J \in C_J$, $\alpha_J \subseteq \alpha_N$, which must hold for every constraint $C_J \in C$.

Since α_N contains a binding for every variable in the CSP, we can think of it as encoding a point in the search space. As the search moves in this space (or some subspace), individual constraints are variously consistent or inconsistent. Whenever a constraint becomes inconsistent, a record of the inconsistency is made in the form of a nogood.

Definition 5: The negation of an inconsistent tuple, written $\neg\alpha_J$, is called a *nogood*. This assignment of values to variables X_J is known not to satisfy some constraint(s) in C.

Nogoods are constructed either by the failure of a given constraint or by resolution from existing nogoods. If the empty nogood is derived (containing no bindings) then the CSP is unsatisfiable. For details, see for example [Ginsberg&McAllester 94].

Definition 6: (*culprit selection rule*) In any nonempty nogood there is a distinguished binding called the *culprit* which is the most recent binding made in the ordering of variables. In the nogood $\neg\alpha_J = \{ \alpha_j \}_{j \in J}$, the culprit is binding $\alpha_t \in \alpha_J$ such that $t \geq j$ for all $j \in J$.

Definition 7: A nogood expressed in *culprit form* is $\neg\alpha_J = \neg(\alpha_K \alpha_t)$, where α_t is the culprit binding according to the culprit selection rule and α_K, $K=J-\{t\}$, is the *antecedent*.

A nogood in culprit form can also be expressed equivalently as the implication $(\alpha_K \Rightarrow \neg\alpha_t)$ such as used by [McAllester&Ginsberg, 94]. In general, let Γ_i be the nogood cache for agent "i" containing the set of nogoods derived for culprit variable X_i. The global nogood cache Γ is simply the union of all the agent's local stores, $\Gamma = \cup\Gamma_i$, $i \in N$.

Definition 8: The subset $\Delta_i \subseteq D_i$ is called the *live domain* of variable X_i which represents those values in its domain D_i which are consistent with the current partial solution.

The live domain for X_i is then those values $\alpha_i \in D_i$ which are not precluded by any existing nogood whose antecedent is currently contained in the global point α_N. More precisely:

$$\Delta_i = \{\alpha_i \in D_i \mid \forall \neg(\alpha_K \alpha_i) \in \Gamma_i, \alpha_K \not\subset \alpha_N\} \tag{1}$$

Initially since there are no nogoods, every value in the domain is also in the live domain. Note that the live domain can change radically as the search moves point α_N in the search space. The values of nogood antecedents α_K are only true when $\alpha_K \subset \alpha_N$. Our challenge is to manage the nogood cache (and hence the live domains) efficiently as the search proceeds.

Definition 9: A variable X_i whose live domain $\Delta_i = \{\}$ is called a *bottom variable* and written
$X_i = \perp$.

3. Dynamic Backtracking

A major research goal of DB is the maximum "freedom of movement" in the search space while maintaining a systematic and complete search. The authors argue that DB is a balance between these two conflicting criteria. In particular, the caching scheme employed by DB is based on the notion of an "acceptable assignment" (hereafter the *AA-rule*) which limits the size of the nogood database as the search proceeds through the search space. However, there is a direct conflict between freedom of motion in the search and retention of nogoods. It is known that this caching rule preemptively discards nogoods which must be recomputed repeatedly [Baker 95]. For distributed algorithms, we argue that this conflict is debilitating because it unnecessarily resets the states of agents not involved in the backtracking. The problem is exacerbated in the network environment where we seek to minimize communication between agents.

3.1 The Acceptable AssignmentRule

Definition 10:   *(AA-rule) an acceptable assignment* is a point α_N that encodes <u>every</u> antecedent in Γ and <u>none</u> of the culprits [Ginsberg&McAllester 1994].

More precisely,

$$\forall \neg(\alpha_K \alpha_t) \in \Gamma, \ \alpha_K \subset \alpha_N \text{ and } \alpha_t \not\in \alpha_N \tag{2}$$

which says that every nogood, $\neg(\alpha_K \alpha_t)$, in the store must obey the following: 1) the antecedent α_K must be currently true (contained in the current global point, α_N) and; 2) α_N cannot contain any binding α_t precluded by such a nogood. The second condition makes sense because it eliminates any point α_N in the search space which is known to be inconsistent given the other bindings α_K contained in this same point.

The first condition is more problematic. It says that any nogood α_K whose antecedent is currently false (*i.e.* $\alpha_K \not\subset \alpha_N$) must be deleted from Γ. This is the basis for the polynomial space bound on the nogood store. The rule has also been called "1-relevance learning" since the cache contains nogoods which differ from α_N in at most one binding (*i.e.* the culprit) [Bayardo& Miranker 96].

```
Cache(¬α_J) ≡
    If α_J=∅ then Halt.
    Γ ← Γ∪{¬α_J}
    let (α_K α_t) = α_J
    for every ¬(α_H α_i)∈Γ such that α_t∈α_H,
        Γ ← Γ-{¬(α_H α_i)}
    if X_t=⊥ then
        let α^⊥={α_H |¬(α_H α_t)∈Γ and α_H⊂α_N}
        Cache(¬α^⊥)
    end.
```

Algorithm 1: DB procedure Cache

Algorithm 1 gives the nogood caching procedure for DB[1]. This procedure is called whenever a new nogood, $\neg\alpha_J$, is discovered during the search. Cache checks for the empty nogood (in which case the CSP is unsatisfiable) and otherwise adds $\neg\alpha_J$ to Γ. Let the nogood have an antecedent α_K and culprit α_t. Then the procedure deletes from Γ every other nogood $\neg(\alpha_H \alpha_i)$ which contains culprit α_t in its antecedent α_H. Finally, if this additional nogood forces variable $X_t=\bot$, then a new nogood $\alpha^\bot$ is resolved

---

1. Recoded from procedure "simp" in [Ginsberg&McAllester 94].

from the antecedents α_H of every nogood on X_t and Cache called recursively on this new nogood.

3.2 A Problematic Example for DB Cache

How will this procedure Cache based on the AA-rule effect the efficiency of the AB search? Please consider the following example shown in Figure 1.

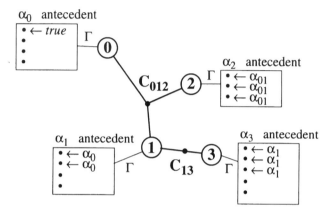

Figure 1: A Problematic Example for DB Cache

We have a DCSP with four agents (variables) and two constraints. Constraint C_{13} relates variables X_1 and X_3 while constraint C_{012} relates variables X_0, X_1 and X_2. Attached to each variable is the corresponding nogood store Γ. Each bullet in the store represents some value α from its domain and the arrows indicates some existing nogood whose antecedent has eliminated that value from its live domain. For example, variable X_1 has four domain values, two of which have been eliminated by nogoods whose singleton antecedents are the binding α_0 for variable X_0.

For illustration, we assume that the agents for X_0 and X_1 have communicated their bindings to the agents for variables X_2 and X_3. Thereafter however, constraints C_{012} and C_{13} repeatedly fail on these bindings generating new nogoods of the form $\neg(\alpha_{01}\alpha_2)$ and $\neg(\alpha_1\alpha_3)$ respectively. Successive domain values for X_2 and X_3 are thus ruled out as illustrated. Suppose eventually $X_2 = \bot$ since its live domain has been completely eliminated thus inducing a new nogood $\neg(\alpha_0\alpha_1)$. The AA-rule then forces the removal of every nogood with culprit α_1 in its antecedent. Thus, neither X_2 nor X_3 will have any nogoods remaining in Γ and their live domains will be fully restored.

The assumption here is that discarded nogoods can be derived again later if required. This is the basis of the polynomial space bound for Γ. But these discarded nogoods will be rediscovered and then discarded again an exponential number of times in the worst case [Baker 95]. Another problem is that some nogoods will never be discovered. Suppose always X_2 reaches bottom before X_3 (e.g. $|D_2| \ll |D_3|$) then never will any nogoods be induced from $X_3 = \bot$. This is because the AA-rule will "reset" the work done by X_3 each time X_2 cycles its live domain asserting the new nogood $\neg(\alpha_0\,\alpha_1)$.

4. Improved NoGood Caching Schemes

In this section, we offer two alternate caching algorithms suitable for the DCSP. The first has an unrestricted cache size while the second imposes an arbitrary bound. The basic idea of both schemes is to keep nogoods in the cache whose antecedents are <u>not</u> necessarily contained in the current state (thus violating the AA-rule) but still delete unnecessary nogoods whenever possible. We will allow multiple nogoods to have the same culprit but different antecedents (*i.e.* (α_H, α_t) and (β_H, α_t)). More precisely, we have the following relaxed rule:[2]

$$\forall \neg(\alpha_K \alpha_t) \in \Gamma, \ \alpha_K \subset \alpha_N \Rightarrow \alpha_t \notin \alpha_N \tag{3}$$

which says that for every nogood $\neg(\alpha_K \alpha_t)$ in Γ, the current point α_N must not contain this culprit α_t if the antecedent α_K is contained in this point. However, Γ may contain nogoods whose antecedents are not currently true. We will define other mechanisms for removing these nogoods.

```
Cache(¬α_J, X_i) ≡
    If α_J=∅ then Halt.
    Γ ← Γ∪{¬α_J}
    let (α_K α_t)=α_J
    if X_i ≠ nil then
        for every ¬(α_H α_i)∈Γ such that α_t∈α_H,
            Γ ← Γ-{¬(α_H α_i)}
    if X_t=⊥ then
        let α^⊥={α_H |¬(α_H α_t)∈Γ and α_H⊂α_N}
        Cache(¬α^⊥, X_t)
    end.
```

Algorithm 2: unrestricted procedure Cache.

Our first new cache algorithm is based on the fact that the only reason for keeping the antecedents of nogoods is to resolve them into a new nogood when the variable reaches bottom. Thereafter, we can discard any of these nogoods. Algorithm-2 above maintains the cache for each variable until it reaches bottom then discards selectively those nogoods for that variable whose antecedents contain the new culprit derived from the bottom variable.

This version of Cache takes two arguments, the new nogood $\neg\alpha_J$ and the bottom variable X_i inducing $\neg\alpha_J$ (or nil if the new constraint was caused by a constraint failure). Like the previous version, Cache first checks for the empty nogood. Otherwise, the new nogood $\neg\alpha_J$ is added to Γ. Let the nogood have an antecedent α_K and culprit α_t. If $X_i \neq$ nil then delete every nogood $\neg(\alpha_H \alpha_i)$ from Γ which containts culprit α_t in its antecedent α_H. If variable X_t is now bottom then perform the following. Resolve a new nogood $\alpha^\perp$ from those nogoods in Γ whose culprit is α_t and whose antecedent

---

2. This rule and Algorithm-2 differ significantly from those appearing in [Havens97].

is currently true (*i.e.* contained in the current point). Finally, recursively cache this new nogood $\alpha^{\perp}$.

Let's consider the example of Figure-1 again using this new caching algorithm. Constraints C_{012} and C_{13} repeatedly fail generating new nogoods of form $(\alpha_0 \alpha_2)$ and $(\alpha_1 \alpha_2)$ respectively. Successive bindings for X_2 and X_3 are ruled out. Eventually $X_2 = \perp$ inducing a new nogood $(\alpha_0 \, \alpha_1)$. The new Cache algorithm removes <u>only</u> nogoods for X_2 (since X_2 is bottom) which have antecedents containing the culprit α_1. This removes all the nogoods on variable X_2 but leaves all existing nogoods on variable X_3 intact. Any subsequent nogoods derived for X_2 and X_3 will be of the form $(\beta_{01} \, \alpha_2)$ and $(\beta_1 \, \alpha_3)$ respectively (since the binding now of X_1 has necessarily changed). We note that the nogoods are now (possibly) disjunctive for each culprit. Suppose eventually $X_3 = \perp$ for some antecedent (say β_1) and a new nogood $(\varnothing \, \beta_1)$ is derived which means that the algorithm will conclude that the current value β_1 for X_1 is globally inconsistent (since the antecedent is null).

Algorithm-2 is an improvement over the original DB version of Cache since it achieves our goal of maintaining autonomy among agents solving the DCSP. However, we have also lost the desirable space bound provided by DB. Can this bound be reclaimed? We note that there are a wide variety of caching schemes in use (*e.g.* virtual memory, disk caches). Most of these schemes do not preemptively empty their caches (like the AA-rule) <u>before</u> the cache is actually full!

```
Cache(¬α_J)  ≡
    If  α_J=∅ then Halt.
    Γ ← Γ∪{¬α_J}
    let  (α_K α_t) = α_J
    if  |Γ| ≥ Max then
        for every ¬(α_H α_i) ∈ Γ such that α_t ∈ α_H,
            Γ ← Γ - {¬(α_H α_i)}
    if X_t=⊥ then
        let α^⊥ = {α_H | ¬(α_H α_t) ∈ Γ and  α_H ⊂ α_N}
        Cache(¬α^⊥)
    end.
```

Algorithm 3: Improved procedure Cache with fixed space bound.

From this observation, we offer a third caching algorithm which imposes an external constraint on the size of the nogood store. Algorithm-3 above looks very similar to Algorithm-1 except that it refrains from preemptively emptying the cache until the size of Γ is greater than some predetermined value "Max". Then it removes every nogood $\neg(\alpha_H \alpha_i)$ in Γ whose antecedent α_H contains the new culprit α_t (according to the AA-rule). Otherwise, nogoods are retained in the cache in an unrestricted fashion. The value of Max could be set by how much memory is available or on some other external criterion.

5. Experimental Results

Our preliminary results are encouraging. All three caching algorithms were coded in C++ and tested in a simulated multiagent environment. Both constraints and variables are repeatedly polled in a round-robin scheme. Whenever a constraint is inconsistent on the current point α_N or a variable becomes bottom, a new nogood is generated and the cache algorithm called. This loop is repeated until all variables have consistent bindings (indicating a solution) or the empty nogood is generated (indicating failure).

For our experiments, we generated 100 random CSPs with 20 variables each and a uniform domain size of 10 values per variable. Binary constraints were asserted between random pairs of variables. It is known that there is a phase transition phenomenon in CSPs where the hard problems reside. Recently a parameter κ has been introduced which estimates this phase transition point at $\kappa = 1.0$ for various values of constraint probability p1 and constraint tightness p2 [Gent *et.al.* 96]. We chose p1=0.40 and p2=0.45 yielding a reasonable distribution of satisfiable and unsatisfiable hard problems.

NoGood Caching	Algorithm-1 (DB preemptive)	Algorithm-2 (unrestricted)	Algorithm-3 (bounded)
avg. nogoods created	335,167	139,469	215,569
avg. nogoods deleted	335,045	127,823	211,922
avg. max cache size	268	11,767	3,779
worst case cache size	304	31,599	3,828
avg. active nogoods	121	11,645	3,646

Table 1: Comparison of NoGood Caching Algorithms

Table 1 shows our preliminary results. For each cache algorithm, we measure the average number of nogoods created and subsequently destroyed. Creating a nogood corresponds to a backtrack point for the culprit variable (agent) involved. It can be seen that Algorithm-2 backtracks far less than Algorithm-1 by a factor of about 2.4. This is a significant improvement. Remembering nogoods whose antecedents are not contained in the current point is very effective in reducing backtracking in multiagent search as we suspected. However, Algorithm-2 maintains a substantial cache, averaging almost 12K nogoods. In the worst case, it stores about 31.5K nodes. Algorithm-1 has an average maximum cache size of only 268 nogoods.

Algorithm-3 presents a good comprimise between the number of backtracks and maximum cache size. Here we have arbitrarily set the value of Max = 3800 nogoods. When this threshold is reached, Algorithm-3 reverts to the preemptive discarding strategy of Algorithm-1.[3] We can see that Algorithm-3 performs about midway between the other two algorithms. However its cache size is effectively bounded as desired.[4] The average maximum cache size is 3,779 and its worst case size is only 3,828.

6. Conclusion

In this paper, we gave a new view of intelligent backtracking in the multiagent context. Dynamic backtracking was examined from this perspective. Very little research has been reported previously on the problem of storing and maintaining nogoods. The existing caching scheme defined for dynamic backtracking was argued inappropriate in the multiagent context. We showed that this caching scheme discards and forces the recomputation of nogoods for each agent repeatedly. This phenomenon exists for both sequential and parallel implementations but is exacerbated in the multiagent case. We conjecture this is because dynamic backtracking depends on a strict depth-first search order. All possible values are tried for the culprit variable before backtracking to any variable appearing in its antecedent. The AA-rule relies on this strict precedence. It cannot work so well for algorithms which impose no ordering on which variables are backtracked (as in the multiagent case).

Two new nogood caching algorithms were suggested which alleviate the problem. Neither algorithm preemptively nor unnecessarily empties the cache. Preliminary experimental evidence was given for both algorithms. The first new algorithm generated significantly fewer backtracks than dynamic backtracking but has an unrestricted space bound. The second algorithm is also better but has a fixed bound on nogood cache size. Certainly other caching schemes are also possible. Our current research seeks to identify some of these improvements.

Acknowledgments

This research was supported by the Canadian Natural Sciences and Engineering Research Council. Thanks to Norman Foo for his hospitality to me while a visiting scholar in his laboratory. Aditya Ghose and Ken Jackson provided useful feedback in the preparation of this manuscript.

References

Baker, A.B. 1995. Intelligent Backtracking on Constraint Satisfaction Problems: Experimental and Theoretical Results. Ph.D. thesis, Dept. of Computer and Information Systems, Univ. of Oregon.

Bayardo, R.J. & Miranker, D.P. 1996. A Complexity Analysis of Space-Bounded Learning Algorithms for the Constraint Satisfaction Problem. In proc. AAAI-96: 13th National Conf. on Artificial Intelligence, Portland, Oregon, 298-304.

---

3. Hence it can generate a linear O[nd] number of nogoods beyond the Max threshold.
4. In [Havens97], we argued that Algorithm-3 exhibits the same polynomial bound as Algorithm-1 for Max = n(n-1)d. This is not true but the algorithm does operate effectively with a fixed upper bound on its cache size as demonstrated here experimentally.

Dechter, R. 1992. Constraint Networks. In *Encyclopedia of Artificial Intelligence*, 2nd ed., 276-285. Wiley.

Gent, I.P.; MacIntyre, E.; Prosser, P. & Walsh, T. 1996. The Constrainedness of Search. In proc. AAAI-96: 13th National Conf. on Artificial Intelligence, Portland, Oregon.

Ginsberg, M. L. 1993. Dynamic Backtracking. *Journal of A.I. Research 1*, Morgan-Kaufmann, 25-46.

Ginsberg, M. L. & McAllester, D. 1994. GSAT and Dynamic Backtracking, In proc. 2nd Workshop on Principles and Practice of Constraint Programming, Orcas Island, WA.

Havens, W. S. 1997. NoGood Caching for MultiAgent Backtrack Search. proc. AAAI-97 Constraints and Agents Workshop, American Assn. for Artifical Intelligence national conf., Providence, Rhode Island, 1997 July 26.

Yokoo, M.; Ishida, T.; Durfee, E. H. & Kuwabara, K. 1992. Distributed Constraint Satisfaction for Formalizing Distributed Problem Solving, In proc. 12th IEEE Int. Conf. of Distributed Computing Systems, 614-621.

Yokoo, M. 1993. Dynamic Variable/Value Ordering Heuristics for Solving Large-Scale Distributed Constraint Satisfaction Problems. In proc. 12th Int. Workshop on Distributed Artificial Intelligence

Constraint-Directed Backtracking

Wanlin Pang * and Scott D. Goodwin

Department of Computer Science, University of Regina,
Regina, Saskatchewan, Canada S4P 0A2

Abstract. We propose a new backtracking algorithm called *constraint-directed backtracking (CDBT)* for solving general constraint-satisfaction problems (CSPs). CDBT searches for an assignment to variables in a variable set from a given constraint posed on that variable set and appends it to an existing partial solution, in contrast with the *naive backtracking (BT)* which searches for an assignment of one variable from its domain. In this way, CDBT has a more limited search space and it actually visits fewer nodes than BT. Like BT, CDBT can be improved by incorporating other tree seach techniques such as *backjumping* or *forward checking* and consistency techniques such as the *ω-consistency algorithm*.

1 Introduction

Backtracking (BT) ([4, 1]) is a powerful technique used for solving search problems, optimization problems, decision problems, etc., which can be stated as the general problem of determining a vector $(x_1, x_2, \ldots, x_n)$ from the Cartesian product space $D_1 \times D_2 \times \ldots \times D_n$ that maximizes the criterion function $p(x_1, x_2, \ldots, x_n)$. The idea of backtracking is to build up a vector one component at a time and to use modified criterion functions to test if the formed partial vector still has a chance of success. The strength of this method consists in its ability to cut off a subregion of the product space whenever it detects a suboptimal partial vector. The search space of the problem can be seen as an n-level complete tree, where each level corresponds to a component, the root (at the 0th level) is a nil-vector, every node at the ith ($1 \leq i < n$) level is a possible i-ary vector from $D_1 \times \ldots \times D_i$, and the leaves (at the nth level) are whole vectors including solutions. BT searches for a solution by exploring the search tree in a depth-first manner one level at a time, until it encounters a suboptimal partial vector (in which case it backtracks) or reaches a solution that is one of the leaves. In the context of using BT to solve a constraint satisfaction problem, *to maximize the criterion function* means satisfying all the constraints; *to build up a vector one component at a time* means assigning a variable with a value selected from its domain; and *to test a partial vector with modified criterion functions* means testing whether the partial vector satisfies every constraint restricted to this vector. It is wasteful to use all the given constraints merely as

---

* Current address: Institute for Information Technology, National Research Council of Canada, Ottawa, Ontario, Canada K1A 0R6

criterion functions in consistency checking. When an ordering is specified on the variable set of a CSP, the search space with respect to the variable ordering is the same n-level complete tree. Since all solutions are at the highest level of the search tree, it is possible, and intuitively more efficient, to search for a solution by exploring the search tree more than one level at a time. Constraints in CSPs can be used to direct such multi-level explorations instead of being used solely to check consistency.

The idea of constraint-directed backtracking (CDBT) is to search for assignments to variable subsets from given constraints on these variable subsets, in contrast with BT which searches for assignments to variables from their domains. The rest of this paper presents the detailed CDBT algorithm. The analytical and empirical results show that CDBT inherits the strength of BT in cutting off subregions of the search space to avoid exhaustive search. It also demonstrates that CDBT has a more limited search space than BT does, and therefore it has potential to solve general CSPs more effectively. The similarity between CDBT and BT allows CDBT to be augmented with other tree search techniques, such as backjumping [3] forward checking [6] or consistency techniques such as the ω-consistency algorithm [9] to further improve its performance.

2 Preliminaries

A *constraint satisfaction problem (CSP)* is a structure (X, D, V, S). Here, $X = \{X_1, X_2, \ldots, X_n\}$ is a set of variables that may take on values from a set of domains $D = \{D_1, D_2, \ldots, D_n\}$, and $V = \{V_1, V_2, \ldots, V_m\}^2$ is a family of ordered subsets of X called *constraint schemes*. Each $V_i = \{X_{i_1}, X_{i_2}, \ldots, X_{i_{r_i}}\}$ is associated with a set of tuples $S_i \subseteq D_{i_1} \times D_{i_2} \times \ldots \times D_{i_{r_i}}$ called *constraint instance*, and $S = \{S_1, S_2, \ldots, S_m\}$ is a family of such constraint instances. Together, a pair (V_i, S_i) is a *constraint* which permits the variables in V_i to take only value combinations in S_i.

Let $V_K = \{X_{k_1}, \ldots, X_{k_l}\}$ be a subset of X. An l-tuple $(x_{k_1}, \ldots, x_{k_l})$ from $D_{k_1} \times \ldots \times D_{k_l}$ is called an *instantiation* of variables in V_K. An instantiation is said to be *consistent* if it satisfies all the constraints restricted in V_K. An consistent instantiation of all variables in X is a *solution*. The task of solving a CSP is to find one or all solutions. The set of all solution is denoted by $\rho(X)$.

We will use some conventional relational operators. Let $C_i = (V_i, S_i)$ and $C_j = (V_j, S_j)$ be two constraints, $t_i \in S_i$ and $t_j \in S_j$ two tuples, and V_h a subset of V_i. The *projection* of t_i on V_h, denoted by $t_i[V_h]$, is a tuple consisting of only the components of t_i that correspond to variables in V_h. The projection of S_i on V_h is a set of tuples denoted by $\Pi_{V_h}(S_i)$, and the projection of C_i on V_h is a constraint denoted by $\Pi_{V_h}(C_i) = (V_h, \Pi_{V_h}(S_i))$. We say that t_i and t_j are *compatible* if $t_i[V_i \cap V_j] = t_j[V_i \cap V_j]$. If t_i and t_j are compatible, the *join* of t_i and t_j, denoted by $t_i \bowtie t_j$, is a tuple such that $(t_i \bowtie t_j)[V_i] = t_i$ and $(t_i \bowtie t_j)[V_j] = t_j$.

---

[2] Throughout this paper, we assume that $\forall i, j (V_i \in V \wedge V_j \in V \wedge i \neq j \Rightarrow V_i \not\subseteq V_j \wedge V_j \not\subseteq V_i)$.

Let V_I and V_J be two subsets of X. A subset of constraint schemes $vks(V_I, V_J) = \{V_h \in V | V_h \subseteq V_I \cup V_J\}$ is called the *variable check-set of V_I and V_J*. Accordingly, a subset of constraints $cks(V_I, V_J) = \{C_h = (V_h, S_h) \in C | V_h \in vks(V_I, V_J)\}$ is called the *constraint check-set of V_I and V_J*. We may also use $vks(V_I \cup V_J)$ and $cks(V_I \cup V_J)$ to denote $vks(V_I, V_J)$ and $cks(V_I, V_J)$. Let tuple t_I be an instantiation of variables in V_I. An *extension of t_I to variables in $V_I \cup V_J$* is a joined tuple $t_I \bowtie t_J$, where t_J is an instantiation of variables in V_J, and t_I and t_J are compatible. The tuple $t_I \bowtie t_J$ is said to be a *consistent extension of t_I* if $t_I \bowtie t_J$ is consistent, that is, it satisfies all constrains in $cks(V_I, V_J)$.

3 Constraint-Directed Backtracking Algorithm

Given a CSP $P = (X, D, V, S)$, and let $C = \{C_i = (V_i, S_i) | V_i \in V, S_i \in S\}$ be a set of constraints. The task is to find a solution if one exists, or to report that the problem is unsatisfiable.

The CDBT algorithm consists of two recursive functions, *forward* and *goback*. Suppose that we have already found a consistent instantiation tup_I of variables in $V_{k_1}, V_{k_2}, \ldots, V_{k_i}$ (for simplicity, we rename them $V_1, V_2, \ldots, V_i$ and denote $\cup_{j=1}^{i} V_j$ by V_I), function *forward* extends this instantiation by appending to it an instantiation of variables in a selected variable set on which there exists a constraint. It first selects[3] a constraint, say, $C_{i+1} = (V_{i+1}, S_{i+1})$, from the given constraint set C such that C_{i+1} has not been selected before, then it chooses a tuple tup from S_{i+1}^* as an instantiation of variables in V_{i+1} and joins tup and tup_I to form a new tuple tup_{I+1}, which is tested to see if it is consistent. Notice that the subset S_{i+1}^* contains those tuples in S_{i+1} that are compatible with tup_I. If tup_{I+1} is consistent, then *forward* is called recursively to extend tup_{I+1}; otherwise, another tuple from S_{i+1}^* is tried. If no tuples are left in S_{i+1}^*, *goback* is called to re-instantiate variables in variable set V_i.

Function *goback* tries to re-instantiate variables in V_i and to form another consistent instantiation of variables in $V_I = \cup_{j=1}^{i} V_j$. It first chooses another tuple from S_i^* and forms a new tuple tup_I which is tested to see if it is consistent. If tup_I is consistent, then *forward* is called to extend tup_I; otherwise, another tuple from S_i^* is tried. If S_i^* is empty, then *goback* is called recursively to re-instantiate variables in variable set V_{i-1}.

Functions *forward* and *goback* are defined as follows:

forward(P, V_I, tup_I)

1. **begin**
2.   **if** $|V_I| = n$ **then return** tup_I;
3.   select $C_{i+1} = (V_{i+1}, S_{i+1})$ from C s.t. $V_{i+1} \not\subseteq V_I$;
4. $cks(V_{I+1}) \leftarrow \{C_h | C_h \in C, V_h \neq V_{i+1}, V_h \not\subseteq V_I, V_h \subset V_{I+1}\}$;
5. $S_{i+1}^* \leftarrow \{tup | tup \in S_{i+1}, tup[V_I \cap V_{i+1}] = tup_I[V_I \cap V_{i+1}]\}$;

---

[3] We assume a deterministic selection procedure that always selects the same constraint from the same constraint subset.

6.   **while** $S_{i+1}^* \neq \emptyset$ **do**
7. $tup \leftarrow$ one tuple taken from S_{i+1}^*;
8. $tup_{I+1} \leftarrow tup_I \bowtie tup$;
9.   **if** $test(tup_{I+1}, cks(V_{I+1}))$ **then return** $forward(\mathbb{P}, V_{I+1}, tup_{I+1})$;
10.   **end while**
11.   **return** $goback(\mathbb{P}, V_I, tup_I)$;
12. **end**

$goback(\mathbb{P}, V_I, tup_I)$

1. **begin**
2.   **if** $|V_I| = 0$ **then return** *unsatisfiable*;
3.   **while** $S_i^* \neq \emptyset$ **do**
4. $tup \leftarrow$ one tuple taken from S_i^*;
5. $tup_I \leftarrow tup_{I-1} \bowtie tup$;
6.   **if** $test(tup_I, cks(V_I))$ **then return** $forward(\mathbb{P}, V_I, tup_I)$;
7.   **end while**
8.   **return** $goback(\mathbb{P}, V_{I-1}, tup_{I-1})$;
9. **end**

Function $test(tup_I, cks(V_I))$ returns *true* if tuple tup_I satisfies all the constraints in $cks(V_I)$ and *false* otherwise. It is defined as follows:

$test(tup_I, cks(V_I))$

1. **begin**
2.   **for** each $C_h = (V_h, S_h)$ in $cks(V_I)$ **do**
3.   **if** $tup_I[V_h] \notin S_h$ **then return** *false*;
4.   **return** *true*;
5. **end**

To find a solution to a given $\mathbb{P} = (X, D, V, S)$, we simply call $forward(\mathbb{P}, \emptyset, \emptyset)$.

Example. We consider the 4-queens problem, which can be formulated as a binary CSP with four variables $X = \{X_1, X_2, X_3, X_4\}$. Each variable has a domain $\{1, 2, 3, 4\}$ and there are six constraints $C = \{C_{12}, C_{13}, C_{14}, C_{23}, C_{24}, C_{34}\}$, where $V_{12} = \{X_1, X_2\}$, $V_{13} = \{X_1, X_3\}$, $V_{14} = \{X_1, X_4\}$, $V_{23} = \{X_2, X_3\}$, $V_{24} = \{X_2, X_4\}$, $V_{34} = \{X_3, X_4\}$; $S_{12} = S_{23} = S_{34} = \{(13), (14), (24), (31), (41), (42)\}$, $S_{13} = S_{24} = \{(12), (14), (21), (23), (32), (34), (42), (43)\}$, and $S_{14} = \{(12), (13), (21), (23), (24), (31), (32), (34), (42), (43)\}$.

Suppose that CDBT chooses constraints in the order C_{12}, C_{23}, C_{34} in function *forward* and backtracks to the most recently instantiated variable set. It first calls $forward(\mathbb{P}, \emptyset, \emptyset)$.

Function *forward* selects C_{12} from C, takes $tup_{12} = (13)$ from $S_{12}^* = S_{12}$ as an instantiation of X_1 and X_2, which is consistent since $cks(V_{12})$ is empty. Then $forward(\mathbb{P}, V_{12}, (13))$ is called to extend this partial assignment.

This time Function *forward* selects C_{23} in C, then V_{I+1} is $\{V_{12}, V_{23}\}$, $cks(V_{123})$ is $\{C_{13}\}$, and S_{23}^* is $\{(31)\}$. The pair (31) in S_{23}^* is taken as an instantiation of X_2 and X_3. By joining (13) and (31), it has a tuple (131) which is tested but does not satisfy C_{13} in $cks(V_{123})$, so it tries to chooses another pair in S_{23}^*. Since S_{23}^* is empty, $goback(\mathbb{P}, V_{12}, (13))$ is called to re-instantiate variables in V_{12}.

Function *goback* takes another pair (14) from S_{12}^* as a new instantiation of X_1 and X_2. Since it is consistent, $forward(\mathbb{P}, V_{12}, (14))$ is called to extend this partial solution.

This process repeats until CDBT finds the first solution (2413). It then reports the solution and stops. The process of *forward* and *goback* is illustrated by a *backtrack tree* in Figure 1, where up-down arrows indicate forward moves and down-up arrows backward moves. The inner nodes of the backtrack tree correspond to consistent partial assignments and the leaves correspond to inconsistent assignments except for the last one which is a solution (2413).

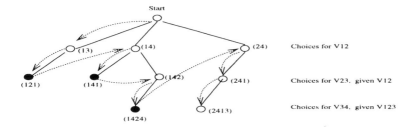

Fig. 1. A CDBT backtrack tree for the 4-queens problem

4 Correctness of CDBT

A CSP algorithm is correct [7] if it is sound, complete, and it terminates. An algorithm is sound if every solution returned by it is a solution. An algorithm is complete if every solution can be found by it.

We consider the situation where CDBT is used repeatedly to find all solutions; that is, at the second line of *forward*, instead of *returning* a solution, it outputs a solution and continues to call *goback* to find another one, until it stops at the second line of *goback*.

When CDBT is used to solve a CSP (X, D, V, S), it selects a constraint subset $C' = \{C_{k_1}, C_{k_2}, \ldots, C_{k_l}\}$ and searches for an assignment to variables in V_{k_i} from S_{k_i}. For the ordered subset of constraint schemes $\{V_{k_1}, V_{k_2}, \ldots, V_{k_l}\}$ such that $\cup_{j=1}^{l} V_{k_j} = X$, we construct an l-level search tree, each level corresponds to a variable set, the root (at the 0th level) corresponds to a nil-assignment, each node at the first level is a tuple from $S_{k_1}^* = S_{k_1}$, and each node at the ith $(i = 2, \ldots, l)$ level is a tuple $tup_I = tup_{I-1} \bowtie tup_i$ where tup_{I-1} is the label of the parent node and $tup_i \in S_{k_i}^*$. The tree can be seen as a search space of CDBT with respect to the selected constraint subset. CDBT searches for a solution by systematically exploring the search tree in the depth-first manner one level at a time and prunes the tree whenever an inconsistent node is reached. Therefore, CDBT only explores a subtree induced by the nodes visited by CDBT during *forward* and *goback*. This subtree is called a *CDBT backtrack tree*.

A node is called a *consistent node* if it corresponds to a consistent instantiation of variables involved; otherwise, it is *inconsistent*.

For proving the correctness of CDBT, we need a few technical lemmas, which have been proved in [8].

Lemma 1. *If a node is inconsistent, then any of its child nodes is inconsistent.*

Lemma 2. *If a node at the ith level ($i \neq l$) is consistent, then its child nodes includes all its consistent extensions.*

Lemma 3. *For any consistent instantiation tup_I of variables in V_I, there is a node tup_I at the ith level in the search tree.*

Lemma 4. *If CDBT visits a consistent node in the search tree, then it visits all its child nodes.*

Lemma 5. *CDBT visits all the consistent nodes in the search tree.*

Lemma 6. *Any inner node of a CDBT backtrack tree is a consistent node. Any leaf is either an inconsistent node or a solution.*

Theorem 7. *The CDBT algorithm is correct.*

Proof: We prove that CDBT is sound, complete, and it terminates. If CDBT outputs a whole assignment, then every inner node on the path from the root to the last visited node is consistent. In particular, the parent node of the last node is consistent, and *test* guarantees that this whole assignment is a consistent extension of its parent node, so it is a solution. This proves the soundness.

The completeness follows directly from Lemma 5. CDBT visits all consistent nodes which include all solutions.

The size of the search tree is limited and since CDBT never visits any nodes twice, it terminates. □

5 Comparison with BT

It is not difficult to see that CDBT has a search space which is a partial subtree of the BT search space. In this section, we show that CDBT actually visits fewer nodes in its search space; that is, the size of CDBT backtrack tree is less than the size of BT backtrack tree. We also describe our test of CDBT and BT on the n-queens problem.

The worst-case complexity of backtracking algorithms is exponential in the size of the problem, and it is difficult to estimate the average cost since the performance of backtracking algorithms depends heavily on the problem being solved. To compare different backtracking algorithms, the number of nodes in the backtrack tree and the number of consistency checks are usually used as a standard measure of efficiency [7].

As an example, when BT and CDBT are used to find the first solution to the 4-queens problem with the variable ordering X_1, X_2, X_3, X_4 and the constraint ordering C_{12}, C_{23}, C_{34}, the nodes visited by BT is all the nodes in the BT backtrack tree shown in Figure 2, whereas CDBT visits only some of them (see Figure 1).

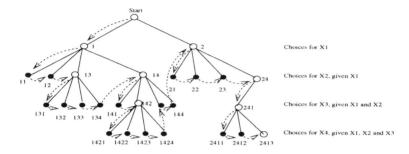

Fig. 2. A BT backtrack tree for the 4-queens problem

In general, for a variable ordering $X_1, X_2, \ldots, X_n$, there is a constraint ordering $C_{k_1}, C_{k_2}, \ldots, C_{k_l}$, such that for $X_p \in V_{k_i}$ and $X_q \in V_{k_j}$, if $V_{k_i} < V_{k_j}$ then $X_p < X_q$. Considering CDBT with the constraint ordering, BT and its search space with respect to the variable ordering, we have:

Theorem 8. *BT visits every consistent node that CDBT visits.*

Proof: It is known that BT visits all consistent nodes and all the child nodes of every consistent node in its search space. We showed that CDBT visits all consistent nodes in CDBT search space. Since every consistent node in CDBT search space is also a consistent node in BT search space, BT visits all consistent nodes that CDBT visits. □

In general, there is no guarantee that every inconsistent node visited by CDBT will be visited by BT. For a consistent node tup_I, CDBT visits its child node $tup_I \bowtie tup_{i+1}$ where $tup_{i+1} = (x_{k_1}, \ldots, x_{k_r}) \in S_{i+1}^*$. BT will not visit node $tup_I \bowtie tup_{i+1}$ if $tup_I \bowtie (x_{k_1}, \ldots, x_{k_j})$ is already inconsistent for $j < r$. However, if CDBT uses a simple constraint selection strategy (line 3 of *forward*), say, it always selects a $C_{i+1} = (V_{i+1}, S_{i+1})$ such that $V_I \cap V_{i+1}$ is maximal, then every node visited by CDBT will be visited by BT. In this case, if tup_I is consistent then every nodes $tup_I \bowtie (x_{k_1}, \ldots, x_{k_j})$ is consistent for all $j < r$, thus will be visited by BT. Node $tup_I \bowtie tup_{i+1}$ will be visited by BT even if it is not consistent, since its parent node is consistent.

For an empirical study, we tested CDBT on the *n-queens* problem, where n varies from 3 to 10, and compared it to a BT program. The n-queens problem is chosen simply because there is a Prolog program of BT on the n-queens available in [11]. We implemented the basic CDBT for the n-queens problem, where the variable pairs $\{V_{n-1,n}, V_{n-2,n-1}, \ldots, V_{2,1}\}$ are chosen in function *forward* and it backtracks to the most recently instantiated variable pair when a dead-end occurs. The order of variables to be instantiated and the order of values to be chosen are the same for both programs, so that they give the same output. We first use the programs to find the first solution and then to find all solutions. The number of nodes visited and the number of consistency checks are recorded and summarized in Table 1. The table shows that the number of nodes and checks recorded from CDBT is significantly smaller than that from BT.

no. of	First Solution				All Solutions				
var-	BT		CDBT		no. of	BT		CDBT	
ables	nodes	checks	nodes	checks	solutions	nodes	checks	nodes	checks
3	18	17	4	2	0	18	17	4	2
4	26	31	9	7	2	68	84	22	18
5	15	22	6	8	10	270	453	104	132
6	171	314	89	145	4	918	1754	488	820
7	42	87	21	46	40	3864	8791	2180	4478
8	876	2205	564	1330	92	16456	42296	10266	24570
9	333	935	229	603	352	75546	216149	49856	134082
10	975	2987	692	2013	724	355390	1115840	249976	743716

Table 1. The result of solving n-queens problem with BT and CDBT

Notice that we only compared CDBT with naive BT, not with other advanced BT techniques, such as BJ, CBJ, or FC. Since CDBT and BT share a similar style of instantiating and re-instantiating variables, these techniques can be incorporated into CDBT [8]. In addition, CDBT's advantages are more pronounced when it is used to solve general CSPs. Unfortunately, we did not find experimental data of naive backtrack or other BT programs on general CSPs.

6 CDBT vs. Decomposition Methods

Decomposition techniques attempt to find solutions more efficiently by decomposing a CSP into several simply-connected sub-CSPs. Each sub-CSP is solved separately and then a new CSP is formed based on connections among these sub-CSPs. The original variable set involved in each sub-CSP is taken as one singleton variable in the new CSP. In a way that CDBT also treats a selected V_i as a singleton variable, CDBT can be seen as a decomposition method. In this section, we compare CDBT with two well-known decomposition methods, the *Tree Clustering Scheme* (TC) [2] and the *Hinge Decomposition Scheme* (HD) [5].

To see the similarity and the difference among them, we first give an uniform description of decomposition methods.

Let (X, D, V, S) be a CSP, let Ψ be a family of subset of X. $\Psi = \{\Psi_1, \Psi_2, \ldots, \Psi_p\}$, such that $\Psi_i \subseteq X$ for $1 \leq i \leq p$ and $\cup_{i=1}^{p} \Psi_i = X$, and let Φ be a family of subsets of V, $\Phi = \{\Phi_1, \Phi_2, \ldots, \Phi_p\}$, such that $\Phi_i = \{V_k \in V | V_k \subseteq \Psi_i\}$ for $1 \leq i \leq p$.

In general, a decomposition algorithm works as follows:

1. find a Ψ and construct a graph $G = (\Psi, E^{\Psi})$ whose nodes are those $\Psi_i \in \Psi$, and if $\Psi_i \cap \Psi_j \neq \emptyset$ then there exists in G a chain $\Psi_i = \Psi_{p_1}, \Psi_{p_2}, \ldots, \Psi_{p_q} = \Psi_j$ such that $(\Psi_{p_k}, \Psi_{p_{k+1}}) \in E^{\Psi}$ and $\Psi_i \cap \Psi_j \subseteq \Psi_{p_k} \cap \Psi_{p_{k+1}}$ for all $1 \leq k < q$;
2. for each $\Psi_i \in \Psi$, construct a sub-CSP $(\Psi_i, D^{\Psi_i}, \Phi_i, S^{\Phi_i})$, where $\Psi_i \subseteq X$ is a subset of variables, $D_i^{\Psi} \subseteq D$ is a set of domains of variables in Ψ_i, $\Phi_i \subseteq V$ is a subset of constraint schemes, and $S_i^{\Phi} \subseteq S$ is a subset of relations;
3. for each sub-CSP related to Ψ_i, use any method to find all its solutions $\rho(\Psi_i)$;
4. form a new CSP $(\Psi, \Gamma, E^{\Psi}, R^{\Psi})$, where each $\Psi_i \in \Psi$ is considered a singleton variable, Γ is a set of $\rho(\Psi_i)$ that is considered a domain for Ψ_i, E^{Ψ} is a set of constraint schemes that are edges of the constraint graph G, and R^{Ψ} is a set of relations $\{\rho(\Psi_i) \bowtie \rho(\Psi_i) | (\Psi_i, \Psi_j) \in E^{\Psi}\}$;
5. solve the new CSP with any method (usually, search).

Most decomposition methods require that $G = (\Psi, E^{\Psi})$ should be a tree so that a solution to the new CSP $(\Psi, \Gamma, E^{\Psi}, R^{\Psi})$ can be found without backtracking. This is always feasible, since choosing $\Psi = \{\{X\}\}$ we have a tree-structured graph $G = (\{X\}, \emptyset)$ with only one node. Under the premise that $G = (\Psi, E^{\Psi})$ is a tree, those techniques try to find a Ψ such that $max_{i=1}^p\{|\Psi_i|\}$ is minimal, so that the time and space complexity of finding all solutions to each sub-CSP $(\Psi_i, D^{\Psi_i}, \Phi_i, S^{\Phi_i})$ can be bounded somehow. However, $max_{i=1}^p\{|\Psi_i|\}$ depends on the constraint structure of the CSP, and it is still an open question if the minimal one can be found in polynomial time. Different methods mainly differ in that which Ψ is chosen. For instance, TC chooses a set of maximal cliques of the triangulated primal graph as Ψ, whereas HD chooses a set of minimal hinges as Ψ.

CDBT can be seen as a decomposition method in which each Ψ_i is an existing constraint scheme V_{k_i}. It does not require that graph $G = (\Psi, E^{\Psi})$ be a tree, so it cannot guarantee that the newly formed CSP $(\Psi, \Gamma, E^{\Psi}, R^{\Psi})$ can be solved without backtracking. However, for each $\Psi_i = V_{k_i}$, all solutions to each sub-CSP $(\Psi_i, D^{\Psi_i}, \Phi_i, S^{\Phi_i})$ is given, i.e., $\rho(\Psi_i) = S_{k_i}$. Consequently, no effort is needed to solve them.

For both TC and HD schemes, in the case that the cardinality of maximal clique or minimal hinge is huge, (e.g., it is close to $|X|$ for hard 3SAT problems), finding all solutions to the subproblems is quite inefficient and unnecessary. For those CSPs (e.g., n-queens problem) with only one maximal clique or only one minimal hinge (i.e., the whole variable set X), both TC and HD degenerate into whichever method that is used in the third step and lose all advantage. On the one hand, CDBT is a general method that can be applied to any kind of problems without losing its advantage. On the other hand, the join tree or the hinge tree may serve as a constraint ordering heuristics for selecting constraints in function *forward* so that backtracking (if it has to backtrack) can be limited within certain areas of the search space. Without finding all solutions to subproblems, CDBT can be modified to perform tree search at different level and may be implemented parallelly [8].

7 Conclusions

We presented a new backtracking algorithm CDBT for solving general constraint-satisfaction problems. CDBT searches for a solution in a more limited search space, and is potentially more effective than BT. In addition, combining other tree search methods [10] with CDBT can lead to further improvements in efficiency. Variants of the CDBT algorithm augmented with some of these techniques are given in [8].

The CDBT algorithm also inherits some undesirable aspects of BT such as the *thrashing* problem. Local consistency for general CSPs needs to be considered in order to eliminate some inconsistent value combinations. Another issue is that with different constraint selection strategies CDBT selects different constraint subsets which may significantly affect its performance. Constraint selection is related to the constraint structure, that is, which variables may be constrained by which other variables. The detailed discusseion on constraint structure and local consistencies in general CSPs and how to use them to improve CDBT can be found in [8].

References

1. J. R. Bitner and E. M. Reingold. Backtrack programming techniques. *Communications of the ACM*, 18(11):651–656, 1975.
2. R. Dechter and J. Pearl. Tree clustering for constraint networks. *Artificial Intelligence*, 38:353–366, 1989.
3. J. Gaschnig. A general backtrack algorithm that eliminates most redundant tests. In *Proceedings of IJCAI-77*, page 457, Cambridge, MA, 1977.
4. S. W. Golomb and L. D. Baumert. Backtrack programming. *Journal of the ACM*, 12(4):516–524, 1965.
5. M. Gyssens, P. G. Jeavons, and D. A. Cohen. Decomposing constraint satisfaction problems using database techniques. *Artificial Intelligence*, 66:57–89, 1994.
6. R. Haralick and G. Elliott. Increasing tree search efficiency for constraint satisfaction problems. *Artificial Intelligence*, 14:263–313, 1980.
7. G. Kondrak and P. van Beek. A theoretical evaluation of selected backtracking algorithms. In *Proceedings of IJCAI-95*, pages 541–547, Montreal, Canada, 1995.
8. W. Pang. *Constraint-Directed Approach for Analyzing and Solving General Constraint Satisfaction Problems*. PhD thesis, University of Regina, Saskatchewan, Canada, 1997.
9. W. Pang and S. D. Goodwin. A revised sufficient condition for backtrack-free search. In *Proceedings of 10th Florida AI Research Symposium*, pages 52–56, Daytona Beach, FL, May 1997.
10. P. Prosser. Hybrid algorithms for the constrain satisfaction problem. *Computational Intelligence*, 9(3):268–299, 1993.
11. E. Tsang. *Foundations of Constraint Satisfaction*. Academic Press, San Diego, CA, 1993.

Applied Partial Constraint Satisfaction Using Weighted Iterative Repair

JohnThornton[1] and Abdul Sattar[2]

[1] School of Information Technology, Griffith University Gold Coast,
Parklands Drive, Southport, Qld 4215
e-mail: j.thornton@eas.gu.edu.au

[2] School of Computing and Information Technology, Griffith University,
Kessels Road, Nathan, Qld, 4111
email: sattar@cit.gu.edu.au

Abstract. Many real-world constraint satisfaction problems (CSPs) can be over-constrained or too large to solve using a standard constructive/ backtracking approach. Instead, faster heuristic techniques have been proposed that perform a partial search of all possible solutions using an iterative repair or hill-climbing approach. The main problem with such approaches is that they can become stuck in local minima. Consequently, various strategies or *meta-heuristics* have been developed to escape from local minima. This paper investigates the application of one such meta-heuristic, *weighted iterative repair*, to solving a real-world problem of scheduling nurses at an Australian hospital. Weighted iterative repair has already proved successful in solving various binary CSPs. The current research extends this work by looking at a non-binary problem formulation, and partial constraint satisfaction involving hard and soft constraints. This has lead to the development of a *soft constraint heuristic* to improve the level of soft constraint optimisation and an extension of the original weighted iterative repair that avoids certain forms of cyclic behaviour. It is also demonstrated that weighted iterative repair can learn from repeatedly solving the same problem. and that restarting the algorithm on the same problem can result in faster execution times. The overall results show that weighted iterative repair finds better quality solutions than a standard iterative repair, whilst approaching near optimal solutions in less time than an alternative integer programming approach.

1 Introduction

A constraint satisfaction problem (CSP) consists of a set of variables, $v_i \in V$, each with a domain of possible values D_i, and a set of constraints between variables. A CSP solution is an assignment of variable values which satisfy *all* the problem constraints [12]. However, many real-world CSPs are either too large to be solved completely, or are over-constrained so that a solution that satisfies all constraints is not possible. Such problems can be treated as *partial constraint satisfaction problems* (PCSPs), as only a partial subset of constraints can be or are satisfied in a solution [5]. The objective of partial constraint satisfaction is to solve a problem that is *as close as possible* to the original CSP. The distance between problems can be measured using a *constraint hierarchy* [2], which defines weights or costs for constraint violations and categorises constraints as either *hard* (having to be satisfied) or *soft* (can be violated).

The presence of hard and soft constraints and of various levels of constraint weighting is typical of many large, over-constrained real-world scheduling problems. Examples include job-shop scheduling [4], university timetabling [6], telescope scheduling [8] and nurse rostering [3]. Such problems can be solved using standard constructive/backtracking techniques, if selected constraints are first relaxed so the problem is no longer over-constrained [4,3]. The difficulty here is recognising which constraints to relax (as some may be relaxed unnecessarily). Freuder and Wallace [5] propose a branch and bound algorithm for PCSPs which parallels the constructive approach but is able to find an optimum level of constraint relaxation. Alternatively, PCSPs can be expressed as optimisation problems and solved using integer and goal programming techniques [13]. However, in the worst case, all the above techniques use exponential time algorithms, and as problem size increases their use becomes more impractical.

Recent studies have indicated that heuristic algorithms can efficiently find optimal solutions to PCSPs [12,8]. Interest has focused on iterative repair techniques, which start with a complete but inconsistent solution and attempt to improve or repair the solution by changing individual variable assignments. The main problem with iterative repair is that it can become 'stuck' on a local optimum solution and fail to find the global optimum. For this reason several *meta-heuristic* schemes have been proposed to guide iterative repair beyond local minimum solutions. These include randomising variable assignments [1], restarting the repair from different positions [9], and adding weights to violated constraints until a local minimum is exceeded [9,10]. Of these techniques, constraint weighting has had the greater success in solving various classical binary constraint problems, and particularly in solving Conjunctive Normal Form (CNF) satisfiability problems (see [9] and [10]).

The current research introduces an independently developed constraint weighting algorithm (*weighted iterative repair*) that parallels the work of Morris [9] and Selman and Kautz [10]. The paper extends earlier research by looking at a real-world over-constrained problem with non-binary constraints, and introduces a *soft constraint* heuristic to handle hard and soft constraints, and a modified weighting heuristic that avoids certain types of cyclic behaviour. Experimentation has also revealed the heuristic has a limited learning ability which can be exploited by restarting a problem using previously learned weightings. The weighted iterative repair is tested against a standard iterative repair algorithm using a set of real-world nurse rostering problems. In addition, an integer programming application is used to *optimally* solve the rostering problems, and so provide an absolute standard from which the quality of other solutions can be evaluated.

The next section gives an introduction to the algorithms developed in the study. Section 3 describes the nurse rostering problem and details the experimental methods used to evaluate the algorithms. Section 4 gives the results of comparisons between algorithms and section 5 presents a discussion of these results. Finally, section 6 presents the conclusions.

2 Algorithms

2.1 Basic Iterative Repair

The approach of iterative repair is to improve on an existing inconsistent solution by selectively changing variable assignments until a consistent solution or a terminating condition is reached. In the basic iterative repair used in the study, each variable $v_i \in V$ is sequentially selected and all elements x in the domain D_i of v_i are tried in the solution S. The cost of S for each new x value is calculated by summing the current constraint violations, with the lowest cost x finally being assigned to v_i. If there is more than one lowest cost value then x is chosen randomly from the candidates. The domain values for the next variable are then tried and the process continues until no further improvement in S is possible. If S has not reached the desired cost, the algorithm is restarted with a different variable ordering, until a maximum number of restarts have occurred or a desired cost solution is reached.

The basic iterative repair algorithm can be categorised as a *local search* or a *cyclic descent* algorithm [7], and is similar to Johnson and Minton's min-conflicts heuristic [8], except that *hard* and *soft non-binary* constraints are considered. The hard and soft constraints are initially distinguished by being given different weights or penalties when calculating the cost of S. Weights are set so that the sum of all possible soft constraint violations cannot exceed the cost of a single hard constraint violation. This reflects the priority that the hard constraints *must* be satisfied.

2.2 Weighted Iterative Repair

The fundamental problem with a standard iterative repair is that it tends to get `stuck' in non-optimal solutions. This occurs when a superior solution can only be reached through a series of moves that involve at least one *cost-increasing* move. One strategy to exceed a local minimum is to restart the algorithm at a new position each time it gets stuck (as in section 2.1). However, given a complicated cost surface, this can be a slow process and information from previous searches is lost (see [9]). Other strategies proposed to escape local minima include randomised move selection (as in simulated annealing [1]) and the selection of the best move that does not repeat a previous move (as in tabu search [6]). Both these approaches are complete, but they are also relatively slow. A more recently proposed strategy is to change the shape of the cost surface by dynamically increasing the weights of any violated constraints [9]. Whilst not complete, this approach has had promising results on various classical and random binary CSP's. The weighted iterative repair used in the current paper is an independently developed adaptation of earlier weighting algorithms, specifically designed to solve partial constraint satisfaction problems with hard and soft constraints. The basic iterative repair described in section 2.1 is adapted so that each time a local minimum is encountered, a fixed quantity is added to the weight of each violated constraint (see fig 1). This changes the cost of the current solution until another *neighbouring* solution becomes preferred and the algorithm moves on. In effect, by recording weights against constraints the algorithm is *learning* which constraints are hardest to satisfy. These difficult constraints tend to be become satisfied so the algorithm finds spaces where there is more freedom of movement. If a particular search space is unpromising, the combined weights of the newly violated constraints will eventually cause a previously "difficult" constraint to become violated and a new area will be explored.

The Soft Constraint Heuristic. As weighted iterative repair is continually changing constraint weights, any initial weight settings will soon become blurred and disappear. This can result in soft constraints acquiring equal or greater weighting than hard constraints and the unnecessary exploration of infeasible solutions. One answer is to only increment the weights of hard constraints, but this can mean little or no attempt is made to optimise the soft constraints. This is especially the case in problems where feasible solutions are difficult to find and little movement is possible to optimise soft constraints. To remedy this behaviour a *soft constraint heuristic* is proposed (see fig 1). The heuristic causes an iterative repair to consider all the moves that *reduce* the hard constraint cost and to accept the move that has the best soft constraint cost. This means the best overall cost assignment is not necessarily chosen. Instead, assignments are selected that improve hard constraint violations at the *least cost* to the soft constraints.

```
procedure WeightedIterativeRepair
begin
    StuckCounter ← 0, set variables to initial assignments
    while weighted cost of current state > DesiredCost do
        if current state is not a local minima then
            Improve ← False
            for each variable
                Moves ← select moves that reduce the hard constraint cost
                SoftMoves ← select moves that do not increase the total cost
                if Moves not empty then
                    perform move from Moves that has least soft constraint cost
                    Improve ← True
                else perform move from SoftMoves that has the least total cost
            end for
        else if Improve = True then
            increase weights of all violated hard constraints
            StuckCounter ← StuckCounter + 1
        else
            increase weight of hard constraint with greatest weighted violation
            StuckCounter ← StuckCounter + 1
        if StuckCounter > MaxStucks then
            reset variables to initial assignments
    end while
end
```

Fig. 1. The Weighted Iterative Repair Algorithm

Avoiding Cyclic Weight Escalation. Morris [9] demonstrated that cyclic behaviour is theoretically possible in weighted iterative repair giving an example of a Boolean Satisfiability problem with four variables, w, x, y, z, and the clause $w \lor x \lor y \lor z$ together with the 12 clauses:

$$\neg w \lor x, \neg w \lor y, \neg w \lor z, \neg x \lor w \; \neg x \lor y, \neg x \lor z,$$
$$\neg y \lor w, \neg y \lor x, \neg y \lor z, \neg z \lor w, \neg z \lor x, \neg z \lor y$$

The clauses have a single solution where all variables are *true*. Given all variables start as *false*, a weighted iterative repair will continually try each variable as *true* but will never arrive at a situation where two or more variables are *true* because two *true* instantiations are always more expensive than one. In more general problems, a group of interrelated constraints can have their weights repeatedly incremented before a better solution is found, where the weighting of a *single* constraint would have broken the deadlock immediately. A heuristic which solves both of these problems is to increment the weights of all violated constraints the *first time* a local minimum is encountered (see fig 1). Then, if no reduced cost move is found only the highest weighted constraint is incremented (breaking ties randomly).

3 Experimental Study

The algorithms described in the previous section were evaluated on a real-world problem of rostering nurses in an Australian public hospital. The problem was chosen firstly because it represents a practical, complex, over-constrained problem, and secondly because an optimal integer programming algorithm already exists for the problem [13]. The complexity of the problem means a simplistic heuristic approach is inadequate, while the availability of optimal problem solutions provides a standard by which more sophisticated heuristics can be evaluated.

3.1 Nurse Rostering

Nurse rostering can be considered as a *partial constraint satisfaction problem*. The task is to find a consistent allocation of shift values, for a group of nurses, over a fixed period of time, that satisfy *as many as possible* of a set of rostering constraints. There are two basic types of constraints: (i) *schedule constraints* defining acceptable shift combinations for each nurse and (ii) *staff constraints* defining acceptable overall staffing levels for each day in the roster. Research into nurse rostering has focused on optimising integer programming solutions [13], and non-optimal heuristic solutions [7]. More recent attention has been placed on constraint programming with selective constraint relaxation [3]. The iterative repair approach developed in the current study most closely resembles the heuristic *coordinate cyclic descent algorithm* for nurse rostering first proposed by Miller *et al* [7]. For this reason it was decided to follow Miller's modelling of the problem. This involves considering each nurse as a variable, with the variable domain being the set of schedules that the nurse is able to work

[13,7]. The task is then to select a schedule from the set of all possible schedules for each nurse such that the best possible roster is generated (fig 2).

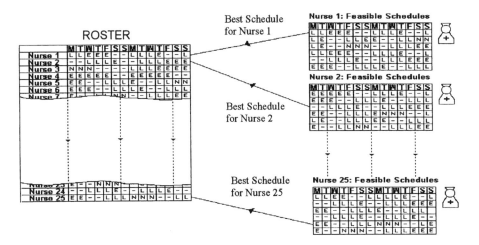

Fig. 2. The Possible Schedule Selection Approach to Rostering

In the current problem, a 30 bed medical ward is considered, employing between 25 to 37 nurses in each roster. There are three shift values covering a 24-hour period (an early, late and night shift) and each roster lasts 14 days. Nurses are allowed to request particular shifts or days off, with part-time *and* full-time staff included in the roster. Staff are further divided into five levels of seniority with maximum, minimum and desired staff constraints defined for each day of the roster and for each seniority level of nurse. Hard schedule constraints are defined specifying the type of schedule each nurse can work. These constraints are then used in a separate *schedule generation program* which builds all possible schedules for each nurse.

In addition, soft schedule constraints are defined to express which schedules a nurse would *prefer* to work. Based on interviews with nursing staff, weights were defined for each level of deviation for each constraint, and two roster quality measures were developed. The first equals the sum of all hard staff constraint violations for a roster, and the second equals the sum of all soft schedule constraint violations for a roster.

3.2 Experimental Methods

The study evaluates the two algorithms described in section 2 with a comparison of results generated from solving a test bed of 25 rostering problems. These problems were reconstructed from rosters actually worked on a hospital ward during 1993. The results were further compared with the original manually generated solutions and with *optimal* solutions generated using an Integer Programming (IP) package [13]. The soft constraint heuristic was tested by running the weighted iterative repair over the same problems twice, firstly with the heuristic activated and secondly by only selecting the lowest overall cost moves (in neither case are the soft constraint weights incremented). In addition the weighted iterative repair algorithm was used to repeatedly solve identical roster problems, with the weight settings from one solution acting as the starting weights for the next solution. This was intended to test whether the algorithm can *learn* from past weightings and so find solutions more quickly.

4 Results

Table 1 summarises the experimental results. The iterative repair algorithms were set to stop at the first minimum that satisfies all hard constraints, and in the event of not finding a minimum, the basic iterative repair was set to stop after 50 restarts. Feasible solutions are defined as solutions that match the level of hard constraint satisfaction obtained from the integer programming algorithm. One integer programming solution was discarded because the execution time was in excess of 4 hours (execution times represent processor time in seconds for a 486 DX50 PC running linux).

	Weight + Soft	Weight - Soft	Basic	Integer	Manual
Mean Execution Time (secs)	93.8	81.24	305.9	576.7	n/a
Mean Soft Constraint Cost	390.7	399.1	390.2	340.5	519.2
% Feasible Solutions Found	100.0	100.0	60.0	96.0	48.0

Weight = weighted iterative repair, Soft = soft constraint heuristic, Basic = basic iterative repair
Integer = integer programming, Manual = manually solved rosters

Table 1. Mean scores for each roster generation method

The graph in figure 3 shows the results of using weighted iterative repair to solve each roster problem 20 times in succession with the weights from one solution acting as the start weights for the next. The normalised time is found by transforming the solution times for each of the 20 runs for a problem onto a scale of 0 to 1000 (0 for the fastest, 1000 for the slowest). Then solution 1 normalised time is the mean of the transformed first solution times for all 25 roster problems, and solution 2 normalised time is the mean of the transformed second solution times for all 25 roster problems, and so on.

5 Discussion

5.1 Execution Time

The experimental results show that weighted iterative repair is significantly faster than the other methods considered (this was confirmed with a further statistical analysis). Weighted iterative repair was also the only method that could reliably solve all 25 problems within a reasonable time frame (basic iterative repair was unable to solve 10 of the problems even after allowing an additional 50 restarts or approximately 2 hours of execution time per problem). In an attempt to improve the basic iterative repair, the algorithm was allowed greater freedom to search *sideways* by making moves of equal cost (as with GSAT [10]), but no improvement in the search was observed.

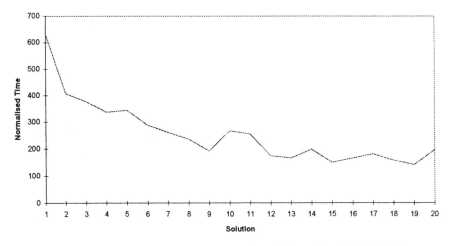

Fig. 3. Normalised times for repeated problem solving with weight feedback

5.2 Soft Constraint Cost

All the algorithmic techniques were able to convincingly improve on the soft constraint costs for the manual solutions (see table 1). This was practically confirmed by the use of an operational iterative repair system on the hospital ward during 1994-5. In addition, the soft constraint heuristic was found to make a small improvement in the soft constraint cost, without causing a large increase in execution time (this was verified by repeated solving of the test problems). The iterative repair algorithms were also able to *approach* optimal levels of soft constraint satisfaction, although the integer programming costs were significantly better.

5.3 Learning

The graph in figure 3 demonstrates that feeding back constraint weights from a solution into a repeated attempt to solve the same problem does cause execution times to reduce. This indicates the constraint weights do *learn* which constraints are hardest to satisfy, and that this information is useful in guiding a new search. The weighted iterative repair algorithm exploits this information by restarting after a fixed number of minima, whilst maintaining the current weightings (see fig 1). This differs from a normal restart strategy because information about the previous search is passed on to the next search. The restart strategy was developed because in 4 of the test problems a non-restarting algorithm occasionally became 'lost' and seemed unable to find a solution even after several hours of execution. After adding a restart strategy this behaviour was eliminated. These results suggest the learning property of the weighted iterative repair could also be exploited to solve a series of very similar problems[1].

5.4 Overall

As a tool to solve nurse rostering problems, weighted iterative repair has proved most useful in practice. This is because rostering problems are generally solved repeatedly, due to initial infeasibilities and last minute changes in staff availabilities. In such circumstances, a fast response time and an ability to find the best *infeasible* solution are important. A capability to learn from a previous similar problem is also useful.

Overall, the application of weighted iterative repair to an over-constrained non-binary CSP has proved successful. However, results from using the soft constraint heuristic are inconclusive. A small improvement was found, but at the expense of a slightly reduced execution time.

6 Conclusions

The study of real-world over-constrained problems is important to extend the theoretical work already published on iterative repair and binary CSPs. The current work shows that weighted iterative repair has practical value in efficiently solving a real-world scheduling problem. The idea of constraint weighting has been extended to handle a non-binary system with hard and soft constraints, and the weighting algorithm has been extended to include a restart facility, a cycle avoidance strategy and a soft constraint heuristic.

Promising areas for further research include the exploitation and refinement of the learning ability of weighted iterative repair and the further exploration of heuristics to optimise soft constraint satisfaction.

References

1. D. Abramson. A very high speed architecture for simulated annealing. *IEEE Comp.*, May:27-36, 1992.
2. A. Borning, B. Freeman-Benson and M. Wilson. Constraint hierarchies. In M. Jampel, E. Freuder and M. Maher, editors, *Over-Constrained Systems*, pages 23-62. Springer-Verlag, 1996.
3. B. Cheng, J. Lee and J. Wu. A constraint-based nurse rostering system using a redundant modeling approach. In *Proc. of the 8th IEEE International Conference on Tools with AI*, 1996.
4. M. S. Fox. ISIS: A Retrospective. In M. Zweben and M. S. Fox, editors, *Intelligent Scheduling*, pages 3-28. Morgan Kaufman, 1994.

---

[1]Paul Morris came to a similar conclusion in looking at the Zebra problem (personal communication).

5. E. C. Freuder and R. J. Wallace. Partial constraint satisfaction. *Artif. Intell.*, 58(1-3):21-70, 1992.

6. F. Glover. Tabu search - part 1. *ORSA Journal on Computing*, 1(3):190-206, 1989.

7. H. E. Miller, W. P. Pierskalla and G. J. Rath. Nurse scheduling using mathematical programming. *Ops. Res.*, 24(5):857-870, 1976.

8. S. Minton, M. D. Johnston, A. B. Philips and P. Laird. Minimizing conflicts: a heuristic repair method for constraint satisfaction and scheduling problems. *Artif. Intell.*, 58:161-205, 1992.

9. P. Morris. The breakout method for escaping local from minima. In *Proc.of AAAI'93*, pages 40-45, 1993.

10. B. Selman and H. Kautz. Domain independent extensions to GSAT: Solving large structured satisfiability problems. In *Proc.of IJCAI'93*, pages 290-295, 1993.

11. J. R. Thornton and A. Sattar. An integer programming-based nurse rostering system. In *Proc. of ASIAN '96*, pages 357-358, Singapore, 1996.

12. R. J. Wallace and E. C. Freuder. Heuristic methods for over-constrained constraint satisfaction problems. In M. Jampel, E. Freuder and M. Maher, editors, *Over-Constrained Systems*, pages 207-216. Springer-Verlag, 1996.

13. D. M. Warner. Scheduling nursing personnel according to nursing preference: A mathematical programming approach. *Ops. Res.* 24(5):842-856, 1976.

The Application of Mutual Information to the Registration of Stereo and Temporal Images of the Retina

Nicola Ritter[1]*, Robyn Owens[2], K. Yogesan[3], and P. van Saarloos[3]

[1] Centre for Opathalmology and Visual Science, University of Western Australia, Nedlands, 6907, Australia
[2] Department of Computer Science, University of Western Australia, Nedlands, 6907, Australia
[3] Lions Eye Institute, 2 Verdun St, Nedlands, 6009, Australia

Abstract. We present a new use of mutual information as a similarity technique for the registration of images. Unlike prior work we find that no more than two resolutions are necessary to gain sub-pixel accuracy and that classical optimisation techniques such as gradient descent or Powell's minimisation are not appropriate. Our results show that mutual information combined with a low resolution simulated annealing search yields very fast first approximations to the registration over a wide range of rigid transformations. The method is particularly robust in terms of changes in colour, intensity and noise between images. This makes it particularly useful for multi-modal and temporal image registration. The method was applied successfully to stereo and temporal retinal image pairs.

1 Introduction

Image registration is a task required in many applications of image processing where one must take measurements that involve multiple images. It involves taking two or more images and aligning them so as to either eliminate differences between them or highlight the salient differences for the purpose of study. The former situation occurs within such areas as target matching and the latter when producing depth information from stereo pairs or mapping changes over time etc. [2].

There are essentially four different types of registration [2]:

1. multi-modal registration, where the images have been taken by different types of sensors, for example computed tomography (CT), positron emission tomography (PET) and magnetic resonance (MR) images of the brain;
2. template registration, where a reference image is to be found inside a larger image, for example the location of a specific feature on a map;

---

* All correspondence to nritter@cs.uwa.edu.au

3. viewpoint registration, where the same object is imaged with two similar sensors at the same moment but from different positions, for example stereo imaging, and

4. temporal registration, where the same object is photographed from the same viewpoint but at different times, for example retinal images for the study of glaucoma.

A major area of use of bio-medical image registration is for retinal images [6, 5, 7]. When stereo images of the eye have been taken, the task is to map the two images as closely as possible. These can then be looked at through special glasses that allow the clinician to gain a three dimensional view of the retina and optic nerve which allows a more detailed study of the eye [1]. More pairs of images are then taken regularly over a passage of time and the comparison between them used to map changes in the eye due to glaucoma or other diseases.

For such registrations the pixel intensities as well as structures within the two images, are used to find a geometric transformation that maps one image on to the other. We have worked with rigid transformations only, however the method could be extended to affine transformations if required.

2 Literature Review

The registration of two images, I_1 and I_2 using an affine transformation can be defined as follows. Let Σ be the set of all transformations T_α, where α is some generalised index. T^* is then the T_α that optimises the similarity measure $S(I_1, T_\alpha(I_2))$. In the case where S should be minimised we say:

$$T^* = arg\left\{\min_\alpha\left[S(I_1, T_\alpha(I_2))\right]\right\} \quad . \tag{1}$$

Therefore the process of image registration can be seen as having two distinct parts: the determination of the search technique to be used to find the optimum value of the similarity measure S, and defining the similarity measure itself [2].

2.1 Search Techniques

Most common search strategies have been used in image registration problems. For example, Ritter *et al.* [8] use an exhaustive search, Viola *et al.* [9] use gradient descent and Collignon *et al.* [3] use Powell's minimisation. One thing common to most strategies is a multi-resolution approach, where the search is performed at increasingly higher resolutions. This reduces the chances of the search getting caught in local minima, however it increases the time taken.

Another common technique is the pre-processing of the image to detect such features as edges [6] and feature distance information [5]. Although this speeds up the actual registration and is designed to make it more likely to succeed, it adds a time overhead and makes the problem more complex.

2.2 Similarity Measures

The similarity measure is the calculation used to judge the closeness of fit between the two images. The most common measure used in the past has been cross-correlation (see for example [6]). Other measures used include correlation, root mean square difference, and phase based methods [2].

All of these methods suffer from one or more of the following problems:

1. they do not work well when the pixel intensities are different in the two images;
2. they have trouble dealing with multi-modal data which may have quite different colours;
3. they do not work or are too expensive to use when the misalignment between the images is large;
4. they are not robust towards noise.

A more recent similarity method suggested specifically for retinal images is that of *edge point coordinate detection* [6]. This method involves using classical edge detection techniques on the two images and then quantifying this data as two matrices for each image: one giving the edge positions found for each image column and the other giving the edge positions for each image row. Registration then becomes the task of lining up the two matrices to get the best fit possible, the measure of fit being calculated from the addition of the matches between the model and registration image matrices.

To do the actual registration, a template area is chosen from the model matrices and then matched within the image matrices by exhaustive search. Whilst this similarity method clearly solves the problem of different intensities, it leaves two major problems unsolved: it only deals with translation, not rotation or scale changes, and it does not give any information on how to choose the template to be matched.

Whilst the largest type of misalignment of retinal images is translational, there will be some cases where the eye is not situated at exactly the same distance from the camera or the subject's head is tilted differently. These effects can lead to scale and rotation changes in the image data.

Problems can occur if the retinal images are from glaucoma patients as the template chosen could be a portion in which changes have occurred due to the disease.

A new similarity measure has recently emerged from two separate sources ([9] and [3]). This technique is based on the statistical measurement called Mutual Information, described in detail in Sect. 3.1. In essence it works on the basis of how well one image 'explains' the other.

Mutual information has several major advantages over other similarity measures: it is robust towards changes in light intensity, pixel colour and noise; it can find transformations that are much larger than those easily found with other methods, and it works well where there is occlusion. It also works extremely well for multi-modal registration where the images have been taken from different sensors, such as for magnetic resonance (MR) and computer tomography (CT) registration. Viola and Wells [9] give excellent results for images with occlusion and for video tracking.

There are two disadvantages with the technique they describe. Firstly, the method used to calculate the mutual information involves *Parzen windowing* which is computationally expensive. Secondly the optimisation algorithm used is gradient descent which is not the best method for the kind of function formed by mutual information (see discussion in Sect. 3.2 and Fig. 2).

Collignon *et al.* [3] use a better method for calculating the mutual information (that described in Sect. 3.1) than do Viola *et al.* [9], however they use Powell's minimisation to find the best fit. We have found this method to be unstable when the algorithm's parameters are not altered to fit the image. The probable reason for this is explained in Sect. 3.2 below. However the results they give clearly show the usefulness of mutual information as a similarity measure when used for MR-CT multi-modal registration.

We have advanced this prior work by testing out the use of mutual information on a variety of images, studying the shape of the mutual information function and suggesting a search strategy that takes into account this shape. A further difference between the work of [9, 3] and ours is that they find it necessary to use multiple resolutions to gain their results whereas we find that two resolutions only are enough to achieve sub-pixel accuracy.

3 Method

3.1 Mutual Information

A detailed discussion of mutual information can be found in Cover and Thomas [4].

Consider a set, $\mathbf{M}$, of disjoint events $M_1, M_2, ..., M_m$. The *uncertainty function* or *entropy* measure is then described as

$$h(p_1, p_2, ..., p_m) = -\sum_{i=1}^{m} p_i \log p_i \; , \tag{2}$$

where p_i is the probability of the ith event. Note that one can use logarithms of any base, as this simply changes the units in which the entropy is measured. The use of base 2 gives units of 'bits' and the use of natural logarithms gives units of 'nats'.

The mutual information, J, between two sets $\mathbf{M}$ and $\mathbf{N}$ is then described as the amount of information that one of the sets gives us about the other. It is a measure of how well $\mathbf{M}$ is explained by $\mathbf{N}$, and is calculated using the following formula:

$$J(\mathbf{M}; \mathbf{N}) = h(\mathbf{M}) - h(\mathbf{M}|\mathbf{N})$$

$$= \sum_{m,n} p(m,n) \log_2 \frac{p(m,n)}{p(m)p(n)} \; . \tag{3}$$

Given that we have a model M and a registration image I and that we are trying to find the transformation T^* that gives the best registration over the set Σ of transformations T_α:

$$T^* = arg \left\{ \min_{\alpha} \left[-\sum_{i \in s} p(M_i, I_i) \log_2 \left(\frac{p(M_i I_i)}{p(M_i)p(I_i)} \right) \right] \right\} , \quad (4)$$

where s is a sample of coordinates from the registration image I, I_i refers to the pixel grey level value of a sample point of that image and M_i refers to the grey level value of the model at the position given by the transformed registration image point, thus $M_i = T_\alpha(I_i)$.

Calculation of the probabilities is most easily done (as described in [3]) by using the distribution of pixel pairs and pixel values across the common part of the model and registration image.

Thus

$$p(M_i, I_i) = \frac{H(M_i, I_i)}{n} , \quad (5)$$

where H is the value of the joint histogram at the point (M_i, I_i) and n is the number of points in the common part of the sample space s.

To ensure that the histograms contain useable data, it is advisable to rescale both the registration image and the model before processing [3], using the following formula:

$$\forall i \in O, \qquad I = \frac{O_i - O_{\min}}{f} , \quad (6)$$

where I is the image or model to be used in the calculations, O is the original image or model, $O_{\min}$ is the minimum grey-level in that image and f is a factor which allows 'binning' of the grey scales. For most image pairs a binning factor of 4 is found to be optimal.

3.2 Search Strategy

The shape of the mutual information function affects the method of optimisation. Figure 2 shows three mutual information graphs for the retinal images shown in Figs. 1(a) and 1(c). The surfaces are "cross-sections" through the manifold formed by the four parameters of rotation, scaling, x translation and y translation. All three graphs show x translation versus y translation, with Fig. 2(a) giving a cross-section where rotation and scaling are very incorrect, Fig. 2(b) a cross-section where rotation and scaling are slightly incorrect and the third figure in the set showing the cross-section where rotation and scaling are almost accurate.

As can be seen from these graphs, mutual information has many local minima and occasional deep "trenches" along the values of best fit. For this reason more classical optimisation methods that rely on smoother functions, such as gradient descent or Powell's minimisation, are likely to fail. A better search engine for this kind of data is simulated annealing.

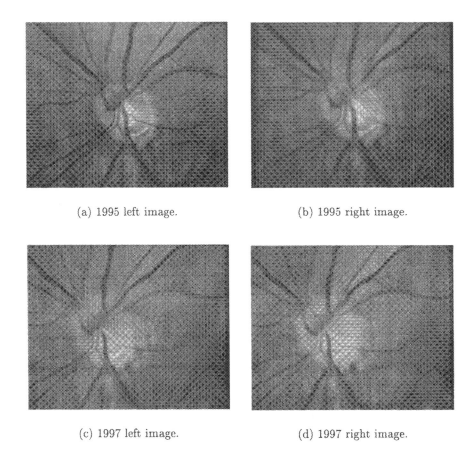

(a) 1995 left image.

(b) 1995 right image.

(c) 1997 left image.

(d) 1997 right image.

Fig. 1: Stereo pairs of the retina of a patient's left eye, taken in 1995 and 1997 using a Nidek stereo fundus camera. The original images were taken in colour, the images used for registration were 255 greyscale.

3.3 Simulated Annealing

Simulated annealing [10] is a process that uses random jumps of decreasing size to find possible other function positions. There are several possible *generation functions* for the random numbers, the most common being a gaussian. The reduction in size of the jump space or 'temperature' is controlled by an *annealing schedule*:

$$T_k = \frac{T_0}{1+k} \ , \tag{7}$$

where T_0 is the initial temperature and k is the iteration counter. This function allows a high initial temperature that ensures jumps to minima that are a long distance from the starting values as well as giving a long tail allowing

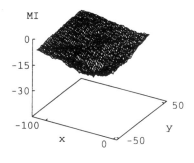

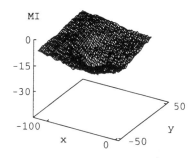

(a) r = 8 deg. and s = 108%.

(b) r = 4 deg. and s = 104%.

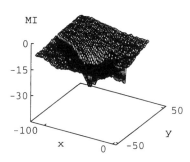

(c) r = 0 deg. and s = 100%.

Fig. 2: "Cross-sections" of the mutual information manifold formed by the parameters of rotation, scaling and x & y translation, for the retinal images in Figs. 1(a) and 1(c). From (a) to (c) the scale and rotation become closer to the correct values. A sampling of 1 in 8 pixels was used.

refinement around the very steep absolute minimum. The temperature is the standard deviation of the gaussian.

When a new position is found the probability of actually moving to that place in the function is determined with an *acceptance probability function* that ensures that the search will occasionally accept a higher mutual information value to allow it to escape from local minima. The most common acceptance function is

$$A_k = \frac{1}{1 + exp\left(\frac{J_k - J_{k-1}}{cT_k}\right)} , \qquad (8)$$

where J_k is the mutual information of the new point, J_{k-1} the mutual information of the current point, c is a constant and T_k is the temperature of the current iteration, k.

4 Results

The registration was tested on a number of artificial and real pairs of images with success. These included simple geometric shapes as well as real images such as scissors and lena, transformed by known amounts. Examples of some of the scissors images tested are shown in Fig. 3. Results from these images, which were all registered successfully, show mutual information combined with simulated annealing to be a fast method for finding a solution to a registration problem even when dealing with several parameters, large transformations and changes in intensity.

Table 1 shows average results obtained for the two pairs of eye images shown in Fig. 1. The use of simulated annealing and a 1 in 8 pixel resolution took an average of 2.5 minutes running on a 200 Mz Pentium and resulted in values that were grouped within a small area. Figure 4 shows two images that result from subtraction of the model and registered images, showing the depth information given by the stereo registration and the changes between the temporal images. The search could now be repeated using super-sampling and a smaller initial temperature to gain more accurate results if required, however as super-sampling calculations for mutual information are very slow, results for this have not been included.

Table 1: Results.

Type	Figs.		Average Results ($n = 5$)				Range				Time	
	Md.	Im.	x pix.	y pix.	r deg.	s %	x pix.	y pix.	r deg.	s %	Average m:secs	Rng. secs
Stereo	1(a)	1(b)	2.75	0.06	-0.01	99.95	5.61	0.52	0.03	0.22	2:36.75	0.70
Stereo	1(c)	1(d)	-6.63	0.05	-0.58	99.34	1.92	1.05	0.31	1.38	2:30.79	0.81
Temporal	1(a)	1(c)	65.64	-1.59	-0.27	98.25	0.68	1.87	0.46	1.56	2:21.64	0.98
Temporal	1(b)	1(d)	59.39	5.49	-0.30	99.40	1.90	2.53	0.80	1.82	2:35.26	2.77

5 Conclusion

The use of mutual information and simulated annealing is shown to be a robust and fast method for finding near approximations to the parameters of translation,

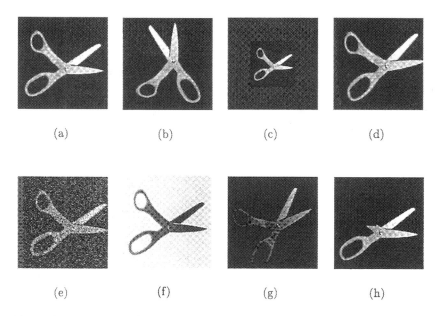

(a)   (b)   (c)   (d)

(e)   (f)   (g)   (h)

Fig. 3: Images created from the scissors image of figure 3(a) by changing the grey level intensities, performing a rigid transformation and/or occluding part of the image.

rotation and scaling for a variety of image pairs. It copes exceptionally well when the average intensities of the images are different and can deal with a large search space over several parameters.

The speed of searching is vastly improved over prior methods, however the results are not accurate to sub-pixel level. Greater accuracy can be gained using super-sampling and interpolation, however this is very costly. It is suggested that mutual information and simulated annealing be used to find a first approximation to the registration and then some other method be used to refine the solution to sub-pixel accuracy. Suggested possibilities for future work include phase-based methods, optical flow, genetic algorithms, curve fitting and more advanced simulated annealing algorithms.

Acknowledgment

I would like to thank the McCusker Glaucoma Foundation for making available the images of the retina.

References

1. Barry, C., House, P., Cuypers, M., and Eikelboom, R.: Flicker stereo chronoscopy in glaucoma: a preliminary report. part2: Method, results and discussion. J. of Bio. Imag. **3** (1997) 4–9.

(a) Stereo registration. (b) Temporal registration.

Fig. 4: Images produced by subtracting model and registered images. (a) shows a result for the stereo image pair in Figs. 1(a) and 1(b), clearly showing depth information and (b) shows a result for the temporal image pair given in Figs. 1(a) and 1(c), indicating changes in the eye over time.

2. Brown, L.: A survey of image registration techniques. ACM Comp. Surv. **24** (1992) 325–375.
3. Collignon, A., Maes, F., Delaere, D., Vandermeulen, D., Suetens, P., and Marchal, G.: Automated multi-modality image registration based on information theory. In Information Processing in Medical Imaging (1995) Y. Bizais, Ed. Kluwer Academic Publishers 263–274.
4. Cover, T., and Thomas, J.: Elements in Information Theory. (1991) John Wiley and Sons, New York.
5. Hart, W., and Goldbaum, M.: Registering retinal images using automatically selected control point pairs. In Proc. of the 1st Int. Conf. on Image Proc. (1994) 576–580.
6. Mendonça, A., Campilho, A., and Nunes, J.: A new similarity criterion for retinal image registration. In Proc. of the 1st Int. Conf. on Image Proc. (1994) 696–700.
7. Noack, J., and Sutton, D.: An algorithm for the fast registration of image sequences obtained with a scanning laser opthalmoscope. Phys. in Med. and Biol. **39** (1994) 907–915.
8. Ritter, N., and Owens, R.: The application of mutual information to image registration. In Yanchep '97 1997 Departmental Research Conference (1997) University of Western Australia 103–117.
9. Viola, P., and Wells, W. M.: Alignment by maximisation of mutual information. In Proc. of the 5th Int. Conf. on Comp. Vis. (1995) 16–23.
10. Yao, X.: A new simulated annealing algorithm. Int. J. of Comp. Math. **56** (1995) 161–168.

Kalman Filtering
from a Phase Based Optical Flow Operator

J. R. Cooper* and R. O. Hastings**

Edith Cowan University, Perth, Western Australia, Australia, 6050

Abstract. We present an optical flow operator composed of a phase based point disparity measurement combined with a Kalman filter that integrates flow information across the scene to obtain two constraints on the optical flow. The point optical flow value is computed as the time derivative of phase divided by the space derivative.

We maximize the efficiency of the algorithm by using causal filters that respond to a wide range of orientation of features so that we only need to convolve each frame with two filters, with the horizontal and vertical components of optical flow being computed separately.

We obtain simple expressions for computing the uncertainty in the phase of the filter response, and note that the uncertainty in the real and imaginary components are uncorrelated. Thus we are able to compute the uncertainty in the phase of the complex filter response and hence the uncertainty in component optical flow measurement. We note that two causal filters cannot directly provide all of the uncertainty information and so we must settle for the assumption that the information we do have is a single constraint whose orientation we estimate. This allows us to compute an uncertainty covariance matrix.

1 Introduction

The understanding of visual motion in a scene is an essential part of many applications such as surveillance, video indexing, real time vision and so on. As a first step, we might consider determining the optical flow at each location of the scene. However, there is a trade off between resolution and the ability to obtain unambiguous optical flow information. This is because the image data in any small neighborhood of a pixel can only give a single constraint on the disparity at that point.

With a derivative based optical flow operator, it is possible to compute the uncertainty in the computed optical flow as an uncertainty covariance matrix [2]. The Kalman filter is then used to compute the second constraint on disparity at a point by combining optical flow information from moving edges with different orientations. Although the resulting Kalman filer based flow technique produces reliable flow estimates along with uncertainty at each point, the optical derivative

---

* j.cooper@cowan.edu.au
** r.hastings@cowan.edu.au

based flow operator reported in [2] has two problems that severely limit its application.

Firstly, changes from frame to frame in scene illumination contribute to the computed flow values, because derivative based flow operators assume that changes in pixel values are due only to movement of features in the scene. Secondly, the derivative operator requires that image edges that provide the flow information appear at the point of application of the operator in both frames of the image pair on which the flow is to be computed. This means that in order to deal with flows of more than about 2 pixels per frame images must be severely blurred to get results. Thus, the ability to deal with large scale image flow requires a reduction in resolution.

The current paper deals with the first problem by use of a modification of the method of [2]. Specifically, we replace the derivative based flow operator with a phase based operator, which is not sensitive to changes in lighting between frames.

2 Method

To develop the phase based operator, we follow the approach of Fleet [4] in convolving the image data with causal filters and then using the phase of the response to compute feature velocity in the flow operator.

2.1 Calculating Pixel Velocity

We convolve the image data with a Gabor filter whose real and imaginary parts are given by

$$G_x(x,y) = \frac{1}{\sqrt{2\pi}w} e^{\frac{-x^2}{2w^2}} (\cos(xk) + i\sin(xk)) \tag{1}$$

and

$$G_y(x,y) = \frac{1}{\sqrt{2\pi}w} e^{\frac{-y^2}{2w^2}} (\cos(yk) + i\sin(yk)) \tag{2}$$

where k and w are respectively the peak frequency and the spread of the Gabor. Note the infinite spread of the filters in the direction orthogonal to the direction of changing phase. The objective is i miminize compution by computing components of velocity with only two Gabor filters – one with horizontal orientation and the other with vertical orientation.

The optical flow velocity $\tilde{v}_t$ can be calculated with

$$\tilde{v}_t = \begin{pmatrix} v_x \\ v_y \end{pmatrix}$$

where

$$v_x = -\frac{\delta\phi/\delta t}{\delta\phi/\delta x} \tag{3}$$

It should be noted that although 'phase based' and 'classical derivative based' optical flow methods are often presented as different paradigms, they are actually very similar. We could convert the phase based operator to a classical flow operator by taking derivatives of the magnitude of the Gabor instead of the phase and propagating flow information across the scene with relaxation instead of Kalman filtering.

2.2 Dealing with Uncertainty

To deal with uncertainty in the optical flow, we need to make some assumptions such as 'locally smooth flow' [6] or 'rigid body translation' [3] about the underlying scene. The assumption is incorporated in techniques such as the Hough transform [1], Kalman filtering [2] and relaxation [7] that integrate flow information across the scene.

We follow the method of [2], using the Kalman filter to compute an optimal estimate of flow in a small region of the scene. In this section we briefly present the Kalman filter formulation and then investigate the error behavior of the system in more detail. The interested reader might compare our approach with the method of [8], who uses a Kalman filter to propagate information from neighboring pixels and a second Kalman filtering operation to propagate information from frame to frame at each point in the scene.

To calculate the optical flow between a pair of frames in a small region, we assume that the region corresponds to a patch of the scene that is moving with no rotation or distortion. We treat the calculation of optical flow at each pixel as a separate measurement of the optical flow of the region, with associated uncertainty, which can be calculated from the image data. We use a Kalman filter formulated as follows to estimate the optical flow of the region.

2.3 Kalman Filter Formulation

Consider a partucular mesuement number t, with optical flow velocity $\tilde{r}_t$ and associated uncertainty covariance $u_{r,t}$. The state equation is given by

$$r_t = \Phi_{t-1} r_{t-1} + N(0, u_{r,t}).$$

Here, Φ is an identity matrix (localy smooth motion) and $N(0, X)$ is a two dimensional normal distribution with mean $(0, 0)$ and covariance X. The measurement of the new optical flow vector at pixel P, with measured velocity $\tilde{v}_t$ and associated uncertainty covariance $u_{p,t}$ is given by

$$\tilde{v}_t = H_{t-1} r_{t-1} + N(0, u_{p,t}),$$

where H is an identity matrix, since we are mesuring the quantitiy we are estimating. The initial prediction of uncertainty is given by

$$P_0 = u_{r,t}$$

and the Kalman gain is given by

$$K_t = P_t^{-1} H_t^T \left[H_t P_t^- H_t^T + u_{p,t} \right],$$

where the region velocity uncertainty covariance matrix is updated as

$$u_{r,t+1} = \left[I - K_t H_t \right] u_{r,t}$$

and the region velocity estimate is updated as

$$r_{t+1} = r_t + K_t \left[P_t - H_t r_t \right]$$

For this to work, we need be able to estimate the pixel velocity $\tilde{v}_t$ as well as the uncertainty $u_{p,t}$ in that estimate.

2.4 Uncertainty in the Flow

We need to estimate the uncertainty in this measurement. In this section we derive the uncertainty in our estimate of v_x.

We have an image function that is subject to uncorrelated additive Gaussian noise with mean zero and standard deviation σ_s. We convolve this image function with a Gabor kernel, defined by

$$K(x; w, k) = G(x; w)(\cos(xk) + i \sin(xk))$$

where

$$G(x; w) = \frac{1}{\sqrt{2\pi}w} e^{\frac{-x^2}{2w^2}}$$

and k and w are respectively the peak frequency and the spread of the Gabor.

The real and imaginary parts of the filter response are subject to uncertainty that can be expressed as the covariance matrix

$$\begin{pmatrix} \sigma_{rr}^2 & \sigma_{ri}^2 \\ \sigma_{ir}^2 & \sigma_{ii}^2 \end{pmatrix}$$

where

$$\begin{aligned}
\sigma_{rr}^2 &= \int \sigma_s^2 \left[G(x; w) \cos(xk) \right]^2 dx \\
&= \frac{\sigma_s^2}{2} \int G^2(x; w) + \frac{1}{2} \int G^2(x; w) \cos(2kx) dx,
\end{aligned} \tag{4}$$

$$\begin{aligned}
\sigma_{ii}^2 &= \int \sigma_s^2 \left[G(x; w) \sin(xk) \right]^2 dx \\
&= \frac{\sigma_s^2}{2} \int G^2(x; w) - \frac{1}{2} \int G^2(x; w) \cos(2kx) dx,
\end{aligned} \tag{5}$$

where σ_s^2 is the variance of the pixel greylevel noise and

$$\sigma_{ri}^2 = \sigma_{ir}^2 = \int \sigma_s^2 \left(G(x;w)\cos(kx)G(x;w)\sin(kx) \right) dx$$

$$= \frac{\sigma_s^2}{2\pi w} \int \cos(xk)\sin(xk) \left(e^{\frac{-x^2}{2w^2}} \right)^2 dx$$

$$= 0$$

and in each case, the limits of integration are $(-\infty, \infty)$. Note that the value of σ_{ri}^2 is zero since the integral evaluates to zero, so uncertainty in the real and imaginary components of the filter response are uncorrelated.

We obtain the values of σ_{rr}^2 and σ_{ii}^2 indirectly by obtaining two equations relating the values. Using (4) and (5) we have

$$\sigma_{rr}^2 + \sigma_{ii}^2 = \sigma_s^2 \left(\int \left[\frac{1}{\sqrt{2\pi}w} e^{\frac{-x^2}{2w^2}} \right]^2 (\cos^2(xk) + \sin^2(xk)) \right) dx$$

$$= \frac{\sigma_s^2}{2w\sqrt{\pi}} \tag{6}$$

and also from (4) and (5) we have

$$\sigma_{rr}^2 - \sigma_{ii}^2 = \frac{\sigma_s^2}{2\sqrt{\pi}w} \int G(x;w)\cos(\frac{\sqrt{2}px}{w}) dx \tag{7}$$

where $p = wk$. We design our filters so that $p = wk = 3.05$ and thus, we define the filter shape. Numerical evaluation of (7) then gives

$$\sigma_{rr}^2 - \sigma_{ii}^2 \approx 0.000026 \frac{\sigma_s^2}{w}, \tag{8}$$

which is close enough to zero to allow us to consider σ_{rr}^2 and σ_{ii}^2 to be approximately equal. From (6) and (8) we have

$$\sigma_{rr}^2 \approx \sigma_{ii}^2 = \frac{\sigma_s^2}{4\sqrt{\pi}w}. \tag{9}$$

Thus, the uncertainty in the filter response is inversely proportional to the filter width.

Given that the off-diagonal elements of the covariance matrix are zero, we can represent the filter response and uncertainty in that value with the diagram of Fig. 1.

If we calculate the magnitude of the filter response at point (x, y) in frame t as $\rho(x, y, t)$, then the uncertainty in the phase of the filter response can be calculated with

$$\sigma_\phi(x, y, t) = \tan^{-1} \left(\frac{\sigma_{rr}}{\sqrt{\rho^2(x, y, t) - \sigma_{rr}^2}} \right) \tag{10}$$

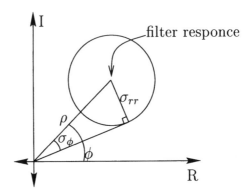

Fig. 1. A graphical representation of the uncertainty in the filter response. The circle represents the (uncorrelated) uncertainty in the real and imaginary components of the response.

where σ_{rr} is obtained using (9). When the magnitude of the filter response is close to the size of the uncertainty in that value, the uncertainty goes to infinity. When the magnitude of the filter response is large in comparison with the uncertainty, the uncertainty is approximated by $\sigma_{rr}/\rho(x,y,t)$.

Recall that we estimate the space and time derivatives of the phase as the difference between two such calculated phase values, and then estimate the x and y components of the flow velocity with (3). Thus, the uncertainty in the x component of the estimated flow can be estimated with

$$\sigma_{vx} = \frac{\sigma_t}{|\Delta\phi_x|} + \frac{|\Delta\phi_t|\sigma_x}{\Delta\phi_x^2} \tag{11}$$

where

$$\Delta\phi_x(x,y,t) = (\phi_x(x-1,y,t) - \phi_x(x+1,y,t))/2$$

with $\phi_x(x,y,t)$ being the phase of the filter response and

$$\sigma_x(x,y,t) = \sqrt{\sigma_\phi^2(x-1,y,t) + \sigma_\phi^2(x+1,y,t)}/2.$$

Similar expressions describe $\Delta\phi_t(x,y,t)$ and σ_t and a similar analysis applies to the estimation of uncertainty in the y component of velocity.

2.5 The Uncertainty Matrix

A full estimation of uncertainty in the behavior of this expression is more complicated than with an intensity gradient method because the real and imaginary parts of the causal filter provide constraint information related to the second and first derivative respectively of the image. At points in the image function coinciding to a greylevel corner, the two filters will provide good constraints that are orthogonal to each other. At image features corresponding to straight edges, the constraints will be parallel.

We convolve each frame in the image sequence with the filters G_x and G_y described in (1) and (2). There is not enough information to determine the constraint provided by the even part of the filters, since that constraint is a second derivative value, which is defined by a covariance matrix with three independent terms and we have taken measurements from only two filters.

However, we can estimate the direction of the constraint provided by the odd part of the filter. In keeping with the method of [2], we assume the large eigenvalue of our uncertainty is infinity. We estimate the small eigenvalue of our velocity as the minimum of uncertainties calculated from the response of G_x and G_y. For the eigenvectors, we observe that the vector composed of the phase of the two filter responses $(\phi_x, \phi_y)^{\mathsf{T}}$ is roughly orthogonal to the edge direction and we do not compute velocities at palaces in the scene where the magnitude of this vector is small. This happens where only the even parts of the filters are responding.

Thus, we have the velocity uncertainty

$$P = Q\Lambda Q^{\mathsf{T}} = \begin{pmatrix} \phi_x & -\phi_y \\ \phi_y & \phi_x \end{pmatrix} \begin{pmatrix} \lambda_1 & 0 \\ 0 & \lambda_2 \end{pmatrix} \begin{pmatrix} \phi_x & -\phi_y \\ \phi_y & \phi_x \end{pmatrix}^{\mathsf{T}}$$

with $\lambda_1 = \min(\sigma_{vx}^2, \sigma_{vy}^2)$ and $\lambda_2 = \infty$.

3 Results

The Kalman and phase based flow operator described above were used to compute an optical velocity and associated uncertainty covariance matrix (UCM) in windows of size 5×5. We display the result in a needle diagram showing the flow values for each window. One such flow diagram is shown in Fig. 2(a), where we have displayed velocities only where the determinant of the UCM is less than 0.01. Only at places in the scene where there is enough information to calculate meaningful flow values are they displayed. The result might be thought of as an elaborate texture detector.

We can demonstrate that the operator produces results suitable for segmentation by using the flow results to remove components of the scene as follows.

Integration of the two dimensional unit volume Gaussian gives a cumulative probability function of

$$p(r < R) = 1 - e^{\frac{-R^2}{2\sigma^2}}. \tag{12}$$

So with a two component random variable whose probability distribution conforms to a symmetric two dimensional Gaussian, 98.9% of the vectors lie within 3σ of the center.

Suppose we know in advance that an object in the scene is moving with velocity $\tilde{v}_o$. For individual windows we can compute flow outputs of the form

(a) Only points of no information removed.

(b) Background removed.

Fig. 2. Phase based Kalman filtered flow with 5×5 windows

$(\tilde{v_w}, \sigma_w)$ where σ_w^2 is the larger of the eigenvalues in the UCM for the window. From (12), if our estimates of σ_w^2 are accurate we would expect to delete 98.9% of the needles corresponding to object o when we deleted the needle for each window where

$$|\tilde{v_o} - \tilde{v_w}| < 3\sigma_w.$$

The background scene is one such object and in the taxi sequence used here its velocity is zero. The result of using this technique to identify flow windows belonging to the background is shown in Fig. 2(b). Production of Fig. 2(b) removed 1342 needles, leaving an estimated 42 needles that should belong to the background. Thus, we removed 96.9% of the background flow values. This indicates a small underestimate of the flow uncertainties.

We have used this technique to identify the flow windows corresponding to three moving objects in Figs. 3(a), 3(b) and 3(c) to demonstrate that we could in principle segment this scene on the basis of optical flow. In practice, we will need a clustering operation to identify the flow velocities of the various objects.

In the cases of moving objects only about 50% of the features associated with the moving objects were removed. Some experimenting with (12) indicates that we have under estimated the uncertainty in the flows of the objects by a factor of about 3.5.

This comes in part from the fact that when we use the phase calculations from the moving objects we do so as though the objects are not moving. This means that at some places we are computing a time difference of phase using features belonging to one part of the object/background combination in one frame and ones belonging to a different combination in the other because the underlying object has moved. To solve this problem we plan to use a multi-scale flow operator – where the small scale calculations use the input of larger scale calculations to target the correct image locations for phase differencing. A report on a one dimensional implementation of the multi-scale flow operator is given in the companion paper [5]. A second source of error is that the calculated direction

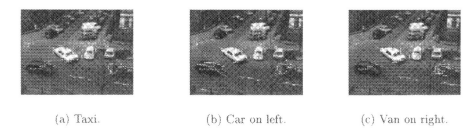

(a) Taxi.   (b) Car on left.   (c) Van on right.

Fig. 3. Segmentation of taxi scene using flow and uncertainty only. In each case an attempt has been made to remove all needles except those corresponding to the named object.

of the constraint has an associated uncertainty, which we have not accounted for in the uncertainty covariance matrix.

The effect of these two problems is similar to adding a small random flow vector with zero mean. Thus although the flow vectors corresponding to the (stationary) background are apparently unaffected, all the object velocities are underestimated by a factor of about 1.3. This needs to be changed.

4 Conclusion

We have demonstrated that the Kalman filter can be used with a phase based optical flow operator to propagate flow information across the scene. In the current work, we use only two causal filters, with horizontal and vertical orientations respectively. However, we show that at least three causal filters need to be used to do a full error analysis of the flow estimates.

We have demonstrated that our method has the potential for use as a source of information for motion based scene segmentation.

Acknowledgment

The Authors wish to thank Dr's Pender Pedler and Ute Mueller for their helpful comments regarding the mathematics behind this work.

References

1. Ballard, D. H.: Generalizing the Hough transform to detect arbitrary shapes. Pat. Rec. **13** (1981) 111–122.
2. Cooper, J., and Venkatesh, S.: Uncertainty in the optical flow using the kalman filter. In Fourth Int. Conf. on Cont., Auto., Rob. and Vis. (1996) vol. 3 1681–1686.
3. Fennema, C. L., and Thompson, W. B.: Velocity determination in scenes containing several moving objects. Comp. Graph. and Im. Proc. **9** (1979) 301–315.

4. Fleet, D. J.: Measurement of Image Velocity. Kluwer Academic Publishers:Boston, USA 1992.

5. Hastings, R., and Cooper, J.: Multi scale phase based velocity tuned flow operators. In these proceedings (1997).

6. Horn, B. K. P., and Schunck, B. G.: Determining optical flow. Artif. Int. **17** (1981) 185–203.

7. Schunck, B. G.: Image flow segmentation and estimation by constraint line clustering. IEEE Trans. on Pat. Anal. and Mach. Intel. **PAMI-11** (1989) 1010–1027.

8. Singh, A.: Incremental estimation of image-flow using a kalman filter. In IEEE Workshop on Vis. Mot. (1991) IEEE Computer Society Press 36–43.

Adaptive Constraint Restoration and Error Analysis Using a Neural Network

Stuart W. Perry and Ling Guan

Department of Electrical Engineering,
University of Sydney
Sydney, NSW 2006 Australia.
sperry@ee.usyd.edu.au
ling@ee.usyd.edu.au

Abstract. In this paper we present a restoration technique aimed at correcting image degradations by consideration of human visual criteria. A neural network model with an adaptive constraint factor is used. By considering local statistical information about regions within an image, the value of constraint factor can be selected which produces an optimal trade-off between noise suppression and edge preservation in each statistically homogeneous region. In addition a novel image error measure is presented which takes into account the statistical matching of homogeneous regions and its effect on human visual appraisal of image quality.

1 Introduction

Image restoration is an important step in low level vision. The restoration of an image degraded in some way is usually approached in terms of a multidimensional optimisation problem. Theoretically, a degraded image may be restored by the creation of an algorithm which minimises a measure of image quality such as mean square error. A Hopfield neural network based algorithm is often used to optimise cost functions such as those involved in image restoration by equating the terms in the quadratic cost function to the terms in the formula for the energy of the neural network [ZC1], [PK1]. This is achieved by correctly choosing the neuron bias inputs and interconnection weights. In this way the cost function may be optimised as the neural network minimises its energy, hence restoring a degraded image.

In the event of a noisy image, or one suffering space-variant [PG1] or unknown distortion, the approach of optimising a quality measure can produce ringing effects and enhance noise in the restored image. To avoid this problem, a constraint factor is added to the restoration quality measure. The constraint factor effectively trades image sharpness for increased suppression of noise and ringing effects. Choosing the best value of the constraint factor is often difficult as too low a constraint will allow noise artifacts to appear, whereas too high a constraint factor will result in an image which is severely blurred [GK1], [TB1], [KV1].

A constant value of constraint factor does not match well the concepts involved in human visual appraisal of image quality. In general, noise artifacts are more noticable in smooth regions of the image, such as the background, where detail is naturally low. On the other hand, blurring is most noticeable when it occurs in the high detail regions of an image, where noise is least disturbing. In light of this, it is desirable to develop an algorithm which uses higher values of constraint in smooth regions, to favour the suppression of noise, and lower values of constraint in highly textured regions to favour the restoration of fine details.

The method presented in this paper involves choosing the optimal value of constraint factor based on local image statistics, such as variance, in the neighbourhood of the pixel being examined. The local image variance is related to constraint values before the restoration procedure begins.

This paper also investigates the problem of identifying an error measure which gives an evaluation of the difference between two images with consideration to human preferences. Classical image error measures such as mean-square error and signal to noise ratio are purely mathematical and do not take into account the factors involved with human visual appraisal of image quality as mentioned above. We present a novel image error measure which attempts to quantify the statistical differences between regions in an image rather than the differences between individual pixels.

2   The Restoration Model

Considering an M by M input image, in most cases the image degradation model is a linear distortion described by the equation [ZC1], [PK1]:

$$g = Hf + n \tag{1}$$

where f and g are the lexicographically organised original and degraded image vectors of length M^2, respectively, H is a matrix distortion operator and n is an additive noise vector. The matrix H is an arrangement of the elements in the degrading point spread function (PSF) such that equation (1) holds. In the case of space-invariant distortion, H may have a Block-Toeplitz form. This model is used here to describe images degraded by space-invariant distortion. When attempting to deconvolve a distorted image, one method is to minimise an error measure such as the constrained least square error function:

$$SE = \left\| g - H\hat{f} \right\|^2 + \left(\frac{1}{2} \right) \lambda \left\| D\hat{f} \right\|^2 \tag{2}$$

where $\hat{f}$ is the restored image estimate and λ is the constraint factor. The matrix D is of the same nature as H and acts as a high pass filter. The first term in the equation is minimised when $\hat{f}$ is equal to the original image whereas the second term in (2) increases in the presence of noise and is minimised for a smooth image estimate. Equation (2) applies the same λ value and D matrix to all pixels in the image and hence a value of λ large enough to fully suppress noise in the smooth regions of the image may blur fine details.

3 Neural Network Algorithm

Neural network image restoration approaches are designed to minimise a quadratic programming problem. The general form of a quadratic programming problem can be stated as:

Minimise energy function E given by:

$$E = \hat{f}^T W \hat{f} + b^T \hat{f} + c \tag{3}$$

In terms of a neural network energy function, the (i,j)th element of W corresponds to the interconnection strength between neurons (pixels) i and j in the network. Similarly, vector b corresponds to the bias input to each neuron, while vector $\hat{f}$ corresponds to the state of each neuron in the network. To solve the quadratic error measure given by (2) we relate W, b and c to H, λ, D, g and n, and $\hat{f}$ to the image estimate.

For an image where each pixel is able to take on any integer intensity between 0 and S, we assign each pixel in the image to a single neuron able to take any real value between 0 and S. Equating the formula for the energy of a neural network with equation (2) the bias inputs and interconnection strengths can be found. From Zhou, *et al.* [ZC1], Setting $L = M^2$, the interconnection strengths and bias inputs were shown to be:

$$w_{ij} = -\sum_{p=1}^{L} h_{pi} h_{pj} - \lambda \sum_{p=1}^{L} d_{pi} d_{pj} \tag{4}$$

$$b_i = \sum_{p=1}^{L} g_p h_{pi} \tag{5}$$

where w_{ij} is the interconnection strength between pixels i and j, and b_i is the bias input to neuron (pixel) i. Note that, h_{ij} is the (i,j)th element of matrix H from equation (1) and d_{ij} is the (i,j)th element of matrix D from equation (2).

4 Adaptive Constraint Restoration

As already stated, noise is most noticeable in smooth regions of an image, whereas blurring is the most disturbing in highly textured regions. For this reason higher values of constraint are best in smooth regions and lower values of constraint are best in high texture regions. Since smooth regions are characterised by having low variances and textured regions are characterised by having higher values of variance, it seems reasonable to select each pixels associated value of λ by examining the variance of pixel intensities in the neighbourhood of the current pixel. To speed up the restoration procedure, the elements of matrix W are computed beforehand for a range of possible values of λ. This produces a number of alternative W matrices. Each different value of λ is associated with a variance range before the algorithm commences operating on the image. The current pixel being acted upon has the variance of its local neighbourhood determined and the correct W matrix is chosen based on that variance. If the variance level is less than a threshold, the pixel's value is not changed. This further suppresses noise in the smooth regions of the image without adversely affecting the resultant image quality.

In addition, an increase in speed may be achieved by pre-associating each pixel in the image with a value of λ before the image is restored. This concept assumes that the constraint values chosen during the first iteration of the algorithm are the most accurate. Precomputing the optimal constraint level for each pixel will help to avoid incorrect constraint selection due to oscillations in pixel intensity during the course of the restoration procedure.

5   Image Error Measurement

Classical image error measures such as Mean Square Error (MSE) or Signal to Noise Ratio (SNR) compare images on a pixel to pixel basis, and in effect make statements about the power of the noise signal of created by the subtraction of the two images to be compared. This kind of information is mathematically useful. However it favours slow variations in the image and bears very little relationship to the manner in which humans view the differences between two images. Humans tend to concentrate attention upon sharp differences in intensity within an image, for example edges or noise in background regions. Hence an error measure should take into account the concept that low variance regions in the original image should remain low variance regions in the restored image, and high variance regions in the original image should likewise remain high variance regions in the restored image. This implies that noise should be at a minimum in background regions, where it is most noticeable, but noise suppression should not be as important in highly textured regions where image sharpness should be the dominate consideration.

We introduce an error measurement, Local Standard Deviation Mean Square Error (LSMSE), which incorporates human perception into error evaluation. LSMSE is calculated by comparing the local standard deviations in the neighbourhood of each pixel in the images we wish to compare. The mean square error between these two standard deviations gives an indication of the degree of similarity between the two images.

Define the local standard deviation in the A by A neighbourhood of pixel (x, y) in image f as:

$$\sigma_A (f(x,y)) = \sqrt{\sum_{i = x - \frac{A}{2}}^{x + \frac{A}{2}} \sum_{j = y - \frac{A}{2}}^{y + \frac{A}{2}} \frac{\left(f(i,j) - M_A (f(x,y))\right)^2}{A^2}} \tag{6}$$

where the local mean of the A by A neighbourhood of pixel (x, y) in image f is defined as:

$$M_A\left(f(x, y)\right) = \sum_{i = x - \frac{A}{2}}^{x + \frac{A}{2}} \sum_{j = y - \frac{A}{2}}^{y + \frac{A}{2}} \frac{f(i, j)}{A^2} \tag{7}$$

Using the above conventions, we define the LSMSE between two $N \times M$ images f and g as:

$$LSMSE_A(f, g) = \sum_{x = 0}^{N-1} \sum_{y = 0}^{M-1} \frac{\left(\sigma_A\left(f(x, y)\right) - \sigma_A\left(g(x, y)\right)\right)^2}{NM} \tag{8}$$

6   Experiments

An image containing a mixture of smooth and rough regions was distorted using a 5 by 5 Gaussian PSF with standard deviation 2.0. Various levels of noise were added to the degraded image, with variances equal to 4.23, 18.49 and 42.53. The following formula was used to estimate the signal to noise ratios of the images in this paper.

$$SNR = 20\log\frac{\sigma_f}{\sigma_n} \tag{9}$$

where σ_f is the standard deviation of the original image and σ_n is the standard deviation of the noise image created by subtracting the image to be analysed from the original image. Table 1 shows the SNR and LSMSE between the original images, degraded images, images restored with a constant value of λ, and images restored using an adaptive λ value. Table 2 shows the regularisation parameters used in the experiment.

Table 1: Statistics of degraded and restored images for various levels of noise.

Noise Variance	SNR (dB)			LSMSE		
	DI	NA	AD	DI	NA	AD
4.23	12.61	13.29	13.14	42.98	14.58	13.10
18.49	12.25	12.81	12.57	38.65	17.45	15.89
42.52	11.73	12.34	11.89	34.17	18.42	16.29

Legend: DI = Degraded Image; NA = Non-Adaptively restored image; AD = image restored using adaptive algorithm.

Table 2: Adaptive constraint restoration details

Degraded Image Noise variance	Constraint Parameter choices for Adaptive Algorithm	Constraint Parameter Choice for Non-Adaptive Algorithm
4.23	0.0004 0.0005 0.001	0.0007
18.49	0.0001 0.002 0.003	0.002
42.52	0.0015 0.002 0.003	0.003

Table 1 indicates that using the adaptive algorithm produces images with an improved LSMSE. This is despite a decrease in SNR when compared to the images produced by the non-adaptive algorithm. A set of figures are used to demonstrate the performance of the method for the case corresponding to the second data row in the two tables. Figure 1 shows the original image and Figure 2 shows the degraded one. Figure 3 shows Figure 2 restored using a constant λ value of 0.002. Figure 4 shows Figure 2 restored using the adaptive approach. Although Figure 4 is slightly sharper than Figure 3 and has better noise suppression in background regions, it has a SNR lower than that of Figure 3. However LSMSE agrees with observation and is lower for the adaptively restored image. This indicates that the local statistics of regions in the adaptively restored image better match the original image compared to the image restored using the classical approach.

An important observation is the agreement of the LSMSE measurement with human perception. The figures show that the restored images are closer to the original one than the blurred image, however the SNR measurement regards the quality of the distorted and restored images as similar. The LSMSE measurement agrees with observation and shows a marked difference between the quality of the restored and degraded images when compared to the original.

7   Conclusion

In this paper a method for the restoration of images suffering space-invariant distortion and additive noise by consideration of human visual quality criteria was presented. This technique is based on a constrained least square error image restoration method, with a constraint factor which varies spatially across the image. The variation of the constraint factor is performed to favour noise suppression in the smooth areas of the image, while favouring restoration sharpness in the high contrast regions of the image. The method investigated selected the constraint factor value based on the local image statistics in the neighbourhood of the pixel being examined. It was found that the images restored using these techniques were of a higher quality than those obtained using the non-adaptive method.

In addition a novel image error measure (LSMSE) was presented which attempts to quantify the difference between two images by comparison of their local regional statistics. It was found that this methodology is a better match for human visual criteria than MSE or SNR.

References

1.   Zhou, Y., Chellappa, R., Vaid, A., Jenkins, B.: Image restoration using a neural network. IEEE Trans. Acoust., Speech, Sig. Proc. **36-7** (1988) 1141-1151

2.   Paik, J., Katsaggelos, A.: Image restoration using a modified Hopfield network. IEEE Trans. Image Proc. **1-1** (1992) 49-63

3.   Perry S., Guan, L.: Neural network restoration of images suffering space-variant distortion. Electronic Letters. **31-16** (1995) 1358-1359

4.   Galatsanos, N., Katsaggelos, A.: Methods for choosing the regularization parameter and estimating the noise variance in image restoration and their relation. IEEE Trans. Image Proc. **1** (1992) 322-336

5.   Thompson, A., Brown, J., Kay, J., Titterington, D.: A study of methods of choosing the smoothing parameter in image restoration by regularization. IEEE Trans. Pattern Anal. Machine Intell. **13** (1991) 703-714

6.   Karayiannis, N., Venetsanopoulos, A.: Regularization theory in image restoration-The stabilizing functional approach. IEEE Trans. Acoust., Speech, Sig. Proc. **38-7** (1990) 1155-1179

Fig. 1. Original image.

Fig. 2. Degraded image.

Fig. 3. Image restored using constant $\lambda = 0.002$.

Fig. 4. Image restored using adaptive method.

Exploring Agent Cooperation:
Studies with a Simple Pursuit Game

Christopher Grinton, Liz Sonenberg, and Leon Sterling

Department of Computer Science
The University of Melbourne
Parkville Vic. 3052
Australia
{cgg, eas, leon}@cs.mu.oz.au

Abstract. This paper concerns cooperation and dynamic team formation in multi-agent systems, where agents inform their activity by observing the world and by communicating with each other. We have developed a testbed where pursuer agents work in teams to catch individual targets. The experiments reported here explore the effect of some simple cooperative behaviors, the level of commitedness of agents to a team goal, and different models of communication.

1 Introduction

This paper describes preliminary work on understanding the complex interactions between characteristics of the environment and attributes of agents, in particular concerning cooperating agents and dynamic team formation. We follow an approach similar to that illustrated in [2, 3, 9, 12, 13] of conducting controlled experimentation in an artificial world. Our world is populated by multiple agents of different types. Agents play a pursuit game, where pursuer agents work in teams to catch individual (stationary) targets. The game is implemented in a testbed environment which is highly parameterised [5]. The use of pursuit games for investigating coordination and cooperation is not new, e.g., [1], and, of course, one needs to take care in generalising results obtained from an artificial environment and interpreting them in a "real-world" setting [6]. Nevertheless, such empirical explorations can inform the design of multi-agent systems. For example, the various formal analyses of commitment do not directly address the problems that agent designers face of what to commit to, when to commit to it, and how to undo commitments. The experimental work in the mentioned studies complements these theoretical perspectives to provide insight into the trade-offs necessary to achieve appropriate behaviours in dynamic situations.

We report preliminary empirical work aimed towards increased understanding of dynamic, task specific, team formation c.f., [14]. We have adopted Jennings' framework of *commitments* and *conventions* [8]. A *commitment* is a promise or pledge to undertake a particular course of action, generally in the future. Such a pledge is made by an individual agent to itself or other agents in the community. Commitments made by a team of agents are called *joint commitments*. A *convention* has two components: (a) a specification of the situations under which an agent should re-evaluate the validity of its current commitments; and (b) the actions that the agent should perform when it does such a re-evaluation. For example, conventions can provide an agreed method by which an agent drops a commitment when it believes it to be unachievable [1].

We introduce the testbed environment and the game and outline some of the experiments we have conducted. The experiments reported here establish that the chosen game environment is sufficiently 'robust' to enable exploration of high level agent characteristics (such as commitment) and lower level issues concerning adopted conventions (such as those concerning communication methods). Our results concerning commitment echo those of Kinny and Georgeff [9], Pollack *et al.* [12], and Clarke, Irwig and Wobcke [3] as discussed in Section 3.3. Our final discussion concerns the use of different communication conventions in the presence of a certain kind of unreliable communication. In this way we begin to address issues which are of importance in realistic environments.

2   The Game

The aim of our game is for one group of agents (the *pursuers*), to locate and catch individual stationary *targets*. The game is designed so that it would be almost impossible for pursuer agents to be effective in catching targets without cooperating. The testbed and resulting game environment are similar to those used in Tileworld [3, 9, 12] and MICE [4]. The testbed provides a discrete event simulation in a simple grid-based world, where events and actions take some amount of simulated time, communication is reliable but is carried out over limited bandwidth channels which can be set up between arbitrary groups of agents. Agents may operate at different speeds, have different sensing ranges and other attributes. We limit our description here to the particular design decisions adopted in the experimental scenarios, but note that the testbed itself, which is written in C++, allows easy adoption of other design decisions.

The game world consists of a rectangular array of hexagonal cells which wraps around at the edges. The *distance* between two cells is the minimum number of single steps that must be made to move from one cell to the other. Each cell can either be empty or contain a single agent.

Targets and pursuers are typed. Each target must be caught by a set of pursuers of particular types. Multiple pursuer agents of a given type may be required to catch a target. A target is *caught* when the required numbers of pursuers of all the types required to catch it are adjacent to the target. Since each cell only has six neighbours, no more than six pursuer agents can be used to catch any single target type.

Targets appear randomly in the world. They disappear either when they are caught, or at random *age*. Each target has a *score* which is awarded to the pursuers if they catch that target. Pursuers are able to observe and identify any target or pursuer which is within their *sensing range*. Pursuers are able to detect the types of pursuers and targets, and the scores of targets which they can observe. Different types of pursuers may move at different *speeds*.

Pursuers do not have individual goals of maximising the scores of the targets they catch; their only incentive is to work together in an effort to maximise the score gained by the group of pursuers as a whole. The *effectiveness* of the pursuer agents is calculated as the ratio of the score of all the targets that have been caught to the score of *all* targets that have disappeared (either naturally or because they were caught) during the simulation. Thus if the pursuers catch most of the targets that appear, their effectiveness will be close to 1.0; but if the environment is changing quickly, an optimal performance does *not* necessarily correspond to an effectiveness of 1.0.

The pursuers have a flat organisation and control structure, with each pursuer having the same authority as any other pursuer. There are situations where allowing team hierarchy has considerable advantages [14], and the testbed is sufficiently flexible to admit experiments of this kind, but we have not yet looked at this. Detailed discussion of the design of the particular pursuers used in the reported experiments, and the various algorithms implemented in the game, appears elsewhere [5].

Pursuers have two primary sources of knowledge: direct observation and notification by other pursuers. Pursuers communicate using a limited range, limited bandwidth communication channel. Pursuer agents record information which is received through either of these sources for use in their later reasoning and decision-making. Due to the limited sensing range, time taken for messages to be sent between pursuers, and the limit on the distance which messages may be sent, the pursuers' knowledge, while correct at the time of observation/report can be both inaccurate and incomplete.

Joint commitments to catch individual targets at a specified time are made by teams of pursuers [2]. Based on their knowledge of the state of the world individual pursuers send one or more *commitment proposals* to all other pursuers within range specifying a time interval during which the pursuer could commit to be adjacent to the target. Each pursuer who has made a proposal calculates (based on their knowledge of the other proposed commitments) times at which the target can be caught, and whether or not they are actually required in the chasing team. The shift from a proposed commitment to a *confirmed commitment* comes after individual evaluation of the known information, and sending of appropriate messages to the other pursuers[3]. In general a proposal will not be made which conflicts with existing commitments (the experiment in Section 3.3 discusses situations where proposals conflicting with current commitments can be made).

Conventions specify when a pursuer should reevaluate a commitment or proposed commitment to catch a target, and what it should do in those situations. The conventions used in the experiments follow the general rule that each pursuer is to drop a commitment or commitment proposal if it ever discovers either that it has been satisfied or that it cannot be satisfied.

3 Experiments and Analysis

Experiments with such an environment fall into two categories. Firstly, experiments which illustrate that the environment behaves in accord with one's intuition and so give some confidence in the viability of the testbed—we did three of these, two of which are presented here (3.1, 3.2). Secondly, experiments designed to explore certain concepts and tradeoffs where behaviours are less easily predictable—we did five of these and two are presented in outline (3.3, 3.4).

Before embarking on a discussion of results, we present some preliminary information about the conduct of the experiments. All simulations are reproducible in that given the same parameters the same sequence of events will occur. A *trial* is a single run of a simulation with specified parameters (which includes a seed value for the random number generator). An *experiment* is a number of trials with related parameter values. Default parameters were determined for the experiments, to keep things manageable. Experiments are run in a square grid of 400 cells. There is only one pursuer type and one target type. Unless otherwise specified, a target needs three pursuers to be caught. Simulation length was settled, after observation and experimentation, at 100 trials of 500,000 time units each. Over this time, around 250 targets can be expected to appear. Each target has a score of 1, and in this case effectiveness corresponds to calculating the proportion of targets which were caught. Other defaults deal with target age, target appearance times, pursuer sensing and communication ranges.

3.1 Number and Speed of Pursuers

The number of pursuers and their speed are parameters which one would expect to significantly affect effectiveness. The graph in Figure 1 plots effectiveness against operation speed, with from $n = 3$ to $n = 9$ pursuers in the world.

Plausible explanations for the increase in effectiveness with a larger numbers of pursuers evident in this graph, come from the observations that: (a) the more pursuers there are in the world, the more targets can be chased simultaneously; and (b) having more pursuers in the world leads to a higher density of pursuers—when a new target appears, the distance which pursuers have to travel to catch it will (on average) be smaller.

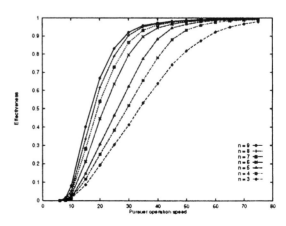

Fig. 1. Effectiveness with different numbers of pursuers

Unsurprisingly, moving from 5 to 6 pursuers, i.e. to allow two complete teams working in parallel, has a significant influence on performance. For example, at a speed of around 30, adding the 6th pursuer increases the overall effectiveness of the pursuers by almost 0.2 (that is, almost 2 more out of every 10 targets are caught by 6 pursuers than by 5 pursuers). Somewhat curiously, the addition of a 9th pursuer does not seem to cause a similar large increase in effectiveness—moving from 8 to 9 pursuers in the world, the difference between "not quite" 3 complete teams and 3 complete teams is not as significant as the difference caused by adding the 6th pursuer.

3.2 Cooperative Behaviour

Once a pursuer has reached a cell adjacent to a target it is chasing, the simplest behaviour is to remain stationary. A more cooperative behaviour would be to attempt to move out of the way of other pursuers in the team which are not yet adjacent to the target. Figure 2 illustrates the relative effectiveness of pursuers with and without this simple cooperative behaviour. The ten lines of the graph show the effectiveness against the operation speed of the pursuers, with from $n = 2$ to $n = 6$ pursuers required to catch each target, both with and without the cooperative behaviour ($c = $ yes/no).

When only two pursuers are required to catch a target, there is no noticeable difference in effectiveness between the cooperative and the non-cooperative pursuers. Most likely this is because the chance of one pursuer being in the way of the other incoming pursuer is not very high. However, when more pursuers are required, it can be quite advantageous for pursuers to adopt this simple cooperative behaviour. For example, at an operation speed of 70, with

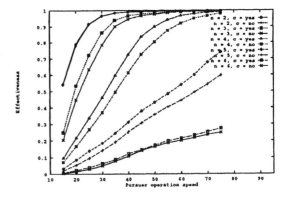

Fig. 2. Effect of simple cooperative behaviour

5 pursuers required to catch a target, the pursuers are about 20% more effective at catching targets with, as opposed to without, the cooperative behaviour. At lower operation speeds, this effect is not so pronounced, as the pursuers are simply not working fast enough to catch many targets, and so the cooperative behaviour is not used as often. Similarly, the cooperation does not have much impact at high operation speeds, as the pursuers operate quickly enough to catch the targets, even if they do waste some time making extra movements.

3.3 Level of Committedness

The experiments reported in this section are similar in character to others working with Tileworld [3, 9, 12] which looked at when to re-deliberate about acting as opposed to proceeding with previously commenced actions, i.e. how 'committed' to be to the previously selected course of action. That work involved working with individual agents or fixed teams. We are more interested in the interaction between commitment and dynamic team formation and reformation [14] and the testbed is set up to facilitate such experimentation.

In the context of teamwork, an agent must determine how committed it is to its team's goals. A high level of commitment will ensure that each agent can rely on other agents to complete the tasks they have agreed to. However, in situations where some tasks can be more important than others, it may be beneficial for an agent to drop a commitment to a task which is not very important in order to ensure the successful completion of a more important task (even if that means the less-important task will not be completed). This form of 'disloyalty' to a group of agents is justified by a utilitarian analysis of the agent community, as the measure of effectiveness we use involves the total score of captured targets!

In the pursuit game setting, the score of each target corresponds to the importance of catching that target: missing a target with a high score has a more detrimental effect on the pursuers' effectiveness than missing a low-valued target. To parameterise the pursuers' level of committedness, an heuristic based on the difference between two targets' scores was introduced. This heuristic allows pursuers to make proposals to catch targets which conflict with current commitments to catch other targets, if the inequality (new target - current target $\geq$ *score-threshold*) holds. A high value of *score-threshold* corresponds to pursuers being very committed (the difference in target scores must be large to make a conflicting proposal), while a low value makes the pursuers not very committed (conflicting proposals will be made for targets of similar scores).

The *score-threshold* is similar to the *override threshold* used by Pollack *et al.* as a filter to determine which tasks should be further considered for action in a single-agent environment. Pollack *et al.* show that it can be useful for agents in a dynamic environment to make commitments and then tend to filter from consideration options which conflict with those commitments. However, when high priority tasks emerge, it is useful to be able to override the filtering strategy, i.e. extreme commitment is not helpful.

Two (proposed or confirmed) commitments are considered to be *consistent* with each other if satisfying either commitment does not cause the other commitment to be unsatisfiable. The commitment proposal generation algorithm used in the earlier experiments excluded the possibility of making proposals inconsistent with existing commitments. The algorithm was modified for this experiment to allow conflicting proposals. Confirmed commitments are still required to be consistent, so sometimes earlier commitments will be dropped.

In an initial experiment to determine if the use of the *score-threshold* parameter was useful, an environment was chosen where there were two types of targets (or tasks): one type of task was not very important (targets had a score of 1), and occurred frequently (these tasks accounted for 90% of all the tasks which appeared); (b) the other type of task was significantly more important (targets had a score of 100), but occurred only 10% of the time.

With an appropriate choice for the *score-threshold* parameter pursuers can spend most of their time chasing the plentiful but low-valued targets, but then make conflicting proposals to catch the high scored targets when they appear. The effectiveness of pursuers using a threshold of 50 is compared to that of pursuers without the threshold in Figure 3 (error bars indicate the estimated errors—which are quite large compared to errors in other experiments, although small enough to show that the trends are significant).

This graph illustrates the expected behaviour that at low operation speeds, pursuers with the threshold perform significantly better than those without. At such speeds, the pursuers are not catching many targets and so there tend to be quite a few targets in the world at any time. Without the threshold, when a new high-valued target appears, proposals (and commitments) are generally made for reasonably distant times into the future. By the time the earlier commitments are eventually satisfied, the

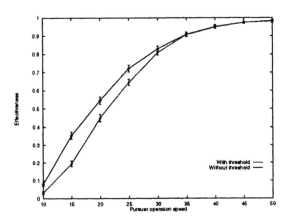

Fig. 3. Effectiveness with and without a threshold

target has often disappeared. When the threshold is used, pursuers are more successful. At high operation speeds, pursuers catch most targets anyway, and so using the *score-threshold* parameter is not as helpful.

We also looked at the effect of varying the *score-threshold* parameter, using targets whose score were chosen randomly in the range 1 to 100. It turns out that being very strongly committed is *not* optimal; in fact, being fully committed (*score-threshold* = 100) is even worse than being able to make proposals conflicting with targets of equal scores (*score-threshold* = 0). This result indicates that the value of being strongly committed to a team is not necessarily as high as having a strategy of making as many proposals as possible while making sure that previous commitments to complete more important tasks are maintained. This last result is consistent with the conclusions in the Tileworld experiments about the tradeoff between stability of commitments and reactivity (or opportunism) of agents.

3.4 Communication and Team Behaviour

A key part of the Cohen and Levesque [10] view of commitment is that if an individual member of a team comes to believe that the team's goal is unachievable, the team member then has an individual responsibility to make that belief a mutual belief amongst all team members. Our pursuers attempt to achieve this by communication and we explored alternative communication protocols which can increase the reliability of communication, at the cost of additional messaging.

When the communication range does not cover the whole world, sending a message once without any regard for who has received it could lead to pursuers with very inaccurate information. In further experiments [5, 11] we explored the following four communication models, with a range of different communication and computation costs: (a) **Single-broadcast:** This is the current pursuer behaviour, where all messages are broadcast once to all other pursuers. (b) **Multiple-broadcast:** Each pursuer periodically rebroadcasts messages containing information about its current proposals and commitments. (c) **Smart messages:** Each message sent by a pursuer is initially broadcast to all other pursuers. The message is then periodically resent to *individual* pursuers which have not indicated that they have received the message. When a pursuer receives a message, it immediately sends an "acknowledgment" message to the original message sender. (d) **Rebroadcast:** Pursuers rebroadcast the contents of any messages that they receive. Messages are only rebroadcast once; that is, if pursuer A sends a message which is received by pursuers B and C, both of those pursuers will rebroadcast the message. However, any pursuers which receive the rebroadcast message from B or C do *not* rebroadcast the message further.

The results to date explore trade-offs between the relative costs of the various options (numbers of messages sent, communication time, amount of computation involved) without reaching any definitive conclusions.

4 Discussion and Conclusions

This paper has described a parameterised testbed which can be used for simulating multi-agent activity, and a particular multi-agent pursuit game. We have explored a few parts of the parameter space of the pursuit game, and a number of experimental results have been reported.

The design of our testbed, especially the extensive parameter set, was of course influenced by consideration of the types of cooperative behaviours that we wished to be able to explore. Features were provided to enable individual agents to work with local or global information about themselves, the targets, and other agents.

Some results (for example, observing an increase in effectiveness as pursuer operation speed increases or as the number of pursuers in the world increases) are simply confirmation of the expected intuitive behaviour of the system. However they do provide useful checks on the viability of the testbed. The more complex aspects addressed in Section 3.3 (commitment) and Section 3.4 (communication options) begin to address realistic issues of concern to agent designers. In relation to communication, it would also be interesting to consider conventions for commitment abandonment which avoid or reduce the need for explicit communication, for example as discussed by Huber and Durfee [7].

The results concerning commitment are very much in line with others obtained using Tileworld with individual agents or fixed teams, which say that in balancing reaction against deliberation in situations with limited resources, it is important to adopt a strategy which takes account of the relative importance of newly arriving tasks. That work essentially dealt with single agents, and with characteristics which could be described using terms such as *bold* and *cautious*. Related work looking at group issues such as social dependencies and power relationships is illustrated in the papers of Cesta *et al.*, e.g. [2], where descriptors such as *selfish* and *parasitic* are used.

These various investigations are seeking to understand, as we are, overall properties of systems which emerge from the behaviours of agents with fixed strategies for interacting with other agents, and the environment. A more elaborate exercise would be to look at system properties when agents may contextually modify their strategies, e.g., following the work of Sen and Durfee [13] which looked at commitment strategies in the setting of distributed task scheduling.

Acknowledgments

Thanks for useful discussions to David Kinny from the Australian Artificial Intelligence Institute, and to Gil Tidhar, of the Department of Computer Science, Melbourne University. Thanks also to Michael Niemann who worked with the testbed to produce some of the results alluded to in section 3.4.

Notes

1. As Levesque *et al.* [10] point out, a joint commitment to an action is more than just the sum of the team members' individual commitments to perform their part of the action. In particular, team members must be aware of and concerned about the status of the team as a whole. For example, under the Cohen and Levesque model, before an agent can drop its commitment to the action, it must act to bring about a mutual belief of this unachievability—by communication. Other approaches achieve similar effects without communication [7], but we restrict our algorithms here to those which use explicit communication.

2. Pursuers negotiate new advance commitments while they are searching for or chasing targets. Note that commitments in this paper include promises to commence an action at some distant time in the future. Such commitments have a somewhat different flavour from the commitments used in discussions of BDI agents.

3. Pursuers assume (perhaps incorrectly) that all the other pursuers they consider necessary for the team have the same information as they do, and thus will also consider themselves necessary and make a commitment to catch the target at the same time. At the time a pursuer makes an individual commitment, a corresponding joint commitment is considered to have come into existence.

References

1. Miroslav Benda, Vasudevan Jagannathan, and Rajendra Dodhiawala. On optimal cooperation of knowledge sources. Technical Report BCS-G2010-28, Boeing AI Center, Boeing Computer Services, Seattle, WA, November 1985.

2. Amedeo Cesta, Maria Miceli, and Paola Rizzo. Effects of different interaction attitudes on a multi-agent system performance. In W van de Velde and J W Perrams, editors, *Agents Breaking Away: Proceedings of the 7th European Workshop on Modelling Autonomous Agents in a Multi-Agent World, MAAMAW'96*, pages 128–138. Lecture Notes in Computer Science 1038, Eindhoven, The Netherlands, 1996.

3. Malcolm Clark, Kevin Irwig, and Wayne Wobcke. Emergent properties of teams of agents in the tileworld. In L. Cavedon, A. Rao, and W Wobcke, editors, *Intelligent Agent Systems: Theoretical and Practical Issues*, pages 164–176. Springer Lecture Notes in Artificial Intelligence 1209, 1997.

4. Edmund H. Durfee and Thomas A. Montgomery. Using MICE to study intelligence dynamic coordination. In *Proceedings of the Second Computer Society International Conference on Tools for Artificial Intelligence*, pages 438–444, Washington, D.C.; November 1990.

5. Christopher G Grinton. A testbed for investigating agent effectiveness in a multi-agent pursuit game. BSc(Hons) thesis, Department of Computer Science, The University of Melbourne, 1996.

6. Steve Hanks, Martha E. Pollack, and Paul R. Cohen. Benchmarks, test beds, controlled experimentation, and the design of agent architectures. *AI Magazine*, 14(4):17–42, 1993.

7. Marcus J. Huber and Edmund H. Durfee. On acting together: Without communication. In *AAAI Spring Symposium on Representing Mental States and Mechanisms*, pages 60–71, Stanford, CA, March 1995. AAAI Press. Available from ftp://ftp.eecs.umich.edu/people/durfee/aaaisss95-hd.ps.Z.

8. Nick R. Jennings. Commitments and conventions: The foundation of coordination in multi-agent systems. *The Knowledge Engineering Review*, 8(3):223–250, 1993.

9. D. N. Kinny and M. P. Georgeff. Commitment and effectiveness of situated agents. In *Proceedings of the Twelfth International Joint Conference on Artificial Intelligence*, pages 82–88, Sydney, Australia, 1991.

10. Hector J. Levesque, Philip R. Cohen, and José H. T. Nunes. On acting together. In *Proceedings of the Eighth National Conference on Artificial Intelligence*, pages 94–99, Boston, MA, 1990.

11. Michael Niemann. Further experiments on agent co-operation using a multi-agent pursuit game testbed. Summer student report, Department of Computer Science, The University of Melbourne, 1996.

12. Martha E. Pollack, David Joslin, Arthur Nunes, Sigalit Ur, and Eithan Ephrati. Experimental investigation of an agent commitment strategy. Technical Report 94-31, Department of Computer Science, University of Pittsburgh, Pittsburgh, Pennsylvania, June 1994. Available from http://bert.cs.pitt.edu/~pollack/distrib/tw.ps.

13. Sandip Sen and Edmund H Durfee. The role of commitment in cooperative negotiation. *International Journal on Intelligent and Cooperative Information Systems*, 3(1):67–81, 1994.

14. Gil Tidhar, Anand S Rao, and Elizabeth A Sonenberg. Guided team selection. In M Tokoro, editor, *Proceedings of the Second International Conference on Multi-Agent Systems (ICMAS96)*, pages 369–376. AAAI Press, December 1996.

The Serializability Problem
in a Parallel Rule-Based System:
A Solution by Distributed Coordination

M.A. Abtroun   S. Hassas

Laboratoire d'Ingénierie des Systèmes d'Information
Université Claude Bernard et INSA de Lyon
43 Boulevard du 11 Novembre 1918
F-69622 Villeurbanne, Cedex
{mabtroun, hassas}@lisisun.univ-lyon1.fr

Abstract. In this paper, we focus on the control problems related to
the evaluation of a parallel rule-based systems (RBS), especially on the
serializability and rules execution order issues. We express these problems
in terms of a coordination problem between certain agents for a common
decision-making, and for which we suggest a totally distributed solution
using a focal points algorithm [4].

1   Introduction

Speeding up rule-based systems (RBSs) has been an active area of research
in the last decade and many parallelization approaches have been investigated
[10, 8, 11]. However, the success of parallel RBSs is implicitly related to the
guarantee of their results correctness. For this purpose, any parallelization approach must be endowed with effective control means. Our work deals with this
issue by focusing in particular on the problems of serializability and rules execution order in a parallel RBS. In our approach, the RBS is modeled by a society
of autonomous interacting agents (rule agents and fact agents) evolving in an
environment materialized by a set of processors. We express the serializability
problem as a coordination problem between certain agents in order to get the
same decision-making without any explicit information exchange. Our solution
is based mainly on a focal points algorithm, proposed by Fenster and al. [4].
In section 2, we present control issues in parallel RBSs. Section 3 is devoted to
the related works. In section 4, we describe briefly our approach for parallelizing
the RBS and in which our work takes place. We describe in section 5 the method
for resolving the two considered problems. A simulation example is then given
in section 6. In section 7 we give the results before concluding in section 8.

2   Control issues in parallel RBSs

2.1   Serializability

The execution of a set of rules is parallelizable if and only if, the results produced
in parallel are equivalent to the results produced by some serial execution (i.e.,
on a single processor) of the same set.

- **The problem's causes** : There are two dependency relations among rules which prevent their concurrent execution.
    1. **Disabling relation** : A rule R_i disables a rule R_j if firing R_i adds or deletes facts so that R_j is no longer satisfied. The results of co-executing a set of rules which contain a cycle of disabling relations may not be serializable.
    2. **Clashing relation** : Two rules R_i and R_j are clashing if firing R_i deletes (adds) a fact which is added (deleted) by firing R_j. The results of co-executing a pair of clashing rules may not be serializable.
- **Example** :

$$WM = \{+A < 1 >, +B < 1 >, -C < 1 >\}$$
$$R_1 \; : \; +A < x >, \; -C < y > \; \rightarrow \; -B < x >, \; +F < y >$$
$$R_2 \; : \; +A < x >, \; +B < x > \; \rightarrow \; +C < x >, \; +E < x >$$

In this example, we have a mutual disabling relation between two rules. In a serial system, only one of the two rules will be fired, whereas in a parallel system, both rules will be fired if they are each on a different processor.

2.2 Rules execution order

During the execution of a parallel RBS, sometimes it is needed to impose an order on firing the rules to make sure that the system follows a specified strategy of resolution. In practice, this is performed during the conflicts resolution step.

- **The problem's causes** : For performance considerations, the conflict resolution step is eliminated in parallel RBS resulting in the RBS following different execution paths and not always the desired one.
- **Example** :

$$WM = \{+A < 2 >, \; +B < 2 >, \; +D < 2 >\}$$
$$R_1 \; : \; +A < x >, \; +B < x > \; \rightarrow \; +C < x >$$
$$R_2 \; : \; +A < x >, \; +B < x >, \; +D < x > \; \rightarrow \; +C < x >, \; -B < x >$$

In a parallel RBS with a conflict resolution step, only one rule will be fired and the other one will no longer be satisfied. Whereas in a parallel asynchronous system, both rules will be fired if each is on a different processor.

3 Related work

The first and the most important work is that of Ishida and Stolfo (I&S) [5]. To guarantee that a set of rules fired in parallel produces a correct result, they use a compatibility matrix where rules which could potentially interfere with each other are labelled as incompatible. At run-time, this table was used to prevent incompatible rules from being fired simultaneously. Schmolze adopted the serializability criterion and developped a number of algorithms [9, 10] that determined, with various degrees of precision and cost, the conditions under which rules and instances of rules could be allowed to co-execute. Neiman in his dissertation [8] offers a fast locking scheme similar to that for database management systems. Its mechanism prevents most interferences but without checks for negative conditions. More recently, Ishida proposed in [6] an organization of distributed production system (DPS) agents where all rules are fired asynchronously and the interferences among rules which violate the serializability are avoided by local synchronizations between specific agents. The structure proposed in [6] is capable of self-organization. Related to the problem of control, may be the most relevant approach is that of Stolfo and al. [11] with PARULEL. The designers of PARULEL reject conventional conflict resolution control mechanism in favor of a meta-rule oriented approach. These meta-rules redact or eliminate offending rules from the conflict set. However, there are some problems with this approach like for example, the resolution of conflicts at the meta-rules level.

In conclusion, most of the approaches reported in the litterature do a statical allocation of rules over the processors, use an off-line form of rule-interaction analysis to detect interferences between rules and most of them prevent instance parallelism. To guarantee serializability, control is either centralized on a single processor (the leader) or is distributed over all processors but with global information. The approach we are going to describe differs from other approaches precisely on these points.

4 A brieve description of the approach

4.1 Context and goals

Mainly, the self-organizational approach [3] advocated to the parallel evaluation of an RBS has two goals:

- RBS's evaluation with the maximum of parallelism (both parallel matching and firing at instance level).
- To achieve no longer a statical allocation of rules and facts over processors but rather a run-time one.

4.2 The evaluation method

This approach is "agents based". Rules and objects (facts) of the system are represented by entities which are able to move, to duplicate and to interact with each other by exchanging informations indirectly. A rule agent R partitions its LHS into many parts called schemes of the rule R. An object agent O creates agents that represent its global scheme (the set of its valued attributes). When a scheme of a rule R meets a scheme of an object O which matches it, an instantiation mechanism creates a rule partial instance (RPI) agent, which is a specialization of the initial rule R. The RPI agent will continue progressively to instantiate its schemes until it becomes completely instantiated. it then produces, a rule complete instance (RCI) agent, which is ready to fire.

4.3 Control issues in our approach

In addition to the problems of serializability and rules execution order, in our setting, other difficulties may arise like the temporary inconsistencies of the database and more specifically, the problem of duplicate computation and data redundancy. These two later problems are out of the paper focus.

5 A solution to serializability and rules firing order

Our concern is to guarantee serializability of rules executions while begining first with rules with high priorities[1] every time that a choice situation occurs.

5.1 The environment

The environment is represented by a set of ($n \times m$ grid) of processors (the proposed solution is independant from topology). Several rule agents may be located on the same processor. The environment is opened in the sense that a new agent may join the system as well as an already existing one may leave it.

5.2 Control area

The control area is a physically connected part of the environment, composed of a set of processors called control processors. RCI agents with serializability problems have to go to this area to solve them. The location of this area is a global information and is unknown locally. Each control processor has a queue called SERIALIZABILITY_QUEUE which sequentializes the access to the control area exploration. A control processor contains also two memory areas called GO_TRACE and BACK_TRACE which are used by RCI agents for leaving their traces (implicit informations for other agents) or taking them off.

5.3 Agents types

Related to the serializability problem, we identify different types of RCI agents according to certain features of their creating rules. Therefore, we introduce for each rule agent R, two attributes INTERPOS(R) and INTERNEG(R) defined as follows:

$$INTERPOS(R) = \{set\ of\ rules\ which\ R\ possibly\ invalidates\}$$
$$INTERNEG(R) = \{set\ of\ rules\ which\ possibly\ invalidate\ R\}$$

---

[1] Priority affectation is the mechanism used to express the rules firing order.

For each rule agent, the values taken by both the attributes are determined during the statical (off-line) analysis[2]. Each RPI/RCI agent inherits the values of these attributes from its creating rule. Precisely, according to the respective values of INTERPOS(R) and INTERNEG(R), we identify three types of RCI agents for a given rule agent R:

. **Safe RCI agent (or green RCI agent)** : An agent RCI_i is said to be safe (green agent) if and only if:

$$INTERPOS(R_i) = \emptyset \ and \ INTERNEG(R_i) = \emptyset$$

Since its creating rule R_i does not invalidate any rule, nor is invalidated by any other one, this agent has no risk to violate serializability and so, it can execute.

. **RCI agent with minor risks (or orange RCI agent)** : An agent RCI_i is said to be with minor risks (orange agent) if and only if:

$$INTERNEG(R_i) = \emptyset \ and \ INTERPOS(R_i) \neq \emptyset$$

Since its creating rule R_i is not invalidated by any other one, it is authorized to execute. However, as its creating rule possibly invalidates other rules, it can execute only on a control processor.

. **RCI agent with major risks (or red RCI agent)** : An agent RCI_i is said to be with major risks (red agent) if and only if:

$$INTERNEG(R_i) \neq \emptyset$$

Since its creating rule R_i can be invalidated by other rules, this agent is not only obliged to reach the control area but it has also to interact in this area with other red agents and eventually to coordinate its actions with theirs, so as to know whether it can finally execute or not.

A red/orange RCI agent has a local memory where it saves the path which has been explored. This is useful during the process of looking for the control area as well as when exploring this area to know when it has completely visited it.

5.4 Agents moving mode

An agent moves from the processor where it is located to a direct neighbour processor in a totally random manner, except when it is located on a processor which has only one control processor among its neighbours. In that case, it goes directly to it.

---

[2] Possible invalidations are detected according to Disabling/Clashing relations but at this step, they are not effective since not all rules variables are instantiated.

5.5 Agents communication mode

Since that the agent has a local view of the environment, a direct communication mode seems impossible. This is why, the adopted communication mode is based on a mecanism of "traces left" by each RCI agent at each control processor. It is a stigmergic-like communication mode [7, 2] based on the modification of the environment (in our case, certain control processor's variables).

5.6 Agents behaviours

We describe below the behaviour of each RCI agent according to its type:

- **Green RCI agent's behaviour** : Its behaviour consists in putting down the content of its RHS on the processor where it is located initially.
- **Orange RCI agent's behaviour** : Its behaviour consists first in reaching the control area and then in putting down the content of its RHS.
- **Red RCI agent's behaviour** : The agent has to decide as quickly as possible whether it can compute or not. To do so, it has to reach the control area and then, to join a group of similar agents (if the group still can take its arrival into account before making decision) which are engaged in a *decision making process*, or to wait for the creation of a new *decision making group*. The *decision making group* : is the set of red RCI agents present in the SERI-ALIZABILITY_QUEUE of the different control processors before the starting of the *decision making process*.

  The decision making process : for making a common decision (which set of rules is authorized to compute) between the set of present red RCIs. This decision is done without explicit exchange of information between agents. Each agent engaged in the *decision making process* has to restore a kind of global vision by identifying the *decision making group* (let's say the set X). After that, it constructs the set W of the greatest subsets of X, containing only compatible[3] agents (parallelizable subsets). If the set W, contains one single element, the *decision making process* is simple, since the only possible choice is this element. If the set W contains more than one element, a selection is done according to the highest priorities, resulting in a new set V[4]. If such a selection returns more than one element, the agents have to coordinate their decision making in order to ensure that only one subset (the same for all agents) will compute in the distributed environment.

5.7 Agents coordination

The *decision making process* uses a coordination mechanism based on a focal point algorithm [4], which is a coordination heuristic advocated for common decision-making, without any prior consultation between agents.

---

[3] Without any clashing/disabling relation.

[4] This selection allows for taking into account the specified order of rules computation.

- **Description of the algorithm** Given a global set of objects (denoted by $Term$), given a subset $Focus \subseteq Term$ out of which the agents must choose one object and given a set $Pred$ of predicates such that for each predicate $P \in Pred$, each object o_i of $Term$ has a value from the set $Value_P$. The restricted version of the focal point algorithm to a subset of focus is:

Focal-point-algorithm (IN: $Term$, $Focus \subseteq Term$, $Pred$; OUT: $FPAV_{Focus}^{Term}$)

- For all objects $o_i \in Focus$, compute the focal point value $F(o_i)$ by considering all the objects of $Term$ and by using this equation:

$$F(o_i) = \sum_{P \in Pred} R(o_i)^P + 0.5 * E(o_i)^{P, \leq, >}$$

$R(o_i)^P$ is the rarity of o_i with respect to predicate P, i.e, how rare is the value of o_i relative to the other objects of $Term$, and $E(o_i)^P$ is the extremeness of o_i with respect to predicate P, i.e., how close, relative to the other objects of $Term$, is the value of o_i to one of the extreme values that predicate P takes in this particular world[5]. Formally, assume $P(o_i) = x$, the order on $Value_P$ denoted by $\leq$ and $>$, and let $MAX(o_i, P)$ be the largest of the following numbers: (1) number of objects of $Term$ that have the value x or less for predicate P; (2) number of objects of $Term$ that have a value greater than x for predicate P. Then:

$$R(o_i)^P = \frac{100}{|\{o_{i'} \in Term | P(o_{i'}) = x\}|}, \quad E(o_i)^{P, \leq, >} = \frac{100 * MAX(o_i, P)}{|Term|}$$

- Construct the set UFP_{Focus}^{Term} defined by:

$$UFP_{Focus}^{Term} = \{o_i \mid o_i \in Focus, \forall(o_{i'} \neq o_i) \in Focus, \ F(o_i) \neq F(o_{i'})\}$$

- If $UFP_{Focus}^{Term} \neq \emptyset$ then return the focal point algoritm value $FPAV_{Focus}^{Term}$ which is the object of UFP_{Focus}^{Term} which maximizes F in this set i.e., $FPAV_{Focus}^{Term} = o_k \in UFP_{Focus}^{Term} \mid \forall(o_i \neq o_k) \in UFP_{Focus}^{Term}, \ F(o_i) < F(o_k)$ else return $FPAV_{Focus}^{Term} = Nil$ (failure case).

We notice that in case of $Focus = Term$, we get the strict version of the focal point algorithm reported in [4].

- **Application of the algorithm in our case :** The function $Func$ used locally by each RCI agent to choose the set of V to be executed consists in fact in:

1. Focal-point-algorithm (IN: $Term = V$, $Focus = V$, $Pred = \{P_1, P_2\}$; OUT: $FPAV_V^V$) where: $P_1(set_i)$ is the total number of condition elements in all LHSs of the set_i; $P_2(set_i)$ is the total number of action elements in all RHSs of the set_i[6]. If the algorithm succeeds, then the $FPAV_V^V$ returned is considered as the set of RCI agents to be executed.

2. If the algorithm fails ($FPAV_V^V = Nil$), then Focal-point-algorithm (IN: $Term = W$[7], $Focus = V$, $Pred = \{P_1, P_2\}$; OUT: $FPAV_V^W$). If the

---

[5] $E(o_i)^{P, \leq, >}$ is only calculated if there is an order on the values of the predicate P.

[6] There is an order on the values of P_1 and P_2, so $E(o_i)^{P, \leq, >}$ can be calculated.

[7] We can show that for two sets $X \subseteq Y$, if $UFP_X^X = \emptyset$ then UFP_X^Y may not be empty.

algorithm succeeds, then the $FPAV_V^W$ returned is considered as the set of RCI agents to be executed.

3. If, once again, the algorithm fails ($FPAV_V^W = Nil$), then the RCI agent takes the intersection's result[8] between all the sets of V which minimize samely F[9] when it called at the first time the focal point algorithm (i.e., $\mathcal{F}ocus = V$). If the intersection does not return an empty set, then the set returned is considered as the set of RCI agents to be executed.

4. In the case where the intersection returns an empty set, each RCI agent will end locally with this result and then each one will decide to not execute and to join again another decision making group.

6 An example of simulation

We consider the following rules (the exponent of each rule represents its priority value in the system):

$$R_1^{[10]} : A < x,y >, \; B < z,u > \; \rightarrow \; -C < x,y >, \; D < x,u >$$
$$R_2^{[8]} : B < x,y >, \; C < u,v > \; \rightarrow \; -B < u,y >$$
$$R_3^{[10]} : A < x,y >, \; -D < x,u > \; \rightarrow \; B < x,u >$$
$$R_4^{[5]} : B < x,y > \; \rightarrow \; E < y,y >$$
$$R_5^{[3]} : A < x,y > \; \rightarrow \; D < y,x >$$
$$R_6^{[1]} : A < x,y > \; \rightarrow \; F < x,x >$$

For each rule, we have:

$$INTERPOS(R_1) = \{R_2, R_3\} \; and \; INTERNEG(R_1) = \{R_2\}$$
$$INTERPOS(R_2) = \{R_1, R_2, R_3, R_4\} \; and \; INTERNEG(R_2) = \{R_1, R_2, R_3\}$$
$$INTERPOS(R_3) = \{R_2\} \; and \; INTERNEG(R_3) = \{R_1, R_2, R_5\}$$
$$INTERPOS(R_4) = \{\} \; and \; INTERNEG(R_4) = \{R_2\}$$
$$INTERPOS(R_5) = \{R_3\} \; and \; INTERNEG(R_5) = \{\}$$
$$INTERPOS(R_6) = \{\} \; and \; INTERNEG(R_6) = \{\}$$

We consider the follwing RCI agents:

$$RCI_1^{[10]} : A < 1,3 >, \; B < 2,4 > \; \rightarrow \; -C < 1,3 >, \; D < 1,4 >$$
$$RCI_2^{[8]} : B < 2,4 >, \; C < 1,3 > \; \rightarrow \; -B < 1,4 >$$
$$RCI_3^{[10]} : A < 1,3 >, \; -D < 1,4 > \; \rightarrow \; B < 1,4 >$$
$$RCI_4^{[5]} : B < 2,4 > \; \rightarrow \; E < 4,4 >$$

---

[8] The intersection operation's result does not depend on the order of its entries.
[9] There is inevitably more than one set, otherwise, UFP_V^W would contain this single set and so would not be empty.

$$RCI_5^{[3]} : A < 1,3 > \rightarrow D < 3,1 >$$
$$RCI_6^{[1]} : A < 1,3 > \rightarrow F < 1,1 >$$

RCI_6 is a green agent, RCI_5 is an orange one while RCI_1, RCI_2, RCI_3 and RCI_4 are all red agents. The simulation of this example on a grid of 24 processors (4x6) with (p9 p10 p15 p16) as the supposed control area gave the following scenario : RCI_6 has computed on the processor where it was initially. RCI_5 has first reached the control area and then has computed. RCI_1, RCI_2, RCI_3 and RCI_4 have reached the control area respectively on P16, P15, P9 and P10. Each one of them has performed the coordination behaviour and each one gets the same contents of the set[10] but in a certain order as it is shown in the table.

	RCI_i (for i= 1 to 4)
X	$\{RCI_1, RCI_2, RCI_3, RCI_4\}$
W	$\{\{RCI_1, RCI_4\}, \{RCI_2, RCI_4\},$ $\{RCI_3, RCI_4\}\}$
V	$\{\{RCI_1, RCI_4\}, \{RCI_3, RCI_4\}\}$
UFP_V^V	$\{\{RCI_1, RCI_4\}, \{RCI_3, RCI_4\}\}$
$FPAV_V^V$	$\{RCI_1, RCI_4\}$

As RCI_1 and RCI_4 belong to the set $FPAV_V^V$ so they executed, while RCI_2 and RCI_3 decided to not execute. Serializability has not been violated and priority has been taken into account.

7 Simulation results

Many tests have been conducted with different configurations. A configuration includes a *decision making group* of size N, a domain of values for rules priorities [1..Z] and a square matrix M[N $\times$ N] of the Disabling/Clashing interactions. For each test, a new configuration has been generated randomly. We present the results of five cases (N = 5, N = 10, N = 20, N = 30, N = 50 with Z fixed to 10). For each case, 1000 tests have been performed. The results obtained are given in the following table[11]:

	PA	PV	PW	PINT	PF
N= 5	92.8	4.7	1.3	1.0	.2
N= 10	91.9	5.5	2.0	.5	.1
N= 20	91.5	5.7	2.3	.4	.1
N= 30	90.1	7.0	2.6	.3	0.0
N= 50	85.7	10.3	3.9	.1	0.0

We notice that by introducing the selection (based on highest priorities), most cases are reduced to a case of a simple decision making (PA)[12].

---

[10] $FPAV_V^V = \{RCI_1, RCI_4\}$ since F($\{RCI_1, RCI_4\}$)= 250 and F($\{RCI_3, RCI_4\}$)= 225.

[11] PA: cases where V contains a single set. PV: cases resolved by the first call of the focal point algorithm. PW: cases resolved by the second call of the focal point algorithm. PI: cases resolved partially by the intersection. PF: failure cases.

[12] Even if these cases decrease smoothly with the increasing of the group size.

8 Conclusion

Our solution guarantees the serializability and the respect of a specified order of rules computation in a completely distributed manner. There is no leader in the system who dictates what behaviour the entities should follow. RCI agents, by interacting with each other in a simple way, succeed in maintaining the system in a "good health". As an improvement, we suggest to endow the control area with means of adaptability to set a certain load balancing. Namely, to face up a high control activity rate, others processors can be appealed to join the control area. Conversely, if it turns out that the control area is too big relatively to the control activity rate, this region will shorten by releasing some procesors.

References

1. M. A. Abtroun, "Etude des Problèmes de Contrôle dans les Systèmes à Base de Règles Parallèles", mémoire de DEA, INSA-UCB Lyon, 1995.
2. E. Bonnabeau, G. Theraulaz, J-L Deneubourg, S. Aron, S. Camazine, "Self-Organization and Alternative Models in Social Insects", published in Trends in Ecology & Evolution, 1995.
3. J. Bonneville, S. Hassas, "Towards a Self-Organizational Approach for a Parallel Computation in a Distributed Production Rule Based System", in Spring Symposium on Adaptation, Co-evolution and Learning in Multi-agent Systems, Stanford University, CA, 1996.
4. M. Fenster, S. Kraus, J. Rosenschein, "Coordination without Communication: Experimental Validation of Focal Point Techniques", First International Conference on Multiagent Systems, pp 102–108, California, USA, June 1995.
5. T. Ishida, S. Stolfo, "Towards the Parallel Execution of Rules in Production System Programs", in Proceedings of the International Conference on Parallel Processing, 1985.
6. T. Ishida, "Parallel Distributed and Multi-Agent Production Systems", in Proceedings of the International Conference on Multi-Agent Systems, San Francisco, 1995.
7. M. Mataric, "Interaction and Intelligent Behaviour", submitted to the Department of Electrical Engineering and Computer Science of the requirements for the degree of Doctor of Philosophy, M.I.T., 1994.
8. D. Neiman, "Design and Control of Parallel Rule-Firing Production Systems", Ph.D thesis, Computer and Information Sciences Department, University of Massachusetts, Amherst, MA, 1992.
9. J. Schmolze, S. Goel, "A Parallel Asynchronous Distributed Production System", in Proceedings of the Eighth National Conference on Artificial Intelligence (AAAI-90), Boston, MA, July 1990.
10. J. Schmolze, "Guaranteeing Serializability in Parallel Production Systems", Parallel Processing for Artificial Intelligence, L. Kanal, V. Kumar, H. Kitano and C. Suttner, editors, Elsevier Science Publishers, 1993.
11. S. Stolfo, O. Wolfson, P.Chan, H. Dewan, L.Woodbury, J. Glasier, D. Ohsie, "PARULEL: Parallel Rule Processing Using Meta-rules for Redaction", Journal of Parallel and Distributed Computing, 13(4): 366-382, 1991.

Optimal Communication Among Team Members

Hung H. Bui*, Dorota Kieronska, and Svetha Venkatesh

Department of Computer Science,
Curtin University of Technology, Perth, WA 6001, Australia
Email: {buihh, dorota, svetha}@cs.curtin.edu.au

Abstract. We present a formal framework based on the theory of game with incomplete information [5] for modelling the coordination and communication problem among team of collaborative agents, and define what it means by optimal communication in this setting. Although computing an optimal communication strategy for the team is hard in general, we illustrate with an example of collaborative negotiation and meeting scheduling that computation can be substantially reduced when domain-dependent assumptions are introduced.

1 Introduction

Multi-agent systems are networks of loosely-coupled computational agents that can interact with one another in solving problems. The distributed nature of such systems means that it is often not feasible for any agent to have complete and up-to-date knowledge about the entire system. These uncertainties can seriously affect the quality of coordination among the agents. Communication can help in reducing these uncertainties, and thus plays an important role in coordinating the agents' actions.

Communication however can be costly due to its time delay and bandwidth demand, and sometimes, due to unwanted revelation of private information. In system such as the contract-net protocol [12], not modelling this cost can result in communication overload which seriously degrades the performance of the system [9]. Thus communication should be subjected to careful cost/benefit analysis, and justified in much the same way as the agents' physical actions are.

The work towards this goal comes under two approaches. The logic-based approach, followed from theory of speech act [10], attempts to give a logical formalisation of the communication process and its relation to the beliefs, goals and intentions of the agent [2, 11]. Alternatively, decision-theoretic approach advises the agent to choose communicative actions that maximise its utilities, which is the difference between the new utility gained by performing the communicative act and the cost of the act [3, 4]. This is similar to the so-called sampling problem in decision theory [7], where one must choose whether or not to spend efforts in gaining more knowledge about a population through sampling.

---

* Supported by Overseas Postgraduate Research Scholarship and Curtin University Postgraduate Scholarship

In this paper, we focus on the communication problem among team members. A group of agents are qualified as a *team* if there is no conflict of interest among themselves, i.e. they share the same goal, e.g. to maximise the entire firm's profits, or to maximise the traffic flow on the entire road network[1]. Even here, coordination is a non-trivial task since the agents might have private information and observations that are unknown to others. Different agents thus would evaluate the same situation differently since their evaluations are conditioned on different sources of information. In this case, communication can be valuable in reconciling their differences, but needs to be weighed against the cost incurred.

We base our analysis of optimal communication on the notion of *team optimality*, i.e. the best a team could do in a team problem, and use game-theoretic tool to formalise it. Team optimality is more suitable in our domain than the agent-centred optimality notion used in decision-theoretic approach [3, 4] since (1) the agents can be assumed to have common knowledge about the team problem, and (2) team optimality insists on a global optimum for the team problem, while an agent-centred optimality could only converge to some local optimum[2].

The paper proceeds as follows. In the next section, we present the framework for coordination in team problems with incomplete information. Next, we enrich the framework with a model of communication and define the notion of optimal communication. Computational issues are considered subsequently, and simplifications in the domain of collaborative negotiation are presented. Finally, we conclude and give directions to possible future work.

2 Model of Coordination with Incomplete Information

2.1 Games and Team Problems

We model a multi-agent interaction as a *game*. Each agent's possible *actions* correspond to its allowed moves in the game. A combination of actions of all agents would bring about some changes in the environment whose effects on the agents might be good or bad. This is modelled by the agent's *utility* for such an action combination. During the game, each agent will act so as to maximise its utility. Formally, a game is a tuple $\Gamma = \langle N, (S_i), (U_i) \rangle$ where N is the set of all agents involved, S_i is the set of actions/strategies available to agent i, U_i is the utility function of agent i and is a function $U_i : \prod_i S_i \to \mathbb{R}$.

A game Γ is a team problem if the utility functions U_i are identical. This represents the case where the agents have no conflict of interests. Ignoring the subscript i in U_i, a team problem Γ has the form $\langle N, (S_i), U \rangle$.

Throughout the paper, we will assume that N, S_i are finite sets. We also adopt the following short-hand notations whenever there is no confusion. N is

---

[1] Such systems are usually referred to in the DAI literature as cooperative. We do not use this term to avoid confusion with the term "cooperative game" in game theory.

[2] For further discussions of decision versus game theoretic approach to coordination, see [1, 6, 8].

informally taken as the set $\{1, 2, \ldots, N\}$ and also used to denote the number of agents present. If x_i are scalars, x represents the vector $(x_1, x_2, \ldots, x_n)$, and x_{-i} represents the vector $(x_1, \ldots, x_{i-1}, x_{i+1}, \ldots, x_n)$. If X_i are sets, X represents the cross products $\prod_i X_i$ and $X_{-i} = \prod_{j \neq i} X_j$. For example, $s \in S$ would represent the action combination $(s_1, \ldots, s_N)$ and s_{-i} would represent the combination of actions of all agents other than i. If z is a random variable on the domain Z, and $f(z)$ is a real-valued function, the notation $E_{p(z)} f(z)$ denotes the expected value of $f(z)$, and is short for $\sum_{z \in Z} p(z) f(z)$.

In the team problem Γ, since there is no conflict of interest, there would be an action combination s^* that maximises the team utility U. Thus optimally, agent i should choose the action s_i^*. We shall term s^* the *team optimal point*[3] (TOP) of the team problem Γ. Formally, we have $s^* \in \arg\max_{s \in S} U(s)$.

2.2 Incomplete Information

The above description of team problem assumes that the agents have enough knowledge at hand to compute their utility for any combination of actions s. In reality, it is often that utility cannot be computed in exact form since it might depend on parameters whose values are unknown to the agent. Thus the agents have to base their actions on expected value of the true utility U. An interesting case is when these parameters are observed in private by the team members. This is likely to happen if the team is a distributed network of agents and data is available in a distributed manner. Since observations change the expected value of U and different agents experience different observations, the agents subjective expectations of U are no longer the same. This introduces new difficulties in coordinating their actions. We term this the incomplete information problem (also known as the asymmetric information problem).

Harsanyi [5] proposed the following ingenious resolution to the above problem[4]. All private information of agent i is summarised into an object called its *type*, denoted by t_i, so that the prior probability distribution of t_i, denoted by p_i is known to all agents. Then, the agents can be thought of as playing the following equivalent game. Firstly, nature or chance choose the agents' type vector t according to the distribution p (t_i is chosen with probability $p_i(t_i)$). Nature then reveals the value t_i to agent i (which now becomes its private information). Finally, each agent i picks an action s_i and receives the utility $U(s, t)$.

Let T_i denote the set of all possible types of agent i (e.g. all possible values of its private observation). We assume that T_i are finite and p_i is a strictly positive distribution on T_i. A team problem with incomplete information can be represented formally as a tuple $\Gamma = \langle N, (S_i), U, (T_i), (p_i) \rangle$ where N, S_i remain as before, U is now a function on both actions and types: $U : S \times T \to \mathbb{R}$. We assume that different agents' types are independent and denote p the joint distribution of p_i: $p(t) = \prod_{i \in N} p_i(t_i)$.

---

[3] A TOP is also a Nash equilibrium, however the opposite is not necessarily true. If multiple TOP's exist for a team problem, they must all yield the same utility, and we assume that the agents will agree on which TOP to follow.

[4] For a more general representation of Harsanyi's idea, readers are referred to [5].

We define an *extended strategy* ψ_i as a rule that tells the agent i which action to choose given its type: $\psi_i : T_i \to S_i$. Let the set of all extended strategies for i be Ψ_i ($\Psi_i = S_i^{|T_i|}$). By letting the agent choose its extended strategy instead of its action, a team problem with incomplete information then can be transformed to one with complete information played within the extended strategy space. The utility assigned to a combination of extended strategies $\psi = (\psi_i)_{i \in N}$ is taken as the expectation of the original utilities: $\bar{U}(\psi) = \mathrm{E}_{p(t)} U((\psi_i(t_i)), t)$. Intuitively, $\bar{U}$ can be viewed as the average utility for the agents if they each employ the extended strategy ψ_i and play the game for many times. Thus the team problem with incomplete information can also be represented as the tuple $\langle N, (\Psi_i), \bar{U} \rangle$.

Having removed the incomplete information, we are now ready to define TOP's for team problems with incomplete information. Given $\Gamma = \langle N, (S_i), U, (T_i), (p_i) \rangle$, its TOP is a combination of extended strategies ψ^* which is simply a TOP of $\langle N, (\Psi_i), (\bar{U}_i) \rangle$. In other words, $\psi^* \in \arg\max_{\psi \in \Psi} \bar{U}(\psi) = \arg\max_{\psi \in \Psi} \mathrm{E}_{p(t)} U((\psi_i(t_i)), t)$.

We call the expected utility resulting from the TOP ψ^* the *value* $v(\Gamma)$ of the team problem. Intuitively, $v(\Gamma)$ is the maximal utility a team can achieve from the team problem Γ:

$$v(\Gamma) = \max_{\psi \in \Psi} \bar{U}(\psi) = \max_{\psi \in \Psi} \mathrm{E}_{p(t)} U((\psi_i(t_i)), t) \tag{1}$$

Finding the TOP ψ^* involves a search in the space of extended strategy combinations $\Psi = \prod_{i \in N} \Psi_i = \prod_{i \in N} S_i^{|T_i|}$. Thus the computational complexity in general would be exponential of the number of agents N, and the number of different types an agent could have assuming a fixed number of possible strategies ($O(\exp(N \max_i |T_i|))$).

We introduce the following notations that will be used in the later sections. Let $\tau = (\tau_i)_{i \in N}$ where τ_i is a subset of T_i. We define the restriction of Γ on τ is the team problem with incomplete information $\Gamma^\tau = \langle N, (S_i), U, (\tau_i), (p_i') \rangle$ where U is restricted to τ_i and $p_i'(t_i) = p(t_i|\tau_i) = \frac{p(t_i)}{\sum_{t_i' \in \tau_i} p(t_i')}, \forall t_i \in \tau_i$.

3 Model of Communication

We want to investigate what would happen if the agents can broadcast information about their private types to others prior to playing the incomplete information game. This is done by considering the extended team problem where the strategy sets of the agents are enlarged to allow for their communication possibilities.

3.1 Communication Strategy

Let M_i be the set of possible messages that can be broadcasted by the agent i to others. We assume that a cost $\pi(m_i)$ would be incurred whenever agent i chooses to broadcast the message $m_i \in M_i$.

We define a *communication strategy* ϕ_i for agent i is a function from the set of its possible types to the set of its possible broadcasting messages: $\phi_i : T_i \to M_i$.

Such a ϕ_i would incur an expected cost $\pi(\phi_i) = E_{p_i}\pi(\phi_i(t_i))$. Let $\phi = (\phi_i)_{i\in N}$ be a combination of communication strategies. The expected cost of ϕ is defined as the sum of the expected costs of all ϕ_i: $\pi(\phi) = \sum_{i\in N}\pi(\phi_i)$.

A communication strategy ϕ_i also partitions T_i into a number of subsets of types that generate identical messages. Formally, let $\mathcal{T}_{\phi_i}$ be the partition of T_i by the communication strategy ϕ_i, we have $\mathcal{T}_{\phi_i} = \{\{t_i|\phi_i(t_i) = m_i\}|m_i \in M_i\}$[5]. Similarly, a combination of communication strategies ϕ partitions T into $\mathcal{T}$, the set of subsets of T that generate identical combination of messages. It can be verified that $\mathcal{T} = \prod_{i\in N}\mathcal{T}_i$.

Intuitively, $\mathcal{T}_i$ defines how much information agent i reveals to other agents through its communication strategy. Let $\tau_i \in \mathcal{T}_i$ and $\phi_i(\tau_i) = m_i$. When other agents receive m_i from i, their uncertainty about t_i will be restricted to τ_i and their updated posterior about t_i will be $p_i'(t_i) = p_i(t_i|\tau_i)$. Thus the effect of a combination of communication strategies ϕ is to break the team problem Γ to a set of team problems $\{\Gamma^\tau|\tau \in \mathcal{T}\}$. We define the value of a communication strategy combination to be the expected values of the team problems in this set:

$$v(\phi) = \sum_{\tau\in\mathcal{T}} p(\tau)v(\Gamma^\tau) \tag{2}$$

It can be shown that the finer the partition $\mathcal{T}$, the higher $v(\phi)$ is. Thus, intuitively, the value of communication is a monotonic non-decreasing function on the amount of information being revealed.

The *worth* of a communication strategy combination is simply the difference between its value and its cost:

$$\omega(\phi) = \sum_{\tau\in\mathcal{T}} p(\tau)v(\Gamma_\tau) - \pi(\phi) \tag{3}$$

We define a communication strategy to be optimal if its worth is maximal:

Definition 1 (Optimal communication). A combination of communication strategies ϕ^* is optimal for Γ iff the worth of ϕ^* is maximal:

$$\phi^* \in \arg\max_{\phi\in\Phi} \omega(\phi)$$

3.2 Team Problem with Communication

In this subsection, we provide concrete rationale for definition 1 by linking it to the TOP of the extended team problem where the agents' action sets are enlarged with communicative action (which we shall term the *team problem with communication*, or TPC).

A team problem with communication (TPC) is modelled in two stages. In the first stage, each agent i broadcasts a message m_i to the rest of the team. In the second stage, the agents proceed to play the original team problem. However, the actions now can be made dependent on the messages received from the other

---

[5] Subsequently, we drop the subscript ϕ in $\mathcal{T}_{\phi_i}$ and write $\mathcal{T}_i$ instead when there is no confusion about which ϕ is being referred to.

agents $m_{-i} = (m_j)_{j \neq i}$. Thus, the strategy for agent i in this TPC is a pair (m_i, r_i) where m_i is the message that would be broadcasted by i, $r_i : M_{-i} \to S_i$ is a plan of what i would do next in reply to the messages m_{-i} received from other agents (if m_{-i} are received, i's action would be $r_i(m_{-i})$). The set of strategies for i is then $M_i \times R_i$, where $R_i = \{r_i : M_{-i} \to S_i\} = S_i^{|M_{-i}|}$ is the set of all such plans. Finally, the agents received their utilities minus the overall communication cost[6]. This is formalised in the following definition of TPC:

Definition 2 (Team problem with communication (TPC)). Let Γ be a team problem $\langle N, (S_i), U, (T_i), (p_i) \rangle$. The TPC Γ^c (extension of Γ) is defined as the team problem $\Gamma^c = \langle N, (S_i^c), U^c, (T_i), (p_i) \rangle$ where $S_i^c = M_i \times R_i$ and $U^c((m_i, r_i)_{i \in N}, t) = U((r_i(m_{-i}))_{i \in N}, t) - \sum_{i \in N} \pi(m_i)$.

Given the TPC Γ^c, agent i's extended strategy is a function $\psi_i^c : T_i \to S_i^c = M_i \times R_i$, and thus is a pair $\psi_i^c = (\phi_i, \lambda_i)$ where $\phi_i : T_i \to M_i$ is a communication strategy, and $\lambda_i : T_i \to R_i$ is a type-dependent action plan for i. Let Φ_i be the set of all possible communication strategies and Λ_i be the set of all type-dependent action plans for i. The set of all i's extended strategies is then $\Psi_i^c = \Phi_i \times \Lambda_i$.

The following theorem provides the rationale for definition 1. It states that the optimal communication strategy is essentially a part of the TOP of the team problem with communication. The proof is omitted here for brevity, but can be found in [1].

Theorem 3. Let $\Gamma^c = \langle N, (S_i^c), U, (T_i), (p_i) \rangle$ be a TPC generated from the team problem Γ. A combination of communication strategies $\phi^* = (\phi_i^*)_{i \in N}$ is optimal for Γ iff it is part of a TOP of Γ^c. That is $\exists$ some $\lambda^* \in \Lambda$ s.t $\psi^{c*} = (\phi^*, \lambda^*)$ is a TOP of Γ^c.

4 Towards Optimal Communication

In this section, we start addressing the issue of computing the agents' optimal communication strategies. This generally involves computing the value and cost of each communication strategy combination, and choosing the one with maximal worth. The complexity then depends on the computation of values and costs, and the number of communication strategies considered. Followingly, we restrict our focus to computing the value of communication strategies. We will assume that the agents would only want to weigh among a small number of different communication strategies, and that their costs can be relatively simple to estimate. We will also adhere to a particular domain, namely the *collaborative negotiation* domain and an example of distributed meeting scheduling.

---

[6] Since the agents are part of a team, it is the overall communication cost that should be minimised, not just their own communication cost.

4.1 Collaborative Negotiation and Meeting Scheduling

As an example of team problem with incomplete information, we consider a collaborative negotiation scenario when a team of agents negotiate to choose an outcome k from a set of possible outcomes $\mathcal{D}$ to maximise the team's objective function F. Each agent also holds a local preference $t_i(k)$ for each outcome k. These local preferences are the agents' private information and constitute the agents' types. Formally, the preferences of agent i are represented by $t_i : \mathcal{D} \to \mathbb{R}$. To make t_i finite, we assume that $\mathcal{D} = \{1, \ldots, K\}$, and $t_i = \{1, \ldots, K\} \to \{1, \ldots, M\}$ for some integers K and M. We can also write t_i in vector form as $t_i = (t_{ik})$ where $t_{ik} = t_i(k)$. F is then defined as a function f combining the preference values

$$F(t_1, \ldots, t_N, k) = f(t_1(k), \ldots, t_N(k)) \tag{4}$$

In the rest of the paper, we assume that f is the summation function: $f(t_1(k), \ldots, t_N(k)) = \sum_{i \in N} t_i(k)$. However, in general, we only need f to be linear w.r.t. each of its variable given the others. Note that in this formulation, the number of types of agent i is $|T_i| = M^K$, and the number of combinations of the agents' types is $|T| = M^{KN}$.

For example, consider a group of agents whose task is to schedule a meeting between their respective users. The set of outcomes $\mathcal{D}$ is the set of tentative time-slots that can be scheduled for the meeting. Each user has his/her own private preferences over the time-slots which represent how free he/she might be during the interval. This data is held by his/her own agent, and not available a priori to the other agents involved. The team objective function is the sum of all users' private preferences: $F(t_1, \ldots, t_N, k) = \sum_{i \in N} t_i(k)$, and the goal for the group of agents is to choose a time-slot to maximise this sum.

To define the agents' strategies S, we need to define a protocol in which the agents can negotiate on the outcome. We assume a simple protocol as follows: the agents simultaneously propose one of the outcomes k in $\mathcal{D}$. If all the proposals are the same, this will be the final agreement. Otherwise, the final agreement will be drawn randomly from the set of proposals such that a proposal k will be selected with probability x/N where x is the number of agents who propose k.

With this negotiation protocol being fixed, the set of actions for the agents coincide with the set of outcomes: $S_i = \mathcal{D}$. The utility of s is the expected utility of the final agreement when the agents follow the protocol and propose s_i respectively[7].

$$U(s, t) = \frac{1}{N} \sum_{i \in N} F(t, s_i) = g[F(t, s_1), \ldots, F(t, s_N)] \tag{5}$$

Now, meeting scheduling can be modelled as a team problem $\Gamma = \langle N, (S_i), U, (T_i), p_i \rangle$ where S, U, T are defined above. The distribution p_i is the prior distribution on T_i, in this case on the set of preferences of user i.

---

[7] This particular protocol is categorised by the function $g((x_i)) = \sum_i x_i/N$. In general g can have the form $g = a_1 x_1 + \ldots + a_N x_N$.

4.2   Value and TOP of Γ

With the above formulation, we show here that Γ has a relatively simple TOP, and derive the formula for $v(\Gamma)$. From (1), we have $v(\Gamma) = \max_\psi \mathrm{E}_{p(t)} U((\psi_i(t_i)), t)$. Substituting the new value for utility from (5) in this, we have:

$$v(\Gamma) = \max_\psi \mathop{\mathrm{E}}_{p(t)} g[F(t, \psi_1(t_1)), \dots, F(t, \psi_N(t_N))]$$

Intuitively, computing $v(\Gamma)$ involves a maximisation over the set of tuples of extended strategies $(\psi_1, \dots, \psi_N)$. However, since g is a linear function, each agent i can independently do a maximisation on the set of its own extended strategies. Given this, the above equation becomes:

$$v(\Gamma) = g[\max_{\psi_1} \mathop{\mathrm{E}}_{p(t)} F(t, \psi_1(t_1)), \dots, \max_{\psi_N} \mathop{\mathrm{E}}_{p(t)} F(t, \psi_N(t_N))]$$

$$= g[v_1(\Gamma), \dots, v_N(\Gamma)] \tag{6}$$

where $v_i(\Gamma) = \max_{\psi_i} \mathrm{E}_{p(t)} F(t, \psi_i(t_i))$ is what agent i needs to compute to find its optimal strategy. Since t_i are independent, this maximisation can be done separately on different values of t_i. Thus, agent i with preferences t_i has the optimal proposal $\psi_i^*(t_i)$ that solves $\max_{k=1}^K \{\mathrm{E}_{p(t_{-i})} F(t, k)\}$, and:

$$v_i(\Gamma) = \mathop{\mathrm{E}}_{p(t_i)} \max_{k=1}^K \{ \mathop{\mathrm{E}}_{p(t_{-i})} F(t, k) \} \tag{7}$$

The expectation $\mathrm{E}_{p(t_{-i})} F(t, k)$ can be interpreted as agent i's *evaluation of its proposal* k, which we shall term z_{ik}. Agent i's best proposal will yield $z_i = \max_k \{z_{ik}\}$. From (4) we have:

$$z_{ik} = \mathop{\mathrm{E}}_{p(t_{-i})} F(t, k) = \mathop{\mathrm{E}}_{p(t_{-i})} f(t_1(k), \dots, t_N(k)) = \mathop{\mathrm{E}}_{p(t_{-i})} f(t_i(k), t_{-i}(k))$$

Since f is a summation function and thus, is linear with respect to each of its variables given the others, we obtain a further simplification:

$$z_{ik} = f\left[t_i(k), (\mathop{\mathrm{E}}_{p(t_{jk})} t_j(k))_{j \neq i} \right] = t_i(k) + \sum_{j \neq i} \mathop{\mathrm{E}}_{p(t_{jk})} t_j(k)$$

Thus agent i's evaluation z_{ik} of a proposal k is the *sum* of i's *own preference* for k together with i's *estimations of the other agents' preferences* for k. The TOP of the team problem Γ advises each agent i to choose its proposal k so that to maximise its evaluations $\{z_{ik}\}$. The value of team problem $v(\Gamma)$ can be obtained from simplifications of (6) and (7) as bellows:

$$v(\Gamma) = g\left[\left(\mathop{\mathrm{E}}_{p(t_i)} z_i \right)_{i \in N} \right] \tag{8}$$

4.3   Simplification of the Value of Communication

Given a communication strategy combination ϕ, its value can be computed using formula (2) as $v(\phi) = \sum_{\tau \in \mathcal{T}} p(\tau) v(\Gamma^\tau)$. However, this involves a summation over all members of the partition $\mathcal{T}$, which could have as many elements as the set of the agents' type vectors T itself. We have mentioned that $|T| = M^{KN}$, thus computing the value of communication by directly using (2) results in an exponential complexity in terms of K and N. Our aim here is to simplify the value of communication $v(\phi)$ gradually until a satisfactory form is reached that can be computed efficiently (with polynomial complexity).

From (8), we have a formula for $v(\Gamma^\tau)$:

$$v(\Gamma^\tau) = g\left[\left(\mathop{E}_{p(t_i|\tau)} z_i\right)_{i \in N}\right]$$

with a similar definition for z_{ik} and z_k as $z_{ik} = t_i(k) + \sum_{j \neq i} e(\tau_j, k)$, $z_i = \max_k\{z_{ik}\}$ where $e(\tau_j, k) = E_{p(t_{jk}|\tau_j)} t_{jk}$ is the expectation of j's preference for k given that j's type is in τ_j.

Substituting the above into (2), we have:

$$v(\phi) = \mathop{E}_{p(\tau)} g\left[\left(\mathop{E}_{p(t_i|\tau)} z_i\right)_{i \in N}\right] = g\left[\left(\mathop{E}_{p(\tau)} \mathop{E}_{p(t_i|\tau)} z_i\right)_{i \in N}\right]$$

$$= g\left[\left(\mathop{E}_{p(\tau_{-i})} \mathop{E}_{p(t_i)} z_i\right)_{i \in N}\right] = g\left[\left(\mathop{E}_{p(t_i, \tau_{-i})} z_i\right)_{i \in N}\right] \tag{9}$$

From this point onward, we proceed by viewing z_i as a random variable whose expectation $\bar{z}_i$ is to be estimated. Let Z_i be its probability distribution: $Z_i(x) = \Pr(z_i \leq x)$, each expectation appearing in (9) can be written as

$$\bar{z}_i = \mathop{E}_{p(t_i, \tau_{-i})} z_i = \int_x x \, dZ_i(x) \tag{10}$$

This can be approximated efficiently if $Z_i(x)$ can be computed efficiently. Since $z_i = \max_k\{z_{ik}\}$, computing Z_i can be greatly simplified when $\{z_{ik}\}_{k=1}^K$ are independent. To satisfy this requirement, we make the following assumptions:

Assumption 1. For all i, $(t_{ik})_{k=1}^K$ are independent, i.e. $p_i(t_i) = \prod_{k=1}^K p_{ik}(t_{ik})$, meaning agent i's preferences for different outcomes are statistically independent.

Assumption 2. ϕ belongs to a class of communication strategy combinations such that the strategy ϕ_i used by agent i reveals information about $t_{i1}, \ldots, t_{iK}$ independently, e.g. no correlation information between t_{ik} and t_{il} such as $t_{ik} \geq t_{il}$ can be revealed. Formally, the partition $\mathcal{T}_i$ by ϕ_i is such that there are some partitions $\mathcal{T}_{ik}$ of T_{ik} such that $\mathcal{T}_i = \prod_k \mathcal{T}_{ik}$.

From assumption 2, $p(\tau_i) = p(t_i \in \tau_i) = p(\forall k, t_{ik} \in \tau_{ik})$. But from assumption 1, this equals to $\prod_{k=1}^K p(t_{ik} \in \tau_{ik}) = \prod_{k=1}^K p(\tau_{ik})$. Thus,

$$p(\tau_i) = \prod_{k=1}^K p(\tau_{ik})$$

which means that $\{\tau_{ik}\}_{k=1}^K$ are independent.

Using assumption 2, we have

$$e(\tau_j, k) = \underset{p(t_{jk}|\tau_j)}{\mathrm{E}} t_{jk} = \underset{p(t_{jk}|\tau_{jk})}{\mathrm{E}} t_{jk} = \bar{\tau}_{jk}$$

and thus $\{e(\tau_j, k)\}_{k=1}^K$ are also independent.

Since z_{ik} is a function of t_{ik} and $\{e(\tau_j, k)\}_{j\neq i}$, the above results implies that $(z_{ik})_{k=1}^K$ are also independent. Thus:

$$Z_i(x) = \mathrm{Pr}(z_i \leq x) = \mathrm{Pr}(\forall k, z_{ik} \leq x) = \prod_{k=1}^K \mathrm{Pr}(z_{ik} \leq x)$$

$$= \prod_{k=1}^K Z_{ik}(x) \tag{11}$$

Recall that $z_{ik} = f[t_i(k), (e(\tau_j, k))_{j\neq i}]$, we have:

$$Z_{ik}(x) = \mathrm{Pr}(f[t_i(k), (e(\tau_j, k))_{j\neq i}] \leq x) = \mathrm{Pr}(t_i(k) + \sum_{j\neq i} e(\tau_j, k) \leq x)$$

We have $\mathrm{Pr}(t_i(k) = x) = p_{ik}(x)$ and let $q_{jk}(x) = \mathrm{Pr}(e(\tau_j, k) = x)$. Since z_{ik} is the sum of N independent random variables $t_i(k)$ and $\{e(\tau_j, k)\}_{j\neq i}$, its density function is the convolution of the density function of these variables. Thus:

$$Z_{ik}(x) = \int_{y \leq x} \mathbf{conv}[p_{ik}, (q_{jk})_{j\neq i}](y)\, dy \tag{12}$$

where **conv** is the convolution operator.

The probability distribution of $e(\tau_j, k) = \bar{\tau}_{jk}$ can be approximated by:

$$q_{jk}(x) \approx \begin{cases} p_{jk}(\tau_{jk}) & : \quad x = \mathrm{round}(\bar{\tau}_{jk}) \text{ for some } \tau_{jk} \in \mathcal{T}_{jk} \\ 0 & : \quad \text{otherwise} \end{cases} \tag{13}$$

Equations (9)–(13) provide the basis for computing $v(\phi)$. Under all the assumptions made, the value of a communication strategy combination $v(\phi)$ can be computed in in $O(KMN^2 \log(MN))$ time. Detailed algorithms and the derivation of this complexity measure will be omitted here, but can be found in [1].

5 Conclusion

In summary, we have presented a formal framework based on of the theory of game with incomplete information for studying the team coordination and communication problem under situations where information is incomplete and asymmetric. The framework allows us to define the notion of team optimality, TOP, to be taken as the ideal solution to the team coordination problem. Communication is considered as an extended team problem where the agents are allowed to broadcast messages prior to acting. We define an appropriate notion of value and cost of a given communicating/broadcasting strategy. Optimal communication then becomes the business of choosing a combination of communication strategies with maximal worth. Our notion of worth has a firm rationale since maximal worth corresponds to the TOP of the extended team problem with communication.

Although computing the optimal communication strategy is very demanding in general, we show that by adding some domain-dependent assumptions computation can be reduced substantially, thus illustrating the practicality of the framework.

Our formalisation here however assumes that the prior probability distributions about the agents' private types are given. One could imagine situation where these distributions are learned by the agents through their repeated interactions with the environment and with one other. The integration of learning into this framework is an interesting possibility and is being considered in our current work.

References

1. H. H. Bui, D. Kieronska, and S. Venkatesh. Coordination and commmunication among team members. Technical Report 2/1997, Department of Computer Science, Curtin University of Technology, Perth, Australia, 1997.
2. P. R. Cohen and H. J. Levesque. Rational interaction as the basis for communication. In J. Morgan P. R. Cohen and M. E. Pollack, editors, *Intentions in Communication*. MIT Press, 1990.
3. Piotr J. Gmytrasiewicz and Edmund H. Durfee. Toward a theory of honesty and trust among communicating agents. *Group Decision and Negotiation*, 2:237–258, 1993.
4. Piotr J. Gmytrasiewicz and Edmund H. Durfee. Rational interaction in multiagent environments: Communication. In submission, 1997.
5. John C. Harsanyi. Games with incomplete information played by Bayesian players 1-3. *Management Science*, 14:159–182,320–334,486–502, 1967-1968.
6. John C. Harsanyi. Subjective probability and the theory of games: Comments. *Management Science*, 28(2):120–124, February 1982.
7. J. Morgan Jones. *Introduction to Decision Theory*. Richard D. Irwin, Inc., 1977.
8. Joseph B. Kadane and Patrick D. Larkey. Subjective probability and the theory of games. *Management Science*, 28(2):113–120, February 1982.
9. Tuomas Sandholm and Victor Lesser. Issues in automated negotiation and electronic commerce: extending the contract net framework. In *Proceedings of the First International Conference on Multiagent Systems (ICMAS-95)*, pages 328–335, San Francisco,, CA, 1995.
10. J. R. Searle. *Speech Acts: An Essay in the Philosophy of Language*. Cambridge University Press, 1969.
11. Ira A. Smith and Philip R. Cohen. Toward a semantics for an agent communications language based on speech-acts. In *Proceedings of the National Conference on Artificial Intelligence (AAAI-96)*, pages 24–31, 1996.
12. R. G. Smith. The contract net protocol: High-level communication and control in a distributed problem solver. *IEEE Transactions on Computers*, 29(12):1104–1113, 1980.

Dominant and Recessive Genes in Evolutionary Systems Applied to Spatial Reasoning

Thorsten Schnier and John Gero

Key Centre of Design Computing
Department of Architectural and Design Science
University of Sydney, NSW, 2006, Australia
fax: +61-2-9351-3031
email : {thorsten,john}@arch.usyd.edu.au

Abstract. Learning genetic representation has been shown to be a useful tool in evolutionary computation. It can reduce the time required to find solutions and it allows the search process to be biased towards more desirable solutions. Learning genetic representation involves the bottom-up creation of evolved genes from either original (basic) genes or from other evolved genes and the introduction of those into the population. The evolved genes effectively protect combinations of genes that have been found useful from being disturbed by the genetic operations (cross-over, mutation).

However, this protection can rapidly lead to situations where evolved genes interlock in such a way that few or no genetic operations are possible on some genotypes. To prevent the interlocking previous implementations only allow the creation of evolved genes from genes that are direct neighbours on the genotype and therefore form continuous blocks.

In this paper it is shown that the notion of dominant and recessive genes can be used to remove this limitation. Using more than one gene at a single location makes it possible to construct genetic operations that can separate interlocking evolved genes. This allows the use of non-continuous evolved genes with only minimal violations of the protection of evolved genes from those operations.

As an example, this paper shows how evolved genes with dominant and recessive genes can be used to learn features from a set of Mondrian paintings. The representation can then be used to create new designs that contain features of the examples. The Mondrian paintings can be coded as a tree, where every node represents a rectangle division, with values for direction, position, linewidth and colour. The modified evolutionary operations allow the system to create non-continuous evolved genes, for example associate two divisions with thin lines, without specifying other values. Analysis of the behaviour of the system shows that about one in ten genes is a dominant/recessive gene pair. This shows that while dominant and recessive genes are important to allow the use of non-continuous evolved genes, they do not occur often enough to seriously violate the protection of evolved genes from genetic operations.

1 Learning Genetic Representations

Evolutionary systems, where random and probability-driven choices play an important part, are strongly influenced by the representation used. Instead of trying to create a neutral representation and to minimize any influence on the outcome of the process, previous work has shown that it can make sense to intentionally introduce a bias into the representation. This can improve the generation of solutions in optimization problems, and can also be used to bias the results of an evolutionary system so that it produces more desirable results.

Starting with a simple representation, a 'conventional' evolutionary system is used to create individuals according to an application-specific fitness function. At the same time, a process observes how the system is using the initial representation. If sufficiently strong patterns are observed, new, evolved genes that represent these patterns are produced and added to the representation (Schnier & Gero 1995). The new evolved genes are used by the system, and can again be incorporated into other, larger evolved genes.

Using the evolved genes can lead to faster problem solving times. The evolved representation can also be re-used for new applications, where the new solution is expected to share features of the original application (see e.g. Gero & Kazakov 1996).

If the initial system is given a set of examples, and the fitness is set to be a measure of the resemblance to the examples, the evolved coding that is created in this process will represent features of the examples. In a second step, this representation can be used to create new individuals that share features of the examples (Schnier & Gero 1996)

The function of evolved genes is the same in both cases: protection of a set of genes from disruption by evolutionary operations like mutation and cross-over.

2 Interlocking Evolved Genes

Genetic operations are used to permutate the genetic material from one or two individuals, creating a new individual. Cross-over and mutation are the most common operations (see e.g. Michalewicz 1992).

Cross-over operations work by cutting the genotypes into two parts, and then swapping the parts of two parents. Evolved genes, however, can easily interlock and lead to situations where no point can be found where cutting is possible without destroying one or more evolved genes, Fig. 1(a). If the operation was allowed to cut through an evolved gene, the protection of gene groups would be violated and the evolved genes would lose their function.

In previous work, evolved genes have therefore been created by combining only directly adjacent genes on the genotype into higher-level genes. In a bottom-up process, this leads to large, continuous groups of basic genes that are represented by an evolved gene. These genes cannot interlock, and conventional genetic operations thus work with little change, Fig. 1(b).

This 'simple evolved gene' model has been shown to be applicable to a range of applications. However, in some applications its restrictions may be undesirable. Figure 1(c) shows an example: while there is no simple evolved gene that can be established, it is still possible to identify useful evolved genes with non-local neighbours.

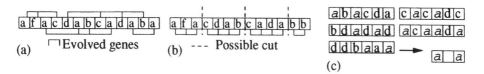

(a) ⌐Evolved genes   (b) --- Possible cut

(c)

Fig. 1. (a) Interlocking evolved genes, (b) simple evolved genes, and (c) example for use of complex evolved genes

3 Using Dominant/Recessive Genes

To allow the use of arbitrary evolved genes, the genetic operations and the method used to create new individuals from evolved genes have to be modified. In doing this it is important to ensure that evolved genes will still be protected. The notion of diploid genetic representations with dominant and recessive genes has been used in genetic algorithms before, but with a very different purposes: a recessive set of genes can act as a memory of previously useful gene sequences, and help the genetic algorithm to adapt in applications with non-stationary fitness functions (Goldberg & Smith 1987, Ng & Wong 1995). Other work has shown that diploidy can help protect genetic algorithms against premature convergence (Greene 1996, Yukiko & Nobue 1994).

3.1 Cross-over

The cross-over operation consists of two steps: cutting the genotypes and re-assembling the two parts. To deal with interlocking evolved genes, the cutting operation has to be modified. It has to cut 'around' the evolved genes. Given a random cutting site, the complex genes spanning the cross-over site can be identified and the genotype cut so that the evolved genes remain completely on either of the two pieces. Figure 2 shows the cuts possible for the genotype in Fig. 1(a).

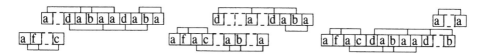

Fig. 2. Possible cross-over cuts for the genotype shown in Fig. 1(a).

The difficulty arises in the reassembly step: if at least one evolved gene spans the cutting site, the ends of the two sections that have to be combined into a new genotype will contain 'holes'. If neither of the ends contains holes, the new genotype can be simply constructed by appending one segment to the other, Fig. 3(a). Similarly, if the holes in both ends happen to 'fit', both segments can be assembled in a 'zipper'-like manner, Fig. 3(b).

In the general case, genes in one end will only partially overlap with holes in the other end. The solution suggested here borrows the notion of recessive and dominant genes in sexual reproduction: allowing genotypes with pairs of genes in some locations of the genotype, with one gene shadowing the other, Fig. 3(c). When the genotype is transformed into a phenotype, one of the genes is expressed, the other ignored. Which gene is expressed is decided when the cross-over operation is executed. Possible criteria are: the gene of the larger evolved gene; the gene of the evolved gene with the higher fitness (see Section 4.3); or one of the two genes randomly selected.

Since some evolved genes are not entirely expressed in the phenotype, the protection of evolved genes is violated. However, this violation is small, since the rest of the evolved gene is still expressed. The important advantage of allowing overlapping, dominant and recessive genes, however, is that all evolved genes involved are still complete units and protected as evolved genes. In further genetic operations they will still be protected from being permutated by the genetic operation. It is also possible that the shadowed parts will be expressed again in an offspring after a cross-over or a mutation.

An interesting special case exists where the holes do not 'fit' but the values of the conflicting genes are equal. This 'continuity' between the two segments, Fig. 3(d), indicates that the new individual might have a higher chance of being successful.

An alternative option to allowing dominant and recessive genes is to append the segments so that 'holes' in the genotype remain, and fill the holes with random basic genes, Fig. 3(e). This adds a larger amount of random genetic material and would only be an option where a high mutation rate is otherwise used. However, it results in very long genotypes, especially once the evolved genes start getting relatively large, maybe spanning 20 or 30 genes. Equally unsatisfying is the option of just rejecting the cross-over: once a high percentage of evolved genes is reached, this would lead to a very strong restriction in possible cross-overs, reducing the performance of the system.

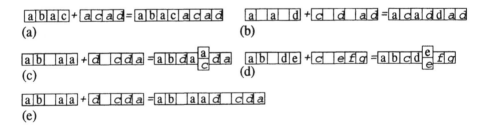

Fig. 3. Different ways to recombine two segments in a cross-over operation.

3.2 Mutation

In a mutation operation, genes in the genotype are randomly swapped with different genes from the current alphabet. While replacing a basic gene by a new basic gene is straightforward, replacing a complex evolved gene with another complex evolved gene is likely to create overlap. If an evolved gene is removed from a genotype, it leaves a pattern of holes; any different evolved gene will probably have genes at different places, and therefore will collide with genes in the genotype.

As with cross-over, using dominant and recessive genes provides a solution. At all places where the new evolved gene collides with an existing evolved gene, both conflicting genes are kept. The set of criteria from Section 3.1 can be used to decide which gene is the dominant and which the recessive. If a collision is caused by a basic gene in the genotype, the basic gene can simply be removed in favour of the evolved gene. To reduce the amount of overlap, one can optionally select the replacement gene as the best fitting one out of a random selection of evolved genes. Remaining holes are filled with basic genes, see Fig. 4. This figure also shows how a recessive gene can become expressed again as the result of a mutation.

Fig. 4. Mutation using complex evolved genes: Evolved gene A is replaced by evolved gene C, one recessive gene of evolved gene B becomes visible, while another one becomes recessive.

3.3 Creating new individuals

If the evolved representation is re-used for a new application, a new initial set of individuals has to be created using this representation. If a set of complex evolved genes is randomly selected from the representation, it is unlikely that they can fit together without holes and overlaps. Re-ordering the evolved genes can minimize the overlaps, but for the remaining overlaps in the individuals the best solution is again to use dominant and recessive genes. Remaining holes can be filled with basic genes.

4 Application Example

The example in this section shows how complex evolved genes can be used to 'learn' features from an example set of Mondrian paintings and to produce new designs that share some of those features.

4.1 Coding Mondrian paintings

A large subset of Mondrian's paintings can be described by recursive rectangle divisions,Fig. 5. These divisions can be mapped into a tree-shaped genotype. Any node in the tree contains a set of attributes that represent the position and direction of the division, the colour of one of the resulting areas, and the thickness of the separating line. As a result, the representation is a mixture of position independent (node) and position dependent (attribute) values.

Without evolved genes, the genetic operations are similar to those used in genetic programming (Koza 1992): the cross-over function swaps branches between two trees and the mutation operation replaces the value for an attribute with a random value. For use with complex evolved gene, these functions are modified to allow dominant and recessive genes.

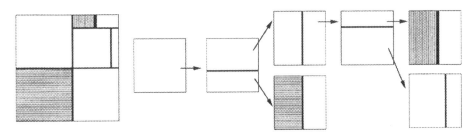

Fig. 5. Representation of a Mondrian painting by a series of rectangle divisions

4.2 Evolving Mondrian genes

In the first step a set of examples is given to the system, Fig. 6; the fitness is a measure of how close the individuals produced are to the examples. This is expressed in a set of Pareto-fitness values for each one of the examples, measuring the number of topologically correct and incorrect divisions, the exactness of the location of the divisions, correctness of colours and of line thicknesses.

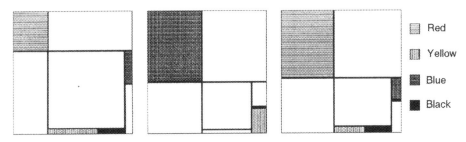

Fig. 6. Example paintings

4.3 Creating complex evolved genes

Ideally, one would want to allow any two genes on the genotype to be combined into an evolved gene. However, with large genotypes and a growing alphabet, this would lead to a combinatorial explosion of possible new evolved genes and would make it very hard to identify the best new gene. Fortunately, genes that are close on the genotype are more likely to be correlated in the fitness than genes that are far away. This allows a limited search by defining a 'search radius': two genes are only considered for gene extraction if they are not more than n steps apart on the genotype. The size of this radius can be selected depending on the application. In this application, two basic genes are only considered for combination if they are on the same node or on directly adjacent nodes. Since every node consists of 4 values, this means that basic genes can be up to 8 values apart. In this way, evolved genes can grow to span a large number of nodes, with each node specifying the value of one or more of the attributes. Evolved genes can be combined with basic genes on any of the nodes that are part of the evolved gene and all nodes directly adjacent. Two evolved genes can be combined if the uppermost node of one of them is a node or directly adjacent to a node of the other evolved gene.

Even with a restriction to a certain search radius, the number of possible new genes can easily be too large. Fortunately, only a small fraction of the possible combinations will occur in the population at any given moment. Since any new evolved gene will obviously have to occur in the population, it is possible to restrict the search to the combinations existing in the population. A hash-table can therefore be used to allow efficient access to the different gene combinations. For the Mondrian application, the table usually contains about 3,000-4,000 entries, and the most common new genes occur about 700 - 800 times in a population of 1,000 individuals.

The fitness of a gene combination is calculated as the sum of the fitnesses of all individuals where this combination occurs. In the same way, a fitness can be calculated for all existing evolved genes. This fitness can be used to select evolved genes for mutation and generation of new individuals, and to decide which gene is the dominant where overlaps are produced.

Use of dominant/recessive gene pairs. Figure 7 is a plot of the average number of dominant/recessive gene pairs per individual during the creation of the evolved genes. It shows that the number of these pairs increases over the time, until about 10% of the genes are dominant/recessive pairs. As a comparison, about 5% of the genes in the final population are basic genes. Further analysis shows that about half the individuals in the final population (one quarter of all evolved genes in the population) have one or more gene that is part of a dominant/recessive gene pair. This shows that those pairs are an important factor in the evolutionary process. On the other hand, about 90% of all genes of evolved genes are expressed into phenotypes. The function of evolved genes to protect groups of genes from the genetic operations is therefore not substantially impaired.

Evolved genes. Figure 8 shows some evolved genes of different sizes created in this application. For example, the complex evolved gene in Fig. 8(a) specifies a division in the upper half of the rectangle (value 0 in first position), with a thin line (value 1 in third position). The other attributes are not specified by this evolved gene, and can be specified by basic genes or other evolved genes. Other evolved genes specify values at two or more nodes, Fig.s 8(c) and (d).

4.4 Creating new designs

The new representation can then be used to create individuals that are adapted to a new fitness function, but show features of the examples. In this example, the fitness function

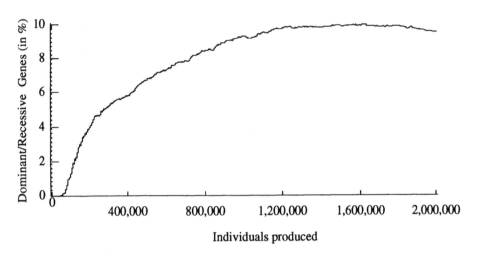

Fig. 7. Percentage of dominant/recessive gene pairs in the population

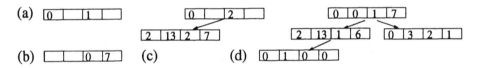

Fig. 8. Evolved genes created from examples, node values are $(direction - position - linewidth - colour)$

is very simple: seven rectangles, three colours and a white rectangle of a certain size in the top right corner. The intention is to make sure that any similarities to the Mondrian examples is caused by the use of the evolved coding, not by the fitness function.

The initial set of individuals is created from the evolved genes as described in Section 3.3. A relatively high rate of dominant/recessive gene pairs is to be expected as a result of an entirely random combination of evolved genes; in fact about 25% of the genes are dominant/recessive pairs. During the course of the evolution, this rate is reduced to about 15%.

Figure 9 shows the top two results of two different runs created with this fitness function without, Figs. 9(a) and 9(b), and with, Figs. 9(c) and 9(d), the use of the evolved coding. All results achieve perfect fitness, the runs without evolved genes converged slightly faster. While the evolved coding helps finding results with features that are present in the examples, it makes finding different features (the small white rectangle) slower. The goal of using the evolved genes, however, is to bias the results towards designs that appear similar to the examples. The success of this can be seen when the results in Figs. 9(c) and 9(d) are compared with the examples in Fig. 6; examples and results use similar colour combinations, line widths, and topological arrangements.

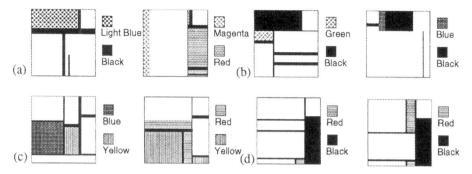

Fig. 9. (a) and (b) New individuals created without evolved genes, (c) and (d) individuals created with evolved genes. The colours used are listed next to the individuals.

5 Conclusion

This paper borrows the notion of dominant and recessive genes from sexual reproduction and applies it to evolutionary systems. It is used to resolve situations where one would like to preserve certain combinations of genes, but permutations from genetic operations lead to conflicts between two of those combinations.

Dominant/recessive genes allows duplicate genes to be kept in the genotype, where always one gene is expressed and the other gene is ignored in the construction of the phenotype, but preserved as part of the individual, and, importantly, as part of an evolved gene. None of the gene combinations therefore has to be destroyed. Moreover, the recessive gene is still part of the genetic material, and may be expressed again after further genetic operations.

Even though the paper focusses on the use of this idea in the context of evolved representation, it is applicable wherever the representation used leads to conflicts during genetic operations.

6 Acknowledgements

This work is supported by a grant from the Australian Research Council and by a University of Sydney Postgraduate Research Award.

References

Gero, J. S. & Kazakov, V. (1996). Spatial layout planning using evolved design genes, *in* C. Dagli, M. Akay, C. Chen, B. Fernandez & J. Ghosh (eds), *Smart Engineering Systems: Neural Networks, Fuzzy Logic and Evolutionary Programming*, ASME Press, New York, pp. 379–384.

Goldberg, D. E. & Smith, R. E. (1987). Nonstationary function optimization using genetic algorithms with dominance and diploidy, *in* J. J. Grefenstette (ed.), *Genetic Algorithms and Their Applications: Proceedings of the Second International Conference on Genetic Algorithms*, Lawrence Erlbaum Associates, Hillsdale, New Jersey, pp. 59 – 68.

Greene, F. (1996). A new approach to diploid/dominance in its effects in stationary genetic search, *in* P. J. A. Lawrence J. Fogel & T. Bäck (eds), *Evolutionary Programming V*, MIT Press, Cambdridge, Massachusetts, pp. 171–176.

Koza, J. R. (1992). *Genetic Programming. On the Programming of Computers by Means of Natural Selection*, Bradford Book, MIT Press, Cambridge, Massachusetts.

Michalewicz, Z. (1992). *Genetic Algorithms + Data Structures= Evolution Programs*, Springer Verlag, Berlin.

Ng, K. P. & Wong, K. C. (1995). A new diploid scheme and dominance change mechanism for non-stationary function optimization, *in* L. J. Eshelman (ed.), *Proceedings of the Sixth International Conference on Genetic Algorithms*, Morgan Kaufmann, San Francisco, pp. 159–166.

Schnier, T. & Gero, J. S. (1995). Learning representations for evolutionary computation, *in* X. Yao (ed.), *Australian Joint Conference on Artificial Intelligence AI '95*, World Scientific, Singapore, pp. 387–394.

Schnier, T. & Gero, J. S. (1996). Learning genetic representations as alternative to hand-coded shape grammars, *in* J. S. Gero & F. Sudweeks (eds), *Artificial Intelligence in Design '96*, Kluwer, Dordrecht, pp. 39–57.

Yukiko, Y. & Nobue, A. (1994). A diploid genetic algorithm for preserving population diversity - pseudo-meiosis ga, *Parallel Problem Solving from Nature - PPSN III*, Springer Verlag, Berlin, pp. 36–45.

Using Multi-chromosomes to Solve a Simple Mixed Integer Problem

Hans J. Pierrot and Robert Hinterding

Department of Computer and Mathematical Sciences
Victoria University of Technology
PO Box 14428 MCMC
Melbourne 8001, Australia
email: hpierrot@acslink.net.au, rhh@matilda.vut.edu.au

Abstract. Multi-chromosomes representations have been used in Genetic Algorithms to decompose complex solution representations into simpler components each of which is represented onto a single chromosome. This paper investigates the effects of distributing similar structures over a number of chromosomes. The solution representation of a simple mixed integer problem is encoded onto one, two, or three chromosomes to measure the effects. Initial results showed large differences, but further investigation showed that most of the differences were due to increased mutation, but multi-chromosome representation can give superior results.

1 Introduction

Multi-chromosome representations are not often used in Genetic Algorithms (GAs), but when they are, each chromosome has been different in structure (Juliff, 1993; Hinterding & Juliff, 1993; Hinterding, 1997; Ronald *et al.*, 1997). To date no work has been done to determine the effect of using multiple chromosomes where each chromosome has the same structure.

The effect of using multi-chromosome representation to solve numeric test functions was investigated in Pierrot (1997). Here a number of scalable functions were solved with the parameters evenly distributed over a varying number of chromosomes. Experiments used one, six and twenty four chromosomes for each of the six functions, and also varied the mutation technique. These experiments show that the method of mutation was the main determinant in deciding if multiple chromosomes were effective or not.

In this paper a simple mixed integer problem representing a manufacturing task is used to investigate the effects of using multi-chromosome representation for mixed numeric representation problems.

The questions addressed here are:

- What is the effect of using multiple chromosomes?
- Does the order of the parameters have an effect? Should the control variables be grouped together or should the variables for each machine be kept together?

– What is the effect of having either real or integer count variables?

Linear constraint problems are traditionally solved by linear programming using the Simplex method. When some of the constraints are integer in form then the problem is defined as a mixed integer problem. Branch and bound techniques are then applied to satisfy the integer constraints. The computation time increases for each integer constraint added, hence integer constraints are kept to a minimum. Therefore both integer and real quantity variables were tested.

The results show that the use of multi-chromosomes can improve the performance of a GA for mixed integer problems. This is attributed to the way that mutation works with this structure.

2 Multi-chromosomes

GAs traditionally use only one chromosome in their representation, and generally a uniform representation is used for each gene. This allows the same reproduction operators to be used for all genes. Suitable standard operators can just be plugged in as required to implement a specific approach.

Complex problems require complex representations. When a complex structure is encapsulated in a single chromosome then this leads to needing to know the structure of the chromosome to be able to operate on it. For example, Davidor (1991) uses complex gene representation to define the path of a robot arm. There is one allele in the gene for each link of the robot arm. Each gene represents one position, or arm configuration on the movement path of the robot arm. The chromosome contains as many genes as required to describe a particular path for the tip of the robot arm. Special mutation and crossover operators were needed for this representation.

This is an instance of using multi-component chromosomes. That is chromosomes where all the genes are placed in one chromosome and the representation of the genes is either not homogeneous or the gene has a compound representation. This increased complexity in the gene or chromosome structure increases the complexity of the genetic operators and forces the creation of special versions of these operators.

One way of overcoming these difficulties is to use a multi-chromosome representation. Here an individual would contain more than one chromosome where each chromosome could have its own representation. The genes in an individual chromosome would then have a homogeneous representation. This would result in each chromosome having its own genetic operators. These could then be chosen from the standard operators.

An example of this is Juliff (1993), who uses multiple chromosomes to represent the structure of pallet loads. The problem is to optimise the loading of trucks, placing pallets in such a way as to minimise unloading time. There are a number of constraints on how the load can be constructed determined by layer content and pallet limits. Initially a single chromosome GA with order based representation was used with disappointing results.

A multi-chromosome GA was then created which carried additional information in the second and third chromosomes, these chromosomes contained information about the position of the pallets on the truck and how many of each different pallet type was to be used. This resulted in a better exploration of the problem space and improved the results. Because of the extra information the decoder could build different loads even though the information in the first chromosome was the same. The results for the multi-chromosome GA outperformed the single chromosome GA.

Hinterding (1997) used multi-chromosome representation to solve the Cutting Stock Problem with a GA using self-adaptation. One chromosome has the group based parameters for the problem. The second chromosome is used to hold the self-adaptive parameters, and each chromosome has its own reproduction operators. This is needed as the group based chromosome needs to be manipulated in an entirely different way to the numeric chromosome which holds the self-adaptation parameters.

Ronald (1997) used a multi-chromosome representation to solve a modified Travelling Salesperson Problem. The normal TSP problem was augmented by the need to consider the cost of transport and a penalty for changing from one mode of transport to another. Different modes of transport were optimal for different distances. Two chromosomes were used. The first chromosome encoded the standard TSP and used permutation encoding to describe the circuit of the cities. The second chromosome described the method of transport when leaving each city. This separation of the parameters into two chromosomes allowed simple genetic operators to be used for each of the two chromosomes.

Using multi-chromosome representation allows the representation of an individual to be decomposed or factored into simple and easy to manipulate components where each chromosome can use simple genetic operators suited to the simple and homogeneous genes in that chromosome.

3   Multi-chromosomes and Mixed Integer Problems

A simple mixed integer problem was found representing a manufacturing task. This was coded as a GA using a penalty function for constraint handling. This mixed integer GA was tested using a varying number of chromosomes.

The Crosby Company is contracted to produce 500 fittings next week for one of its customers. Crosby has three machines in its machine shop that can produce the fittings, but at different variable and fixed costs. These costs and weekly production limits are shown in Table 1. The fixed cost is incurred only if the machine is set up to produce the fitting. The objective is to determine how to produce 500 fittings at minimal cost.

This problem is usually solved as a mixed integer problem using a linear program. The control variables which determine if a machine will be used must be integers. The quantity to be produced on each machine can be represented by either an integer or a real variable. If this was to be solved using a linear program then these values would be treated as reals to speed up the solution

Table 1. List of production costs for each machine

Machine	per unit production cost	fixed set up cost	weekly production limit
1	$1.12	$60	300
2	$1.40	$55	250
3	$1.23	$50	270

process. For this reason it was decided to try using both integers and reals for the quantity variables.

The optimal answer to the problem is to set up only machines 1 and 3, and to produce 300 fittings on machine 1, and 200 on machine 3. This gives a minimal cost of $692.

3.1 Representation

The initial idea was to use separate chromosomes for the two different types of variables; that is one chromosome for the real variables and another for the integer variables. This followed the ideas of Juliff (1993) in the truck loading problem.

Hence a chromosome would represent all integer or all real variables, but it was realised that by recording the length and the value range for each gene in a chromosome, it did not matter if the gene represented an integer or a fixed point real. Some minor changes were needed for the Gaussian mutation operator as it operates on genes (function variables), but the crossover operator was not affected at all. As a result a single chromosome could represent any mixture of integer and real values.

In all tests run, the control variables were treated as one bit integers. A value of one meant that the relevant machine was set up and a value of zero meant that the machine was not set up. The number of units produced was represented by a real value encoded using 10 bits, or by an integer value using 9 bits. Further tests were run changing the order of the variables to see if having the control variables next to the count variables was better than having all control variables together and then all the count variables.

The control variables for machine 1, 2 and 3 are $f1$, $f2$ and $f3$ respectively and the count variables for the three machines are $x1$, $x2$ and $x3$. Figures 1 & 2 show how the variables were distributed across the chromosomes for the various test cases.

The common parameter settings for the GA are shown in Figure 3. A new individual is produced by either crossover or mutation but not both. For the initial tests each chromosome was mutated once when the mutation function was invoked and Poisson based mutation was not used. This means that only one gene was mutated in each chromosome.

one chromosome					
$f1$	$f2$	$f3$	$x1$	$x2$	$x3$

chrom. 1			chrom. 2		
$f1$	$f2$	$f3$	$x1$	$x2$	$x3$

chrom. 1		chrom. 2		chrom. 3	
$f1$	$f2$	$f3$	$x1$	$x2$	$x3$

Fig. 1. Representation: chromosomes with parameters grouped

one chromosome					
$f1$	$x1$	$f2$	$x2$	$f3$	$x3$

chrom. 1			chrom. 2		
$f1$	$x1$	$f2$	$x2$	$f3$	$x3$

chrom. 1		chrom. 2		chrom. 3	
$f1$	$x1$	$f2$	$x2$	$f3$	$x3$

Fig. 2. Representation: chromosomes with parameters intermixed

3.2 Gaussian Mutation

Gaussian mutation is used for all of the experiments and is implemented by adding Gaussian noise to the value of the gene similar to that used in Evolution Strategies. The difference being that there is only one rate and not one for each function parameter as in Evolution Strategies. We use a default std. dev. parameter of 0.1.

3.3 Evaluation Function

The evaluation function had to perform two tasks. One, calculate the cost of producing the fittings given by the the function:

$$(f1 * 60) + (f2 * 55) + (f3 * 50) + (x1 * 1.12) + (x2 * 1.40) + (x3 * 1.23)$$

Here $f1$ is set to one if machine 1 is in use and zero if not in use. Similarly $f2$ is one if machine 2 is in use and $f3$ is one if machine 3 is in use. $x1$ represents the number of units being produced by machine 1, $x2$ represents the number of units produced by machine 2 and $x3$ represents the units produced on machine 3.

Population size of 50	No duplicates allowed
Binary Gray encoding	replacement rate of 90%
crossover rate of 60%	Gaussian mutation
number of evaluations $= 12000$	

Fig. 3. GA parameters used for the mixed integer problem

The second task is to compute the penalty function to model the constraints in the problem. The constraints are:

$$x1 \leq 300 \qquad x2 \leq 240 \qquad x3 \leq 270$$
$$x1 + x2 + x3 \geq 500 \qquad M = 300$$
$$x1 \leq M * f1 \qquad x2 \leq M * f2 \qquad x3 \leq M * f3$$
$$f1, f2, f3 \in \{0, 1\}$$

The first three constraints are easily met when they are defined as real values within a defined range. If they are integer values, they can hold any value between 0 and 511. The evaluation function returns a fitness value which is the sum of the cost and the penalty functions.

3.4 The Penalty Function

The penalty method used is a simplification of the method of Homaifar *et al.* (1994). They suggest that a family of intervals should determine appropriate penalty values. A penalty coefficient should be attached to each level and multiplied by the error value. A single level was employed in this GA for each constraint.

In most cases the GA first finds a local optimal solution using all three machines. Sometimes it gets stuck there, otherwise it will find a solution with machine 2 turned off and then approaches the solution near the true minimal cost of $692 when machine 1 produces 300 units and machine 3 produces 200 units.

4 Results

The results shown in Tables 2 & 3 give the average results from batches of 40 runs. The figures show how many times in the batch of 40 runs the cost was reduced to be less than 700 (optimal cost is 692). All other runs gave an answer near the local optima of 747. The plot in Figure 4 shows the way the results are distributed in a typical test. The results have been sorted into ascending sequence to better show how results are distributed.

Two sets of tests were run using the 1, 2 or 3 chromosome representations, and using real or integer values for the count variables. One set had the three control parameters first followed by the variables for the number of units produced. The other set of tests had each control variable next to the matching number of units produced. These representations are shown in Figures 1 & 2.

It can be seen in Table 2 that more chromosomes give a better result. Using integers gives a better result in the one and two chromosome cases. It can also be seen that having related genes close together does not give a clear improvement. Therefore the position of each gene is not particularly important for this specific problem.

What are the differences between the one chromosome and three chromosome representation? The first is the way that crossover takes place: in the one

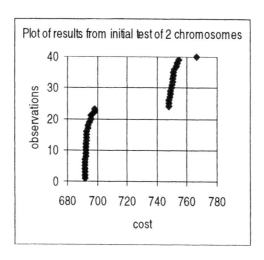

Fig. 4. Distribution of results (40 runs)

chromosome representation this is standard two point crossover; in the three chromosome representation crossover takes place on each chromosome, hence it is like six point crossover.

The other difference is the effect of mutation. In multi-chromosome representations each chromosome is mutated, hence with the three chromosome representation three genes are mutated, while only one gene is mutated in the single chromosome representation.

To verify this further tests were run. The multi-chromosome representations were tested with only one chromosome being mutated. Six point crossover and higher levels of mutation were performed on the single chromosome representation. To increase the mutation rate, Poisson mutation was enabled. Now a Poisson probability function was sampled to determine how many genes would mutate. The mutation tests were run with a mean (λ) of 1, 2 and 3.

Table 2. Summary of results of mixed integer tests

Rep.	No. Chroms	Control then count variables	Paired control and count variables
real	one	3	6
integer	one	13	10
real	two	23	22
integer	two	28	31
real	three	26	38
integer	three	37	37

The results of these tests showed that six point crossover gave a small improvement to the effectiveness of the single chromosome representation. Increasing the mutation rate by using Poisson mutation had a larger effect and combining the two was even more significant. However this still did not equal the results for the three chromosome representation.

Using multi-chromosome representations with only one chromosome being mutated did not give good results. The three chromosome result was very close to the six point crossover result for the single chromosome representation as expected.

To reduce mutation in the multi-chromosome representations Poisson mutation was used and the mean mutation rate divided by the number of chromosomes. When reducing mutation in this manner the results for the two chromosome representation are the best. The three chromosome results are not as good as those obtained when Poisson mutation is not used. This would indicate that a steady mutation of one variable per chromosome gives a better result than the average of one mutated variable per chromosome. This is caused by the way that mutation takes place when Poisson mutation is used. Each time that mutation is invoked a Poisson random number is generated, for low values of λ, a significant number of samples will be zero, and a chromosome identical to the parent chromosome will be produced.

Table 3. Results: varying crossover for integer representation

Mutation	Poisson 2.7				No Poisson			
No. chrom.	% Crossover				% Crossover			
	0	20	40	60	0	20	40	60
1	**38**	36	32	30	28	24	15	12
2	36	**39**	35	33	40	36	37	28
3	24	35	**37**	36	39	39	**40**	37

As mutation appears to have such a major effect on the problem further runs were conducted varying the crossover rate to decrease crossover and therefore increase the proportion of the population produced by mutation. Table 3 shows the results for the integer representations with the best values found for λ (the Poisson mean) as well as the results when Poisson mutation is not used. Using one chromosome representation the best results are obtained when Poisson mutation is used. For multi-chromosome representations the best results are obtained when Poisson mutation is turned off, hence a regular mutation rate of 1 mutation per chromosome is used. There also appears to be a pattern in the crossover rate. The one chromosome representation appears to do best at the crossover rate of 20% whereas the multi-chromosome representation appears to do best at a crossover rate of 40%. This is most likely due to multi-chromosome representations using crossover more effectively and the effect of a steady mutation rate when Poisson mutation is not being used in this representation. The results for the real variables are similar to the above numbers though in most cases lower in value than for the integer tests.

Up to this point the cost of 700 has been used as a cut off in deciding which representation is the better. Using this method the multi-chromosomes are better by a small margin. The close results obtained in the final tests when the mutation rate was increased prompted a closer look at what happened at cut off points different to a cost of less than 700. An examination of a range of cut off values from 700 down to 692.1, the perfect score, showed that reducing

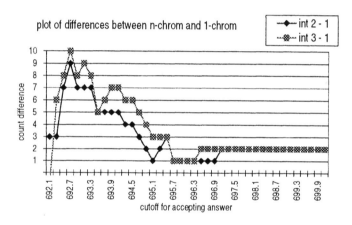

Fig. 5. Differences in results for multi and single chroms.

To get a better feel for what was happening the best answer for each of the three representations for both integer and real quantity variables were determined and plotted. This showed that there was a marked variance between the different representations. To highlight these a plot of the difference between the one chromosome and the multi-chromosome representation was produced. The graph in Figure 5 shows the difference between the one chromosome representation and the Multi-chromosome representations for the integer tests. The comparison between the one and two chromosome representations is labelled *int 2-1* and the comparison between the one and three chromosome representations is labelled *int 3-1*. These represent the differences between the best number of answers for each cut off value. Examination of this plot shows that making the cut off too close to the actual optimum gives a non typical picture. Values from 692.3 through 694.5 show a significant advantage to using a multi-chromosome representation. The results for the real quantity variables were similar but only went as high as 693.5 before falling off dramatically.

5 Conclusions and Discussion

This investigation looked at a simple mixed integer problem as a vehicle for determining if a multi-chromosome representation would bring any benefits. We show that using multiple chromosomes can give superior results to a single chromosome representation for mixed integer problems.

Contributing factors to these improvements are:-

- the increase in crossover points which is similar to a six point crossover when comparing the three chromosome configuration to the single chromosome configuration.
- the increased mutation provided by mutating each chromosome.

While these factors account for some of the improvement, the multi-chromosome representation still has real benefits as far as simplicity and effectiveness are concerned.

The other questions investigated appear to have the following results:-

- the order of the genes does not appear to have any clear cut impact on the solution.
- the use of integer variables for the count variables appear to give improved results. This is in contrast to the traditional linear program where it is more efficient to code variables as reals to avoid the extra computation of the branch and bound process.

References

Davidor, Y.: *Genetic Algorithms And Robotics - A Heuristic Strategy For Optimization.* Singapore: World Scientific Publishing, 1991.

Hinterding, R.: Self-adaptation using Multi-chromosomes. *In: Proceedings of the 4th IEEE International Conference on Evolutionary Computation.* IEEE Press. 1997, pp 87–91.

Hinterding, R., & Juliff, K.: *A Genetic Algorithm for Stock Cutting: An exploration of Mapping Schemes.* Technical Report 24COMP3. Department of Computer and Mathematical Sciences, Victoria University of Technology, Victoria Australia, 1993.

Homaifar, A., Lai, S. H. Y., & Qi, X.: Constrained Optimization via Genetic Algorithms. *Simulations,* **Vol. 62**, 1994, pp. 242–254.

Juliff, K.: A multi-chromosome genetic algorithm for pallet loading. *In: Proceedings of the Fifth International Conference on Genetic Algorithms.* 1993, pp. 476–73.

Pierrot, H. J.: *An investigation of Multi-chromosome Genetic Algorithms.* Masters Thesis, Victoria University of Technology, Melbourne, Australia, 1997.

Ronald, S., Kirkby, S., & Eklund, P.: Multi-chromosome Mixed Encodings for Heterogeneous Problems. *In: Proceedings of the 4th IEEE International Conference on Evolutionary Computation.* IEEE Press. 1997, pp 37–42.

Hierarchical and Feed-Forward Fuzzy Logic for Financial Modelling and Prediction

Masoud Mohammadian
School of Computing & Information
Technology
Monash University
Churchill, Australia
masoud.mohammadian@fcit.monash.edu.au

Mark Kingham
Department of Computer Science
Edith Cowan University,
Perth, Western Australia
mkingham@scorpion.cowan.edu.au

Abstract : In this paper, the development of a Hierarchical and Feed-Forward intelligent Fuzzy Logic system using Genetic Algorithms for prediction and modelling of fluctuations in interest rates in Australia is discussed. The system developed is used to predict quarterly and half yearly interest rates using fuzzy logic. The fuzzy rules for fuzzy logic predictor are unknown. A knowledge base must be created from the available data. In the paper Genetic Algorithm is proposed as a method for learning the fuzzy rules of the fuzzy logic predictor. A Hierarchical and Feed-Forward Fuzzy Logic system consisting of five fuzzy knowledge bases is developed to solve the prediction problem.

1. Introduction

In the past, the prediction and modelling of uncertain dynamic systems, such as prediction of economic indicators (Interest Rates), has relied on complex mathematical models to describe the dynamic of the system to be modelled. These models work well provided the system meets the requirement and assumption of synthesis techniques. However due to the uncertainty or sheer complexity of these systems, they are difficult to model and not easily adaptable to changes in the system which they were not designed for [3, 4].

Recently, new Intelligent System techniques such as Fuzzy Logic (FL), Genetic Algorithms (GAs) and Neural Networks have been successfully used in the place of the complex mathematical systems [2, 4, 10, 11]. These new techniques are capable of responding quickly and efficiently to the uncertainty and ambiguity of the system. Fuzzy Logic is an active research area [4, 5, 6, 8, 10, 11]. Fuzzy modelling or fuzzy identification, has numerous practical applications in control, prediction and inference. It has been found useful when the system is either difficult to predict and or difficult to model by conventional methods. Fuzzy set theory provides a means for representing uncertainties. The underlying power of fuzzy logic is its ability to represent imprecise values in an understandable form. The majority of Fuzzy Logic systems (FLs) to date have been static and based upon knowledge derived from imprecise heuristic knowledge of experienced operators, and where applicable also upon physical laws that governs the dynamics of the process.

Although its application to industrial problems has often produced results superior to classical control [4, 6, 10], the design procedures are limited by the heuristic rules of the system. It is simply assumed that the rules for the system are readily available or can be obtained. This implicit assumption limits the application of FL to the cases of the system with a few parameters. The number of parameters of a system could be large. The number of fuzzy rules of the system are directly dependant on these parameters. As the number of parameters increase, the number of fuzzy rules of the system grows exponentially [7, 12]. By using a Hierarchical Fuzzy Logic (HFL) architecture the number of fuzzy rules in the system are reduced thereby reducing the computational time while maintaining the systems robustness and efficiency.

In this paper the development of a intelligent hierarchical FL system using GAs to model and predict economic fluctuations in real world situations is considered. GAs are employed as an adaptive method for selection of fuzzy rules of a FL system. By integrating FL system and GAs it is found that the proposed integrated architecture is able to generate comprehensible and reliable fuzzy rules for FL system by a self-learning adaptive method. The GAs is applied to learn the fuzzy rules of FL system for prediction of interest rate.

2. Integration of FL and GAs

GAs [9], are powerful search algorithms based on the mechanism of natural selection and use operations of reproduction, crossover, and mutation on a population of strings. A set (population) of possible solutions, in this case, a coding of the fuzzy rules of a FL system, represented as a string of numbers. New strings are produced every generation by the repetition of a two step cycle. First each individual string is decoded and its ability to solve the problem is assessed. Each string is assigned a fitness, depending on how well it performed. In the second stage the fittest strings are preferentially chosen for recombination to form the next generation. Recombination involves the selection of two strings, the choice of a cross-over point in the string, and the switching of the segments to the right of this point, between the two strings (the cross-over operation).

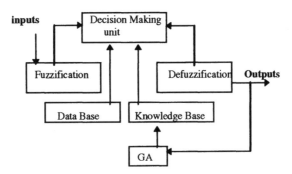

Fig. 1. combination of FL and GAs for fuzzy rule generation.

Mutation is used to maintain genetic diversity within a small population of strings. There is a small probability that any allele in a string will be flipped from its present value to another value within a specific range. This prevents certain allele's becoming fixed at a specific value due to every string in the population having that value, often a cause of premature convergence to a non-optimal solution. Figure 1 shows the combination of FL and GAs for generating fuzzy rules.

3. Encoding and Decoding of Fuzzy rules by GAs

First the input parameters of the FL system is divided into fuzzy sets. Assume that the FL system has two inputs α and β and a single output δ. Assume also that the inputs and output of the system is divided into 5 fuzzy sets. Therefore a maximum of twenty five fuzzy rules can be written for the FL system. The consequent for each fuzzy rule is determined by genetic evolution. In order to do so, the output fuzzy sets are encoded. It is not necessary to encode the input fuzzy sets because the input fuzzy sets are static and do not change. The fuzzy rules relating the input variables (α and β) to the output variable (δ) have twenty five possible combinations. The consequent of each fuzzy rule can be any one of the five output fuzzy sets. Assume that the parameter (δ) is has five fuzzy sets with the following fuzzy linguistic variable: **NB** (Negative Big), **NS** (Negative Small), **ZE** (Zero), **PS** (Positive Small), and **PB** (Positive big). The output fuzzy sets are encoded by assigning 1 = **NB** (Negative Big), 2 = **NS** (Negative Small), 3 = **ZE** (Zero), 4 = **PS** (Positive Small), and 5 = **PB** (Positive Big). GAs randomly encode each output fuzzy set into a number ranging from 1 to 5 for all possible combinations of the input fuzzy variables. A string encoded this way can be represented as:

Each individual string is then decoded into the output linguistic terms. The set of fuzzy rules thus developed, is evaluated by the FL system based upon a fitness value which is specific to the system. At the end of each generation, two copies of the best performing string from the parent generation is included in the next generation to ensure that the best performing strings are not lost. GA then performs the process of selection, crossover and mutation on the rest of the individual strings. Selection and crossover are the same as a simple GAs while the mutation operation is modified.

Crossover and mutation take place based on the probability of crossover and mutation respectively. Mutation operator is changed to suit this problem. For mutation, an allele is selected at random and it is replaced by a random number ranging from 1 to 5. The process of selection, crossover and mutation are repeated for a number of generations till a satisfactory fuzzy rule base is obtained. We define a satisfactory rule base as one whose fitness value differs from the desired output of the system by a very small value.

4. Interest Rate Prediction using Integrated FL and GAs

Investors and governments alike are interested in the ability to predict future interest rate fluctuations from current economic data. Investors are trying to maximise their gains on the capital markets, while government departments need to know the current position of the economy and where it is likely to be in the near future for the well being of a countries people.

Economists, and investors, have been unable to find all the factors that influence interest rate fluctuations. However, there are some major economic indicators released by the government [1] that are commonly used to determine the current position of the economy. These indicators used in this paper and they are as follows.

- *Interest Rate which is the indicator being predicted. The Interest Rate used here is the Australian Commonwealth government 10-year treasury bonds.*
- *Job Vacancies is where a position is available for immediate filling or for which recruitment action has been taken.*
- *The Unemployment Rate is the percentage of the labour force actively looking for work in the country.*
- *Gross Domestic Product is an average aggregate measure of the value of economic production in a given period.*
- *The Consumer Price Index is a general indicator of the rate of change in prices paid by consumers for goods and services.*
- *Household Saving Ratio is the ratio of household income saved to households disposable income.*
- *Home Loans measure the supply of finance for home loans, not the demand for housing.*
- *Average Weekly Earnings is the average amount of wages that a full time worker takes home before any taxes.*
- *Current Account is the sum of the balances on merchandise trade, services trade, income and unrequited transfers.*
- *Trade Weighted Index measures changes in our currency relative to the currencies of our main trading partners.*
- *RBA Commodity Price Index provides an early indication of trends in Australia's export Prices.*
- *All Industrial Index provides an indication of price movements on the Australian Stock Market.*
- *Company Profits are defined as net operating profits or losses before income tax .*
- *New Motor Vehicles is the number of new vehicles registered in Australia.*

A FL system is developed uses the above indicators as its inputs. Each input of the FL is split into five fuzzy sets. Using the above indicators as the inputs of FL, we need a fuzzy knowledge base (FKB) consisting of over six billion rules. This would be unmanageable in both size and execution speed, so a better way in which all the relevant indicators can be used in a more efficient manner must be found. The first step to achieve this is to divide the indicators into smaller-related groups and then to develop a FL system for each group. In final stage the FL systems are combined to predict the interest rate. By breaking down the system into smaller system the number of fuzzy rules in the system is reduced and the execution speed of the system is improved. The division of the above indicators to small-related groups are shown below:

1. *Employment* (Job Vacancies, Unemployment Rate)
2. *Country* (Gross Domestic Product, Consumer Price Index)
3. *Savings* (Household Saving Ratio, Home Loans, Average Weekly Earnings)
4. *Foreign* (Current Account, RBA Index, Trade Weighted Index)
5. *Company* (All Industrial Index, Company Profit, New Motor Vehicles)

The Interest Rate is then included with each of the groups. Two methods for predicting interest rate fluctuations for quarterly data using a Hierarchical Fuzzy Logic (HFL) structure and a Feed-forward Fuzzy Logic (FFL)structure is developed. Both methods are used for prediction of the interest rate. GAs was used to learn the Fuzzy rules for Fuzzy Knowledge Base (FKB) for each group. The GAs had a population size of 150 with a crossover rate of 0.6 and a mutation rate of 0.01. It was run for 10000 generations over a period of 40 quarters (10 years). Fitness was calculated as the sum of the absolute differences from the predicted quarter and the actual quarters interest rate. The aim is to minimise the difference between the predicted interest rate and actual interest rate. The fitness was subtracted from an 'optimal' fitness amount, which was decided to be 30 as it is unlikely the error amount would be higher than 30 over 10 year data used for training of the system. The fitness of the system is calculated by the following formula

$$fitness = 30 - \sum_{i=0}^{30} abs(PI_i - I_{i+1})$$

The closer the fitness to 30, the better the population generated by the GAs. An Elitist strategy was used in that the best solution in a population generated is saved and entered in the next generation. This procedure prevents a good solution being lost by the probabilistic nature of reproduction and speeds convergence to a good solution [9]. It should be noted that there are a number of ways in which the data can be represented to the integrated FL and GAs. The data can be the actual amounts (such as dollar values, number of new cars, etc) or it could be the difference between the current value of an indicator and its past value. In this research study the difference between the current value and the previous quarter is used for all data except the interest rate. In this case the actual interest rate is predicted.

5. Hierarchical Fuzzy Logic for Prediction of Interest Rate

A FL system is developed for each of the five groups (see Figure 2). Each group is trained using integrated FL and GAs to predict the quarterly interest rate. The number of fuzzy rules for each group is shown below:

Employment group	125 fuzzy rules
Country group	125 fuzzy rules
Savings group	625 fuzzy rules
Foreign group	625 fuzzy rules
Company group	625 fuzzy rules

Five FL systems are developed for the five the groups. These FL systems are than combined to form the top layer of the HFL as shown in Figure 2.

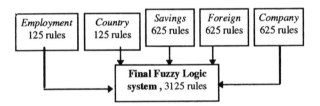

Fig. 2. HFL system developed from combination of the 5 FL systems

All five FL are connected together to form a HFL system. The output of all the five groups is then feed into a FL system called Final Fuzzy Logic system to predict the interest rate. The Final FL system contains 3125 rules giving the total number of rules learnt to be 5250. This is a significant reduction from the 6 billion rules that would have been used previously. Therefore training time is reduced and the need for huge computer resources is eliminated. The fuzzy rules for each of the FL system for the five groups are learnt separately. Figure 3 shows the interest rate prediction of each of the FL groups separately. All FL systems were trained for 40 quarters (10 years data) and tested for another 18 quarters (4 and half years).

Simulation results (Figure 3 (a) to (e)) show that each of five FL system is able to predict the interest rate with some degree of accuracy. However, the prediction error between the predicted interest rate and the actual is still large in some cases. For the prediction to be reliable for government and investors the prediction error must be reduced. By combining the five FL system into a HFL system as shown in Figure 2, the performance of the system is improved and a more accurate prediction is obtained.

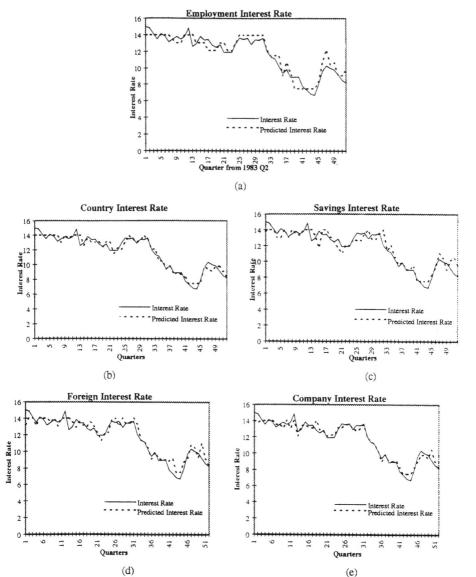

Fig. 3. (a) Predicted Interest Rate using FL of Employment group
(b) Predicted Interest Rate using FL of Country group
(c) Predicted Interest Rate using FL of Savings group
(d) Predicted Interest Rate using FL of Foreign group
(e) Predicted Interest Rate using FL of Company group

To show the improvement in prediction using HFL system some experiments were performed. First three FL systems are combined and the prediction of the system is evaluated then four FL systems and finally all of the FL systems are combined. The way in which different combination of FL systems are performed is shown below:

Combined 3 FL systems	**Combined 4 FL systems**	**Combined 5 FL systems**
Employment FL system	Employment FL system	Employment FL system
Country FL system	Country FL system	Country FL system
Savings FL system	Savings FL system	Savings FL system
	Foreign FL system	Foreign FL system
		Company FL system

Figure 4 ((a) to (c)) shows the results of combining the FL systems into the HFL system for prediction of interest rate. As it can be seen from the simulation results the prediction results are improved with the increase in combined FL system. This suggests that by combing FL systems in a hierarchical fashion the performance of the prediction is improved. The results have become increasingly reliable by using more economic indicators, without the extreme overheads of combining every indicator together to build a single FL system

Next we consider a new architecture for combining FL systems. We combine FL systems in a new fashion called Feed-forward FL system. In this case the output of each FL system sent as input into the next FL system to obtain a more accurate prediction. We also consider the performance of the HFL system and the Feed-forward FL system for prediction of interest rate.

6. Feed-forward Fuzzy Logic for Prediction of Interest Rate

A Feed-forward FL system is developed to test the prediction capabilities of the such a system. In Feed-forward FL, the predicted interest rate from one FL is fed as an input into the next FL system. The structure of the Feed-forward FL system for interest rate prediction is shown in Figure 5.

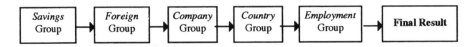

Fig. 5. Feed-forward FL system

Figure 4 (d) shows the results from the Feed-forward FL system for prediction of interest rate. From this Figure, it can be seen that the Feed-forward FL system predicts interest rates more accurately than the single FL system, but is not as accurate as the HFL system (see Figure 4 (c)).

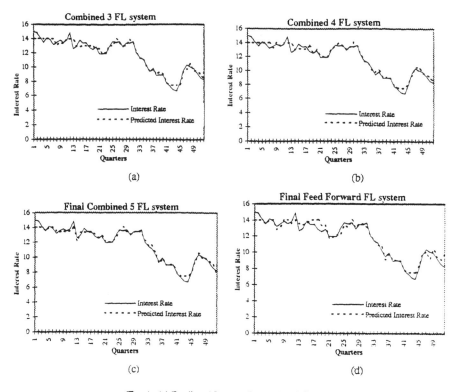

Fig. 4. (a) Predicted Interest Rate using 3 Combined FL
(b) Predicted Interest Rate using 4 Combined FL
(c) Predicted Interest Rate using 5 Combined FL
(d) Predicted Interest Rates using Feedfoward FL

7. Conclusions

In this paper the development of an intelligent FLs using GAs for prediction of interest rates is proposed. By using a HFL system consisting of five FL systems the number of fuzzy rules of the system is reduced significantly, hence computational times is decreased resulting in a more efficient system. The application of the proposed method to modelling and prediction of interest rate using Australian economic indicators is considered. GAs are used to obtain the fuzzy rules for each FL system as well as the mapping between different FL systems.

When the separate FL systems are combined to form a HFL system, there is a definite improvement in the accuracy of the results. Simulation results show that there is a gradual improvement in predicted results as we move from combining 3 FL systems to the final combined 5 FL systems in the hierarchy. The HFL system was tested for accuracy of its prediction by using both training data sets and testing data sets. It was found that the system is capable of making accurate predictions even for the cases not trained for.

A new structure to combine FL system called Feed-forward FL system was also considered. The results of Feed-forward FL system are not as encouraging as the HFL system. The Feed-forward FL system is unable to predict the interest rate with the same degree of accuracy as the HFL system. Although, the results of Feed-forward FL system are still promising in that the overall trends of the interest rate movement have been captured. There may be some merit in using a combination of Feed-forward FL systems and the HFL system. This is subject of future research. In conclusion both HFL systems and Feed-forward FL systems proposed are adaptive and show some generalisation capability.

References

1. Madden, R., *Measuring Australian Economy* , Australian Bureau of Statistics, Catalogue No 1360.0, 1995.
2. Welstead, T., *Neural networks and fuzzy logic applications in C/C++*. Wiley, New York, 1994.
3. Croughanowr, D. R. & Koppel, L. B., *Process Systems Analysis and Control.* New York: McGraw-Hill, 1965.
4. Kosko, B., *Neural networks and fuzzy systems, a dynamic system.* Prentice-Hall: Englewood Cliff, 1992.
5. Karr, C., Adaptive Control with Fuzzy Logic and Genetic Algorithms, *Fuzzy Sets and Neural Networks, and Soft Computing*, Edited by R. R. Yager, L. A. Zadeh, Van Nostrand ReinHold, NY, USA, 1994.
6. Lee, C. C., Fuzzy Logic in Control Systems: Fuzzy Controllers - part I, part II. IEEE Transactions on Systems, Man and Cybernetics., Vol 2092, pg 404-435, 1990.
7. Raju, G. V. S. & Zhou, J., Adaptive Hierarchical Fuzzy Controller, IEEE Transactions on Systems, Man & Cybernetics, Vol 23, No 4, pg 973-980, 1993.
8. Zadeh, L., Fuzzy Sets. Inf. Control, vol 8, pg 338-353, 1965.
9. Goldberg, D., *Genetic Algorithms in Search, Optimisation and Machine Learning.* Reading, Massachusetts: Addison Wesley, 1989.
10. Goonatilake, S. & Treleaven, P. (editors)., *Intelligent Systems for Finance and Business.* Jihn Wiley & Sons, 1995.
11. Furuhashi, T. (editor)., *Advances in Fuzzy Logic, Neural Networks and Genetic Algorithms*, Lecture Notes in Artificial Intelligence, Springer Verlag, 1994.
12. Stonier, R. J. & Mohammadian, M., Evolutionary Learning in Fuzzy Control System", Complex96 Conference, NSW, Australia, 1996.

A Knowledge-Based System for Workflow Management Using the World Wide Web

John Debenham

Key Centre for Advanced Computing Sciences, University of Technology, Sydney,
PO Box 123, NSW 2007, Australia
debenham@socs.uts.edu.au

Abstract: A knowledge-based system acts as an intelligent agent to manage workflows. This knowledge-based system represents both organisational rules and cultural factors, as well as the state of the decision making environment. An experimental intelligent workflow system has been built to manage the processing of applications received by a university department from potential research students. This particular workflow was selected because it involves a range of different types of interaction with the players that interact with the system. This experimental system uses no physical documents. Interactive documents are available on the world wide web; 'read only' documents are sent by electronic mail. Principles for designing intelligent workflow systems have emerged from this experiment. As a result of this experiment a second version of this intelligent workflow system is being constructed in a distributed environment. Intelligent workflow systems admit considerable flexibility in the formation of decision making bodies. The exploitation of innovative forms of decision making bodies can form the basis of efficient decision making environments that can not be realised in traditional systems.

1. Introduction

The effectiveness of workflow processing is central to the success of any organisation. An increase in the effectiveness of workflow processing will improve corporate competitiveness. Workflow management is concerned with the design of workflow systems and their infrastructure so as to achieve effectiveness. Strategic workflow management is concerned with the control of the effectiveness of workflow systems. The effectiveness of a strategic workflow system is the extent to which is reflects corporate strategy. An essential component of a strategic workflow system is sufficient reporting to enable the control of corporate strategic variables. Key issues within strategic workflow management are:

• the representation of organisational knowledge so that it can both manage workflows and contribute to decision making,
• the representation of strategic variables such as the desired and the actual quality and cost of workflow processing,
• the presentation of an useable reporting/control loop to enable corporate strategies to govern the management of workflows, and
• the development of intelligent agents to support the users of the system.

Artificial intelligence, in particular knowledge-based systems and distributed AI, is central to these issues.

Workflow processing involves decision making during each segment of the workflow. The cost of using a workflow system is the cost of workflow processing though that system subject to constraints. For example, these constraints could be that a given minimum quality of decision making should be achieved, and that processing delays are acceptable. A crucial issue in strategic workflow management is balancing the cost of processing against the quality of the decisions made. In a strategic workflow management system the desired quality of decision making is a variable that should be controlled explicitly. The quality of the decisions made during a workflow will be related to the quality of the decision making environment. Strategic workflow management should enable workflow systems to be constructed so that the cost of processing workflows can be tuned to reflect corporate goals. A continual challenge for workflow management is to maintain a decision making environment in which high quality decision making can be achieved for low processing cost. An aspect of this challenge is to make the best use of information technology in providing both a good decision making environment and a management infrastructure that enables the effectiveness of workflow processing to be controlled. Many organisations are now able to communicate using the world wide web. The world wide web is the first example of a truly global, platform independent, distributed systems technology enabling the development of cooperative systems (Bentley & Applet, 1997). An experiment in strategic workflow management is described here in which an experimental workflow system has been constructed using knowledge technology, world wide web technology (Ames et al, 1997) and electronic mail technology.

Most early workflow systems supported planned work which called for standard tasks at each step in the belief that this guaranteed good quality outcomes by following pre-specified rules. The trend in the workplace now is towards more complex processes calling for workflow systems that no longer rely on pre-specified actions (Hawryszkiewycz & Gorton, 1996). The trend from planned to situated work (Suchman, 1987) requires new kinds of workflow support. This change is due to a number of factors, including:

- individual workflows can vary and should be given appropriate treatment, there are always exceptions;
- there is increasing emphasis on the use of ad hoc groups to make decisions rather than formal statutory committees;
- if urgent workflows are being processed in a stable organisation then personnel may not always available, and
- the decision making environment is constantly changing, and workflows should adapt to these changes.

Strategic workflow management attempts to address these factors and to manage workflows so as to reflect current corporate strategies.

2. Workflow Management

An *instance* is the representation of pieces of information in either electronic or physical form; an instance cannot be altered as such. In other words, if an instance is altered it becomes another instance. A *workflow segment* consists of: a set of instances called the *segment inputs*, a specification of the possible outcomes of the workflow segment, an agent who is responsible for determining the correct outcome for the given segment input and for representing that outcome as a set of instances called the *segment outputs*, on the basis of specified criteria. Given a workflow segment, a *workflow* for that segment is that segment together with the set of other workflow segments that have generated all of that segment's inputs. A *workflow graph* shows the agents as nodes that are joined by arcs representing the workflows. A workflow graph can be cyclic; in simple applications it may have a linear or a tree structure (Barthelmess & Wainer, 1995).

Workflows can be specified imperatively or declaratively. An imperative specification will describe *how* a workflow is to be performed. A declarative specification will describe *what* has to be achieved in a workflow; it then being left to the workflow management system to deduce the 'how' from the 'what'. For example, a workflow segment could be specified imperatively as "the given form is sent to person X who will mark that form to show whether particular aspects of that form are correct". Alternatively, the goal of a workflow segment could be specified declaratively as "for a given form decide whether that form has been completed correctly"; it then being left to the workflow management system to determine how this goal should be achieved and who should be responsible for achieving it (Bogia & Kaplan, 1995).

A *pre-planned workflow* specifies precisely what will happen in each workflow segment before the workflow commences (Suchman, 1987). Pre-planned workflows are specified imperatively. A pre-planned workflow can be specified in terms of the roles of the people involved in the workflow. Adaptive workflows are more flexible that pre-planned workflows. An *adaptive workflow* determines what will happen in a workflow segment on the basis of both the goal of that segment and knowledge of the current state of the decision making environment (Kwan & Balasubramanian, 1997). Once the segment output is determined, an adaptive workflow system will derive the goal for the next workflow segment. Adaptive workflows are specified declaratively. An adaptive workflow management system should take account of day-to-day changes in the environment and should continually review each workflow in the context of the current state of its environment. Adaptive workflow management systems thus rely on an understanding of the relationship of workflows to their environment. A specification of the *environment* is a specification of the "organisational rules", the "cultural factors" and the "processing capacity" of the organisation. For each workflow segment an adaptive workflow management system will determine how the goal of that segment may be achieved. The *organisational rules* describe how an enterprise fits together and how it operates. Organisational rules describe who is responsible to whom and for what. Organisational rules describe who is authorised to do what in the name and business of the organisation. Organisational rules also specify procedures for carrying out tasks. The *cultural factors* of an organisation are the "knowledge of how things work". This includes rules of thumb about "who is a good person to ask about certain difficult situations", or who is to be consulted so that a decision may be accepted. If workflow management is to be effective then it must take account of the cultural factors. The *processing capacity* includes a specification of "which agent is available when to do what".

Workflow management is concerned with the design of workflow systems and their infrastructure so as to achieve effective workflow processing. The cost of using a workflow system is the cost of workflow processing though that system subject to constraints. If the constraints include that a given minimum acceptable quality of decision making that should be achieved then the specification of the possible outcomes of each workflow segment should include the required quality of that outcome, and a strategic workflow management system should include the ability to modify these measures of quality to reflect strategic targets. The specification of a workflow often contains a statement of the urgency of that workflow. A *strategic workflow management system* determines adaptive workflows on the basis the environment using the "strategic variables". A strategic workflow management system will "report" on its performance. This *strategic reporting* may contain, for example, the cost of processing workflows, the recorded quality of workflow processing and the time taken to process workflows. The strategic reporting will enable the performance of the workflow system to be tuned by controlling the values of the strategic variables whilst attempting to process workflows so that their reported performance is within the tolerance specified by constraints. The *strategic variables* are of two types the "control variables" and the "report variables". The *report variables* are a sufficient set of variables to describe the effectiveness of workflow processing. The *control variables* are a sufficient set of variables to control the effectiveness of workflow processing. The strategic variables could include the urgency of a workflow or the quality of a workflow. The report variables enable the control variables to be determined.

3. Experimental System

A highly simplified description of the external operation of an experimental system follows. Prospective research students are directed to a world wide web page that contains explanatory material and a form. If the prospective student chooses to complete this form, the completed form is submitted. When a form is submitted it is screened automatically to check for obvious errors such as leaving the section "Please suggest a brief title for your proposed research project." blank. If the form fails the automatic screening then an email message is sent to the prospective student to request that the detected errors should be rectified. When this initial screening is complete an email message is sent to a senior academic in the department advising that a form has been screened. This academic will then check the form to ascertain whether the interests of the prospective student are relevant to the interests of the department. If the academic indicates that the interests of the prospective student are relevant then that academic marks the form with any potential supervisors who are clearly well suited to supervise the proposed work. The form is then released. When a form is released the system refers to a database containing the research interests of all academic staff and forms a prioritised list of appropriate candidate supervisors. The form is then circulated to these candidate supervisors until either two supervisors are found or no two supervisors can be found.

This particular application was chosen for the following reasons. The application involves three important types of interaction with players. The first type of player is the "client", ie the prospective student, who should be "kept happy" with sufficiently frequent and detailed communication to give the impression that "something is happening" whilst not giving the impression of a system that is generating unnecessary "junk mail". The second type of player is employees with whom the system communicates; the system should assist these employees to do

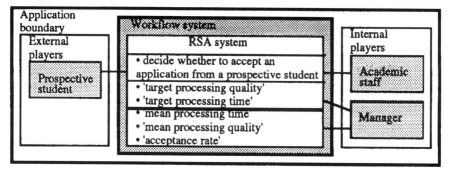

Figure 1 Context diagram for experimental RSA system

their job with a minimum of fuss. The third type of player is the "dynamic committee" with which the system interacts during the search for a potential supervisor. In a *dynamic committee* a workflow is considered collectively by a continually changing group of people or agents whose reactions to that workflow may be influenced by the decisions already made, and by the decisions presently being made. For example, "I'll take this person on as a research student if you will" is an example of a reaction influenced by a decision that is presently being made. If any group is to be an effective decision making body then appropriate levels of communication between the active members of that group, and between the active members and any previous members, is required.

Despite its inherent interest, the application chosen is limited. First, the basic input document is an application form that is subsequently annotated but otherwise remains fixed. In other words, there is not a significant versioning problem to be managed through the workflow. Second, the flow structure is basically linear. Third, the application is based on a "single document workflow". In a *single document workflow* the relevant sections of a single document are available to all players during processing. In a single document workflow the single document may grow during processing, and it may contain sections that are confidential to particular players. The restriction to single document workflows simplifies system design. This restriction does not prevent the use of asynchronous parallel processing.

4. System Design

Experience with the experimental system has suggested an approach to strategic workflow systems design for single document workflows. The first three steps in this approach are described. First determine the context diagram. Second design the top level system object. Third decompose the top level system object (Debenham, 1996b).

The first step is to determine the overall context of the workflow system including the players, the environment, the strategic variables and the strategic reporting. This is represented in a *context diagram* for each workflow system. A context diagram for the experimental system is shown in Figure 1. The context diagram shows the workflow system, the external players and the internal players. A context diagram for a workflow system consists of the workflow name, the role of the workflow, the strategic variables and the strategic reporting. In Figure 1 the

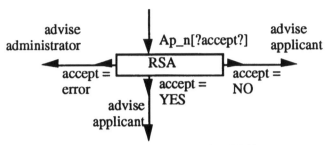

Figure 2 Workflow graph for 'RSA'

workflow system *name* is 'RSA system' (ie Research Student Application). The *role* of the RSA system is to "decide whether to accept an application from a prospective student". The *strategic variables* for RSA are 'target processing quality' (ie the target quality of the decision making for this workflow system) and 'target processing time' (ie the target mean time for processing), and the *strategic reporting* for RSA consists of monthly values for the variables 'mean processing time', 'mean processing quality' and 'acceptance rate' (ie the proportion of applications that are accepted).

The second step is to design the top level system object. The complete design will consist of a set of nested knowledge-based objects (Dellen et al, 1997), where each knowledge-based object represents a sub-system. Each *object* has of a *name*, a set of *sub-objects*, a set of *rules* that state how those sub-objects are to be used to achieve one or more workflow goals, and a *reporting mechanism*. Each workflow is given a *name*. At each stage in the processing each workflow has a "status". A workflow *status* is either a "goal" or a "result". The status of a workflow may be changed either by a rule or by an agent. A *goal* is a variable whose value is to be determined possibly subject to given values of variables (denoted by either "?<variable name>?" or "?<variable name>(<list of values>)?"). A *result* is the value of a variable that has occurred in a goal (denoted by "<variable name> = <value>"). The rules for the RSA system are shown informally on a workflow graph in Figure 2 (Georgakopolous & Hornick, 1995). Formally the rules have the form: IF <condition> THEN <action>. Examples of rules will be given during the third design step. The reporting mechanism is also expressed in terms of rules. In this example this is achieved by recording events on local "blackboards" within objects. The reporting mechanism will not be described here.

The third step is to decompose the top level system object. In the RSA system suppose that the way in which workflows will be processed is determined substantially by the specified 'target processing time'. Suppose that if the 'target processing time' ≥ 6 days then 'regular processing' is prescribed. The RSA object could then have two sub-objects 'find_stat_vars' and 'regular_proc'; where 'find_stat_vars' looks for the current values of the strategic variables, and 'regular_proc' aims to process an application in a given time that is six or more days. The 'find_stat_vars' object will refer to the Manager's files to determine the current value of 'target processing quality' and 'target processing time'. The rules for this decomposition of the RSA object are shown in summary only on a flow graph in Figure 3. Formally two of the rules for the RSA object are:

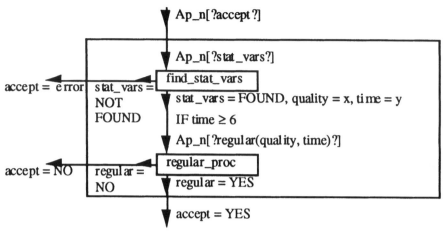

Figure 3 Decomposition of 'RSA' for 'time' ≥ 6 only

IF status of Ap_n is '?accept?' THEN
                status of Ap_n is '?stat_vars?' AND
                PASS Ap_n to 'find_stat_vars'

IF status of Ap_n is 'stat_vars = FOUND, quality = x, time = y'
AND time ≥ 6 THEN
                status of Ap_n is '?regular(quality, time)?' AND
                PASS Ap_n to 'regular_proc'

As before, the reporting mechanism is not discussed here.

The decomposition of the 'regular_proc' object is more complex. Suppose that the desired procedure for regular processing requires that the 'regular_proc' object should have three sub-objects 'check_fields', 'check_relevance' and 'find_supervisors'; where 'check_fields' is a quick automatic check of the completed form to check for "silly omissions", 'check_relevance' is a check by a senior academic of the completed form to ensure that it is relevant, and 'find_supervisors' attempts to find two potential supervisors for the applicant. The rules for this decomposition of the 'regular_proc' object are shown in summary only on a flow graph in Figure 4. In Figure 4 the object 'check_fields' will be implemented as a knowledge base, the object 'check_relevance' is substantially implemented by reference to a person, and the object 'find_supervisors' is substantially implemented by a dynamic committee which, in the experiment, was constrained to contain either two or three people at any time. The analysis does not need to specify these different forms of implementation.

As workflows are specified in terms of goals, the decomposition procedure (Debenham, 1996a) generates an AND/OR structure of sub-objects. The workflow processing described so far has been sequential. Consider the simple piece of organisational culture that "all applications in Knowledge-Based Systems (KBS) go to Professor X who may accept them directly"; this piece of culture is in addition to the organisational rules in the regular procedure 'regular_proc' shown in Figure 4.

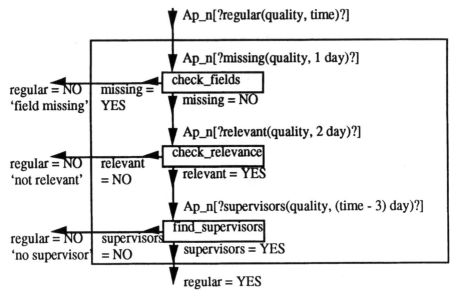

Figure 4 Decomposition of 'regular_proc' using three sub-objects

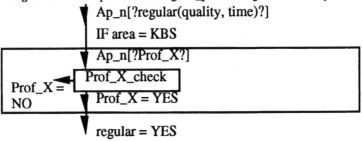

Figure 5 Organisational culture is included

The object 'Prof_X_check' is shown in Figure 5, and is included with the objects shown in Figure 4. If the application is in the Knowledge-Based Systems area then the 'Prof_X_check' object and the 'regular_proc' object are processed asynchronously in parallel. This parallel execution causes no conflict. For example suppose that control is with 'check_relevance' in Figure 4 at the same time Professor X is looking at the form in 'Prof_X_check'. If Professor X makes the decision to accept the applicant then the goal of the workflow is changed to 'Prof_X = YES' and then to 'regular = YES'. If the person who is attending to 'check_relevance' subsequently attempts to enter a decision then that decision will be ignored because that person can only change the workflow goal *from* 'relevant(quality, 2 day)?' *to* something else. In this example conflict has been avoided by restricting the workflow to a single document. If different values of the strategic variables lead to different modes of processing then the resulting systems may be highly parallel.

The description of the experimental system given here has focussed on the knowledge-based systems aspect of the system. The cooperative aspects of the system are equally important and are responsible for providing a good decision making environment (Swenson et al, 1994).

5. Conclusion

The principal conclusions from this experiment are that:

• a simple workflow system that delivers good performance for a modest cost can be constructed using a knowledge-base, the world wide web, email and database technologies.

• the experimental system was constructed in two months by a programmer who had some artificial intelligence experience; in excess of half of this time was spent developing the world wide web / database gateway and the knowledge base / email gateway.

• those involved in the experimental system were encouraged by the quality of the performance of the experimental system which contained approximately twenty rules; in this application a little knowledge delivered good performance.

• if a knowledge base is used to drive workflow systems then the distinction between organisational rules and cultural factors is made in the design but not necessarily in the representation.

• the experiment failed to support the decision making environment (Abbott & Sarin, 1994) by providing easy access to historic information, for example the regulations governing research students and a convenient history of applicants.

• the experiment failed to provide a good decision making environment by providing an appropriate level of communication both with and between the players. The incorporation of cooperative systems software is being considered for the next generation of the system.

• the experimental system treated all users in the same way and did not permit users to 'control' the way in which the system behaved. The development of a distributed AI environment containing intelligent agents that assist with the management of each internal player's system is being considered for the next generation of the system.

• the design methodology used was for single document workflows; the extension of the design work to include multi-document workflows is being considered. The flow structure in multi-document workflows may rely on inputs from other workflows, and thus requires the scheduling of segment processing.

• the 'dynamic committee' proved to be an effective decision making environment. Intelligent workflow systems in a cooperative systems environment present great flexibility in the formation of decision making bodies. Experiments will be conducted to explore the effectiveness of innovative decision making bodies, and criteria will be derived for identifying appropriate decision making bodies for given types of decision.

In short the experiment proved to be worthwhile. A second version of the system is presently being implemented.

References

Abbott, K.R. and Sarin, K.S. (1994): "Experiences with Workflow Management: Issues for the Next Generation" in Furuta, R., Neuwirth, C. (eds.): proceedings *Conference on Computer Supported Cooperative Work, CSCW94*, ACM Press, pp. 113-120.

Ames, C.K., Burleigh, S.C. and Mitchell, S.J. (1997) "WWWorkflow: World Wide Web based Workflow" in proceedings *Thirteenth Annual IEEE Hawaii International Conference on System Science.*

Barthelmess, P. and Wainer, J. (1995) "Workflow Systems: a few definitions and a few suggestions" in proceedings *1995 ACM Conference on Organisational Computing Systems (COOCS'95)*, N. Comstock and C.A. Ellis (eds.), pp 138-147, Milpitas, California, 1995.

Bentley, R. and Applet, W. (1997) "Designing a Systems for Cooperative Work on the World-Wide Web: Experiences with the BSCW System" in proceedings *Thirteenth Annual IEEE Hawaii International Conference on System Science.*

Bogia, D.P. and Kaplan, S.M. (1995) "Flexibility and Control for Dynamic Workflows in the Worlds Environment" in proceedings *Conference on Organisational Computing Systems* (COOCS'95), N. Comstock and C.A. Ellis (eds.), pp 148-159, Milpitas, California, 1995.

Debenham, J.K. (1996a) "Knowledge Simplification", in proceedings *9th International Symposium on Methodologies for Intelligent Systems ISMIS'96*, Zakopane, Poland, June 1996, pp305-314.

Debenham, J.K. (1996b) "Unification of Knowledge Acquisition and Knowledge Representation", in proceedings *International Conference on Information Processing and Management of Uncertainty in Knowledge Based Systems IPMU'96*, Granada, Spain, July 1996, pp897-902.

Dellen, B., Maurer, F. and Pews G. (1997) "Knowledge Based Techniques to Increase the Flexibility of Workflow Management" in *Data and Knowledge Engineering Journal* (North Holland) 1997.

Georgakopolous, D. and Hornick, M. (1995) "An Overview of Workflow Management: From Process Modelling to Workflow Automation Infrastructure" in *Distributed and Parallel Databases* 3, pp 119-153.

Hawryszkiewycz, I.T., and Gorton, I. (1996): "Workflow Support for Change Management and Concurrency" *Proceedings of the Conference on Software Engineering: Education and Practice*, Dunedin, New Zealand, pp. 181-188.

Kwan, M.M. and Balasubramanian, P.R. (1997) "Dynamic Workflow Management: A Framework for Modelling Workflows" in proceedings *Thirteenth Annual IEEE Hawaii International Conference on System Science.*

Suchman, L. (1987): *"Plans and Situated Action: The Problem of Human-Machine Communication"* Cambridge University Press, Cambridge.

Swenson, K.D., Maxwell, R.J., Matsumoto, T., Saghari, B. and Irwin, K. (1994) "A Business Process Environment Supporting Collaborative Planning" in proceedings *CSCW'94*, ACM, 1994.

Use of Partial Functional Dependencies to make Practical Approximate Translations Among Forms of Propositional Expert Systems

Robert M. Colomb. and Phoebe Yi-Ping Chen

School of Information Technology,
The University of Queensland, Brisbane, QLD 4072, Australia
e-mail: {colomb, yiping}@it.uq.edu.au.

Abstract. Decision tables and decision trees have long been used to describe and implement computer programs which classify cases. It also is known that there is a close relationship between them. This however, is mediated by algorithms which tend to be exponential.Decision tables and decision trees can be viewed as propositional system; so can most expert systems. Knowledge-based systems therefore give rise to very large decision tables or trees. Further, it is often convenient to transform an object from one representation to another, so that the exponential algorithms become impracticable. In this paper, we first formalise decision tables, decision trees, cases and rules and the well known relationships among them. We then introduce the concept of equivalence with respect to a set of cases, which enables us to make transformations with algorithms which are linear in the number of cases. Then we introduce the concept of equivalence with respect to a set of constraints(rules), which enables us to perform transformations with algorithms in a sounder, less ad hoc way. The paper evaluates these algorithms by applying them to a large example. These new algorithms permit computationally effective and practically useful transformations for large problems.

1 Introduction

There is a large class of expert systems whose purpose is essentially to classify cases, for example to diagnose disease from symptoms. Several different methods are used to represent the knowledge in such systems and to form the basis of computer implementations; in particular propositional production rules, decision tables and decision trees.

It has been known for some time that these representations are equivalent, in that a system represented in one can be automatically translated into another, exactly preserving the input-output behaviour of the original representation. This issue is addressed in detail by Colomb and Chung(1995). Translatability means that a body of knowledge can be represented in different ways for different purposes. For example, an expert system may be built by experts as a set of rules, which might be a natural way for humans to understand the knowledge; but a decision table representation can make it much easier to perform an analysis of the vulnerability of the knowledge base to measurement errors (Colomb 1992); and a decision tree representation may give a fast bounded time implementation (Shwayder 1971, 1974). On the other hand, an expert system may be built originally as a decision tree, say by induction from a set of cases (Quinlan 1982, 1986), but be translated into one of the other forms for analysis or understandability. Since these various representations of knowledge are interchangeable, we will call them all decision objects.

However, even though the translations can be automatically performed by simple algorithms, there is a severe practical difficulty, namely that the translated representation can be very much larger than the original. Furthermore, most of the constituent parts of the translated object may not be used in practice, even if all the parts of the original are. A decision object will be described as compact if most of its rules, rows or leaves are exercised in practice. We have observed that, in general, the transformation does not preserve compactness. An extreme case analysed in Colomb (1993) shows that an object in one form which is compact and of size 1000 is transformed into a very non-compact object of size 400 million. We will call this loss of compactness inflation.

Colomb and Sienkiewicz (1995) have shown that this inflation is caused by the way decision objects are built. A particular knowledge base is designed for a particular classification task. The cases to be classified are represented by a collection of attributes. If we consider each attribute as a dimension in attribute space, the decision object is regarded as a function mapping attribute space into a classification space. The representations of the classification functions are typically total, in that any combination of selections of values for attributes will be assigned a classification by the decision object, whether it is a sensible case or an impossible combination.

The problem arises from the fact that in very many applications, nearly any random assignment of values to attributes will result in an absurd case. In other words, in practice the process generating real cases will generate points in a tiny region of the attribute space. The decision object is a total function, so would give absurd results over most of the attribute space. Construction of decision objects as total functions works in practice because the process generating cases never generates absurd cases, so cases lying outside what we will call the permitted region are never encountered.

In this paper, we show that we can use a description of the permitted region to approximate the source decision object in the target representation in such a way that any case occurring in the permitted region is correctly classified, but the translated object may behave differently outside that region. This approximate translation can be much more compact, and therefore much more practically useful.

We first present an algorithm from the literature which translates a decision table into a decision tree, showing how the inflation occurs. Next, we show from earlier work how the algorithm can be modified to use a set of cases as a description of the permitted region, resulting an a compact approximate transformation. This approximation is not entirely satisfactory, since the description of the permitted region by a set of cases is ad hoc, and its reliability is difficult to assess. Finally, we present the key result, namely that we can use a description of the permitted region based on partial functional dependencies estimated from a set of cases to make a much more reliable approximate transformation. The paper concludes with a discussion of some of the implications of the main result. The results of this paper have been tested using the well-known Garvan ES1 data set (Horn, et al. 1985), which was a successful thyroid hormone pathology laboratory system in clinical use for several years. The decision object associated with that data set was a decision table with 653 rows. The data set includes a collection of 9805 cases, which represents a full year's clinical use.

2 Decision Table to Decision Tree

Firstly, we formalize decision tables, decision trees, cases and the well-known relationships among them.

2.1 Definition

Decision table: An *elementary proposition* consists of an attribute and a set of zero or more admissible values from the value set belonging to that attribute. Typical elementary propositions would be sex in {female} or sex in {female, male}(the latter is a "don't care" elementary proposition, it will be designated " Ø"). A *decision table* consists of a set of rows r_i. Each row is a conjunction of elementary propositions in which each attribute is represented exactly once. Associated with the row r_i is a result k_i, which is so far uninterpreted. A decision table is *unambiguous* if two rows with different results are inconsistent: $(k_i \neq k_j) \supset (r_i \& r_j \supset false)$. If the table is unambiguous there will be at most one result associated with any case. A decision table is intended to be applied to a *case* which is an assignment to each attribute of a member of its value set. Each elementary proposition in each row is interpreted as a test on the value of its associated attribute in the case. The table is said to *classify* the case: if case c_j is consistent with r_i, then k_i is assigned to the case. If a table is complete, there will be at least one result associated with every case. We will assume that our decision tables are unambiguous, but not necessary complete. A *trivial decision table* has no attributes, only a result. It fires on all cases, assigning its result.

Decision tree: A *decision* is a non-trivial elementary proposition. A *decision tree* is a finite tree; each of its nodes consists of a decision, and each of its leaves consists of a result. The path leaving each node is called an arc. A *decision node* consists of a attribute and an arc for each value in its value set. Each arc is therefore associated with an *arc proposition*. If the decision reaches a node, and one of its arc propositions is true, then the arc is said to *fire*. The decision at a node for a case will be designated the arc proposition associated with the case. If a leaf node fires for a case, the tree is said to *classify* the case. It is easy to show that a decision tree is complete and unambiguous. Since a decision tree is necessarily complete, it is not possible to translate an incomplete decision table into decision tree. Since we wish to do so, we will extend the definition of a decision tree to include propositions at its leaf nodes. If L is a leaf node, the associated *leaf proposition* will be P_L. If the leaf L fires, then P_L is evaluated. If P_L is true then the result associated with the leaf is assigned to the case, otherwise, the reserved result "Not Classified" is assigned. We will call this modified decision tree a *conditional decision tree*.

If P_L is a tautology, then the leaf always classifies. (A conditional decision tree all of whose leaf propositions are tautologies reduces to the original definition of a decision tree). This sort of leaf will be called an *normal leaf node*. If P_L is inconsistent, then the leaf can never classify, and will be called an *else node*. Otherwise, the leaf will be called a *rule node*.

2.2 Relationship Between Tables, Trees and Cases in Theorem 1

Theorem 1: *An unambiguous decision table is equivalent to a conditional decision tree. The decision tree is unconditional only if the table is complete.* (We prove Theorem 1 by induction on the number of distinct attributes.)

Proof:

Basis step:

- If the number of attributes is equal to zero then the algorithm terminates, and a leaf node is created. The decision table is trivial so it has a single conclusion, which is assigned to the normal leaf node. The proof can terminate in other situations: if all rows in the table have the same result then create a rule leaf node with that result whose leaf proposition is the disjunction of the rows; if the number of rows in the table is equal to zero then the algorithm terminates and an else leaf node is created.

Induction step:

- There is at least one attribute. Choose an attribute A_i to become a decision node in the tree by some selection procedure.

- Denote by m the number of values in its value set, each value being a branch under the decision node.

- Construct the set of *associated tables*(each associated table belongs to the branch) T_j for $j=1,...,m$, where T_j is the rows of T where v_{ij} from row i is in the set of admissible values of A_i.

The tree is unconditional only if all of its leaf propositions are tautologies. Leaf propositions are created only in the basis step. The proposition created by the "no attributes" stopping rule is a tautology, resulting from the trivial decision table, which is complete. The proposition created by the "all same result" criterion is a tautology only in case the table is complete. The "no rows" criterion reflects a table with attributes but no rows, which is necessarily incomplete.☐

An Algorithm can be easily be created from Theorem 1. Its practical utility depends on the selection heuristic used in the induction step. Shwayder(1974) gives a selection procedure based on information. The selection procedure of Quinlan(1983) could also be used.

3   How inflation arises in Theorem 1

The algorithm derived from Theorem 1 can create many more leaf nodes than there are rows in the original table. The problem arises in the induction step, when the associated tables are created for the various branches of the tree node. A row in the table having a don't care condition in the selected attribute will generate a row in more than one of the tables associated with the branches of the tree. The total number of rows in the associated tables can therefore be more than the number of rows in the table. For example(see Figure 1), the decision table below has 2 rows, but the total number of rows of the two associated tables is 3. The second row generates rows in each associated table.

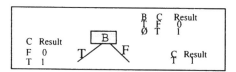

Fig. 1. Example for don't care value existing in the row

3.1 A not very satisfactory cure for inflation using cases

Colomb (1993) presented a method of reducing inflation by taking advantage of a set of cases. We will say that a decision object D1 is *equivalent with respect to a set C of cases* to another decision object D2 if for every case in C, D1 and D2 assign the same result. That work reported a modification of Theorem 1.

Theorem 2: *A decision table is equivalent with respect to a set C of cases to a conditional decision tree which has no more leaves than there are cases.*

Proof: We associate with each row r_i of the table a subset C_i of cases in C which are consistent with r_i.(These are the cases which would be classified by r_i.) If two rows have different results, then their sets of associated cases are disjoint, since we have assumed that the table is unambiguous. If a case is consistent with two rows having the same result, we assign the case arbitrarily. The family $\{C_i\}$ is therefore a partition of C.

The proof of Theorem 2 is similar to Theorem 1. The basis step is the same. In the induction step, when a row r_i in the decision table has a don't care condition in the selected attribute A_j, we partition the set C_i into a family $\{C_{ik}\}$, where C_{ik} is the set of rows consistent with r_i with the don't care condition replaced by $A_j = v_k$. A row is created in the table associated with branch T_k only if C_{ik} is not empty. The resulting tree is a conditional tree. Since there is always at least one case associated with each branch-associated table and cases are never duplicated, there are no more leaves than cases. Finally, the tree is equivalent with respect to C since each case in C is associated with a leaf of the tree which classifies the case in the same way as the table does.☐

This result cures the inflation problem, but is not entirely satisfactory. It relies on a set of cases. Should the process generate a case not in the reference set, the behaviour of the tree is not specified. Further, the smaller the set of cases, the smaller the tree. If we think of the pruning of the decision tree as being the result of additional information provided by the set of cases, then the less information we have (the fewer cases), the more we prune, which is the reverse of what we would like.

4 Curing inflation using partial functional dependencies

4.1 Partial function dependencies

One feature of the theory of rough sets is an analysis of functional and partial functional dependencies among attribute functions derived from a set of cases. The partial functional dependencies are called value reducts, and a specific combination of attribute/ value pairs in the domain of a dependency with an attribute/value pair in its range is called a rule. For the algorithms to compute a set of rules derived from the value reducts of a set of cases see Pawlak(1991).

Colomb and Sienkiewicz (1995) applied the value reduct algorithm to the set of 9805 cases in the Garvan data set, resulting in a set K of constraints of the form $A_i = v_{i1}$ => $A_j = v_{j1}$. (This process is essentially the same as Agrawal (1995)'s association rules with 100% confidence; in other words none of the cases presented a counterexample to the constraint.) The set of constraints was limited to those with a support level of 10 or more (at least 10 cases provided positive examples of the constraint). The experiment applied to the Garvan data set resulted in a set of 332 constraints.

In that work, the set K of constraints was interpreted as an estimate of the definition of the permitted region for the process generating cases. This estimate is more suitable than the cases themselves, since as the number of cases increases, the reliability of K increases. (As a limiting situation, if there are no cases, then K is empty and there are no constraints on the permitted region. In Theorem 2, we would end up with an empty tree, which is not of much use.) The key result of the present work is presented in the following section, in which the set of constraints rather than the set of cases is used to prune the decision tree.

4.2 A better cure for inflation

We will say that decision object D1 is *equivalent with respect to a set K of constraints* with decision object D2 if every case consistent with K is assigned the same result by both D1 and D2.

Theorem 3: *An unambiguous decision table T is equivalent with respect to a set of constraints to a conditional decision tree.*

Proof: As with Theorem 2, the basis step is the same as for Theorem 1. We modify the induction step of Theorem 2 so that where a row has a don't care condition, a row is placed in the table associated with a branch only if it is consistent with K. The resulting tree is a conditional decision tree. Every case consistent with K is clearly classified the same by the table and the tree, so the two are equivalent with respect to K.□

Note that the number of leaves in the tree is not specifically limited as it was in Theorem 2. However, it is reasonable to expect the size of the tree to be smaller if K is highly constraining. Colomb and Sienkiewicz estimated that the 332 constraints from the Garvan data restricted the permitted region to 10^{-6} of the attribute space (if 1 million cases were generated at random, we would expect on the average that only 1 would be consistent with K). The algorithm derived from Theorem 3 was applied to the Garvan data set, together with the collection of 332 rules from Colomb and Sienkiewicz(1995). The resulting number of leaves in the decision table was 4562, which is more than that resulting from Theorem 2 but far less than that resulting from Theorem 1. The three methods are compared in Table 1. A more complete analysis appears in the following. We can conclude that use of a derived rule set gives a practical approximate translation method.

Pruning Method	Decision Tree	Theorem
No Pruning	46378 leaves	1
Cases	985 leaves	2
Partial FD	4562 leaves	3

Table 1. Comparison of the number of leaves resulting from 653 rows decision table

In Theorem 1, the resulting tree was unconditional if the table was complete. Theorems 2 and 3 do not preserve this property, since they work by pruning the decision tree, introducing else nodes.

Statistic	T1	T3
Number Decision Nodes	30282	2362
Number Pruned Branches	0	9231
Number Rule Leaf Nodes	36817	3103
Number Else Leaf Nodes	9561	1459
Total Number Different Rule Nodes Fired	877	404
Total Number Different Else Nodes Fired	108	122

Table 2. Comparison of Theorem 1 and Theorem 3 in Garvan data set

Table 2 shows a more complete comparison of the application of Theorem 1 and Theorem 3 to the Garvan data set. Note that there were a large number of branches pruned using Theorem 3, and the resulting number of decision nodes and leaves of both kinds is much less. Both resulting trees were used to classify the 9805 cases. Of the leaves resulting from Theorem 1, only about 2% fired on the year's cases, while of the leaves resulting from Theorem 3, 11.5% fired on the year's cases, a much more compact result.

5 Example

In this section, we will use a simple example to explain the difference between Theorem 1 and Theorem 3. At the same time, we can also see better how Theorem 1 and Theorem 3 work.

A	B	C	Result
F	T	F	0
F	Ø	T	1

Table 3. Sample decision table

Table 3 shows a decision table which will be used in the example. In this prototypical case the attributes are boolean with values {true, false}, but other value sets are possible. In particular, the attribute B of the second row includes "Ø", so this attribute value could be "T" or "F". The result column determines classifications for data when a table is applied to a case. Figure 2 shows how the decision table shown in Table 3 translates to a decision tree. The decision tree was constructed using a choice of attributes introduced to illustrate the algorithm and its properties.

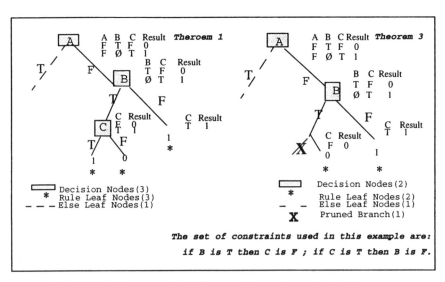

Fig. 2. Using Theorem 1 and Theorem 3 transformation decision tree

The difference between left-hand and right-hand in Figure2 illustrates the difference between Theorem 1 and Theorem 3. In Theorem 3 when a row with a don't care condition is encountered while partitioning the table into the decision tree, Theorem 3 will check whether each specialization of the row satisfies the set of constraints(rules). If the specialization does not satisfy the set of constraints then this row will not be included in the partition.

For the A="F" followed by B="T" followed by C="T" ,where the existing branch has only one row in Figure. 2, the row "F T T" in Figure 2 failed for the set of constraints so the branch is pruned from the tree. The "B" node can no longer belong to the node in the tree. So the numbers of nodes in the decision tree and the number of rule leaf node will be both decreased by 1. The tree in Figure 2(using Theorem 3) has 2 decision nodes, 1 else leaf node, 2 rule leaf nodes and has had one branch pruned.

6 Conclusions

This paper began with the fact that the several representations of propositional expert systems are intertranslatable, but that some of the translations result in objects which are unnecessarily large, sometimes impractically large. This inflation is a consequence of decision objects designed for processes occupying a small portion of their attribute space being implemented as total functions.

We have shown that it is possible to make use of a characterisation of the permitted region of a process in the form of a set of constraints expressed as partial functional dependencies to produce a much more practicable approximate translation which agrees with the original on the subspace of the attribute space defined by the set of constraints. The utility of this approximate translation has been demonstrated by its application to a large real system.

The ability to represent a decision object as a partial function in a number of different forms will make it easier to develop classification systems which are understandable to the experts, are reliable, and which have desirable execution properties, including suitability for real-time operation. One would expect that use of partial functional dependencies would also control inflation in rules to table(Colomb and Chung 1995), and ripple-down rule trees to decision tables(Colomb 1993).

References

Agrawal, R. and Srikant, R.(1995), Mining Generalized Association Rules, VLDB'95, pp.407-419.

Colomb, R.M. (1992), Computational stability of expert systems, Expert Systems With Applications 5(2/3), pp. 411-419.

Colomb, R.M. (1993), Decision Tables, Decision Trees and Cases: Propositional Knowledge-Based Systems Technical Report 266, Department of Computer Science, The University of Queensland, Australia.

Colomb, R.M. and Chung, C.Y. (1995), "Strategies for Building Propositional Expert Systems" International Journal of Intelligent Systems Vol. 10, No.3, pp 295ff.

Colomb, R.M. and Sienkiewicz, J. (1995), "Analysis of Redundancy in Expert Systems Case Data" Eighth Australian Joint Conference on Artificial Intelligence, World Scientific, pp. 395-402.

Horn, K. A., Compton P., Lazarus L. and Quinlan J. R. (1985), An expert computer system for the interpretation of thyroid assays in a clinical laboratory, Australian Computer Journal, 17(1) (1985) pp. 7-11.

Pawlak, Z. (1991), Rough Sets: Theoretical Aspects of Reasoning About Data Kluwer Academic Publishers.

Quinlan, J.R. (1986), Introduction of decision trees, Machine Learning, 1(1) pp. 81-106.

Quinlan, J.R.(1982), Semi-autonomous acquisition of pattern based knowledge, in Hayes, Michie J.E.,D.and Pao,Y-H eds Machine Intelligence 10, (Ellis Horwood, London, 1982) pp. 159-172.

Shwayder,K.(1974), Extending the information theory approach to converting limited-entry decision tables to computer programs, Communications of the ACM 17(9) pp.532-537.

Shwayder, K.(1971), Conversion of limited-entry decision tables to computer programs-a proposed modification to Pollack's algorithm,Communications of the ACM 14(2) pp.69-73.

NRDR for the Acquisition of Search Knowledge

Ghassan Beydoun and Achim Hoffmann
School of Computer Science and Engineering
University of New South Wales
Sydney, NSW 2052, Australia
Email: {ghassan,achim}@cse.unsw.edu.au

Abstract

The contribution of this paper is three-fold: It substantially extends Ripple Down Rules, a proven effective method for building large knowledge bases without a knowledge engineer. Furthermore, we propose to develop highly effective heuristics searchers for combinatorial problems by a knowledge acquisition approach to acquire human search knowledge. Finally, our initial experimental results suggest, that this approach may allow experts to stepwise articulate their introspectively inaccessible knowledge.

The development of highly effective heuristics for search problems is a difficult and time-consuming task. We present a knowledge acquisition approach to incrementally model expert search processes. Though, experts do not normally have introspective access to that knowledge, their explanations of actual search considerations seems very valuable in constructing a knowledge level model of their search skills.

Furthermore, for the basis of our knowledge acquisition approach, we substantially extend Ripple Down Rules [1], a proven effective method for building large knowledge bases without a knowledge engineer: The conditions may involve yet undefined terms which can be incrementally defined during both, the knowledge acquisition as well as the knowledge maintenance process. The resulting framework is called Nested Ripple Down Rules.

Our extension greatly enhances the applicability of Ripple Down Rules. Furthermore, for the acquisition of search knowledge, we developed our system SmS1.2 using our new Nested Ripple Down Rules, which has been employed for the acquisition of expert chess knowledge for performing a highly pruned tree search. Our first experimental results in the chess domain are promising for our knowledge acquisition approach to build heuristic searchers which perform a much more restricted tree search than programs like Deep Blue.

1   Introduction

In most application areas of computer science the satisfactory treatment of search problems is of primary importance. The efficient and effective solution of these problems has a major impact on today's economy, the environment as well as on technological advances. Unfortunately, many such problems are known to be **NP**-complete or **NP**-hard, which means that no really fast algorithm for optimal solutions can be expected to be found.

Opposed to that, it is well-known that human experts are often surprisingly good in finding better solutions to a given optimisation problem then existing heuristic programs. For example in the area of circuit design, human engineers often intervene into the automatic design steps performed by highly specialised design programs in order to optimise the overall result.

In this paper, we describe an approach to incrementally acquire expert search control knowledge. We developed a workbench which consults the expert on search problems and takes advice of what search steps should be taken in which search state. The first results we obtained are very encouraging and provide evidence that our approach may be suitable for a general framework of building high-performance problem-specific search heuristics for combinatorial problems.

1.1   Knowledge on search heuristics

Most knowledge based systems perform a search process when applying the knowledge stored in the knowledge base to a given problem. In this paper, the effective performance of such a search process itself becomes the domain of expertise. In many activities of human intellectual endeavour, some sort of search within a set of potential solutions can be said to take place. E.g. in design processes, engineers will evaluate partial designs on their fitness for a vantage point to complete the design successfully. If a partial design seems unfit, an alternative partial design is selected etc. Capturing the expertise being employed for such skilled search processes is a difficult task.

Although there are plenty of applications of more relevance, let us consider the expert search processes in chess playing for illustration purposes. De Groot [3] conducted systematic psychological studies into the thought processes involved in master chess play. A master chess player, thinking aloud, may report the following:

> ... Let me try to attack the pawn on f2. Ok, I can move my bishop to c5 attacking this pawn. Possibly, my opponent will move his knight to e4 defending the pawn and simultaneously attacking my bishop on c5, such that I am forced to move the bishop again. This is unpleasant - so let me see whether this problem can be fixed. Maybe, I can avoid the knight move to e4. Oh well, first I can attack the knight by moving my pawn to b4 forcing it to move to another square. If it does not move to e4, then moving my bishop to c5 is much better. ...

Obviously, such an expert search process involves more complex reasoning than just the association of move sequences which were useful in other chess positions. E.g. it involves some causal reasoning on a rather abstract level. However, it seems difficult to devise a general inference mechanism, which could accommodate such expert reasoning. This is particularly the case, since much of such reasoning will not be at a conscious level to the expert.

1.2 Acquiring Search Knowledge

Our approach targets at acquiring such knowledge through close interaction of an expert with a system performing the search on an actual problem instance. Knowledge Acquisition is widely considered as a modelling activity [8]. What is modelled is the expertise of a domain expert. Such a model is attempted to be described at the Knowledge level [6]. Building such models is largely attempted by prior detailed conceptual analysis of the domain and the available knowledge.

Opposed to that is our approach, which targets to skip the time-consuming process of analysing the expertise and the problem domain by a knowledge engineer, as it has been advocated, e.g. in [2]. It rather allows the experts themselves to communicate their expertise to the system. Since also experts usually need to perform some structuring of their knowledge themselves in order to articulate it, the system should allow to specify knowledge 'on the fly' and to restructure or rephrase or refine it later on. Thus, we allow the expert to develop the structure of the knowledge they want to communicate to the system during the knowledge acquisition and maintenance process. Structure means essentially the concepts being used to express the knowledge and, thus, also the hierarchy of concepts being defined.

We envisage a spiral process of knowledge acquisition of coming stepwise closer and closer to an operationalisation of the knowledge in question. Our approach follows the work by Compton et al. on knowledge acquisition which allows knowledge acquisition and maintenance without a knowledge engineer; see e.g. [1, 5].

We believe, that experts are usually able to explain their reasoning process on a particular problem instance in rather general terms that cover at least the given concrete next step in their search process. However, their explanation may be quite inaccurate in the sense that for other search states their explanation would not deliver the search step they would actually take. Either their explanation would not cover the step they would take or their explanation would suggest search steps they would actually not consider. Thus, we pursue an approach to incrementally acquire concept definitions without demanding an operational concept definition from the expert. Rather, the expert is merely required to judge whether the concept applies to particular instances, which is a much more natural task for an expert.

The paper is organised as follows: In the next section 2, we present our knowledge acquisition approach of Nested Ripple Down Rules, substantial extension to Ripple Down Rules [1]. In section 3, we present the design of our knowledge acquisition workbench and initial experiments in the domain of chess. The final section 4 presents a discussion of the achieved results and future directions of research.

2   Nested Ripple Down Rules

In this section, we introduce Nested Ripple Down Rules, which represent a substantial extension to Ripple Down Rules, as introduced by Compton et al., see e.g. [1]. Nested Ripple-Down Rules (NRDRs) represent a powerful framework for the incremental development and maintenance of complex knowledge bases without a knowledge engineer.

The original conception of Ripple Down Rules allows the incremental definition of a concept by an expert as follows: Initially, a default class is given, which applies to all objects and forms the root of a decision tree which will represent the final concept definition. The expert monitors the application of the concept while objects are considered by the system. When the expert disagrees with the system's classification of an object x, s/he will give the system an explanation for why x needs to be differently classified. This explanation is a conjunction of one or more conditions being met by x, where each condition is a specified value range for one of the object's attributes. This explanation is transformed into an exception rule r, i.e. a branching condition, to be appended to the terminal node n, which gave the incorrect classification. The object x becomes a cornerstone case for the rule r. For later amendments, this cornerstone case will be recalled to support the expert in providing conditions for further exception rules. Due to the fact, that each amendment to the tree has only local effect, i.e. only changes the classification of those objects, which are passed down that particular path, the tree always classifies those objects correctly, which have already been seen by the expert. In practice it turned out, that this approach allows an expert to easily specify conditions which characterise necessary exception rules fairly well and with minimal effort. Furthermore, possible mistakes in the specification of such rules are easily corrected later on. Compare also [1, 4, 2].

In this paper we introduce our NRDRs as follows: For explaining the classification of an object, we allow besides the choice of an attribute value range also the use of other user-defined concepts. In fact, those concepts are also incrementally defined as a Ripple Down Rule. Since our approach results in the definition of a hierarchy of concepts, each represented by a Ripple Down Rule, we call our framework Nested Ripple Down Rules (NRDRs). To allow the expert to define a hierarchy of concepts seems for the acquisition of search knowledge absolutely indispensable, since experts use abstract concepts to explain their way of searching a problem space. In search domains, the 'raw representation' of the search space and a particular search state is much too primitive to allow a suitable description of the expert's knowledge.

Unfortunately, the introduction of concepts as conditions in other concept definitions is not as straight forward as it may seem: The essential property of the Ripple Down Rules approach of keeping effortlessly the concept definitions consistent with the objects already seen cannot easily be maintained with NRDRs. See figure 1 for an illustration. Given an instance where the knowledge base does not agree with the expert, the modification of the knowledge base can occur in a number of places. For example, let in figure 1 a case X satisfies conditions $A1$ and $B1$ in rule $C1.1$ but the expert thinks that case X is not $C1$. Hence, the knowledge base needs to be modified to reflect this. A rule can

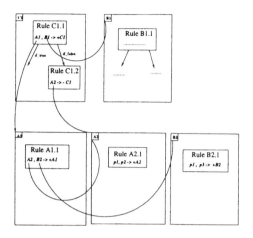
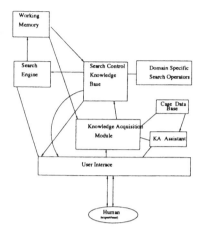

(a) A simple example of nested rules. An update in concept A2 can cause modifications in the meaning of rules C1.1, C1.2, and A1.1 of the knowledge base.

(b) SmS1.2 Architecture.

Figure 1: (a) An example of NRDRs. (b) SmS1.2's architecture.

be added as an exception for the RDR tree describing $C1$, or alternatively, the meaning of attribute $A1$ can be modified by updating the definition of $A1$, or, the meaning of $A2$ in rule $A1.1$ can be modified; and so forth. The number of possibilities depends on the depth of the concept hierarchy in the knowledge base.

Assume, the expert wants to modify the definition of A1 by modifying the definition of concept A2 in rule A1.1. This may cause an unwanted modification in the definition of rule C1.2 which contains A2 as condition. This problem is in conflict with the very idea of Ripple Down Rules of never becoming inconsistent with the seen objects. To ensure this consistency of NRDRs, we developed a knowledge acquisition assistant, which checks after each change to the knowledge base caused by an object x, whether any object y already seen may become incorrectly classified. If so, then the expert is informed of that, so that an alternative modification due to x may be chosen. Otherwise a further modification of the knowledge base can be done to correct the classification of y. This may cause a subsequent correction... However, the number of required changes is limited and depends on the depth of the concept hierarchy.

3   System Design and Experiments

See figure 1(b) for SmS's architecture. The Knowledge Acquisition Module together with the Case Data Base and the KA Assistant are responsible for the incremental development of an NRDR knowledge base which is always consistent with the seen cases. The Search Engine and the Working Memory are conducting the actual search. Which search states are visited is determined by the Domain Specific Search Operators Module and the Search Control Knowledge Base which functions as a filter on all applicable search operators. The progress of the search is stored in the working memory. This progress is often used by the expert to explain his decisions.

All cases classified by the expert are stored in the case data base. They are used by the knowledge acquisition assistant to check the consistency. All interactions between the user and the system are facilitated by the graphical interface, see figure 2. It allows to view and to modify the various concept definitions, as well as it shows traces of which concepts apply to the current case and why.

Experimental results with chess as a search domain

To demonstrate our approach, we discuss an example of the typical knowledge acquisition cycle in the domain of chess. The objective is to develop a search knowledge base which produces a search process that resembles a human expert search process as much as possible. To do that, we defined concepts which approve moves to be considered in a min-max tree search, which in turn determines the actual move to be taken. In order to keep the searched tree small, it is important to approve only those moves which are really worthwhile considering any further. On the other hand, no critical move on either side should be excluded from the tree search in order to ensure high quality play. The knowledge acquisition process attempts to develop a concept 'good move', which applies to exactly those moves which should be considered for the tree search. Initially, no search operator in any search state will qualify, i.e. no move in any chess position will be classified as 'good move' and, hence, no tree search takes place.

In figure 3 and 4 there is a pawn to be captured on e3. Our human expert considers and even plays for black Nd5xP. The expert considers it as a good move because he wins a piece. He introduces a new rule "If Win-Piece then Good". Subsequently, he needs to explain the meaning of the newly used attribute "WinPiece" in the form of a new RDR for which the expert enters "If WinPawn then WinPiece" as a root node. Similarly for "WinPawn".... Eventually, the concepts are defined in domain-dependent primitive terms, which are supplied to the system as C-

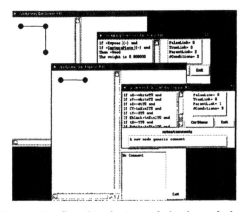

Figure 2: Graphical view of the knowledge base. Concept definitions are given in separate windows.

functions. Now, assume it was white's turn, and white played Re1. SmS1.2

(a) White pawn on e3 can be captured.

(b) Black captured Pawn on e3.

Figure 3: Black to play. Free pawn on e3.

considers Ne3xP as a good move because it wins a piece [because it wins a pawn]. The expert disagrees with this because Ne3xP is not a safe move as the black knight on e3 can be captured by a rook on e1. So the knowledge base must be modified. At this point, there are three rules available for modification. At the highest level, the expert can add "If not SafeMove then Not Good" on the true link of "If WinPiece then Good". Or, he can change the meaning of "WinPiece" by adding "If not SafeMove then Not WinPiece". Finally, he can also change the meaning of "WinPawn" in the "WinPiece" Ripple Down Rule tree by adding "If Not SafeMove then Not WinPawn". The choice of the point of modification is part of the knowledge acquisition process. In this particular example any of the modifications is valid. The expert chooses the last option.

A concept definition may also include a parameter.[1] For instance, in figure 4(b) the pawn on e3 is protected by the rook on e1, hence, Ne3xP is not currently considered a good move by the system. However, that move exposes the white knight on d4 to the black bishop on g7. So, the expert enters the rule "If Expose then Good" is added on the highest level. He explains the concept Expose(X) as capturing an opponent piece Y, such that Y has been protecting another piece X for the last two positions, i.e. the move exposed X to an attack. This parameter X is a variable used in the primitives explaining the concept "Expose". It is made visible outside the concept definition. The expert refers in his explanation to the game progress stored in the working memory. In position 5(a), white plays the bishop to b2 to protect the knight on d4. Hence, capturing the pawn on e3 no longer exposes the knight. Furthermore, the knowledge base needs to be altered again. In particular, inside the Ripple Down Rule tree describing the "Expose" concept.

---

[1]We actually extended RDRs also to allow first-order conditions, which was not possible before.

(a) Re1: Ne3xP (bad unsafe play).

(b) P on e3 is worth capturing.

Figure 4: White attempts to protect pawn on e3.

Chess is a two players game. The search tree nodes alternate for the two players. To look ahead further than one half move, the knowledge base must be large enough to account for the responses of the opponent. The expert plays for white explaining the option he takes. Thus, for figure 3(a) the expert plays Re1 to protect the pawn on e3, and for figure 4(b), he plays Bb2 to protect the knight on d4. The knowledge base is developed by the expert's input. The concept of "DefendingPiece" is introduced. As for black's sake who is required to find some good moves in the absence of possible killer moves- i.e. capturing and/or exposing white's pieces, the knowledge base is extended to cover more strategic moves such as strengthen one's defence or attack. As a result, in our knowledge acquisition session, our knowledge base evolved to 20 rules and 11 concepts, with a depth of the concept hierarchy of up to four. In position 3(a) with white to play, the evolved knowledge base lead to a tree search of depth five involving 47 nodes. This is opposed to the blind min-max tree search of several million of nodes for this position. The pruned tree reflected largely the expert's decisions on which moves are worthwhile to investigate further. The computer play with a pruned tree of depth three is also shown below figure 5. The play shown resulted in the computer gaining the upper hand against an average human player.

4 Discussion and future work directions

In this paper, we presented a substantial extension to Ripple Down Rules, our Nested Ripple Down Rules. This greatly enhances the applicability of the RDR approach to the development of complex knowledge bases without a knowledge engineer.

We built our NRDR framework into our Workbench SmS1.2 for the acquisition of search control knowledge. To our knowledge, this is a novel approach to

(a) P should not be taken after White plays Bb2.

(b) White to play against SmS1.2.

(c) The resulting position.

Figure 5: b) and c): Average human player against our system SmS1.2. Left: Starting position. After the move sequence of 1. Re1 Rd8 2. h3 Bf6 3. Nd4 Nxe3 4. Rxe3 Bxd4 5. Ke2 ... the right position was reached.

acquire effective search heuristics and to describe search skills at the Knowledge Level. Initial experiments in the domain of chess are encouraging and indicate that the development of our approach to the acquisition of search knowledge should be pursued further. Furthermore, our results, so far, suggest that it is possible for an expert to articulate introspectively inaccessible knowledge when forced to explain the outcome of that knowledge in sufficient detail.

Future work will address a deeper theoretical penetration of the structure and properties of nested Ripple-Down Rules. Initial theoretical studies of 'plain' RDRs just began [7], which is a yet a far away from the study of NRDRs.

Acknowledgement: The work reported in this paper was supported by the Australian Research Council.

References

[1] P. Compton and R. Jansen. A philosophical basis for knowledge acquisition. *Knowledge Acquisition*, 2:241–257, 1990.

[2] P. Compton, B. Kang, P. Preston, and M. Mulholland. Knowledge acquisition without knowledge analysis. In *Proceedings of the European Knowledge Acquisition Workshop*, pages 277–299. Springer-Verlag, 1993.

[3] A. de Groot. Thought and choice in chess. Mouton, Paris, 1965.

[4] B. Gaines. Induction and visualisation of rules with exceptions. In *Proceedings of the 6th AAAI-sponsored Banff Knowledge Acquisition for Knowledge Based Systems Workshop*, pages 7.1–7.17, 1991.

[5] B. Kang, P. Compton, and P. Preston. Multiple classification ripple down rules: Evaluation and possibilities. In *Proceedings of the 9th AAAI-sponsored Banff Knowledge Acquisition for Knowledge Based Systems Workshop*, pages 17.1–17.20, 1995.

[6] A. Newell. The knowledge level. *Artificial Intelligence*, 18:87–127, 1982.

[7] T. Scheffer. Algebraic foundations and improved methods of induction or ripple-down rules. In *Proceedings of the 2nd Pacific Rim Knowledge Acquisition Workshop*, 1996.

[8] T. Schreiber, B. Wielinga, J. Akkermans, W. van de Velde, and R. de Hoog. CommonKADS: A comprehensive methodology for KBS. *IEEE Expert*, 9(6):28–37, 1994.

Rapid Prototyping of Executable Problem Solving Methods Using MODEL-ECS

Gavin Lawson and Dickson Lukose

Distributed Artificial Intelligence Centre (DAIC)
Department of Mathematics, Statistics, and Computing Science
University of New England, Armidale, N.S.W., Australia, 2351

Email: {glawson I lukose}@peirce.une.edu.au

Abstract: This paper demonstrates the capability of MODEL-ECS to support domain users in rapid prototyping of executable problem solving methods (PSMs) (i.e., known as inference structures in the KADS models of expertise). MODEL-ECS is a graphically based conceptual modeling language that is made up of Conceptual Graphs [14] and Actors [6]. In addition to being highly formal and considerably sophisticated, the PSMs resulting from modeling using MODEL-ECS is executable (i.e., executable prototypes). This enables the knowledge engineer to immediately test, and if necessary re-design his knowledge model. This is a major advantage of the contemporary approach of performing the modeling process, and then carrying out the prototyping activity (where one builds a prototype knowledge based system). This paper attempts to demonstrate the capabilities of MODEL-ECS by modeling a simple PSM for Audio System Diagnosis.

1. Introduction

Rapid prototyping of "executable" problem solving methods (PSMs) have always been a goal of the knowledge modeling and enterprise modeling community. Prototyping PSM is necessary to increase productivity of a knowledge engineer. To achieve this, two mechanisms must be available. They are: a *knowledge modeling methodology*, and a *knowledge-modeling tool*. In the 1980's, many efforts were directed into developing knowledge modeling methodologies, in particular: Component of Expertise [15]; Knowledge Analysis and Design Support (KADS) [19]; and Generic Tasks [1]. The most predominant among them is the KADS methodology (especially in Europe).

The KADS methodology utilizes the principle of multiple models and the principle of knowledge-level modeling as a way to describe problem-solving expertise in an implementation-independent way [11]. KADS treats a knowledge-based system as an operational model that exhibits some desired behavior observed in terms of a real-world phenomenon. KADS distinguishes the following models: the *organizational model*, the *application model*, the *task model*, the *model of cooperation*, the *model of expertise*, the *conceptual model*, and the *design model*. The idea of knowledge-level description is incorporated into the KADS approach through the introduction of models of expertise (i.e., these models can be used to analyze and specify the required problem-solving behavior in a knowledge based system application domain). Models of expertise are composed of four categories of knowledge: *strategic knowledge*, *task knowledge*, *inference knowledge*, and *domain theories*. Building the model of expertise of a particular domain expert involves the modeling of these four categories of knowledge, and their complex interactions. In recent years, many efforts have been directed into building knowledge modeling tools that support the KADS methodology. Among them are ML^2 [16], KARL [2], FORKADS [18], OMOS [5], MODEL-K [17], CG-DESIRE [13], CG-KADS [12], and MODEL-ECS [9].

MODEL-ECS is a graphically based (i.e., visual) conceptual modeling language that is made up of Conceptual Graphs [14] and Actors [6]. It is composed of two forms of abstractions, and a set of complex modeling constructs [4]. The two forms of abstractions are: the *Primitive Conceptual Structures*; and the *Executable Conceptual Structures*. There are two types of Primitive Conceptual Structures. They are: *Conceptual Graphs*; and *Actors*. There are also two types of Executable Conceptual Structures. They are: *Actor Graphs*; and *Problem Maps*. In addition to being highly formal and considerably sophisticated, the PSMs resulting from modeling using MODEL-ECS is executable (i.e., executable prototypes). This enables the knowledge engineer to immediately test, and if necessary re-design his knowledge model. This is a major advantage to the contemporary approach of performing the modeling process, and then carrying out the prototyping activity (where one builds prototype knowledge based systems).

From our observation, it is apparent that most people (i.e., non-knowledge engineers or computer scientist) adopt a procedural approach to modeling a problem solving method. Procedural approach seems to be more intuitive to most people [4]. Therefore, we first look at a model of a PSM in procedural form, then review its equivalent procedural representation in MODEL-ECS. The main contribution of this paper is in demonstrating the capabilities of MODEL-ECS to graphically model an "executable" procedural representation of a PSM (i.e., for Audio System Diagnosis).

The outline of this paper is as follows: In Section 2, we will briefly describe the Audio System Diagnosis Domain, and the inference structure resulting from knowledge modeling process. The overall knowledge analysis and domain theory modeling process is beyond the scope of this paper. In Section 3, we will show the pseudo code (procedural) representation of the inference structure, and in Section 4, we will describe the MODEL-ECS representation of the same. In Section 5, we list the sample run of this PSM. Finally, in Section 6, we conclude this paper by highlighting the significance of the contribution of this paper, and lists future research directions.

2 Audio System Diagnosis Domain

The knowledge level modeling of a particular domain involved building the model of expertise of the domain. The Audio Systems Diagnosis is a simple domain that is used by Wielinga et al. [11], and is also used in our study. In this paper, we are not concerned with the modeling of the strategic knowledge and the domain theories. We will concentrate on the modeling of the task knowledge, leading to the formation of the inference structure of the necessary PSM. Once the task decomposition, tasks dependencies and task distribution process is completed, the task tree for "Systematic Diagnosis" is depicted in Figure 2.1, and the corresponding inference structure (i.e., PSM) is shown in Figure 2.2.

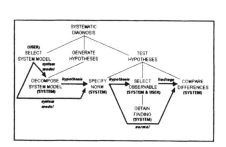

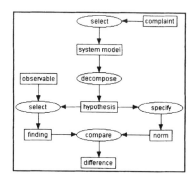

Fig. 2.1. Task Tree for "Systematic Diagnosis"

Fig. 2.2. Inference Structure for "Systematic Diagnosis"

3. Algorithmic Representation of Systematic Diagnosis

If one analyses the PSM (i.e., Systematic Diagnosis in Figure 2.2) from a procedurally, this PSM can be broken down into several smaller methods, and can be represented by the procedural pseudo code listed in Figure 3.1.

The input parameter for this procedure is *Complaint*, for which a solution (i.e., difference) is sought. All complaints are in the audio system domain (i.e., this is not a generalized problem solver). A *Difference_List* is returned to the caller. The complaint maps to a list of system components in the audio system. For instance, if the complaint related to a power problem, every component that had a relationship to (POWER) might be selected (e.g., AMPLIFIER, TAPE_DECK, TUNER, CD). We see no reason why the complaint could not be tightened to "TAPE_DECK has no POWER", rather than no power somewhere in the AUDIO_SYSTEM. In reality, we see this as some sort of database lookup, rather than some procedural encoding. The *Decompose (Component, Hypothesis_List)* returns a list of hypothesis (i.e., sub-components). Each AUDIO_SYSTEM component may have several observable norms. The *Specify_Norm (Hypothesis_Item, Norm_List)* identifies these norms. *Select_Obs_Value (Hypothesis_Item, Norm_Item, Observation)* returns the observed value for a particular component (i.e., *Hypothesis_Item* and *Norm_Item*). The *Compare(Norm, Observation, Difference_List)* identifies any differences between actual values and expected values, and these differences are added to the *Difference_List*.

```
Main(Complaint, Difference_List)
Select_System_Model(Complaint, System_Model_List)
While System_Model_List not empty
        Component = next_item(System_Model_List)
        Decompose(Component, Hypothesis_List)
        While Hypothesis_List not empty
                Hypothesis_Item = next_item(Hypothesis_List)
                Specify_Norm(Hypothesis_Item, Norm_List)
                While Norm_List is not empty
                        Norm_Item = next_item(Norm_List)
                        Norm = value(Norm_Item)
                        Select_Obs_Value(Hypothesis_Item,   Norm_Item,
Observation)
                        Compare(Norm, Observation, Difference_List)
                End While
        End While
End While
```

Fig. 3.1. Pseudo Code for the Procedural Representation of "Systematic Diagrnosis"

4. MODEL-ECS Representation of Systematic Diagnosis

The "Systematic Diagnosis" PSM can also be modeled by using the MODEL-ECS (a graphical based executable conceptual modeling language). Table 4.1 lists the conceptual constructs used in modeling executable problem solving methods. Detailed description on the complex constructs available in MODEL-ECS is found in Lukose [10]. In-depth description of MODEL-ECS is beyond the scope of this paper.

Conceptual Constructs	Descriptions
(FBS)	Conceptual Relation to indicate *sequence*.
(SWS)	Conceptual Relation to indicate *concurrence*.
[PM]	Concept to represent *Problem Map*.
[KS]	Concept to represent *Knowledge Source*.
[TRUE_TEST]	Actor Graph to indicate *positive* test.
[FALSE_TEST]	Actor Graph to indicate *negative* test.
[LT]	Actor Graph to check *less than* condition.
[GT]	Actor Graph to check *greater than* condition.
[LTEQ]	Actor Graph to check *less than* or *equal to* condition.
[GTEQ]	Actor Graph to *check greater* than or *equal to* condition.
[ASSERT]	Actor Graph to *assert* a predicate into the working memory.
[RETRACT]	Actor Graph to *retract* a predicate from the working memory.
[INCREMENT]	Actor Graph to *increment* a variable predicate.
[DECREMENT]	Actor Graph to *decrement* a variable predicate.

Table 4.1. Conceptual Constructs

When using MODEL-ECS, the domain theories are represented using Conceptual Graphs, the knowledge sources are represented using Actor Graphs, and the PSM (i.e., inference structure) is represented by an abstraction called Problem Map [8][9]. In this paper, we will only concentrate on the representation of the Knowledge Source (using Actor Graphs) and Inference Structure (using Problem Maps).

From the analysis of this domain (modeling task knowledge and building the inference structure), the following knowledge source has been identified: SELECT (two different types of this knowledge source), DECOMPOSE, SPECIFY, and COMPARE. Each of these knowledge sources have to be modeled using Actor Graphs. Note that an actor graph consists of three components: (1) Differential Graph; (2) Methods; and (3) Pre-condition, Post-conditions, and Delete List of conceptual graphs. The methods in each of the actor graphs are the same (i.e., inherited from its genus (i.e., actor graph called ACT)). The method simply checks the memory of the knowledge based system for the pre-condition graphs, and if they exist in the memory, then, this method will add the graphs from the post-condition list and remove the graph listed in the delete list. An example (i.e., SELECT) of an actor graphs is shown in Figure 4.1.

```
[SELECT] -
        -> (OBJ) -> [SYSTEM_MODEL:*a]
        -> (ARG) -> [COMPLAINT: *c] ]
        -> (RSLT) -> [SYSTEM_MODEL_LIST: *d]
--------------------------------------------------------------------
Method(s) to project on COMPLAINT to determine system model(s)
--------------------------------------------------------------------
Pre Graphs List: pre([p1]) :       { [COMPLAINT: *c] }
Post Graphs List:post([p2]):       { [SYSTEM_MODEL_LIST: *a] }
Delete Graphs List:del([])   :     { [COMPLAINT: *c] }
```

Fig. 4.1. Actor Graph for SELECT

By using the knowledge sources (i.e., in the form of Actor Graphs) similar to the one described above, we are able to model the inference structure depicted in Figure 2.2, using MODEL-ECS. Example of this model is listed in Figure 4.2.

We have used a slightly unconventional way to represent the actor graphs in Figure 4.2. Here, when we have a knowledge source of the following form: [KS: [Select: [System_Model]]], we are in fact representing a knowledge source of the following form:

```
[KS: [SELECT] -
        -> (OBJ) -> [SYSTEM_MODEL: *a]
        -> (ARG) -> [COMPLAINT: *c]
        -> (RSLT) -> [SYSTEM_MODEL_LIST: *d]
    ]
```

```
[PM: [KS: [Select: [System_Model]]] -
    -> (FBS) ->[PM: {[KS:[FALSE_TEST: [System_Model_List: { }]]] -
              -> (FBS) -> [KS: [Next_Item: [System_Model_List]]] -
              -> (FBS) -> [KS: [Decompose]] -
              -> (FBS) -> [PM: {[KS:[FALSE_TEST: [Hypoth_List: { }]]] -
                       -> (FBS) -> [KS: [Next_Item: [Hypothesis]]] -
                              -> (FBS) -> [KS: [Specify: [Norm]]] -
                              -> (FBS) -> [PM: { [KS: [FALSE_TEST: [Norm_List: { }]]] -
                                            -> (FBS) -> [KS: [Next_Item: [Norm_List]]] -
                                            -> (FBS) -> [KS: [Select: [Obs_Value]]] -
                                                       -> (FBS) -> [KS: [Compare]] -
                                                       -> (FBS) -> [PM:*],
                                                           [KS: [TURE_TEST: [Norm_List: { }]]]
                                                                  }
                                                             ]
                                            [KS: [TRUE_TEST: [Hypoth_List: { }]]]
                                       }
                                 ] -> (FBS) -> [PM:*]
                       [KS:[TRUE_TEST: [System_Model_List: { }]]]
                  }
              ]
]
```

Fig. 4.2. MODEL-ECS Representation of the Inference Structure of "Systematic Diagnosis"

An actor graph is invoked when it receives a message. Messages passing mechanism enable messages (in the form of conceptual graphs) to be sent from the user (or an actor graph) to another actor graph [7]. For example, consider a message graph shown below that is sent to the above actor graphs:

```
[SELECT] -
        -> (OBJ) -> [SYSTEM_MODEL]
        -> (ARG) -> [COMPLAINT:#51402]
        -> (RSLT) -> [SYSTEM_MODEL_LIST]
```

Assume that [COMPLAINT: #51402] represents "no power". The technique used by the actor graphs SELECT to comprehend the incoming message is to project its differential graph (see Figure 4.1) shown below onto the message graph.

```
[SELECT] -
        -> (OBJ) -> [SYSTEM_MODEL:*a]
        -> (ARG) -> [COMPLAINT: *c]
        -> (RSLT) -> [SYSTEM_MODEL_LIST: *d]
```

The resultant graph shown below will replace the differential graph in the actor graph, thus specializing the actor graph SELECT to the problem at hand. Due to the co-referencing that exist between the differential graph and the graphs in the pre/post/delete list, these graphs will also be specialized. The newly specialized actor graph is shown in Figure 4.3.

```
[SELECT] -
    -> (OBJ) -> [SYSTEM_MODEL:*a]
        -> (ARG) -> [COMPLAINT: #51402]
        -> (RSLT) -> [SYSTEM_MODEL_LIST: *d]
-------------------------------------------------------------------------
Method(s) to project on COMPLAINT to determine system model(s)
-------------------------------------------------------------------------
Pre Graphs List: pre([p1]) :        { [COMPLAINT: #51402]          }
Post Graphs List:post([p2]):        { [SYSTEM_MODEL_LIST: *d]      }
Delete Graphs List:del([])  :       { [COMPLAINT: #51402]          }
```

Fig. 4.3. Specialized Actor Graph for SELECT

The next stage of actor graph processing is to check the blackboard (working memory of the system) for the existence of the graphs in the pre-condition list (i.e., [COMPLAINT: #51402]). Assuming they exist, the actor graph will execute the method in its body by projecting the COMPLAINT to determine the system models that may experience this type COMPLAINT. The actor graph then asserts all of these system models (e.g, [CD:#1235], [TAPE_DECK:#5463], etc.) into the working memory. These individuals are then collected together into a list and then this actor graph will assert the graph [SYSTEM_MODEL_LIST: {#1235, #5463, etc.}] into the working memory. Finally, the actor graph removes the [COMPLAINT: #51402] from the working memory.

5. Simple Simulation

In this section, we will list a simple scenario and take the reader through the process that will be engaged by the Problem Map that was modeled in the last section. Each of the steps of this problem solving is listed below:

1. A complaint is detected in the audio system and given an identifier. For instance, [COMPLAINT:#51402] might represent "no power". Assume it is in the tape deck.

2. The message graph m_0 (below) is sent to the actor graph SELECT.

```
[SELECT] -                                              (m_0)
        -> (OBJ) -> [SYSTEM_MODEL:*a]
        -> (ARG) -> [COMPLAINT:#51402]
        -> (RSLT) -> [SYSTEM_MODEL_LIST]
```

3. The differential graph for SELECT projects onto m_0, and the updated pre/post/del graphs reflect the specialization of the complaint.

4. Processes within SELECT ensure that [COMPLAINT:#51402] is on the blackboard. A list of AUDIO_SYSTEM components that are associated with (POWER) complaints are generated onto the domain theory for SELECT;

```
[AMPLIFIER] -> (OCCURS) -> [COMPLAINT:#51402]
[TUNER]     -> (OCCURS) -> [COMPLAINT:#51402]
```

```
[CD]      -> (OCCURS) -> [COMPLAINT:51402]
[TAPE_DECK] -> (OCCURS) -> [COMPLAINT:51402]
```

Thus, [SYSTEM_MODEL:*a] could be [AMPLIFIER: #667], [TUNER: #343], [CD: #1235] or [TAPE_DECK: #5463]. The graphs are added to the blackboard.

5. Each of the above components are decomposed by [DECOMPOSE] to add the following to the blackboard:

```
[AMPLIFIER: #667] -> (PART_OF) -> [INPUT_SELECTOR: #445]
[AMPLIFIER: #667] -> (PART_OF) -> [POWER_SWITCH: #447]
[TAPE_DECK: #5463] -> (PART_OF) -> [POWER_SWITCH: #448]
[TUNER: #343] -> (PART_OF) -> [POWER_SWITCH: #449]
[CD: #1235] -> (PART_OF) -> [POWER_SWITCH: #450]
```

6. [SPECIFY] identifies the [NORM] for each of the components. For example the [NORM] for [POWER_SWITCH: #448] may be a state [PRESSED]. On the other hand, the [INPUT_SELECTOR: #445] could have some other [NORM] value.

7. The second [SELECT] would add [OBSERVABLE] observations to the blackboard. Graphs such as;

```
[TAPE_DECK: #4563]->(PART_OF)->[POWER_SWITCH: #448]->(STAT)->[NOT_PRESSED]
```

now exist on the blackboard.

8. Finally, the [COMPARE] will detect the [DIFFERENCE] between the [NORM] (i.e., [PRESSED]) and [FINDING] (i.e., [NOT_PRESSED]) for the [TAPE_DECK: #5463].

6. Conclusion

This paper demonstrates the practical use of MODEL-ECS to rapidly prototype a PSM in a well-known problem domain (i.e., the audio diagnosis problem). Traditionally, the KADS methodology requires the description of the Model of Expertise before creating the design model. Creation of the Design Model involves transforming the Model of Expertise (and Model of Cooperation?) to use the programming language (and data structures?) selected for the Design Model. Such an approach has obvious disadvantages for rapid prototyping of a PSM. When using MODEL-ECS we do not have to transform the Conceptual Model to the Design Model. The Model of Expertise (plus the Model of Cooperation = Conceptual Model) is represented using MODEL-ECS constructs are "executable". Domain knowledge is captured in the conceptual graphs of MODEL-ECS, while inference and task knowledge is represented in the actor graphs of MODEL-ECS. We demonstrated the applicability of MODEL-ECS in the audio system diagnosis domain. We also list a simple simulation of the PSM built using MODEL-ECS. The significant contribution of this paper is to demonstrate the procedural modeling of PSMs using MODEL-ECS.

For "Systematic Diagnosis", the requirements for Strategic Knowledge are limited. However, we see an obvious need to be able to cater for Strategic Knowledge in other domains. To this end, work is required to ensure that MODEL-ECS can model strategic knowledge. The future direction of this work is in the modeling of strategic knowledge. In contemporary literature, strategic knowledge can usually represented as production rules. We are currently investigating ways of modeling them using the *if-then* construct of MODEL-ECS. Further, Kremer et al. [4] are investigating the use of a graphical interface to MODEL-ECS, using the meta-level Concept Map specification language called Constraint Graphs [3].

References

[1] Chandrasekaran, B., and Johnson, T. Generic tasks and Tasks Structures: History, Critique and New Directions, in J.M. David, J.P. Krivine, and R. Simmons (Eds.), *Second Generation Expert Systems*, Springer Verlag, Berlin, Germany, 1993.

[2] Fensel, D., Angele, J., and Landes, D. Knowledge Representation and Acquisition Language (KARL), in *Proceedings of the 11th International Workshop on Expert Systems and Their Applications (Volume: Tools and Techniques)*, Avignon, France, 1991.

[3] Kremer, R. A Graphical Meta-Language for Knowledge Representation, PhD Dissertation, University of Calgary, Canada, 1997.

[4] Kremer, R., Lukose, D., and Gaines, B. Knowledge Modeling using Annotated Flow Chart, in Proceedings of the International Conference on Conceptual Structures (ICCS'97), Seattle, August 4 - 8, 1997.

[5] Linster, M. Using OMOS to Represent KADS Conceptual Model, in Schreiber, G., Wielinga, B., and Breuker, J., (Eds.), *KADS: A Principles Approach to Knowledge-Based System Development*, Academic Press, London, UK, 1993.

[6] Lukose, D. Executable Conceptual Structures, in G.W. Mineau, B. Moulin and J.F. Sowa (Eds.), *Conceptual Graphs for Knowledge Representation, Lecture Notes in Artificial Intelligence (699)*, Springer- Verlag, Berlin, Germany, 1993.

[7] Lukose, D. Projection Based Invocation Mechanism for Actor Graphs, in Proceedings of the 2nd Australia and New Zealand Conference on Intelligent Information Systems, Brisbane, Queensland, Australia, 1994.

[8] Lukose, D. Using Executable Conceptual Structures for Modeling Expertise, in *Proceedings of the 9th Banff Knowledge Acquisition For Knowledge-Based Systems Workshop (KAW'95)*, Banff Conference Centre, Banff, Alberta, Canada, 1995.

[9] Lukose, D. MODEL-ECS: Executable Conceptual Modeling Language, in *Proceedings of the Knowledge Acquisition for Knowledge Based Systems Workshop (KAW'96)*, Banff, Canada, 9 - 14 November, 1996.

[10] Lukose, D. Complex Modeling Constructs in MODEL-ECS, in *Proceedings if the Fifth International Conference on Conceptual Structures (ICCS'97)*, Seattle, USA., August 3-8, 1997.

[11] Schreiber, B. Wielinga, and J. Breuker. *KADS: A Principles Approach to Knowledge-Based System Development*, Academic Press, 1993.

[12] Moller, J-U. Operationalisation of KADS Models by using Conceptual Graph Modules, in Proceedings of the 9th Banff Knowledge Acquisition For Knowledge-Based Systems Workshop, Banff Conference Centre, Banff, Alberta, Canada, 1995.

[13] Moller, J-U., and Willems, M. CG-DESIRE: Formal Specification Using Conceptual Graphs, in Proceedings of the 9th Banff Knowledge Acquisition For Knowledge-Based Systems Workshop, Banff Conference Centre, Banff, Alberta, Canada, 1995.

[14] Sowa, J.F. *Conceptual Structures: Information Processing in Mind and Machine*, Addison Wesley, Reading, Mass., USA, 1984.

[15] Steels, L. Components of Expertise, AI Magazine, 11(2), 1990.

[16] van Harmelen, F., and Balder, J. (ML)2: A Formal Language for KADS Models of Expertise, in G. Wielinga, B., Schreiber, A.T., and Breuker, J.A. *Modeling Expertise, in KADS: A Principled Approach to Knowledge-Based System Development*, Academic Press, London, UK, 1993.

[17] VoB, A., and Karbach, W. MODEL-K: Making KADS Run, in G. Schreiber, B. Wielinga, and J. Breuker (Eds.), *KADS: A Principles Approach to Knowledge-Based System Development*, Academic Press, London, UK, 1993.

[18] Wetter, T. First-Order Logic Foundation of the KADS Conceptual Model. in B. Wielinga, J. Boose, B. Gaines, G. Schreiber, and M. van Someren (Eds.), *Current Trends in Knowledge Acquisition*, Amsterdam, The Netherlands, IOS Press, 1990.

[19] Wielinga, B., Schreiber, A.T., and Breuker, J.A. KADS: A Modelling Approach to Knowledge Engineering, in The KADS Approach to Knowledge Engineering Special Issue, *Knowledge Acquisition*, 4(1), Academic Press, London, UK, 1992.

Preferential Semantics for Causal Fixpoints

Pavlos Peppas[1], Maurice Pagnucco[2], Mikhail Prokopenko[3], and Norman Foo[2]

[1] Knowledge Systems Group, Department of Computing, School of MPCE,
Macquarie University, NSW 2109, Australia. Email: pavlos@mpce.mq.edu.au.
[2] Knowledge Systems Group, School of Computer Science and Engineering,
University of New South Wales, NSW 2052, Australia.
Email: {morri, norman}@cse.unsw.edu.au.
[3] Knowledge Systems Group, CSIRO Mathematical and Information Sciences,
Locked Bag 17, North Ryde, NSW 2113, Australia.
Email: mikhail.prokopenko@cmis.csiro.au.

Abstract. In this paper we concentrate on the causal theory of action developed by McCain and Turner [2] for computing *ramifications*. Our aim here is to characterise this theory of action in terms of a *preferential-style semantics* in the spirit of Shoham [4]. Such a result would not only place McCain and Turner's theory in a uniform setting, facilitating comparison with other logics of action, but also give a clearer insight into the nature and behaviour of causality captured by their framework. We first show that this objective is not attainable via a traditional preferential semantics. However, preferential semantics is not abandoned entirely. Rather, it is augmented to arrive at the desired result. We maintain that two components — minimal change and causality — are essential in providing a (concise) solution to the frame and ramification problems.

1 Introduction

An early, landmark, development in the field of reasoning about action was Shoham's *preferential semantics* [4]. It provides a semantics for a class of (non-monotonic) logics in which an ordering is imposed over the class of interpretations and the models relating to a particular entailment are subsequently identified as the minimal models under this ordering. Intuitively, the ordering indicates a preference or likelihood over interpretations with only the most preferred being considered in the final outcome (thus sanctioning more inferences than the corresponding classical semantics). The *principle of minimal change* — taking the minimal ("most preferred") models — is the overriding tenet of this approach. Needless to say, work on reasoning about action has progressed but preferential semantics remains an important and intuitive idea.

Currently, a topic of much interest is the role of *causality* in reasoning about action, especially in connection to the *ramification problem*. Over the last few years it has become apparent that *domain constraints* alone are not sufficient to determine the indirect effects of actions and the notion of causality has been suggested as one way of addressing this problem.

In this paper we concentrate on one particular approach that is based on causality, advanced by McCain and Turner [2]. They replace traditional domain constraints by causal associations between formulae $\phi \Rightarrow \psi$ known as *causal laws*. Intuitively, we can think of such a formula as expressing that ϕ *causes* ψ. As such, causal laws express "a relation of determination between the states of affairs that make ϕ and ψ true" [2, p. 1979]. One important aspect of causal laws is that the contrapositive (i.e., $\neg\psi \Rightarrow \neg\phi$) does not hold in general.

The main aim of this paper is to furnish a preferential-style semantics for McCain and Turner's causal theory of action. In particular, the contributions offered are, at least, twofold. Firstly, we show that preferential semantics *per se* cannot capture McCain and Turner's causal theory (Section 4). Secondly, as a result of this, we augment preferential semantics to obtain the desired characterisation. This is achieved by introducing two state selection mechanisms: *state transition systems* (Section 7) which augment the preference structure with a binary relation on states to give the requisite preferential-style semantics and *state elimination systems* (Section 6) which function as an intermediary between causal systems and state transition systems. State elimination systems should not only be viewed as a stepping stone but as providing a clearer picture of the underlying nature of causality.

There are a number of advantages to be gained from these results. They will place causal theories, in the spirit of McCain and Turner's approach, in the context of action theories and (nonmonotonic) logics having a preferential semantics, facilitating a clear comparison between the two. They will give a clearer insight into the nature of causality as captured by these systems. Previous work has shown that minimal change and causality are interreducible under certain conditions (e.g., [1]). One may be tempted to suggest that such a result can be generalised. We maintain that this is not the case but that the two coexist and, in fact, complement each other.

2 Technical Preliminaries

Throughout this paper we will be working with a fixed finitary propositional language $\mathcal{L}$ whose propositional letters we will call *fluents*. The set of all fluents is denoted by $\mathcal{F}$. A *literal* is a fluent or the negation of a fluent. A *state* (or *world*) is defined as a maximal consistent set of literals. The set of all states will be denoted $\mathcal{W}$ and the set of all literals by $\mathcal{N}$. By $[\phi]$ we denote all states consistent with the sentence $\phi \in \mathcal{L}$ (i.e., $[\phi] = \{w \in \mathcal{W} : w \vdash \phi\}$). Occasionally we will refer to $[\phi]$ as ϕ-*states*.

3 Causal Systems

In this section we briefly review the basic concepts underlying McCain and Turner's [2] causal theory of action. This will help to further fix some notation and spell out more clearly the precise objective of this paper.

McCain and Turner introduce a new connective $\Rightarrow$ between sentences φ, ψ of $\mathcal{L}$, and call expressions of the form $\varphi \Rightarrow \psi$ *causal laws* (or *causal rules*).[1] A set of causal laws $\mathcal{D}$ is called a *causal system*. For a set of sentences $\Gamma \subseteq \mathcal{L}$ and a causal system $\mathcal{D}$, the *closure of Γ in $\mathcal{D}$*, denoted $C_{\mathcal{D}}(\Gamma)$, is defined as the smallest superset of Γ that is closed under logical implication, and it is such that for any $(\varphi \Rightarrow \psi) \in \mathcal{D}$, if $\varphi \in C_{\mathcal{D}}(\Gamma)$ then $\psi \in C_{\mathcal{D}}(\Gamma)$. We shall say that Γ *causally entails* φ with respect to $\mathcal{D}$, denoted $\Gamma \vdash_{\mathcal{D}} \varphi$, iff $\varphi \in C_{\mathcal{D}}(\Gamma)$.

One further notion we require is that of a *legitimate state* (wrt a causal system $\mathcal{D}$). A state r is called legitimate with respect to $\mathcal{D}$ if and only if $r = C_{\mathcal{D}}(r) \cap \mathcal{N}$. Intuitively, a state is legitimate if and only if it does not violate any of the causal laws in $\mathcal{D}$. We denote the set of legitimate states (wrt $\mathcal{D}$) by $Legit_{\mathcal{D}}$.

Now McCain and Turner's aim is to determine, given an initial state w and sentence E representing the direct effects (or post-conditions) of an action[2], the set of possible next states $\mathrm{Res}_{\mathcal{D}}(E, w)$. More formally, to any causal system $\mathcal{D}$ we associate a function $\mathrm{Res}_{\mathcal{D}}$ mapping a legitimate state w (the initial state) and sentence E to the set of states $\mathrm{Res}_{\mathcal{D}}(E, w)$ defined as follows:

$$\mathrm{Res}_{\mathcal{D}}(E, w) = \{r \in [E] : r = \{\mathtt{f} : (w \cap r) \cup \{E\} \vdash_{\mathcal{D}} \mathtt{f}\} \}$$

Often we shall refer to the members of $\mathrm{Res}_{\mathcal{D}}(E, w)$ as *causal fixpoints*. Intuitively, resultant states are those E-states at which the only changes are the ones that are causally justified.

The aim of this paper can now be seen clearly. Put simply, it is to provide a preferential-style semantics capturing $\mathrm{Res}(E, w)$ for any legitimate state w and sentence E. In other words, to mimic McCain and Turner's fixpoint definition with a process involving a preference ordering imposed over states.

4   Counterexample

At first glance it may seem that all that has to be done to achieve our aims is to determine the restrictions that need to be placed on an ordering $<$ over states to effect the desired result. However, in this section we present an example showing that this straightforward approach will not work in general.

Suppose we are given an initial state $w \in \mathcal{W}$ and a (strict) preference ordering $<_w \subseteq \mathcal{W} \times \mathcal{W}$ on states with the only proviso that $<_w$ satisfy transitivity. In the spirit of preferential semantics [4] we would like to define the states resulting from the occurrence at w of an action with postcondition E, as the minimal E-states wrt $<_w$:

(P) $\mathrm{Res}_{\mathcal{D}}(E, w) = min([E], <_w)$

---

[1] For simplicity, throughout this paper we assume that the antecedent of any causal law is consistent.

[2] Since actions play no immediate role in this framework we shall not refer to them explicitly but only through their direct effects.

In McCain and Turner's approach it is not necessary to consider illegitimate states as possible resultant states since they violate the causal laws. Therefore, we first concentrate on the following variant of (P).

(P') $\text{Res}_D(E, w) = min([E], <_w) \cap \text{Legit}_D$

The first result shows that (P') cannot be satisfied in general.

Theorem 1. *There exists a causal system D and (initial) state w such that no ordering on states satisfies (P').*

Proof: Assume that $\mathcal{L}$ has five propositional letters a, b, c, d, e. Let the initial state be $w = \{a, b, c, d, e\}$ and define s_1, s_2 and s_3 to be the following states: $s_1 = \{\neg a, \neg b, c, d, \neg e\}$, $s_2 = \{a, \neg b, \neg c, d, \neg e\}$ and $s_3 = \{a, \neg b, c, \neg d, e\}$. Finally let D be the following causal system: $D = \{\bigwedge s_i \Rightarrow false \text{ (for } s_i \neq w, s_1, s_2, s_3), \neg a \Rightarrow \neg b, \neg d \Rightarrow \neg b\}$.

Consider now the following direct effects (post-conditions) of actions. $\Delta_1 = (\neg a \vee \neg c) \wedge \neg e$, $\Delta_2 = (\neg a \vee \neg d)$ and $\Delta_3 = (\bigwedge s_2) \vee (\bigwedge s_3)$. Clearly, state s_1 satisfies Δ_1 and Δ_2; s_2 satisfies Δ_1 and Δ_3; and, s_3 satisfies Δ_2 and Δ_3.

Suppose a (transitive) ordering on states $<_w$ satisfying condition (P') exists. Now, the following is easily (albeit tediously) verified. $\text{Res}_D(\Delta_1, w) = s_1$ from which we conclude $s_1 <_w s_2$. $\text{Res}_D(\Delta_2, w) = s_3$, therefore $s_3 <_w s_1$. By the transitivity of $<_w$ we infer that $s_3 <_w s_2$. However, $\text{Res}_D(\Delta_3, w) = \{s_2, s_3\}$ from which it follows that $s_3 \not<_w s_2$ contradicting the above. ∎

Returning our attention to (P) which is a closer rendering of preferential semantics than (P'), the result above can now be used to show Theorem 2 below.[3] We therefore conclude that a traditional preferential semantics (characterised by condition (P)) cannot, in general, be supplied for McCain and Turner's causal theory of action.

Theorem 2. *There exists a causal system D and (initial) state w such that no ordering on states satisfies (P).*

This will not lead us to abandon preferential semantics entirely. Our strategy will be to retain as much of the spirit of preferential semantics as possible and augment it with a further mechanism that takes into account the presence of causality.

5   Three State-Selection Mechanisms

From a purely technical point of view, McCain and Turner's causal theory of action can be regarded as nothing more than a state-selection mechanism. More precisely, given some background knowledge expressed in the form of *causal laws*, McCain and Turner provide a method for selecting, for any state w and any sentence E representing the initial state and direct effects respectively, a

---

[3] Proofs will generally be omitted due to lack of space.

subset $\text{Res}_D(E, w)$ of $[E]$. The intention is of course that $\text{Res}_D(E, w)$ contains precisely those states that can possibly result from the occurrence of an action with post-condition E at the initial state w.

However, we can adopt a more abstract perspective and view it simply as a selection function. On this view $\text{Res}_D(E, w)$ is just a function selecting the "best" states from among E (wrt w). In this paper, we now proceed as follows. Firstly, in addition to McCain and Turner's selection mechanism, we present two other types of systems that provide means for selecting states which we call respectively *state elimination systems* and a *state transition systems*. State transition systems constitute the preferential-like semantics characterising McCain and Turner's causal theory of action.

The desired characterisation is achieved in two steps: we first show how to translate from causal rules to state elimination systems (while preserving the selection function). Then we show how (under certain conditions) we can move from state elimination systems to state transition systems (again in a way that preserves the selection function). Let us now take a more detailed look at each of these systems.

6 State Elimination Systems

The performing of an action with known direct effects E makes certain states — the E-states (or a subset of them) — entertainable as possible resultant states. The basic idea behind state elimination systems is the use of certain elimination rules to reject states from further consideration. Any state rejected through the application of an elimination rule violates a causal relationship deemed to hold in the world.

Definition 3. (State elimination rule)
A *state elimination rule* (or simply, *elimination rule*) is an expression of the form $\{r_1, r_2, \cdots, r_k, r_{k+1}, \cdots, r_n\} \rhd \{r_1, r_2, \cdots, r_k\}$ where each r_i is a state.

Intuitively a state elimination rule works as follows. Assume that, according to your current beliefs, the states you consider possible are among $\{r_1, \cdots, r_n\}$. Then the above rule allows you to eliminate or disregard the worlds $r_{k+1}, \cdots, r_n$. A state elimination system $\mathcal{S}$ is a set of elimination rules.

In a state elimination system we are working with a set of states; the states currently being entertained. Applying elimination rules to such a set of states potentially allows us to rule out illegitimate states and concentrate our attention on the remaining ones. All elimination rules would, of course, need to be applied in turn in order to ensure that no illegitimate states are considered possible.

Definition 4. ($\leadsto$ and $\overset{*}{\leadsto}$)
Given a state elimination system $\mathcal{S}$, we shall say that a set of states Q *yields in one step* a set of states R, which we denote by $Q \leadsto R$, iff there is an elimination rule $X \rhd Y$ such that $Q \subseteq X$ and $R = Q \cap Y$. We define $\overset{*}{\leadsto}$ to be the reflexive transitive closure of $\leadsto$.

At some point the set of entertained states will reach a point of *equilibrium*. That is, the application of any further rules will no longer eliminate states.

Definition 5. (Compact state)
We shall say that a set of states Q is *compact* (in S) iff for any R such that $Q \overset{*}{\leadsto} R$, $Q = R$. If Q is a singleton and compact, we will also call the state in Q compact.

Before presenting the state selection mechanism associated with elimination systems, we need one more definition.

Definition 6. (*E*-predecessor)
For any two states w, r and any sentence E, we define the E-predecessors of r with respect to w, to be the set $\langle r, E \rangle_w = \{r' : r' \in [E] \text{ and } Diff(w, r') \subseteq Diff(w, r)\}$ (where $Diff(w, r)$ represents the symmetric difference of r and w (i.e., $(r \setminus w) \cup (w \setminus r)$) as in the PMA [5]).

Clearly any $r \in [E]$ is an E-predecessor of itself with respect to w (i.e., $r \in \langle r, E \rangle_w$). The E-predecessors of r with respect to w are simply those E-states which agree with w on at least those fluents where w and r agree and possibly others. If one considers a PMA ordering [5] of states $\leq_w$ (i.e., $r \leq_w s$ iff $Diff(w, r) \subseteq Diff(w, s)$), then the E-predecessors are simply those E-states closer to w than r.

We now define the state selection mechanism at the heart of state elimination systems.

Definition 7. ($\text{Next}_S(E, w)$)
To any state elimination system S we associate a function Next_S (mapping a compact (in S) state w and a sentence E to the set of states $\text{Next}_S(E, w)$) defined as follows: $\text{Next}_S(E, w) = \{r \in [E] : r \text{ is compact (in } S) \text{ and } \langle r, E \rangle_w \overset{*}{\leadsto} \{r\}\}$

As we shall see in section 6.1, $\text{Next}_S(E, w)$ will be used to capture $\text{Res}_D(E, w)$ in terms of state elimination systems. Intuitively, r is a permissible next state if all its E-predecessors with respect to w are eliminated by the rules in S but r <u>alone</u> survives. If r is eliminated then, as indicated above, it must violate some causal law. On the other hand, if r survives together with some other state(s), then it means that there is some ambiguity for which causality cannot account. More to the point, since our intention is not to abandon the principle of minimal change entirely but merely to augment it with causality, then it means that there is some closer state (i.e., a state admitting "less change") which is consistent with the causal laws being considered. This is precisely why we need only consider the E-predecessors of a state r when determining its membership in $\text{Next}_S(E, w)$. We want to know whether a state is illegitimate or whether there is a "closer" state satisfying the causal forces at work. If so, we need no longer entertain it as a permissible resultant state.

6.1 Causal Systems and State Elimination Systems

In this section we define mappings from causal systems to state elimination systems and vice versa. This will serve to identify the interrelationship between the two. For this purpose we require the following definition.

Definition 8. (Selection-equivalent)
We shall say that a causal system $\mathcal{D}$ is *selection-equivalent* to a state elimination system $\mathcal{S}$ iff $\mathrm{Res}_{\mathcal{D}}(E, w) = \mathrm{Next}_{\mathcal{S}}(E, w)$, for every sentence E and state w.

The term selection-equivalent will also be used to relate (in the obvious way) not just a causal system and a state elimination system, but any two state selection mechanisms (for example, a causal system and a state transition system, two different state elimination systems, etc.).

The main result of this section — an exact characterisation of McCain and Turner's causal theory of action in terms of state elimination systems – can now be established.

Theorem 9. *For every causal system there is a selection-equivalent state elimination system. Conversely, for every state elimination system there is a selection-equivalent causal system.*

Proof (Sketch)
$(\Rightarrow)$
Let $\mathcal{D}$ be an arbitrary causal system. For every causal law $\varphi \Rightarrow \psi$ in $\mathcal{D}$, produce the elimination rule $[\varphi] \triangleright [\varphi \wedge \psi]$. Call $\mathcal{S}$ the set of elimination rules so produced. It is not hard to verify that for any legitimate state w and sentence E, $\mathrm{Res}_{\mathcal{D}}(E, w) = \mathrm{Next}_{\mathcal{S}}(E, w)$ (simply notice that for any state r, $[(w \cap r) \cup \{E\}] = \langle r, E \rangle_w$).
$(\Leftarrow)$
Let $\mathcal{S}$ be an arbitrary state elimination system. For every elimination rule $X \triangleright Y$ produce the causal law $\varphi \Rightarrow \psi$, where φ, ψ are such that $[\varphi] = X$ and $[\psi] = Y$ (since our language is a finitary propositional one, such φ and ψ always exist). The set of causal laws so produced, call it $\mathcal{D}$, is selection-equivalent to $\mathcal{S}$.
∎

Note, in this proof, the relationship between causal laws and elimination rules: $\phi \Rightarrow \psi$ if and only if $[\phi] \triangleright [\phi \wedge \psi]$ (or, equivalently, $[\phi] \triangleright [\phi] \cap [\psi]$).

The following two definitions will be important for the next section but we introduce them here in order to highlight a relationship that exists between a certain class of state elimination systems and a class of causal systems.

Definition 10. ($\mathcal{S}$ Closed under union)
We shall say that a state elimination system $\mathcal{S}$ is *closed under union* iff whenever $(X \triangleright Y)$ and $(Q \triangleright R)$ are in $\mathcal{S}$ then $(X \cup Q) \triangleright (Y \cup R)$ is also in $\mathcal{S}$.

Definition 11. ($\mathcal{D}$ Closed under disjunction)
We shall say that a causal system $\mathcal{D}$ is *closed under disjunction* iff whenever $\varphi \Rightarrow \psi$ and $\chi \Rightarrow \zeta$ are in $\mathcal{D}$ then $(\varphi \vee \chi) \Rightarrow (\psi \vee \zeta)$ is also in $\mathcal{D}$.

The relationship is given by the following result.

Theorem 12. *Every causal system closed under disjunction is selection-equivalent to a state elimination system closed under union. Conversely, every state elimination system closed under union is selection-equivalent to a causal system closed under disjunction.*

To see this rather quickly, note that disjunction in terms of sentences $(\phi \vee \psi)$ corresponds to union in terms of states $([\phi \vee \psi] = [\phi] \cup [\psi])$.

7 State Transition Systems

A state transition system consists of a binary relation over states which, as the name suggests, represents transitions between states. We group together some definitions required in the context of such systems.

Definition 13. A *state transition system* $\mathcal{M}$ is a binary relation on the set W of states (i.e., $\mathcal{M} \subseteq W \times W$). Whenever $\langle r, r' \rangle \in \mathcal{M}$ we will write $r \to r'$. We define $\overset{*}{\to}$ to be the reflexive transitive closure of $\to$. Whenever $r \overset{*}{\to} r'$ we shall say that r' is *reachable* from r. We shall say that a state r is *final* (in $\mathcal{M}$) iff for any r' such that $r \overset{*}{\to} r'$, $r = r'$.

Intuitively, $\mathcal{M}$ represents transitions between states due to the presence of causality.

We shall now define the notion of *successor states* $\text{Succ}_{\mathcal{M}}(E, w)$ for a state transition system $\mathcal{M}$, initial state w and direct effects E of an action. This identifies the resultant states and it is this that will be used to capture $\text{Res}_D(E, w)$ (and $\text{Next}_S(E, w)$).

Definition 14. $(\text{Succ}_{\mathcal{M}}(E, w))$
To any state transition system $\mathcal{M}$ we associate a function $\text{Succ}_{\mathcal{M}}$ (mapping a final (in $\mathcal{M}$) state w and a sentence E to the set of states $\text{Succ}_{\mathcal{M}}(E, w)$) defined as follows: $\text{Succ}_{\mathcal{M}}(E, w) = \{r' \in [E] : r' \text{ is final (in } \mathcal{M}) \text{ and } r \overset{*}{\to} r' \text{ for all } r \in \langle\!\langle r', E \rangle\!\rangle_w \}$.

There are some important points to note about $\text{Succ}_{\mathcal{M}}(E, w)$ that are at the very heart of our preferential-style semantics. Notice that $\text{Succ}_{\mathcal{M}}(E, w)$ relies on two very important components. Firstly, a preference ordering over states used to determine the E-predecessors of r' (wrt w — i.e., $\langle\!\langle r', E \rangle\!\rangle_w$). In fact, it is a PMA ordering as previously noted. Secondly, the binary relation $\mathcal{M}$ on states. *The former embodies the principle of minimal change while the latter captures the notion of causality.* Again, only the E-predecessors of r' (wrt w) need be considered due to our desire to adhere to the principle of minimal change as much as possible. Also note that a resultant state must be reachable via "causality" from all of its E-predecessors. If it were not, then there must be a state "closer" to w consistent with the causal laws and the minimality/causality duo would be violated.

7.1 State Elimination Systems and State Transition Systems

In this section we obtain mappings between state elimination systems and state transition systems and vice versa. Then, using the results of section 6.1, we obtain a correspondence between causal systems and state transition systems; thus a preferential-style semantics for McCain and Turner's causal theory of actions.

Theorem 15. *For every state elimination system S that is closed under union, there exists a selection-equivalent state transition system M. Conversely, for every state transition system M there is a selection-equivalent state elimination system S that is closed under union.*

Proof. (Sketch)

($\Rightarrow$)

Let S be a state elimination system closed under union. Let S' be a unary state elimination system that is selection-equivalent to S. From S' we shall construct a selection-equivalent state transition system M. First however we need some definitions.

Consider an arbitrary set of states Q with cardinality $n+1$. We shall say that the string of elimination rules $\sigma_1; \sigma_2; \cdots; \sigma_n$ *dissolves* Q iff after applying these rule successively (in that order), all but one of the states of Q are eliminated and, moreover, the one remaining state is compact.

Assume that $\sigma_1; \sigma_2; \cdots; \sigma_n$ dissolves Q and for all $1 \leq i \leq n$, let r_i be the state of Q that is eliminated by the rule σ_i; let us also call w the one state of Q that is not eliminated. We shall call the sequence $r_1; r_2; \cdots; r_n; w$ a *trace* for Q (in S').

We now construct from S' a state transition system M as follows. For any two states r, r', $\langle r, r' \rangle \in M$ iff there is a dissolvable set of states Q containing r and r', such that for some trace of Q in S', r' appears immediately after r. It can be shown that M is selection-equivalent to S'.

($\Leftarrow$)

Proved by essentially reversing the construction presented above. ∎

By combining theorems 12 and 15 we derive the following corollary, which is the central result of this article.

Corollary 16. *For every causal system D closed under disjunction, there exists a selection-equivalent state transition system M. Conversely, for every state transition system M there exists a selection-equivalent causal system D which is closed under disjunction.*

This says that our preferential-style semantics in terms of state transition systems — consisting of a preference ordering (in this case, PMA ordering) over states augmented by a binary relation on states — exactly characterises McCain and Turner causal systems where the causal laws are closed under disjunction.

8 Conclusion and Future Work

In this article we provided an augmented preferential semantics for McCain and Turner's causal theory of action. In doing so, we first demonstrated that traditional preferential semantics using the principle of minimal change cannot achieve this task alone. To remedy this we did not abandon minimal change but rather we enhanced preferential semantics with a binary relation capturing the force of causality. That is, causal laws were transformed (via state elimination systems) into a binary relation on states. Moreover, we maintain that these two components – minimal change and causality – are both essential in providing a (concise) solution to the frame and ramification problems.

Placing McCain and Turner's causal theory of action in the uniform setting of preferential-style semantics facilitates comparison with other logics of action. This is clearly an interesting avenue for future work. Another equally important research direction is a comparison between the state transition semantics introduced herein, and the *causal propagation semantics* proposed by Sandewall [3]. Establishing a link between the two will indirectly connect (by means of the results reported herein) Sandewall's semantics with McCain and Turner's theory of action, thus giving a clearer insight into the nature of causality captured by these various formalisms.

References

1. Joakim Gustafsson and Patrick Doherty. Embracing occlusion in specifying the indirect effects of actions. In L. Aiello, J. Doyle, and S. Shapiro, editors, *Proceedings of the Fifth International Conference on Knowledge Representation and Reasoning.* Morgan-Kaufmann, 1996.
2. Norman McCain and Hudson Turner. A causal theory of ramifications and qualifications. In *Proceedings of the Fourteenth International Joint Conference on Artificial Intelligence*, pages 1978–1984. Montreal, 1995.
3. Erik Sandewall. Assessments of ramification methods that use static domain constraints. In L. Aiello, J. Doyle, and S. Shapiro, editors, *Proceedings of the Fifth International Conference on Knowledge Representation and Reasoning.* Morgan-Kaufmann, 1996.
4. Yoav Shoham. *Reasoning About Change.* MIT Press, Cambridge, Massachusetts, 1988.
5. Marianne Winslett. Reasoning about actions using a possible models approach. In *Proceedings of the Seventh National Artificial Intelligence Conference*, San Mateo, CA., 1988. Morgan Kaufmann Publishers.

Belief Update, the Markovian Situation Calculus, and Discrete Event Systems

Tyrone O'Neill and Norman Foo

Knowledge Systems Group
Department of Artificial Intelligence
University of New South Wales
Australia

Abstract. Imposing a markovian condition on the situation calculus enables the embedding of situation calculus theories into the DEVS (discrete event system specification) modelling and simulation framework. DEVS has an algebraic formalism relying on classical systems theory, and has been used to good effect in practical domains. The demonstrated correspondence between the situation calculus and DEVS is based upon an independently interesting translation from the semantics of circumscription into a simpler semantics based on belief updates.

1 Introduction

A markovian situation calculus is one for which the history of the transitions caused by event occurrence is functionally irrelevant to determining the future transitions of the system. Markovian systems are of fundamental importance in systems theory and control. Unfortunately, much of the attention given to the situation calculus has either explicity assumed a non-markovian system or ignored the issue altogether. The research described in this paper is motivated by the observation that engineering issues must be addressed if formalisms for reasoning about action are to be made useful. We have demonstrated a correspondence between situation calculus theories and specifications of discrete event systems - a map which will allow the situation calculus and related formalisms to use the well-tested results of systems engineering manifest in discrete event systems methodologies.

Our map is constructed in three stages. First, we show how the circumscriptive closure often used for situation calculus theories can be simplified at the semantic level, using a belief update representation. Second, we present an augmented version of the situation calculus with an explicit temporal representation. The third stage uses the results of the first two to complete the process: models of a situation calculus theory, first closed via a belief update technique which replaces circumscription and then augmented with a temporal ordering, are represented as discrete event systems.

An important and independently interesting corollary of this process is that the standard (Baker) circumscription policy is shown to imply a markovian condition.

This work has been motivated by five objectives enumerated as follows. 1. Imposing markovian conditions on the situation calculus provides the basis for further work on integrating common sense reasoning formalisms with the classical theory of systems and control, a well developed branch of engineering. 2. Representing the circumscribed situation calculus as a a form of belief update itself constitutes on theoretical grounds a useful and intuitive tool for reasoning about the effects of circumscription, and further illuminates the relationship between belief update/revision and circumscriptive approaches. 3. Apart from the intrinsic interest of understanding the connections between these two approaches to reasoning about action, demonstrating a correspondence between the situation calculus and DEVS is useful because, unlike most first-order frameworks, the DEVS methodology is geared closely towards efficient implementation, thus the established correspondence provides a well understood basis for implementation of situation calculus (and related) formalisms. 4. Recent work in representing continuous change in the situation calculus can thereby be grounded in the well-understood modelling and simulation approach to the same phenomenon. 5. The DEVS principles of object-orientation, modularity of models and systems design can then be applied to the situation calculus (and other logic formalisms), enabling issues like granularity and encapsulation, for both epistemic and computational purposes, to be better understood.

It seems to us that the logic of actions on the one hand is strong in its explication of issues like soundness and completeness but weak in applications of realistic engineering scale, while algebraic systems like DEVS are the opposite. Establishing a connection between the two is useful for both. Indeed, an immediate goal of our research is the investigation of situation calculus theories in an object-oriented discrete event environment (similar to that described by Zeigler ([Zei90]). Conversely, we will use logic to provide justifications for various DEVS computational rules that have hitherto been heuristic.

2 The Situation Calculus

We imagine that most readers will be familiar with the situation calculus. Our assumed semantics for the situation calculus is that of first-order theories[1].

If we let A, F, and S denote the sorts for actions, fluents, and situations respectively, then a situation calculus theory contains as a minimum the follows components:

Individual Constants: $s0$ $(\in S)$
Individual Variables: a, $a1$, $a2$, $a3$, ... $(\in A)$; f, $f1$, $f2$, $f3$, ... $(\in F)$;
$\quad\quad\quad\quad s$, $s1$, $s2$, $s3$, ... $(\in S)$
Predicates: $Holds$ $(\in F \times S)$
Functions: $Result$ $(\in A \times S \mapsto S)$
Very often an Ab predicate (for 'Abnormality') is introduced into the language to

---
[1] We construe the situation calculus as a language *schema* identifying an infinite class of languages for classical, three-sorted, first-order theories.

facilitate non-monotonic reasoning. Therefore a situation calculus interpretation is a tuple $<S,F,A,Holds,Result,Ab,s_0>$.

We assume that situation calculus theories used for reasoning about actions contain proper axioms of three types: domain constraints (DC), effect axioms (EA), and observation statements (OS), a well-known classification discussed at some length by authors such as Shanahan ([Sha97]).

One of the major difficulties in working with the situation calculus is that there exists significant disagreement over the way in which the calculus should be used for common sense reasoning. This disagreement manifests itself most pivotally in the metaphysical status given to situations; this status is evident in the identity conditions for situations. The three main competing interpretations are the *markovian* interpretation, in which two situations are identical when they have the same fluents holding; the *arboreal* interpretation, in which two situations are identical when not only do they have the same fluents holding but when also the situations are the result of the exactly the same sequence of actions from the initial situation; and the *agnostic* interpretation, in which no particular conditions are imposed on the identity of situations.

While the agnostic interpretation is (mostly by default) the most commonly used, it is the arboreal interpretation which, primarily in the hands of Ray Reiter (e.g., [Rei94]), has had the most detailed exposition and defence. The central axioms of the arboreal interpretation (as named by Shanahan ([Sha97])) are as follows:

A1. $(\forall a1,a2)(\forall s1,s2)(Result(a1,s1)=Result(a1,s2) \Rightarrow (a1=a2 \wedge s1=s2))$

A2. $(\forall a)(\forall s)\neg(s_0=Result(a,s))$

In direct opposition to the arboreal axioms are the markovian axioms:

M1. $(\forall s_1,s_2)(((\forall f)(Holds(f,s_1)\ )\Leftrightarrow Holds(f,s_2))) \Rightarrow s_1=s_2)$

M2. $(\forall s_1,s_2)(\forall f)Holds(f,s_1) \Leftrightarrow Holds(f,s_2)) \Rightarrow$
$\qquad (\forall a)(\forall f)(Holds(f,Result(a,s_1)) \Leftrightarrow Holds(f,Result(a,s_2)))$

M1 clearly implies M2, but inclusion of either one in a situation calculus theory achieve a markovian effect, namely, that the identity of situations is independent of the history of transition between situations.

3 Baker's Solution to the Frame Problem

Andrew Baker's solution to the frame problem ([Bak91]), which remains in a slightly modified form a benchmark for non-monotonic solutions to the frame problem, contains some unrecognised and unexplored markovian assumptions which in the next two sections we will make explicit and develop.

Baker's solution relies on circumscription, a technique which, as most readers would be aware, selects models of a theory ϕ through the employment of a preference relation. The preference relation for calculating $CIRC[\phi;P;Q_1,\ldots,Q_n]$ (the circumscription of P in ϕ, allowing $Q_1,\ldots,Q_n$ to vary) is defined for models M_i and M_j thus:

$M_i < M_j$ iff:
   (i) $M_i[P] \subseteq M_j[P]$, and

(ii) M_i and M_j agree on everything, including their universe of
interpretation, besides possibly P and $Q_1,\ldots,Q_n$.

Selected models are those which are minimal with respect to this preference relation. The circumscription policy used by Baker minimises, as is usual, the Ab predicate, the smaller bound of which is specified in the condition:

SC1.$\neg(Holds(f,s) \Leftrightarrow Holds(f,Result(a,s))) \Rightarrow Ab(f,a,s)$

Thus condition (i) of the circumscription preference relation definition would for Baker's policy read '$M_i[Ab] \subseteq M_j[Ab]$'. His policy, which for a situation calculus theory ϕ=DC $\cup$ EA $\cup$ OS we shall denote CIRC$_{Baker}(\phi)$, is more completely referred to as CIRC[DC∧EA∧EOS∧UNA∧SC1; Ab; Result]∧OS, where 'EOS' refers to the existence-of-situations axiom, which requires that every model contain at least one situation for every combination of fluents satisfying the domain constraints, and 'UNA' refers to the uniqueness-of-names assumption for actions and fluents (see Baker's paper for details). Observation statements, OS, are not included in the circumscribed theory itself, but instead are conjoined to the circumscribed theory, thus eliminating models incompatible with the observations; this separation is a modification of Baker's original theory first suggested by Sandewall under the name *occlusion*[2] ([San89]) to eliminate anomalies in the calculation of circumscription.

4 A Belief Update Representation of Circumscription

Fortunately, both for the purposes of comprehensibility and for the facilitation of proof, Baker's circumscription policy can be translated into an equivalent, more easily understood, model-based structure. The structure into which we will translate Baker's policy is based on those used in the belief update/revision literature ([KM91]). Marianne Winslett ([Win89]) has previously demonstrated that circumscription and update are related, by showing that update can be represented as circumscription. This translation goes the other way.

A *worlds-structure* is a tuple W = <K,P,E,T,I> where: K is a set of 'worlds', members of which are themselves subsets of P ('propositions'); there exists a transition function T:E×K↦K which, for each w∈K and each a∈E ('events'), specifies the effect of performing action a in world w; the 'initial' world (a member of K) is denoted 'I'.

We will show that for any situation calculus interpretation, there exists an equivalent worlds-structure. Let us refer to the translation from situation calculus interpretations to worlds-structures as ψ. Recall that a situation calculus interpretation is a tuple $<S,F,A,Holds,Result,Ab,s_0>$. ψ is defined for entire situation calculus interpretations via its definition for components, thus:

$\psi(s) = \{f| \; Holds(f,s)\}$
$K = \{\psi(s)| \; s \in S\}$
$P = \psi(F) = F$
$E = \psi(A) = A$

---

[2] Occlusion is now often referred to as 'filtering', following the nomenclature of Kartha ([Kar94]).

$I = \psi(s_0)$

$T(a,w) = \{v|\ \text{Result}(a,s_1)=s_2\ \wedge e=\psi(a)\ \wedge w = \psi(s_1)\ \wedge v = \psi(s_2)\}$

Note that the 'worlds' (members) of K are complete: a proposition failing to hold in any world implies that the propositions's negation holds in that world. *Ab* is so far lost in the translation—although we shall soon see that *Ab* can be recovered without loss of inferential capacity. This recovery, central to the translation of the effects of circumscription, is where the interest begins.

A very important feature of the translation is that because worlds in K are defined in terms of set-membership (each K is a subset of P), any two situations s_i, s_j with the same fluents holding map to exactly the same world-structure, i.e., $\psi(s_i)=\psi(s_j)$. Thus the space of situations defined for situation calculus models is partitioned into equivalence classes with respect to fluents holding in situations; one 'world' represents each partition. (Such a condition tacitly enforces the (M2) condition for situation calculus theories.) This consolidation of the space of situations forms the intuitive basis of the rest of the section.

Consider the worlds-structure W = <K,P,E,T,I> achieved after the foregoing translation from the situation calculus model M. For each world w∈K, define a partial pre-order $<_w$ on the members of K based on the symmetric difference between propositions holding in worlds[3]:

$w_i <_w w_j$ iff $\text{Diff}(w_i,w) \subseteq \text{Diff}(w_j,w)$

where $\text{Diff}(w_1,w_2) = \{p\in P|\ \neg(p\in w_1 \Leftrightarrow p\in w_2)\}$.

A *globalised PMA* preference relation between worlds-structures $W_1 = <K_1, P_1, E_1, T_1, I_1>$ and $W_2 = <K_2, P_2, E_2, T_2, I_2>$ is defined as follows: $W_i < W_2$ iff:

(I) $(\forall w\in K_1)(\forall e\in E_1)(T_1(a,w) \leq_w T_2(a,w))$, and

(II) $K_1=K_2$, $P_1=P_2$, $E_1=E_2$, $I_1=I_2$.

This preference relation for worlds-structures captures exactly the Baker circumscription preference relation for the situation calculus. Selected worlds-structures are those which are minimal with respect to the preference relation and, as Theorem 1 (below) demonstrates, the preferred situation calculus models match exactly the preferred worlds-structures. Two lemmas, each of which have straightforward proofs, lead directly to the Theorem.

Lemma 1: Consider any situation calculus theory ϕ. Then for any model M of $\text{CIRC}_{Baker}(\phi)$: $M\models (\forall f,a,s)(Ab(f,a,s)\Leftrightarrow\neg(Holds(f,s)\Leftrightarrow Holds(f,Result(a,s))))$.

Lemma 2: Let GlobalDiff(W_i) for any worlds-structure W_i be defined as:

$\{p\in P|\ (\exists w\in K_i)(\exists e\in E_i)\neg(p\in w \Leftrightarrow p\in T_i(e,w))\}$

For any worlds-structures W_1 and W_2, $W_1<W_2$ for the globalised-PMA preference relation defined above iff:

(i) GlobalDiff(W_1)$\subseteq$GlobalDiff(W_2), and

(ii) W_1 and W_2 are identical apart from T.

---

[3] Note that this is the PMA ordering, as defined by Winslett ([Win88]).

Theorem 1: Let $\{M_1,\ldots,M_n\}$ denote the set of models of a situation calculus theory ϕ which are minimal for the preference relation specified by Baker's circumscription policy. Then the minimal set according to the globalised-PMA preference relation defined above for the translated structure $\psi(\phi)$ is exactly the set $\{\psi(M_1),\ldots,\psi(M_n)\}$.

It is important to note that the cardinality of the set $\{\psi(M_1),\ldots,\psi(M_n)\}$ will very often be significantly less than n, due to the conflating effect of the translation.

Theorem 1 demonstrates the correctness of the translation between Baker's circumscription policy applied to situation calculus theories and globalised PMA update as defined in this paper.

The markovian nature of the worlds-structures into which the situation calculus theories have been translated is obvious, but the following corollary of Theorem 1 makes this explicit.

Corollary 1: For any situation calculus theory ϕ,
$$\mathrm{CIRC}_{Baker}(\phi) \models (\forall s_1, s_2)(\forall a)((\forall f)(Holds(f,s_1) \Leftrightarrow Holds(f,s_2)) \Rightarrow$$
$$(\forall f)(Holds(f,Result(a,s_1)) \Leftrightarrow Holds(f,Result(a,s_2))))$$

This result is the formal expression of the previously mentioned partioning of the set of situations into equivalence classes with respect to fluents holding. It follows that imposing the stronger markovian condition, $M1$—$(\forall s_1, s_2)$ $(\forall a)$ $((\forall f)$ $(Holds(f,s_1) \Leftrightarrow Holds(f,s_2)) \Rightarrow s_1 = s_2)$—on situation calculus theories will not affect the sentences modelled by the Baker closure of the theory.

5 A Temporal Ordering for Situations

Miller and Shanahan ([MS94]) and Pinto and Reiter ([PR95]) have suggested two different ways of introducing a temporal ordering into the situation calculus to allow narrative reasoning to be performed[4]. The fundamental difference between the two approaches is that Miller and Shanahan associate a situation with each time point in the temporal range, whereas Pinto and Reiter associate a time point with each situation in the situation space. For present purposes we choose to adopt Miller and Shanahan's approach.

Miller and Shanahan introduce a temporal ordering into the situation calculus in an attempt to introduce what they call *narratives*. Whereas the standard situation calculus is based upon *hypothetical* reasoning, in which the whole range of possibilities of states and actions are accounted for, narrative-based formalisms specify one particular *actual* course of events and intervening states. A narrative is some particular actual course of events, and the standard situation calculus does not allow representation of narratives; Miller and Shanahan augment the calculus to so allow. They begin by introducing a new sort for times ranging

---

[4] See Shanahan ([Sha97]) for a useful discussion of the relative advantages of each approach.

over the non-negative reals with variables t and $t_1,\ldots,t_n$, and two new predicates: *Happens(a,t)*, which states that an action of type a occurs at time t; and *Initially(f)*, which states that fluent f holds in the initial state. Through the use of *Initially* and *Happens* an actual course of events is specified. Note that hypothetical reasoning is still possible in this augmented situation calculus. To conveniently distinguish between the standard situation calculus and Miller and Shanahan's augmented version we shall call the latter the *narrative situation calculus* (NSC).

The formal machinery underpinning the function of the NSC is based on a new function, *State(t)*, which is defined to refer to the situation holding true at time t:

NSC1. *Initially(f)* $\Leftrightarrow$ *Holds(f,State(0))*

NSC2. *State (t1)* $=$ *State(0)* $\Rightarrow \neg(\exists a)(\exists t2)(Happens(a,t2) \wedge t2< t1)$

NSC3. *State(t1)* $=$ *Result(a1,State(t2))* $\Rightarrow$

    (Happens(a1,t2) $\wedge t2< t1 \wedge \neg(\exists a2)(\exists t3)(Happens(a2,t3)$ $\wedge t2< t3< t1))$

A fourth axiom defines the predicate *HoldsAt(f,t)*, which states that fluent f holds at time t:

NSC4. *HoldsAt(f,t)* $\Leftrightarrow$ *Holds(f,State(t))*

A standard situation calculus theory comprises DC $\cup$ EA $\cup$ OS. Due to the introduction of narrative representation, a narrative situation calculus theory comprises DC $\cup$ EA $\cup$ OS $\cup$ HA $\cup$ IS, where 'HA' are *Happens* Statements, and 'IS' are *Initially* statements. And whereas SC models are a tuple $<S,F,A,Holds,Result,Ab,s_0>$, NSC models are of the form $<S,F,A,Holds,Result, Ab,s_0,Happens>$. *Initially* statements are used to impose conditions on s_0 and so do not appear explicity in the model.

Using the NSC, which, it should be noted, is a conservative extension of the standard situation calculus, we now present the relationship between the situation calculus and the DEVS framework.

6 Discrete Event Systems

In his classic text on discrete event systems, Zeigler ([Zei76]) contrasts discrete event systems with both differential equation systems, in which system changes are specified by differential equations, and discrete time systems, in which system changes occur only at fixed time points (such as at the start or beginning of regular intervals of a given duration). Discrete event systems are those which change in state only through the occurrence of some event; that these events are discrete rather than continous means that events occur, or at least begin occurring, at specifiable time points when the system changes in quantum-like 'leaps'.

Such systems are described in a discrete event system specification (DEVS), an eight-tuple of the form $<X,Y,S,ta,Q,\delta_{int},\delta_{ext},\lambda>$ where:

X is a set of external input types

Y is a set of external output types

S is a set of sequential system states

$ta: S \mapsto \Re^+$, specifies the duration of state $s \in S$

$Q = \{(s,t) | \ s \in S \ and \ 0 \leq t \leq ta(s)\}$, specifies the set of total system states

$\delta_{int}: S \mapsto S$, specifies the internal transition function

$\delta_{ext}: Q \times X \mapsto S$, specifies the external transition function

$\lambda: Q \mapsto Y$, specifies the (observable) output function

Note that Q is defined completely in terms of other components of the DEVS. The system's dynamism is specified in the two transition functions, δ_{int} and δ_{ext}, the first of which specifies changes of a continous (non discrete) kind which occur within a particular discrete state, and the second of which is the state transition function for discrete changes in the system. An initial state is normally specified when the system is actually being simulated. DEVS is normally used in the process of modelling and simulation as a formal specification of the system being simulated, and has been used to great success in real world problem domains.

Now we turn to translating between the narrative situation calculus and DEVS. It happens that the situation calculus, even when augmented with a temporal ordering, is less expressive than DEVS. Therefore the translation we will demonstrate is between the situation calculus and a subclass of DEVS specifications. Let us call a *basic DEVS* a tuple $<X,Y,S,ta,\delta_{ext},\lambda>$ - it is a DEVS without the internal transition function δ_{int}. The reason why δ_{int} has been omitted is because it enables specification of *continuous change*, something beyond the scope of this paper (but which we plan to address in future work). Components of a basic DEVS are defined as above for a complete DEVS except that for a basic DEVS the occurrences of Q in the definitions of the next-state and output functions (δ_{ext} and λ respectively) are replaced by X, because Q is no longer required (as no change takes place within states). A basic DEVS is essentially a temporally specified finite state machine, and we will now show that any basic DEVS is equivalent to some interpretation for a corresponding narrative situation calculus theory. For the purposes of the translation, we introduce a new function:

$TimeofNextEvent(t) = t'$ iff

$\qquad (\exists a)(Happens(a,t') \wedge \neg (\exists a')(Happens(a',t'') \wedge t<t''<t'))$

Consider any basic DEVS $<X,Y,S_{DEVS},ta,\delta_{ext},\lambda>$. The corresponding NSC model (which is determined by a translation which we shall denote θ) $<S_{NSC},F,A,$ $Holds,Result,Ab,s_0>$ is defined through the following relationship of components:

$X=A$

$Y=F$

$S_{DEVS}=S_{NSC}$

$ta(s)=\{t \ |\theta(s_{NSC})=s_{DEVS} \wedge (\exists a)(\exists t')(Happens(a,t') \wedge TimetoNextState(t')=t)\}$

$\delta_{ext}(s_{DEVS},x) = \{Result(a,s_{NSC}) \ | \ \theta(s_{NSC})=s_{DEVS} \wedge \theta(x)=a)\}$

$\lambda(s_{DEVS})=\{y \ | \ (\exists t)(\theta(s_{NSC})=s_{DEVS} \wedge t=ta(s_{NSC}) \wedge HoldsAt(f,t) \wedge \theta(f)=y)\}$

With regard to the translation, note that the *Holds* component of a NSC model is contained in the corresponding DEVS through the *HoldsAt* predicate (which itself is defined in terms of *State* and *Holds*). Thus apart from s_0, which we shall ignore (since DEVS implementations specify initial states during simulation itself), the only component of the NSC model not translated is the Ab predicate. Here is where Section 4 finds its use. By applying the update semantics outlined in that section, the effect of using the Ab predicate in the NSC is maintained for the DEVS internal transition. This correspondence succeeds only because of Theorem 1 of Section 4—as DEVS works on a purely markovian basis, the situation calculus would not be representable in DEVS without fluent-equivalent situations being conflated.

Theorem 2: The correspondence θ establishes an equivalence between NSC models and DEVS.

The above translation takes a single NSC model and produces a single corresponding DEVS, but we need to provide a translation from NSC theories (or sets of models) to sets of DEVS. (Note that if a model of a system is supposed to be contained in a single DEVS, it is assumed that the description of the system is complete; therefore, since agent knowledge of systems is normally incomplete, a set of DEVS is needed to represent the agent's knowledge of the system.)

Take some NSC theory ϕ with models $M_1, \ldots, M_n$. Using the translation of Section 4, determine the set of worlds-structures $\phi(M_1), \ldots, \phi(M_n)$, then according to the globalised PMA preferece relation determine the set of minimal worlds-structures $\phi(M_{i(1)}), \ldots, \phi(M_{i(m)})$. Now take (any) corresponding situation calculus models $M_{i(1)}, \ldots, M_{i(m)}$ of the minimal worlds-structures and translate each to a DEVS using the above translation. Call this translation between NSC theories and sets of DEVS Θ.

Theorem 3: The correspondence Θ establishes an equivalence between NSC theories and sets of DEVS.

Thus the circumscriptive closure of a situation calculus theory, after being augmented with a time-line and translated through a belief-update mechanism, can be represented as a family (or set) of DEVS. The reason why it is useful to work with a set of DEVS is that in a simulation framework, when the model of a system is known to be uncertain or imprecise, as is the case with common sense knowledge, *multiple runs* of the simulation are performed to achieve the desired result. Each of the runs corresponds to a different complete closure of the incomplete knowledge of the system. Thus it is normal to specify an imperfectly apprehended discrete event system as a family of DEVS.

7   Conclusion

A markovian situation calculus can be very useful if common sense temporal reasoning is to be integrated into classical systems-theoretic frameworks. We have shown that Baker circumscription can be replaced with an intuitively simpler belief-update model which explicitly affirms a markovian ontology for situations; the markovian ontology supports the construction of translation between the situation calculus and DEVS.

Future research will be two-fold. In one direction we will use object-oriented DEVS implementations as benchmarks for common sense temporal reasoning problems, and to motivate the construction of event logics with realistic structure and scale. In the other direction, the practice of modelling and simulation can benefit from correctness ideas from event logics that justify heuristics.

8 Acknowledgements

We are indebted to the members of the Knowledge Systems Group, especially Maurice Pagnucco and Pavlos Peppas, and to an anonymous reviewer, for their helpful responses to draft versions of this paper.

References

[Bak91] Andrew B. Baker. Nonmonotonic reasoning in the framework of the situation calculus. *Artificial Intelligence*, 49:5–23, 1991.

[Kar94] G. Neelakantan Kartha. Two counterexamples related to baker's approach to the frame proble m. *Artificial Intelligence*, 69:379–391, 1994.

[KM91] Hirofumi Katsuno and Alberto O. Mendelzon. On the difference between updating a knowledge and revising it. In Peter Gardenfors, editor, *Belief Revision*. Cambridge U.P., 1991.

[MS94] Rob Miller and Murray Shanahan. Narratives in the situation calculus. *Journal of Logic & Computation*, 4(5):513–530, October 1994.

[PR95] Javier Pinto and Raymond Reiter. Reasoning about time in the situation calculus. *Annals of Mathematical and Artifical Intelligence*, 14:251–268, September 1995.

[Rei94] Raymond Reiter. Proving properties of states in the situation calculus. *Artifical Intelligence*, 64:337–351, 1994.

[San89] Erik Sandewall. Filter preferential entailmentfor the logic of action in almost con tinuous worlds. In *Proceedings of IJCAI '89*. Morgan Kaufmann, 1989.

[Sha97] Murray Shanahan. *Solving the Frame Problem*. MIT Press, 1997.

[Win88] Marianne Winslett. Reasoning about action using a possible models approach. In *Proceedings of the American Association for Artifical Intelligence Conference*, pages 89–93, 1988.

[Win89] Marianne Winslett. Sometimes updates are circumscription. In *Proceedings of the International Joint Conference for Artifical Intelligence*, pages 859–863, 1989.

[Zei76] Bernard P. Zeigler. *Theory of Modelling and Simulation*. Wiley, New York, 1976.

[Zei90] Bernard P. Zeigler. *Object-oriented simulation with hierarchical, modular models: intelligent agents and endomorphic systems*. Academic Press, Boston, 1990.

A Notion of Correctness with Theories Containing Theoretical Terms

Rex Bing Hung Kwok[1], Abhaya Nayak[1], and Norman Foo[1]

Knowledge Systems Group, School of Computer Science and Engineering, University of New South Wales, NSW 2052, Australia.
Email: {rkwok, abhaya, norman}@cse.unsw.edu.au.

Abstract. This paper considers how theories containing theoretical terms can be tested with experiments which only give results in observable terms. An agent will be defined which makes predictions about the effect of actions. To test such an agent, the predictions of the agents will measured against an experimental frame. With the experimental frame a result will be presented demonstrating when some theoretical vocabulary is necessary. Further, the correctness of an agent will be defined and results showing the correspondence between beliefs containing theoretical terms and the experimental frame will be presented.

1 Introduction

Most scientific theories use theoretical terms, terms such as "electron", "gene" and "black hole". These terms differ from other terms such as "rock", "skeleton" "star" in that while rocks, skeletons and stars are observable under normal conditions, the theoretical terms refer to unobservable entities. In the philosophy of science literature, the utility of theoretical terms has been the focus of much debate. Despite Craig's famous result [1] to the effect that theoretical terms can, in principle, be replaced by strings of "observational vocabulary", the role of theoretical terms in formation, replacement and systematisation of scientific theories remains unchallenged. From the vantage point of Artificial Intelligence, however, what is important is not a debate on the ontological status of what theoretical terms refer to, but rather the design of near automatic processes for generating *appropriate* theoretical terms when, and if, required. Theoretical terms and theory formation have drawn their fair share of attention from the AI research community. For instance, [4] [8] have formalised the work of Gregor Mendel relating the discovery of genes in order to validate their methods for creating and using new terms. Muggleton [5] and Ling [4] have used inverse resolution to generate theoretical terms. In fact, Muggleton [6] has maintained in the past that theoretical entities (the referents of theoretical terms) are mere convenient fictions. Taking a different approach, Shen's work [7] concerns the creation of theoretical terms in a dynamic framework. The guiding idea behind this work is that if a dynamic system responds to a given action non-deterministically, some hitherto unaccounted-for (theoretical) entity/property is perhaps responsible for this anomalous behaviour, whereby creation of a new theoretical term is warranted. This is closely related to the problem of hidden variables in quantum mechanics. Shen has demonstrated the efficacy of this method via the formalisation of the discovery of genes. Kwok [3] has examined this method a little more closely and has established the conditions under which this method works.

The current work aims at investigating the correctness of theories containing theoretical terms. We assume a dynamic framework in which an agent, with a fixed repertoire of actions and a prediction function, is situated in an "experimental frame". The agent predicts in advance the result of performing a given action sequence and is in a position to compare the prediction with the observed effect of the performed action sequence in question. A considerable body of work has accumulated dealing with the problems related to reasoning about change (for example, [9]). The purpose of this paper is not to devise a logic of action but to consider how the role of theoretical terms may fit into a general system which reasons about change. In Section 2 we provide a precise definition of an agent in terms of an action-repertoire/prediction-function pair and offer a brief discussion there of. In Section 3 we model an experimental frame that the agent is situated in as a Kripke-structure. Such a model is in fact similar to the Kripke-structures used as models in dynamic logics [2]. This provides us with the necessary semantic machinery to precisely define crucial notions such as *experiment* and *empirical adequacy*. More notably, at the end of this section we characterise a sufficient (by no means necessary) condition under which the agent is warranted to invent a new theoretical term. Section 4, on the other hand, relates our investigation into the notion of correctness appropriate to evaluate the theoretical terms (or rather the entities they denote) postulated in order to address the perceived need for one. Apart from defining correctness in rigorous terms, we establish, among other results, that under separability assumptions for the experimental frame, if the agent has attained a correct set of beliefs via a sequence of actions (read experiments) performed, then this sequence of actions must correspond to a fixed structure in the experimental frame. Finally, we conclude with a brief summary.

2   The Agent

An agent makes predictions about the effects of actions given a set of initial conditions. These conditions and predictions may contain theoretical terms. While much of the research into reasoning about actions is concerned with how predictions are made, the central concern of this paper is with what predictions are made and how such predictions compare with an experimental frame. With most logics of action, an action is equated with a formula called the postcondition which represents what must hold after the performance of an action. However, this represents an assumption about the nature of actions and may be too restrictive; especially when dealing with theoretical terms. For instance, consider a home pregnancy test kit. The performance of such a test can result in one of two different and opposite outcomes. Yet, for each outcome, the action performed in carrying out the test is the same. To avoid the possibility that such an assumption is restrictive, actions are represented by a set of action symbols. The predictor function of an agent takes three arguments: a set of sentences from the language of theories – representing the beliefs of an agent prior to an action, an action symbol – representing the action the predictor will determine the effect of, and a set of sentences from the observational language – representing a possible observational outcome. While the first two arguments of the predictor function are uncontroversial, the third argument is novel and requires elaboration. Such an argument is a set of observational sentences because, as will be seen later in the experimental frame, the agent can only gain feedback about the status of observational sentences. Once again, consider the example of the pregnancy test kit where pregnancy is a theoretical property. If it were not possible to specify any possible outcomes, as is the case in most logics of action, there is nothing that can be said about the result of the action. However, if the result of the test is 'blue' then the diagnosis of the experiment is that the patient is pregnant. If the result were 'red', the diagnosis is that the patient is not pregnant. In science, the entities to which terms refer to tend to vary in the degree to which they are considered theoretical or observational. For example, the entities referred to by the term "enzyme" may be thought of as being more observational than the entities referred to by the term "quark". An assumption made in this paper about the nature of theoretical terms is that they do not intersect with the set of observational terms. This simplifying assumption means that no terms are both observational and theoretical. Two first order languages are used: $\mathcal{L}_o$, the observational language and $\mathcal{L}$, the language of theories which is a superset of the observational language. An agent is defined as follows:

Definition 2.1: An agent is a tuple, $X = (A, P)$, where A is a set of action symbols and P is a function $P : 2^{\mathcal{L}} \times A \times 2^{\mathcal{L}_o} \to 2^{\mathcal{L}}$.

With the pregnancy test example, the predictor function behaves as follows:

$P(\{\}, \text{pregnancy\_test}, \{\}) = \{\}$
$P(\{\}, \text{pregnancy\_test}, \{\text{blue}\}) = \{\text{blue, pregnant}\}$
$P(\{\}, \text{pregnancy\_test}, \{\text{red}\}) = \{\text{red}, \neg\text{pregnant}\}$

Reasoning about the possible outcomes of actions is common in many fields of science where experiments are used to gain theoretical information. These experiments range from determining whether an athlete is taking performance enhancing drugs to the sequencing of DNA. Although nothing can be directly predicted about the outcome of a pregnancy test, the knowledge that each outcome leads to the conclusion of pregnancy or non-pregnancy needs to be represented. Before proceeding, the following conventions will be adopted to simplify the notation:

Definition 2.2: Given an agent, $X = (A, P)$, for every $K \in 2^{\mathcal{L}}, a \in A, O \in 2^{\mathcal{L}_o}$

1. $P(K, a, O) = K(a, O)$.
2. $A^* = \{ \mathbf{a} \mid \mathbf{a} = \langle(a_1, O_1), (a_2, O_2), ..., (a_n, O_n)\rangle$ and for each $i, a_i \in A$ and $O_i \in 2^{\mathcal{L}_o}\}$.
3. For every $\mathbf{a} = \langle(a_1, O_1), (a_2, O_2), ..., (a_n, O_n)\rangle \in A^*$,
   $K\mathbf{a} = K(a_1, O_1)(a_2, O_2)...(a_n, O_n)$.

4. $Cn(K) = \{\alpha \mid K \models \alpha\}$.
5. $A(K) = \{(O, \mathbf{a}) \mid O \in 2^{\mathcal{L}_o}$ and $\mathbf{a} \in A^*$ and $Cn(K) = Cn(O\mathbf{a})\}$.

These definitions abbreviate the notation describing the predictor behaviour under composition. With the first definition, the effect of the predictor is now represented by a postfix operator, (a, O), acting on a belief set K. The set, A^*, contains all finite sequences of pairs with an action symbol and a possible outcome. Elements of each sequence, (O, a) say, are called *conditional actions* as each pair contains an action symbol, a, and a possible or conditional outcome, O. The sequences themselves are called *sequences of conditional actions*. The third definition is the standard closure operator and forms the set of all formulae entailed by a set of sentences. The final definition forms the set of pairs, a set of observational sentences and a sequence of conditional actions, which are possible histories of K. This is the *attaining* set of a belief set.

3 The Experimental Frame

The aim of this section is to define an experimental frame which can be used to test the adequacy of agent predictions and to establish conditions under which an agent will require some theoretical vocabulary. The experimental frame used to test the accuracy of an agent is a Kripke possible worlds structure in the observational language. From such a structure, experiments and experimental results can be extracted and compared with the predictions of an agent. It may be argued that scientific experiments can yield direct knowledge of theoretical factors. However, such knowledge is actually due to the interpretation of observational facts with methods developed and refined through experience. For example, in using gel electrophoresis to sequence DNA pairs, a geneticist may predict that a person suffers from sickle cell anaemia. However, the procedure only produces photographs with columns of irregularly spaced bands. The ability of a scientist to make such predictions is based upon a background theory about inheritance and genetics.

As a motivating example for the work that follows, consider the experimental frame depicted in Figure 1 (only positive literals are shown). In this frame, odour and colour are observable. Considered in isolation, the action of placing lit tapers in containers with colourless and odourless air produces a number of outcomes: the flame may die out, burn as before and then die out gradually, or the flame may suddenly flare. Very little can be predicted about the result of such experiments. However, when combined in sequence, a more deterministic outcome is observed. When calcium carbonate is heated, a colourless and odourless air is evolved and when lit tapers are placed in containers with this air, the flame quickly extinguishes. Chemists of the late 18th century dubbed such an air, 'fixed air', and this gas is known as carbon dioxide today. This then, represents a theoretical property of colourless and odourless gases.

A Kripke possible worlds structure consists of a set of worlds, a set of binary relations between worlds, and a valuation function which determines the formulae satisfied by each world. Each binary relation reflects how an action transforms a world. With the framework to be used, an experimental frame is relative to

Fig. 1. Producing CO_2 and testing with a lit taper.

an agent in that there is a bijective correspondence between the action symbols of an agent and the accessibility relations of the experimental frame. Further, the observational language of the agent and the experimental frame are the same.

Definition 3.1: For an agent, $X = (A, P)$, with an observational language, $\mathcal{L}_o$, there is a Kripke possible worlds structure, $EF_X = (S, R, V)$, which is the experimental frame of an agent X where S is a set of worlds, R is a set of accessibility relations (each relation a subset of $S \times S$), and V is a valuation function for $\mathcal{L}_o$. Further, for every $\mathbf{a} = \langle (a_1, O_1), (a_2, O_2), ..., (a_n, O_n) \rangle \in A^*$

(i) $R_{\mathbf{a}} = \{(s_0, s_n) \mid$ there exists $s_1, s_2, ..., s_{n-1}$ for every $i, 1 \le i \le n, (s_{i-1}, s_i) \in R_{a_i}$ and $s_i \models O_i\}$.

(ii) $W(S_1, \mathbf{a}) = \{s' \mid$ there exists $s \in S_1 ((s, s') \in R_{\mathbf{a}})\}$ for every $S_1 \subseteq S$.

This definition generalises the set of accessibility relations in a Kripke structure to include all sequences of conditional actions. It shows that as individual actions can be viewed as accessibility relations so can any sequence of actions with conditional outcomes. Further, $W(S_1, \mathbf{a})$ defines the set of worlds that are reachable from a set of worlds, S_1, via $R_{\mathbf{a}}$. Within this framework, the agent is assumed to have complete control over initial observational conditions. As such, the initial conditions of an experiment are specified by a set of observational sentences. From such initial conditions, any sequence of conditional actions may be executed. An experiment, then, is a trace in the experimental frame from an initial world satisfying the initial conditions to a final world accessible from the initial world via the accessibility relation corresponding to the sequence of conditional actions. An experimental result would then be the observational formulae satisfied by the final world in the trace. An example of an experiment in the carbon dioxide scenario would be $(\{\text{colourless\_air, odourless\_air}\}, \text{lit\_taper}, \{\text{flame\_flares}\})$.

Definition 3.2: A triple $(O, \mathbf{a}, O')$ where $O, O' \in 2^{\mathcal{L}_o}$, $\mathbf{a} \in A^*$ is an *experiment* if and only if there exists $s, s' \in S (s \models O$ and $(s, s') \in R_{\mathbf{a}}$ and for every $\alpha \in \mathcal{L}_o (s' \models \alpha \Leftrightarrow O' \models \alpha))$.

The possibly nondeterministic nature of the experimental frame means that for any set of initial conditions there may be multiple experimental outcomes for any sequence of conditional actions. The commonality of all experimental outcomes is called the *effect* of an action sequence $\mathbf{a}$ on O. For example, the effect of $\langle (\text{heat}, \{\}), (\text{lit\_taper}, \{\}) \rangle$ on $\{\text{calcium\_carbonate}\}$ would be $\{\text{flame\_dies}\}$. An agent, then, is described as being *empirically adequate* for an action sequence $\mathbf{a}$ on O just when the predictions of $\mathbf{a}$ from O coincide with the effect of $\mathbf{a}$ on O.

Definition 3.3: For any $O \in 2^{\mathcal{L}_o}, \mathbf{a} \in A^*$ the *effect* of $\mathbf{a}$ on $O, E(O, \mathbf{a})$, is defined by $E(O, \mathbf{a}) = \{\alpha \mid$ for every experiment $(O, \mathbf{a}, O')(O' \models \alpha)\}$.

Definition 3.4: For any $O \in 2^{\mathcal{L}_o}, \mathbf{a} \in A^*$, an agent is *empirically adequate* for $\mathbf{a}$ from O if and only if for every $\alpha \in \mathcal{L}_o$ ($O\mathbf{a} \models \alpha \Leftrightarrow E(O, \mathbf{a}) \models \alpha$).

A consequence of using a Kripke structure to represent the experimental frame is that there are occasions when an agent requires some theoretical vocabulary.

Lemma 3.5: For any $\mathbf{a} = \langle (a_1, O_1), (a_2, O_2), ..., (a_n, O_n) \rangle \in A^*, O \in 2^{\mathcal{L}_o}$

$$E(O, \langle (a_1, O_1), (a_2, O_2), ..., (a_n, O_n) \rangle) \supseteq$$
$$E(E(O, \langle (a_1, O_1) \rangle), \langle (a_2, O_2), ..., (a_n, O_n) \rangle) \supseteq \cdots \supseteq$$
$$E(E(O, \langle (a_1, O_1), (a_2, O_2), ..., (a_{n-1}, O_{n-1}) \rangle), \langle (a_n, O_n) \rangle)$$

This result shows that longer sequences of actions have more effects. Performing a sequence of actions has at least the effect of starting from the effect of some subsequence and performing the rest of the sequence. The interesting case arises when a sequence of actions strictly produces more effects than those produced by starting from the effect of a subsequence and performing the rest of the sequence. To demonstrate this, suppose the following:

$$E(O, \langle (a_1, O_1), (a_2, O_2) \rangle) \supset E(E(O, \langle (a_1, O_1) \rangle), \langle (a_2, O_2) \rangle)$$

This assumption means that the effect of performing two actions sequentially produces more effects than performing the second action on the effect of the first action. The worlds satisfying the effect of the first action is always a superset of the set of intermediate worlds encountered after the first action when both actions are performed sequentially. As such, the final worlds encountered on performing the second action on the effect of the first is a superset of those on performing both actions sequentially. This difference in the set of final worlds may by realised observationally as a difference in the effects. This is the case in the carbon dioxide scenario. The effect of heating calcium carbonate is to produce a odourless and colourless air. When a lit taper is placed with colourless and odourless gases the effect is that the flame may flare, gradually die, or quickly extinguish. However, the effect of placing a lit taper in the colourless and odourless air produced by heating calcium carbonate is that the flame dies quickly. One necessary assumption for the following result is that an agent makes the same predictions from belief sets which entail the same formulae. Such an agent is said to satisfy the principle of the *irrelevance of syntax*.

Observation 3.6: For an agent satisfying the principle of the irrelevance of syntax with no theoretical vocabulary and an experimental frame in which $E(O, \langle (a_1, O_1), (a_2, O_2) \rangle) \supset E(E(O, \langle (a_1, O_1) \rangle), \langle (a_2, O_2) \rangle)$ if the agent is empirically adequate for $\langle (a_1, O_1) \rangle$ on O and $\langle (a_2, O_2) \rangle$ on $E(O, \langle (a_1, O_1) \rangle)$ then the agent is *not* empirically adequate for $\langle (a_1, O_1), (a_2, O_2) \rangle$ on O.

Proof: Since the agent has no theoretical vocabulary and is empirically adequate for (a_1, O_1) on O, $Cn(O(a_1, O_1)) = E(O, \langle(a_1, O_1)\rangle)$. Similarly, since the agent is empirically adequate for (a_2, O_2) on $E(O, \langle(a_1, O_1)\rangle)$,
$Cn((E(O, \langle(a_1, O_1)\rangle))(a_2, O_2)) = E(E(O, \langle(a_1, O_1)\rangle), \langle(a_2, O_2)\rangle)$. Thus,
$Cn(O(a_1, O_1)(a_2, O_2)) = Cn((E(O, \langle(a_1, O_1)\rangle))(a_2, O_2))$
$= E(E(O, \langle(a_1, O_1)\rangle), \langle(a_2, O_2)\rangle) \subset E(O, \langle(a_1, O_1), (a_2, O_2)\rangle)$. Therefore, the predicted outcome is a strict subset of the effect which means that the agent is not empirically adequate for $\langle(a_1, O_1), (a_2, O_2)\rangle$ on O.

The reason for this is that the agent has no theoretical vocabulary to differentiate between the intermediate worlds traversed when performing two actions sequentially from the worlds satisfying the effect of the first action. In order to rectify the situation, the agent must obtain some extra beliefs involving theoretical terms after the performance of the first action in order to stand a chance at being empirically adequate for the sequence of actions. In the carbon dioxide scenario, the agent requires some theoretical beliefs about the colourless and odourless air produced on heating calcium carbonate.

4   Correctness and Theoretical Terms

Given the definitions of the agent and the experimental frame, the purpose of this section is to define when an agent correctly uses a belief set containing theoretical terms and to show that such a belief set corresponds to a fixed set of worlds in the experimental frame. The example used in the preceding section recalls how the theoretical property of 'fixed air' was hypothesised to account for the different effects of colourless and odourless gases on lit tapers. Such a method may seem *ad hoc* because new terms may be created for each anomalous sequence of actions. However, the same beliefs may be attained through many pathways and there may be any number of experiments to test such beliefs. It is this principle which will form the basis for defining when a belief set containing theoretical terms is used correctly. The example involving 'fixed air' can be elaborated as shown in Figure 2. As can be seen in the diagram, there are now two actions which require a belief in 'fixed air' and two ways to differentiate 'fixed air' from other odourless and colourless gases. The burning of charcoal results in the production of fixed air and when mice are placed in containers with this air they suffocate quickly. This increases the testability of the notion of fixed air as there are now four experimental pathways involving a belief in fixed air.

The idea, then, is to consider all action sequences which lead the agent to attain a belief set and consider all action sequences which test that belief set. This is formally defined as follows:

Definition 4.1: A belief set, $K \in 2^{\mathcal{L}}$, is *correct* if and only if for every $\mathbf{a}$, $\mathbf{b} \in A^*, O \in 2^{\mathcal{L}_\circ}((O, \mathbf{a}) \in A(K)) \Rightarrow$ the agent is empirically adequate on $\mathbf{a} \circ \mathbf{b}$ from O, where $\mathbf{a} \circ \mathbf{b}$ is the concatenation of $\mathbf{a}$ by $\mathbf{b}$.

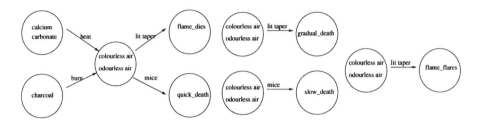

Fig. 2. Producing and testing CO_2.

From the definition, a belief set is correct when the agent is empirically adequate for every sequence of conditional actions of the form **aob** on observational sentences O when $(O,\mathbf{a})$ attains the belief set. One example in science which resembles this definition are the postulates formulated by Robert Koch in the late 19th century for determining when an animal suffers from a disease caused by bacteria. Koch discovered the bacteria responsible for anthrax, tuberculosis, and cholera using the following defining guidelines:

1. An animal suffers from the disease if and only if the organism is present in the animal.
2. The organism can be isolated and cultured away from the animal.
3. Inoculation of such cultures to susceptible animals cause the disease.
4. The process of isolation, culture, and inoculation should be repeatable any number of times.

The first postulate suggests that an agent is forced to have some theoretical vocabulary to account for the anomaly of disease. The remaining postulates generate an infinite number of experiments to test the theoretical belief in bacterial infection. This is equivalent to the **b** part of action sequences in the definition above. Valid though the postulates are still, it is infeasible to continually transfer bacteria from animal to animal in an attempt to prove that the original animal was infected. This is exactly the problem of induction and points to the pragmatic aspect of science where the number of testing experiments is limited. Having established such a definition it was hoped that it would imply that a correct belief set would always correspond to a fixed set of worlds in the experimental frame. However, the following condition proved necessary:

Definition 4.2 A Kripke structure is *separable* when for every $S_1, S_2 \subseteq S$, $S_1 = S_2$ whenever for every $\mathbf{a} \in A^*, \alpha \in \mathcal{L}_o$
$((\text{for every } s^{'} \in W(S_1, \mathbf{a}) \ (s^{'} \models \alpha)) \Leftrightarrow ((\text{for every } s^{'} \in W(S_2, \mathbf{a}) \ (s^{'} \models \alpha)))$.

The above definition requires that any two sets of worlds in a Kripke structure be the same if and only if the effects of any sequence of conditional actions starting from both sets of worlds are the same. In fact, for Kripke structures, when two sets of worlds are the same it necessarily follows that all sequences of actions produce the same effects. The definition describes a Kripke structure as *separable* because whenever two subsets of worlds are different then some sequence of conditional actions will produce effects with an observational difference starting from both sets of worlds. Using this definition, the following theorem can be established:

Theorem 4.3: For any set of observational sentences, O, let $[O] = \{s \mid s \models O\}$. Given an agent, $X = (A, P)$, and an experimental frame $EF_X = (S, R, V)$, which is separable then for any correct $K \in 2^{\mathcal{L}}, (O, \mathbf{a}), (O', \mathbf{b}) \in A(K)$ $(W([O], \mathbf{a}) = W([O'], \mathbf{b}))$

This result means that for any correctly used belief set, whenever the agent attains such a belief set the sequence of conditional actions given the initial conditions correspond to a fixed set of worlds in the experimental frame. For any correct belief set, K, this set of worlds can be denoted by W_K. Further results show that this theorem is reasonable:

Corollary 4.4: For any belief set, K, let $O(K) = \{\alpha \mid K \models \alpha \text{ and } \alpha \in \mathcal{L}_o\}$. For an agent with a separable experimental frame,

1. For every $O \in 2^{\mathcal{L}_o}$, if O is correct then $W_O = [O]$
2. For any correct K, $O(K)$ $(W_K \subseteq W_{O(K)})$

The first part shows that when a set of observational sentences is correct then the worlds corresponding to those sentences are exactly the worlds satisfying those sentences. With the second part, worlds corresponding to a belief set are always a subset of the worlds corresponding to the observational content of the belief set. This is intuitive as the extra beliefs involving theoretical terms would represent additional information on top of the observational beliefs. When W_K is a strict subset of $W_{O(K)}$ then the observational vocabulary is insufficient to capture the dynamic behaviour of the W_K worlds. As such, the theoretical content of K is necessary in generating extra predictions about the dynamic behaviour of W_K worlds.

Theorem 4.3 establishes that attaining a correct belief set corresponds to a fixed set of worlds. However, the converse should also be considered. Whenever a number of sequences of conditional actions always reaches a fixed set of worlds, what belief sets might those sequences correspond to? To gain the result that these sequences correspond to the same belief set, a separability assumption is required for an agent:

Definition 4.5: A agent is *separable* if and only if for every $K, K' \in 2^{\mathcal{L}}$ (for every $\mathbf{a} \in A^*, Cn(K\mathbf{a}) = Cn(K'\mathbf{a})) \Leftrightarrow Cn(K) = Cn(K')$.

This definition stipulates that whenever an agent has belief sets which act the same way under the predictor function then the belief sets entail the same formulae. Such a stipulation implies the following corollary:

Corollary 4.6: For a separable agent and experimental frame, for every $O, O' \in 2^{\mathcal{L}_o}, \mathbf{a}, \mathbf{b} \in A^*$ $(W([O], \mathbf{a}) = W([O'], \mathbf{b})$ and the agent is correct on $O\mathbf{a}$ and $O'\mathbf{b}$ $\Rightarrow Cn(O\mathbf{a}) = Cn(O'\mathbf{b})$.

5 Conclusion and Summary

This paper has defined a notion of the correctness belief sets containing theoretical terms and has shown that a correct belief set corresponds to a fixed set of worlds in a model of the experimental frame. In order to gain such a correspondence, several conditions are necessary and this suggests that the use of theoretical terms is more than a matter of convenience. However, this does not mean that any one theory containing one set of theoretical terms is any better or worse than another. In fact, it may be possible, given any theoretical vocabulary to manufacture an empirically correct agent. Scientific revolutions often result in the overthrow of one set of theoretical terms in favour of another. This is an important facet of science and it will be interesting to consider notions that rank empirically adequate agents with different theoretical vocabularies.

The ideas used in this paper have parallels in systems theory. In systems theory, a state is a convenient abbreviation for an equivalence class of input sequences for which any member input sequence produces the same output from the system for any future concatenation of further input sequences. Such input sequences are analogous to the sequences of actions which lead an agent to attain a belief set while the concatenations correspond to the sequences of actions which concatenate to the attaining sequence and test the belief set. The separability assumption about the experimental frame is parallelled in automata theory where such a notion leads to minimal state machines in which no two states behave in the same way. Further, such an assumption is necessary for the learnability of automata. It will be interesting to considers the parallels this might have with the treatment of theoretical terms in this paper.

References

1. W. Craig. On axiomatizability within a system. In *The Journal of Symbolic Logic vol. 18*, 1953.
2. Robert Goldblatt. *Logics of Time and Computation*. Center for the Study of Language and Information (CLSI), Leland Stanford Junior University, 1992.
3. R. Kwok. Creating theoretical terms for non-deterministic actions. In *Proceedings of the 4th Pacific Rim International Conference on Artificial Intelligence*, pages 510–521, 1996.
4. X. C. Ling. Inventing necessary theoretical terms to overcome representation bias. In *Proceedings of Machine Learning 1992 Workshop on Inductive Learning*. Morgan Kaufman, 1992.
5. S. Muggleton. Predicate invention and utilization. In *Journal of Experimental and Theoretical Artificial Intelligence 6*, pages 121–130, 1994.
6. S. Muggleton and W. Buntine. Machine invention of first-order predicates by inverting resolution. In *Proceedings of the 5th International Machine Learning Workshop*, pages 339–352. Morgan Kaufman, 1988.
7. Wei-Min Shen. Discovery as automomous learning from the environment. In *Machine Learning, 12*, pages 145–165. Kluwer, 1993.
8. Wei-Min Shen and Herbert A. Simon. Rule creation and rule learning through environmental exploration. In *Proceedings of the Eleventh International Joint Conference on Artificial Intelligence*. Morgan Kaufman, 1989.
9. Y. Shoham. *Reasoning About Change*. MIT Press, Cambridge, Massachusetts, 1988.

Inductive Properties of States

Norman Foo[1], Pavlos Peppas[2], and Yan Zhang[3]

[1] Knowledge Systems Group, School of Computer Science and Engineering,
University of New South Wales, NSW 2052, Australia.
Email: norman@cse.unsw.edu.au
[2] Knowledge Systems Group, Department of Computing, School of MPCE,
Macquarie University, NSW 2109, Australia.
Email: pavlos@mpce.mq.edu.au.
[3] Knowledge Systems Group, Department of Computing, University of Western
Sydney, Nepean NSW 2747, Australia.
E-mail: yan@st.nepean.uws.edu.au.

Abstract. In the situation calculus states are often distinguished from situations by the assumption that situations are paths in a rooted tree while a state is a particular truth assignment to the fluents. It is then possible that two situations have end points that agree on all fluents, i.e., are the same state, and yet be distinct from the perspective of situations. This has the merit of making inductive proofs simple as it introduces two axioms amounting to enforcing the rooted tree structure that are used as trivial bases for the inductions. In this paper we show that the tree structure is dispensable for induction when the underlying system is deterministic, thus elevating the state perspective to equal status.

Keywords: situation calculus, states, induction, automaton, actions.

1 Introduction

The situation calculus approach to reasoning about actions is so deeply entrenched that other approaches have difficulty in being accepted as viable alternatives. Yet, a recent monograph [6] has shown that this calculus has to be enhanced and refined in several directions in order for it to be practically useful. In one direction the enhancements classify constraints into different kinds, e.g., passive vs. causal. In another direction, time intervals are introduced. The direction that we examine in this paper is one that is intended to model deterministic actions [3,5], and has applications in reasoning about constraints, databases, and situated robotics. The organization of the paper is as follows. In section 2 we show how to reduce the deterministic situation calculus to classical automata theory, thereby clarifying a widespread confusion between situations and states. In section 3 we examine three induction postulates for proving properties of states to compare their strengths. Section 4 shows that by adopting the state-transition perspective we can reproduce the basic results of [5] without appeal to the foundational axioms used in that paper; as a consequence the transition graphs of the systems being modelled are not constrained to be acyclic. We close in section 5 with remarks on the generalizations needed to relax the determinism assumption.

2 Situations vs States

We take as primitive the two types *Sit* and *Act*, the binary predicate *poss* which has signature $Act \times Sit \to Bool$, and the binary operation *do* with signature $Act \times Sit \to Sit$. The *starting situation* s_0 is identifiable with a zero-ary operation (a constant). The intuition behind these assumptions are that *Act* formalizes the set of possible actions in a system, and *Sit* is the set of traces (history) of action sequences on the states of the system. The starting situation s_0 is intuitively the initial state of the system prior to any action. The literature on the situation calculus seems to be ambivalent about the interpretation of situations as states. We see our first task to be one that clears up this confusion.

Systems theory [1] is the appropriate machinery for this clarification. Consider the *term algebra* generated by the operations s_0 and *do*. Two examples of these terms are s_0 and $do(a, (do(b, s_0))$ where a and b are in *Act*. We can identify the type *Sit* with this algebra, and an explicit way to do this via logic programs is to define a predicate *Sit* as follows:

Definition 1. The situations *potentially reachable* from starting situation s_0, denoted by $C(s_0)$, is the least fixed point of the logic program:

$$Sit(s_0) \leftarrow$$

$$Sit(do(A, s)) \leftarrow Sit(s)$$

where the variable A in the second clause is to be bound to action symbols.

From this, $C(s_0)$ is precisely the type *Sit*. Now, system states usually come with *observables*, or in the parlance of the situation calculus, *fluents*. Fluents are state variables, and they correspond to system properties that can change with time or as a result of actions, or for both reasons. Because we restrict attention in this paper to *deterministic* systems, we can assume that Boolean fluents have signature $Sit \to Bool$, and non-Boolean fluents signature $Sit \to Val_i$ where Val_i is the range of values that can be assumed by the i-th fluent. A typical example of a Boolean fluent is *alive-fred* representing the alive/dead status of Fred. A typical example of a deterministic non-Boolean fluent is *color-of-block-A* which may take values in the set $\{blue, red, green\}$. A fluent applied to a situation $do(a_n, (do(a_{n-1}, (\ldots, (do(a_1, s_0) \ldots)$ intuitively yields its observed value(s) at the *end* of the sequence $a_1 \ldots a_n$ of actions. So, if s is a situation $F(s)$ will denote the value of fluent F in (at the end of) s.

A sequence $a_1 \ldots a_n$ of actions can be represented in a natural way by the 'string' $a_1 \cdots a_n$. Indeed, in systems theory such strings constitute *semigroup acts* on the initial situation, and the *concatenation* of two strings $a_1 \cdots a_n$ and $b_1 \cdots b_m$ has the obvious intended meaning of 'apply the sequence $a_1 \ldots a_n$ then apply the sequence $b_1 \ldots b_m$'. Denote the action concatenation operation by $\circ$, and arbitrary sequences of actions by ω (subscripted if necessary). More formally, the set of all strings is the free monoid semigroup generated by the action symbols with $\circ$ as the binary operation and the null string as the identity element. As all situations are presumed to start at s_0, we will identify the situation $do(a_n, (do(a_{n-1}, (\ldots, (do(a_1, s_0) \ldots)$ with the string $a_1 \cdots a_n$, and the starting situation s_0 with the null string. The reason for writing the string 'backwards' is that it will be more natural to use right-composition in the sequel.

Definition 2. Two (situation) terms ω_1, ω_2 in *Sit* are Nerode equivalent, written $\omega_1 N \omega_2$ iff for all fluents F and all action sequences ω, $F(\omega_1 \circ \omega) = F(\omega_2 \circ \omega)$.

It is well-known [1] that the equivalence N is in fact a right-congruence relation respecting the composition operation $\circ$. Moreover, it induces a *minimal state representation* for the system describable in a style familiar from automata theory [1] that is perhaps necessary to recall. An automaton is a quintuple $\langle I, Q, \delta, \lambda, Y \rangle$ where I is the input set, Q is the state set, $\delta : Q \times I \to Q$ is the state-transition function, Y is the output set, and $\lambda : Q \to Y$ is the output function. Among all automata that have the same input-output behavior $F(\omega)$ on action sequences ω, the minimal one is that with the smallest state set. One would not be misled if an automaton is modelled as a directed graph (digraph) in which the nodes are states, the arcs are state transitions labelled by inputs, and each node (state) is associated with symbols that are the outputs for that state. In section 3 we will appeal to this model.

Suppose we now make the following identifications using situations, actions, fluents and the Nerode equivalence:

1. the state set Q is $\{[s] | s \text{ is in } C(s_0)\}$ where $[s]$ is the Nerode equivalence class of situation s;
2. the input set I is the set of actions A;
3. the state transition function is defined by $\delta([s], a) = [s']$ where s' is the situation $s \circ a$;
4. the output set is the cartesian product $\prod Val_i$ of the fluent value sets;
5. the output function is defined by $\lambda(s) = \langle v_1, \ldots, v_k \rangle$ where v_i is the value of fluent F_i in situation s.

The identification in item 3 is well-defined due to the right conguence property of the Nerode equivalence. The following is a consequence of a well-known result in systems theory [1].

Theorem 3. *The identification above defines a minimal automaton whose input-output behavior coincides with the system described by situations, actions and fluents.*

The *potentially reachable* states should be distinguished from the *actually reachable* by introducing "tests" on the applicability of actions a in situations

s via the *poss* predicate. Informally, *poss* is a guard that blocks inappropriate actions because of pre-condition failure — read "action a is possible in state s" for $poss(a, s)$. With this refinement, the state transitions are restricted to those defined as follows.

Abbreviation:(Transitions)

$$trans(s, a, s') \equiv poss(a, s) \wedge do(a, s) = s'$$

Definition 4.

$$s_1 <^0 s_2 \equiv s_1 = s_2$$

$$s_1 <^1 s_2 \equiv \exists A \; trans(s_1, A, s_2)$$

$$s_1 <^{n+1} s_2 \equiv \exists s_3 \; (s_1 <^1 s_3 \wedge s_3 <^n s_2)$$

$$s_1 < s_2 \equiv \exists n \; s_1 <^n s_2$$

$$s_1 \leq s_2 \equiv s_1 = s_2 \vee s_1 < s_2$$

$$s_1 \leq^n s_2 \equiv s_1 = s_2 \vee s_1 <^n s_2$$

The following observations are consequences of these definitions. $<$ is the transitive closure of the trans relation, and $\leq$ is its reflexive transitive closure. Also, for $m + n = k$, if $s_1 <^m s_3$ and $s_3 <^n s_2$ then $s_1 <^k s_3$. A special case of this using compositional notation is $<^{n+1} = <^n \circ <^1 = <^1 \circ <^n$.

We note that while the $<^n$ relation is first-order definable for any particular instance of n, there is no *uniform* first-order formula that can define it in which n is a variable. The Appendix reviews the well-known argument for this. Consequently, its transitive closure $<$ is also not first-order definable. In logic programming, the way to meet this difficulty is to resort to the second-order notion of *fixed points* [4] which has a natural operational (proof-theoretic) interpretation. Indeed an alternative way to define $<$ exploiting fixed points is the following:

Definition 5. The transitive closure of the *trans* relation is $<$, which is the least fixed point of the logic program:

$$s_1 < s_2 \leftarrow trans(s_1, A, s_2)$$

$$s_1 < s_2 \leftarrow s_1 < s_3 \wedge trans(s_3, A, s_2)$$

where the variable A is to be bound to action symbols.

Corollary 6. $s_1 \leq s_2$ iff either $s_1 = s_2$ or there is a finite chain $trans(s_1, a_1, t_1), \ldots,$ $trans(t_{n-1}, a_n, s_2)$.

3 Three Induction Postulates

In [5] Reiter inroduced an induction postulate (called R-induction below) to mirror the usual inductive postulate on numbers (called N-induction below). He showed that his postulate can be used with two foundational axioms (see section 4) to establish inductive properties of states. In this section we examine these induction postulates and also introduce another one that is a relativized version of R-induction.

R-Induction (Reiter induction)

$$\forall P\{[P(s_0) \wedge \forall(a, s)][(P(s) \to P(do(a, s)))] \to \forall s P(s)\}$$

T-Induction (Transition induction)

$$\forall P\{[P(s_1) \wedge \forall(a, s)][(P(s) \wedge trans(s, a, s') \to P(s'))]$$

$$\to \forall s(s_1 \leq s \to P(s))\}$$

N-Induction (Numeric induction)

$$\{\phi(0) \wedge (\phi(N) \to \phi(N + 1))\} \to \forall N \phi(N)$$

It is important to specify what is admissible for P and ϕ in these postulates. Reiter's work [5] allows P to be strong enough to eliminate non-standard models. In this spirit, ϕ in schema N can denote any subset of the natural numbers, and not necessarily just the first-order expressible ones. We will therefore assume this level of generality, but the remarks that follow theorem 7 should be noted.

Theorem 7. *N-Induction implies T-induction.*

Proof: In schema N let $\phi(n)$ be the subset of numbers satisfying $\forall s[s_1 \leq^n s \supset P(s)]$. Then $\phi(0)$ is equivalent to $P(s_1)$, which is the basis case for schema T. The antecedent of the inductive hypothesis of schema N is $\forall s[s_1 \leq^n s \supset P(s)]$. Its conclusion is $\forall s'[s_1 \leq^{n+1} s' \supset P(s')]$, which turns out to follow from the inductive step of schema T. To see this, we use the observations following definition 4 to decompose its antecedent $s_1 \leq^{n+1} s'$ into its equivalent $s_1 \leq^n s_2 \wedge s_2 \leq^1 s'$, and then note that by the inductive hypothesis of N the first conjunct implies $P(s_2)$, and therefore the conjunction implies $P(s_2) \wedge s_2 \leq^1 s'$. By the inductive hypotheis of schema T, this in turn implies $P(s')$. Thus the inductive step of N is established, and its conclusion $\forall n\{\forall s[s_1 \leq^n s \supset P(s)]\}$ follows. By definition 4 this is equivalent to the conclusion of schema T.

In this proof we did not say that $\phi(n)$ is a *formula* defining $\forall s[s_1 \leq^n s \supset P(s)]$ for the simple reason that there may be no such formula even when P is an expressible predicate. The intuitive reason for this is that any such formula would be one that has parameters including s_1 and n, the second of which cannot be a variable (see the Appendix for details).

R-induction appears to be stronger than T-induction, and this is indeed so for at least the following reason.

Theorem 8. *The R-schema implies that the least fixed point $C(s_0)$ in definition 1 are all the situations that exist.*

Proof: To see this, let $P(s)$ denote the set $C(s_0)$. Then certainly $P(s_0)$ holds by the first clause of definition 1. That $(P(s) \to P(do(a, s))$ also holds is a consequence of the second clause. Hence from schema R, every situation is in $C(s_0)$.

Schema R therefore restricts transition digraphs to have only one component. When this is so, schema T is in fact equivalent to schema R, which we record as the next theorem.

Theorem 9. *If all situations are reachable from one situation s_0, then R is a special case of T with $s_1 = s_0$ and $trans(s, a, s') \equiv true \wedge do(a, s) = s'$.*

It is instructive to see what kinds of models are admitted by schema T in terms of transition digraphs. Consider a predicate P in the in the schema. Let G be such a digraph. Write $P(v)$ $(\neg P(v))$ if P is true (false) in state (vertex) v. Say that a path is *P-stable from* v if for every vertex u such that $v \leq u$, it is the case that $P(u)$. A path is P-stable if it is so from some vertex v. The following is immediate.

Theorem 10. *Every digraph of schema T has only P-stable paths.*

Corollary 11. *If a digraph of schema T has a cycle L, then either P is false in every vertex in L, or true in every vertex in it (i.e, no P "swithches" are possible).*

Corollary 12. *In any linear (acyclic) path a digraph of schema T, these are the only possibilities: (i) P is true at all vertices (ii) P is false at all vertices, or (iii) P is false up to vertex v, and then true beyond it.*

The principal use of theorem 10 and its corollaries is in establishing system constraints as indicated at the end of section 4. In that section we will use either schema T or N in re-establishing the main results proved by Reiter [5] using schema R. In using schema N, we will be reasoning about the number n in the relation $<^n$, which will be seen to be equivalent to reasoning about the number of invocations of the logic program rules assumed in the propositions or theorems. As this assumes the least fixed point semantics for such programs it is not first-order; but on the other hand it is computable, i.e., the $<$ relation is recursively enumerable and indeed recursive when the reachable set is finite.

4   Consequences of Induction

In [5] Reiter established a number of fundamental results using schema R and two *foundational axioms*:

$$\forall s(\neg s < S_0) \tag{1}$$

$$\forall a, s, s'(s < do(a, s') \equiv poss(a, s') \land s \le s' \tag{2}$$

These have the respective effects of preventing looping back to the initial state s_0, and preventing two states from transiting to the same next state. Presumably these are desired in the interpretation of states as *situations* — which are really paths in a rooted tree (with S_0 as root). If states are more traditionally interpreted in accordance with systems theory [1], the foundational axioms will not hold. The question then is how many of the fundamental results of Reiter's can be established using the T (or N) schemas without appeal to the foundational axioms. The main purpose of this paper is to show that nothing is lost.

In order to make comparisons and reference easy, we will cite the propositions in [5] that we will re-establish in the form "R-proposition (R-theorem) X.Y" where X.Y is the proposition (theorem) number as it appears in [5]. We will take some liberties with the re-statement of these propositions (theorems) using our terminology and notation, and rely on the reader to verify the faithfulnes of the translation.

Proposition 13. *(R-proposition 3.1) The statement $s < s'$ is equivalent to the assertion that for all predicates P the atom $P(s, s')$ is a logical consequence of the logic program*

$$P(s_1, s_2) \leftarrow s_1 <^1 s_2$$

$$P(s_1, s_3) \leftarrow P(s_1, s_2) \land s_2 <^1 s_3$$

Proof: In the backward direction, it is similar to that given by Reiter, i.e., let P be $<$, and we use definition 4. In the forward direction we use N-induction with induction variable n in $s <^n s'$. The base case of $n = 1$ is guaranteed by the first clause of the program. For the inductive step if $s <^{n+1} s'$, then by definition 4 for some s'', $s <^n s''$ and $s'' <^1 s'$, so by the induction hypothesis $P(s, s'')$ is a logical consequence of the program. Then by the second clause, $P(s, s')$ is also a logical consequence of it.

Theorem 14. *(R-theorem 3.2) $\forall W\{W(s_0) \land \forall a, s[s_0 \le s \land trans(s, a, s') \land W(s) \rightarrow W(s')] \rightarrow \forall s[s_0 \le s \rightarrow W(s)]\}$*

Proof: This is vitually a transcription of the T-schema with the substitution of $W(s) \land s_0 \le s$ for $P(s)$ in T. The properties of $\le$ in definition 4 are essential.

Theorem 15. *(R-theorem 3.3) If $s_0 \le s \le s'$ then for any predicate R, $R(s, s')$ is a logical consequence of the logic program:*

$$R(s_0, s_0) \leftarrow$$

$$R(s', s') \leftarrow s_0 \le s \land R(s, s) \land s <^1 s'$$

$$R(s, s'') \leftarrow s_0 \le s \land s \le s' \land R(s, s') \land s' <^1 s''$$

Proof: We use course-of values N-induction on the induction variable n in $s_0 \leq^m s \leq^k s'$, where $m + k = n$. For $n = 0$, this is simply s_0, of which the first gives $R(s_0, s_0)$ as a logical consequence. For the inductive step, we assume that for all s, s' $R(s, s')$ is a logical consequence of the program whenever $s_0 \leq^m s \leq^k s'$ and $m + k < n$. Then suppose $s_0 \leq^m s \leq^k s'$ and $m + k = n$. There are several cases to consider: (i) $m = 0$ (ii) $k = 0$ (iii) $m \geq 1$ and $k \geq 1$.

Case (i): This is when $s_0 = s$ and therefore $R(s, s')$ is $R(s_0, s')$, with $s = s_0 < s'$. We now require a sub-induction to show that if $s_0 \leq t$ for any t, $R(s_0, t)$ is a logical consequence of the program. But this is immediate from the transitivity of $\leq$, and the first and third clauses of the program.

Case (ii): This is the case when $s_0 \leq s = s'$, so we need to show that when $s_0 \leq s'$, $R(s', s')$ is a logical consequence of the program. But again a sub-induction using the first two clauses immediately yields this.

Case (iii): Here we have $s_0 \leq^m s \leq^k s'$ and $m + k = n$, with $m \neq 0$ and $k \neq 0$. Therefore there is s'' such that $s_0 \leq^m s \leq^{k-1} s'' \leq^1 s'$ (where possibly $s = s''$). Since $m + k - 1 < n$, the induction hypothesis says that $R(s, s'')$ is a logical consequence of the program, and then by $s'' \leq^1 s'$ and the third clause, $R(s, s')$ is also its logical consequence.

This concludes our main aim, which is that there is a framework for proving inductive properties of states without the restriction of the Reiter foundational axioms, thus freeing the digraph of state transitions to have loops and merges. All of Reiter's example applications using his induction axiom are therefore valid using our approach without the restriction. In an extended version of this paper we will show how other inductive properties of states can be established by appeal to schema T, particularly those which have to do with state constraints derivable from action invariants.

5   Conclusion

We have shown that classical automata theory coupled with logic program semantics suffices to establish the inductive properties of states without the foundational axioms of situation calculus. However, while deterministic systems abound in practice, the logic of actions has to address non-determinism in order to account for commonsense inferences when information is incomplete. The reduction of situations to states for non-deterministic systems is not simple, so the results in this paper will not carry over to such systems without major modifications. We hope to report progress on this problem soon.

References

1. Arbib, M.A., "Automata theory: the rapprochement with control theory" (Chapter 6, pp 163-184), and "Basic notions of automata and semigroups" (Chapter 7, pp 185-20), in *Topics in Mathematical Systems Theory*, ed. R.E.Kalman, P.L.Falb, and M.A.Arbib, McGraw-Hill, 1969.

2. Boolos, G. and Jeffrey, R. "Computability and Logic", Cambridge University Press, 1989.
3. Baral, C., Gelfond, M. and Provetti, A., "Representing Actions: Laws, Observations, and Hypotheses", To appear in the Journal of Logic Programming, 1997.
4. Lloyd, J., "Foundations of Logic Programming", Springer-Verlag, 1984.
5. Reiter, R., "Proving Properties of States in the Situation Calculus", *Artificial Intelligence*, 64 (1993), 337-351.
6. Shananhan, M., "Solving the Frame Problem", book manuscript, 1996.

Appendix

It is well known [2] that there is no sound and complete finite axiomatization of arithmetic, the usual proof being the existence of a non-standard denumerable model in which there is one point that is not reachable from zero by finitely many applications of the successor function. From this it easily follows that there is no first-order formula $\psi(x,y)$ that denotes the relation *for some* n $x <^n y$. For, if $\psi(x,y)$ is first-order, in the use of schema N as a *first-order* induction schema we let $\phi(N)$ be $\psi(0,N)$, and interpret $<^1$ as the successor function, and $<^0$ as the identity. Then it will follow from schema N that $\forall N \psi(0,N)$, which enforces the standard model. Hence, parametrising the path length n in $<^n$ in a predicate makes the predicate second-order.

Describing Plan Recognition as Nonmonotonic Reasoning and Belief Revision

Paweł Jachowicz and Randy Goebel

Department of Computing Science
University of Alberta
Edmonton, Alberta, Canada
{pavel,goebel}@cs.ualberta.ca

Abstract. We provide a characterization of plan recognition in terms of a general framework of belief revision and non-monotonic reasoning. We adopt a generalization of classical belief revision to describe a competence model of plan recognition which supports dynamic change to all aspects of a plan recognition knowledge base, including background knowledge, action descriptions and their relationship to named plans, and accumulating sets of observations on agent actions.

Our plan recognition model exploits the underlying belief revision model to assimilate observations, and answer queries about an agent's intended plans and actions. Supporting belief states are determined by observed actions and non-monotonic assumptions consistent with background knowledge and action descriptions.

Our intent is to demonstrate the connections between a general plan recognition model and important concepts of belief revision and nonmonotonic reasoning, to help establish a basis for improving the specification and development of specialized plan recognition systems.

1 Introduction

Knowing the plan an agent is pursuing is important for several reasons. It allows us to predict actions the agent might take in the future, and it allows us to aid or hamper the agent by suggesting or even taking action alternatives.

In its simplest conception, a plan explains a sequence of actions if they comprise the plan. To recognize an observed set of actions as a plan first requires that one establish a representation of plans as a named or similarly identified set or sequence of actions. With this plan representation and given a set of observed actions, a plan recognition system constructs the set of possible plans which explain the specified actions [7].

Like all recognition tasks, the object to be recognized has to be described in terms of some number of components. Sentences are sequences of words, programs are sequences of instructions, and plans might simply be conceived as named sequences of actions. The concept of "sequence" is typically too simple however, and can be elaborated along at least two dimensions. First, a plan of any practical complexity will likely include alternative actions to accomplish the same subgoals (which turns any plan description into a tree or lattice). Second, any set of actions to accomplish any particular plan will typically have optional actions which serve only to embellish the goal; so there will be necessary and contingent actions for any practical plan.

Within this kind of situation, a plan recognition system must be able to use incomplete information to provide the required flexibility. A general plan recognition system must be able to perpetually accept revised descriptions of a world in which actions take place, including changes to the observed relationships amongst actions and plans. To anticipate the behaviour of agents acting in a dynamic observable world, the plan recognition system must be able to hypothesize consistent plans. Within this kind of framework, it is unsurprising that non-monotonic reasoning and belief revision will provide a basis for reasoning in this kind of incomplete information context.

At least four different general plan recognition strategies exist in literature: parsing [15], inference under uncertainty [2], plausible inference [1] and circumscribing a hierarchical representation of plans using deduction [7].

The method proposed here uses ideas related to at least the last three of these methods, developed within a framework for managing and reasoning about beliefs. We use the Ghose-Goebel belief change model to maintain a dynamic set of assertions that represent actions and relationships amongst actions and plans. This method explicitly supports reasoning with incomplete knowledge and revision of the belief base with newly observed facts. Observed actions are assimilated within the belief revision system and, together with current beliefs about actions and their affects, constrain the plans that can be recognized. Additionally, the Ghose-Goebel reasoning framework supports the maintenance of multiple mutually inconsistent states of the world, providing a basis to assume alternative hypothetical completions of plans.

2 What Must Plan Recognition Do?

To help make our intuition clear, and as a basis for elaborating specific details, we begin by assuming that any plan recognition system has to be able to both accept observations about a changing world, and make predictions about what could plausibly take place in that world. To help make these ideas concrete, we first assume that we could use a goal-directed logic programming reasoning system like Prolog to define the top level functionality of a generic belief revision system.

This generic system would have to interpret the following relations:

- *observe(Action, Situation)* We can assert that a particular action has been observed in a particular situation.
- *predict(Action, Situation)* We can query the system to determine if it is reasonable to expect a certain action in a particular situation.

Note that the idea of being able to predict the next anticipated action can be elaborated to the more familiar plan recognition relation as follows: if we assume that plan recognition takes place in the context of a plan library consisting of named sequences of actions, e.g.,

$$plan(planName, [a_1, a_2, ..., a_n]) \qquad (1)$$

then we can generalize $predict(Action, Situation)$ to the more familiar output of conventional plan recognition systems, namely

$$predictPlan(Plan, Situation) \qquad (2)$$

We expect our nonmonotonic reasoning system to assume consistent hypotheses based on observations, and to provide us with the names of plans that could plausibly be considered as those intended by an agent that had carried out some number of the actions in the given situation.

Here we want the underlying belief revision system to process observations as expansions, contractions or revisions, and then be able to produce predictions based on existing plan libraries. The predictions could be in the form of guessing what action might be next attempted by an observable agent, or in the form of a named plan, whose actions somehow consistently subsume those already observed.

To be a little more specific, we can begin with the following definitions:

- $observedAction(Action, Situation)$. True when Action has been observed in Situation, e.g., $observedAction(getGun, s_1)$.
- $observedFluent(Fluent, Situation)$. True when Fluent has been observed in Situation, e.g., $observedFluent(isInBank, s_3)$.
- $predictAction(Action, Situation)$. True if a belief state consistent with Situation and Action is possible in that state. e.g., $Action = goToBank$, $Situation = result(getGun, s_2)$
- $predictPlan(Plan, Situation)$. True if the plan library contains a definition of $Plan$ in a form which associates Plan with a list of actions which comprise it: $plan(Plan, [a_0, a_1, \ldots, a_n])$. Furthermore, the preconditions or consequences of actions comprising the plan but not yet observed must hold or be assumable.

To explore the ideas of how non-monotonic reasoning plays a role in plan recognition, note that if the preconditions or consequences of unobserved actions are at least assumable, the the plans associated with those actions are plausible.

$$predictPlan(Plan, Situation) \Leftarrow \qquad (3)$$
$$(plan(Plan, [a_0, a_1, \ldots, a_i, a_{i+1}, \ldots, a_n])),$$
$$arePossibleOrAssumable([a_0, a_1, \ldots, a_i, a_{i+1}, \ldots, a_n],$$
$$Situation)$$

If the $actions$ $a_1, \ldots, a_i$ have been observed, it may be nonmonotonically feasible to assume that $Plan$ is a plan if it can be verified that the actions $a_{i+1}, \ldots, a_n$ may be taken from $Situation$, or that the consequences of required but unobserved actions are themselves assumable. As long as no information contradicts such assumptions for actions $a_{i+1}, \ldots, a_n$, $Plan$ is plausible. This is analogous to saying that the enabling conditions and effects are not required to hold or be observed, but only to be possible. This is true if nothing would make these actions impossible [10].

3 Motivation for Plan Recognition Competence Based on Belief Revision and Nonmonotonic Reasoning

Current techniques used for solving the plan recognition problem deal with static knowledge bases, where a plan library already exists and the relationships amongst its comprising actions are known. In such systems, certain heuristics are applied to recognize viable plans. Carberry's focusing heuristic [1] hypothesizes a set of viable plans, selects the "best" one and incorporates it into the context model. Kautz [7] presents yet another heuristic used for selecting plans amongst multiple plausible plans.

The Ghose-Goebel belief revision framework allows the maintenance of all feasible plans which are recognizable, based on given observations. Eventually, and in any practical situation, such preferences for particular plans will be captured as epistemic entrenchment conditions [11]. We claim it is unnecessary and in fact dangerous to make a premature commitment to some plausible plan, when in fact all the possible plans ought to be presented to reflect the competence of a plan recognition system. This is consistent with the belief revision principle of informational economy which states that belief states should change in such a way as to maintain the maximal amount of information from state to state [3].

By using the techniques developed in belief revision, we explicitly allow for our knowledge base to consist of incomplete knowledge. We incorporate new observations into our knowledge base using the belief revision expansion, revision and contraction operators [3, 4, 12]. Our plan library is therefore dynamic. This mimics a more natural temporal varying behaviour of beliefs: in every reasonable possible world changes occur. As observations are made, the plausibly inferred plans are reflected in incrementally determined belief states.

4 Notation

Before discussing further details, we informally describe some of the key components of our chosen representation. We use a version of situation calculus syntax based roughly on work by Lifschitz [9] and Kowalski [8].

We make use of three predicates: *holds, observed* and *goal*. The predicate *holds* allows us to describe each state in terms of fluents which are claimed to be true in a state.

A *knowledge base* or *plan library* is a collection of axioms. These axioms describe actions, action effects, and relationships amongst fluents, actions, and plans. A *belief state* is a situation represented by constant symbols, e.g., s_0 or by composite terms $result(a, s_0)$ when a denotes an action. A *fluent* is a truth function defined on a state: $holds(hasGun(Fred), s_0)$ is a fluent denoting the fact that Fred has a gun in state s_0, while $\neg holds(isInBank(Fred), s_2)$

is a fluent denoting the fact that in state s_2 Fred is not in the bank. An *action* is an *n*-ary function from states to states, e.g., as in the agent named "Fred" in the action *getGun*, here asserted to have taken place in state s_1: $holds(hasGun(Fred), result(getGun(Fred), s_1))$. The simplest form of a *plan* is a sequence of actions leading from some state to some subsequent state. Actions are contained in a plan if a plan explains them: e.g., $goal(toHunt, s_0) \leftarrow holds(getGun(Fred), s_0)$; this simple one action plan "to hunt" is one explanation for the the "get a gun" action [9].

The *holds* relation also allows us to describe relations amongst actions and fluents by specifying state axioms, effect axioms and frame axioms. See examples 7, 8 and 9.

The *observed* fluent serves the purpose of distinguishing facts which we have not "seen" an agent perform from facts which we have already included into our knowledge base. See example 10.

Finally, the predicate *goal* allows us to define a relationship between plan names and a situation, and can be viewed as a plan recognition-specific instance of a non-monotonic derivability relation like that used, for example, in hypothetical reasoning systems like Theorist [13, 14]. Example 11 expresses the relation that it is plausible that one has the goal *robBank*, in the situation resulting from the actions of getting a gun and going to a bank.

5   Integrating Plan Recognition with Belief Revision

5.1   The Ghose-Goebel Reasoning Model

Ghose and Goebel [5] developed a framework for the dynamics of belief change based on the idea that all observations (including mutually contradictory observations) are retained in a compact representation of multiple mutually inconsistent belief sets based on a nonmonotonic representation system.

Among other properties, this model has the property that all new beliefs are retained and simply treated as constraints on a possibly infinite set of consistent belief states. In terms of support for plan recognition, the intuition is that accumulating observations about actions are treated as constraints on possible belief states.

Unlike conventional belief revision systems, where each new observation forces a commitment to one new unique belief state, the model we adopt for plan recognition maintains multiple consistent belief states constrained by accumulating observations (see Figure 1).

This formalization of belief is guided by the following observations:

- A belief state should be represented not as a single theory, but as a collection of theories, each one representative of a possible outcome of a belief revision operation. Thus $K = \{Th1, Th2, \ldots\}$.
- *Minimal change* should act as the guiding principle for belief revision. All possible outcomes of a belief revision operation should therefore be retained,

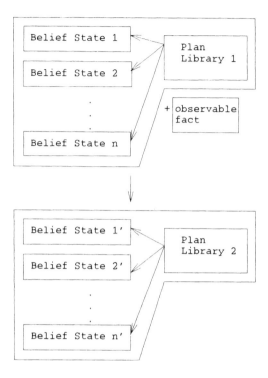

Fig. 1. Belief State Transformation

thus eliminating the possibility of discarding possibly valuable beliefs. This would ensure minimal change.

– A record of all revisions and contractions ought to be kept in order to maintain the results of some previous belief change operation. This allows information to persist unless contrary evidence is exists.

See [4, 5] for details.

5.2 Belief Revision Operations

Belief revision is the process of changing a belief state according to some new information. As mentioned previously, there exist three operators which may be used to deal with changing beliefs in a belief state.

Expansion (equation 4) deals with adding a new observation to the knowledge base. This might be a new action, some new relationships between actions and their effects, or even a new plan. The idea lies in appending the knowledge base with new information which does not result in any portion of the knowledge base becoming inconsistent.

If a theory K is expanded by a fact x, commonly written K_x^+, then there is formed a union between the consequences of K and the new fact x.

$$Cn(K)_x^+ = Cn(Cn(K) \cup \{x\}) = Cn(K \cup \{x\}) \tag{4}$$

Contraction (equation 5) deals with removing a fact x from theory K in such a way as to eliminate from K the possibility of deriving x. Therefore if x is accepted in K_x^-, it ought also be accepted in the intersection of K and K_x^*. This is known as the *Harper identity* and defines contraction in terms of revision. The idea lies in trying to eliminate from the knowledge base some fact which we see being invalidated through observation of the agent. If no evidence points towards the removal of a fact after its addition to a theory, such a fact ought not to be abandoned.

$$Cn(K)_x^- = Cn(Cn(K) \cap Cn(K_x^*)) \tag{5}$$

Revision (equation 6) deals with adding a new fact x to a theory K as long as the new theory K_x^* is consistent and closed under logical consequence [12]. It should be noted that minimal changes ought to be made to the theory which is being revised, in order to preserve the postulate of informational economy. The *Levi identity* may be employed to define revision in terms of contraction and expansion. It is important to keep in mind that revision will most likely result in multiple logical theories within our knowledge base, because there will most likely be multiple ways of contracting x.

$$Cn(K)_x^* = Cn((K_{\neg x}^-) \cup \{x\}) \tag{6}$$

6 Representing Plans and Actions

To provide a concrete example, we provide further details based, again, on the style of Kowalski. Under that scheme, state description axioms are used to describe the status of all fluents of a state. This information is used to determine which actions are possible in a state. The axioms here are roughly based on the problem discussed by Hanks and McDermott [6]. In this case, three fluents are true: Fred is in the bank, has a gun, and the gun is loaded. This state of affairs is particular to state s_0.

$$holds(isInBank(Fred), s_0) \tag{7}$$
$$holds(hasGun(Fred), s_0)$$
$$holds(isLoaded, s_0)$$

Effect axioms consist of action preconditions and postconditions. It is possible that certain preconditions and postconditions of actions be left unstated or will change from state to state based on observations of the agent's behaviour. Here described are the actions *getGun*, *goToBank* and *ioadGun*.

$$\neg holds(hasGun(X), S) \Rightarrow \tag{8}$$
$$holds(hasGun(X), result(getGun(X), S))$$
$$\neg holds(isInBank(X), S) \Rightarrow$$
$$holds(isInBank(X), result(goToBank(X), S))$$
$$\neg holds(isLoaded, S) \Rightarrow$$
$$holds(isLoaded, result(loadGun, S))$$

Frame axioms specify fluents which remain unchanged from state to state. The action *getGun* does not influence the fluents *isInBank* and *isLoaded*. Frame relationships not explicitly stated can be dealt with by using non-monotonic assumptions [5].

$$holds(isInBank(X), S) \wedge holds(isLoaded, S) \Rightarrow$$
$$holds(isInBank(X), result(getGun(X), S)) \wedge$$
$$holds(isLoaded, result(getGun(X), S)) \tag{9}$$

7 Plan Recognition System Behaviour as Belief Revision

The most basic operation which the plan library will undergo is *Expansion* or the addition of some new piece of information to the plan library. Before the consequences of *Expansion* can be analyzed, it is necessary to define the type of new information which could be appended to the plan library.

Based on the notation of section 4 the plan library may be expanded with the following pieces of information:

- A new *Description Axiom*. This is a fluent which is consistent with all other fluents, yet provides new information to the plan library.
- A new *State Axiom*. This is an axiom which defines new universally true knowledge pertaining to each state of the world.
- A new *Effect Axiom*. This is also an axiom which defines the properties of actions. New preconditions or postconditions are added which change the behaviour of actions.
- A new *Frame Axiom*. This axiom specifies unchanging fluents over an action.
- A New Plan. This is a new named sequence of allowable actions.

To continue our example, we assume an initial plan library (including the axioms specified in section 6) to demonstrate an operator of belief revision. To understand the intricacies of *Expansion*, the plan library must contain a set of fluents, axioms and plans which will be appended with each of the above mentioned new types of information.

The following example shows the relationships between what is observed in one state and what holds in the next state.

$$holds(isInBank(Fred), s_1) \Leftarrow$$
$$observedFluent(isInBank(Fred), s_0) \wedge$$
$$s_0 \leq s_1 \tag{10}$$

Revision and contraction are accomplished similarly, except that it is up to the belief revision system to maintain all information which has been revised, without unnecessarily discarding any information (see [5]).

8   Plan Recognition

One way a plan is fulfilled is if all of the postconditions of actions which comprise the plan have been fulfilled. To recognize possible plans in any given state, the postconditions of previously observed actions must be examined. These are expressed in terms of fluents which describe any given state. In our case, the set of recognized plans will include all the plans whose comprising actions' postconditions are at least partially fulfilled, as our nonmonotonic interpretation of the goal predicate supports the "completion" of plans by consistent assumption.

As an example, consider the plan library consisting of the fluents in example 7 and effect axioms in example 8. The three fluents are postconditions of the actions: goToBank, getGun and loadGun as shown by the effect axioms.

Also given the following three plans: robBank, toHunt, toSwim; it is possible to recognize some of these plans based on the state description axioms provided.

$$goal(robBank, result(goToBank(X), \tag{11}$$
$$result(getGun(X), s_0)))$$
$$goal(toHunt, result(goToForest(X),$$
$$result(getGun(X), s_0)))$$
$$goal(toSwim, result(goToPool(X), s_0))$$

The state description axiom $holds(isLoaded, s_0)$ does not play any role in recognizing plans, since it is not a postcondition of any actions which comprise the three plans. The axiom $holds(hasGun(X), s_0)$ is the postcondition of the action $getGun$ which is a part of two plans. The plans $robBank$ and $toHunt$ must therefore be recognized since there exists evidence which supports both of them. Furthermore, the axiom $holds(isInBank(Fred), s_0)$ is a postcondition of the action $goToBank$, which gives even more evidence for recognizing the plan $robBank$.

Given this information, it is possible to recognize two of the three plans, because evidence exists which supports these two plans. The plan $robBank$ has most evidence (two postconditions are satisfied), the plan $goHunt$ has only one postcondition satisfied. Both plans should however be recognized because evidence supporting both of them is present. Some form of epistemic entrenchment [11] would provide the basis for ranking plausible plans.

9 Conclusion and Future Work

This sketch of plan recognition as belief revision only begins the investigation of various classes of specific plan recognition systems. These systems arise from making assumptions about what can be assumed. For example, can one assume only a subset of actions (like abducibles in [13])?

At least a partial implementation for examining details of simple problems will help reveal further interesting assumptions that can be used to build a classification of plan recognition.

References

1. S. Carberry. Modelling the user's plans and goals. *Computational Linguistics*, 14:23–27, 1988.
2. E. Charniak and R. Goldman. A bayesian model of plan recognition. *Artficial Intelligence*, 64:53–79, 1993.
3. P. Gärdenfors. Belief revision: An introduction. In *Belief Revision*, pages 1–28. Cambridge University Press, 1992.
4. A. Ghose. *Practical Belief Change*. PhD thesis, University of Alberta, Department of Computing Science, 1995.
5. A. Ghose, P. Hadjinian, A. Sattar, J. You, and R. Goebel. Iterated belief change: a preliminary report. In *Proceedings of the Sixth Australian Joint Conference on Artificial Intelligence*, pages 39–44, Melbourne, Australia, November 17–19 1993.
6. S. Hanks and D. McDermott. Default reasoning, nonmonotonic logics and the frame problem. In *Proceedings of AAAI-86*, pages 328–333, 1986.
7. H. Kautz. *A Formal Theory of Plan Recognition*. PhD thesis, University of Rochester, Department of Computer Science, 1987.
8. R. Kowalski. *Logic for Problem Solving*. Elsevier North Holland, Inc., 1979.
9. V. Lifschitz. Formal theories of action. In *Proceedings of the Tenth International Joint Conference on Artificial Intelligence*, volume 2, pages 966–972, 1987.
10. D. Lin and R. Goebel. A message passing algorithm for plan recognition. In *Proceedings of the Twelfth International Joint Conference on Artificial Intelligence*, pages 280–285, 1991.
11. A. Nayak, N. Foo, M. Pagnucco, and A. Sattar. Entrenchment kinematics 101. In *Proceedings of the 7th Australian Joint Conference on Artificial Intelligence*, pages 157–164, 1994.
12. B. Nebel. *Reasoning and Revision in Hybrid Representation Systems*. Springer-Verlag, first edition, 1990.
13. D. Poole. A logical framework for default reasoning. *Artfical Intelligence*, 36(1):27–47, 1988.
14. D. Poole, R. Goebel, and R. Aleliunas. Theorist: A logical reasoning system for defaults and diagnosis. In N.J. Cercone and G. McCalla, editors, *The Knowledge Frontier: Essays in the Representation of Knowledge*, pages 331–352. Springer Verlag, New York, 1987.
15. M. Villain. Getting serious about parsing plans: A grammatical analysis of plan recognition. In *Proceedings of the Eighth National Conference on Artificial Intelligence*, pages 190–197, 1990.

Specification Morphisms for Nonmonotonic Knowledge Systems

C K MacNish[1] and Grigoris Antoniou[2]

[1] Department of Computer Science, University of Western Australia,
Nedlands, WA 6907, Australia
`kym@cs.uwa.edu.au`
[2] School of Computing & Information Technology, Griffith University
QLD 4111, Australia
`ga@cit.gu.edu.au`

Abstract. Conservative extensions of (classical) logical theories play an important role in software engineering, because they provide a formal basis for program refinement and guarantee the integrity and transparency of modules and objects. Similarly specification morphisms play a central role for information hiding and combining modules. Surprisingly, while the use of nonmonotonic theories for describing knowledge systems which may contain incomplete or uncertain data has been advocated for some time now, the above concepts have yet to be applied in this area.

The aim of this work is to develop and apply analogues of these concepts in a nonmonotonic context. This paper builds on previous results, which focus on conservative extensions, extending the ideas to the more general case of specification morphisms.

1 Introduction

Formal specification of software and the software development (or refinement) process is vital in improving the integrity and reliability of software in general, and knowledge representation systems in particular. An important aspect of this methodology is its view of what it means for one specification S' to be a refinement of another S. One interpretation of this relationship, for example, is that S' is an implementation of S, so S' "has more detail" than S. Turski and Maibaum [8] advocate the idea that this be modelled in two steps: (i) regard S and S' as logical theories, and (ii) let S' be a *conservative extension* of S. The latter means (assuming closure of S and S') that every formula in S' that has only terms in the language of S is actually included in S.

In knowledge representation the analogue of a specification in the above sense is the knowledge base. While knowledge bases have traditionally been represented by sets of logical formulae, modern defeasible knowledge bases also include a means of specifying defaults for incomplete knowledge, along with a nonmonotonic consequence relation. This makes the task of analysing refinement more complex (and more interesting). It is the interplay of refinements and nonmonotonicity that is investigated by this body of work. Our hope is that an understanding of this interplay will yield dividends for knowledge system design similar to those that accrued for software engineering.

In previous work [1] we have developed conservative expansion[1] concepts corresponding to the three main interpretations of default logics — the *sceptical approach* (the intersection of all extensions), the *credulous approach* (the union of all extensions), and the *choice approach* (specific extensions) — and investigated the interrelations between them. Interestingly, they uncover a property that distinguishes Reiter's default logic from some important variants, namely Justified Default Logic [4], Constrained Default Logic [2] and Rational Default Logic [6].

In this paper we generalize these concepts and results by turning to *specification morphisms*. Such morphisms play a central role in the interplay of different modules, and in stepwise refinement. Their idea is to map desired functions or predicates to functions or predicates that have already been implemented. The important feature is that the properties of the already available operations are strong enough to derive the desired properties of the new operations; this makes clear the close relationship to the idea of conservative extensions — in fact conservative extensions are a special case of specification morphisms.

Before presenting our development of specification morphisms for nonmonotonic systems in Section 3, we briefly cover some requisite technical definitions. Section 4 concludes the paper with a summary of the results.

2 Technical Preliminaries

We assume that the reader is familiar with the basics of classical logic. In this paper we restrict our attention to propositional nonmonotonic theories, and hence propositional classical theories. We denote the deductive closure of a set of formulae S by $Th(S)$ and the conjunction of (a finite set) S by $\bigwedge S$.

A *signature* Σ is a set of atoms. For signatures Σ and Σ' with $\Sigma \subseteq \Sigma'$, and a set of Σ'-formulae T', the *restriction* of T' wrt Σ is the set of Σ-formulae in T', and is denoted by T'/Σ. We will also consider deductive closures with respect to different signatures. This is discussed in more detail in Section 3.

Nonmonotonic logics provide a way of reasoning with incomplete information by allowing the incorporation of assumptions, or defaults, about missing data. The nonmonotonic system considered in this paper is *default logic*, originally proposed by Reiter [7]. This is one of the best known systems — it has been widely studied and a number of variants proposed (for example[2,4,6]).

Default logic extends classical logic with *defaults* of the form

$$\delta = \frac{\varphi : \psi_1, \ldots, \psi_n}{\chi}$$

where φ, $\psi_1, \ldots$ and ψ_n, χ are classical formulae. φ is called the *prerequisite*, denoted $pre(\delta)$, $\psi_1, \ldots, \psi_n$ the *justifications*, $just(\delta)$, and χ the *consequent*,

---

[1] We use the terminology conservative *expansions* to avoid misunderstandings with extensions of default theories.

$cons(\delta)$. Roughly speaking, the default states that the consequent may be believed providing the prerequisite is believed and the justification is not violated.

A *default theory* T is a pair (W, D) consisting of a set of classical formulae W (the set of facts) and a countable set of defaults D. T is *finite* if D is finite. The meaning of a default theory is given in terms of *extensions* — world views or beliefs (represented by deductively closed sets of formulae) that are sanctioned by the given facts and defaults. A default theory may have none, one or several extensions. A detailed definition of extensions and discussion of their properties is given in [7].

We will make use of an equivalent characterisation of extensions in terms of *augmentations* [5] — minimal sets of formulae, or *bases*, that generate individual extensions. In practice it is augmentations rather than extensions that we wish to manipulate, since the bases are finite and computable for finite default theories and decidable first–order subclasses. A set of formulae A is an *augmentation* of T iff A is equal to a minimal set A' such that

$$A' = W \cup \{ \chi \mid \frac{\varphi : \psi_1, \ldots, \psi_n}{\chi} \in D, \ A' \vdash \varphi \ \text{ and } \ A \not\vdash \neg\psi_1, \ldots, A \not\vdash \neg\psi_n \}.^2$$

The set of all augmentations of T is denoted by $aug(T)$, and the set of extensions by $ext(T)$.

The relationship between augmentations and extensions is formalised by the following result:

Theorem 1. *[5] Let T be a default theory. Then E is an extension of T iff $E = Th(A)$ where A is an augmentation of T.*

We will make use of this result later in the paper.

3 Specification Morphisms

We now turn to the more general case of specification morphisms. Specification morphisms are mappings from one specification S to another S'. They are more general than conservative extensions, in that they allow the use of different symbol names in S and S', and that several symbols of S may be mapped to one symbol of S'. Thus they provide increased flexibility for system development. Specification morphisms are therefore a central concept of the algebraic methodology [3].

In this section we first develop specification morphism concepts for default logic through analogy with the classical case. This requires some development of the conditions for classical morphisms. We then look at the relationships between various definitions of default logic morphisms.

---

[2] Note that this defines a fixed-point — it is not sufficient to define a minimal set based on A alone.

3.1 Morphisms of Classical Specifications

If h is a specification morphism from S to S', then the translation of the proper axioms of S under h follow from the axioms of S'. Formally:

Definition 2. Let $h : \Sigma \to \Sigma'$ be a function mapping atoms from signature Σ to signature Σ'. h is extended to formulae and theories in the obvious way. Let S and S' be propositional theories (specifications) over Σ and Σ' respectively. Then h is a *(specification) morphism* from S to S' iff

$$h(S) \subseteq Th(S'). \tag{1}$$

For example, let $S = \{p \vee q\}$, $h : p, q \mapsto r$, and $S' = \{r \wedge s\}$. Then $h(p \vee q) = r \vee r$, which follows from S'. Thus h is a specification morphism from S to S'.

Note that in what follows we assume that h is a total function; that is, $h(\alpha) \in \Sigma'$ for all $\alpha \in \Sigma$.

3.2 Morphisms of Default Specifications

We would like to carry the idea of classical specification morphisms over to non-monotonic knowledge systems, in which we associate specifications with default theories. Unfortunately this cannot be achieved by direct analogy with (1) for the following reason.

In a classical system, a theory such as S, $h(S)$ or S' represents a concise specification of a system, while the closure $Th(S)$, $Th(h(S))$ or $Th(S')$ contains all the consequences, or beliefs, that follow from that specification. The corresponding concise specification in a default system is a default theory $T = (W, D)$. The corresponding closure or set of beliefs in a default system is either an intersection, union, or selection from extensions of T, depending on whether the skeptical, credulous or choice approach is adopted.

The immediate problem with (1) is that it compares (by way of inclusion) a specification with the closure of a specification. This is possible in a classical setting because both are of the same type (that is, sets of formulae). It is not possible in a default setting since a specification and its closure are of different types (that is, a default theory and a set of formulae).

In order to overcome this problem, we first demonstrate an alternative form of (1) which contains only closed specifications. We give this result in two stages, since the first stage (Theorem 3) is also used later in the paper.

Note that we will use Th to denote closures over various signatures. Where the signature is important and not obvious from the context, we will add it as a subscript. Thus, in the examples above, $Th(S)$ can be regarded as shorthand for $Th_\Sigma(S)$, while $Th(S')$ is short for $Th_{\Sigma'}(S')$. $Th(h(S))$ could indicate either of the closures $Th_{h(\Sigma)}(h(S))$ or $Th_{\Sigma'}(h(S))$.

In the first stage we demonstrate that, given an appropriate change of signature, the mapping h can be moved inside (or "distributed over") deductive closure:

Theorem 3. *Let* $h : \Sigma \rightarrow \Sigma'$ *and* A *be a (propositional) theory over* Σ. *Then*

$$h(Th_\Sigma(A)) = Th_{h(\Sigma)}(h(A)).$$

Proof. We assume (w.l.o.g.) Hilbert deductions.

(a) $h(Th_\Sigma(A)) \subseteq Th_{h(\Sigma)}(h(A))$

We need to show that for any formula $\varphi \in Th_\Sigma(A)$, $h(\varphi) \in Th_{h(\Sigma)}(h(A))$. There are three possibilities for $\varphi \in Th_\Sigma(A)$:

1. φ is an instance of an axiom scheme. Since h simply maps atoms and h is total, $h(\varphi)$ will also be an instance of the axiom scheme, and therefore $h(\varphi) \in Th_{h(\Sigma)}(h(A))$.
2. $\varphi \in A$. Then $h(\varphi) \in h(A)$ and hence $h(\varphi) \in Th_{h(\Sigma)}(h(A))$.
3. φ follows by modus ponens from two earlier formulae in the deduction, γ and $\gamma \rightarrow \varphi$. It is easily shown by induction that $h(\gamma) \in Th_{h(\Sigma)}(h(A))$ and $h(\gamma \rightarrow \varphi) \in Th_{h(\Sigma)}(h(A))$. Since $h(\gamma \rightarrow \varphi) = h(\gamma) \rightarrow h(\varphi)$, it follows by modus ponens that $h(\varphi) \in Th_{h(\Sigma)}(h(A))$.

(b) $h(Th_\Sigma(A)) \supseteq Th_{h(\Sigma)}(h(A))$

We need to show that for any formula $\varphi \in Th_{h(\Sigma)}(h(A))$ there exists $\varphi' \in Th_\Sigma(A)$ such that $h(\varphi') = \varphi$. There are three possibilities for $\varphi \in Th_{h(\Sigma)}(h(A))$:

1. φ is an instance of an axiom scheme constructed from atoms in $h(\Sigma)$. Since each atom maps from an atom in Σ, we can construct an instance φ' of the axiom in Σ that maps to φ.
2. $\varphi \in h(A)$. Then by definition there exists $\varphi' \in A$ such that $h(\varphi') = \varphi$.
3. φ follows by modus ponens from two earlier formulae in the deduction, γ and $\gamma \rightarrow \varphi$. By induction there exists γ' and $\gamma' \rightarrow \varphi'$ in $Th_\Sigma(A)$ such that $h(\gamma') = \gamma$, $h(\gamma' \rightarrow \varphi') = \gamma \rightarrow \varphi$ and $h(\varphi') = \varphi$. Therefore by modus ponens $\varphi' \in Th_\Sigma(A)$.

$\square$

We can now give our alternative form of (1):

Theorem 4. h *is a specification morphism from* S *to* S' *iff*

$$h(Th(S)) \subseteq Th(S'). \tag{2}$$

Proof. From Definition 2 we have $h(S) \subseteq Th_{\Sigma'}(S')$. Since the r.h.s. is deductively closed, clearly $Th_{\Sigma'}(h(S)) \subseteq Th_{\Sigma'}(S')$, and since $h(\Sigma) \subseteq \Sigma'$, $Th_{h(\Sigma)}h(S) \subseteq Th_{\Sigma'}(S')$. Finally, from Theorem 3, $h(Th_\Sigma(S)) \subseteq Th_{\Sigma'}(S')$. $\square$

Given this result, if we adopt the choice approach to default reasoning there is a clear analogue of (2): we will define h to be a morphism from T (on Σ) to T' (on Σ') if it maps extensions of T to subsets of extensions of T'.

For the skeptical and credulous approaches there is another decision to be made — whether the mapping takes place before or after taking intersections or unions. Here it is less clear what the classical case suggests as there is no definite analogue. We will take the following intuitive view.

Following the original intent in [7], a single extension represents the set of beliefs ("closure" in the above sense) that result from a default theory. The intersection or union of extensions, on the other hand, is an additional (or "meta") step taken in order to *use* the information in the various extensions in a more skeptical or less skeptical way. The spirit of (2) is therefore followed more closely by mapping the extensions directly.

On the basis of this we define default logic morphisms as follows:

Definition 5. Let $h : \Sigma \to \Sigma'$ be a function mapping atoms from signature Σ to signature Σ', extended to formulae and theories in the obvious way. Let T and T' be propositional default theories over Σ and Σ' respectively. Then h is a *default logic morphism*, of Type 1, 2 or 3 respectively, from T to T' iff:

M1 $\bigcap_{E \in ext(T)} h(E) \subseteq \bigcap_{E' \in ext(T')} E'$
M2 $\bigcup_{E \in ext(T)} h(E) \subseteq \bigcup_{E' \in ext(T')} E'$
M3 $\forall E \in ext(T) \; \exists E' \in ext(T') \quad h(E) \subseteq E'$.

As a simple example, let T consist of just the default $\frac{true:p}{p \vee q}$. Suppose $h : p \mapsto p$ and $h : q \mapsto r$. Finally let T' contain the single fact r. Then T has the single extension $E = Th(\{p \vee q\})$, and T' has the single extension $E' = Th(\{r\})$. Thus $h(E) = Th(\{p \vee r\}) \subseteq E'$, and all three conditions of a default logic morphism are satisfied.

3.3 Properties of Default Logic Morphisms

Having identified three candidates for default logic morphisms it is important to establish their inter-relationships — are they indeed unique, or in other words, does the *concept* of a default logic morphism differ between the different styles of default reasoning? And, if they are not equivalent, are there morphisms of one kind that imply morphisms of another?

We will show, in the remainder of this paper, that M2 and M3 are in fact equivalent, whereas M1 is completely distinct, neither implying or being implied by the other two.

In order to prove these relationships we require two further intermediate results. Like Theorem 3, both results allow us to express sets in terms of deductive closures of smaller (finite) sets or (finite) *bases*. The first essentially moves intersection inwards through deductive closure. While the proof is trivial (and follows from a more general result) it is included as motivation for Theorem 8.

Lemma 6. *Let A and B be finite sets of (propositional) formulae. Then there exists a finite set C such that*

$$Th(A) \cap Th(B) = Th(C).$$

Proof. $C = \{\bigwedge A \vee \bigwedge B\}$ is such a set since for any formula α, both $\bigwedge A \vdash \alpha$ and $\bigwedge B \vdash \alpha$ are true iff $\bigwedge A \vee \bigwedge B \vdash \alpha$. $\qquad\square$

The second, which is a little more complex, essentially moves restriction inwards through deductive closure, in the context of restricted extensions. A finite base is found by extending the idea of disjoining conjunctions, as used in Lemma 6 above, to disjunctive normal forms:

Definition 7. For a formula φ, define $dnf(\varphi)$ to be the disjunctive normal form of φ, and $dnf(\varphi)/\Sigma_{tr}$ to be the formula obtained by replacing each literal appearing in $dnf(\varphi)$ but not in the signature Σ with the formula *true*. This definition is extended to sets of formulae in a natural way.

The following theorem shows that $dnf(A')/\Sigma_{tr}$ provides the finite base we require.

Theorem 8. *Let A' be a finite propositional theory over Σ' and $\Sigma \subseteq \Sigma'$. Then $Th_{\Sigma'}(A')/\Sigma = Th_\Sigma(dnf(A')/\Sigma_{tr})$.*[3]

Proof. Assume $\alpha \in Th_{\Sigma'}(A')/\Sigma$. Then $\alpha \in \Sigma$ and $A' \models \alpha$. Thus $dnf(A') \models \alpha$, or α is true in all Σ'-models of $dnf(A')$. α must also be true in all Σ'-models of $dnf(A')/\Sigma_{tr}$ since Σ_{tr} increases the number of models only by allowing non-Σ conjuncts to take alternative truth values. Further, α is true in all Σ-models of $dnf(A')/\Sigma_{tr}$ since these agree with the Σ'-models on Σ-formulae. Therefore $\alpha \in Th_\Sigma(dnf(A')/\Sigma_{tr})$.

Conversely, assume $\alpha \in Th_\Sigma(dnf(A')/\Sigma_{tr})$, or α is true in the Σ-models of $dnf(A')/\Sigma_{tr}$. Then α is true in the Σ'-models of $dnf(A')/\Sigma_{tr}$ since they agree on Σ-formulae. α is also true in all Σ'-models of $dnf(A')$ since these are a subset of the models of $dnf(A')/\Sigma_{tr}$. Thus $\alpha \in Th_{\Sigma'}(A')/\Sigma$. $\qquad\square$

We are now able to prove our central result:

Theorem 9. *The following hold for Reiter, Constrained, Justified and Rational Default Logic.*

(a) $M2$ and $M3$ are equivalent.
(b) $M1$ does not imply $M2$ (or $M3$), and $M2$ (or $M3$) does not imply $M1$.

Proof. **(a)** $M3$ implies $M2$ is trivial. For the reverse implication, assume $M2$ is satisfied, but not $M3$. Then for any $E \in ext(T)$ there exists a set $E'_1 \in ext(T')$ such that:

1. $h(E) \cap E'_1$ is maximal w.r.t. set inclusion. (That is, there is no $E'_2 \in ext(T')$ such that $h(E) \cap E'_1 \subset h(E) \cap E'_2$. Since T, T' are finite there is a finite number of extensions and therefore such a set must exist.)

---

[3] Closure over Σ is necessary to avoid tautologies from $\Sigma' - \Sigma$ on the r.h.s. Note that this result appears in [1] but is not proven there.

2. For some formula $\alpha \in h(E)$, $\alpha \notin E_1'$.

From Theorem 1, $E = Th_\Sigma(A)$ for some finite set A over Σ, and therefore from Theorem 3, $h(E) = Th_{h(\Sigma)}(h(A))$, where $h(A)$ is a finite set over $h(\Sigma)$. Also from Theorem 1, $E_1' = Th_{\Sigma'}(A')$ for some finite set A' over Σ', and therefore from Theorem 8, $E_1'/h(\Sigma) = Th_{h(\Sigma)}(A'')$, for some finite set A'' over $h(\Sigma)$. Therefore, by Lemma 6, $h(E) \cap E_1'/h(\Sigma)$ is the deductive closure of a finite set. Let I be such a set.

Since $I \cup \{\alpha\} \subseteq h(E)$ and $h(E)$ is deductively closed, $\bigwedge(I \cup \{\alpha\}) \in h(E)$. On the other hand, since $\alpha \notin E_1'$ and E_1' is deductively closed, $\bigwedge(I \cup \{\alpha\}) \notin E_1'$. However, every formula in $h(E)$ is included in some $E' \in ext(T')$ (by $M2$), so there must be some $E_2' \in ext(T')$ such that $\bigwedge(I \cup \{\alpha\}) \in E_2'$ and hence $I \cup \{\alpha\} \subseteq E_2'$. Therefore $I \cup \{\alpha\} \subseteq h(E) \cap E_2'$, and since $\alpha \notin h(E) \cap E_1'$, $h(E) \cap E_1' \subset h(E) \cap E_2'$, contradicting the assumption that $E \cap E_1'$ is maximal.

(b) Take $\Sigma = \Sigma' = \{a\}$, $W = W' = \emptyset$, $h = id$, $D = \{\frac{true:a}{a}, \frac{true:\neg a}{\neg a}\}$, $D' = \{\frac{true:a}{a}\}$. T has the extensions $Th(\{a\})$ and $Th(\{\neg a\})$, whereas T' only the extension $Th(\{a\})$. Thus $M1$ is satisfied, but not $M2$.

Now consider $W = W' = \emptyset$, $\Sigma = \{a\}$, $\Sigma' = \{a, b\}$, $h = id$, $D = \{\frac{true:a}{a}\}$, $D' = \{\frac{true:a\wedge b}{a\wedge b}, \frac{true:\neg a}{\neg a}\}$. $T = (W, D)$ has the extension $Th(\{a\})$, $T' = (W', D')$ has the extensions $Th(\{a, b\})$ and $Th(\{\neg a\})$. Thus $M2$ is satisfied, but $M1$ is not.

Given the equivalence in Part (a), the same results apply to $M3$.

Also note that since Theorem 1 applies to Justified, Rational and Constrained default logics, the result applies to all variants. $\qquad\square$

4 Conclusions

This work is part of an ongoing investigation into the possibility of applying formal specification techniques in the context of nonmonotonic representations. We have developed and analysed conservative expansion concepts for default logic settings and, in this paper, extended this idea to the more general case of specification morphisms. This involved developing the classical definition so that direct analogies in the nonmonotonic setting could be found, and analysing the relationships between the different possibilities that arise from the treatment of multiple extensions. These relationships are summarised diagrammatically in Figure 1.

The ultimate goal of this research effort is the integration of default reasoning with software engineering methods, and in particular with object orientation, both regarding knowledge representation and the development process. To do so, we have to introduce and adapt concepts which have been proven important in software engineering — conservative extensions and specification morphisms are such concepts.

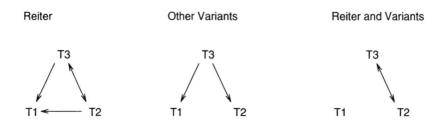

Conservative Expansions

Reiter Other Variants

Specification Morphisms

Reiter and Variants

Fig. 1. Relationships between specification refinement concepts as a result of alternative approaches to the multiple extension problem.

References

1. G. Antoniou, C. K. MacNish and N. Y. Foo. Conservative Expansion Concepts for Default Theories. In *Proc. PRICAI'96*, Springer 1996, LNAI 1114, 522–533
2. J.P. Delgrande, T. Schaub and W.K. Jackson. Alternative Approaches to default logic. *Artificial Intelligence* 70 (1994): 167–237
3. H. Ehrig and B. Mahr. *Fundamentals of Algebraic Specification Vol. 2*. Springer 1990
4. W. Lukaszewicz. Considerations of default logic: an alternative approach. *Computational Intelligence* 4,1(1988): 1–16
5. C. MacNish. Hierarchical default logic. In *Symbolic and Quantitative Approaches to Uncertainty: Proc. European Conference*. Springer-Verlag Lecture Notes in Computer Science 548, pp 246–253, 1991
6. A. Mikitiuk and M. Truszczynski. Constrained and rational default logics. In *Proc. International Joint Conference on Artificial Intelligence* 1995
7. R. Reiter. A logic for default reasoning. *Artificial Intelligence* 13(1980): 81–132
8. W.M. Turski and T.S.E. Maibaum. *The Specification of Computer Programs*. Addison-Wesley, Reading Massachusetts, 1987

Representation Results for Default Logics

Grigoris Antoniou

Griffith University, CIT, QLD 4111, Australia

ga@cit.gu.edu.au

Abstract

Normal forms play an important role in computer science, for example in the areas of logic and databases. This paper provides a study of normal forms for some prominent logics for default reasoning. In particular we show that in Constrained and in Justified Default Logic, semi–normal default theories can represent arbitrary default theories. The main result for Justified Default Logic requires the signature (logical language) to be enhanced in order to obtain the desired outcome.

1 Introduction

Normal forms play an important role in computer science. They help restrict the study of some properties to specific classes of items, and thus make the task at hand easier. Examples of areas where normal forms have proved fruitful include logic, where normal forms of formulae are used both for the proof of theoretical results and in theorem proving, and relational databases [2], where normal forms have been the driving force in the development of database theory and principles of good data modeling.

In this paper we study normal forms in the context of default reasoning. The results we derive are of the following form: Knowledge bases can be represented by syntactically simpler bases in such a way that the semantics is preserved.

We will be focusing on a family of approaches which originated from the seminal work of Reiter [7]. In default logic a knowledge base is also called a *default theory*, and consists of two kinds of information, certain information in the form of predicate logic formulae, and default rules. The semantics of a knowledge base is given in terms of so–called *extensions*, which represent alternative world views based on the given information. Our task can now be characterized more precisely as follows: Derive results showing that default theories can be represented by syntactically simpler default theories in such a way that extensions are preserved.

In fact such a representation theory was presented by Marek and Truszczynski [5] for Reiter's default logic. This paper will provide a similar analysis for other default logics, which have been developed to overcome some of the drawbacks of Reiter's original approach. In particular, we will study Lukaszewicz' Justified Default Logic [4] whose motivation was to ensure the existence of extensions, and Schaub's Constrained Default Logic [8, 3] which forbids an extension to be based on a contradictory set of assumptions.

2 Basics of default logics

We assume that the reader is familar with notation and basic notions of predicate logic. A *default* δ has the form $\frac{\varphi : \psi_1, \ldots, \psi_n}{\chi}$ with closed first–order formulae φ, $\psi_1, \ldots, \psi_n$, χ. φ is the *prerequisite pre*(δ), $\psi_1, \ldots, \psi_n$ the *justifications just*(δ), and χ the *consequent cons*(δ) of δ. A *default theory* T is a pair (W, D) consisting of a set of formulae W (the set of facts) and a countable set D of defaults. A default of the form $\frac{\varphi : \chi}{\chi}$ is called *normal*; a default is called *semi–normal* iff it has the form $\frac{\varphi : \psi \wedge \chi}{\chi}$. A default theory consisting only of normal defaults is called normal. A default theory consisting only of normal, semi–normal or justification–free defaults is called semi–normal.

First we give a definition of extensions in Justified Default Logic (JDL). Let $\delta = \frac{\varphi : \psi_1, \ldots, \psi_n}{\chi}$ be a default, and E a deductively closed set of formulae. We say that δ *is applicable to* E iff φ is included in E, and $\neg\psi_1, \ldots, \neg\psi_n$ are not included in E. Sometimes the following generalization is needed: δ is applicable to E w.r.t. a set of formulae F iff $\varphi \in E$ and $\neg\psi_1 \notin F, \ldots, \neg\psi_n \notin F$.

Let $T = (W, D)$ be a default theory and $\Pi = (\delta_0, \delta_1, \delta_2, \ldots)$ a finite or infinite sequence of defaults from D without multiple occurrences (modelling an application order of defaults from D). We denote by $\Pi[k]$ the initial segment of Π of length k, provided the length of Π is at least k. We define: $In(\Pi) = Th(W \cup \{cons(\delta) \mid \delta \text{ occurs in } \Pi\})$[1]. $Out(\Pi) = \{\neg\psi \mid \psi \in just(\delta), \delta \text{ occurs in } \Pi\}$. Π is called a *process of* T iff δ_k is applicable to $In(\Pi[k])$, for every k such that δ_k occurs in Π. Π is *successful* iff $In(\Pi) \cap Out(\Pi) = \emptyset$, otherwise it is *failed*. Note that in case Π is successful, every justification ψ of a default in Π is consistent with $In(\Pi)$.

[1] shows that the original definition of extensions in JDL is equivalent to the following one: A set of formulae E is an *extension* of a default theory T iff there is a maximally successful process Π of T such that $E = In(\Pi)$.

Sometimes we are interested in the set of defaults occurring in a process Π; we denote that set by *defaults*(Π). Note that by the definition of applicability, $In(\Pi)$ and $Out(\Pi)$ depend only on $defaults(\Pi)$ and not on the order of the defaults. Therefore the concept of success is meaningful for $defaults(\Pi)$, and we will feel free to apply this term to sets of defaults whenever it is convenient. Also note what it means for a process Π of T to be maximally successful: Π is successful, and there exists no successful process Π' of T such that $defaults(\Pi) \subset defaults(\Pi')$.

Now we turn our attention to Constrained Default Logic (CDL). Let $\delta =$

---

[1]where $Th(M)$ denotes the deductive closure of the set M of formulae.

$\frac{\varphi:\psi_1,\ldots,\psi_n}{\chi}$ be a default, and E and C deductively closed sets of formulae. δ is *constrained applicable to* (E, C) iff $\varphi \in E$, and $\{\psi_1, \ldots, \psi_n, \chi\} \cup C$ is consistent.

Let $T = (W, D)$ be a default theory and $\Pi = (\delta_0, \delta_1, \ldots)$ a sequence of defaults from D without multiple occurrences. $Con(\Pi) = Th(\{\psi_1 \wedge \ldots \wedge \psi_n \wedge \chi \mid \{\psi_1, \ldots, \psi_n\} = just(\delta)$ and $\chi = cons(\delta)$, for a default δ occurring in $\Pi\})$. Π is a *constrained process* iff δ_k is constrained applicable to $(In(\Pi[k]), Con(\Pi[k]))$, for all k such that $\Pi[k]$ is defined. In fact, in a constrained process Π, every default δ_k is constrained applicable to $(In(\Pi[k]), Con(\Pi))$. Π is *closed* iff every $\delta \in D$ which is constrained applicable to $(In(\Pi), Con(\Pi))$ already occurs in Π.

[1] shows that the original definition of extensions in CDL is equivalent to the following one: A set of formulae E is a *constrained extension* of a default theory T iff there is a closed constrained process Π of T such that $E = In(\Pi)^2$.

3 Representation results for CDL

We define two default theories T and T' to be *equivalent*, denoted by $T \sim T'$, iff T and T' have exactly the same constrained extensions. Obviously $\sim$ is an equivalence relation.

As an example, consider the default theories $T = (W, D)$ with $W = \{p\}$ and $D = \{\frac{p:q}{q}, \frac{true:r}{r}\}$, and $T' = (W', D')$ with $W' = \emptyset$ and $D' = \{\frac{true:p}{p}\} \cup D$. Both have the single constrained extension $Th(\{p, q, r\})$, therefore they are equivalent.

We say that a class of default theories $\mathcal{C}$ *represents* another class of default theories $\mathcal{C}'$ iff for every default theory T' in $\mathcal{C}'$ there exists a default theory T in $\mathcal{C}$ such that $T \sim T'$.

The following two results show that results known from Reiter's default logic (see [5]) do not carry over to Constrained Default Logic (nor to Justified Default Logic, as we will see later).

Observation 3.1 *Let* $\delta_0 = \frac{\varphi:\psi_1,\ldots,\psi_n}{\chi_1 \wedge \chi_2}, \delta_1 = \frac{\varphi:\psi_1,\ldots,\psi_n}{\chi_1}$, *and* $\delta_2 = \frac{\varphi:\psi_1,\ldots,\psi_n}{\chi_2}$. *Let* W *be a set of formulae,* D *a countable set of defaults,* $T_1 = (W, D \cup \{\delta_0\})$ *and* $T_2 = (W, D \cup \{\delta_1, \delta_2\})$. *It is not necessarily the case that* $T_1 \sim T_2$.

Proof: Consider the following example: $W = D = \emptyset$, $\delta_0 = \frac{true:\neg p}{p \wedge q}$, $\delta_1 = \frac{true:\neg p}{p}$ and $\delta_2 = \frac{true:\neg p}{q}$. The default theory consisting only of δ_0 has the single constrained extension $Th(\emptyset)$, but the default theory consisting of defaults δ_1 and δ_2 has the constrained extension $Th(\{q\})$. ∎

Theorem 3.2 *Let* $\delta_0 = \frac{\varphi:(\alpha_1 \vee \alpha_2),\psi_1,\ldots,\psi_n}{\chi}, \delta_1 = \frac{\varphi:\alpha_1,\psi_1,\ldots,\psi_n}{\chi}$, *and* $\delta_2 = \frac{\varphi:\alpha_2,\psi_1,\ldots,\psi_n}{\chi}$. *Let* W *be a set of formulae,* D *a countable set of defaults,* $T_1 = (W, D \cup \{\delta_0\})$ *and* $T_2 = (W, D \cup \{\delta_1, \delta_2\})$. *It is not necessarily the case that* $T_1 \sim T_2$. *But every constrained extension of* T_1 *is a constrained extension of* T_2.

---

[2]The original definition of CDL defined constrained extensions to be pairs (E, C) of sets of formulae, E corresponding to what we just defined to be a constrained extension, and C being the set of underlying beliefs. In that context $(E, C) = (In(\Pi), Con(\Pi))$ for a closed constrained process Π. In section 3 we will focus on the first component E.

Proof: Consider $\delta_0 = \frac{true:p \vee q}{r}, \delta_1 = \frac{true:p}{r}, \delta_2 = \frac{true:q}{r}$, and $\delta_3 = \frac{true:\neg p}{\neg p}$. T_1 consists of the defaults δ_0 and δ_3, and has the single constrained extension $Th(\{\neg p, r\})$. On the other hand T_2 consists of the defaults δ_1, δ_2 and δ_3, and has two constrained extensions, $Th(\{\neg p, r\})$ and $Th(\{r\})$. This shows that T_1 and T_2 are not equivalent.

Let E be a constrained extension of T_1, and $\Pi = (\gamma_0, \gamma_1, \ldots)$ a closed constrained process of T_1 such that $E = In(\Pi)$.

Case 1: δ_0 does not occur in Π. Then either $\varphi \notin In(\Pi)$ or $\{\alpha_1 \vee \alpha_2, \psi_1, \ldots, \psi_n, \chi\} \cup Con(\Pi)$ is inconsistent. In both cases it follows immediately that the defaults δ_1 and δ_2 are not constrained applicable to $(In(\Pi), Con(\Pi))$. Therefore Π is a closed constrained process of T_2, and $E = In(\Pi)$ a constrained extension of T_2.

Case 2: Let δ_0 be the default γ_k in Π. Then, by definition, $\varphi \in In(\Pi[k])$ and $\{\alpha_1 \vee \alpha_2, \psi_1, \ldots, \psi_n, \chi\} \cup Con(\Pi)$ is consistent (the latter by the definition of a constrained process). Since all formulae involved are closed (those stemming from defaults, by definition, while the facts can be viewed to be universally quantified) it follows that $\{\alpha_1, \psi_1, \ldots, \psi_n, \chi\} \cup Con(\Pi)$ or $\{\alpha_2, \psi_1, \ldots, \psi_n, \chi\} \cup Con(\Pi)$ is consistent. In the following we consider the case that only one of them is consistent. The case that both are consistent can be treated in a very similar way: in the definition of Π' below replace δ by δ_1 followed by δ_2.

If $\{\alpha_1, \psi_1, \ldots, \psi_n, \chi\} \cup Con(\Pi)$ is consistent then define $\delta = \delta_1$ and $\beta = \alpha_1$, otherwise define $\delta = \delta_2$ and $\beta = \alpha_2$. We note that

$$\{\beta, \psi_1, \ldots, \psi_n, \chi\} \cup Con(\Pi) \text{ is consistent} \tag{1}$$

$$\delta \text{ is applicable to } (In(\Pi[k], Con(\Pi)) \tag{2}$$

Now define $\Pi' = (\gamma_0, \ldots, \gamma_{k-1}, \delta, \gamma_{k+1}, \ldots)$. First we observe that $In(\Pi'[l]) = In(\Pi[l])$ for all numbers l. Therefore we also have $In(\Pi) = In(\Pi')$. Furthermore $Con(\Pi') = Th(\{\beta\} \cup Con(\Pi))$. We conclude the proof by showing that Π' is a closed constrained process of T_2; then $E = In(\Pi) = In(\Pi')$ is a constrained extension of T_2.

Suppose that Π' is not a constrained process of T_2. Because of (2) there must be a default γ_l with $l > k$ such that γ_l is not applicable to $(In(\Pi[l]), Con(\Pi[l]))$ (for $l < k$, applicability follows from the property that Π is a process). In that case, $just(\gamma_l) \cup \{cons(\gamma_l)\} \cup Con(\Pi'[l])$ is inconsistent (because $ptr(\delta_l) \in In(\Pi'[j]) = In(\Pi[l])$). Therefore we also get that $Con(\Pi')$ is inconsistent. But this is a contradiction: We have already observed that $Con(\Pi') = Th(\{\beta\} \cup Con(\Pi))$, so, by (1), $Con(\Pi')$ must be consistent. Therefore our assumption was wrong, and Π' is a constrained process of T_2. Finally Π' is closed, because Π was a closed constrained process of T_1, and Π' constains the "new" default δ_1 or δ_2, which can be added consistently (as mentioned before, the proof for the case that both δ_1 and δ_2 can be added consistently is treated in a very similar way). The important point is that $Con(\Pi')$ is logically stronger than $Con(\Pi)$, so less defaults can be applied. ∎

Next we make the remark that the class of normal default theories cannot represent all default theories. The reason is simple. Consider the default theory consisting of the two defaults $\frac{true:p}{q}$ and $\frac{true:\neg p}{r}$; it has two constrained extensions, $E = Th(\{q\})$ and $F = Th(\{r\})$. $E \cup F$ is consistent, so there cannot be a normal default theory with exactly the two constrained extensions E and F[3].

Observation 3.3 *In CDL, the class of normal default theories cannot represent the class of all default theories.*

Since normal defaults are not expressive enough, we turn our attention to semi–normal defaults. If we take any default $\delta = \frac{\varphi : \psi_1, \ldots, \psi_n}{\chi}$ and replace it by the semi–normal default $c(\delta) = \frac{\varphi : \psi_1 \wedge \ldots \wedge \psi_n \wedge \chi}{\chi}$, the resulting default theory exhibits exactly the same behaviour. The reason is that in CDL, by definition, the default δ is constrained applicable to (E, C) if, and only if, $c(\delta)$ is constrained applicable to (E, C). Thus we have the following:

Theorem 3.4 *In CDL, the class of semi–normal default theories represents the class of all default theories. Therefore the class of default theories in which defaults have exactly one justification, represents the class of all default theories.*

4 Representation results for JDL

The concepts of equivalence and representation can be carried over from CDL in an obvious way (use "extension" instead of "constrained extension").

Observation 4.1 *Let* $\delta_0 = \frac{\varphi : \psi_1, \ldots, \psi_n}{\chi_1 \wedge \chi_2}, \delta_1 = \frac{\varphi : \psi_1, \ldots, \psi_n}{\chi_1}$, *and* $\delta_2 = \frac{\varphi : \psi_1, \ldots, \psi_n}{\chi_2}$. *Let* W *be a set of formulae, D a countable set of defaults, $T_1 = (W, D \cup \{\delta_0\})$ and $T_2 = (W, D \cup \{\delta_1, \delta_2\})$. It is not necessarily the case that $T_1 \sim T_2$.*

Proof: Consider the default theory T_1 consisting of the two defaults $\frac{true : p}{q}$ and $\frac{true : r}{\neg p \wedge r}$. T has two extensions, $Th(\{q\})$ and $Th(\{\neg p, r\})$. Now let us consider T_2 consisting of the defaults $\frac{true : p}{q}$, $\frac{true : r}{\neg p}$ and $\frac{true : r}{r}$. T_2 has two extensions, $Th(\{q, r\})$ and $Th(\{\neg p, r\})$. Obviously T_1 and T_2 have different sets of extensions. ∎

Theorem 4.2 *Let* $\delta_0 = \frac{\varphi : (\alpha_1 \vee \alpha_2), \psi_1, \ldots, \psi_n}{\chi}, \delta_1 = \frac{\varphi : \alpha_1, \psi_1, \ldots, \psi_n}{\chi}$, *and* $\delta_2 = \frac{\varphi : \alpha_2, \psi_1, \ldots, \psi_n}{\chi}$. *Let W be a set of formulae, D a countable set of defaults, $T_1 = (W, D \cup \{\delta_0\})$ and $T_2 = (W, D \cup \{\delta_1, \delta_2\})$. Then it is not necessarily true that $T_1 \sim T_2$. But every extension of T_1 is an extension of T_2.*

The proof is similar to that of Theorem 3.2. As for CDL, normal defaults cannot represent all default theories in JDL. Consider the default theory consisting of the two defaults $\frac{true : p}{q \wedge r}$ and $\frac{true : \neg q}{r}$. It has two extensions, $E = Th(\{q, r\})$ and $F = Th(\{r\})$. $E \cup F$ is consistent. Given that normal default theories in JDL have exactly the same properties as in Reiter default logic (since they have the same extensions in both logics [1]), there is no normal theory with exactly the extensions E and F.

Observation 4.3 *In JDL, the class of normal default theories cannot represent the class of all default theories.*

---

[3]It is known that normal theories satisfy the orthogonality property in Reiter default logic, and that constrained extensions and Reiter extensions coincide for normal theories [1].

5 A semi–representability result for JDL

Compared with the results for Constrained Default Logic, what we have to sort out for Justified Default Logic is whether the class of semi–normal default theories can represent any default theory. In the following we will derive a somewhat weaker result. We will show that an arbitrary default theory can be represented by a semi–normal default theory, provided that the logical language can be extended by new atoms.

Formally, we say that a default theory T over signature Σ is *semi–representable* in a class of default theories $\mathcal{C}$ iff there is an expansion Σ' of Σ and a default theory T' (over signature Σ') in the class $\mathcal{C}$, such that the following property holds: E is an extension of T iff there is an extension E' of T' such that the restriction of E' to Σ equals E. The main result of this paper is the following.

Theorem 5.1 *In JDL, every default theory T' is semi–representable in the class of semi–normal default theories.*

The basic idea of the proof (used for Reiter's default logic in [5]) is to "simulate" a default

$$\delta = \frac{\varphi : \psi_1, \ldots, \psi_n}{\chi}$$

by the following collection of defaults:

$$\alpha_1(\delta) = \frac{\varphi : \psi_1 \wedge c_{1,\delta}}{c_{1,\delta}}, \ldots, \alpha_n(\delta) = \frac{\varphi : \psi_n \wedge c_{n,\delta}}{c_{n,\delta}}$$

$$\beta(\delta) = \frac{c_{1,\delta} \wedge \ldots \wedge c_{n,\delta} :}{\chi}$$

where all $c_{i,\delta}$ are different *new atoms* not occurring elsewhere in the default theory. In case δ has no justification, we still use one α–default $\alpha_1(\delta) = \frac{\varphi : c_{1,\delta}}{c_{1,\delta}}$ along with the associated β–default $\beta(\delta)$. Applying the above construction to all defaults of a default theory T over a signature Σ, we obtain a default theory T' over a signature Σ' which expands Σ by all the new atoms c.

Proof of Theorem 5.1: In one direction, we assume that E is an extension of $T = (W, D)$, and we have to show that there exists an extension E' of T', such that E'/Σ, the restriction of E' to the signature Σ, is precisely E. Let $E = In(\Pi)$ for a maximally successful process $\Pi = (\delta_0, \delta_1, \ldots)$ of T. We define a sequence of defaults from T' as follows:

$$\Pi' = (\alpha_1(\delta_0), \ldots, \alpha_{n_0}(\delta_0), \beta(\delta_0), \alpha_1(\delta_1), \ldots, \alpha_{n_1}(\delta_1), \beta(\delta_1), \ldots).$$

Intuitively, we wish to simulate the defaults from D by the α– and β–defaults, while maintaining the order given by Π. Using the property that Π is a successful process of T, we will show that Π' is a successful process of T'. First we make the following observations, which follow directly from the construction:

(a) $In(\Pi'[n_0+\ldots+n_k+k+1]) = Th(In(\Pi[k+1]) \cup \{c_{1,\delta_0}, \ldots, c_{n_0,\delta_0}, \ldots, c_{n_k,\delta_k}\})$,
where n_i is the number of α–defaults corresponding to δ_i. This property

says that if we apply the defaults of Π' "in blocks" corresponding to the single defaults of Π, we obtain the same In–set as the corresponding steps in Π would, plus the additional atoms $c_{i,\delta}$.

(b) $In(\Pi'[n_0 + \ldots + n_k + k + 1])/\Sigma = In(\Pi[k + 1])$.

(c) $In(\Pi')/\Sigma = In(\Pi)$.

Now we show that $\alpha_i(\delta_k) = \frac{\varphi : \psi_i \wedge c_{i,\delta_k}}{c_{i,\delta_k}}$ (for some $\alpha_i(\delta_k)$ in Π') is applicable to $M = In(\Pi'[n_0 + \ldots + n_{k-1} + k + i - 1])$ which is the In–set when the default $\alpha_i(\delta_k)$ has to be applied in Π'. Since Π is a process and $\delta_k = \frac{\varphi : \psi_1, \ldots, \psi_{n_k}}{\chi}$, we know that $\varphi \in In(\Pi[k])$. Since $In(\Pi[k]) \subseteq M$ by (a), it follows $\varphi \in M$. Furthermore we know that ψ_i is consistent with $In(\Pi[k])$. We know that ψ_i is a Σ–formula, and that $M/\Sigma = In(\Pi[k])$ by property (b) above. Therefore ψ_i is consistent to M. Finally, c_{i,δ_k} is a new atom, therefore $\psi_i \wedge c_{i,\delta_k}$ is also consistent with M. Thus the applicability of $\alpha_i(\delta_k)$ has been shown.

Applicability of the β–defaults in Π' is obvious: They have no justification, so no consistency check is required, and their prerequisite is the conjunction of the consequents of all α–defaults associated with the same default from Π. Since these α–defaults precede the β–default in Π', the applicability is clear.

Thus we have shown that Π' is a process of T'. Next we show that Π' is successful. Assume, to the contrary, that Π' is failed. Then there must be a justification $\psi_i \wedge c_{i,\delta_k}$ of a default $\alpha_i(\delta_k)$ such that $\neg(\psi_i \wedge c_{i,\delta_k}) \in In(\Pi')$. By property (b) above and because c_{i,δ_k} is a new atom, $\neg c_{i,\delta_k} \notin In(\Pi')$. Therefore $\neg \psi_i \in In(\Pi')$. Since $\neg \psi_i$ is a Σ–formula, it follows from property (c) above that $\neg \psi_i \in In(\Pi)$. But $\neg \psi_i \in Out(\Pi)$, too, since it is a justification of the default δ_k which occurs in Π. Thus Π is failed, which is a contradiction.

Π' may not be a maximally successful process of T' because some more α–defaults may be applicable. But we know that it is included in a maximally successful process Π'' of T'. That means, $defaults(\Pi') \subseteq defaults(\Pi'')$, and the defaults of Π' appear in Π'' in the same order. We complete the proof in this direction by showing that $In(\Pi'')/\Sigma = In(\Pi')/\Sigma$. Then we are done, because it follows from property (c) that $In(\Pi'')/\Sigma = In(\Pi) = E$. Since Π'' is a maximally successful process of T', $In(\Pi'')$ is an extension of T', and we have proven the one direction of the theorem.

We show $In(\Pi'')/\Sigma = In(\Pi')/\Sigma$ by demonstrating that no β–default can be included in $defaults(\Pi'') - defaults(\Pi')$. Suppose, to the contrary, that this were not the case, and let $\beta(\delta)$ be the *first* such default appearing in Π''; let $\delta = \frac{\varphi : \psi_1, \ldots, \psi_n}{\chi}$. For $\beta(\delta)$ to be applicable (which is necessary since Π'' is a process of T') the corresponding α–defaults must precede $\beta(\delta)$. Let $\alpha_i(\delta) = \frac{\varphi : \psi_i \wedge c_{i,\delta}}{c_{i,\delta}}$ be the first such default appearing in Π''. By the choice of this default, all defaults from $defaults(\Pi'') - defaults(\Pi')$ preceding $\alpha_i(\delta)$ in Π'' are of the α–form. Therefore, the applicability of $\alpha_i(\delta)$ implies that $\varphi \in In(\Pi')$, and also

$$\varphi \in In(\Pi) \tag{$*$}$$

because φ is a Σ–formula. Furthermore we know that Π'' is successful, so $In(\Pi'') \cup Out(\Pi'')$ is consistent. Combining the information

$\chi \in In(\Pi'')$
$In(\Pi) \subseteq In(\Pi'')$ and
$\neg(\psi_j \wedge c_{j,\delta}) \in Out(\Pi'')$ for all $j = 1, \ldots, n$

we conclude $\neg\psi_j \vee \neg c_{j,\delta} \notin Th(In(\Pi) \cup \{\chi\})$. Therefore

$$\neg\psi_j \notin Th(In(\Pi) \cup \{\chi\}) \text{ for all } j = 1, \ldots, n \tag{$**$}$$

From ($*$) and ($**$) we conclude that δ is applicable to Π, and (together with the success of Π'') that $defaults(\Pi) \cup \{\delta\}$ is successful. So Π is not a maximally successful process of T, which is a contradiction.

In the opposite direction, let E' be an extension of $T' = (W, D')$. We have to show that E/Σ is an extension of T. Let $\Pi' = (\delta'_0, \delta'_1, \ldots)$ be a maximally successful process of T' such that $E' = In(\Pi')$. Now we define a sequence $\Pi = tr(\Pi') = (\delta_0, \delta_1, \ldots)$. For all i (such that $\Pi[i]$ is defined) the following property holds: Of the defaults δ in $D - defaults(\Pi[i])$, let δ_i be the first default such that $\beta(\delta_i)$ appears in Π'.

We will show that $\Pi = tr(\Pi')$ is a maximally successful process of T with $In(\Pi')/\Sigma = In(\Pi)$. Then the proof is completed. We begin by showing that Π is a process of T. Let $\delta_i = \frac{\varphi:\psi_1,\ldots,\psi_n}{\chi}$. The associated defaults in Π' are $\alpha_1(\delta_i) = \frac{\varphi:\psi_1 \wedge c_{1,\delta_i}}{c_{1,\delta_i}}, \ldots, \alpha_n(\delta_i) = \frac{\varphi:\psi_n \wedge c_{n,\delta_i}}{c_{n,\delta_i}}, \beta(\delta_i) = \frac{c_{1,\delta_i} \wedge \ldots \wedge c_{n,\delta_i}}{\chi}$. Let k be the number with $\delta'_k = \beta(\delta_i)$. Since Π' is a process all α–defaults associated with δ_i must precede δ'_k in Π'. Furthermore, since all c atoms are new and don't belong to Σ,

$$In(\Pi'[k])/\Sigma = In(\Pi[i]) \tag{1}.$$

Π' is a process of T', therefore δ'_k must be applicable to $In(\Pi'[k])$. Therefore $\varphi \in In(\Pi'[k])$, and so

$$\varphi \in In(\Pi[i]) \tag{2}$$

by property (1), since φ is a Σ–formula. Also, Π' is successful, so $\neg(\psi_1 \wedge c_{1,\delta_i}), \ldots, \neg(\psi_n \wedge c_{n,\delta_i}) \notin In(\Pi')$. So $\neg\psi_1, \ldots, \neg\psi_n \notin In(\Pi')$. Since $In(\Pi[i]) \subseteq In(\Pi')$, it follows

$$\neg\psi_1, \ldots, \neg\psi_n \notin In(\Pi[i]) \tag{3}$$

Properties (2) and (3) show that δ_i is applicable to $In(\Pi[i])$, so Π is a process of T. Next we show that Π is successful. Suppose, to the contrary, that there exists a justification ψ_j of a default δ_i such that $\neg\psi_j \in In(\Pi) \cap Out(\Pi)$. $\neg\psi_j \in In(\Pi)$, therefore $(\neg\psi_j \vee \neg c_{j,\delta_i}) \in In(\Pi')$. But $\psi_j \wedge c_{j,\delta_i}$ is the justification of $\alpha_j(\delta_i)$, therefore $(\neg\psi_j \vee \neg c_{j,\delta_i}) \in Out(\Pi')$ (this follows from the following argument: $\delta_i \in defaults(\Pi)$, therefore $\beta(\delta_i) \in defaults(\Pi')$; but $\beta(\delta_i)$ can only be applied if all corresponding α–defaults precede it in Π'; therefore $\alpha_j(\delta_i) \in defaults(\Pi')$). Thus $In(\Pi') \cap Out(\Pi') \neq \emptyset$, and Π' is failed, which is a contradiction.

Finally we show that Π is a maximally successful process of T. Assume, to the contrary, that this is not the case. Then there must be a default $\delta =$

$\frac{\varphi:\psi_1,\ldots,\psi_n}{\chi} \in D$ such that δ does not occur in Π, is applicable to $In(\Pi)$, and $defaults(\Pi) \cup \{\delta\}$ is successful. Thus we know

$$\varphi \in In(\Pi) \tag{4}$$
$$In(\Pi) \cup \{\psi_i\} \text{ is consistent, for all } i = 1, \ldots, n \tag{5}$$
$$defaults(\Pi) \cup \{\delta\} \text{ is successful} \tag{6}$$

Since all atoms c are new, we conclude from (5) that $In(\Pi) \cup \{c_{j,\delta'} \mid \delta' \in defaults(D)\} \cup \{\psi_i\}$ is consistent, for all $i = 1, \ldots, n$. From (1) it follows that $In(\Pi') \cup \{\psi_i \wedge c_{i,\delta}\}$ is consistent, for all $i = 1, \ldots, n$. From (4) we also know that $\varphi \in In(\Pi')$. Therefore $\alpha_i(\delta) = \frac{\varphi:\psi_i \wedge c_{i,\delta}}{c_{i,\delta}}$ is applicable to $In(\Pi')$. Moreover $\Pi' \cup \{\alpha_i(\delta)\}$ is successful (since the c atoms are new). Since Π' is a maximally successful process of T', all $\alpha_i(\delta)$ must occur in Π'.

But then $\beta(\delta)$ is applicable to $In(\Pi')$, by the definition of β–defaults. From (6) it follows easily that $defaults(\Pi') \cup \{\beta(\delta)\}$ is successful (follows immediately from (6) if we take into account that all c atoms are new and pairwise disjoint, and appear only positively in any defaults of Π'; and that $In(\Pi')/\Sigma = In(\Pi)$, by construction). Since Π' is a maximally successful process, it follows that $\beta(\delta)$ must occur in Π'. But then, by the definition of Π, δ must occur in Π. But we assumed that δ does not occur in Π, and this gives us a contradiction. $\blacksquare$

In fact we can show something more than the previous theorem says: there exists a one–to–one correspondence between the extensions of T and the extensions of T'. Formally:

Theorem 5.2 *Let E and F be extensions of T' (defined above) such that $E/\Sigma = F/\Sigma$. Then $E = F$.*

Lemma 5.3 *Let E be an extension of a default theory T, and Π, Π' two maximally successful processes of T such that $E = In(\Pi) = In(\Pi')$. Then $defaults(\Pi) = defaults(\Pi')$.*

Proof: Let $\delta = \frac{\varphi:\psi_1,\ldots,\psi_n}{\chi} \in defaults(\Pi)$, and suppose that $\delta \notin defaults(\Pi')$. Since Π is a process we know that $\varphi \in In(\Pi)$ and $\neg\psi_1, \ldots, \neg\psi_n \notin In(\Pi)$. Since $In(\Pi) = In(\Pi')$, it follows that δ is applicable to $In(\Pi')$.

For Π' to be maximally successful, $defaults(\Pi') \cup \{\delta\}$ must be failed. We know $\chi \in In(\Pi)$ since $\delta \in defaults(\Pi)$, therefore $\chi \in In(\Pi')$. Therefore $In(defaults(\Pi') \cup \{\delta\}) = In(\Pi')$. Furthermore $Out(defaults(\Pi') \cup \{\delta\}) = Out(\Pi') \cup \{\neg\psi_1, \ldots, \neg\psi_n\}$. Since $defaults(\Pi') \cup \{\delta\}$ is failed, there must be a $\psi_i \in just(\delta)$ such that $\neg\psi_i \in In(\Pi')$. But since $In(\Pi') = In(\Pi)$ we conclude $\neg\psi_i \in In(\Pi)$. But δ occurs in Π, so $\neg\psi_i$ is also included in $Out(\Pi)$. Therefore $In(\Pi) \cap Out(\Pi) \neq \emptyset$, which contradicts the assumption that Π be a succeeful process of Π.

So $defaults(\Pi) \subseteq defaults(\Pi')$. By a symmetric argument we can also show $defaults(\Pi') \subseteq defaults(\Pi)$. Therefore $defaults(\Pi) = defaults(\Pi')$. $\blacksquare$

Proof of Theorem 5.2: Since E and F are extensions of T' there must be maximally successful processes Π and Π' such that $E = In(\Pi)$ and $F = In(\Pi')$. If we build the processes $tr(\Pi)$ and $tr(\Pi')$ as described in the proof of Theorem 5.1, we conclude that $In(tr(\Pi)) = In(\Pi)/\Sigma = E/\Sigma = F/\Sigma =$

$In(\Pi')/\Sigma = In(tr(\Pi'))$. By Lemma 5.2 we conclude that $defaults(tr(\Pi)) = defaults(tr(\Pi'))$. By construction of tr, Π and Π' include the same β-defaults.

We conclude that they also contain the same α-defaults. Let $\alpha_i(\delta) = \frac{\varphi : \psi_i \wedge c_{i,\delta}}{c_{i,\delta}}$ be a default occurring in Π. Then $\varphi \in In(\Pi)$ and $\neg(\psi_i \wedge c_{i,\delta}) \notin In(\Pi)$. Because $In(\Pi)/\Sigma = In(\Pi')/\Sigma$, we know that

$$\varphi \in In(\Pi') \tag{1}$$
$$\neg\psi_i \notin In(\Pi') \tag{2}$$

Furthermore we note that $c_{i,\delta}$ is a new atom which does not occur negatively anywhere Π' or in ψ_i. Therefore we can strengthen (2) to

$$\neg(\psi_i \wedge c_{i,\delta}) \notin In(\Pi') \tag{3}$$

(1) and (3) show that $\alpha_i(\delta)$ is applicable to $In(\Pi')$. Since $c_{i,\delta}$ is a new atom it cannot cause failure when added to Π', so $\Pi' \cup \{\alpha_i(\delta)\}$ is successful. Π' is a maximally successful process of T', so $\alpha_i(\delta)$ occurs in Π'.

By the definition of T', Π and Π' consist only of α- and β-defaults. Thus we have shown $defaults(\Pi) \subseteq defaults(\Pi')$. By a symmetric argument we can show the other direction, and thus establish $defaults(\Pi) = defaults(\Pi')$. Therefore $E = In(\Pi) = In(\Pi') = F$, which is what we had to show. ∎

6   Conclusion

This paper presented a representation theory for two popular logics for default reasoning, Constrained and Justified Default Logic. We started with simple observations and moved to more complex results, culminating in the semi–representability result for Justified Default Logic. A similar result was recently established for another default logic variant, Rational Default Logic [6].

References

[1] G. Antoniou. *Nonmonotonic Reasoning*. MIT Press 1997 (in press)

[2] E.F. Codd. Further Normalization of the Data Base Relational Model. In *Data Base Systems, Courant Computer Science Symposia Series 6*, Prentice Hall 1972

[3] J.P. Delgrande, T. Schaub and W.K. Jackson. Alternative Approaches to default logic. *Artificial Intelligence* 70 (1994): 167–237

[4] W. Lukaszewicz. Considerations of default logic: an alternative approach. *Computational Intelligence* 4,1(1988): 1–16

[5] V. Marek and M. Truszczynski. *Nonmonotonic Logic*. Springer 1993

[6] A. Mikitiuk. Semi–representability of default theories in rational default logic. In the *Proceedings of the 5th European Workshop on Logics in AI (JELIA '96)* (in press)

[7] R. Reiter. A logic for default reasoning. *Artificial Intelligence* 13(1980): 81–132

[8] T. Schaub. On Constrained Default Theories. In the *Proceedings of the 10th European Conference on Artificial Intelligence*, Wiley 1992, 304–308

Proving Quantified Literals in Defeasible Logic

David Billington
School of Computing and Information Technology,
Griffith University,
Nathan, Brisbane, Queensland, 4111, Australia.
e-mail: db@cit.gu.edu.au
facsimile: +61 7 3875 5051
telephone: +61 7 3875 5052

Abstract

Defeasible Logic is a nonmonotonic reasoning approach which has an efficient implementation. Currently Defeasible Logic can only prove ground literals. We describe a version of Defeasible Logic which is capable of proving existentially and universally closed literals, as well as ground literals. The intuition motivating the formalism is presented, as are some of its properties.

Keywords

Quantified literals, Defeasible logic, Nonmonotonic reasoning.

1. Introduction

People reason nonmonotonically. That is, they may change their minds when new information becomes known. Nonmonotonic reasoning is an accepted part of knowledge representation, in particular, and artificial intelligence in general, as is evidenced by the inclusion of sections on nonmonotonic reasoning in several introductory textbooks on artificial intelligence. Good introductions to many of the formalisations of nonmonotonic, or commonsense, reasoning can be found in Lukaszewicz [1990], Brewka [1991], and Antoniou [1997]. Three well known formalisations are Default Logic, Autoepistemic Logic, and Circumscription.

It is desirable to have a nonmonotonic reasoning formalism or logic with the following four properties.

1) There is a well defined proof theory.

2) The proof theory is easy to use.

3) The logic has an efficient implementation.

4) The logic gives intuitive answers for any nonmonotonic reasoning problem which can be formulated in the logic.

The three nonmonotonic logics mentioned above do not satisfy properties 2 or 3.

Nute [1988a, 1988b, 1992, 1994a, 1994b] has defined a family of nonmonotonic logics called Defeasible Logic which satisfies all four of the above properties. From the very beginning Defeasible Logic was designed to be implemented, see for example [Nute and Lewis 1986], [Nute 1988a], [Nute, Mann, and Brewer 1990], and [Fordyce and Billington 1992]. That Defeasible Logic is useful in controlling expert system recommendations is shown in [Nute, Mann, and Brewer 1990]. Billington, De Coster, and Nute [1990] have shown that semantic networks can be regarded as simple Defeasible Logics. The application of Defeasible Logic to many nonmonotonic reasoning problems is shown in [Nute 1994b]. Many mathematical properties of Defeasible Logic are proved in [Billington 1993]. It will be convenient to denote the Defeasible Logic defined in [Billington 1993] by DL.

In classical logic, we can regard Prolog as an efficient implementation of (part of) first-order logic. Similarly in nonmonotonic logic we can regard Defeasible Logic as an efficient implementation of (part of) a yet to be defined first-order Defeasible Logic. Just as first-order logic is a useful extension of Prolog, so we believe a first-order Defeasible Logic will be a useful extension of DL. Since DL can only prove ground literals, and hence their conjunctions, a first step along the path to the definition of a first-order Defeasible Logic was the extension of DL in [Billington 1994] so that disjunctions of ground literals could also be proved. Previous Defeasible Logics have been essentially propositional, in that an expression containing variables could be replaced by all ground instances of that expression. Such variables could be called removable variables. In this paper we shall extend DL so that the variables are not removable, and existentially and universally closed literals, as well as ground literals, can be proved. We shall denote this extension by DL(q).

Defeasible Logic does not (yet) have a model theory. So we need to discuss and justify our claim that existentially and universally closed literals can be proved. This is done in section 4. DL(q) is described in section 3, and uses the syntax given in section 2. The detailed presentation of definitions, theorems, lemmas, proofs, and examples have been omitted due to the length limitations. However all the details are in [Billington 1996].

2. Syntax

Since our formal language is not very familiar, we shall define it from the beginning.

Our *alphabet* $\mathcal{A}$ is the union of the following eight pairwise disjoint sets of symbols: a non-empty countable set of predicate symbols; a countable set of function symbols; a countable set of constant symbols; a countable set, Var, of variable symbols; the set $\{\neg, \rightarrow, \Rightarrow, \rightsquigarrow\}$ of connectives; the set $\{\forall, \exists\}$ of quantifiers; the set $\{+, -, \Delta, \partial\}$ of positive, negative, definite, and defeasible proof symbols; and the set of punctuation marks consisting of the comma, braces and parentheses.

A *term* (over $\mathcal{A}$) is a variable symbol, or a constant symbol, or a function symbol applied to the appropriate finite number of terms. An *atomic formula* (over $\mathcal{A}$) is a predicate symbol applied to the appropriate finite number of terms. A *literal* (over $\mathcal{A}$) is either an atomic formula, called a *positive literal* (over $\mathcal{A}$); or the negation of an atomic formula, called a *negative literal* (over $\mathcal{A}$). The negation of the atomic formula, p, is denoted by ¬p. If p is a positive literal then the *complement* of p is ¬p; and the *complement* of ¬p is p. If q is any literal then the complement of q is denoted by ~q.

A *formula* (over $\mathcal{A}$) is defined recursively as follows.

(F1) Any literal is a formula.

(F2) If x is a variable which occurs freely in a formula, f, then both $\forall xf$ and $\exists xf$ are formulas.

(F3) Every formula can be built using F1 and F2 a finite number of times.

Thus formulas are literals and quantified literals. If q is a literal we denote the *universal closure* of q by $\forall(q)$, and the *existential closure* of q by $\exists(q)$. As usual, if q does not contain any variables then $\forall(q) = q = \exists(q)$.

A *rule* (over $\mathcal{A}$) has three parts: a finite set of literals on the left, an arrow in the middle, and a literal on the right. The set on the left of the arrow is called the *antecedent* of the rule, and the literal on the right of the arrow is called the *consequent* of the rule. Rules which contain the *strict arrow* →, for example A→ q, are called *strict rules* (over $\mathcal{A}$). The intuition is that whenever all the literals in A are accepted then q must be accepted. Rules which contain the *defeasible arrow* ⇒, for example A ⇒ q, are called *defeasible rules* (over $\mathcal{A}$). If all the literals in A are accepted then q is accepted provided that there is insufficient evidence against q. Rules which contain the *defeater arrow* ↝, for example A ↝ ~q, are called *defeating rules* (over $\mathcal{A}$) or *defeaters* (over $\mathcal{A}$). If all the literals in A are accepted then A ↝ ~q is evidence against q, but not for ~q. It should be noted that the antecedent of a rule can be the empty set, which is denoted by { }. This facility is useful because it enables us to express presumptions, for example, if p is a presumption then we can write this as { } ⇒ p. When the antecedent of a rule is just a singleton set, say {p}, we usually omit the set braces around p.

By an *expression* (over $\mathcal{A}$) we mean a term, or a formula, or a rule. A *ground* expression is an expression which does not contain any variables.

A *substitution* (over $\mathcal{A}$) is a function from the set of variables, Var, to the set of all terms. Substitutions are denoted by lower case Greek letters. A *ground substitution* (over $\mathcal{A}$) is a function from Var to the set of all ground terms over $\mathcal{A}$. The set of all ground substitutions over $\mathcal{A}$ is denoted by Γ. Let σ be any substitution and e be any expression in which no quantifiers occur. We define $e\sigma$ to be the expression formed from e by just simultaneously replacing each occurrence of a variable in e by its image under σ. We say that $e\sigma$ is an *instance* of e.

The positive, negative, definite, and defeasible proof symbols are explained in section 3.

If m and n are integers then we define $[m..n] = \{i \in \mathbb{Z} : m \leq i \leq n\}$, where $\mathbb{Z}$ is the set of all integers.

3. Defeasible Logic

If R is a set of rules then a *superiority relation* on R is any asymmetric binary relation, >, on R. That is, if $t \in R$ and $s \in R$ and $t > s$ then not $(s > t)$. We read t > s as t *is superior to* s, or equivalently, as s *is inferior to* t. The superiority relation enables us to use (or fire) one rule from a set of usable rules.

A *Defeasible theory* over $\mathcal{A}$ with an explicitly defined superiority relation is a triple (F, R, >) such that DT1, DT2, and DT3 hold.

(DT1) F is a finite set of literals over $\mathcal{A}$, often referred to as facts; and

(DT2) R is a finite set of rules over $\mathcal{A}$; and

(DT3) > is a superiority relation on R.

A Defeasible theory over $\mathcal{A}$ together with a suitable deducibility relation, $\vdash$, is called a *Defeasible Logic* over $\mathcal{A}$.

We now begin to describe a suitable deducibility relation $\vdash$. Ground literals, universally closed literals, and existentially closed literals are called *p-formulas*, because these are the only formulas for which the notion of proof is defined. P-formulas can be proved definitely, in which case new information will not defeat the proof, or defeasibly, in which case new information might defeat the proof. Moreover we need to be able to indicate that we can prove that p-formulas can not be proved. To distinguish these cases we define a *tagged p-formula* to be a tag followed by a p-formula. A *tag* consists of two symbols; the first symbol is either + or −, and the second symbol is either Δ or ∂. Let f be a p-formula. In a proof $+\Delta f$ indicates that f is proved definitely, $-\Delta f$ indicates that it is proved that f can not be proved definitely, $+\partial f$ indicates that f is proved defeasibly, and $-\partial f$ indicates that it is proved that f can not be proved defeasibly.

In order to prove universally quantified literals, we need to augment our alphabet $\mathcal{A}$ by some new constant symbols. Formally for each variable $x \in Var$ define c_x to be a new constant symbol not occurring in $\mathcal{A}$. Let $Var^* = \{c_x : x \in Var\}$ and define $\mathcal{A}^* = \mathcal{A} \cup Var^*$. The idea is that to prove $\forall x P(x)$ we prove $P(c_x)$ instead. Since c_x is new it will only unify with variables. So if we substitute any ground term g for c_x in a proof of $P(c_x)$ we should get a proof of $P(g)$. That is, a proof of $\forall x P(x)$ should be a template into which we can substitute any ground term g to get a proof of $P(g)$. Theorem 4.1 shows that this is essentially correct. We shall say more about what proving an existentially or a universally quantified literal means in section 4.

Let (F, R, >) be a Defeasible theory over $\mathcal{A}$. A finite sequence, $P = (P(1), ..., P(n))$, of tagged p-formulas over $\mathcal{A}^*$ is called a *proof* in (F, R, >) if and only if for each $i \in [0..n-1]$ the eight inference conditions $+\Delta\exists$, $-\Delta\exists$, $+\Delta\forall$, $-\Delta\forall$, $+\partial\exists$, $-\partial\exists$, $+\partial\forall$, and $-\partial\forall$ all hold. These conditions formalise the above intuitions. The detailed statement of these conditions is in [Billington 1996]. The elements of a proof are called *lines* of the proof.

We are now able to define a suitable deducibility relation, $\vdash$. If f is a tagged p-formula then $(F, R, >) \vdash f$ if and only if f is a line in a proof in $(F, R, >)$.

Since we want proofs to be finite, we restrict the language of Defeasible Logic so that it only contains finitely many ground terms. This means that there are no function symbols and only finitely many constant symbols.

We conclude this section with two simple examples, the details of which are in [Billington 1996]. The Defeasible Logic is given on the left with an English translation on the right. In the English translation we use "defeasibly" rather than "usually", or "normally", or "typically" because we want to convey the idea that if the antecedent of a defeasible rule is accepted then the consequent will be accepted provided that there is insuffient evidence to the contrary. The words "usually", or "normally", or "typically" can also convey this idea, but they can also convey the idea that in more than 50% of cases if the antecedent is accepted then the consequent will be accepted. We do not want to limit ourselves to this probabilistic interpretation.

Example 3.1

Facts

F1: Red(A)	Block A is red.
F2: Red(B)	Block B is red.

Rules

R1: Red(y) $\Rightarrow$ OnTable(y)	Red blocks are defeasibly on the table.
R2: Red(B) $\rightsquigarrow \neg$OnTable(B)	B may be an exception to this rule.

Superiority Relation

{}	There is no superiority relation between R1 and R2.

In this situation commonsense would lead us to behave as if there is a block on the table. Defeasible Logic arrives at the same conclusion by proving $+\partial\exists x\,\text{OnTable}(x)$. The four line formal proof, P, of this is found by starting with the goal, $+\partial\exists x\,\text{OnTable}(x)$, and using inference condition $+\partial\exists$ to generate subgoals. These subgoals are further reduced by using the inference conditions until they can be lines in the proof P. The formal proof P is

P(1)	$-\Delta\neg\text{OnTable}(A)$	It is not the case that A is not on the table.
P(2)	$+\Delta\text{Red}(A)$	A is red.
P(3)	$+\partial\text{Red}(A)$	Defeasibly A is red.
P(4)	$+\partial\exists x\,\text{OnTable}(x)$	Defeasibly there is a block on the table.

Example 3.2
Facts

F1: Red(y)   All blocks are red.

Rules

R1: $Red(z) \Rightarrow OnTable(z)$ Red blocks are defeasibly on the table.

Superiority Relation

{}   There is no superiority relation.

In this situation commonsense would lead us to behave as if all blocks are on the table. Defeasible Logic arrives at the same conclusion by proving $+\partial \forall x\, OnTable(x)$. The four line formal proof, P, of this is found by starting with the goal, $+\partial \forall x\, OnTable(x)$, and using inference condition $+\partial \forall$ to generate subgoals. These subgoals are further reduced by using the inference conditions until they can be lines in the proof P. The formal proof P is

P(1) $-\Delta \exists x \neg OnTable(x)$ It is not the case that there is a block not on the table.

P(2) $+\Delta Red(c_x)$ All blocks are red.

P(3) $+\partial Red(c_x)$ Defeasibly all blocks are red.

P(4) $+\partial \forall x\, OnTable(x)$ Defeasibly all blocks are on the table.

4. Quantifier Behaviour

In the previous section we described a proof theory which involved the symbols $\exists$ and $\forall$. The purpose of this section is to show that $\exists$ behaves like an existential quantifier and $\forall$ behaves like a universal quantifier.

In the absense of any model theory, what behaviour or property characterises the existential quantifier? We propose the following property E1 as such a characterisation.

(E1) If an instance of a formula can be proved then
the existential closure of that formula can be proved.

Theorem 4.2(1 & 3) shows that E1 holds, and so we are justified in calling $\exists$ an existential quantifier.

The classical first-order logic existential quantifier satisfies E1 but not the converse of E1. This is because the first-order language may not have a name for the individual or witness whose existence is proclaimed by the existential quantifier. However the logic described in the previous section, DL(q), does satisfy the converse of E1, as is shown by Theorem 4.2(2 and 4). This means that the existential quantifier of DL(q) is stronger than the classical first-order logic existential quantifier.

In the absense of any model theory, what behaviour or property characterises the universal quantifier? We propose the following property U1 as such a characterisation.

(U1) If the universal closure of a formula can be proved then
all instances of that formula can be proved.

Theorem 4.2(5 & 6) shows that U1 holds, and so we are justified in calling $\forall$ a universal quantifier. However the converse of U1 does not hold, as the following simple example shows. Let $F = \{P(a)\}$, and let R and > be empty. The details of this example are worked out in [Billington 1996].

The classical first-order logic universal quantifier satisfies U1 but not the converse of U1. Indeed the converse of U1 is not desirable because merely proving all instances of a formula need not necessarily enable us to prove that these are all the instances.

We note that $(F, R, >) \vdash +\partial \forall x\, Q(x)$ means that we have a proof of $\forall x\, Q(x)$ using defeasible rules. It does not mean we can prove $Q(x)$ for almost all x. So the "weakness" signalled by ∂ applies to the proof, not the quantifier.

Theorem 4.1

A proof of $\forall x P(x)$ is essentially a template into which we can substitute any ground term g to get a proof of $P(g)$.

Theorem 4.2

Let q be any literal over $\mathcal{A}$, and suppose that there is a ground term. Recall that Γ is the set of all ground substitutions over $\mathcal{A}$.
(1) If $\gamma \in \Gamma$ and $(F, R, >) \vdash +\Delta q\gamma$ then $(F, R, >) \vdash +\Delta \exists(q)$.
(2) If $(F, R, >) \vdash +\Delta \exists(q)$ then there exists $\gamma \in \Gamma$ such that $(F, R, >) \vdash +\Delta q\gamma$.
(3) If $\gamma \in \Gamma$ and $(F, R, >) \vdash +\partial q\gamma$ then $(F, R, >) \vdash +\partial \exists(q)$.
(4) If $(F, R, >) \vdash +\partial \exists(q)$ then there exists $\gamma \in \Gamma$ such that $(F, R, >) \vdash +\partial q\gamma$.
(5) If $(F, R, >) \vdash +\Delta \forall(q)$ then for all $\gamma \in \Gamma$, $(F, R, >) \vdash +\Delta q\gamma$.
(6) If $(F, R, >) \vdash +\partial \forall(q)$ then for all $\gamma \in \Gamma$, $(F, R, >) \vdash +\partial q\gamma$.

The proofs of these results, and their many preliminary definitions and lemmas, are in [Billington 1996].

5. Conclusion

We have described DL(q) which is an extension of the Defeasible Logic DL defined in [Billington 1993]. DL(q) adds to the expressive power of DL by enabling existentially and universally closed literals, as well as ground literals, to be proved.

We have shown that the universal quantifier behaves like its classical counterpart. However the existential quantifier is stronger than its classical counterpart, in that every witness that is proclaimed to exist has a name.

This paper is an important step towards a first-order Defeasible Logic. The next step is to eliminate the restriction that there are only finitely many ground terms. However it is likely that removing this restriction will increase the computational complexity. Hence DL(q) may be a good compromise between expressive power and computational efficiency.

After the definition of a first-order Defeasible Logic, the two most important theoretical developments for Defeasible Logic are (1) a model theory for (the various versions of) Defeasible Logic; and (2) the establishment of a relationship between Defeasible Logic and one of the three well-known nonmonotonic logics mentioned in the introduction.

Although the theory of nonmonotonic logics is worthwhile and interesting, it is their practical application which is sorely needed. Defeasible Logic's implementability and ease of use makes it a prime candidate for the preferred applied nonmonotonic logic, and hence makes its theoretical development even more important.

References

G. Antoniou [1997] "*Nonmonotonic Reasoning*", MIT Press, Cambridge, Massachusetts, USA.

D. Billington, K. De Coster, and D. Nute [1990] "A Modular Translation from Defeasible Nets to Defeasible Logics", *Journal of Experimental and Theoretical Artificial Intelligence*, **2**, 151-177.

D. Billington [1993] "Defeasible Logic is Stable", *Journal of Logic and Computation* **3**, 379-400.

D. Billington [1994] "Adding Disjunction to Defeasible Logic", *Proceedings of the 7th Australian Joint Conference on Artificial Intelligence*, World Scientific, 259-266.

D. Billington [1996] "A Defeasible Logic with Quantifiers", Griffith University, School of Computing and Information Technology, research report.

G. Brewka [1991] "*Nonmonotonic Reasoning: Logical Foundations of Commonsense*", Cambridge University Press.

R. Fordyce and D. Billington [1992] "DLog(e): An Implementation of Defeasible Logic", *Proceedings of the 5th Australian Joint Conference on Artificial Intelligence*, 284-289.

W. Lukaszewicz [1990] "*Non-monotonic Reasoning Formalization of Commonsense Reasoning*", Ellis Horwood.

D. Nute [1988a] "Defeasible Reasoning: A Philosophical Analysis in Prolog", in J.H. Fetzer (ed.) *"Aspects of Artificial Intelligence"*, Kluwer, 251-288.

D. Nute [1988b] "Defeasible Reasoning and Decision Support Systems", *Decision Support Systems* **4**, 97-110.

D. Nute, R.I.Mann, and B.F.Brewer [1990] "Controlling Expert System Recommendations with Defeasible Logic", *Decision Support Systems* **6**, 153-164.

D. Nute [1992] "Basic Defeasible Logic", in L.F.D. Cerro and M. Penttonen (eds.) *"Intensional Logics for Programming"*, Clarendon Press, Oxford, 125-154.

D. Nute [1994a] "Defeasible Logic", in D.M. Gabbay, C.J. Hogger, and J.A. Robinson (eds.) *Handbook of Logic in Artificial Intelligence and Logic Programming vol.3*. Clarendon Press, Oxford, 353-395.

D. Nute [1994b] "A Decidable Quantified Defeasible Logic", in D.Prawitz, B.Skyrms, and D.Westerståhl (eds.) *Logic, Methodology and Philosophy of Science IX*. Elsevier Science B.V., 263-284.

D. Nute and M. Lewis [1986] "A users' Manual for d-Prolog" Technical Report 01-0016, The Artificial Intelligence Center, Rm 111 GSRC, The University of Georgia, Athens, GA, 30602-7415, USA.

Fuzzy Hierarchical Pattern Recognition
for Robotics Applications

Yoshinori ARAI[1] and Kaoru HIROTA[2]

[1] Tokyo Institute of Polytechnics, 1583 Iiyama, Atsugi, Kanagawa
243-02, Japan (arai@t-kougei.ac.jp)
[2] Tokyo Institue of Technology, 4259 Nagatsuda, Midori-ku,
Yokohama, Kanagawa 226, Japan (hirota@hrt.dis.titech.ac.jp)

Abstract. Two approaches of pattern recognition for robotics applications are introduced. The first study is concerned with a method of efficient pattern classification for moving objects using a discriminant tree. The second study is about three dimensional pattern classifications. Both studies use fuzzy logic and hierarchical knowledge base. In the first study, the experimental system shows the robot-arm system which is able to recognize a moving pattern (parts shape recognition) and to manipulate a moving object on a belt-conveyer at a various speed. And in the second study, the experimental system provideds a car-name recognition system which is able to recognize various car-name (trade name) from image data of minicars.

Keywords: Robotics Vision, Fuzzy Inference, Parts shape recognition,
Car-name recognition

1 Introduction

We have a lot of problems which must be solved for robot permeate into human community. In this paper, we introduce two approaches of pattern recognition which solved one of these problems. The first study provides a method of efficient pattern recognition of two dimensional known patterns using a concept of fuzzy discriminant tree. And second study is about method three dimensional and more delicate pattern classifications using fuzzy inference. Both studies use fuzzy logic and hierarchical knowledge representation.

The first experimental system [1] provides the robot-arm system which is able to recognize a moving pattern (parts shape recognition) and to manipulate (grasping and putting) a moving object on a belt-conveyer at a various speed. And in the second study, the experimental system aims a car-name recognition system which is able to identify various car-name (trade name) from image data of minicars. These image data are taken from several views of each of different models of minicar. This system used method of "fuzzy hierarchical pattern recognition using fixation feedback" which was proposed by the authors [2], [3].

2 Robotics Vision in Assembling Line

2.1 Outline of the System

A robot-arm system which is able to recognize a moving pattern and to manipulate a moving object on a belt-convveyer at a various speed has been built [1].

The algorithm which was proposed in this system can apply a rule to a case of autonomous mobile robots. For example, a robot will be able to be recognize special moving object, and chase, close and catch it.

Fig. 1 shows overview of this system. The robot-arm system is able to recognize a moving pattern (parts shape recognition) and to manipulate (grasping and putting) a moving object on a belt-convveyer at a various speed. That is, the robot-arm system is able to grasp a specified shape object which is indicated by an operator, and to putting on specified shape mark which is indicated by an operator.

This system consists of two parts. The first part is related to recognizing patterns. In this part, a method of constructing a discriminant tree is proposed. The robot-arm system is able to recognize the shape and the size of moving patterns on a belt-conveyor based on the discriminant tree.

The second part is concerned with replacing a moving object (i.e., grasping a moving object and putting it on an indicated moving mark) based on fuzzy-inference rules with the aid of image-processing technique. The second part consists of the following 6 blocks; (1) observation block, (2) quantization block, (3) fuzzy inference block, (4) interpretation block, (5) robot control block, (6) action (grasping/putting) block.

The first part is mentioned a little bit precisely in the followings becouse this part is concerned with robotics vision.

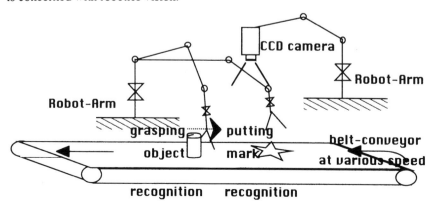

Fig. 1. overview of robot-arm system

2.2 Fuzzy Discriminant Tree

In dynamic pattern recognition, one of the most important thing is a discriminant tree. The discriminant tree distinguishes patterns using features. Each of the end nodes (leaves) corresponds to one pattern category. The method using discriminant tree has been a fundamental approach in real time pattern recognition. In general, however, how to construct the discriminant tree depends on the experience of researchers. Although various features of patterns have been studied, construction methods of discriminant trees have not been studies enough.

In the paper [1], a new approach concerning how to construct an efficient discriminant tree is proposed first. Necessary information for choosing minimum features' set which is used to construct an efficient discriminant tree is the frequency of appearance of each pattern category, the features themselves, and the computing time of extracting each feature. Shape recognition using the discriminat tree and size recognition based on fuzzy logic are applied to distinguish moving patterns on a belt-convveyer. In the proposed system an object or a mark moves on a belt-convveyer, and the robot grasps an indicated object and puts it on indicated mark.

2.3 Experimental Results

It should be noted that only one 16 bit personal computer controls the whole system (i.e., real time image processings of CCD camera data, fuzzy inference, and robot control of 2 robot arms (one is for manipulate a moving object, another is for take pictures with CCD camera) are done by this 16bit personal computer alone.) Through a lot of processing time and memory are required in general to realize a robot control system with a visual sensor (e.g., CCD camera, only lower level devices were successfully utilized in this system to construct a real time robot system equipped with a visual function. It is realized by applying the fuzzy inference method with vagueness to rather insufficient visual information from a CCD camera. Such a system has not been realized by other methods.

3 Fuzzy Hierarchical Patern Recognition System using Fixation Feedback

3.1 Outline of the System

Pattern identification of three dimensional objects by machine (computer and robot) is not enough to investigate. For example in our modern automobile-society many models of cars have been produced. Even for humans, it is difficult to distinguish specific models, and for a computer / robot this is an extremely difficult problem. There have been many studies of discrimination among vehicles, but most of these studies [4] simply tried to distinguish between trucks, buses, passenger cars, and so forth. The focus of this paper is on discriminating among different models of cars such as Cedric, MarkII, Celica, GTO, etc.

When humans try to identify car models, the following steps are observed; First they sort the cars by major features. Second, they look for the characteristic features of the likely models. Finally, they decide on the specific model. The algorithm of "fuzzy hierarchical pattern recognition using fixation feedback (FHPR/FF)"[2] attempts to emulate this human process.

Generally, in the case of 'automatic recognition' of a kind of car by machine, the "Template matching" or "Construction matching" methods are used. However, if the template matching method is chosen, many templates will be necessary, which makes it difficult to observe which car is the indicated three dimensional object. Therefore, it is very difficult to recognize some kinds of cars.

If the Construction Matching Method (which distinguishes by observing the features of certain parts) is chosen, the same problem occurs. It is difficult to unify information and build up rules (knowledge), because the discriminate-tree is too complex. When common, human observed features are simulated by a machine (using the image processing technique) the process becomes arduous and is not realistic. In the past, there have seen many studies using pattern recognition to discriminate kinds of cars [4]. However, the aims of those studies were to discriminate between trucks, buses, passenger cars, and so on.

On the other hand, pattern recognition can be used to discriminate between groups of trade names like Cedric, MarkII, Celica, GTO, etc. Accordingly, it is difficult to develop a system that will measure information accurately. It has to develop image-understanding methods that are able to recognize using several combined and various features without inaccurate observation.

This paper introduces an algorithm of "fuzzy hierarchical pattern recognition using fixation feedback (FHPR/FF)"[2] and the system[3] can be used to recognize various trade names of car models from image data based on the algorithm. This FHPR/FF method provides a framework for efficient recognition without high-level image processing devices. The recognition templates use fourteen models of minicar. In experiments, this system can recognize its model from image data which are shot from several different directions.

3.2 Fuzzy Hierarchical Pattern Recognition System using Fixation Feedback

In this section the framework of the fuzzy hierarchical pattern recognition system using fixation feedback is introduced.

At first, humans make subjective judgments, organizing the possible objects hier-

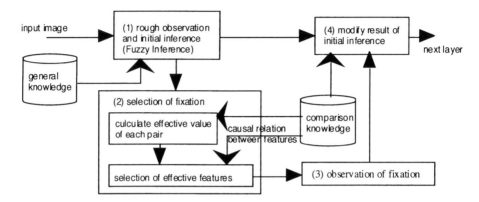

Fig. 2. concept of FHPR/FF

archically even before beginning the discrimination task. For example, in this pattern recognition task for different models of cars, the entire set of possible objects was divided into two hierarchies. In the first hierarchy, cars are classified in clusters such as standard passenger cars (X), hatchbacks (Y), and so on based on general types of cars. In a second hierarchy, the terminal nodes are specific sets of models of car's trade name, such as X = (Cedric, MarkII, Silvia,...), Y = (Celica, GTO,....).

The FHPR/FF consists of four parts (See Figure 2). The outline of one hierarchy is described here, but for each hierarchy the process is almost the same.

(1) rough observation and initial inference

The system guesses which class an object belongs in by making a rough observation. The patterns used for recognition of various models are based on general knowledge reported by human subjects. Here is one sample rule: if l is big and m is short, then X = 0.9, Y = 0.5 and Z = 0.1, where l is the angle of rear-glass and m is the height of the car.

Applying the fuzzy inference step at this stage results in X = 0.7 and Y = 0.6, Z = 0.2, for example.

(2) selection of fixation

A fixation here refers to a part of the car which has become the focus of more precise estimation because it is evaluated to contribute toword the success of the discrimination task. The fixation is a kind of feature of the car in this system, not just a part of the car.

The effective value of each pair of features was calculated based on how effective this pair of features was in discriminating between the clusters. Actually in this system, each effective value was combined from two different effectiveness.

In this system, the effective value was calculated as an algebraic sum from these effectiveness.

An example of the combined results of the calculations is followed; effective value is 1.0 between X and Y, and is 0.8 between Y and Z.

Next, the actual features to use as fixations are selected using the calculated effective values combined with the causal relation between each features . Causal relation was made from knowledge (rule) of making comparisons. An example of causal relation is as followes; l and m are needed for clasified X and Y. And an example of knowledge of making comparisons is; [causal relation between X and Y] if feature value of l is long, then X is true and Y is false.

Accordingly, for this example, it is necessary that we observe l and m to discriminate between X and Y. And effective value to observe them is 0.8. Applying it step at this stage example results in l = 1.8 and m = 1.55, n = 1.35.

(3) observation of fixation

Then the system focuses on the selected features, and observes them.

(4) modify the result of the initial inference

The result of the initial inference was modified based on the observed values of the features as fixations, using the knowledge of how to compare the causal relation between features. Thereby, the system is able to achieve higher accuracy in discriminating among models of car. Modified result is X = 0.7 and Y = 0.6, Z = 0.2 for example.

3.3 Experimental Results

The system which is able to recognize a kind of car was constructed. It is run on Sun SS5 workstation. The recognition templates for this experiment used 85 images data that was shot from several views of each of 14 different models of minicar. These models of minicar were divided into 3 categories: "type of Standard Passenger car", "type of Hatchback car", and "type of Recreational Vehicle (RV)". And car-names of minicars are "Celica", "GTO", "Supra", "Z", etc. Fig. 3 shows examples of the original input images which is a type of Standard Pssenger car and model of Silvia (the trade name of the car).

Fig. 3 example of original image data (Silvia)

This system can identify and observe fifteen features (ex. length of bonnet and trunk, thickness of front and rear, angle of front and rear glass, etc.). However, at first, the system observes two features: "direction" and "total length". These two features were used in calculating the standardization of the other fifteen features.

Table 1 shows accuracy rates of recognition in all experimental results using the eighty-five different images. Table 1 shows initial inference results and modified results in each step. In these experimental results, we obtain that the average accuracy rate of recognition is 58%. In summary, the results obtained approximately agreed with the expected results. In some cases, accurate feature values could not be determined because of the poor quality of the image data. However, even with poor quality images, the system was able to recognize with a high degree of accuracy.

The system uses 94.8% features in first hierarchy, but uses only average 72.6% features in second hierarchy. In these experiments, we did not measure running time, however, the average rate of non-necessity features was 27.4%. The inference is that this method provides a framework for efficient recognition.

This method described here a human-like process of selecting significant features is used, reducing unnecessary observations and increasing efficiency. When the observations are ambiguous, we can still classify appropriately.

Table 1. accuracy rates of recognition

original image (number)	1st hierarchy (type)		2nd hierarchy (trade name)	
	rough inf.	modified	rough inf.	modified
hatch-back car (x25)	48% (12/25)	60% (15/25)	47% (7/15)	67% (10/15)
standard passenger car (x 29)	45% (13/29)	59% (17/29)	35% (6/17)	53% (9/17)
RV car (x 31)	45% (14/31)	58% (18/31)	44% (8/18)	56% (10/18)
average (x 85)	46% (39/85)	59% (50/85)	42% (21/50)	58% (29/50)

4 Conclusion

In this paper, we introduced two systems which approached to pattern recognition for robotics. One system is the robot-arm system which is able to recognize a moving pattern (parts shape recognition) and to manipulate (grasping and putting) a moving object on a belt-convveyer at a various speed. This system was able to realize an efficient pattern recognition of two dimensional known patterns. And the second system is the car-name recognition system which is able to identy various car-name (trade name) from image data of minicars used "fuzzy hierarchical pattern recognition using fixation feedback" (FHPR/FF) method.

Techniques of fuzzy logic and hierarchical knowledge representation led to solve a problem. These techniques lead to develop other fields including clustering shown in [2].

Reference

1. K. Hirota, Y. Arai, S. Hachisu: "Moving Mark Recognition and Moving Object Manipulation in Fuzzy Controlled Robot", CTAT, Vol.2, No3, pp.399-418, 1986
2. K. Hirota, Y. Arai, Y. Nakagawa: "Pattern Recognition & Image Understanding based on Fuzzy Technology", Int. Workshop on BOFL'96, 56-61, 1996
3. Y. Arai, G. Sekiguchi, K. Hirota: "Fuzzy Hierarchical Car-model Pattern Recognition System Using Fixation Feedback", Int. Conf on KES '97, 154-158, 1997
4. H. Kono: "Simulator System for Automatic Pattern Recognition of Motorcar Shape", IFAC 8th. Triennial World Congress, Vol.4, p2003, 1982

Adaptive Curvature-Based Topography for Learning Symbolic Descriptions of Terrain Maps

Adrian R. Pearce[1], Terry Caelli[1], and Simon Goss[2]

[1] School of Computing, Curtin University, Perth WA 6845, Australia
[2] Aeronautical and Maritime Research Laboratories, DSTO, Melbourne, Australia.

Abstract. We present an adaptive curvature scale space technique for extracting symbolic topographical descriptions from image data such as that of three dimensional digital terrain maps where specific image interpretation constraints play a significant role in defining the scale of analysis. In our approach we use machine learning techniques to *learn* efficient segmentation of image data, the *Topograph*, which satisfies the constraints of the application task and guarantees the quality of the solutions returned. The Topograph representation is evaluated empirically using a flight trajectory planning application where the problem involves minimising the integral under the path (sum of altitude) while satisfying the constraints of flight. It is shown how the Topograph hierarchy can be used to guarantee lower bounds on solutions for search problems of this nature by incorporating multiple resolution states and using dynamic programming techniques.

1 Introduction

Many matching and planning processes are often computationally expensive or intractable when applied to digital terrain data. In the case of aeronautical flight trajectory planning, finding the optimal flight trajectory involves minimising some cost function while satisfying the constraints of navigation. Digital terrain map data is comprised of elevation data for a rectilinear grid. Each grid element typically comprises one arc second of longitude and latitude on the Earth's surface. One solution to generating these paths involves formulating the problem in state-space. Each state is described by the aircraft's position, orientation and speed, while the cost associated with the state is a function of threat, terrain and the aircraft's manoeuvre required to change state.

If the aim is to simply minimise altitude (the integral under the curve) solutions can be found using minimum spanning tree techniques. However, minimum clearance for plausible flight manoeuvres and factors such as the desire to avoid certain areas adds additional complexity to the problem. Further, the problem is computationally expensive when applied to large maps, particularly when multiple states (heading and speed) are maintained for each grid location. Under these conditions some form of segmentation is required.

In order to use topographical regions to reduce the search the cardinality of the problem must be reduced by segmenting groups of grid elements into generalised symbolic regions. However, the search must still satisfy both the cost function and navigational constraints. Although segmentation methods are often used, they have not necessarily produced regions which are meaningful or optimised in terms which are critical to the quality of the solution demanded by the particular task. For example, in flight trajectory planning segmentation may unfortunately produce symbolic regions which are impossible to traverse due to the constraints of the physics of flight.

The use of classical clustering procedures such as Leader or K-means [7] are reliant on certain threshold values and these result in variable fragmentation size according to the local surface topology. A simple clustering scheme for digital terrain maps based on altitude slicing may arbitrarily divide regions which are homogeneous, and thus does not guarantee appropriate size and scale requirements for navigation. Clustering schemes operate on global image characteristics (the histogram) and do not explicitly utilise local spatial information of the image. From computer vision, there has been a move to structural descriptions which incorporate shape information in the form of symbolic descriptions [11].

For navigation purposes, it is most important to have a representation for the shape which is invariant to view direction - given that the region is visible. Fortunately, the surface mean(H) and Gaussian(K) curvatures have such characteristics and have the property that they are invariant to viewer position (pose) and offer descriptions of regions according to locally homogeneous surface types [3]. Examples of these are ridges, valleys or planes.

The application of differential curvature-based techniques, alone, to digital terrain images results in over-fragmentation since there is no notion of resolution scale, and every pit and undulation in the terrain is exposed. This has been addressed using multiple scale-space [6] and hierarchical descriptions using hypergraphs [13]. To date, there has been no efficient way of generating and evaluating symbolic regions which offer meaningful generalisation with respect to different surface types while satisfying appropriate size and scale requirements of an application process - from either three dimensional (depth) or two-dimensional (intensity) images. Machine Learning techniques have been used to generate symbolic hierarchies using information theoretic techniques. Such techniques have been based on minimum entropy methods [10] and in general, are applied *after* the Segmentation stage.

In our approach we use machine learning techniques to *learn* efficient segmentation of image data which satisfies the constraints of the application task. Our technique combines differential curvature and multi-resolution methods from Computer Vision with information theoretic foundations of Machine Learning and produces a symbolic hierarchy *during the segmentation process*.

2   The Topograph Hierarchy

We have developed an efficient generalisation of the topography which optimises the ability of the regions to represent different surface types while maximising the generalisation through the description of symbolic regions. An adaptive seg-

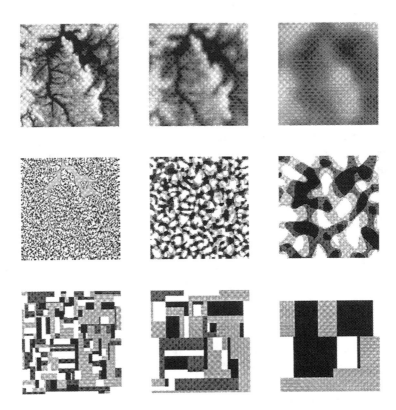

Fig. 1. Top: A multi-resolution scale space is shown for digital terrain images using low pass (Gaussian) smoothing at varying resolution. **Middle:** Segmented regions are shown below based on the different surface types using the zero crossings of the mean and Gaussian curvature measurements. **Bottom:** The topograph representation is shown at different cardinalities. Regions are shown for the three grouped surface types ridge (white), valley (black) and planar (grey).

mentation scheme is developed which combines adaptive curvature scale with a segmentation procedure to split the image into convex regions. The technique relies on producing a *Topograph* through the adaptive (recursive) application of three basic principles:

1. Surface descriptions based on differential curvature types,
2. Adaptive resolution scale through image smoothing,
3. Symbolic region extraction based on minimum entropy partitioning.

First, our method uses Gaussian (low pass) filtering together with differential curvature determination to recursively smooth the images (see Figure 1 Top). Mean (H) and Gaussian (K) curvatures can be calculated at varying scales

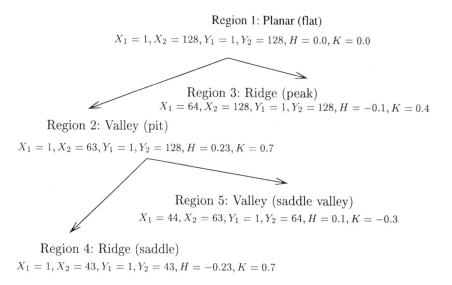

Region 1: Planar (flat)
$X_1 = 1, X_2 = 128, Y_1 = 1, Y_2 = 128, H = 0.0, K = 0.0$

Region 3: Ridge (peak)
$X_1 = 64, X_2 = 128, Y_1 = 1, Y_2 = 128, H = -0.1, K = 0.4$

Region 2: Valley (pit)
$X_1 = 1, X_2 = 63, Y_1 = 1, Y_2 = 128, H = 0.23, K = 0.7$

Region 5: Valley (saddle valley)
$X_1 = 44, X_2 = 63, Y_1 = 1, Y_2 = 64, H = 0.1, K = -0.3$

Region 4: Ridge (saddle)
$X_1 = 1, X_2 = 43, Y_1 = 1, Y_2 = 43, H = -0.23, K = 0.7$

Fig. 2. The symbolic Topograph hierarchy is shown for different regions of different surface types. The region coordinates (X_1, X_2, Y_1, Y_2) and mean (H) and Gaussian (K) curvatures are also shown.

until the scale and size resolution factors for the surface descriptors, relevant to the application process, are reached [4, 5]. Eight fundamental surface types can be determined according to the signs of H and K (zero, positive or negative). The seven actually possible surface types: peak, pit, ridge, flat, valley, saddle, minimal surface and saddle valley are too fine for navigational purposes, so the zero-crossings of the determinant of the Hessian (numerator of Gaussian curvature operator) are used,

$$f_{xx} f_{yy} - f_{xy}^2$$

as the segmentation procedure, where f_{uv} refers to partial differentiation of f with respect to u ($u = x$) and v ($v = y$) and $f(x, y)$ to the view-dependent range image. This determines grouped surface types ridge (peak or ridge), valley (pit, saddle or saddle valley) and planar regions (flat, saddle or minimal surface) in a way which minimises noise amplification which typically occurs when full curvature zero-crossings are evaluated. Such a segmentation procedure is invariant to rigid motions [1] (see Figure 1 Middle).

Once these segments have been extracted, an entropy-based information metric [7] is used to partition the image resulting in a graph representation - the Topograph. This procedure recursively splits image regions into new regions based on moving a linear partition to minimise the joint entropy sum according to the surface types on either side of the spilt. It is related to Quad tree representation where regions are recursively partitioned into four new equal regions [12, 14]. However, it differs in that it adaptively adjusts the boundaries. Further,

---

Topograph generation Algorithm:

1. Set medial axis and height range thresholds (minimum width, max climb/descent rates for flight).
2. Initialise smoothing threshold schedule (decreasing smoothing with i).
3. Maintain a queue of regions (initially one) ordered by variance of image to smoothed region.
4. While desired cardinality not reached
   (a) Select region from queue and calculate surface types for each pixel at current scale.
   (b) Split region by finding the minimum entropy partition with respect to surface type.
   (c) if region is greater than medial axis threshold AND height range is greater than height threshold then re-split using smoothing threshold schedule[i+1].

Fig. 3. The Topograph algorithm

Topographs uses two thresholds-medial axis of convex regions and height difference to adjacent regions. These correspond to the minimum width and maximum climb/descent rates for flight (see Figure 1 Bottom).

The procedure is an adaptation of machine learning decision tree techniques [2, 10] for producing convex spatial regions. Consider splitting a region R along a spatial dimension F. The elements of R are first sorted by their differential surface type $f(r)$ (convex, concave and planar), and then all possible cut points T midway between successive feature values in the sorted sequence are evaluated. For each cut point T, the elements of R are partitioned into two new regions, $P_1 = \{r \mid f(r) \leq T\}$ with n_1 elements and $P_2 = \{r \mid f(r) > T\}$ with n_2 elements. We define the partition entropy $H_P(T)$ as

$$H_P(T) = n_1 H(P_1) + n_2 H(P_2) \tag{1}$$

The cut point T_F that minimises $H_P(T_F)$ is considered the best point for splitting region R along spatial dimension F. The best split of region R is considered the one along the spatial dimension F that minimises T_F.

Here, we have a scalable view independent procedure that produces the most general "fit" or description of the landscape within certain depth and width thresholds - according to the constraints of the application, such as legal flight trajectories. This result in a hierarchy of regions as shown in Figure 2. The procedure recursively adapts the smoothing resolution to the local area to satisfy the constraints of width and depth. The algorithm is shown in Figure 3.

3 A Flight Trajectory Planning Example

The Topograph representation was tested using unprocessed digital terrain map images for the complexity and quality of solution to the flight trajectory planning

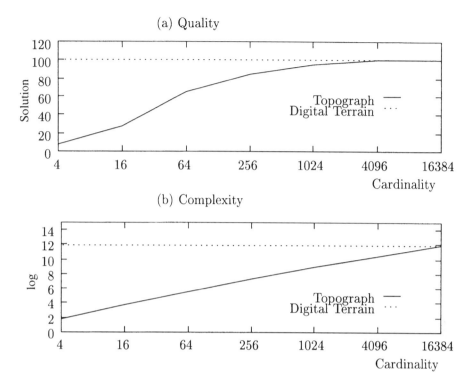

Fig. 4. Evaluation of Representation for 128 × 128 digital terrain map. (a) The quality of the solutions as determined by Equation 2 are compared. (b) The worst case complexity of the flight trajectory solution is compared for the Topograph and unprocessed Digital terrain map representations at different cardinalities (numbers of regions).

problem. A solution to the problem involves finding a path through the map from start to finish. In our case we have set the cost function to the integral under the path (sum of altitude).

Instead of representing the problem as an adjacency graph, as in the traditional minimum spanning tree problem, each position is an enumeration of different heading "layers". In the scheme you can only traverse between your current x,y,direction node and other nodes which are both adjacent and legally possible according to the constraints of motion and flight clearance. The quality of the solution is determined by the percentage of the best possible solution, obtainable using all the grid elements, when using the generalised symbolic regions in the Topograph. The quality of the solution, using a Topograph of cardinality t, is obtained using

$$quality(t)\% = 100 \left(1 - \frac{\int path_t - \int path_n}{\int path_s}\right) \qquad (2)$$

where $\int p_t$ is the integral under the solution in the topograph at cardinality t, $\int p_o$ is the integral of the optimum path integral using all n grid elements and $\int path_s$ is the integral under a straight line connecting the start and finish. A trade off is possible between the complexity versus the lower bound on the quality of the solution (see Figure 4(a)). This demonstrates the ability of the technique to preserve important spatial features with respect to homogeneity of types. In the topograph representation each region is characterised by the curvature information rather than the mean, as in pixelation.

The complexity of the problem is $O(nblog(nb))$ in the worst case, for n grid elements and branching factor b. The worst case number of search steps required to find the minimum cost trajectory using the Topograph is compared with that of unprocessed digital terrain map images (see Figure 4(b)).

4 Discussion

In the Topograph approach we have shown how machine learning techniques can be used to *learn* efficient segmentation of image data which satisfies the constraints of the application task. With the Topograph scheme, regions themselves are modelled according to the application requirements.

The Topograph hierarchy guarantees lower bounds on the quality of the solution to flight trajectories by requiring regions to satisfy application dependent thresholds. In addition, an optimal version of the search can be used by utilising dynamic programming principles, specifically the A^* search strategy [8], to formulate estimates of distance remaining based on symbolic region information.

A metric for homogeneity of the topography can also be established using an combined entropy measure over the Topograph representation based on the depth of the recursive splits needed to describe the topography. This also serves to establish the degree of generalisation achieved according to application defined constraints.

Other application areas include the segmentation of two dimensional intensity or depth images for pattern recognition, geographic information surveying applications and water shed problems for water routing. The topography representation could be extrapolated to include conditional edges between regions. Techniques could be investigated for generating more sophisticated graphs or lattices using relational learning techniques [9].

References

1. Besl, P., Jain, R.: Segmentation through variable-order surface fitting. IEEE Trans. Pattern Anal. Machine Intell. **10** (1988) 167–192
2. Bischof, W. F., Caelli, T.: Learning structural descriptions of patterns: A new technique for conditional clustering and rule generation. Pattern Recognition. **27**(5) (1994) 689–97
3. Caelli, T., Dreier, A.: Variations on the evidence-based object recognition theme. Pattern Recognition. **27** (1994) 185–204
4. Fan, T., Medioni, G., Nevatia, R.: Segmented descriptions of 3-D surfaces. IEEE Journal of Robotics and Automation. **RA-3** (1987) 527–538

5. Fan, T., Medioni, G., Nevatia, R.: Recognizing 3-D objects using surface descriptions. IEEE Transactions on Pattern Analysis and Machine Intelligence. **11**(11) (1989).
6. Gauch, J. M., Pizer, S. M.: Multiresolution analysis of ridges and valleys in grey-scale images. IEEE Transactions on Pattern Analysis and Machine Intelligence. **15**(6) (1993) 635–646
7. Jain, A. K., Dubes, R. C.: Algorithms for Clustering Data. Prentice Hall. (1988)
8. Nilsson, N. J.: Problem-Solving methods in artificial intelligence. McGraw-Hill Book Company. (1971)
9. Pearce, A., Caelli, T. Bischof, W. F.: Claret: A new relational learning algorithm for interpretation in spatial domains. In Proceedings of the Fourth International Conference on Control, Automation, Robotics and Vision (ICARV'96), Singapore. (1996) 650–654
10. Quinlan, J. R.: C4.5 Programs for Machine Learning. Morgan Kaufmann (1993)
11. Shapiro, L. G. Haralick, R. M.: Structural descriptions and inexact matching. IEEE Transactions on Pattern Analysis and Machine Intelligence. **3**(5) (1981) 504–519
12. Suzuki, T. Mori, S.: A thinning method based on cell structure. In Proc. Int. Workshop Frontiers Handwriting Recognition, Montreal, Canada. (1990) 39 – 52
13. Wong, A. K. C., Lu, S. W., Rioux, M.: Recognition and shape synthesis of 3-D objects based on attribute hypergraphs. IEEE Transactions on Pattern Analysis and Machine Intelligence. **11** 3 (1989) 279–290
14. Zelinsky, A.: A mobile robot exploration algorithm. IEEE Trans. on Robotics and Automation. **8**(6) (1992) 707–717

A Computer Assisted Image Analysis System for Diagnosing Movement Disorders

R Chang,[1] L Guan[1] & JA Burne[2]

[1] Department of Electrical Engineering, University of Sydney

[2] Department of Biomedical Science, University of Sydney

Abstract. Video image analysis is able to provide quantitative data on postural and movement abnormalities and thus has an important application in neurological diagnosis and management. The conventional techniques require patients to be videoed while wearing markers in a highly structured laboratory environment. This restricts the utility of video in routine clinical practice. We have begun development of intelligent software able to extract complete human profiles from video frames, to fit skeletal frameworks to the profiles and derive joint angles and local curvatures. By this means a given posture is reduced to a set of basic parameters that can provide input to a neural network classifier.

To test the system's performance, we videoed patients with dopa-responsive Parkinson's and age matched normals during several gait cycles, to yield 61 patient and 49 normal postures. These postures were reduced to their basic parameters and fed to the neural network classifier in various combinations. The optimal parameter sets (consisting of both swing distances and joint angles) yielded successful classification of normals and patients with an accuracy above 90%. This result demonstrated the feasibility of the approach. The technique has the potential to guide clinicians on the relative sensitivity of specific postural /gait features in diagnosis.

1. INTRODUCTION

Conventional diagnosis of many neurological and musculoskeletal disorders, involves the examination of posture and movement. The examination of a subject's gait, in particular, is a central part of current visual diagnostic procedures. It is carried out by trained clinicians, but is still subjective. There is a lack of quantitative criteria. Computer based video image analysis systems are able to provide an interface for precisely recording, quantifying and analysing of events otherwise dependent on subjective evaluation by human inspectors. They may thus assist in visual diagnosis.

Video image analysis can be applied in this context to capture abnormal human postures and movements, to reduce them to basic parameters, such as joint angles, swing distances and curvatures, etc. and to assess abnormal features against existing disability criteria. Common human conditions producing disabled posture and /or movement include stroke, cerebral palsy, muscular dystrophy, spinal injury, joint and bone disorders, fitting of prostheses, degenerative diseases and ageing.

A simple form of image analysis has already been applied to the problem of quantising human gait and posture[DLD1][LDAJSL1][KRW1][MCJJ1][KSLR1][MB1][NJL1].This method requires subjects to be videoed against a calibrated background while wearing small high contrast markers on the body segments of interest. It is thus restricted to a highly structured laboratory situation. The image processing component of this method is trivial and confined to identification of the location of the markers within the video frame.

In this paper, we present a computer-assisted system for diagnosing abnormal gait in a neurological disorder. By incorporating our knowledge of neurology and biomedical engineering into video image processing, we aim at achieving a flexible tool that can be applied to a less restricted environment, thereby assisting clinicians in analysing and diagnosing neurological disorders quantitatively and objectively. This requires the development of intelligent software that has the capability of identifying and quantifying human posture and movement. This paper reports some pioneer development and work in this project. The analysis of static postures is presented. The objective of static posture analysis is twofold: a) to assess the feasibility of video image processing in human posture and movement analysis and in the application of diagnosis of neurological disorder; b) to identify the postures in a gait cycle which carry more sensitive features to be used in a more advanced gait analysis.

The paper is organised in the following sections. In Section 2, the structure of the system is introduced. Details of the processing techniques are described in Section 3. Preliminary experimental results are given in Section 4. Section 5 summarises the current work and points out some future research directions.

2. SYSTEM STRUCTURE

The image analysis system is composed of three subsystem: image acquisition, image processing and decision making. The digital image acquisition subsystem consists of a video camera, a video recorder, and a frame grabber. This subsystem also contains the necessary software to interface the PC to the hardware, which also assists in acquiring an image from a selected part of a subject's gait and storing it in a specified image format. The images can then be processed in the next stage.

The image processing subsystem is software based. This software performs the required processing to extract important visual information (features) from the images digitised in the previous stage, which can then be used for classification in the next stage. In this paper, ten features are extracted: two knee joint angles, two ankle joint angles, two sole to floor's angles and four swing distances which are all defined in the next section.

The decision-making subsystem consists of a neural network that has been trained using the joint angles and swing distances extracted from the processing subsystem. This network is used to classify new and unseen samples in the patient group and those in the normal control group.

3. PROCESSING TECHNIQUES

The observation of gait in particular, provides a sensitive measure of generalised disability. It is thus a central part of current neurological assessment procedures. Fig. 1 shows two standing postures, one from a patient and the another from a normal person.

The characteristics of the two are quite distinct to each other. We will thus focus on the analysis of abnormal gait as well as standing posture.

The steps in the collection and analysis of the video images are summarised in Fig. 2. They consist of acquisition and storage of video frames on tape and image analysis of selected frames to outline the captured postures, fit axes to them and make estimates of sensitive features from the axes (including angles about each joint, the distances between the tips of the upper limbs and the body, and the length of stride). Each member of the resulting sets of features will be statistically weighted according to its ability to discriminate between the experimental groups. By this process, the reliability of individual gait features, as well as various combinations of features, in discriminating between groups will be discovered. Particular techniques adapted in this research are described in details in the following subsections.

3.1 Image Acquisition and Preprocessing

Stationary postures and gait cycles are colour videoed using a single colour camera and stored on tape. Individual frames are then selected and loaded to a colour frame grabber (Datatranslations DT2871) under computer control.

Due to technical synchronization problems, there were unwanted vertical noise in some frames. It was effective to use a low-pass filter to clean this type of noise. For impulse noise, the median filter was more effective, because it was able to reduce noise without much blurring. In order to minimise the effect of background, the size of the image is cut down to contain principally the subject of interest only.

3.2 Image Segmentation

Segmentation is critical stage in the processing. The images captured from videos are normally of poor quality. This gives difficulties in segmenting human subjects from the background, even when the subject wears a costume against a uniform background. For the current work, a specially designed costume consisting of three colours (Black, White, Red), and a single background colour are used. Typical examples are shown in Fig. 1. It may be feasible to use relatively simple threshold measures to segment the image in this setting. However, because of lighting and shadow effects and the poor quality of the images, simple thresholding results in poor segmentation.

Therefore, a combined edge detection and thresholding algorithm was studied and implemented. The algorithm consists of two steps. The first step is edge detection. A edge detector was used to get the outline of the subject to be processed. Then the outline was used to erase the background. There exist many edge detection operators. In our system, The Sobel edge operator was applied, which results in a wide range of grey-scale levels of edges in the edge map as given in Fig -3.a. In order to obtain the close boundary of the subject, segmentation of the edge map based on a low threshold value was then used. The result is illustrated in Fig. 3.b. Since the segmented edge map contains a lot of noise, the prior knowledge of the position of the subject is used to clear some of the noise. Finally, the image region which contains the subject of interest is identified as shown in Fig. 3.c.

In Step1, the image region found is represented still in grey scale levels with background being set to certain value, which means that different parts i.e. legs, torso, arms, of the body have not been segmented. The second step is to segment the image regions for different parts of the body from the image obtained in Step 1, so that the features can be extracted. To do this, a scheme is used that adaptively choose the threshold using a histogram of the image obtained in Step 1. Basically there are three colour zooms in the grey-scale level image of the subject to be segmented, which represent the main body part(black), one leg(white) and two arms (red, but transparent). First of all, the histogram of the grey scale levels of the image is applied. According to the histogram shown in Fig. 4, it can be seen that the pixels of the black area representing the main body part stands at the low end of the horizontal axis and the pixels of the white area mainly distribute at the upper end of the axis. According to prior knowledge, the peaks respectively corresponding to black region and white region can be found. The lower threshold for the black region and the upper threshold for the white region can be easily set, because they just simply stand at the two ends of the horizontal axis. It is assumed that the grey-scale levels of the pixels follow a Gaussian distribution. Because the peaks and one end threshold are known, the thresholds of other ends for both cases are determined geometrically. Finally, because of environmental variation, such as in lighing, the distance and angle between video camera and subject, some tolerance is needed. Hence adaptive thresholding is used. After finding the thresholds for the black and white regions, these two image regions are segmented. To erase the bright outline of the subject which mixes with the white leg, the dilation and erosion operations are applied. To segment the two arms from the regions (including head and face) left from the above segmentation, the relative position knowledge of the human body is used. Final result of segmentation is shown Fig. 3.d

3.3 Image Analysis

After segmentation, the areas of interest were separated from the background. In order to extract features (joints angles and the distance between the ends of the limbs), image analysis techniques, such as, border tracing, region filling, and skeletonization were applied.

Since tight clothes were worn, the boundary of the subject quite accurately represents the postural information of the subject. Thus the boundary of the subject was used in joint angle calculation (The details will be discussed in section 3.4.1). To obtain the border of the subject, a border tracing algorithm was used [SHB1]. The border tracing algorithm starts from an arbitrarily selected edge point. It uses an 8-connection search scheme to continuously find connecting edge point, until the whole border line being traced. The result is shown in Fig. 3.e.

The segmented image may contain some small holes. This can cause problems when applying a skeleton algorithm. To overcome this problem, a region filling algorithm adopted from [8] was applied to eliminate the holes. The method is based on set dilations, complementing, intersections and other morphological processing techniques.Shapes, especially the elongated ones, are sufficiently well described by their thinned versions consisting of connected lines that, ideally, run along the medial axes of object limbs. These unit-width lines are closely related to object skeleton. To obtain the skeleton of the object, thinning techniques are required. Thinning can be defined heuristically as a set of successive erosions of the outermost layers of a shape, until a connected unit-width set of lines(skeleton) is obtained. Thus, thinning algorithms are iterative algorithms that 'peel off' border pixels. Connectivity is an important property that must be preserved in the thinned object. Therefore, border pixels are deleted in such a way that object connectivity is maintained. Thinning algorithms satisfy the following two constraints:

1. They maintain connectivity at each iteration.
2. They do not shorten the end of thinned shape limbs.

There are many thinning algorithms available. In our system, Jang's structuring templates algorithm [JC1]] is used.

3.4 Feature Calculation and Analysis

3.4.1 Feature Calculation

From observation of the gait in normal people and patients with Parkinson's disease, it becomes apparent that the stretching and joint flexibility of the limbs of human subjects are key features to explain the different gait patterns between the two groups. So two types of features, distances and angles are calculated to distinguish the two groups: normal people and patients with Parkinson's disease. In the distance group, four features are calculated, including:

- Front hand to median axis of torso i.e feature 8;
- Back hand to median axis of torso i.e. feature 9:
- Front hand to back hand i.e feature 10
- Front heel to back toe i.e feature 7

All the distances are scaled by the height of the subject. In the joint angle group, six features are extracted, including:

- Two knee joint angles (including the front leg's knee angle (feature 1) and the back leg's one (feature 4));
- Two ankle joint angles (front: feature 2; back: feature 4);
- Two angles of the soles to the floor (front: feature 3; back: feature 6)

The advantages of using the distances are that they are easy to obtain, robust to noise and more accurate than angles obtained by the current method.

Measurement of distances is based on the skeleton calculated, since skeleton quite accurately represents the structure of the human subject. We first identify the endpoints of limbs from the skeleton, and then calculate the distance.

The original approach to measure the joint angles is also based on the skeleton representation of the subject, which can be defined by its medial axis transformation. However, later studies show that there is some extent of distortion as shown in Fig. 3.f. The angles between two arms are typical examples. Because of the stretchable clothes worn by the subject, the boundary of the subject provides a more reliable information source and is thus used to calculate the joint angles instead of using the skeleton representation.

3.4.2 Feature Analysis

After calculating the ten features, the importance of them in term of the intended task is studied. First, principal component analysis(PCA) is applied [GW1] to find the relative importance of the feature. The results are tabulated in Table1. In the table Fi stands for feature i.

From the table, it can be seen that the variances corresponding to the last four features (the distances) are more significant than the ones corresponding to the first six features (the angles). However, our experimental results shows that the discriminating ability of the less significant features are not in the order of the list given by PCA. One explanation is that PCA is a linear analyser and it assumes Gaussian distribution. In real world applications like ours, neither of the assumptions is true. PCA can pick up the prominent features correctly in the nonlinear and/or the nonGuassian cases, since the linear model used by PCA approximates the dominate characteristics represented by the most significant features. It fails to work out the relative importance of the less significant features, since the nonlinearity represented by those features can not be correctly modelled by a linear PCA. To analyse the less important but contributing features, we introduce a novel strategy based on histogram analysis.

Table1

	F1	F2	F3	F4	F5	F6	F7	F8	F9	F10
NORMAL & PATIENT	28.1	26.7	17.3	7.1	3.7	48.2	94.7	475	729	2469

To start with, we calculated the histograms of all the ten features in the two classes. Observation of the histograms clearly indicates the order of importance of the features. The nonoverlap distributions of features 7, 8, 9, 10 indicate that they are the features with significant discriminating power. This is consistent with the result of the PCA. However, the histograms also tell us that, among features 1-6, features 1 and 3 are the next important features. For example, in the histogram of feature1, the normal group is mainly spread above 0.6, while the patient group is largely distributed below 0.6. Histograms of some typical features are displayed in Fig. 5. Hence in our feature analysis, we first use PCA to identify the most important features and then use histogram analysis to obtain some supplementary features.

3.5 CLASSIFICATION BY NEURAL NETWORKS

Neural network is adopted in object identification. A neural network is equivalent to a non-parametric statistical method which addresses problems not by means of pre-specified algorithms but rather by "learning" from examples that are presented repeatedly. The reason to use neural networks is primarily due to their apparent ability to make decisions and draw conclusions when presented with "noisy", or partial information and to adapt their behaviour to the nature of the training data. Since they do not need an exact model as the linear statistical methods do, neural network methods have the potential to resolve nonlinear classification problems such as posture and movement analysis.

Classification is performed by a back-propagation neural network. The network consists of an input layer that has a number of processing elements (the optimal number decided by the experiments), a hidden layer and an output layer that has two processing elements. The number of nodes in the hidden layer is determined by the following formula [Ma1]

$$N_h = N_o \times \sqrt{N_i}$$

Where N_h is the number of hidden nodes, N_o is the number of output nodes, and N_i is the number of input nodes.

4. EXPERIMENTS

The experimental data were collected from two groups, normal people and patients with Parkinson's disease. Both of the two groups were in same age range(45-55). The total number of samples was 109, including 48 from normal people and 61 from patients.Samples in the two groups were evenly divided into four subgroups: NA, NB, PA and PB(N for normal and P for patient). Then Data group A and group B were made up by NA, PA and NB, PB respectively. Group A and B excluded each other. When the group A was used as testing data, the group B is used as training data, and vice versa.

Four experiments were conducted using the features extracted and analysised in the last section. The results are listed in Table 2

- In Test 1, inputs consisted of the six angle features.
- In Test 2, inputs were the four distance features.
- In Test 3, inputs were combined by four distance features and two angle features (front leg's knee angle and sole to floor angle) chosen by histogram analysis. The histograms tell us that the other four angle features have little classification power, if any.
- In Test 4, the six most significant features identified by the PCA, features 1,6,7,8,9,10 were used as inputs.
- In Test 5, inputs were the total ten features.

From Table 2, the following facts were observed:

- Only angle features can not characterise the problem effectively.This result does not rule out the importance of the joint angles, but suggests that more robust processing techniques and angle measurements are required.

- Although there are only the four distance features, they are indeed the key to success. This confirms our claim about the robustness of the distance features.
- By combining the power of PCA and histogram analysis, Test 3 is in theory the optimal decision making strategy and it does provide the best classification results.
- By comparing Test 3 and Test 4, it is very clear that PCA does not rank the secondary significant features correctly.
- It is interesting to note that "junking" all the extracted features into decision making does not give the best performance, as we compare Test 3 and Test 5. Since the neural network addresses the problem by "learning" i.e being trained by the training data, if the feature does not indicate clearly the differences between the two groups, it will not contribute positively.

Table 2

	Test 1	Test 2	Test 3	Test 4	Test 5
Group A	76.5	80.4	92.2	84.3	86.3
Group B	60.7	87.5	91.1	91.1	87.5

5. CONCLUSION AND FUTURE WORK

We present an image processing based computer-aided system to quantitatively analysing human posture and movement. A complete processing and analysis procedure is defined and implemented to extract and analyse joint angles and swing distances, two groups of prominent features characterising neurological disorders. Preliminary experiment results show that, by incorporating intelligent processing techniques, the system is able to provide valuable information to clinicians in diagnosing neurological disorders.

The classification accuracy that had been obtained indicated that diagnosis of neurological disorder based on joint angles and swing distances is promising and feasible. Since the features of swing distances are introduced, it makes the whole system more reliable and robust to noise, particularly to tolerance of the accuracy of joint angles. The more significant point is that it is feasible to process the images with normal clothes, because only the ends of limbs are needed to measure the swing distance. In order to improve the accuracy of the classification and enhance the reliability of the system, the following research directions are suggested

- Introduce a straight-line finding algorithm such as Hough transform to improve the accuracy of the joint angles.
- Instead of using only the features from a single static posture in the analysis, a set of postures from a gait cycle will be selected. Dynamic features representing transitions between the postures and human movement will be studied to improve the performance of the system.

After further improvement, the system is potentially useful in the following areas:
- Assist the process of diagnosing patients with neurological disorders;

- Quantitative analysis of the walking movement of human subjects
- Rating the severity of the patient with movement disorder by quantitative analysis.
- An objective basis for identifying the most and less significant features in diagnostic observation, a potentially valuable training aid.

References

1.Embry, D. G.,Yates, L. and Mott, D. H.: Effects of Neur-Developmental Treatment and Orthoses on Knee Flexion During Gait: A Single Subject Design. Physical Therapy 70(10): 1990.

2.Gunderson, L. A., Valle, D. R., Barr, A. E., Danoff, J. V., Stanhope, S. J. and Snyder-Mackler, L.: Bilateral Analysis of the Knee and Ankle During Gait: An Examination of the Relationship Between Lateral Dominance and Symmetry. Physical Therapy 69(8):640-650, 1989.

3. Kadaba, MP., Ramakrishnan, HK. and Wooten, ME.: Measurement of Lower Extremity Kinematice During Level Walking. Journal of Orthopaedic Research 8(3): 383-392,1990.

4. Kassover, M., Tauber, C., Au, J. and Pugh, J.: Auditory Biofeedback in Spastic Diplegia. Journal of Orthopaedic Research 4(2);246-249, 1986

5. Kepple, TM., Stanhope, SJ., Lohmann, KN. and Roman, NL.: A Video-Based Technique for Measuring Ankle-Subtaler Motion During Stance. Journal of Biomedical Engineering 12(4):273-280, 1990.

6. Martinez-Martin, P., Bermejo-Parejo, F.: Rating Scales in Parkinson's Disease.In: Jankovic Joseph and Tolosa Eduardo, ed. Parkinson's Disease and Movement Disorders. Baltimore-Munich: Urban and Schwarzenberg, pp.235-242, 1988.

7. Nuzzo, R.M., Jllly, J. and Langrana, NA.: contralateral Compensation with Knee Impairment.Clenicl Orthopaedics and Related Research No.223:225-236, 1987.

8.Gonzlez, R. C., Woods, R. E.: Digital Image Processing No.148-156; No.532-533. Addison-Wesley, New York, U.S.A. 1992

9.Sonka, M., Hlavac, V., Boyle, R.: Image Processing, analysis and Machine Vision No. 129-131. University Press, Cambridge, U.K.1993.

10. Jang, B., Chin, R. T.: Analysis of Thinning Algorithms Using Mathematical Morphology, IEEE Transactions on Pattern Analysis and Machine Intelligence,Vol.12, No. 6, June 1990.

11. Masters, R. T.: Practical Neural Network Recipes in C++, Academic Press, Boston, U.S.A. 1993.

Acknowledgement

This work is partially supported by a ARC Small Grant.

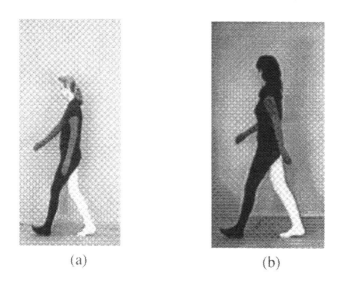

(a)   (b)

Fig. 1. Original images from patients group and normal control group. (a) Patient. (b) normal.

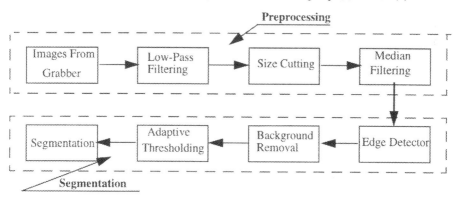

Fig. 2. Image processing procedures.

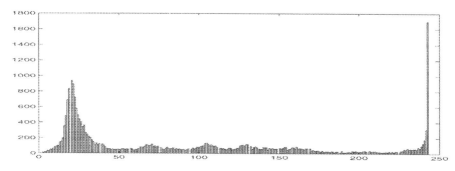

Fig. 4. The histogram of grey scale levels of the image region, only including the real body parts.

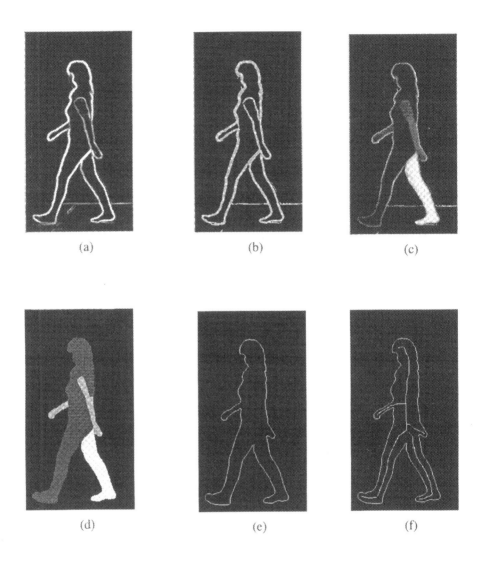

Fig. 3. The results of each procedures: (a) the result of the edge detector; (b) the result of the thresholding on edge map; (c) the image with the background being set on certain value; (d) the final result of the segmentation; (e) the boundary of the body; (f) the overlap of the boundary and the skeleton of the body.

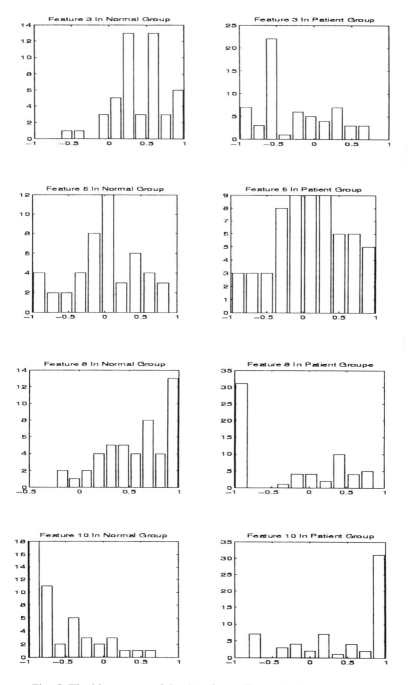

Fig. 5. The histograms of the data from all samples for some feature.

Vowel Recognition for Speaker Independent Chinese Speech Recognition[1]

YIN Baolin, YU Tao

Department of Computer Science
Beijing University of Aeronautics & Astronautics
Beijing, China 100083

Abstract

Vowel recognition is essential in Chinese speech recognition, especially in the speaker independent tasks. In this paper, the authors argued that the fixed length frame segmentation of the speech signal makes the feature extracting process lose essential features and introduces some irrelevant information so that the extracted features may be less expressive and consistent. Using the pitch-based dynamically adaptive frames will improve the process of extracting the speech features so that they can be more expressive for the phonemes to be recognized, and more consistent among different speakers. The algorithm for dynamically segmenting the speech signals is discussed, and a variety of features has been tested with the pitch-based adaptive frames, and a new type of feature, the FFT magnitude pattern, shows that it is very expressive and consistent and may help to simplify the recognition models. By the use of the FFT magnitude patterns, definite algorithms can be adopted at the recognition stage. This will simplify the calculation and speed up the process. The experiment is done using a finite-state machine model. The results showed that the pitch-based FFT magnitude patterns are more expressive and consistent than other features and suitable for speaker independent Chinese speech recognition tasks.

1. Introduction

Speech recognition, as an input method, has more significance in the Chinese community than in the English world. This is because that Chinese is not an alphabetic language but a character based one. Although many methods have been developed for the input of Chinese characters, none of them has been very successful and accepted by most of the users. In fact, the majority of these methods are different coding systems designed for the users to input Chinese characters by using the ordinary key board. These methods are either too complicated, too slow, or need special training which are only suitable for specialized typists. This makes the speech recognition to be an attractive method for Chinese input.

---

[1] This work was supported by the Trans-Century Training Programme Foundation for the Talents by the State Education Commission, China.

Much work has been done on Chinese speech recognition and some systems have been published. However, not much has been achieved in the area of speaker independent large vocabulary recognition. The literature (e.g. [1, 2, 3]) shows that the average recognition rate is around 80% for a speaker independent task. The main reason for this is that the techniques used are not suitable for spoken Chinese, especially the techniques for recognizing the basic speech unit.

2. The Special Characteristics of Chinese Speech

In Chinese language, all the characters are mono-syllabic with one of the four lexical tones, and different tones basically represent the changes of the pitch of a syllable. This is a nice feature for character detection and segmentation, but it also causes difficult problems in character recognition.

There are 21 consonants and 35 vowels and some 1,300 phonologically allowed syllables in the concurrent standard Chinese pronunciation. A syllable usually consists of a consonant and a vowel. In some syllables there may be no consonants, but any syllable must end with either a vowel or a vowel plus a nasal such as -n or -ng. If the differences among the syllables caused only by lexical tones are disregarded, there are only 408 distinguished syllables allowed in Chinese. Meanwhile, there are about 8,000 commonly used Chinese characters. This means that there are in average 20 homonym characters for each syllable.

The large number of homonym characters for each syllable makes some techniques which have been successfully used in English recognition not suitable for Chinese. In addition to this, the constitution rules for Chinese words are quite flexible. The 8,000 Chinese characters can make up more than 50,000 words with each word containing two, three, four or even up to seven characters. Some characters can also be independent one-character words by themselves. Because of the flexibility of the Chinese morphology and grammar, it is not easy to apply any higher level knowledge in recognizing a syllable in a Chinese speech sequence. In fact, even when a correct sequence of syllables is given, the interpretation may be ambiguous in many ways: in segmenting the syllable sequence into words, in selecting a word from its homonyms, etc.. At this stage, interaction between the user and the system is inevitable. Therefore, it is essential for the syllable recognition sub-system to provide high recognition rate by itself without using much high level knowledge and the user interaction.

3. The Recognition Features

In Chinese speech recognition, the commonly used units are syllables and words. The process for extracting the features is as follows: first, the speech signal is divided into frames. Each frame has a fixed length and consecutive frames overlap. The LPC based cepstral coefficients are calculated for each frame. Then vector quantization (VQ) is applied to the LPC cepstrum to convert the real vectors into symbols. The symbols are then used in a Hidden Markov Model (HMM) for training and recognition respectively.

The LPC based cepstral coefficients extracted this way seems to be efficient in many English speech recognition systems. As the speech signals are smoothed by using overlapped frames and smooth windows, the extracted features are insensitive to the noise and signal distortions. However, as the frames are of fixed length, they will cover different articulation segments for speeches with different pitches. The smoothing techniques make the features insensitive to the noise and undesired signal inconsistency, but they also filter out the useful information for distinguishing the speech units. Thus, in most systems, the LPC based vectors should be compensated by other information. This will increase the calculation burden in the quantization stage. The inaccuracy of the feature extraction is also compensated by vast training for the HMM. Although these measures are taken, the recognition rate for the speech unit is still not high enough for Chinese speech recognition. Even for a speaker dependent task, the recognition rate is between 70% to 80%, depending upon the type of the HMM used[4].

4. The Framework of the Vowel Recognition System

In the following sections, a new method for the vowel recognition will be described. This method differs from the existing ones mainly in two aspects. First, it segments the speech signals into frames in an adaptive way by the use of the pitch information so that the discrepancy caused by the pitch differences of different speakers will be filtered out. Second, a new type of feature is adopted which is more expressive than the LPC based ones, and this makes the recognition process more effective. As spoken Chinese is a mono-syllable based language, this method can be used in both the discrete and continuous speech recognition.

4.1. Selecting the Phoneme as the Recognition Unit

For a speaker independent task, both the speech unit and the features selected for recognition should be expressive, consistent and efficient. In a Chinese syllable, the consonant is very short compared with the vowel. While the vowel is a quasi-periodic signal fragment with the characteristics of short time steadiness and occupies most of the duration of a syllable, the consonant is more irregular and volatile. Therefore, it is better to use a phoneme as a speech unit, that is, to recognize the consonant and the vowel separately. With the selection of the phoneme as the unit, the size of the recognition task will be reduced dramatically from 408 syllables to 56 phonemes, 21 for consonants and 35 for vowels, and the knowledge of the phonologically allowed syllables may also be used in the recognition task.

4.2. The Adaptive Frame for a Speaker Independent Vowel Recognition

In order to fulfil the speaker independent recognition task, it is important to find out and make use of intrinsic speaker independent features of the speech signal. When a fixed length frame is used, the starting point of the frame is at a random position with respect to the speech signal, and the frame covers a random number of cycles of the speech signal which is usually not an integer. Therefore, although there are some similarities among the utterances of different speakers, the segmented speech signals seems quite different from the view point of the feature extraction. This makes the smoothing techniques necessary. As the frames have a fixed length, the pitch will be extracted as a part of the features. Since different speakers have different pitches, the features extracted this way will inevitably vary significantly from speaker to speaker. This in turn makes extensive training and complicated HMM necessary. Training makes the feature extraction less sensitive to the differences caused by speakers, but also loses some useful information for distinguishing the speech units. This explains why sometimes extensive training will reduce the recognition rate.

When a dynamically adaptive frame is used to accommodate the speaker's pitch, it can be considered as a normalization in the time domain. The frame length is determined dynamically by the pitch to be processed and each frame contains only one pitch cycle. In this way, the extracted features will no longer contain the pitch related information. Thus, the insensitiveness to the pitch is no longer a factor for selecting the feature extracting algorithm, and a more effective algorithm for extracting more expressive features can be adopted without considering the insensitivity to the factors caused by fixed length segmentation. The features extracted this way will be more consistent for different speakers, and more expressive for the vowels.

4.3. Pitch Determination and Frame Segmentation

In order to select an adaptive frame to accommodate the pitch, the pitch period must be determined. This is done in two steps. First, the starting point of a pitch is selected, and second, the pitch is calculated.

The pitch interval is determined by the elapsed time between two successive glottal pulses. Each time the vocal cords is stimulated, a declining signal is generated. As the starting point of a pitch (SPP) is corresponding to the starting of the stimulation of the pulse, its signal should have the largest local magnitude change. Therefore, the starting point of a pitch must lie at a rising zero-cross point (RZP) which separates the last valley of the last pitch and the first (usually the largest) peak of the current pitch. However, because of the inconsistency of the articulation, the first peak may not be the largest one in some cases. In order to determine the starting point of a pitch correctly, other features should be taken into account.

It is discovered that the energy of the valley which is adjacent to the SPP is usually the largest among the valleys in a whole pitch cycle. Therefore, only when an RZP is adjacent to a high following peak and a large leading valley, can it be a candidate of the SPP. The search for the SPP will be done among these candidates by comparing their corresponding peaks and valleys. Occasionally, an SPP does not meet this criterion. In this case, the correlation of the extracted pitch interval and the pitch interval determined by the candidate RZPs will be calculated. The one with the largest correlation coefficient will be selected as the SPP.

In order to describe the algorithm for extracting the pitch period, the cross-correlation coefficient between voice signals $x(t)$ and $y(t)$ is defined as follows.

$$r_{t0} = \frac{\sum\limits_{t=0}^{N} x(t)y(t)w(t-t_o)}{\sqrt{\sum\limits_{t=0}^{N} x^2(t)w(t-t_o)\sum\limits_{t=0}^{N} y^2(t)w(t-t_o)}}$$

where t_0 is the starting point, w is a rectangular window of length p:

$$w(t) = \quad 1 \quad 0 \leq t \leq p$$
$$0 \quad otherwise$$

For the voice signal s(t) at each time instance t_0 two signals are defined as follows:

$$x_p(t, t_o) = s(t)w(t - t_o)$$
$$y_p(t, t_o) = s(t+p)w(t - t_o)$$

The algorithm for detecting the pitch period is as follows: From the starting point t_0 which must be an RZP,

1) The correlation coefficient r(p) is calculated within the range p = [Pmin, Pmax] for each RZP, where Pmin and Pmax are the minimum and maximum possible period of the pitch respectively.
2) Selecting peaks r(p1), r(p2), ..., r(pn) among $rt_0(p)$.
3) For the set P = [p1, p2, ..., pn], the following operations are applied.
   a. if $p2 \cong np_1$, where $n \in N$, (N is the set of the natural numbers) then the short time energy for xp1(t, to) and yp1(t, to) Exp1 and Eyp1 are calculated. If $\frac{|Exp_1 - Eyp_1|}{Exp_1 + Eyp_1}$ is greater than a threshold, then p1 must be PP/m where PP is the pitch period and $m \in N$. So p1 is removed from P. Otherwise p2 must be qPP where $q \in N$, and p2 is removed from P.
   b. if $p2 = fp_1, f \notin N$, then the one with smaller r(p) is to be removed from P.
   c. The above operation will be repeated until there is only one element p_i left in P. p_i will be selected as the pitch period.

Because the correlation coefficient is only calculated at the RZPs, the number of the calculation is dramatically reduced and the algorithm is more efficient than that described in [5].

5. Selecting Effective Features

Using the dynamically adaptive frames, experiments were conducted for selecting the effective features for vowel recognition. Three types of features have been tested. They are the LPC cepstrum based coefficients, the FFT magnitude coefficients and the FFT magnitude patterns. The testing data were uttered by 20 male speakers, with each vowel being articulated five times. Experiments were done on a subset of the total 35 vowels. The tested vowels included all the six uni-vowels and ten dual-vowels with 17 tri-vowels left untested. These vowels were selected because they are the essential and representative ones and presents typical characteristics of the Chinese vowels. The sample rate for the speech signal was 22KHz, and this provides better results in feature extraction then the lower rates.

The testing on the LPC based features were done in two stages. In the first stage, the extracted feature vectors were clustered. Both the LGB algorithm and the self-adaptive neural network were tried for the clustering and showed similar results, but the neural network system worked faster than the LGB one. The clustering resulted in 4 codebooks for the LPC cepstrum based coefficients, each with 128 codewords. Then the VQ was done to the testing data and the sequences of the codewords were recorded. It is observed that under the adaptive frames, the LPC based features show that they are more consistent among different speakers. In the second stage, an HMM was trained and the vector quantizer was connected directly to a discrete HMM for recognition. The recognition rate for the trained data is over 99% while that for the untrained data is 82%.

The testing on the FFT coefficients was done using the first 30 coefficients. For the purpose of simplicity, only the magnitude is used. The VQ and the HMM were trained and tested the same as the LPC based features, except there was only one codebook with the size of 128. The results were also quite similar to that of the LPC based features. It demonstrated that using the dynamically adaptive frames, the FFT features are also consistent among the speakers. Because of this, the size of the codebook need not to be large, and the smaller size of the codebook will speed up the process of VQ. The recognition rate using this type of feature is 98% for trained data about 80% for untrained data.

The third type of features tested was the FFT magnitude patterns. The magnitude patterns were derived from the top 7 FFT magnitude coefficients. For each frame, the FFT magnitude coefficients were calculated and the magnitude patterns generated by magnitude normalization and sorting. This type of feature has a very good consistency among different speakers. In fact, as few as 16 patterns will be able to cover almost all the sample data of the 15 tested vowels. For each uni-vowel, there are usually only two or three patterns appeared in the feature sequence. Another good characteristics of this type of feature is that it expresses the compound vowels very well. In our experiments, many dual-vowels were recognized using the patterns for the uni-vowels of [a], [o], [e], [i], [u] and [ü] only without introducing any new patterns. Using this type of feature, the combination and the transition process of a compound vowel can be seen clearly.

Compared with the LPC based features and FFT magnitude coefficients, the FFT magnitude pattern seems more expressive for the vowel and more consistent among speakers than the other two. In fact, for most testing samples, it can almost be seen straightforward from the patterns which vowels they are. In addition to this, it is also less intensive in calculation.

One of the shortcomings of the FFT magnitude patterns is that it has some difficulties in distinguish the nasals. In our experiments, the vowels [an] and [ang], [en] and [eng] are the two most confusing pairs. The end patterns for the nasals in each pair are quite similar. It is hard to distinguish one from the other using this type of feature and therefore only [an] and [en] were formally tested.

6. Recognizing a Vowel with FFT Patterns and Finite-State Machine

Currently, the most commonly used recognition methods are HMM based ones. These algorithms are calculation intensive. They are adopted mainly because that the features provided to the recognition phase are less expressive. There are many uncertainties in the features and the phonemes cannot be determined just by using the features themselves with simple rules. Extensive search is needed with the guidance of some types of higher level knowledge. This makes the recognition quite time consuming.

With more expressive features, it may no longer be necessary to use the complicated recognition methods mentioned above. As there is less speaker dependent information in the features, it can be expected that the features for a phoneme will be clustered more closely and thus different phonemes can be distinguished more easily in the domain of the features. Therefore, some definite algorithms can be used to determine the phonemes without calculating the probabilities in a vast searching network. In our experiment, a finite-state machine (FSM) model was tested. The general model of the FSM used in our experiment is as follows:

Fig. 1. The general model of the finite-state machine

For different vowels, the number of the states and the feature pattern set for each state are different. There is a feature pattern set for each state. The recognition process is as follows. First, the voice signal is segmented into pitch frames, and the FFT feature pattern is extracted. At the end of this stage, the voice signal has been transformed into a stream of pitch-based feature patterns. This stream is pumped into the FSM, and the FSM will decide whether it will stay at the current state, jump into the next state, or quit the current model. This process will repeat until either the FSM reaches its final state or quit. In the first case, the input stream is recognized as the vowel represented by the current model. In the latter case, another model will be tested until either a match is found or all the models have been tried. If all the models have been tried without a match, the input stream is recognized as unknown.

The duration of each part of the same vowel varies from sample to sample. In order to adapt to the variation, a limited time warping is adopted by recording the duration of each state of the FSM model during recognition. The recorded duration will be taken into account for deciding which model the pattern stream of a voice sample belongs to. This technique has been proven to be effective in distinguishing some vowel model which are otherwise confusing.

As the uni-vowels are relatively simple, the FSM model used for them have only three states: one for the starting state, one for the dominant (steady) state and another for the ending state. The followings are the set of the feature patterns for each state.

Vowel\State	state 1	state 2	state 3
a	[noise, unknown]	[a]	[noise, unknown, n]
e	[noise, unknown]	[e]	[noise, unknown, n]
i	[noise, unknown]	[i]	[noise, unknown, n]
u	[noise, unknown]	[u]	[noise, unknown, n]
ü	[noise, unknown]	[ü]	[noise, unknown, n]

The dual-vowels are more complicated than the uni-vowels. It can be seen from the observation that there are usually two dominant patterns with a transition stage between them in each dual-vowel . Therefore the model for the dual-vowels are of five states. The followings are the set of the feature patterns for each state in the dual-vowel FSM models.

Vowel\State	state 1	state 2	state 3	state 4	state 5
ai	[noise, unknown]	[a, ae]	[e, ao]	[ai, i]	[noise, unknown]
ei	[noise, unknown]	[e]	[ei]	[i]	[noise, unknown]
ao	[noise, unknown]	[a]	[ao, e]	[ou, u]	[noise, unknown]
ou	[noise, unknown]	[e, ao]	[ou]	[u]	[noise, unknown]
an	[noise, unknown]	[a, an]	[e]	[n]	[noise, unknown]
en	[noise, unknown]	[e, ou]	[n]	/	[noise, unknown]
ia	[noise, unknown]	[i]	[ia, ai]	[a]	[noise, unknown]
ua	[noise, unknown]	[u, ou]	[ao, ae]	[a]	[noise, unknown]
ü e	[noise, unknown]	[ü]	[ai, e]	/	[noise, unknown]
o	[noise, unknown]	[u]	[ou]	[e]	[noise, unknown]

The recognition rate of the finite state machine is 97% for the trained data and 93% for the untrained ones. It can be seen that the recognition rate is quite high for the untrained samples. Another obvious advantage of this model is that it is not a probability one and does not need vast search. Therefore it runs much faster than the HMM. As the finite state machine model is quite simple, it was implemented without using any training but just by observing the feature sequences with some modification in the test.

A discrete HMM using the FFT pattern features was also implemented for the purpose of comparison. The recognition rate of this model is 98% for the trained data and 91% for the untrained data. It can be seen that the recognition rate is almost the same as that of the finite state machine model. As there are only 16 possible codewords as the input symbols for the HMM, the storage space is much smaller than that which uses ordinary LPC features and usually needs 128 or 256 codewords, and therefore both training and recognition processes are faster.

7. Conclusions

In the previous sections, the disadvantages of the fixed length framing were discussed and a new type of technique for segmentation, the dynamically adaptive framing, introduced. Using this technique, a variety of features has been tested and a new type of features, the FFT magnitude pattern, showed to be expressive for the vowels and consistent among different speakers. Compared with the LPC based features extracted using the fix length frames, the FFT magnitude patterns resulted in a more consistent feature set. In all our experiments with the FFT magnitude patterns, this type of features was adopted without other features such as the energy based ones. The results showed that with this type of features, even a simple model such as a finite state machine may generate acceptable results. Even when the HMM is still desired because of its power and advantages in other aspects, such as the tolerance to the noise and the capability of automatic training, the search area will be much smaller with the FFT magnitude patterns than using the fixed length frame features, since the features are more convergent. It can be expected that with further improvement and combination with other features, the adaptive framing and the FFT magnitude pattern features will generate better results in vowel recognition.

References

[1] Xu Bo, et al.: Large Vocabulary Isolated-Word Chinese Speech recognition Based on HMM/VQ. Proc. of National Conf. on Man-Machine Sound Communication-94, pp146-152, Oct, 1994, Chongqing, China

[2] Baosheng Yuan, et al.: An Unlimited Vocabulary Speaker-Dependent Chinese Speech Recognition System. Proc. NCMMSC-94 pp157-160, Oct, 1994, Chongqing, China

[3] Ji Tianying, et al. Continuous Speech Recognition on Chinese Limited Commands. Proc. NCMMSC-94 pp273-276, Oct, 1994, Chongqing, China

[4] Lin-shan Lee, et al. Golden Mandarin (I)---A Real Time Mandarin Speech Dictation Machine for Chinese Language with Very Large Vocabulary, IEEE Trans. Speech & Audio Processing, Vol.1 No 2, April 1993

[5] Yoav Medan, et al: Super Resolution Pitch Determination of Speech Signals, IEEE Trans. on Signal Processing. Vol.39, No. 1. pp40-48, Jan. 1991.

Beat Induction and Rhythm Recognition

Simon Dixon

Department of Computer Science, Flinders University of South Australia, GPO Box
2100, Adelaide SA 5001. dixon@cs.flinders.edu.au

Abstract. Most people have no difficulty in picking out the beat in a piece of music,
and even if they cannot define what it is they have detected, they can tap their feet
in time with the music. This ability is called *beat induction*. A more difficult task,
which we call *rhythm recognition*, involves uncovering the hierarchical structure of the
timing relationships in the music, at a higher level than the frequencies of vibration
of individual notes and chords, but at a lower level than the musical form and phrase
structure. In this paper, we present a bottom-up approach to the recognition and
transcription of musical rhythms from acoustic signals. We assume no a priori high-level
knowledge of the music such as the time signature or tempo, but attempt to derive this
information from the timing patterns of detected note onsets. The problem of rhythm
recognition is divided into three stages: firstly, finding the main beat or rhythmic pulse
of the music; secondly, discovering the rhythmic structure, a hierarchical arrangement
of units consisting of multiples and submultiples of beats; and thirdly, mapping the
note onsets to musical timings and durations. We compare our methods with other
work presented in the literature and with commercial products which purport to solve
the same problems. This work forms part of an automatic music transcription system
currently under development by the author.

1 Introduction: Human Rhythm Perception

Most people have no difficulty in picking out the beat[1] in a piece of music.
Although we may be unable to give a precise definition of what it is that we have
detected, we can clap or dance in time with this beat. In fact, when listening
to music we often subconsciously tap a foot in time with the beat. This ability
is called *beat induction*. On the other hand, understanding the rhythm of a
piece of music is a more difficult task, which involves uncovering the hierarchical
structure of the timing relationships in the music. These relationships exist at a
higher level than the frequencies of vibration of individual notes and chords, but
at a lower level than the musical form and phrase structure [10]. The process of
extracting these relationships is called *rhythm recognition*.

Although we do not attempt to model or describe the cognitive mechanisms
involved in human rhythm perception, we do note certain features which motivate an ambitious unsupervised approach to the problem. Firstly, human rhythm
perception sets its own parameters; the tempo and the metrical structure are
not specified explicitly at the beginning of a piece, and if they change suddenly

---

[1] Or, more precisely, the *tactus*.

during the piece, the perceptual system is able to adjust itself within seconds to the new listening framework. Secondly, it copes well with "noise" in the input, that is, deviations from precise timing are allowed, as are variations in speed, without disturbing the overall perception of the music. Thirdly, it is able to cope with a degree of syncopation, that is, sections of music where no audible event occurs at the time of the beat, but where events still occur at other times between the beats. Rather than ignoring such parts as erroneous, they are perceived as rhythmically interesting sections of the music.

In contrast with these capabilities, computer music software does not cope well with any of these situations. Commercial sequencing and transcription programs require the beat to be declared explicitly before the music is processed, so that all data can then be indexed relative to this given beat. Even recent research systems are limited by the fact that once they get out of synchronisation with the music, it is very difficult for them to recover and resume correct interpretation of the rhythmic structure [3]. The robustness of human perception is one feature which is extremely difficult to reproduce in a computer system.

In this paper, we present a bottom-up approach to the recognition and transcription of musical rhythms from acoustic signals. We assume no a priori high-level knowledge of the music such as the time signature or tempo, but attempt to derive this information from the timing patterns of detected note onsets. Our approach breaks the problem of rhythm recognition into three subproblems: finding the main beat, or rhythmic pulse, of the music; discovering the structure of the rhythm, that is, units containing multiples and submultiples of beats; and mapping the note onsets to musical timings and durations. We present a solution to the first two stages, and discuss how we intend to tackle the final stage of processing.

We conclude this section with a brief outline of this paper: section 2 describes our approach to onset detection using multiple resolution Fourier analysis; the following section contains our beat induction algorithm which maps inter-onset intervals into equivalence classes, keeping track of the relative frequency of each class; then, in section 4, we describe the structural information that can be drawn from the onsets times and the induced beat to solve the first two stages of the rhythm recognition problem; section 5 discusses quantisation, the mapping of absolute time to relative time (in musical notation); and we conclude the paper with a review of related work followed by a discussion of achievements and future research directions.

2 Onset Detection

The input to the rhythm recognition system is a digitally sampled acoustic signal, stored in a single channel 16 bit linear pulse code modulated (PCM) format. Various sampling rates (8-48kHz) may be used. In the experiments described in this paper, solo jazz guitar CDs were used for the acoustic input, sampled at 8kHz. The loss of frequency range caused by using a low sampling rate did not affect the results of this work, but provided significant savings in memory and processing time.

The first stage in rhythm perception is the detection of the beginnings of notes, which are called *onsets*. (Similarly, the end of a note is called its *offset*.) Note onsets define the rhythm of a piece of music, whereas the offsets have almost no bearing on the perceived rhythm, except to alter the smoothness or connectedness of the notes. On percussive instruments (e.g. piano, guitar), it is not even possible to specify when a note offset occurs, as notes decay exponentially, so notes are often already inaudible before they are physically released. Also, it is rare for offsets to be performed as notated in music; in fact, many works for wind instruments or voice would not give the performers sufficient time to breathe if the offsets were played strictly as written!

We use a sliding window short-time Fourier transform to create a frequency-time representation of the music, and search each frequency band for sudden increases in amplitude which may correspond to note onsets. By using a very small window length for the transform, we are able to achieve a high degree of time resolution, at the expense of a corresponding loss in frequency resolution. For this paper we used a window size of 16ms (128 samples), which gives a sufficiently high time resolution (and certainly finer than human perception), but gives a frequency resolution of 62.5Hz, more than an order of magnitude too coarse for accurate note identification across all frequencies of interest. Since we are interested in music transcription, it is important that our approach to rhythm recognition does not preclude correct note identification. To obtain a high enough frequency resolution to distinguish notes to the nearest semitone, we perform another Fourier transform on the acoustic data, using a much larger time window (usually 100-200ms). The loss in time resolution by using the larger window does not damage our results, as we already have an accurate estimate of note onset times from the small window transform. A more detailed discussion of our approach to note identification can be found in [7].

To guard against false detections of onsets, we correlate possible onsets across frequency bands, noting that most musical notes begin with a transient of indeterminate pitch, which produces a peak across a large range of frequencies at the beginning of the note (see Figure 1). On the contrary, we do not get a high degree of correlation between the frequencies at which the onsets are detected and the frequencies of the notes to which the onsets belong, but the information from the transients is useful in discriminating true onsets from spurious peaks in the data. Another method that is used to filter out spurious peaks is by insisting that each note has a sufficiently long duration that its frequency can be determined by the auditory system. This condition is checked when the longer window Fourier transform is calculated. It is probable that this condition will have to be relaxed if the system is required to process music containing drum sounds.

The final stage that remains is to correlate the two transforms of the data, which is done by analysing each high resolution frequency band around the time of each detected onset. For peak detection, we use a search for local maxima

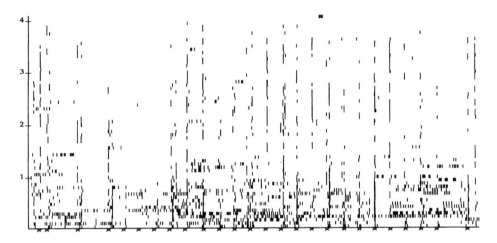

Fig. 1. Amplitude peaks in short window spectrogram; vertical axis is frequency in kHz; horizontal axis is time with note onsets marked by (x).

within a small band of frequencies, (usually one or two bands either side), and also require that the amplitude is above a minimum threshold level. The resulting peaks are used as a second check for false detections, and any onset which doesn't have a corresponding note to attach to is deleted at this stage.

It is difficult to evaluate the results for onset detection separately, as it is intricately related to our note identification algorithm. We note that in a small test (24 notes) where the data was analysed manually, there were two false positives detected, both of which corresponded to notes ending abruptly, causing a spike in the frequency-time distribution. These onsets are easily eliminated when it is found that there is no corresponding frequency components which begin or increase suddenly around these times. There were also three missed notes, all of which had small peaks but were below threshold. These are harder to correct, because they are surrounded by notes of much higher amplitude, so that the note identification stage will also have the same difficulties in detecting the onset.

The onset detection method may miss detecting valid onsets in cases where the initial transient is not as pronounced, such as with electronically produced sounds, or notes which are produced via a gradual change from another note. To date, this possible source of problems has not caused any missed detections, but we flag it for further investigation.

We note that by analysing the data at two independent levels of resolution, we are performing a similar type of analysis as occurs in the ear, which has mechanisms for detecting sound at both high and low resolutions of frequency (the inner and outer hair cells on the Organ of Corti). It is assumed that the brain correlates these data to produce a clearer overall picture of the properties of the source sound. The approach of performing spectral analysis at multiple resolutions is also a standard technique in engineering.

3 Beat Induction

Once the onsets have been detected and spurious peaks removed, we analyse the time durations between near pairs of notes. Using results from psychoacoustic research, we are able to use limits on the accuracy of production and perception of timing information in music to set parameters for this analysis. It is known that in musical performances, deviations of up to 30-40ms from the timing indicated in the score are not uncommon, and often go unnoticed by listeners [15]. This allows us to construct classes of inter-onset intervals (IOI's) which are sufficiently similar to be perceived as the same duration. These classes are characterised by the average duration of their members, and new members are added if their durations are close enough to this average. Closeness is defined in absolute terms by the constant *MaxError* (see algorithm below). If an IOI does not fit into any existing class, a new class is created.

Algorithm: Generate_Classes
For each pair of onset times t_1, t_2 (with $t_1 < t_2$)
    If $t_2 - t_1 < D$ (maximum distance between intervals)
        Let $I = t_2 - t_1$
        Find class C_n such that $|Average(C_n) - I|$ is minimum
        If $|Average(C_n) - I| < MaxError$ then
            $C_n := C_n \cup \{I\}$
        Else
            Create new class $C_m := \{I\}$
        End If
    End If
End For

Note that the process of adding an IOI to a class automatically adjusts the average of the members, so that the class boundaries are not rigid, but may drift over a period of time. For this reason it is important that these classes are not constructed over too long a time interval, or else variations in the tempo will corrupt the accuracy of the results. That is, we are looking to develop a local model of the tempo, and use that to determine the local structure. Having done this, the next local area may be calculated, with the added constraint of continuity, that is, the local tempo will not normally change between areas.

For each equivalence class, we calculate a score based on the number of intervals in the class and the agreement of the durations of the intervals. This gives us a ranking of classes, most of which are integer multiples or submultiples of the beat. Each score is adjusted to reflect the scores of other intervals which are related in this way, and a final best estimate of the period of the beat is determined.

The algorithm described above was tested on a collection of samples of solo jazz guitar music (acoustic and electric). These were chosen for their difficultly for beat induction, because of the high level of syncopation and because the performers take liberties with the rhythm. In order to deal with changing tempos, it is essential that the beat induction algorithm works on small amounts of data, so we tested the algorithm with samples of only 5 seconds to test whether the system can find the local tempo at any point in a piece of music. Our results for the first 24 5-second segments of one piece of music are presented below, with a comparison to an autocorrelation function (see section 6). Each row represents a time interval expressed as a fraction or multiple of the correct beat. The table entries represent the number of samples which were assigned this time interval as their beat.

Interval (beats)	Autocorrelation	Our algorithm
$\frac{1}{3}$	1	1
$\frac{1}{2}$	1	0
$\frac{2}{3}$	2	0
1	12	22
$\frac{4}{3}$	1	1
2	3	0
other	4	0

In the two cases where our algorithm failed to choose the correct beat, it chose the correct beat as the second and third most likely choices respectively. Using the assumption of continuity of tempo between adjacent time frames, these errors would be corrected easily.

4 Deriving Structural Information

The ranked estimates discussed in the previous section give us more than just an estimate of the period of the beat. They also provide us with structural information in the form of the multiples and submultiples of beats which occur commonly in the music. The system recognises that pieces in simple time have a highly ranked submultiple at half the beat, and pieces in compound time have submultiples at one third and two thirds of the beat. This information has not yet been integrated into the higher level rhythm recognition process.

We also expect that when examining longer samples of music, highly ranked multiples should occur at multiples of the beat corresponding to the length of the bar. Using this information, the hierarchical structure of the rhythm can be extracted without necessarily modelling expected rhythmic patterns. The next stage of the system will incorporate a hierarchy of rhythmic decomposition patterns, sorted by complexity, so that the system is steered towards the more plausible interpretations.

Another method of obtaining higher level structure is by autocorrelation [2], but this relies on precise timing relationships between notes which are not present in our work until after the quantisation stage. Brown's work does not examine performance data, but calculates the autocorrelation function on the IOI's as written in the score. The results in section 3 show that autocorrelation is not suitable for extracting the rhythmic structure of performance data.

5   Quantisation

Once the beat and metre have been established, the next step is to express each of the durations in terms of these parameters. The simplest way to do this is to choose a limit of resolution (a time quantum) and round each onset time to the nearest whole number of quanta. This approach produces musical nonsense, as it fails to distinguish between likely and unlikely rhythmic patterns (Figure 2). (Most commercial music software uses this technique.)

Fig. 2. Left: an implausible rhythm; Right: a similar but more plausible rhythm

The issue here is not one of accuracy — the interpretation on the left of Figure 2 may be a more accurate rendition of a performance than the rhythm on the right. But due to the difficulty for human performers to reproduce such rhythms accurately, it is a matter of musical convention that such rhythms are not notated. Also, the left hand rhythm is likely to have been produced by a performer playing the right hand rhythm and either inadvertently modifying the tempo, or anticipating the beat deliberately for expressive effect.

To solve this problem, we must create a model of the type of rhythmic patterns we expect. One approach is to order the patterns by the degree of syncopation, and then use the quantisation process to minimise the syncopation whilst also minimising the amount that times are adjusted by the quantisation process. This approach is similar to that of Longuet-Higgins and Lee [12], and assuming that the measure of syncopation corresponds to the complexity of expressing the timing information, it also relates to the approach of Tanguiane [16].

The ideal approach must allow the user to specify at some level how the rhythm should be interpreted by the system, that is to specify the user's preference on the tradeoff between accuracy and simplicity. In this way, the system could be used by composers seeking a faster way of producing musical scores, who are more likely to prefer the simpler representation, but also by musicologists studying performance data, who are more likely to want a precise representation of expressive timing variations. Pressing [13] describes an interactive system where the user specifies a menu of allowed syncopations, which provides a precise method of specifying what is meant by the concept of "minimal" syncopation.

6 Related Work

A substantial amount of research has been performed in the area of rhythm recognition by computer, culminating in a display at the 1994 International Computer Music Conference in which a variety of methods were demonstrated by attaching the computer to a shoe which tapped in time with the calculated beat of the music [6]. Many of these methods are difficult to compare, as they rely on different forms of input, or make different assumptions about the nature of the music being analysed, or are limited by a subset of a complete rhythmic language, or rely on a high level of supervision (interaction with the user).

Much of the work in machine perception of rhythm has used MIDI files as input [14, 4, 9], which contain control information but no direct acoustic information. A MIDI file consists of a chronologically ordered sequence of events, such as keys being pressed or released, and timing information in the form of time durations between each pair of events. (Type 1 MIDI files also allow for the encoding of structural information such as the time signature and tempo, but most research in this area presumes that this information is not available to the rhythm recognition program.)

Work using MIDI files views the input as a list of inter-onset intervals (IOI's), and does not attach any rhythmic significance to differences in pitch or volume of notes. That is, each note is treated purely as an uninterpreted event. This ignores potentially useful information which could be gained by separating parts using principles of auditory streaming [1]. This form of input also sidesteps the first difficult issue in rhythm recognition, which is the detection of onsets of notes. Nevertheless, the ideas are still useful, as they can be applied to subsequent stages of analysis.

Notable work using MIDI file input is the emulation of human rhythm perception of [14] which produces multiple hypotheses of possible hierarchical structures in the timing, assigning a score to each hypothesis, corresponding to the likelihood that a human listener would choose that interpretation of the rhythm. This technique gives the system the ability to adjust to changes in tempo and metre, as well as avoiding many of the implausible rhythmic interpretations produced by commercial systems.

A similar approach is advocated by Tanguiane [16], who uses Kolmogorov complexity as the measure of the likelihood of a particular interpretation, with the least complex interpretations being favoured. He presents an information-theoretic account of human perception, and argues that many of the "rules" of music composition and perception can be explained in information-theoretic terms.

Desain [4] compares two different approaches to modelling rhythm perception, the symbolic approach of Longuet-Higgins [11] and the connectionist approach of Desain and Honing [5]. Although this work only models one aspect of rhythm perception, the issue of quantisation, and the results of the comparison do not provide a definitive preference for one style over the other, it does highlight the need to model expectancy, either explicitly or implicitly. Expectancy, as described in the work cited above, is a type of predictive modelling which is particularly relevant to real-time processing as it provides a contextual framework in which subsequent rhythmic patterns can be interpreted with less ambiguity.

An alternative approach uses a nonlinear oscillator to model the expectation created by detecting a regular pulse in the music [9]. A feedback loop controls the frequency of the oscillator so that it can track variations in the rhythm. This system performs quite robustly, but due to its intricate mathematics it does not correspond to any intuitive notion of perception, and in this sense is very similar to connectionist approaches.

One of the few attempts to analyse rhythm in acoustic signals is the Beat Tracking System (BTS) of Goto and Muraoka [8]. This system is designed to follow the beat of pop music in real time (one of the shoe-tapping programs mentioned above). BTS uses frequency histograms to find significant peaks in the low frequency regions, which are presumed to correspond to the bass and snare drums, and then tracks these frequency regions by matching timing patterns in these bands to a small set of pre-stored drum beat patterns. It was found that this method was successful for 42 of the 44 popular songs on which it was tested. Clearly this method could not be used in other styles of music where drums do not keep the beat, or where the rhythmic patterns are less predictable.

Commercial transcription and sequencing programs do not even address the issues covered in these research systems. The tempo and time signature must be explicitly entered before the music is played, and the system then aligns each note with the nearest position on a metrical grid. This grid is computed from the given beat and a resolution limit which is defined to be the shortest allowed note length. Thus these systems often produce implausible rhythmic interpretations, and cannot be used in an unsupervised manner for anything but the simplest rhythms.

7   Discussion and Future Work

It is clear that rhythm identification is not a trivial task, despite the apparent ease with which many humans are able to perform the task. We have described a rhythm recognition process which analyses acoustic data, detecting a sequence of note onsets, and then discovers patterns in the intervals between the onsets, from which the most likely beat is induced.

The rhythm detection system has not yet been completed, but the early stages show promising results. The onset detection and beat induction algorithms have been tested on a number of examples of jazz guitar music, in which the rhythm is quite complex, and have produced correct results for the induced beat. It is expected that similar results shall be obtainable with other instruments and mixed instrument music, as the system does not rely on any features which are peculiar to the guitar, nor to stringed instruments or plucked instruments in general.

The next stage of using structural information for quantisation is currently being addressed, and we are examining some of the techniques discussed in the previous section. A comparison of our approach with connectionist techniques has also begun. The precise direction of future work depends somewhat on the results of these investigations and implementations, with the end goal being an automatic music transcription system.

Other research currently underway includes dynamic modelling of parameters of musical instruments and voices using multidimensional feature spaces, as well as psychoacoustic results from auditory scene analysis, with the aim of separating music into parts in a similar way that a human listener is able to attend to the various instruments playing in an ensemble.

References

1. A.S. Bregman. *Auditory Scene Analysis: The Perceptual Organisation of Sound.* Bradford, MIT Press, 1990.
2. J.C. Brown. Determination of the meter of musical scores by autocorrelation. *Journal of the Acoustical Society of America*, 94(4):1953–1957, 1993.
3. R.B. Dannenberg. Recent work in real-time music understanding by computer. *Proceedings of the International Symposium on Music, Language, Speech and Brain*, 1991.
4. P. Desain. A connectionist and a traditional AI quantizer: Symbolic versus sub-symbolic models of rhythm perception. *Contemporary Music Review*, 9:239–254, 1993.
5. P. Desain and H. Honing. Quantization of musical time: A connectionist approach. *Computer Music Journal*, 13(3), 1989.
6. P. Desain and H. Honing. Foot-tapping: a brief introduction to beat induction. In *Proceedings of the International Computer Music Conference*, pages 78–79. Computer Music Association, San Francisco CA, 1994.
7. S.E. Dixon. Multiphonic note identification. *Australian Computer Science Communications*, 18(1):318–323, 1996.
8. M. Goto and Y. Muraoka. A real-time beat tracking system for audio signals. In *Proceedings of the International Computer Music Conference*. Computer Music Association, San Francisco CA, 1995.
9. E.W. Large. Beat tracking with a nonlinear oscillator. In *Proceedings of the IJCAI Workshop on Artificial Intelligence and Music*, 1995.
10. F. Lerdahl and R. Jackendoff. *A Generative Theory of Tonal Music.* MIT Press, 1983.
11. H.C. Longuet-Higgins. *Mental Processes.* MIT Press, 1987.
12. H.C. Longuet-Higgins and C. Lee. The rhythmic interpretation of monophonic music. *Music Perception*, 1:424–441, 1994.
13. J. Pressing. Personal communication. 1996.
14. D. Rosenthal. Emulation of human rhythm perception. *Computer Music Journal*, 16(1):64–76, 1992.
15. J. Sundberg. *The Science of Musical Sounds.* Academic Press, 1991.
16. A.S. Tanguiane. *Artificial Perception and Music Recognition.* Springer-Verlag, 1993.

Boosting Neural Networks in Real World Applications: An Empirical Study

Hongxing He[1] and Zhexue Huang[2]

[1]Research & Analysis Section,
Health Insurance Commission
134 Reed Street P.O. Box 1001 Tuggeranong ACT 2900
AUSTRALIA
Email: auhic24c@ibmmail.com

[2]Cooperative Research Center for Advanced Computational Systems
CSIRO Mathematical and Information Sciences
GPO Box 664 Canberra ACT 2601 Australia
Email: Zhexue.Huang@cmis.csiro.au

ABSTRACT

Boosting techniques allow the combination of a collection of sequentially trained neural networks into an ensemble whose classification performance is superior to any of the individual neural networks. Empirical studies on the performance of boosting neural networks in optical character recognition have demonstrated significant improvements in classification. In this paper we report on an empirical study of boosting neural networks for classifying business data from real world databases. These data often contain noise and subjective or even contradictory classifications. Therefore, classification of such business data is a hard problem in practical applications. Two boosting algorithms were tested in this empirical study. The experimental results have shown that boosting neural networks indeed improved the classification performance. With one data set, we have achieved to date the best classification result, which had never been achieved using single and committee neural networks.

1. INTRODUCTION

Boosting is a recent technique that combines a collection of sequentially trained classifiers into an ensemble to improve classification accuracy [1][2]. Empirical studies on boosting decision tree algorithms such as CART and C4.5 were recently conducted by several researchers [3][4][5]. The results of these studies have shown that boosting decision trees lead, in many cases, to significant improvements in classification of data in a number of domains. Experiments of boosting neural networks in optical character recognition were also reported [6]. Some dramatic improvements were obtained by boosting, compared with the previous single neural networks with the same data set. Unlike boosting decision trees, however, results of boosting neural networks in other domains have rarely been reported.

In this paper we report on an empirical study of boosting neural networks for classifying business data from real world databases. In this study two data sets were used, one from databases in the Health Insurance Commission (HIC) and one from a credit card database. The first data set describes a set of general medical practitioners

(GP) who were classified by a medical expert into two classes according to their practice profiles. The task was to add boosting to a neural network classification system that is used to identify GPs who may be abusing the public Medicare system. The second data set concerns a set of credit card records which were classified into three classes. The objective was to build a neural network classification system which can predict actions on the candidate card holders, retrieved from the credit card database. Those candidates may match the information of a person to be enquired. An action determines whether a candidate is a match to that person or more than one candidate should be reviewed by reviewers. A common characteristic of the data sets is that both were classified by human experts. Therefore, noise, and subjective and contradictory classifications inevitably exist in these data sets.

We have experimented with two boosting algorithms for classifying these data sets. The first algorithm described in [1][6] uses three sequentially trained neural networks to make the final classification. This algorithm requires a large data set to create training data for the second and third neural networks. We generated the large training data set by adding noise to some independent features of the available training examples.

The second algorithm was initially proposed in [2]. We made a modification to the original algorithm to control the re-sampling rates of misclassified objects by each individual network. Without the modification, classification of the original algorithm was often dominated by the first network because of its dominating weight.

Our initial results have shown that boosting neural networks indeed gave better performance than single neural networks. With one data set, we have achieved to date the best classification result, which had never been achieved using single and committee neural networks [7][8][9].

2. BOOSTING

Boosting [1] is a technique that combines multiple classifiers $\{C(1), ...,C(p)\}$ to form a composite classifier C^* whose accuracy is usually found to be equal to or better than any $C(i)$. Although it uses a voting approach to deciding classes of unseen cases, boosting is different from other techniques such as committee voting [8] and bagging [10] in that $C(1), ...,C(p)$ are trained sequentially. That is, the training data set for $C(i+1)$ is formed from the trained result of $C(i)$.

The general idea of boosting can be expressed as follows. Assume we want to train neural networks on data from a domain with distribution D. If we train each neural network independently, we use training data sampled from the domain with the same distribution D. However, we can train neural networks sequentially. The training data for the $(k+1)$st neural network are resampled based on the performance of the k previous trained neural networks. Therefore, the training data sets for these neural networks have different distributions. This strategy allows a subsequent neural network to be focused more on the examples which were misclassified by its preceding neural networks. Different boosting algorithms use different schemes to vote on the final classification. The detailed discussions of boosting algorithms can be found in [1][2][3].

3. BOOSTING NEURAL NETWORKS

Two boosting algorithms were tested in this study. The difference between these algorithms lies in the resampling methods and the schemes to make the final classification.

3.1 ALGORITHM 1

This algorithm was originally defined in [1] and first used in [6] in optical character recognition. In general, this algorithm can use 3^n neural networks to form an ensemble. As in [6] we used only three networks (n=1) in this study. The algorithm is expressed as follows.

1. The first network C(1) is trained by N_1 training examples from an application domain. After C(1) has been trained, the training set for the second network C(2) is formed in the following way. Generate a uniform distributed random number σ in [0, 1]. If $\sigma > 0.5$, then pass new training examples through C(1) until C(1) misclassifies an example and add this example to the second training set. If $\sigma <= 0.5$, then pass new training examples through C(1) until C(1) correctly classifies an example. Add this example to the second training set. Repeat this process until N_2 training examples are obtained. In the end the second training set contains half examples correctly classified and half incorrectly classified by C(1).

2. The second network C(2) is then trained with the second training set. After C(2) is trained, the third training set is formed as follows. Pass new training examples through C(1) and C(2). If the first two networks disagree on classification of an example, add the example to the third training set, otherwise, ignore the training example. This process continues until N_3 training examples are obtained.

3. The third network C(3) is trained with the N_3 examples.

4. C(1), C(2) and C(3) form a composite classifier C*. C* is used as follows. Pass an unclassified example e to C(1), C(2) and C(3), if C(1) and C(2) produce the same class for e, then e is classified as that class, if C(1) and C(2) produce different classes, then the class of e is determined by C(3).

3.2 ALGORITHM 2

This algorithm was defined in [2]. Different versions of the algorithm exist [1][2][3]. The version we used is called AdaBoost.M1 [2], which is used for solving multi-class classification problems. It is expressed as follows.

ADABOOST.M1

Input: A set of training examples S = {(x_1,y_1), ...(x_i,y_i),... ,(x_N,y_N)} where y_i are class labels of the examples.

Neural Network Training Algorithm *NeuroTrain*

Integer T specifying the number of iterations

Initialize a weight $w^1_i = 1/N$ for each training example

Do for t=1,2,...,T

1. Set the probability p^t_i of training example i as

$$p^t_i = \frac{w^t_i}{\sum\limits_{i=1}^{N} w^t_i} \qquad (1)$$

2. Sample the training set Z(t) from S according to p^t_i
3. Call a *NeuroTrain* to train Net(t) with Z(t)
4. Use Net(t) to classify S and calculate the error rate:

$$\varepsilon_t = \sum\limits_{i=1}^{N} p^t_i \langle h_t(x_i) \neq y_i \rangle \qquad (2)$$

($\langle X \rangle = 1$ if X is true)

If $\varepsilon_t > 1/2$, then set T=t-1 and abort loop.
5. Update the new weights of training examples by

$$\beta_t = \varepsilon_t/(1 - \varepsilon_t) \qquad (3)$$

$$w^{t+1}_i = w^t_i \beta_t^{1-\langle h_t(x_i) \neq y_i \rangle} \qquad (4)$$

6. Endfor
7. Supply a set of test examples to Net(t) for t=1...T and determine the final classes by

$$h_f(x) = \arg \max_{y \in Y} \sum\limits_{t=1}^{T} (\log \frac{1}{\beta_t}) \langle h_t(x) = y \rangle \qquad (5)$$

(Y is the set of class labels)

4. EXPERIMENTS

4.1 DATA SETS

The two boosting algorithms in Section 3 were tested with two real world data sets. One data set consists of 1500 records, each representing the practice profile of a General Practitioner (GP). The 1500 GPs were classified into two classes, one for GPs who provided appropriate services to their patients and one for GPs who provided inappropriate services or say abused the public Medicare system. Several other methods have also been tested on this dataset in HIC[7][8][9].

The other data set was generated from a credit card database. This data set consists of 1393 records, each relating to a credit card holder stored in the database. The credit card database is used to provide information for customers about the creditability of enquired people. When the basic information such as name, address and driver's licence of a person is given, the system often returns several people (candidates) whose information may match the asked person. However, only one candidate can be the person asked. Selection of such candidate is based on the matching scores on names, addresses, driver's licence etc. The records in this data set describe these matching scores. Various actions can be taken according to the matching scores, such as returning one candidate as the exact match to the person asked or forwarding two candidates to a human expert to decide which one is the best match. Three classes were given to these 1393 records by human experts.

A common characteristic of the two data sets is that both were classified by human experts. Therefore, they are noisy and contain subjective and contradictory classifications. The other problem is that the application domains are complicated by a large number of features, but the examples available are limited. This is well known as the curse of dimensionality.

4.2 TRAINING METHODS

Feed forward three layer neural networks were used in the boosting algorithms. The numbers of neurons in the input and output layers were dependent on the numbers of features and classes in the data sets. An multilayer perceptron with error back propagation algorithm[11] was used to train the neural networks. The multilayer perceptron has three layers, namely input layer, hidden layer and output layer. The number of neurons in the input layer is equal to the number of features used. The number of neurons in the output layer is chosen to be equal to the number of classes of the problem. The number of neurons in the hidden layer varies according to the problem. To avoid the over training problem, a weight decay term was added to the error function. The coefficient of the weight decay term was chosen as 0.01[9].

The original data sets were randomly divided into two data sets, one for training (70%) and one for testing (30%). For Algorithm 1, a large pool of training examples was generated by adding noise to some features of the examples in the training data sets. However, the testing data sets were left untouched.

4.3 RESULTS OF ALGORITHM 1

Algorithm 1 requires a large pool of training examples for generating training data for the second and third neural networks. Such a pool was generated by adding noise to one or two independent features of available training examples. The first neural network was trained with N examples randomly sampled from the pool. The second neural network was trained with N examples filtered by the first network and the third network was also trained with N examples filtered by the first two networks (refer to Section 3.1 for the filtering process).

In testing the ensemble of the three networks, we let the three networks classify the test examples. The final classification is determined as follows: if the first two neural networks give the same classification to a test example, then the class is taken as the ensemble class. If the first two disagree on the classification, then the class given by the third neural network is taken as the class given by the ensemble.

Table 1 Results of boosting on HIC Data

Number of Training Samples	Number of Test Samples	Number of Noise Terms	Noise (Low Bound)	Noise (High Bound)	% Correct Rate (Single NNet)	% Correct Rate (Boost)	% Improve-ment
1000	500	1	0.007	0.010	79.00	79.40	0.40
1000	500	2	0.030	0.050	79.60	80.00	0.40
1000	500	2	0.010	0.030	81.20	82.00	0.80

Table 2 Results of boosting on credit card data

Number of Training Samples	Number of Test Samples	Number of Noise Terms	Noise (Low Bound)	Noise (High Bound)	% Correct Rate (Single NNet)	% Correct Rate (Boost)	% Improve-ment
993	400	1	0.010	0.050	74.00	75.75	1.75
993	400	1	0.001	0.070	74.00	75.25	1.25
993	400	2	0.010	0.030	75.00	75.50	0.50

Tables 1 and 2 list the results of running Algorithm 1 on the two data sets. Compared to the single neural network results, the classification accuracy was increased in both data sets. The improvement in the first data set was marginal because this data set is noisier than the second one. The improvement in the second data set was significant and the classification accuracy was more stable. Comparatively, the domain of this data set is simpler, even though it has three classes.

4.4 RESULTS OF ALGORITHM 2

Algorithm 2 was only tested with the credit card data because the first data had only two classes. Our first run of this algorithm resulted in no improvement in classification. The reason was that the final classification was dominated by the first neural network because of the big difference between ε_1 and the error rates of subsequent neural networks. Table 3 lists the error rates and voting weights of the neural networks in a run of the Algorithm 2.

Table 3 List of ε_i and $\log(1/\beta_i)$

i	ε_i	$\log(1/\beta_i)$
1	0.252	0.473
2	0.410	0.158
3	0.470	0.053
4	0.502	-

One can see the voting weight of the first neural network is much larger than the voting weights of other neural networks, i.e, $\log(1/\beta_1) > \log(1/\beta_2)+\log(1/\beta_3)$. Therefore, the classifications of the other two neural networks were ignored.

To overcome this problem, we introduced a exponent γ to equation (4) to include more correctly classified examples in the subsequent training data set, as

$$w_i^{t+1} = w_i^t \beta_t^{\gamma(1-\langle h_t(x_i)\neq y_i\rangle)} \qquad (0<\gamma<1) \qquad (6)$$

The effect of γ was a reduction of the increasing speed of the error rate, which resulted in more neural networks. Table 4 shows the effect of $\gamma=0.5$. In this example the first neural network no longer dominates the final classification.

Table 4 List of ε_i and $\log(1/\beta_i)$, where $\gamma = 0.5$

i	ε_i	$\log(1/\beta_i)$
1	0.264	0.579
2	0.343	0.282
3	0.412	0.154
4	0.418	0.144
5	0.480	0.035
6	0.438	0.108
7	0.453	0.082
8	0.477	0.040
9	0.451	0.085
10	0.489	0.019
11	0.489	0.019
12	0.487	0.022
13	0.521	-

With 12 sequentially trained neural networks ($\gamma=0.5$) the correct rate of the single neural network was 75.60% and the correct rate of the ensemble was 75.80%. The confusion matrix on the test set is listed in table 5. From table 5 we can see that the accuracy in class 3 is the highest (91%) among all three classes, because of the lower classification inconsistency in that class.

Table 5 Confusion matrix of test set using algorithm 2

	Predicted Class 1	Predicted Class 2	Predicted Class 3	Total
Real Class 1	80	23	44	147
Real Class 2	4	95	30	129
Real Class 3	10	10	204	224
Total	94	128	278	500

Although the improvement was marginal, it suggested that some wrongly classified examples by the single neural network were corrected by the ensemble. One reason for the marginal improvement in performance was that the individual neural networks were not optimally trained due to CPU time limits.

5. CONCLUSIONS

In this paper we have presented some initial results of applying boosting techniques to neural networks for classifying business data. These results are encouraging because they have demonstrated that boosting neural networks can improve the classification accuracy of the noisy business data. Classification of such data represents a complex problem in the practical applications of neural networks[7][8][9].

We have experimented with two boosting algorithms, both useful in solving our problems. Introduction of the exponent γ in the second algorithm were proved effective for one data set though theoretical soundness needs to be further investigated. The results reported here are preliminary and a further study is needed to improve the performance of the boosting neural networks.

ACKNOWLEDGMENT

Authors wish to thank P. Milne, G. Williams at CSIRO, M. Ng at Australian National University and Warwick Graco, Dennis Armstrong at HIC for their critical reading of the manuscript, Nick Zaitzieff for his assistance in preparing manuscript in the final form. The second author wishes to acknowledge that part of this work was carried out within ACSys (Advanced Computational Systems) established under the Australian Government's cooperative research centers program.

REFERENCES

[1] Schapire, R. E. (1990) "The Strength of Weak Learnability." Machine Learning, vol. 5, pp. 197-227.

[2] Freund, Y. and Schapire, R. E. (1995) "A Decision-Theoretic Generalization of On-line Learning and an Application to Boosting" AT&T Bell Lab.

[3] Breiman, L. (1996) "Bias, Variance, and Arcing Classifiers." TR-460, Department of Statistics, Univ. of California, Berkeley, CA, USA.

[4] Quinlan, J. R. (1996) "Boosting First-Order Learning." In Proceedings of ALT'96, Lecture Notes in Artificial Intelligence 1160, Springer, pp. 143-155.

[5] Drucker, H. and Cortes, C. (1995) "Boosting Decision Tress." AT&T Bell Lab.

[6] Drucker, H., Schapire, R. E. and Simard, P. (1993) "Boosting Performance in Neural Networks." International Journal of Pattern Recognition and Artificial Intelligence, Vol. 7, No. 4, pp. 705-719.

[7] Luan F., He H. and Graco, W. (1995) "A Comparison of a Number of Supervised-Learning Techniques for Classifying a Sample of General Practitioners' Practice Profiles." Application Stream Proceedings of Eighth Australian Joint Artificial Intelligence Conference, Canberra, Australia, pp.114-133.

[8] He H. (1996)"The Multiple Classifier Approach to a Medical Fraud Detection Problem." Proceedings of Fourth International Conference on Control, Automation, Robotics and Vision, Singapore, pp. 241-244.

[9] He H., Wang J. and Graco W. (1997) "Application of Neural Networks in Medical Fraud Detection." Singapore International Conference on Intelligent Systems, Singapore, pp. 499-506.

[10] Breiman, L. (1994) "Bagging Predictors." TR-421, Department of Statistics, Univ. of California, Berkeley, CA, USA.

[11] Haykin, S. (1994) *Neural Networks,* Macmilan Publishing Company.

Machine Learning of Credible Classifications

Howard J. Hamilton   Ning Shan   Wojciech Ziarko

Department of Computer Science, University of Regina
Regina, Saskatchewan, Canada S4S 0A2
E-Mail: {hamilton,ning,ziarko}@cs.uregina.ca

Abstract. We present an approach to concept discovery in machine learning based on searching for maximally general credible classifications. To be credible, a classification must provide decisions for all or nearly all possible values of the condition attributes, and these decisions must be adequately supported by evidence. Our objective is to find a classification for a domain that meets predefined quality criteria. For example, a classification can be sought whose coverage of the domain exceeds a user-defined threshold and whose decisions are supported by sufficient input instances.

1 Introduction

The standard approach to concept discovery in machine learning, as discussed by many authors, is to attempt to induce a classification from data using inductive algorithms [2, 7, 8, 9, 10, 11]. A *classification* is a partition of the instance space into equivalence classes based upon the condition attributes. A classification is *consistent* if at most one value for the decision attribute is specified for each equivalence class, and a classification is *complete* if at least one value for the decision attribute is specified for each possible combination of the values of the condition attributes. A classification is commonly given as a decision table, a decision tree, or a set of decision rules.

It might be assumed that a complete, consistent classification would be ideal, but we explain why these characteristics are insufficient. Our analysis illuminates a commonly observed problem whereby decision rules learned via inductive algorithms provide insufficient coverage of their domain. We propose a measure called *credibility* for assessing classifications. Informally, a classification is *credible* if it is complete or almost complete with respect to the domain from which the data set was collected and each decision it specifies is supported by input instances. This measure is novel because it assesses the classification as a whole without reference to predictive accuracy.

We observe that (a) data sets are often highly incomplete, that is, many combinations that are possible among the values of the condition attributes in the chosen attribute-value representation are not present in a given data set; and (b) in particular, instances existing in the data set may be insufficient to reliably estimate the probability distribution for the decision attribute. As long as we lack sufficient evidence about the completeness of the classification and the reliability of the associated probability estimates, rule extraction from the data and the application of these rules to the original domain is of limited utility.

The remainder of this paper is organized as follows. Section 2 explains classifications and illustrates various types. In particular, an inadequacy of complete, consistent classifications is demonstrated. In Section 3, we discuss searching for credible classifications in the presence of concept trees, and in Section 4, we present the CredSearch algorithm for doing so. At each step of this algorithm, values for one attribute are generalized, as suggested by that attribute's concept tree, to create a new, less complex classification. We conclude in Section 5.

2   Credible Classifications

We assume that the input consists of a set of instances with m condition (or independent) attributes and a single binary decision (or dependent) attribute. Our method generalizes in a straightforward manner to multiple decision attributes, each with multiple possible discrete values, but this generalization is not germane to the present paper.

In concept discovery, one applies an inductive algorithm to a set of instances drawn from the instance space to produce a classification (or description) drawn from the description space. Suppose that the input instances are as shown below.

red	odd	Y
red	even	N
red	odd	Y
black	odd	Y

The two condition attributes ($m = 2$) are Color and Parity and the decision attribute yields Y or N.

Recall that a *classification* is a partition of the input instances into equivalence classes based only on the condition attributes. As a simple case, all instances that are indistinguishable based on the values of their condition attributes are placed in the same equivalence class. (Other partitions into equivalence classes are discussed in the next section.) For example, a classification for the given instances is shown in Table 1. For later reference, a column has

Color	Parity	Decision	#instances
red	odd	Y	2
red	even	N	1
black	odd	Y	1

Table 1. Classification of the given instances

been added to the classification to show the number of input instances in each equivalence class. The classification is shown in a format similar to a decision table, but a decision tree or a set of decision rules could readily be constructed instead.

Let us assume that the domain of the Color attribute is {red, black} and that of the Parity attribute is {odd, even}. Under this assumption, the given classification is incomplete, because no decision value is suggested for black-even instances. The *coverage* is the fraction of possible combinations of the values for the condition attributes that are classified by the classification. In the example, the coverage is $3/4 = 0.75$.

A complete, consistent classification for the given instances, under the same assumption, is shown in Table 2.

Color	Parity	Decision	#instances
red	odd	Y	2
red	even	N	1
black	odd	Y	1
black	even	Y	0

Table 2. Complete and consistent classification of the given instances

This classification may be appealing because all black instances are classified as Y. On the other hand, choosing N instead of Y for the black-even case yields another complete, consistent classification (not shown), where all even instances are classified as N. The fundamental problem is that the decision for the black-even case is not supported by any evidence.

Informally, a classification is *credible* if a decision is given for all combinations of condition attributes and each decision is supported by input instances. Assuming (say) 30 input instances are required to support the decision for each equivalence class, a credible classification created after obtaining additional input instances is shown in Table 3. We measure credibility based on the levels of

Color	Parity	Decision	#instances
red	odd	Y	32
red	even	N	41
black	odd	Y	31
black	even	N	32

Table 3. Classification after obtaining additional instances

coverage and support. In practice, we may want to relax the requirement that coverage be complete.

The *classificatory complexity* of a classification is the number of equivalence classes in it. In practice, this number is usually not known in advance. If the joint domain $V = V_1 \times \ldots \times V_m$ of the condition attributes is known, an upper bound on the classificatory complexity for a subset A of condition attributes C, can be computed in advance as:

$$CC_{MAX}(A, V) = \prod_{a \in A} card(V_a)$$

The quantity $CC_{MAX}(A, V)$ is called the *maximum classificatory complexity* of the set of attributes A, given the set of values V of the attributes A. If the number of attributes and the size of the domain V_a for each attribute is large, then $CC_{MAX}(A, V)$ grows combinatorily.

Available instances may be insufficient to allow the immediate production of a credible classification. Consider the classification shown in Table 4 (ignore the Q_E and $Cred_E$ columns for now). Province has 10 possible values and Amount

Province	Amount	Decision	Coverage	Q_E	#instances	$Cred_E$
Alberta (AB)	10-20	N	1/80	0.0177	1	0.0044
Alberta (AB)	60-100	Y	1/80	0.0097	1	0.0024
British Columbia (BC)	20-30	N	1/80	0.0177	2	0.0089
Manitoba (MB)	100+	Y	1/80	0.0097	1	0.0024
New Brunswick (NB)	30-40	Y	1/80	0.0097	3	0.0072
Newfoundland (NF)	60-100	N	1/80	0.0177	1	0.0044
Nova Scotia (NS)	40-50	Y	1/80	0.0097	2	0.0048
Ontario	50-60	N	1/80	0.0177	1	0.0044
PEI	40-50	Y	1/80	0.0097	2	0.0048
Quebec	0-10	Y	1/80	0.0097	1	0.0024
Saskatchewan (SK)	60-100	Y	1/80	0.0097	1	0.0024
Saskatchewan (SK)	20-30	N	1/80	0.0177	1	0.0044
Total			12/80	0.1562	17	0.0531

Table 4. Example showing insufficient instances to allow credible classification

has 8, so maximum classificatory complexity $CC_{MAX} = 10 \times 8 = 80$. Only 12 equivalence classes (combinations of values for the Province and Amount attributes) are present in this classification, so coverage is $12/80 = 0.15$. If an instance was chosen at random from the instance space, it would have only a 15% chance of being classified by this classification.

Three relevant factors for credibility are: (1) coverage of the joint domain of the condition attributes, (2) consistency of the decision for each equivalence class, and (3) support for each decision. Formally, we represent the coverage as $P(E)$, the probability of occurrence of the equivalence class E. For the second factor, we start with $P(F|E)$, the conditional probability of the occurrence of the concept F specified by a fixed value (e.g., Y) of the decision attribute conditioned by the occurrence of the equivalence class E. The quality Q of a classification Cl with respect to concept F is evaluated [12]:

$$Q_E(Cl) = \beta P(E) \times |P(F|E) - P(F)|,$$

$$Q(Cl) = \sum_{E \in Cl} Q_E(Cl),$$

where $\beta = \frac{1}{2P(F)(1-P(F))}$. Q represents the average gain in the quality of information, reflected by $P(F|E)$, used to make the classificatory decision F versus $\neg F$. In the absence of classification Cl, the only available information for this decision is the occurrence probability $P(F)$. In Table 4, $P('Y') = 7/12$ since 7 out of 12 instances have Y as their decision value. Thus, without consulting the classification, one could estimate the probability of an instance having decision value Y as $7/12 = 0.6471$. The quantity β is a normalization factor to ensure that Q is always within the range $[0, 1]$, with 1 corresponding to the exact characterization of the concept (that is, when for every equivalence class E, $P(F|E)$ is either 0 or 1) and 0 corresponding to the situation where the distribution of F within every equivalence class E is the same as in the instance space.

The formula for Q takes into account the first two factors discussed above, but not the third. To reflect the intuition that a minimum number of instances MIN should be present for each equivalence class in a credible classification, we use the factor $min(\#instances/MIN, 1)$, where min takes the minimum of its two arguments. This factor ensures that a proportional weight is attached to equivalence classes supported by an inadequate number of input instances. Thus, we define credibility as:

$$Cred_E(Cl) = Q_E(Cl) \times min(\#instances/MIN, 1),$$

$$Cred(Cl) = \sum_{E \in Cl} Cred_E(Cl).$$

(An alternate approach would be to discard all equivalence classes with fewer than MIN instances.) Assuming that $MIN = 4$ (artificially small for the sake of this example), values for Q_E and $Cred_E$ for choosing the decision Y are shown for each equivalence class in the previous table. The totals for these columns give the values for Q and $Cred$ respectively. Further illustrations of the measures are provided in the next section.

3 Searching for Credible Classifications

Every approach to concept learning sanctions some means of generalization. To illustrate the search for credible classifications, we describe how it applies to an inductive algorithm called *attribute-oriented concept tree ascension* [3, 4]. With this algorithm, generalization is guided by concept trees (also called concept hierarchies). Each generalization generalizes the condition attributes to a certain level based on the attribute's *concept tree*, which is provided by knowledge engineers or domain experts. Trivially, the values for any attribute can be represented as a one-level concept tree where the root is the most general value "ANY" and the leaves are the distinct values of the attribute. Each replacement of a value for a condition attribute with a value from higher in the tree generalizes the value to cover more cases than the original one. Generalizing to the root of the concept tree is equivalent to removing the corresponding condition attribute.

Concept trees for the Province and Amount attributes are shown in Fig. 1. The values on the right, e.g., P0, label the depths in the trees, for use in subsequent discussions. The leaf values in a concept tree cover all possible values for the corresponding attribute. A variety of methods for converting continuous values to discrete ones are surveyed and compared in [13].

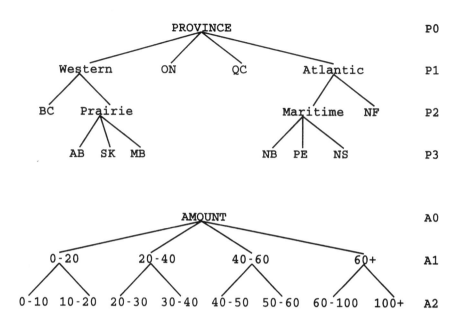

Fig. 1. Concept trees for the Province and Amount attributes

To reduce the classificatory complexity and thus possibly increase the coverage, input instances can be generalized according to the "climbing tree" heuristic. After generalizing the Province attribute once, which generalizes values at depth P3 to depth P2, the resulting classification is as shown in Table 5. The 6 values for

Province	Amount	Decision	Coverage	Q_E	#instances	$Cred_E$
British Columbia	20-30	N	1/48	0.0295	2	0.0148
Maritime	30-40	Y	1/48	0.0161	3	0.0121
Maritime	40-50	Y	1/48	0.0161	4	0.0161
Newfoundland	60-100	N	1/48	0.0295	1	0.0074
Ontario	50-60	N	1/48	0.0295	1	0.0074
Prairie	10-20	N	1/48	0.0295	1	0.0074
Prairie	20-30	N	1/48	0.0295	1	0.0074
Prairie	60-100	Y	1/48	0.0161	2	0.0805
Prairie	100+	Y	1/48	0.0161	1	0.0402
Quebec	0-10	Y	1/48	0.0161	1	0.0402
Total			10/48	0.2281	17	0.0885

Table 5. Classification after generalizing the Province attribute

Province (those at depth P2) and 8 values for Amount give $CC_{MAX} = 6 \times 8 = 48$ possible combinations. With 10 combinations in this classification, coverage is $10/48 = .20$. During this generalization, it happens that decisions for combined instances remained consistent. For example, $\langle \text{Alberta}, 60 - 100, \text{Y} \rangle$ and $\langle \text{Saskatchewan}, 60-100, \text{Y} \rangle$ instances were combined to form $\langle \text{Prairie}, 60-100, \text{Y} \rangle$

instances. Since coverage increased and decisions remained consistent, credibility is increased, in this case, from 0.0531 to 0.0885.

Generalizing the values for Province from depth P2 to P1 and those for Amount from depth A2 to A1, gives the classification shown in Table 6. The

Province	Amount	Decision	Coverage	Q_E	#instances	$Cred_E$
Atlantic	20-40	Y	1/16	0.0483	3	0.0362
Atlantic	40-60	Y	1/16	0.0483	4	0.0483
Atlantic	60+	N	1/16	0.0885	1	0.0221
Ontario	40-60	N	1/16	0.0885	1	0.0221
Quebec	0-20	Y	1/16	0.0483	1	0.0121
Western	0-20	N	1/16	0.0885	1	0.0221
Western	20-40	N	1/16	0.0885	3	0.0664
Western	60+	Y	1/16	0.0483	3	0.0362
Total			8/16	0.5473	17	0.2656

Table 6. Classification after generalizing the Province and Amount attributes

Province and Amount attributes both have 4 possible values, giving $CC_{MAX} = 16$ and a coverage of $8/16 = 0.50$. Coverage is higher than for the initial classification, and decisions are consistent for every equivalence class. Reasonable doubts about the credibility of this classification remain because of the relatively low coverage (50%) and thin support (fewer than 4 instances) for many decisions. The credibility score increased to 0.2656, but it is still low.

Some inductive algorithms, typically those based on decision rules or trees, allow conditions to be pruned. Here, by generalizing Amount for the Ontario and Quebec cases, the coverage of their decisions can be increased, as shown in Table 7. In this case, coverage varies among the equivalence classes. The overall

Province	Amount	Decision	Coverage	Q_E	#instances	$Cred_E$
Atlantic	20-40	Y	1/16	0.0483	3	0.0362
Atlantic	40-60	Y	1/16	0.0483	4	0.0483
Atlantic	60+	N	1/16	0.0885	1	0.0221
Ontario	-	N	4/16	0.3542	1	0.0885
Quebec	-	Y	4/16	0.1932	1	0.0483
Western	0-20	N	1/16	0.0885	1	0.0221
Western	20-40	N	1/16	0.0885	3	0.0664
Western	60+	Y	1/16	0.0483	3	0.0362
Total			14/16	0.9579	17	.3683

Table 7. Classification after generalizing and pruning

coverage is $14/16 = 0.875$, which may be sufficient for the user. Consistency has been maintained since each equivalence class still has a single decision. These factors combine to produce a relatively high score for the Q measure (0.96). Nonetheless, the relatively low credibility measure ($Cred$ is still less than 0.5) shows that the decisions are not adequately supported. Only after the adequacy of coverage, consistency, and support has been determined, can the overall credibility of a classification be asserted.

If a credible classification cannot be derived, we can (1) simply inform the user; (2) ask for additional input instances constrained to match generalized values of the condition attributes that have no coverage or inadequate support; or (3) report probabilistic decision rules with attached descriptions of coverage and support.

4 The CredSearch Algorithm

The following algorithm extracts a classification, i.e., a generalized relation, from an input relation with condition attributes $C_1, C_2, \ldots, C_n$ and decision attribute D. The credibility measure $Cred$, defined in Section 2, guides the algorithm. Condition attributes are generalized by ascending their concept trees until any further ascension would reduce the credibility of the overall classification. For each iteration, one attribute is selected for generalization (this selection can be made in many ways [1]). Here, one step lookahead is used to select the attribute whose next generalization most increases the credibility of the classification. Lower level concepts of the selected attribute are replaced by concepts at the next higher level in the concept tree. Fewer possible values are always present at a higher level of a concept tree than at a lower level, so the maximum classificatory complexity is reduced.

Algorithm CredSearch:
Input: (i) Original relation R with set of condition attributes $C = \{C_1, \ldots, Cn\}$
        and decision attribute D;
      (ii) Set T of concept trees, where each $T_i \in T$ is a concept tree for attribute C_i.
Output: The classification (generalized relation) R'
$R' \leftarrow R$
$C_i \leftarrow Lookahead(R', C, D, T, 0)$
while $C_i \neq \emptyset$ DO
      Replace values for C_i in R' to reduce depth in tree T_i by a level
      Combine rows in R' with identical condition values
      Calculate $Cred$ of R' as described in Section 2.
      $C_i \leftarrow Lookahead(R', C, D, T, Cred)$
endwhile

This hill-climbing algorithm examines a series of classifications by repeatedly using a one-step lookahead function to select an attribute to generalize. When an attribute has been selected, one step of generalization is applied to its values. The one step of generalization is performed by by replacing the attribute's values with corresponding values from one level higher in its concept tree, then combining any rows in the classification that now have the same condition values, and finally recalculating the credibility of the resulting classification. The $Lookahead$ function applies one step of generalization, as just described, separately for each attribute, and determines which causes the greatest increase in the overall credibility. Ties are broken arbitrarily. The algorithm stops when any generalization would result in a decrease in credibility.

Consider the application of Algorithm CredSearch to the data shown in Table 4. Fig. 2 shows the generalization space for this data based on the concept hierarchies in Fig. 1. Each oval is labelled with a possible state of generalization, i.e., a combination of depths from the concept trees for Amount and Province. Each oval also contains the credibility of this state. The original data correspond to the ⟨P3, A2⟩ pair in the lower left of Fig. 2. Generalizing the Amount attribute is equivalent to moving upwards in the space, and generalizing the Province attribute to moving right. Thus, generalizing the data in Table 4 to produce Table 5, is equivalent to moving from ⟨P3, A2⟩ to ⟨P2, A2⟩. Algorithm CredSearch begins by looking ahead and evaluating the credibility of ⟨P2, A2⟩ (*Cred* is 0.0885) and ⟨P3, A1⟩ (0.1063). The algorithm chooses the latter because it results in the greatest improvement in credibility. Next it looks ahead again and chooses ⟨P3, A0⟩ over ⟨P2, A1⟩. Then it chooses to move to ⟨P2, A0⟩. It looks ahead to ⟨P1, A0⟩, but rejects this possibility and stops.

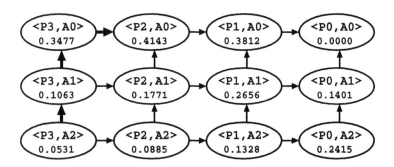

Fig. 2. Generalization space for Table 4

An alternate approach is to generate all possible combinations of levels of generality from the concept trees for the attributes, as is done in [5]. Although this approach is exponential in complexity, a parallel implementation yields satisfactory results for a relatively small number of attributes (< 5) with relatively shallow trees (< 7 levels) for relations with hundreds of thousands of tuples [6]. As with the above algorithm, the credibility could be assessed for each classification and the combination giving the highest credibility selected.

5   Conclusion

We have devised a measure of credibility for classifications. We have described how this measure applies to concept learning in the presence of concept hierarchies. We have also proposed Algorithm CredSearch for searching for the most credible classification, using a hill-climbing approach. Future research will examine variants of the simple hill-climbing technique used and the possible addition of the pruning techniques described in Section 3.

Acknowledgement: The research reported in this paper was supported in part by operating grants from the Natural Sciences and Engineering Research Council of Canada.

References

1. B. Barber and H.J. Hamilton. Attribute selection strategies for attribute-oriented generalization. In *Advances in Artificial Intelligence, 11th Biennial Conference of the Canadian Society for Computational Studies of Intelligence, AI '96*, pages 429–441. Springer, Toronto, 1996.
2. E. Bloedorn and R. Michalski. The AQ17-DCI system for data-driven constructive induction. In *Proc. of Ninth Int'l. Symp. on Methodologies for Intelligent Systems*, pages 108–117, Zakopane, Poland, June 1996.
3. Y.D. Cai, N. Cercone, and J. Han. Attribute-oriented induction in relational databases. In *Knowledge Discovery in Databases*, pages 213–228. AAAI/MIT Press, Cambridge, MA, 1991.
4. C.L. Carter and H.J. Hamilton. Efficient attribute-oriented algorithms for knowledge discovery from large databases. *IEEE Trans. on Knowledge and Data Engineering.* To appear.
5. H.J. Hamilton, R.J. Hilderman, and N. Cercone. Attribute-oriented induction using domain generalization graphs. In *Proceedings of the Eighth IEEE International Conference on Tools with Artificial Intelligence (ICTAI'96)*, pages 246–253, Toulouse, France, November 1996.
6. R.J. Hilderman, H.J. Hamilton, R.J. Kowalchuk, and N. Cercone. Parallel knowledge discovery using domain generalization graphs. In J. Komorowski and J. Zytkow, editors, *Proceedings of the 1st European Conference on the Principles of Data Mining and Knowledge Discovery*, pages 25–35, Trondheim, Norway, June 1997.
7. I.F. Imam. An empirical study on the incompetence of attribute selection criteria. In *Proc. of Ninth Int'l. Symp. on Methodologies for Intelligent Systems*, pages 458–467, Zakopane, Poland, June 1996.
8. S.K. Murthy and S. Salzberg. Decision tree induction: How effective is the greedy heuristic? In *Proceedings of the 2nd International Conference on Knowledge Discovery and Data Mining (KDD-96)*, pages 222–227, Portland, OR, 1996.
9. Z. Pawlak. *Rough Sets: Theoretical Aspects of Reasoning About Data.* Kluwer, 1991.
10. J. R. Quinlan. *C4.5 Programs for Machine Learning.* Morgan Kaufmann, 1993.
11. N. Shan, H.J. Hamilton, and N. Cercone. GRG: Knowledge discovery using information generalization, information reduction, and rule generation. *International Journal of Artificial Intelligence Tools*, 5(1 & 2):99–112, 1996.
12. N. Shan, H.J. Hamilton, W. Ziarko, and N. Cercone. Discovering classification knowledge in databases using rough sets. In *Proc. of the 2nd International Conference on Knowledge Discovery and Data Mining (KDD'96)*, pages 271–274, Portland, OR, 1996.
13. N. Shan, H.J. Hamilton, W. Ziarko, and N. Cercone. Discretization of continuous valued attributes in attribute-value systems. In *Proc. of the Fourth Int'l. Workshop on Rough Sets, Fuzzy Sets, and Machine Discovery (RFSD'96)*, pages 74–81, Tokyo, Japan, 1996.

Mining the Knowledge Mine
The Hot Spots Methodology for Mining Large Real World Databases

Graham J. Williams and Zhexue Huang

Cooperative Research Centre for Advanced Computational Systems
CSIRO Mathematical and Information Sciences
GPO Box 664 Canberra 2601 Australia
Email: Graham.Williams@cmis.csiro.au
Phone: (+61 2) 6216 7042
Fax: (+61 2) 6216 7111

Abstract. As databases grow in size and complexity the task of adding value to the wealth of data becomes difficult. Data mining has emerged as the technology to add value to enormous databases by finding new and important snippets (or nuggets) of knowledge. With large training sets, however, extremely large collections of nuggets are being extracted, leading to much "fools gold" amongst which to fossick for the real gold. Attention is now being directed towards the problem of how to better focus on the most precious nuggets. This paper presents the hot spots methodology, adopting a multi-strategy and interactive approach to help focus on the important nuggets. The methodology first performs data mining and then explores the resulting models to find the important nuggets contained therein. This approach is demonstrated in insurance and fraud applications.

1   Introduction

With the rapid increase in the use of databases together with the dramatic increases in storage capacities and performance many businesses today maintain extremely large databases. NRMA Insurance Ltd, one of Australia's largest general insurers has, for example, many millions of active insurance policies with several million claims being made against those policies each year. Australia's Health Insurance Commission (HIC) maintains a record of every visit every person in Australia has ever made to a medical practitioner since 1975 (Viveros, Nearhos and Rothman 1996).

To be effective and competitive such organisations must continually update their understanding of their core business. This often involves monitoring trends in their client base and attempting to understand and hence predict changes. Although the data is often available to perform such analyses traditional (statistical) approaches are reaching their limits (Mallows and Pregibon 1996). Statistics is not alone in being hamstrung with extremely large and complex datasets. Traditional Machine Learning and Knowledge Acquisition techniques often work well with small datasets but struggle when applied to more than a few thousand records. Run-times of days and weeks are common and the results are often so complex to be of little cognitive use. Such approaches often rely on sampling the data and identifying trends from those samples—necessitated by a lack of processing power. High performance computers now provide the opportunity to analyse all (or at least more) of the data. Hitherto hidden, but important, nuggets of information may now be discovered.

Data Mining (or exploratory data analysis with large and complex datasets) brings together the wealth of knowledge and research in Statistics and Machine Learning for the task of discovering new nuggets of knowledge in very large databases (Fayyad, Piatetsky-Shapiro and Smyth 1996). Visualisation and database research also play a central role in Data Mining. Together, these technologies have demonstrated that they can help businesses better understand their data, to rapidly identify changing trends in the data, and to discover insights that were previously missing.

Data Mining, however, is giving rise to its own peculiar difficulties. When Data Mining techniques are applied to very large databases, the amount of "discovered knowledge" itself can be beyond the capabilities of any person to comprehend and analyse. With a focus on the discovered knowledge rather than on building accurate models of the data, we are again lost in the wealth of information.

In this paper we present the **hot spots** methodology which tackles the specific problem of coming to terms with the large amounts of knowledge that can be discovered from large databases. In essence, we develop the idea of *mining the results of data mining*—turning data mining on itself to focus on the outcomes. The approach taken employs multiple-strategy learning with a post-processing step which automatically discovers hot spots in the discovered knowledge. This step uses additional data and background knowledge that may not have been used in the actual data mining. Traditional tools can be used with no or little modification to identify large collections of patterns, which can then be mined for the key discoveries. We present two case studies which illustrate this general approach to the discovery of hot spots in very large real world databases.

2 Motivation

In many businesses the identification of key client groups is a core concern. Targeting business development towards identified opportunities can give an organisation their competitive edge. Target groups are traditionally identified from market research, past experience, and business intuition. With the advent of very large databases and high performance computers, data mining provides an alternative approach to identifying key customer groups that may in the past have been overlooked, and that may continue to be overlooked by competitors. Such mission critical information we refer to as hot spots. This is information that an organisation needs to know in order to improve its performance or its processes. In general it may not be information that describes large groups of the customer base but more importantly identifies key customer groups—groups which although small, have above average significance to the business of the organisation.

When dealing with extremely large and complex datasets, as we do in data mining, the descriptions and models built, whether from statistical tools or machine learning tools, are often extremely complex. The key knowledge or discoveries may be lost in this wealth of knowledge structures. For example, C4.5 (Quinlan 1993), when used on data with 30 or 40 attributes and many millions of records, will quite happily generate decision trees and rule sets with thousands of nodes or rules (ignoring the issue of over training). While the overall model may represent a good prediction tool it gives us little insight. New techniques are required to assist in the task of taking this model and extracting key "discoveries" from it.

3   The Hot Spot Methodology

We regard a *hot spot* as an identified set of entities which are of some particular, but crucial, importance to the domain of interest. Examples include loyal customer groups in a supermarket dataset or the group of regular high claiming insurance policy holders in a motor vehicle insurance portfolio. The discovery of these hot spots in the data can assist management in targeting their promotional efforts, for example. Simple techniques such as clustering or segmentation can help this task but are often computationally expensive and/or build groups that are not well described. An aim of data mining is to highlight areas of the data in such a way that makes sense to the domain experts—providing human understandable discoveries.

A heuristic approach to this segmentation task that we have empirically found to be effective in many real world problems involves the combination of a clustering tool and a decision tree induction tool. These are augmented with post analysis tools. This methodology we refer to as the hot spots methodology: cluster; rule induction; nugget evaluation.

Suppose we have a dataset $\mathcal{D}$ consisting of a set of real world entities such as a set of policy holders in an insurance company or a set of Medicare patients. We generally assume that $\mathcal{D}$ is relational with only one universal relation $\mathbf{R}(a_1, a_2, \ldots, a_m)$, where the a_i are the attributes of the entities, and are defined by the basic data types such as integers, reals, and strings. The dataset then consists of the set of entities $\mathcal{D} = \{e_1, e_2, \ldots, e_n\}$, with each entity being a tuple $\langle v_1, v_2, \ldots, v_m \rangle$. For real world problems m and n are typically "large" (m may be anywhere from 20 to 1000 and n typically greater than 1 million).

Step 1 The first step of our approach is to develop a raw (and unsupervised) clustering of $\mathcal{D}$. A particular clustering of $\mathcal{D}$ might be $\mathcal{C} = \{C_1, C_2, \ldots, C_p\}$. The clusters are constructed to be complete and disjoint: $\mathcal{D} = \bigcup C_i$ and $C_i \cap C_j = \emptyset, i \neq j$. A mixed data-type clustering algorithm has been used (Huang 1997). This efficient algorithm is based on a k-means clustering algorithm extended to handle categorical attributes. Other clustering algorithms tend to be computationally expensive, particularly in the context of data mining where the datasets are very large. Typically, anywhere between 10 and 1000 clusters may be constructed, depending on the size of the dataset.

Step 2 The second step records with each entity the cluster to which it now belongs. Thus, the entity becomes $\langle v_1, v_2, \ldots, v_m, c \rangle$, where $c \in \{1, 2, \ldots, p\}$. Supervised learning can then be used to build a symbolic description of the clusters. Using C4.5, for example, the resulting decision tree can be converted to a rule set and pruned. The end result is a set of rules, $\mathcal{R} = \{r_1, r_2, \ldots, r_q\}$, usually with $q \geq p$, and usually much greater (since for each of the p clusters multiple rules will be induced). We will refer to a rule as a description of a nugget (or simply as a nugget). Each nugget now corresponds to a subset of the original dataset $\mathcal{D}$. We use the notation r_i to represent both the nugget description and the nugget subset. $\mathcal{R}$ will be referred to more generally as the *nugget set*. Note that the nugget subsets are no longer disjoint: $r_i \cap r_j$ is not necessarily empty for $i \neq j$.

Step 3 The third and final step is to evaluate each nugget in the nugget set to find those of particular importance to the task at hand. We define the function $Eval(r)$ as a mapping from nuggets to a measure of the significance of the particular nugget r. Such a function is very much domain dependent, and is the key to effectively mining the knowledge mine. The nuggets may be evaluated in the context of all discovered nuggets or evaluated for their usefulness, novelty, and validity in the context of the application domain. Evaluation functions can be quite complex.

In the first instance domain experts often provide the most effective form of evaluation of discovered nuggets. Visualisation tools can be a critical component of this evaluation, providing effective presentations of the results of mining. However, as the nugget sets become large, such manual approaches become less effective.

An approach we have found empirically to be effective in evaluating nuggets is based on building statistical summaries of the entities associated with each nugget. Key variables that play an important role in the business problem at hand are characterised for each nugget and filters are developed to pick out those nuggets with profiles that are out of the ordinary. As the data mining exercise proceeds, the filters are refined and further developed.

The end result is a small (manageable) collection of nuggets that can be further investigated using human resources. The approach focuses attention on segments of the business portfolio where important discoveries may be made.

4 Hot Spots for Insurance Premium Setting

We now illustrate the approach with actual real world data in the context of two case studies. In this section we describe a case study involving insurance risk analysis. This is a joint project with NRMA Insurance Limited. The following section describes public fraud detection in the context of Medicare, a joint project with the Australian Health Insurance Commission.

A major task faced by any insurer is to ensure profitability. To oversimplify, the total sum of premiums charged for insurance must be sufficient to cover all claims made against the policies. However, the premiums must also be competitive against other insurers. The actuarial task is usually performed manually with the support of a variety of statistical tools resulting in only a small number of customer attributes being considered and very broad generalisations being made. With more powerful computing resources available many insurers are now looking to perform more detailed and complex analyses to assist them in developing and annually (or even more frequently) refining their premium setting formulae. An approach we have taken with this problem is to identify, describe, and explore customer groups that have significant impact on the insurance portfolio—using the hot spots methodology for insurance risk analysis.

The original data for our task was collected for business purposes other than for data mining. Consequently, considerable effort was required to transform the data for data mining—a common observation of data miners (Williams and Huang 1996). After preprocessing the dataset the three step hot spot methodology was used: clustering; rule induction; nugget evaluation.

For illustration and to protect confidentiality we present an example here consisting of a dataset of just some 72,000 records. This dataset was clustered into some 40 clusters, ranging in size from tens of records to thousands of records. Treating each cluster as a class we can build a decision tree to describe the clusters and then prune the tree through rule generation. This leads to some 60 rules (nugget descriptions). A sample rule is given in Figure 1. For each cluster there may be many such rules that together describe the data records that (mostly) belong to that cluster.

If   NCB < 60 and Age ≤ 24 and Address is Urban and
         Vehicle $\in$ {Utility, Station Wagon}
Then   Cluster $= 1$

Fig. 1. Sample nugget from the motor vehicle insurance dataset.

An evaluation function was developed to identify those nuggets that exhibit "peculiarities" or collections of customers that are important to the business. This is an ongoing task of refinement and exploration, and we present in Tables 1 and 2 an illustration of this process. For these examples the evaluation function identifies nuggets which exhibit characteristics significantly different from the "normal."

The first step was to derive for each nugget a collection of important indicators. For our example we use the number and proportion of claims lodged by the group of clients in the associated nugget subset, and the average and total cost of a claim for each nugget subset. This information is presented in Table 1 for some of the nuggets. For the whole dataset there were 3800 claims in all, representing a proportion of some 5%. The overall average claim cost is $3000, with a total of some $12 million. (Again, because of confidentiality these figures are indicative only.)

Nugget	Claims	Total	Proportion	Average Cost	Total Cost
2	148	1391	**11.90**	**3685**	545,000
3	141	2300	6.51	**3795**	535,000
19	3	25	**13.64**	**4338**	13,015
24	10	123	8.85	**7915**	79,150
34	22	344	6.83	**5293**	116,440
35	64	523	**13.94**	**4386**	280,728
36	3	3	100	**6771**	20,314
40	800	1400	5.9	**3500**	2,800,000
All	3800	72000	5.0	3000	12,000,000

Table 1. Number of claims, number of records, and summary nugget data.

From this "raw" data we define an evaluation function that specifies the conditions under which the nuggets are deemed to be of significant interest for the business problem at hand. The evaluation may, for example, highlight nugget subsets containing a very large number (or proportion) of claims (greater than 10%) is important. Alternatively, any nugget having significantly more than the average for any particular measure may be a candidate for further investigation. Table 2 identifies the nuggets that have higher than average characteristics.

Nugget	By Claims	By Proportion	By Average Cost
2	Y	Y	Y
3	Y	Y	Y
19		Y	Y
24		Y	Y
34	Y	Y	Y
35	Y	Y	Y
36		Y	Y
40	Y		Y

Table 2. Risk Areas by Various Criteria (Y indicates risk area).

By then investigating the associated descriptions of the nuggets, and the associated customers, a better understanding of these key groups can be obtained. This exploration can then be used as a key input to the process of defining the insurance premium setting formulae.

5 Hot Spots for Fraud Detection

Fraud is an area receiving significant attention from data mining. In very large collections of data (such as held by credit card companies, telephone companies, insurance companies, and the tax office), it is often expected that there is a small percentage of customers who are practising fraudulent behaviour. It is not surprising then that data mining has been a player in tackling this problem.

The Health Insurance Commission maintains a large database recording information relating to payments made to doctors and patients from the government's Medicare program. Their database is measured in terms of terabytes, and, if it could be analysed, would paint a very comprehensive picture of the health of Australia.

Like any large and complex payment system, Medicare is open to fraud. The HIC is very active in developing and refining its arsenal for identifying and procedurally eliminating fraud, committed both by doctors and by the public. Data mining is now being used to explore and to bring new tools to the problem of public fraud detection.

Once again we have used the hot spots methodology to identify areas within the very large datasets which may require further investigation. For reasons of confidentiality we will present artificially constructed, but indicative, results.

The dataset for this exercise consisted of some 40,000 Medicare numbers (a small subset of the many millions of Medicare numbers available), with over 30 raw attributes (e.g., age, sex, etc.) and some 20 derived attributes (e.g., number of times a patient visited a doctor over a year, number of different doctors visited, etc.). A variety of clusters have been developed for the exploratory analysis, but we will present results from just two: a clustering consisting of just 10 clusters and a clustering consisting of 100 clusters. For the 10 cluster, Table 3 lists the prototypes for each of the clusters over 5 of the variables, and the size of each cluster.

Cluster:	0	1	2	3	4	5	6	7	8	9
Age	30	30	65	40	30	45	50	10	50	55
Sex	F	F	F	F	M	F	F	M	F	F
Services	15	24	34	33	28	21	15	12	32	47
Benefits	430	841	1288	2233	1390	743	463	360	1125	1912
Weeks	2	4	2	2	1	1	2	2	10	7
Size	9000	150	3000	1000	80	5500	9000	7000	2000	800

Table 3. Prototypes for the 10 clusters.

Rules were generated for each of the clusters using C5.0 (the successor to C4.5). For the "10 cluster", some 280 nuggets (rules) were generated and for the "100 cluster" over 1000 nuggets were generated. Figure 2 gives an indicative example. Once the collection of nuggets gets to these sizes it is not longer feasible to manually scan through them looking for those that are interesting. For the 100

If   Age is between 18 and 25 and Weeks ≥ 10 and
AnkSpc is either X or Y
Then   Cluster = 4

Fig. 2. Sample nugget from the Medicare dataset.

cluster, for example, we can generate a listing of over 1000 lines recording for each nugget the characteristics of that nugget. This might include the average number of claims made on those Medicare numbers in that cluster, the average size of those claims, and so on. Such a listing covers many pages and hides much interesting information. A hot spots evaluation function is used to mine this information to find those nuggets that, for example, have significantly higher rates of claim than the overall average. The evaluation function is tuned iteratively as we (both the data miners and the domain experts) gain more insights and understanding.

The approach has already identified interesting areas in the data that have required further detailed investigation by the Health Insurance Commission.

6 Conclusions

Data Mining has proved to be a useful tool in exploring and discovering interesting and useful knowledge in very large datasets. However, as the datasets get larger the tools being used generally produce significantly more complex models. In this paper we have presented a methodology that we have found useful in deploying data mining in real world problems. The hot spots methodology introduces the idea of mining the knowledge mine. The results of data mining are themselves being "mined" to find those interesting discoveries that are of particular importance to the business problem at hand.

The methodology we have presented employs clustering to provide a first cut segmentation of the data. Decision tree induction and then rule set pruning, using C4.5 and C5.0, deliver symbolic rule sets. Each rule can then be regarded as defining a segment of the dataset. The records from the original dataset associated with each rule are then analysed to find those nuggets that correspond to areas of the data that are significant to the domain problem.

Two case studies have been presented where the approach was used. For NRMA Insurance Limited, key areas of a dataset were those that had significantly greater than average impact on the motor vehicle insurance portfolio. For the Health Insurance Commission, the key areas of the dataset were those that had odd patterns of Medicare claim lodgment or claim amounts. For both case studies these segments of the data were identified for further human investigation, leading to potential refinements to their business.

The Evaluation function is of key importance to the hot spots methodology. Empirically we have found a simple filter approach to be effective so far, but more effort is needed to further develop our skills in defining evaluation functions. Future work will focus on using machine learning approaches, once again, but on the data associated with the nuggets, and incorporating domain knowledge, to derive evaluation formulae from the data.

Acknowledgements

The authors wish to acknowledge that this work was carried out within the Cooperative Research Centre for Advanced Computational Systems established under the Australian Government's Cooperative Research Centres Program.

References

Fayyad, U. M., Piatetsky-Shapiro, G. and Smyth, P.: 1996, From data mining to knowledge discovery: An overview, *in* U. M. Fayyad, G. Piatetsky-Shapiro, P. Smyth and R. Uthurusamy (eds), *Advances in Knowledge Discovery and Data Mining*, AAAI Press / The MIT Press, pp. 1–34.

Huang, Z.: 1997, Clustering large data sets with mixed numeric and categorical values, *in* H.-J. Lu, H. Liu and H. Motoda (eds), *Knowledge discovery and data mining: techniques and applications*, World Scientific.

Mallows, C. and Pregibon, D.: 1996, The analysis of call-detail data, *The Sydney International Statistical Congress*.

Quinlan, J. R.: 1993, *C4.5: Programs for Machine Learning, Morgan Kaufmann, San Mateo, CA, 1993.*, Morgan Kaufmann, San Mateo, CA.

Viveros, M. S., Nearhos, J. P. and Rothman, M. J.: 1996, Applying data mining techniques to a health insurance information system, *Proceedings of the 22nd VLDB Conference*, Mumbai (Bombay), India, pp. 286–293.

Williams, G. J. and Huang, Z.: 1996, A case study in knowledge acquisition for insurance risk assessment using a kdd methodology, *in* P. Compton, R. Mizoguchi, H. Motoda and T. Menzies (eds), *Pacific Knowledge Acquisition Workshop*, pp. 117–129.

Using Decision Trees for Agent Modelling:
A Study on Resolving Conflicting Predictions

Bark Cheung Chiu, Geoffrey I. Webb, and Zijian Zheng

School of Computing and Mathematics, Deakin University, Australia

E-Mail: chiu@deakin.edu.au

Abstract: Input-Output Agent Modelling (IOAM) is an approach to modelling an agent in terms of relationships between the inputs and outputs of the cognitive system. This approach, together with a leading inductive learning algorithm, C4.5, has been adopted to build a subtraction skill modeller, C4.5-IOAM. It models agents' competencies with a set of decision trees. C4.5-IOAM makes no prediction when predictions from different decision trees are contradictory. This paper proposes three techniques for resolving such situations. Two techniques involve selecting the more reliable prediction from a set of competing predictions using a tree quality measure and a leaf quality measure. The other technique merges multiple decision trees into a single tree. This has the additional advantage of producing more comprehensible models. Experimental results, in the domain of modelling elementary subtraction skills, showed that the tree quality and the leaf quality of a decision path provided valuable references for resolving contradicting predictions and a single tree model representation performed nearly equally well to the multi-tree model representation.

1 Introduction

Inductive learning techniques provide approaches to building agent models in the form of knowledge acquisition by observing the agents' behaviors. For example, they can be used in an intelligent tutoring system (ITS) to model a student's competencies. They make hypotheses about a student's knowledge of that problem domain. They learn theories, from examples, like many people do. Decision tree learning or rule learning provides the additional advantage of representing the acquired knowledge in explicit form such that people can interpret it.

The use of inductive learning for agent modelling has been studied previously, e.g. (Desmoulins and Van Labeke, 1996; Gilmore and Self, 1988). An induction based modelling system may require prohibitive resources for implementation if its inductive engine is tightly linked to the cognitive aspects of an agent. An Input-Output Agent Modelling (IOAM) approach allows a system to treat the operation of the cognitive system as a black box and models the operation in terms of the relationships between the inputs and outputs of the system. Therefore, a general-purpose classifier learning algorithm can be employed as an induction engine. Examples of modelling systems which employ the IOAM approach include Feature

Based Modelling (FBM) (Webb and Kuzmycz, 1996), Relational Based Modelling (Kuzmycz, 1995), FFOIL-IOAM and C4.5-IOAM (Chiu et al., 1997). Note that they use different induction engines. C4.5-IOAM uses C4.5 (Quinlan, 1993), a well-known and general-purpose learning algorithm, as its induction engine. It has been used to model students' competencies of elementary subtraction skills with a set of decision trees. Comparative evaluations of C4.5-IOAM against FBM (Webb et al., 1997) and FFOIL-IOAM (Chiu et al., 1997) have shown that the use of C4.5 increased the number of predictions made without significantly altering the accuracy of those predictions.

However, C4.5-IOAM makes no prediction when the individual predictions from different decision trees are contradictory. If C4.5-IOAM is augmented by a mechanism for resolving conflicting predictions, it might make more predictions without affecting the prediction accuracy. Three techniques have been explored for this purpose. Two of them involve selecting the more reliable prediction from a set of competing predictions. The other technique merges multiple decision trees into a single tree. This approach offers the additional advantage of producing more comprehensible models. This paper presents an empirical study of how conflicting predictions can be resolved with these alternative techniques.

2   An overview of C4.5-IOAM Subtraction Modeller

The C4.5-IOAM subtraction modeller manipulates an n-digit subtraction problem by treating it as n separate column problems. In this subtraction modeller, context features and action features, adopted from the FBM (Kuzmycz and Webb, 1992), are used to represent inputs and outputs. Context features describe the problems with which a student is faced. Action features describe aspects of a student's actions for a particular problem. There are eleven action features: Result=M-S, Result=M-S-1, Result=10+M-S, Result=10+M-S-1, Result=M, Result=S, Result=zero, Result=M-S-2, Result=10+M-S-2, Result=S-M and Result=correct, where M and S stand for minuend and subtrahend digits respectively. Action features are not mutually exclusive. That is, a student's action may correspond to more than one action feature. However, C4.5 requires mutually exclusive classes. Thus, C4.5-IOAM uses eleven decision trees to model different aspects of a student's actions (behavior).

The context features of a unit problem are described by 12 attributes. The first four attributes, M_is_0, S_is_0, S_is_9 and S_is_BK (BK stands for blank), are self-explanatory. The rest of them are listed below with their meanings where N stands for Not Available.

- M_vs_S: {G, L, E}, M is greater (G) or less than (L), or equal (E) to S.
- $M\_L\_is\_0$: {T, F, N}, M in the column to the left is zero.
- $M\_L\_is\_1$: {T, F, N}, M in the column to the left is one.
- $M\_R\_is\_0$: {T, F, N}, M in the column to the right is zero.
- $S\_R\_is\_9$: {T, F, N}, S in the column to the right is nine.
- M_S_R: {G, L, E, N}, similar to M_vs_S, but it describes the column to the right.
- M_S_2R: {G, L, E, N}, similar to M_vs_S, but it describes two columns to the right.
- $Column$: {L, I, R}, the current column is left-most (L), inner (I), or right-most (R).

Figure 1 illustrates how 11 training examples, one for each decision tree, are formed from one single column problem. The context features, described by 12 attributes, are extracted based on the problem environment and applied to each example. At the inner column, M (minuend digit) is nine, S (subtrahend digit) is zero, and the student's answer is nine. Two action features, $Result=M-S$, and $Result=M$, correspond to the student's action. These two action features are, therefore, set as T. The other action features are set as F. One 3-digit subtraction problem will generate three training examples for each decision tree. After all examples of a student's subtraction performance are processed, C4.5 is used to infer a decision tree for each training set.

When C4.5-IOAM predicts a student's answer for a problem, the problem context is extracted and used to consult the eleven decision trees. The decision trees being consulted are then confined to those, each predicts the presence of the corresponding action. If these predictions lead to the same digit, the system adopts the digit as the final prediction. Otherwise, the system makes no prediction about the student's answer.

Figure 2 shows a sample theory inferred by C4.5-IOAM. Decision trees with only one leaf labeled F predict the student will not exhibit the corresponding actions. *Tree_M* predicts that if the subtrahend digit is zero, the student will assign the minuend as the answer.

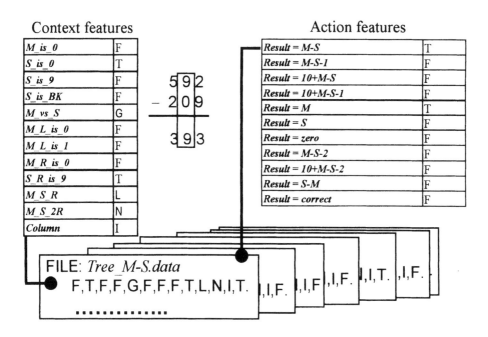

Figure 1. Formation of a column's training examples for decision trees.

Tree_M-S-1	Tree_M-S-2	Tree_10+M-S-1	Tree_10+M-S-2
F	F	F	F

Tree_M	Tree_M-S	Tree_10+M-S	Tree_zero
S_is_0 = F:F	M_vs_S = G:T	M_vs_S = G:F	M_vs_S = G:F
S_is_0 = T:T	M_vs_S = L:F	M_vs_S = L:T	M_vs_S = L:F
	M_vs_S = E:T	M_vs_S = E:F	M_vs_S = E:T

Tree_correct	Tree_S	Tree_S-M
M_S_R = G:T	M_is_0 = T:F	M_vs_S = G:F
M_S_R = L:F	M_is_0 = F:	M_vs_S = E:T
M_S_R = N:T	|---M_L_is_1 = F:F	M_vs_S = L:
M_S_R = E:F	|---M_L_is_1 = N:F	|---M_L_is_1 = T:F
	|---M_L_is_1 = T:T	|---M_L_is_1 = N:F
		|---M_L_is_1 = F:T

Figure 2. A theory inferred by C4.5-IOAM.

3 Techniques for resolving conflicting predictions

The current version of C4.5-IOAM makes no prediction whenever different decision trees make conflicting predictions. The following conflict-resolving techniques are proposed to improve the prediction rate of the current system.

3.1 Using quality measure of a decision tree

The prediction rate of the system can be improved by adopting the predictions from the more reliable decision trees. A conflict resolution technique like voting is not suitable because the decision trees predict different aspects of a student's actions. We assume decision trees making conflicting predictions have different characteristics in terms of measurable quality such as prediction accuracy and prediction error rate. We employed stratified ten-fold cross-validation (Kohavi, 1995) for estimating the error rate of each decision tree. For each action feature, the training examples are randomly divided into ten equal-sized partitions. Each partition, which preserves the original class distribution, is used in turn as test data for the decision tree trained on the remaining nine partitions. The total numbers of correct and incorrect predictions of these tests are then used to estimate the error rate of the decision tree trained on the whole training set. An C4.5-IOAM system can improve its prediction rate by associating decision trees with estimated error rates, and consulting the trees in a ranked order. With this consulting order, the first tree that gives a positive prediction is used to make the system's prediction. This method contrasts to the current system, which consults the trees in parallel.

3.2 Using a leaf quality measure

The error rate of a tree reflects the overall quality of the tree. We know that different leaves have different predictive power because the evidence on which they make predictions are different. A leaf with less support on a high quality tree may make a poorer prediction than a leaf with more support on a tree with a relatively lower quality. A closer look at how C4.5 builds a decision tree may help to explain this. C4.5 builds decision trees by using a divide and conquer strategy. It recursively selects the best attribute, which will generate less complex subtrees, to form branching nodes. Examples of the training set are partitioned based on the selected attribute. This process continues until the training set at a node cannot be further divided, for example, because no significant split exists. In the case that a terminal node (leaf) contains examples of different classes, it takes the majority class as the leaf label. When the tree is used to predict the class of an unseen (test) example, it traverses the unseen example through a decision path and suggests the leaf label of the path as the prediction. The reliability of this prediction can be estimated by examining the distribution of the classes of training examples at the leaf node. We are only concerned with the leaf labeled with T for predicting that a student will exhibit a particular action. Let t denote the total number of examples, and e denote the number of examples labeled with F, at the leaf node with label T, a value based on the Laplace formula, $(e + 1)/(t + 2)$, can be used as the estimated error rate of a leaf. A C4.5-IOAM system can therefore adopt the prediction of a decision tree of which the leaf node of the decision path is associated with a lower error measure.

3.3 Using a single tree instead of multiple trees

The tree and leaf quality approaches attempt to resolve multiple predictions. Another approach is to circumvent the problem by producing only one prediction. We can achieve this by developing a single tree that predicts the most *useful* action feature for predicting an agent's actions in a given context. Such a tree requires a training set labeled with the most useful action feature for each example. We propose a two-phase identification algorithm (see Figure 3) which can be employed at the training stage. For each training example which is accompanied with more than one action feature, each action feature is validated by a lazy Bayesian tree[1] (Zheng and Webb, 1997) trained from all other training examples. The lazy Bayesian tree is used for the sake of computational efficiency. This filtering process reduces the number of examples with multiple action features. At the second stage, those training examples with multiple action features form a temporary test set. A temporary decision tree, trained on examples that each has an unique action feature, predicts the most useful action feature for each example in the test set. The ultimate training set, in which each example is labeled a most useful action feature, or as unknown if a most useful action feature cannot be identified, infers a single tree for the system.

---

[1] For each test example, the Lazy Bayesian Tree learning algorithm generates one relevant decision path. The leaf of the path uses a local naive-Bayesian classifier, instead of a majority class, to classify the test example.

354

Given: raw training set M with N examples, from a single student, in the form of
(Att, undetermined_action) where Att is a set of problem context features;
11 training sets, A_i, each has N examples in the form of (Att, a_i), $a_i \in \{F,T\}$ where
F/T stand for the status, absence/presence, of a corresponding action feature.
Output: a training set of examples in the form of (Att, Action), Action $\in \{$ M-S, M-S-1,..,
correct, unknown}.

FOR n := 1 to N DO
    obtain a status list (a_1 ,...,a_i ,.., a_{11}) from the n-th examples from training sets A_1
    ,..,A_i ,..,A_{11}
    generate an index list, L, of competing actions, where L = (.,i,..) for any $a_i = T$
    IF L has more then one element THEN L = Reduce_ competing_actions (L, n)
    IF L has one element i THEN undetermined_action := $Action_i$
    ELSE IF L is empty THEN undetermined_action : = unknown
    ELSE
        append $example_n$ to undetermined example list U; and
        append L to a list of competing action lists LL

FOR each undetermined example, $example_u$, in U DO
    retrieve the corresponding L from LL
    undetermined_action = Classify_within_competing_actions($example_u$, L)

Process name: Reduce_competing_actions.   */* Phase 1: Internal identification */*
Given: L, an index list of competing actions; n, an index of the current example.
Output: L, a revised index list of competing actions.

    FOR each index i in L DO
    build a lazy Bayesian tree LBT_i based on A_i excluding the $example_n$
    IF the predicted class of the test item, $example_n$, is F
    THEN remove i from L
    RETURN L

Process name: Classify_within_competing_actions. */* Phase 2: Global identification */*
Given: $example_u$, a test example ; L, a list of index of competing actions.
Output: an action, or unknown.

    prepare a temporary training set by copying all examples, for which class labels
    match the actions described by the index in L, from the raw training set
    IF the temporary training set is not empty
    THEN
        build a decision tree D to test $example_u$ and RETURN the action predicted by D
    ELSE
        RETURN unknown

Figure 3. Two-phase identification process.

4 Experiments

The same data set, which has been used to evaluate C4.5-IOAM and other IOAM based subtraction modellers (Webb et al., 1997; Chiu et al., 1997), was used to evaluate experimentally the techniques discussed in Section 3. The data came from 73 primary school students who were administered with five rounds of subtraction-problem tests. For each student, a modelling system used all data from prior rounds to build a student model and used the current round data to test the student model. The data set allows a system to conduct 264 training-testing processes.

The performance of the current version of C4.5-IOAM was used as a baseline. There were a total of 30,474 student answers, of which 3,630 were incorrect answers. The C4.5-IOAM system made 28,700 predictions, of which 26,507 (92%) were correct. Of the system's 1,999 predictions that a subject would provide an incorrect digit for a column, 1,347 (67%) were accurate, predicting the exact digit provided. We used the symbols +Tree_QTY, +Leaf_QTY and Single-tree to represent new versions that were implemented by introducing quality measures on trees and leafs, and merging multiple trees to a single tree respectively. The performance of these new versions was compared with C4.5-IOAM. Table 1 summarises these results.

We used a two-tailed pair-wise t-test to evaluate the statistical significance of the observed differences. The performance differences of the 264 model tests are summarised in Table 2, where the number at the intersection of row A > B and column C represents the number of cases that system A outperformed system B for the performance category C.

All new versions achieved significant improvement in prediction rate while their overall prediction accuracy dropped slightly. However, their numbers of correct predictions were still higher than that of C4.5-IOAM. The introduction of quality measures for decision trees and leaf nodes increased the number of error prediction with an expanse of error prediction accuracy. Again, their numbers of correct predictions were still higher than that of C4.5-IOAM. In this aspect, the difference between the Single-tree version and C4.5-IOAM was not significant.

Regarding the inferred theories generated by these systems, only the Single-tree version generated a single tree for describing a student's problem solving competency. Figure 4 and Figure 5 show the outputs of the single-tree and multi-tree versions when a student's first round performance was captured. Both models exhibited identical performance in predicting the student's next round answers. The multi-tree representation tells the absence and presence of each action in detail. For the Single-tree version, a leaf labeled as correct covers those actions leading to correct answers, while a leaf with other label tells how an erroneous action is predicted. This single model is likely to be easier for teachers and students to understand.

Table 1. Performance of new versions created by three kinds of treatment.

	C4.5-IOAM	+Leaf_QTY	+Tree_QTY	Single-tree
Number of predictions made	28,700	30,093	29,783	30,130
Prediction rate	94.2%	98.7%	97.7%	98.9%
Number of predictions that were correct	26,507	27,543	27,308	27,495
Prediction accuracy	92.4%	91.5%	91.7%	91.3%
Number of error predictions made	1,999	2,173	2,346	2,095
Prediction rate	55.1%	59.9%	64.6%	57.7%
Number of error predictions that were correct	1,347	1,426	1,485	1,373
Prediction accuracy	67.4%	65.6%	63.3%	65.5%

Table 2. Observed differences in performance between new versions and C4.5-IOAM.

	More predictions made	Higher accuracy	More error predictions made	Higher accuracy (for errors)
+Leaf_QTY > C4.5-IOAM	197	73	40	7
C4.5-IOAM > +Leaf_QTY	0	105	0	24
	($p < 0.0001$)	($p = 0.0001$)	($p < 0.0001$)	($p = 0.0081$)
+Tree_QTY > C4.5-IOAM	186	80	79	11
C4.5-IOAM > +Tree_QTY	16	103	1	35
	($p < 0.0001$)	($p = 0.0001$)	($p < 0.0001$)	($p = 0.0029$)
Single-tree > C4.5-IOAM	195	83	48	17
C4.5-IOAM > Single-tree	14	114	33	39
	($p < 0.0001$)	($p < 0.0001$)	($p = 0.2045$)	($p = 0.1460$)

Tree_actions

```
M_S_R = G: correct
M_S_R = N: correct
M_S_R = L:
|---M_vs_S = G: M-S
|---M_vs_S = L: 10+M-S
|---M_vs_S = E: S-M
M_S_R = E:
|---M_S_2R = G: correct
|---M_S_2R = L: M-S
|---M_S_2R = E: correct
|---M_S_2R = N: correct
```

Figure 4. Knowledge representation inferred by a single-tree modeller.

Tree_M-S-1	Tree_M-S-2	Tree_10+M-S-1	Tree_10+M-S-2
F	F	F	F

Tree_M

```
S_is_0 = F: F
S_is_0 = T: T
```

Tree_M-S

```
M_vs_S = G: T
M_vs_S = L: F
M_vs_S = E: T
```

Tree_10+M-S

```
M_vs_S = G: F
M_vs_S = L: T
M_vs_S = E: F
```

Tree_zero

```
M_vs_S = G: F
M_vs_S = L: F
M_vs_S = E: T
```

Tree_correct

```
M_S_R = G: T
M_S_R = L: F
M_S_R = N: T
M_S_R = E:
|---M_S_2R = G: T
|---M_S_2R = L: F
|---M_S_2R = E: F
|---M_S_2R = N: T
```

Tree_S

```
M_is_0 = T: F
M_is_0 = F:
|---M_L_is_1 = F: F
|---M_L_is_1 = N: F
|---M_L_is_1 = T:
    |---S_R_is_9 = F: F
    |---S_R_is_9 = T: T
    |---S_R_is_9 = N: F
```

Tree_S-M

```
M_vs_S = G: F
M_vs_S = E: T
M_vs_S = L:
|---M_L_is_1 = T: F
|---M_L_is_1 = N: F
|---M_L_is_1 = F:
    |---S_is_9 = T: T
    |---S_is_9 = F:
        |---M_R_is_0 = T: F
        |---M_R_is_0 = N: F
        |---M_R_is_0 = F:
            |---M_S_R = G: T
            |---M_S_R = L: F
            |---M_S_R = E: F
            |---M_S_R = N: F
```

Figure 5. Knowledge representation inferred by a multi-tree modeller.

5 Conclusions

The main tasks of modelling systems mentioned in this paper are learning to predict correct and erroneous actions, and generating theories describing agents' behaviors in subtraction problem solving. The main problem discussed in the paper is how to resolve conflicting predictions about an agent's action. We have described and evaluated three techniques for this objective.

Techniques of employing quality measures on decision trees and leaf nodes in resolving conflicting predictions at testing stage have been shown to be effective for this purpose. These two methods cover two aspects of resolving conflicts: adopting a decision from a point of view at global level; and considering the judgement based on local experience. It is quite similar to consulting human experts. While an engineer might have good abstract knowledge but lack sufficient experience for a particular case, an ordinary person could have encountered numerous similar examples and could be an expert for that case. The employment of merging multiple trees into a single tree shifts the conflict resolution to the training stage. The results are also promising. The Single-tree version achieved significant improvement in prediction rate with a slight drop in overall prediction accuracy. However, the number of correct predications was still higher than that of the original system. There was no significant performance difference in predicting incorrect answers, when it was compared with the baseline.

The use of multiple decision trees to represent different aspects of a student's action allows an ITS administrator to diagnose each action in detail. Yet, if a human tutor wants to get the whole picture of a class, thirty students, for example, a picture represented by thirty single trees should be preferable when compared with that involving hundreds of trees.

References

Chiu, B. C., Webb, G. I., and Kuzmycz, M. (1997). A comparison of first-order and zeroth-order induction for Input-Oput Agent Modelling. In Jameson A., Paris C., and Tasso C., eds., *Proceedings of the Sixth International Conference on User Modeling, UM97*, 347-358.

Desmoulins, C., and Van Labeke, N. (1996). Towards student modelling in geometry with inductive logic programming. In Brna, P., Paiva, A., and Self, J., eds., *Proceedings of the European Conference on Artificial Intelligence in Education.*

Gilmore, D., and Self, J. (1988). The application of machine learning to intelligent tutoring systems. In Self, J., ed., *Artificial Intelligence and Human Learning: Intelligent Computer-aided Instruction.* London: Chapman and Hall. 179-196.

Kohavi, R. (1995). A study of cross-validation and bootstrap for accuracy estimation and model selection. *Proceedings of 14th International Joint Conference on Artificial Intelligence*, 1137-1143.

Kuzmycz, M , and Webb, G. I. (1992). Evaluation of Feature Based Modelling in Subtraction. *Proceedings of the Second International Conference in ITS, ITS92*, 269-276.

Kuzmycz, M. (1994). A dynamic vocabulary for student modelling. *Proceedings of the Fourth International Conference on User Modelling*, 185-190.

Quinlan, J. R. (1993). *C4.5: Programs for Machine Learning.* San Mateo, CA: Morgan Kaufmann.

Webb, G. I., Chiu, B. C., and Kuzmycz, M. (1997). A comparative evaluation of the use of C4.5 and Feature Based Modelling as induction engines for Input/Output Agent Modelling. To appear in the *International Journal of Artificial Intelligence in Education.*

Webb, G. I., and Kuzmycz, M. (1996). Feature Based Modelling: A methodology for producing coherent, dynamically changing models of agent's competencies. *User Modelling and User-Adapted Interaction* 5(2):117-150.

Zheng, Z., and Webb, G. I. (1997). Lazy Bayesian Tree. *Technical Report TC97/07*, School of computing and mathematics, Deakin University.

Sample Set Assessment for Providing Personalised Recommendations*

Bhavani Raskutti and Anthony Beitz

Telstra Research Laboratories
Clayton, Victoria 3168, Australia
{b.raskutti,a.beitz}@trl.oz.au

Abstract. An important problem in providing personalised recommendations is how to determine when the sample items are representative of the user's long-term preferences (*user profile*) and when more sample items must be collected before a profile pattern may be identified. In this paper, we present an algorithm to determine if a particular sample set for a user is sufficient to provide personalised recommendations from a large collection. Our algorithm identifies features of items that the user likes, and then determines if these features have sufficient discrimination to extract a small fraction of the collection from which recommendations are provided. The determination is based on Bayesian theory of probability and has the advantage that sample sets can be assessed quickly for their generalisation ability. We demonstrate the usefulness of the algorithm through an empirical evaluation on data collected about movie preferences.

1 Introduction

An important problem in providing personalised recommendations is how to determine when the sample items are representative of the user's long-term preferences (*user profile*) and when more sample items must be collected before a profile pattern may be identified. Providing personalised recommendations is a part of providing easy and personalised access to services. The need for it has arisen in recent years due to the introduction of a large number of computer-network-based information services and the resulting diversity and choice that present navigational difficulties to new and casual users. Personal recommendations are one way of easing the users' difficulties and providing quick access to items preferred by the user.

The problem of providing personalised recommendations has been addressed by a number of researchers [Houseman & Kaskela 1970, Mackay et al. 1989, Allen 1990, Maes 1994, Jennings & Higuchi 1992, Karunanidhi & Alspector 1995, Raskutti & Beitz 1996]. However, the issue of sample requirements has been side-stepped either by using explicit profiles specified by the user [Houseman & Kaskela 1970, Mackay et al. 1989] or by requiring a large number of samples to train a neural network [Jennings & Higuchi 1992, Karunanidhi & Alspector 1995] or by using all of the few samples for comparison and ranking of all the items in

---

* The permission of the Director of Telstra Research Laboratories, to publish this work is gratefully acknowledged.

the collection [Allen 1990, Maes 1994] or by attempting to learn a pattern from a few samples regardless of whether these samples embody a pattern of usage [Raskutti & Beitz 1996].

In this paper, we present an algorithm to determine if a particular sample set for a user is sufficient to provide personalised recommendations from a large collection. Our mechanism identifies common features of items that the user likes, and then determines if these features have sufficient discrimination to extract a small fraction of the collection from which recommendations are to be provided. The determination is based on Bayesian theory of probability and has the advantage that sample sets can be assessed quickly for their generalisation ability.

We begin in the next section by describing the problem of sample assessment when providing personalised recommendations. In Section 3, we provide an overview of our mechanism for determining sufficiency of samples. In Section 4, we discuss the results of an empirical evaluation of our prediction on data collected about movie preferences. Section 5 concludes the discussion with some remarks on future research directions.

2 Sample Assessment for Recommendations

The problem of sample complexity, i.e., determining the number of samples required for learning a hypothesis about the sample set has been addressed for methods that use a large sample size [Solomonoff 1964, Gold 1967, Valiant 1984]. These research efforts have focussed on identifying the sample requirements in the limit and hence, are useful for identifying a theoretical limit to the number of samples required by classification systems. In recommendation systems, however, the emphasis is on selecting a few useful items from a large collection and not necessarily classifying each and every item in the collection correctly. Hence, identifying a theoretical limit that is substantially larger than what is realistically obtainable is not necessarily useful.

Providing personalised recommendations from a large collection $\{C\}$ consists of choosing a small of set of recommended items $\{R\}$ from $\{C\}$ on the basis of a user's habits. The user's habits are defined by a sample set of items $\{S\}$ from $\{C\}$, such that the elements in $\{S\}$ are items the user has experienced and hence, the system is aware of the user's reactions to these items. These reactions may be recorded either as (1) a simple positive or negative reaction or (2) a wider range of quantized reactions, e.g., HATED, DISLIKED, UNSURE, LIKED and LOVED as used in [Raskutti & Beitz 1996], (3) a number from 0 to 10 as used in [Karunanithi & Alspector 1995] or (4) a rating scale as used in [Kay 1995]. Thus, the user's habits ($\{Habits\}$) are encoded as a set of item-reaction pairs.

The recommendations $\{R\}$ are drawn from $\{C\}$ on the basis of the knowledge gained from the user's habits, $\{Habits\}$. In order to recommend items that are acceptable to the user, the elements in $\{Habits\}$ may be used in one of the following methods:

1. Use the features of the items in $\{Habits\}$ to train a neural network, so that a new item may be automatically classified [Jennings & Higuchi 1992, Karunanidhi & Alspector 1995].

2. Use a similarity measure to compare and rank every item in the collection $\{C\}$ either against a stored profile or against the samples themselves [Allen 1990, Maes 1994].

3. Acquire a pattern of the user's preferences on the basis of $\{Habits\}$, and use this to create indices that may be used to select items from $\{C\}$ [Raskutti & Beitz 1996].

One problem with all these methods is that the recommendations can be good only if the samples can be generalised to represent the user's preferences, and the generalisation has sufficient discrimination to choose only a few items from $\{C\}$. Methods based on neural networks solve the generalisation problem by requiring a large number of samples to train on. However, this requirement is unrealistic in the context of services used by a large number of casual users. Methods that use a small sample population (methods 2 and 3) are particularly sensitive to the sample used for training. Hence an initial assessment of whether a particular sample set can be generalised is useful before recommendations are made using that set.

2.1 Sufficiency of Sample

In the information retrieval literature, the quality of retrieval is evaluated in terms of three measures: (1) precision, which measures the fraction of the recommended items that the user likes, (2) fallout, which measures the fraction of the disliked items in the collection that are actually recommended, and (3) recall, which measures the fraction of the liked items in the collection that are actually recommended [Harman 1994]. Typically there must be a trade-off between recall, precision and fallout.

More precisely, let the set $\{R\}$ consist of n_R elements out of which l_R are liked by the user and d_R are disliked by the user. Similarly, the set $\{C\}$ consists of n_C elements out of which l_C are liked by the user and d_C are disliked by the user[2]. Then the three measures for goodness require that the set $\{R\}$ contains (1) a large fraction of items that the user might like (large value for $\frac{l_R}{n_R}$), (2) a small fraction of items that the user might dislike (a small value for $\frac{d_R}{d_C}$), and (3) as many items from $\{C\}$ that the user might like (large value for $\frac{l_R}{l_C}$).

It may be argued that for a recommendation system, good precision is more important than high recall, since there are likely to be a large number of films which any given user will enjoy, but the user does not want to be swamped with possibilities. Further, minimising fallout may be less important than attaining good precision since it is important that the recommendations include some items that the user might like rather than exclude all items that the user might dislike. Hence, our algorithm for assessing if a set of sample is sufficient to make recommendations identifies common features of items that the user likes, and then determines if these features have sufficient discrimination to extract a small fraction of the collection from which recommendations are to be provided. The determination is based on Bayesian theory of probability.

---

[2] Clearly, it is not feasible to require users to classify every item in $\{C\}$, particularly if the collection is large. Hence, the values for l_C, d_C, l_R and d_R are usually not known for a particular user.

3 Determining Sample Sufficiency

Given a sample set $\{S\}$ consisting of elements $s_1, s_2, ..., s_n$, we need to determine if the probability of being able to make recommendations on the basis of this set is high. Since a recommendation system should have precision, we consider a subset $\{SP\}$ of $\{S\}$ such that each entry sp_i in $\{SP\}$ are items that the user has experienced and liked. Further, each entry sp_i has some features from the feature set $\{F\}$ consisting of features $f_1, f_2, ..., f_m$. Suppose that there are several possible hypotheses $H_1, H_2, ..., H_m$, where hypothesis H_i represents the situation that the feature f_i has a positive impact on the user's evaluation of items in the collection. If the event of making good recommendations is denoted X, then we can classify $\{SP\}$ as having the ability to make recommendations by determining whether $P(X|\{SP\})$ is high. Using Bayesian learning, $P(X|\{SP\})$ is given by the following equation:

$$P(X|\{SP\}) = \sum_i P(X|\{SP\}, H_i)P(H_i|\{SP\})$$

$$= \sum_i P(X|H_i)P(H_i|\{SP\})$$

This equation describes full Bayesian learning and is often intractable since it may require the calculation for every hypotheses H_i [Russell & Norvig 1995]. Further, the fact that the probability is high if all hypotheses are taken into account does not mean that each of these hypotheses has a large impact on the probability. The most common approximation to overcome this is to use the most probable hypothesis, i.e., an H_i that maximises $P(H_i|\{SP\})$. This hypothesis is often called a maximum a posteriori or MAP hypothesis (H_{MAP}), and $P(X|\{SP\})$ is now given by the following formula:

$$P(X|\{SP\}) \simeq P(X|H_{MAP})P(H_{MAP}|\{SP\}) \tag{1}$$

The above equation, however, does not take into account the fact that multiple features may be used together to select items from the collection. Hence, in determining $P(X|\{SP\})$, we use

$$P(X|\{SP\}) \simeq \sum_j P(X|H_j)P(H_j|\{SP\}) \tag{2}$$

where the summation is over only those hypotheses that have a large contribution to $P(X|\{SP\})$[3]. Thus, these are the hypotheses that may be identified by a recommendation system as useful for making personalised recommendations.

$P(H_j|\{SP\})$ determines whether the recommendations would be useful if f_j is used to retrieve items from the collection, i.e., whether the feature f_j has a a positive impact on the choice of items. It may be approximated as the fraction of elements in $\{SP\}$ that have the feature f_j. Hence, if SP_{f_j} is the number of items in the set $\{SP\}$ with the feature f_j and $\{SP\}$ has SP_n elements, then $P(H_j|\{SP\})$ is given by the following equation:

$$P(H_j|\{SP\}) = \frac{SP_{f_j}}{SP_n} \tag{3}$$

---

[3] If only one hypothesis makes a large contribution, then the probability estimate will be lower than the standard approximation. However, this is taken into account through a normalization step.

$P(X|H_j)$ represents the probability of making personalised recommendations given that f_j has a large positive impact on the choice of items. This probability depends on the ability of this feature to constrain the collection such that if f_j is used to retrieve items from the collection then the required number of items are retrieved from the collection. Hence, it should be 1 if f_j retrieves exactly the number of items required, and approach 0 as the number of retrieved items deviates from that required. Let C_r be the number of items that should be recommended to the user from the collection which contains C_{f_j} elements with the feature f_j. Then, we use the following formula to determine $P(X|H_j)$:

$$P(X|H_j) = \frac{k}{q^{\left(\frac{C_{f_j}}{C_r} - 1\right)^2}} \qquad (4)$$

where $q > 1$, and k is a normalising constant. According to the above equation, the probability of making personalised recommendations is maximum when the number of retrieved items is C_r, and it falls exponentially as the ratio $\frac{C_{f_j}}{C_r}$ departs from 1. The rate of fall depends on the value of q, higher values providing steeper fall. For the results presented in this paper, q was set to 10 with the result that $P(X|H_j)$ is one tenth of the maximum value when C_{f_j} is 0 or twice C_r.

Substituting equations (3) and (4) into equation (2), the probability of making recommendations given the sample set $\{SP\}$ is calculated as follows:

$$P(X|\{SP\}) \simeq \sum_j \left(\frac{SP_{f_j}}{SP_n}\right) \left(\frac{k}{q^{\left(\frac{C_{f_j}}{C_r} - 1\right)^2}}\right) \qquad (5)$$

As mentioned earlier, the summation is over only those hypotheses that may be used by a recommendation system for providing personalised recommendations, i.e., the hypotheses that have a high probability relative to other hypotheses. In our system, these hypotheses are determined by doing the following steps: (1) Eliminate all hypotheses whose contribution to $P(X|\{SP\})$ is less than an acceptable threshold[4]; (2) Normalise the contribution of the remaining hypotheses so that they add up to 1; (3) Eliminate all those hypotheses whose contribution is less than $ProbWt * EqualProb$, where $EqualProb$ is the contribution if all of the hypotheses remaining after step 1 had equal contribution to $P(X|\{SP\})$, and $ProbWt$ is a weighting constant.

Clearly, the value of $ProbWt$ has a large influence on the hypotheses that remain after step 3. The larger the value of $ProbWt$, the harder it is to obtain hypotheses that are useful for providing recommendations, and hence the smaller the value of $P(X|\{SP\})$. The smaller the value, the larger the number of hypotheses available for recommending selections and hence, the larger the value of $P(X|\{SP\})$. However, the relationship is not as linear as depicted above. For instance, if there is a single hypothesis with a very large contribution to $P(X|\{SP\})$ and it is large enough to be higher than the threshold

---

[4] The threshold for acceptance is configurable, and was set at 0.01 for the results reported in this paper.

Fig. 1. Procedure Check-SampleSet($\{SP\}$)

1	Create the hypotheses set $\{H\}$ by determining all the features f_j in the elements of $\{SP\}$
2	For each hypothesis H_j
3	Compute SP_{f_j}, the number of items in the set $\{SP\}$ with the feature f_j
4	Compute C_{f_j}, the number of items in the collection with the feature f_j,
5	Compute the contribution of H_j to $P(X|\{SP\})$ using SP_{f_j}, C_{f_j}, SP_n, the number of elements in $\{SP\}$ and C_r, the number of elements required in the recommendation set (Equation 5)
6	If contribution is less than 0.01 then
7	delete H_j from $\{H\}$
8	End for
9	Set $P(X|\{SP\})$ to 0
10	For each hypothesis H_j left in $\{H\}$
11	Normalise contributions so they add up to 1
12	If normalised contribution $(CNorm_{H_j}) \geq ProbWt * EqualProb$
13	Add $CNorm_{H_j}$ to $P(X|\{SP\})$
14	End for
15	If $P(X|\{SP\}) \geq AcceptableProb$ then
16	$\{SP\}$ is sufficient sample set for for providing recommendations

$(ProbWt * EqualProb)$ when $ProbWt$ is high, then $P(X|\{SP\})$ is high. This is as should be since this sample set includes a feature that is very useful for providing recommendations.

Once $P(X|\{SP\})$ is determined for a particular sample set $\{SP\}$, then the sample set is classified as able to make recommendations if the probability is greater than $AcceptableProb$. The larger the value of this threshold for acceptance, the more difficult it is for a sample set to be classified as having the ability to provide recommendations.

The algorithm based on the above reasoning is given in Figure 1. The computation time for creating the hypotheses set $\{H\}$ is small since the set $\{SP\}$ and therefore the number of features f_j is small (line 1). For each hypothesis in the set $\{H\}$, the contribution to $P(X|\{SP\})$ is calculated by computing (1) SP_{f_j}, the the number of items in the set $\{SP\}$ with the feature f_j (line 3) and (2) C_{f_j}, the number of items in the collection with the feature f_j (line 4), and using Equation(5). Of these computations, the calculation of C_{f_j} is the only one that analyses all the entries in the collection. In most databases, this calculation is a single data base query.

Hypotheses whose contributions are less than 0.01 are dropped (lines 6 and 7), and the remaining contributions are normalised so that they add up to 1 (line 11). If the normalised probability is not less than $ProbWt * EqualProb$, then it contributes to $P(X|\{SP\})$ (lines 12 and 13). If the total value of $P(X|\{SP\}) \geq AcceptableProb$, then $\{SP\}$ is classified as having the ability to provide recommendations (line 15).

As can be seen from lines 12 and 15 in Figure 1, the two constants, $ProbWt$ and $AcceptableProb$ determine how tolerant the system is in classifying a sample set $\{SP\}$ as having the ability to provide recommendations. Low values of *ProbWt* ensure that features are classified as useful even when they are not. Low values of *AcceptableProb* ensure that a sample set is classified as having the ability to recommend even if it includes few features that are useful. Thus, we would expect the system to be more tolerant in classifying a sample set as useful for providing recommendations, when it uses low values of *ProbWt* and *AcceptableProb*. This reasoning was tested in our evaluation described in the following section.

4 Evaluation of Algorithm

In order to determine if our algorithm is useful for predicting generalisation ability of a sample set, data about movie preferences was collected, and used for testing our algorithm against a movie recommendation system that works on a small sample set. The domain of movie recommendation was chosen due to the following reasons:

- It is easy to obtain data about movie preferences. This is particularly true when the movies are deliberately chosen from popular movies so that a large number of people would be likely to have seen them.
- Data about movies is easily available in the internet, and this data is annotated with features describing the movie, e.g., title, director, producer and genre. Hence, it is easily adaptable to the feature-based prediction used by our algorithm.
- We had access to the movie recommendation system developed by [Raskutti & Beitz 1996], which uses a small sample set (set size between 10 and 20).

The data for evaluation was collected as follows: sixty people were asked to fill out a survey form giving their opinions on a group of sixty popular movies. The survey form asked people to rate the movies on the list by choosing one of the following six options: HATED, DISLIKED, UNSURE, NOT SEEN, LIKED and LOVED. These six options were internally rated as -3, -2, -1, 0, 1 and 2, respectively[5].

In order to evaluate our algorithm, our system used a sample set consisting of five movies that the user LOVED (when available) and five movies that s/he LIKED to predict if this sample set is useful for making recommendations. The ten movies for training were randomly selected from the user's LIKED/LOVED selections. The recommendation system then used these ten movies to learn preferences, and make five recommendations from the remaining fifty movies. Forty repetitions of this test were performed for each user with different training movies, and the entire cycle was performed for 45 users (all the users who had more than 15 films that they LIKED or LOVED). Thus, our algorithm was tested on 1800 sample sets for each of the different combination of *ProbWt* and *AcceptableProb*. For the results presented in this paper, *ProbWt* was varied from 0.75 to 1.75 in increments of 0.25, and *AcceptableProb* was varied from 0.1 to 0.9 in increments of 0.2.

---

[5] The negative reactions were not used in the results described in this paper. They were collected in order to determine how the algorithm should be modified to account for fallout.

4.1 Assessing a single prediction

The prediction of our algorithm is assessed by comparing our prediction against the actual results obtained from the recommendation system that uses the same sample set. The recommendations for each user itself is assessed by comparing the recommendation made at random to the same user. The comparison with a random selector rather than a selector based on movie popularity rating was used based on the following reasoning. Since the movies used for testing and training are all popular movies, these movies would have been recommended by a selector based on popularity rating. A recommendation was considered good if the probability of a random selector recommending the same or more number of items that the user LIKED/LOVED is less than 0.5.

The probability that a random selection of five items from fifty items, l of which the user had either LIKED or LOVED, will include exactly x items out of these l items is given by the hyper geometric probability function [Kreyszig 1983]:

$$Pr(x) = \frac{\binom{l}{x}\binom{50-l}{5-x}}{\binom{50}{5}} \tag{6}$$

The probability that a random selector will include at least 3 items from the l items is then the sum of the above probabilities for $x = 3$, 4 and 5. For $l = 13$, this probability equals 0.102993. Hence, if the recommendation system used a specific sample set and suggested 3 movies that this user liked, then that particular sample set has been useful for recommending items. If our algorithm predicted this, then it has been useful for identifying this sample set correctly.

4.2 Results

Of the 1800 sample sets that the recommendation system was tested on, the system had better than random performance for 1446 tests and worse than random for the remaining. The predictions of our algorithm for the same sample sets for different values of $ProbWt$ and $AcceptableProb$ are plotted in Figure 2.

Figure 2(a) plots the proportion of the sample sets for which our algorithm predicted generalisation capability. These are termed positive predictions, and they decrease with increasing values of $ProbWt$ and $AcceptableProb$. This is in line with our expectation that the tolerance of the algorithm in admitting that a sample set is useful increases when more features are admitted as useful (low $ProbWt$), and the threshold for acceptance is decreased (low $AcceptableProb$).

Figure 2(b) plots the proportion of the sample sets for which our algorithm predicted generalisation capability when the recommendation system actually found no pattern of preference. These are errors of commission in that the recommendation system is being called in even when the sample set has no generalisation capability. These proportions follow the same trend as positive predictions and decrease with increasing values of $ProbWt$ and $AcceptableProb$. This trend is expected since the number of positive predictions is the sum of the number of commission errors and a part of the total number of correct predictions.

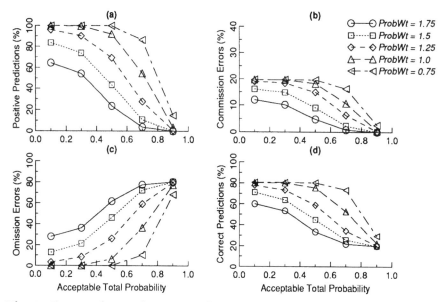

Fig. 2. Comparison of our Predictions against Actual Outcomes

Figure 2(c) plots the proportion of the sample sets for which our algorithm predicted lack of generalisation capability when the recommendation system actually found a pattern of preference. These are errors of omission in that if a prediction algorithm had not been used, the recommendation system would have gone ahead and made recommendations successfully. These proportions increase with increasing values of *ProbWt* and *AcceptableProb*. This is expected since these errors are a part of the total negative predictions provided by the algorithm, and hence follow the trend of negative predictions (which is 100 less the percentage of positive predictions).

Figure 2(d) plots the proportion of the sample sets for which our algorithm and the recommendation system agreed. As can be seen, the accuracy of the prediction algorithm increases with decreasing values of *ProbWt* and *AcceptableProb*. This is expected when the recommendation system has more successful recommendations than unsuccessful ones.

The prediction algorithm performed best when it was most tolerant, i.e., for low values of *ProbWt* and *AcceptableProb*. However, the proportion of omission errors in this case is quite high. Thus, the choice of values for *ProbWt* and *AcceptableProb* will be dictated not merely by overall accuracy, but by the requirements on the prediction algorithm, namely, whether it is necessary to minimise omission errors or commission errors.

5 Conclusion

In this paper, we have presented an algorithm to determine if a particular sample set for a user is sufficient to provide personalised recommendations from a large collection. Our algorithm identifies features of items that the user likes, and then determines if these features have sufficient discrimination to extract a small fraction of the collection from which recommendations are provided. The determination is based on Bayesian theory of probability and has the advantage that sample sets can be assessed quickly for their generalisation ability. The algorithm was assessed through an empirical evaluation on data collected about movie preferences, and the assessment indicates that it is useful for identifying the generalisation capabilities of an individual sample set quickly.

Our future research directions include the following: (1) use of our algorithm for other recommendation systems that use small sample sets, e.g., [Maes 1994]; (2) enhancements to take into account items that the user has disliked and discard features that correlate with user's negative reactions; and (3) use of domain independent features, such as user reactions for each item in the collection so that our algorithm is useful even when the collection items are not annotated with features.

References

R. B. Allen. User Models: Theory, Method and Practice. *International Journal of Man-Machine Studies*, 32: 511-543, 1990.

E. M. Gold. Language Identification in the Limit. *Information and Control*, 10:447-474, 1967.

E. M. Houseman and D. E. Kaskela. State of the Art of Selective Dissemination of Information. *IEEE Transactions on Engineering Writing and Speech III*, 2: 78-83, 1970.

A. Jennings and H. Higuchi. A Personal News Service Based on a User Model Neural Network. In *IEICE Transactions on Information and Systems*, Vol. E75-D, No. 2, pp. 198-209, 1992.

Harman, D.: 1994, 'Overview of the Second Text Retrieval Conference (TREC-2)'. In the Proceedings of the Second Text Retrieval Conference (TREC-2), 1-20.

N. Karunannithi and J. Alspector. A Feature-Based Neural Network Movie Selection Approach. In *Proceedings of the International Workshop on the Applications of Neural Network to Telecommunications* 2, 162-169, 1995.

J. Kay. The UM Toolkit for Cooperative User Modeling. *User Modeling and User Adapted Interaction*, 4(3): 149-196, 1995.

E. Kreyszig. Advanced Engineering Mathematics. Fifth Edition. Wiley, 1983.

W. E. Mackay, T. W. Malone, K. Crowston, R. Rao, D. Rosenblitt, and S. K. Card. How do Experienced Information Lens Users Use Rules? In *Proceedings of ACM CHI '89 Conference on Human Factors in Computing Systems*, 211-216, 1989.

P. Maes. Agents that Reduce Work and Information Overload. *Communications of the ACM*, 37(7): 31-40, 1994.

B. Raskutti and A. Beitz. Acquiring User Preferences for Information Filtering in Interactive Multi-Media Services. In *Proceedings of the PRICAI'96 conference*, 1996.

E. Rich. User Modeling via Stereotypes. *Cognitive Science* 3: 329-354, 1979.

S. Russell and P. Norvig. Artificial Intelligence: A Modern Approach. Prentice Hall Series in Artificial Intelligence, 1995.

R. J. Solomonoff. A Formal Theory of Inductive Inference. *Information and Control*, 7:1-22, 1964.

L. Valiant. A Theory of the Learnable. *Communications of the ACM*, 27:1134-1142, 1984.

Integrated Correction of Ill-Formed Sentences

Kyongho Min and William H. Wilson
School of Computer Science and Engineering
The University of New South Wales
Sydney NSW 2052 Australia
{min,billw}@cse.unsw.edu.au

Abstract

This paper describes a system that performs hierarchical error recovery, and detects and corrects a single error in a sentence at the lexical, syntactic, and/or semantic levels. If the system is unable to repair an erroneous sentence on the assumption that it has a single error, a multiple error recovery system is invoked. The system employs a chart parsing algorithm and uses an augmented context-free grammar, and has subsystems for lexical, syntactic, surface case, and semantic processing, which are controlled by an integrated-agenda system. In the frequent case that there is a choice of possible repairs, the possible repairs are ranked by *penalty scores*. The penalty scores are based on grammar-dependent and grammar-independent heuristics. The grammar-independent ones involve error types, and, at the lexical level, character distance; the grammar-dependent ones involve, at the syntactic level, the significance of the repaired constituent in a local tree, and, at the semantic level, the distance between the semantic form containing the error, and normal act templates. This paper focuses on single error recovery.

1 Introduction

The ill-formedness may be at various levels, including the morphological (also typographical, orthographical, and phonological), syntactic, semantic, and pragmatic levels. Pollock and Zamora (1983) collected spelling errors from approximately 25 million words from seven scientific and scholarly databases, finding an error rate of 2%. These would have been mostly typographical errors. Mitton (1987) found that a large proportion of orthographical errors are real-word errors: *to → too, were → where*.

At the sentential level, Young, Eastman, and Oakman (1991) found that 27% of 426 queries typed into a library search interface had errors: conjunction errors (18%), punctuation errors (7%), and spelling errors (2%). In addition, spelling errors may raise a problem at the sentential level. In 300 email messages analysed by the authors, 0.6% of words were mis-spelt (447/68966), leading to about 12.1% of sentences having errors (451/3728).

Most systems focus on the correction of errors at a *particular level*. In many cases, however, it is impossible to detect the errors at the particular level because the detection and correction of the errors requires higher level knowledge. For example, at the lexical level (Damerau, 1964; Peterson, 1980), the misspelt word *it* is not detected in "I saw a man *it* the park". At the syntactic level, the misspelling of *pork* can not be detected or corrected using lexical and syntactic information in "I saw a man in the *pork*."

Various systems have focused on the recovery of ill-formed text at the morpho-syntactic level (Vosse, 1992), the syntactic level (Irons, 1963; Lyon, 1974), the semantic level (Fass and Wilks, 1983; Carbonell and Hayes, 1983), and the pragmatic level (Granger, 1983). Those systems described how to identify a localised error and how to repair it in various ways, including using grammar-specific rules (meta-rules) (Weischedel and Sondheimer, 1983), least-cost error recovery based on chart parsing (Lyon, 1974; Anderson and Backhouse, 1981), semantic preferences (Fass and Wilks, 1983), conceptual dependency (Granger, 1983), and heuristic approaches based on a shift-reduce parser (Vosse, 1992).

This paper focuses on the automatic correction of ill-formed sentences by a method that integrates information from three levels (lexical, syntactic, and semantic). The system, called CHAPTER (CHArt Parser for Two-stage Error Recovery), performs two-stage error recovery, and employs generalised top-down chart parsing for the syntax phase (cf. Mellish, 1989; Kato, 1994). The system uses an augmented context-free grammar, which covers verb subcategorisations based on the Oxford Advanced Learner's Dictionary classification, passives, yes/no questions (direct), WH-questions, finite relative clauses, and EQUI/SOR phenomena but not conjunctions, comparatives, compound nouns, or topicalisations.

For the semantic phase, it uses a conceptual hierarchy and act templates (cf. Wilks, 1983), with some restrictions represented by a kind of boolean expression (e.g. (NOT HUMAN)). The surface case phase instantiates surface cases, which are used to help in extraction of meaning (cf. Grishman and Peng, 1988). CHAPTER uses an integrated agenda system, which integrates and controls its four levels of language processing: lexical, syntactic, surface case, and semantic.

In contrast to other systems (Mellish, 1989; Kato, 1994), CHAPTER uses syntactic *and* semantic information to correct spelling errors detected, including real-word errors. At the syntactic level, the detection and correction of errors are separated. In addition, suggested syntactic repairs are verified by the semantic processing.

In section 2, the method employed in CHAPTER will be described. Section 3 will describe the results of tests on the system using real world data. Section 4 will describe problems and issues related to CHAPTER and section 5 contains conclusions.

2 Methodology

The system uses separate error detection and correction phases and includes recovery subsystems at three levels: spelling, syntactic, and semantic. The subsystems works together to get the best repair for an ill-formed sentence, up to the semantic level. In case there are alternative repairs, heuristics are employed to select the best repair. In this paper, we will focus on description of the two subsystems (syntactic and semantic level) because of limitation of pages.

2.1 Syntactic Recovery

Syntactic errors may occur because of misspelt words, agreement violations (number, gender, case, and tense), extraneous words, and missing words. These errors are repaired using generalised top-down chart parsing (cf. Mellish, 1989) employing an augmented context-free grammar. Syntactic error recovery is based on the following four processes:

(1) *top-down expectation*: expanding a goal[1] using syntactic rules based on grammar rules;

(2) *bottom-up satisfaction*: searching for an error using a goal and inactive arcs made by the first parser for well-formed sentences, and producing a *need-chart network*;

(3) a *constituent reconstruction engine*: repairing the error and reconstructing local trees by retracing the need-chart network; and

(4) *spelling correction* (see Min and Wilson, 1995).

The first two phases are used to *detect* a single syntactic error and the others are used for *error correction*.

Consider the sentence *I saw a man it the park*. Syntactic error recovery would be as follows:

• Top-down expectation

The initial goal for the sentence is a constituent of category S from 0 to 7. From this first goal, the system can infer the needed constituents for the (repaired) parse of the sentence; this is called top-down expectation. Each goal is expanded using grammar rules, refining information about the error location. For example, the first goal, <goal S is needed from 0 to 7> is expanded to <S needs (NP VP) from 0 to 7> using the grammar rule S → NP VP.

When expanding goals, the MEL (Minimal Extension Length) of the rule is considered, to avoid useless goal production. For example, if there is a goal <NP is needed from 0 to 1>, then NP rules with an MEL > 2 are not retrieved as only a single error is being considered. However, the rule NP → DET NOUN would be retrieved, as it would be assumed that one category is missing: a *deletion error* → *addition correction*.

• Bottom-up satisfaction

After a goal is expanded, the leftmost or rightmost constituent of the expanded goal is looked for among the inactive arcs left behind by the first-stage parser, which is designed to parse a well-formed sentence. Thus this is a bidirectional technique. If inactive arcs for the leftmost constituent are found, then the default process, left-to-right, is employed. Otherwise, if inactive arcs for the rightmost constituent are found, the right-to-left process is employed. If inactive arcs for leftmost/rightmost constituents are found and both constituents are phrasal, then both processes are employed. For example, the expanded goal, <S needs (NP VP) from 0 to 7>, would be processed with two inactive arcs: {NP("I") from 0 to 1} and {VP("park") from 6 to 7}. With the first inactive arc, the left-to-right process is applied: for the expanded goal S, NP ("I") is found from 0 to 1 and VP is needed from 1 to 7: or, more briefly, <S → NP("I") • VP is needed from 1 to 7>. This data structure is called a *need-arc* (see footnote 4). From this need-arc, we can produce another goal, <goal VP is needed from

---

[1]A goal is a partial tree (which may contain one or more syntactic categories), specially a subtree of a syntax tree corresponding to a single context-free rule, and which might contain syntactic errors. For example, the first goal for the ill-formed sentence *I have a bif book* is <S needs from 0 to 5 with its penalty score 4>.

1 to 7>, which will require new top-down expectation and bottom-up satisfaction phases. With the second inactive arc, the right-to-left process is applied: <S → VP ("park") • NP is needed from 0 to 6>.

These two need-arcs are linked to the objects to which they refer, and also passed to the goal production process. The structure created is called a need-chart network; it represents the history of the chart items (i.e. goals, need-arcs[2], and repaired constituents).

• Constituent Reconstruction Engine

After performing top-down expectation and bottom-up satisfaction phases, a localised error is corrected using two types of chart item: a goal and a need-arc. With the goal <goal: needs PREP from 4 to 5>, a substitution error is detected because the goal's constituent is a single lexical category and the number of words which covers the category is 1. Thus this error would be handled by substitution of the constituent {PREP ("in") from 4 to 5} after spelling correction. In terms of the need-chart network, the goal is linked to its parent data structure, a need-arc. Via the need-chart network links, the repaired constituent is used to repair constituents all the way up to the first S goal. The subprocess of CHAPTER that does this is called the *constituent reconstruction engine*.

At the syntactic level, the choice of the best correction depends on two penalty schemes: grammar-independent error-type penalties and grammar-dependent penalties based on the weight (or importance) of the repaired constituent in its local tree. The error-types penalties are 0.5 for substitution errors, and 1 for deletion and addition errors[3]. The weight penalty of a repaired constituent in a local tree is either a head daughter penalty of 0.1, a non-head daughter of 0.5, or a recursive head-daughter (e.g. NP in the right-head side of the rule NP → NP PP) penalty of 0.3. The weight penalty is accumulated while retracing the need-chart network. In effect, the system looks for a best repair with minimal length path from the S goal to the error location in the syntax tree.

Often there is more than one repair suggested. The repaired syntactic structures are interpreted by surface case and semantic processing during syntactic reconstruction. If a syntactic repair does not violate selectional restrictions, then it is acceptable.

2.2 Semantic Recovery

CHAPTER interprets the meaning of a sentence using semantic selectional restrictions based on a concept hierarchy and act templates. Some selectional restrictions are represented by a boolean expression like (NOT HUMAN), which represents any concept that is not a subconcept of HUMAN. This permits fast computation and update. The interpretation of a surface case frame is based on a mapping procedure and a pattern matching algorithm using a concept hierarchy. The mapping procedure converts

---

[2]A need-arc is similar to an active arc, and it includes the following information: which constituents are already found and which constituents are needed for the recovery of a local tree between two positions with its penalty score.

[3]These penalties are somewhat arbitrary. A corpus-based probability estimate would be preferable.

the surface case slots into concept slots, while the pattern matching algorithm constrains filler concepts using ACT templates. The surface cases are mapped to concept slots: subject → agent, verb → act, direct object → theme[4]. Consider the sentence "I parked a car". The mapping is as follows:

SENT1	(subj (value "I"))	→	PARK1	(agent (SPEAKER))
	(verb (value "parked"))	→		(act (PARK))
	(dobj (value "a car"))	→		(theme (CAR))

Semantic errors come in two forms:

(1) an input sentence may be ill-formed at the syntactic level so that there is no complete parse tree and semantic interpretation is not possible;

(2) the sentence may be syntactically acceptable, but semantically ill-formed (e.g. "I parked a *bug* (bus)").

The first type of error is incrementally repaired from the spelling level (if a spelling error is detected) up to semantic level. For errors of a semantic nature, semantic selectional restrictions may be forced onto the error concept to make it fit the template. For example, the sentence "I parked a bug" violates the semantic selectional restrictions on the theme slot of *park*. The template of the verb *park* is (HUMAN PARK VEHICLE). However, the concept BUG, associated with *bug*, is not consistent with the restriction, VEHICLE, on the theme slot. As a result, the sentence is semantically ill-formed, with a semantic penalty of -1 (one slot violates a restriction). To correct the error , the filler concept BUG is forced to satisfy the template concept VEHICLE by invoking the spelling corrector with the word *bug* using the concept VEHICLE. Thus the real word error *bug* would be corrected to *bus*.

In another case, the filler concept itself can be inconsistent. Suppose the sentence "I saw *a pregnant man*." The theme slot of SEE satisfies restrictions. However, the filler concept of the theme slot is inconsistent. In CHAPTER, the attribute concept *pregnant* is identified as an error rather than the head concept *man*. In this case, the attribute concept is relaxed to any attribute concept that can qualify the *man* (i.e. a male person) concept. It is also possible to force the *man* concept to fit to the attribute concept (e.g. by changing it to *woman*). There seems to be no general method to pick the correct component to modify with this type of error: we chose to relax the attribute concept. This problem might be resolved by pragmatic processing.

2.3 The Integrated-Agenda Manager

CHAPTER has two integrated-agenda managers (figure 1): one for the first-stage system that deals with well-formed sentences and one for the error recovery system. The integrated-agenda manager controls all types of parsing items: lexical, syntactic, surface case, and semantic. Thus the agenda system aims to distribute each agenda item to relevant subsystems. For example, if an agenda item is a repaired syntactic node, then the item is distributed to syntactic recovery, to surface case interpretation (if the item can instantiate a surface case frame) and to semantic recovery.

---

[4]See footnote 1.

To **Perform** integrated-agenda control in constituent reconstruction engine
  loop
    while there is an agenda item (i.e. a repaired constituent)
      perform get the next agenda item
      if the agenda item is a syntactic node
      then perform syntactic node control with the item
      else **if** the agenda item is a surface case frame
          then perform surface case frame control with the item
          else **if** the agenda item is a semantic concept
             then perform semantic concept control with the item
             end if
          end if
      end if
    end while
  end loop
  to **perform** syntactic node control with the item
    store the item in syntactic memory.
    case1: the category of the item is S
      perform syntactic, surface case, and semantic recovery
    case2: the category can be used to instantiate a surface case frame
      perform surface case and syntactic recovery
    case3: the category is phrasal
      perform syntactic recovery, then semantic recovery
    case4: the category is lexical
      perform syntactic recovery
    end case
  end perform
  to **perform** surface case frame control with the item
    if the frame is a surface case frame and its label is one of {STMT, WHQ,
    INV, RELS}
    then perform semantic recovery
    else **if** the frame is a surface case frame
          then store the item in surface-case memory.
          end if
    end if
  end perform
  to **perform** semantic concept control with the item
    store the item in semantic memory.
  end perform
end perform

Fig. 1. The integrated-agenda manager algorithm

3 Experimental Results

CHAPTER was implemented and tested using Macintosh Common Lisp 2.0, with 10MB working memory, on a Macintosh IIfx. Real world data were collected, much of it from email messages: it included syntactic errors introduced by substitution of unknown/known word, addition of unknown/known word, deletion of a word, segmentation, apostrophe problems, and semantic errors. The data sets used as a testbed for CHAPTER are referred to as: Wilson (a mix of errors found in novels, electronic mail, and on-line diary); Appling1, and Peters2 (the Birkbeck data from Oxford Text Archive (Mitton, 1987)); and Thesprev[5].

In all, we had 258 ill-formed sentences from various sources as described above: 153 in the Wilson data, 13 in Thesprev, 74 in Appling1 data, and 18 in Peters2. We tested the coverage rate for our grammar on manually corrected versions of these 258 sentences. The syntactic grammar covered 166 (64.3%) of these: 85/153 on Wilson, 9/13 on Thesprev, 54/74 on Appling1, and 18/18 on Peters2. The average parsing time was 3.2 seconds. Syntactic processing produced on average 1.7 parse trees[6], of which 0.4 syntactic parse trees were filtered out by semantic processing. Semantic processing produced 9.3 on average per S node, and 7.3 of them on average were ill-formed. So many were produced because CHAPTER generated a semantic concept whether it was semantically ill-formed or not, to assist with the repair of ill-formed sentence.

Across the four data sets, 34.1% of the well-formed sentences were classified as ill-formed because of a lack of syntactic and semantic information in the grammar and lexicon. The most common reasons they were not parsed as well-formed were that the sentences included a conjunction (e.g. "He places them face down *so that* they are a surprise"), a phrasal verb (e.g. "I *called out* to Fred and went inside"), or a compound noun (e.g. "*PC development tools* are far ahead of *Unix development tools*"). From the 258 original sentences, we selected 182 sentences: Wilson (98/153)[7]; Thesprev (12/13); Appling1(55/74); and Peters2 (17/18).

Data Set	No. of sents tested	Number of repairs	Best repairs	Next repairs	No repairs suggested
Wilson (%)	98	90 (91.8)	64/90 (71.1)	26/90 (28.9)	8 (8.2)
Appling1 (%)	55	52 (94.5)	40/52 (76.9)	12/52 (23.1)	3 (5.5)
Peters2 (%)	17	17 (100)	14/17 (82.4)	3/17 (17.6)	0
Thesprev (%)	12	10 (83.3)	9/10 (90.0)	1/10 (10.0)	2 (16.7)
Average (%)	-	89.9%	79.3%	20.7%	10.1%

Table 1. Performance of CHAPTER on ill-formed sentences

Table 1 shows that 89.9% of these ill-formed sentences were repaired[8]. Among these, CHAPTER ranked the correct repair first or second in 79.3% of cases

---

[5]A scanned version of "Thesis Prevention: Advice to PhD Supervisors: The Siblings of Perpetual Prototyping" 18 October 1991.

[6]There are so few parse trees because of the use of subcategorisation and the augmented context-free grammar (the number of parse trees ranges from 1 to 7).

[7]Compound and compound-complex sentences were split into simple sentences to collect 13 more ill-formed sentences for testing.

[8]The results for the Peters2 data are not considered here because we selected only the sentences that were covered by our grammar, from more than 300 sentence fragments which were either a simple sentence or a phrase. The Peters2 sentences tested were all repaired (100%).

(see 'best repair' column in Table 2). The ranking was based on penalty schemes at three levels: lexical, syntactic, and semantic. If the correct repair was ranked lower than second among the repairs suggested, then it is counted under 'next repairs' in Table 1. In the case of the Wilson data, the 'next repairs' include 11 cases of incorrect repairs (12.2%), introduced by: segmentation error (7 sentences); apostrophe error (1); semantic error (2); and a phrasal verb (1). Thus for about 71% of all ill-formed sentences tested, the correct repair ranked first or second among the repairs suggested. For 19% of the tested sentences, incorrect repairs[9] were ranked as the best repairs.

Table 2 shows further results of repairing ill-formed sentences. CHAPTER took 18.8 seconds on average to repair an ill-formed sentence, and suggested an average of 6.4 repaired parse trees and an average of 3 repairs were filtered out by semantic processing. In the case of semantic processing, an average of 40.3 semantic concepts were suggested for each S node and an average 34.3 concepts per S node were classified as ill-formed. Twenty seven percent of the *'best'* parse trees suggested by CHAPTER's ranking strategy at the syntactic level were filtered out by semantic processing. The remaining 73% of the *'best'* parse trees were judged semantically well-formed.

In the case of the Wilson dataset, 90 ill-formed sentences were repaired. On average: recovery time per sentence was 23.9 seconds; 9.8 repaired S trees per sentence was produced; 4.5 of the 9.8 repaired S trees were semantically well-formed; 95.1 repaired concepts (ill-formed and well-formed) were produced; 8.5 of 95.1 repaired concepts were well-formed; and semantic processing filtered syntactically best repairs, removing 22% of repaired sentences. The number of repaired concepts for S is very large because semantic processing allowed single interpretation of verbal (or verb phrasal) adjuncts. For example, the template of the verb GO allows either a temporal (PRD) or destination (DEST) adjunct only to its template at present: [THING GO DEST] or [THING GO PRD].

Data set	Total sent repaired	Time (sec)	Repair-ed S trees	Semant-ically well-formed parse trees	Repaired concepts for S	Repaired well-formed concepts for S	% of syntactical-ly-best parses filtered
Wilson	90	23.9	9.8	4.5	95.1	8.5	26/90 (22%)
Appling1	52	15.8	4.7	3.3	17.7	5.2	11/52 (20%)
Peters2	17	15.8	6.3	2.5	29.8	5.0	7/17 (41%)
Thesprev	10	19.4	4.9	3.4	18.7	5.3	2/10 (20%)
Average	-	18.8	6.4	3.4	40.3	6.0	46/169 (27%)

Table 2. Results on CHAPTER's performance (average values per sentence)

4 Discussion

4.1 Problems at the syntactic level

The grammar rules need extension to cover the following grammatical phenomena: Compound noun and adjectives; Gerund and TO+VP (infinitive); Conjunctions and

---

[9]A sentence was considered to be "correctly repaired" if any of the suggested corrections was the same as the one obtained by manual correction.

comparatives; and Phrasal verbs and idiomatic sentences. For example, 'in the morning' and 'at midnight' are the well-formed strings as syntactic idioms. However, CHAPTER currently also parses the ill-formed strings like 'in morning', 'at the morning', and 'at morning' as well-formed at the syntactic and semantic levels.

CHAPTER uses prioritised search to detect and correct syntactic errors using the penalty scores of goals. However, the scheme for selecting the best repair did not uncritically use the first detected error found by the prioritised search at the syntactic level, because the best repair might be ill-formed at the semantic level. In fact, the prioritised search strategy did not contribute to the selection scheme, which depended solely on the error type and the importance of the repaired constituent in its local tree.

4.2 Problems at the semantic level

In the current state of CHAPTER's semantic system, the most complex problem is the processing of prepositions, and their conceptual definition. For example, the preposition, 'for', can indicate at least three major concepts: time duration (*for a week*), beneficiary (*for his mother*), and purpose (*for digging holes*). If *for* takes a gerund object, then the concept will specify a purpose or reason (e.g. *It is a machine for slicing bread*).

In addition, the act templates do not allow multiple optional conceptual cases (i.e. relational conceptual cases - LOC for locational concepts, and DEST for destination concepts, etc.) for both prepositional and adverbial phrases. This would increase the number of templates and the computational cost as well. If there is more than one verbal adjunct (PPs and ADVPs) in a sentence, then CHAPTER does not interpret all adjuncts. For example, the sentence "We are supposed to be going *to the restaurant for dinner*" has two PPs. The first PP would be mapped to the optional conceptual case DEST but the second PP would not be mapped to an another conceptual case, for example, PURPOSE, because the act templates of GO do not at present allow multiple optional conceptual cases for an EVENT.

5 Conclusions

This paper has presented a hierarchical error recovery system, CHAPTER, based on a chart parsing algorithm using an augmented context-free grammar. CHAPTER performs a heterarchical procedure, based on an integrated-agenda manager, that invokes subsystems incrementally at four levels: lexical, syntactic, surface case, and semantic. Thus the well-formedness of a sentence has been confirmed and/or repaired after finishing parsing the sentence at four levels.

Semantic processing performed pattern matching using a concept hierarchy and verb templates (which specify semantic selectional restrictions). In addition, procedural semantic constraints represented using a type of boolean expression have been used to improve the efficiency of semantic processing based on a concept hierarchy. However, it increases computational cost.

CHAPTER repaired 89.9% of the ill-formed sentences on which it was tested, and in 79.3% of cases suggested the correct repair (as judged by a human) as the best of its alternatives. CHAPTER's semantic processing filtered out 27% of the best repairs suggested by syntactic recovery system. So it suggested the first correct repair in 73% of cases at both the syntactic and semantic level.

References

Anderson, S. and Backhouse, R. (1981). Locally Least-cost Error Recovery in Earley's Algorithm. *ACM Transactions on Programming Languages and Systems*, **3**(3): 318-347.

Carbonell, J. and Hayes, P. (1983). Recovery Strategies for Parsing Extragrammatical Language. *American Journal of Computational Linguistics*, **9**(3-4): 123-146.

Damerau, F. (1964). A Technique for Computer Detection and Correction of Spelling Errors. *Communications of the ACM*, **7**(3): 171-176.

Fass, D. and Wilks, Y. (1983). Preference Semantics, Ill-formedness, and Metaphor. *American Journal of Computational Linguistics*, **9**(3-4): 178-187.

Grishman, R. and Peng, P. (1988). Responding to Semantically Ill-Formed Input. *The 2nd Conference of Applied Natural Language Processing*, 65-70.

Irons, E. (1963). An Error-Correcting Parse Algorithm. *Communications of the ACM*, **6**(11): 669-673.

Kato, T. (1994). Yet Another Chart-Based Technique for Parsing Ill-formed Input. *The Fourth Conference on Applied Natural Language Processing*, 107-112.

Lyon, G. (1974). Syntax-Directed Least-Errors Analysis for Context-Free Languages: A Practical Approach. *Communications of the ACM*, **17**(1): 3-14.

Mellish, C. (1989). Some Chart-Based Techniques for Parsing Ill-Formed Input. *ACL Proceedings, 27th Annual Meeting*, 102-109.

Min, K. and Wilson, W. H. (1995). Are Efficient Natural Language Parsers Robust?. *Eighth Australian Joint Conference on Artificial Intelligence*; 283-290

Mitton, R. (1987). Spelling Checkers, Spelling Correctors and the Misspellings of Poor Spellers. *Information Processing and Management*, **23**(5): 495-505.

Peterson, J. (1980). Computer Programs for Detecting and Correcting Spelling Errors. *Communications of the ACM*, **23**(12): 676-687.

Vosse, T. (1992). Detecting and Correcting Morpho-Syntactic Errors in Real Texts. *The Third Conference on Applied Natural Language Processing*, 111-118.

Weischedel, R. and Sondheimer, N. (1983). Meta-rules as Basis for Processing Ill-formed Input. *American Journal of Computational Linguistics*, **9**(3-4): 161-177.

Young, C., Eastman, C., and Oakman, R. (1991). An Analysis of Ill-formed Input in Natural Language Queries to Document Retrieval Systems. *Information Processing and Management*, **27**(6): 615-622.

Information Filtering for Context-Sensitive Browsing

Tsukasa Hirashima, Noriyuki Matsuda*, Toyohiro Nomoto*, Jun'ichi Toyoda*

Dept. of Artificial Intelligence, Kyushu Institute of Technology
Kawazu 680-4, Iizuka, 820 JAPAN
e-mail: tsukasa@ai.sanken.osaka-u.ac.jp
*ISIR, Osaka University, 8-1, Mihogaoka, Ibaraki, 567 JAPAN

ABSTRACT

Browsing is one of the most popular ways to gather information in database with hypertext structure. In the browsing, a user continuously searches nodes which include useful information for her/him. Her/his interests, then, often change while the browsing. We call this type of browsing "context-sensitive browsing" in order to distinguish it from browsing with consistent interests. In this paper, we propose a method to filter the links in hypertext based on the user's browsing history. We assume that even when a user browses, following changeable interests without a clear task, the user's current interests are reflected in the content and order of nodes in the browsing history. The filtering method models user's current interests from the user's browsing history and puts the next choices in order of the nearness to the interests. We call the filtering method "context-sensitive filtering". We have developed a browsing support system with this method for an encyclopedia in CD-ROM format. The results of an experimental evaluation, by real users, are also reported.

1. Introduction

Browsing is one of the most popular ways to gather information in database with hypertext structure [4, 10, 12]. In the browsing, a user continuously searches nodes which include useful information for her/him. Her/his interests, then, often change while the browsing. We call this type of browsing "context-sensitive browsing" in order to distinguish it from browsing with consistent interests. The context-sensitive browsing is gaining importance as databases with hypertext structure (for example, digital libraries or WWW), become more widespread. Therefore, the need for an advanced method to assist a user who is browsing with shifting interests in hypertext system is also gaining importance.

There are two issues to be understood in support of the context-sensitive browsing: one is the author links and the other is the excess of choices. In most hypertext, a user has to follow links designed by the author. These links are made based on the author's viewpoint for the content of the hypertext. When the user has the same viewpoint as the author, the user can comfortably browse useful information on the hypertext. However, a user isn't always able to follow the author's point of view. Especially when the user browses with his/her shifting interests, a wide variety of viewpoints should be available. It is impossible for the author to completely cover all aspects.

A solution to this problem is to link each node through indexes [3, 5]. In this method, first, each node is assigned a listing of indexes. When two nodes have the same index, they are linked through that index. This method of connecting a node to every node, which can be associated by indexes included in the node, provides a dense hypertext structure in response to various usages from several viewpoints. Such a hypertext system allows a user to browse freely following her/his interests.

There is a trade-off to this advantage. An excess of choices can occur [3, 5]. When a user is provided several choices at each browsing node, the user is often at a loss and finds it difficult which to choose. This is a typical problem of information filtering [4]. Links designed by the author are filtered from the author's viewpoint, so the quality and number of links are guaranteed to a certain extent. Unfortunately, links which connect nodes through indexes aren't filtered.

In this paper, we propose a method to filter the links which connect nodes through indexes, based on the user's browsing history [9]. We assume that the history can provide a 'blueprint' of the shift in user's interests. Even when a user browses, following changeable interests without a clear task, the browsing is not a haphazard one. It is reasonable to assume that the user's current interests are reflected in the content and order of nodes in the browsing history. The filtering method models user's current interests from the user's browsing history and puts the next choices in order of the nearness to the interests. We call the filtering method "context-sensitive filtering". Here, "context" is used to emphasize that the sequence of nodes in browsing history should be considered.

Model of user's interests depends on the contents of each node and their order in the browsing history. Currently, a list of indexes for each node is used as the description of the contents. When a user visits and accepts a node, two assumptions are made (I) that the user is interested in the indexes for the node, (II) that the user is more interested in an index included in several nodes and in more recently browsed nodes. Based on these assumptions, the model of interests is described as a set of pairs: an index and its current weight. The weight means the user's interest for the index. As the sum total of indexes included in a node, this method calculates the weight of nodes which are choices for the next browsing nodes, and then, judges that the heaviest node is the nearest node for the user's current interest.

We have developed a browsing support system with this method for an encyclopedia, written in Japanese in CD-ROM format [6]. In the encyclopedia, there are 18,892 nodes which were given indexes beforehand. In the indexes, 183,011 words are used. From two to 2,270 nodes (the mean is seven nodes) are connected through one index. The results of an experimental evaluation, by real users, are also reported.

2. Context-Sensitive Filtering

2.1 A Framework of Context-Sensitive Filtering

Figure 1 shows an example of browsing history. Here, an ellipse is a node: letters included in the ellipse are indexes which characterize that node. BN means an already

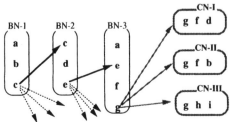

Figure 1. An example of browsing history.

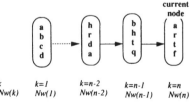

Figure 2. Weight of browsed node after a user browsed n nodes.

browsed node in the browsing history and CN means a candidate node as the next browse node. Assuming that a user browses BN-1, BN-2 and BN-3, in order, the user will then browse the next node through Index-g. The next assumption is that three choices are available, CN-I, CN-II, and CN-III, each of which includes Index-g. The model of the user's interests is composed of the pairs of an index and its weight. The index which is included in the most browsed nodes, and in the most recently browsed nodes (that is, BN-1, BN-2 and BN-3 in order), is the heaviest. Therefore, the heaviest index between Index-a to Index-g is Index-e which is included in BN-2 and BN-3. The lightest index is Index-d which is only included in the oldest node BN-1.

By using the model of the user's interests, the weight of each candidate node (CN-I, CN-II and CN-III) can be calculated. In Figure 1, CN-III has only one index, Index-g, which is included in the browsing history. Other nodes also included Index-g. Because the weight of an index which isn't in the context is zero, the weight of CN-III is lighter than other candidate nodes. The indexes difference between CN-I and CN-II are Index-d and Index-b. Index-d is included in BN-2 and Index-b is included in BN-1. Because BN-2 is more recently browsed than BN-1, Index-d is heavier than Index-b. CN-I, then, is heavier than CN-II. With these results, the three candidate nodes can be ordered CN-I, CN-II and CN-III. Here, if the user browses nodes BN-2, BN-1 and BN-3 in order, the weight of Index-b is heavier than Index-d. In this case, the three candidate nodes are ordered CN-II, CN-I and CN-III. Thus the filtering method is sensitive to user's browsing history.

2.2 Calculation of Weights

The procedure for ordering candidate nodes can be determined by four steps. These are: (1) the retrieval of every candidate node: here, every node, including the index which a user selects in the current node, is retrieved (2) the calculation of weight for each index which is included in the candidate nodes: the weights of each index are calculated based on the browsing history (3) the calculation of weight of each candidate node: here, the weights of each candidate node are calculated as the sum total of weights of all the indexes included in the node (4) the ordering and presentation of candidate nodes: the nodes are presented in order of weight. In this section, we will explain the method to calculate the weight of an index.

We define $Iw(i, n)$, which is the weight of index i after a user browses n nodes, as follows:

$$Iw(i,n)= \frac{\sum_{k'} Nw(k')}{\sum_{k=1}^{k=n} Nw(k)} = \frac{S(i,n)}{T(n)} \tag{1}$$

where $Nw(k)(1 \leq k \leq n)$ is the weight of a node which is the kth node in the browsing history. k' is the number of the nodes which include index i. $S(i, n)$ is the sum total of weight of the nodes, which includes index i. $T(n)$ is the sum total of n nodes in the browsing history.

Figure 2 is an example of a browsing history. Here, an ellipse is a node and each letter is an index. In this history, index "a" is included in the first node, ..., $(n-2)$th and nth node. $Iw("a", n)$, which is the weight of index "a", is then calculated as:

$$Iw("a",n)= \frac{Nw(1)+...+Nw(n-2)+Nw(n)}{\sum_{k=1}^{k=n}Nw(k)} \qquad (2)$$

To calculate the weight of index, $Iw(i, k)$, the weight of node, $Nw(k)$, should be defined. $Nw(k)$ has to satisfy three conditions:

(*Condition-1*) the values of $Nw(k)$ have to increase monotonically. This is because the weight of the latter node should be higher than the weight of the former node. This is a basic condition to reduce the weights of older nodes.

(*Condition-2*) the weight of an index should change following increments of n and shouldn't diverge, even when n becomes a large number. This condition is necessary to be context-sensitive because the user's interests should be influenced and changed by newly collected information.

(*Condition-3*) the computational quantity which is required to renew the weight of an index, should be finite and independent of n. This condition is necessary to be practical. In this method, the weight of kth node should be decreased when one more node is added in the browsing history. This means that every node weight in the history should be recalculated following increments of n. If the recalculations are simply carried out, the recalculations require numerous computational quantities and this method may be not practical.

We use a geometric progression sequence which satisfies these three conditions:

$$Nw(k)= r^{n-k} \; (0< r <1) \qquad (3)$$

where r corresponds to the ratio of decrease of user's interests. When n increases one, the weight of index term i changes depending on whether the nth node include index i or not. The weight of an index can be renewed by a recurrence formula. The verifications are omitted in this paper due to limitations of space.

3. Experimental Evaluation by Real Users

3.1 Browser for Experiment

To evaluate the context-sensitive filtering, we developed a browser which allows a user to browse nodes in CD-ROM encyclopedia as hypertext, where the nodes are linked through indexes. The interface of the browser is shown in Figure 3. The interface is composed of three windows: (1) the Selection Window, (2) the Text Window, and (3) the Index Window. These three windows are explained in more detail.

Text Window: The text window includes three command buttons and one check box, in addition to the area showing the content of selected node. The command buttons and check box are explained as follows:

(1) "Another Candidate Selection" button: When a user clicks this button, he/she can select another candidate again in the selection window.

(2) "Retrieving Candidate Node by Selected Word" button: When a user selects a word in the text by dragging, he/she can click this button. When the word selected is used as an index at several nodes, they are shown in the selection window. If there is no node which includes the word as an index, the browser informs the user of this fact.

(3) "Index Showing" button: When a user clicks this button, indexes of the current node are shown in the index window.

(4) "Useful Node Check" box: This is used to check whether or not the current node includes interesting information for the user. Checking means the node is interesting for the user, and a blank means that the node isn't interesting for the user. When the box is blank, the node displayed in the text window is disregarded in the calculation of weight of nodes. The initial state of this box is checked.

Index Window: The index window is opened by clicking the "index showing" button. It is closed when the node shown in the text window is changed. In the index window, indexes included in the node are displayed. By clicking an index, nodes including the index are shown in the selection window as candidate nodes.

Selection Window: In the selection window, titles of the candidate nodes are shown and a user can select one as the next browse node. Our research objective is to order candidate nodes by relevance to the user's interests inferred from the browsing history. In the list of the candidate nodes, more relevant nodes for the user's interests are placed upward in the list, so the user can select them easily. When the user clicks a title in the list, the node content is shown in the text window.

Figure 3 is the snapshot where a user had read the explanation of "Client Server System" shown in the Text Window. He/she had then checked the "Useful Node Check"

Figure 3. Browser for experiment. This is the snapshot where a user had read the explanation of "Client Server System" shown in the Text Window. He/she had then checked "Useful Node Check" box. In the Index Window, a list of indexes of the "Client Server System" node has been shown. By clicking "personal computer" which is an index shown in the Index Window, the content of the Selection Window is renewed. The Selection Window contains 91 candidate nodes which have "personal computer" as an index, but only 20 can be displayed at any one time. After selecting a node in the Selection Window, the content of the node will be shown in the Text Window.

box. In the Index Window, a list of indexes of the "Client Server System" node has been shown. By clicking "personal computer", which is an index shown in the Index Window, the content of the Selection Window is renewed. The Selection Window contains 91 candidate nodes which have "personal computer" as an index, but only 20 can be displayed at any one time. After selecting a node in the Selection Window, the content of the node will be shown in the Text Window.

3.2 Value of r

The value of common ratio r in Equation 3 corresponds to the ratio of decrease of user's interests. In the case of $r=1$, the weight of every node in the browsing history is one. It means the oldest browsed node has the same influence to the user's current interests as the most recently browsed node. Following this, the weights of the candidate nodes are decided by a set of the browsed nodes, independent of their sequence in the history. On the other hand, in the case of $r=0$, only the current node has weight one, but the weight of all other nodes in the browsing history is zero. Here, the weights of the candidate nodes are decided only by the current node independent of the browsing history. We defined our method in the range of $0 < r < 1$. Reducing the weights of nodes are the characteristics for $r=1$, cumulating in $r=0$.

The reduction and cumulation of the weights of nodes are the essential points of context-sensitive filtering. Currently, a numerical value of r isn't critical point. In the experimental evaluation described in this section, we decided the value of r based on the following consideration. Assuming that following three indexes: "a", "b", and "c": where "a" is included in the current node but isn't included in any nodes in the browsing history, "b" isn't included in the current node but is included in the two most recently browsed nodes without the current node, and "c" isn't included in the current node but is included in the three most recently browsed nodes. It is assumed, then, that the weights of these three indexes are satisfied with the following inequality:

$$Iw("b", n) < Iw("a", n) < Iw("c", n) \qquad (4)$$

The answer of the above inequality is $0.544 < r < 0.614$. Based on this result, we adopted 0.6 as the value of r in the experimental evaluation done by real users. The value is a tentative one. The ways to find adequate values of r are an issue in the future of our work.

3.3 Procedure of the Experiment

When a user selects an index in Text Window or Index Window, a list of nodes which share the index is shown in Selection Window. The context-sensitive filtering is an adaptive ordering method [5] for the list. To evaluate the method, we compared the following three methods:

(Ordering Method-1: OM-1) Our ordering method in the case of $r=0.6$ in Equation 3: This ordering method is the context-sensitive filtering proposed in this paper. The candidate nodes are ordered in response to the user's browsing context.

(Ordering Method-2: OM-2) In the case of $r=0$ in Equation 3: this method orders the candidate nodes by considering only the current node. This means the weight of the candidate nodes is decided statically independent of the browsing history.

(Ordering Method-3: OM-3) The order of the raw results of retrieval.

First, a user is provided a browser which uses one ordering method among the three. The user is asked to browse freely an encyclopedia. After the user has browsed several nodes, he/she is presented a list of candidate nodes in random order. The user is, then, asked to read each of them and to judge whether or not each node is acceptable as the next node. The results are ordered again by the three methods. Each of the three methods is,

Table I. An example of scoring procedures of the three ordering methods.

User's evaluations	Ranking (j)	Score(N=5) ($N-j+1$)	Score of an ordering method		
CN-A	1	5: (N)	CN-D	√	5
CN-B √	2	4: (N-1)	CN-A		
CN-C	3	3: (N-2)	CN-B	√	3
CN-D √	4	2: (N-3)	CN-C		
CN-E	5	1: (N-4)	CN-D		
Total Score			8		

then, evaluated whether or not they can put the accepted candidate nodes higher than the rejected nodes in their lists. This procedure is described in more detail in the next section.

In this experiment, when the user has already browsed more than five nodes and the number of candidate nodes is 30 to 60, he/she is asked to judge the candidate nodes. Each user is asked to browse three times. Every time the ordering method is different; the user, however, isn't informed of the differences. Twelve users participated in this experiment and they were divided into two units. Each unit was formed of six users who used the three methods in different sequences. This was done to balance the order of the use of the three methods. All of the users were graduate and undergraduate students who regularly use e-mail and browsers of WWW.

3.4 Procedure of Evaluation

The scoring procedure of the three ordering methods is explained with Table I. Assuming that five candidate nodes (CNs) are presented to a user in the order in the first column, he/she, then, accepted two nodes as the next browse node, CN-B and CN-D. A check means the accepted node; a blank means the rejected nodes. These nodes are ordered again by each of the three ordering methods. The orders are then, scored. As an example, the score of the fourth column is explained. Each accepted candidate node is given a score dependent on its rank. If the accepted node is ranked higher in the list, it is given a higher score. When the number of candidate nodes is N, the score of each accepted node is calculated as ($N-j+1$), where j is the ranking of the candidate node. In the fourth column, because CN-D is placed first (j=1) and the total number of candidate nodes is five (N=5), its value is five. Similarly, the value of CN-B is three. The score of an ordering method is the sum total of the scores of the accepted nodes. The score of the ordering method used in the fourth column is eight.

These scores are described by number values. The measure of the value, however, is different depending on each browsing context and the regularity of intervals isn't guaranteed. The score differences are dealt with in a ranking scale. Here, two of the three conditions are examined by a two-sided sign test. The results are explained in the next section.

3.5 Results and Discussion

We asked twelve users to browse the hypertext with the browser shown in Figure 3 three times and evaluate a list of the candidate nodes in each time. A total of thirty-six sets of scores was gathered. The results examined by the two-sided sign test are shown in

Table II. OM-1 vs. OM-2.

(* OM: Ordering Method)	OM-1	OM-2	two-sided sign test
The numbers of times when the score of one method is larger than the other	26	8	p = 0.0021

Table III. OM-1 vs. OM-3.

(* OM: Ordering Method)	OM-1	OM-3	two-sided sign test
The numbers of times when the score of one method is larger than the other	31	3	p = 7.0E-07

Table IV. OM-2 vs. OM-3.

(* OM: Ordering Method)	OM-2	OM-3	two-sided sign test
The numbers of times when the score of one method is larger than the other	30	2	p = 2.3E-07

Table V. OM-1 vs. OM-4.

(* OM: Ordering Method)	OM-1	OM-4	two-sided sign test
The numbers of times when the score of one method is larger than the other	24	8	p = 0.0070

Tables II, III and IV. The numbers in the second column are the numbers of times when the score of one method is larger than the other. The cases of equivalent scores are omitted. Based on these results, it is significant that OM-1, the context-sensitive filtering proposed in this paper, is better than OM-2 and OM-3 in ordering the candidate nodes which a user wants to browse upward in the list.

In addition, we implemented one more ordering method which is in the case of $r=1$: OM-4. This method gives equivalent weight to every node independent of the time order in the history, in contrast to OM-1, which reduces the weight of nodes following the sequence in the history. By using the browsing histories collected in the above experiment, the scores of OM-4 for each browsing history were calculated. The scores were then compared with OM-1 in the same way. The result is shown in Table V. It is significant that OM-1 is better than OM-4.

The OM-1, -2 and -4 use the browsing history in their own way to infer user's interests. It is significant that OM-1, -2, and -4 are better than OM-3, which uses raw results of retrieval. This fact suggests that the browsing history is a useful source to infer the user's interests.

In OM-2 ($r = 0$), only the current node has weight one but the weight of all other nodes in the browsing history is zero. It means the weights of the candidate nodes can be decided statically independent of the browsing history. On the other hand, in OM-4 ($r = 1$), the weight of every node in the browsing history is one. It means the weights of the candidate nodes are decided by a set of the browsed nodes independent of their sequence in the history. The main characteristics of OM-1 ($r = 0.6$) are (1) reducing the weights of the nodes to deal with their sequence in the history, and (2) cumulating their weights to deal with the history. It is significant that OM-1 is better than both OM-2 and -4. This fact suggests that the two characteristics are suitable to support the browsing.

The above, however, are only statical results. In not all cases, OM-1 is better than other methods. When the user's interests change frequently, OM-2 may be better. In contrast, when the user's interests are stable in long term, OM-4 may be better. During the interests shift gradually depending on the local context, OM-1 has an advantage over the other methods. OM-1, overall, is significantly better than the other methods because browsing behaviors, which are suitable to be supported by OM-1, are more frequent than others. This type of browsing is "context-sensitive browsing."

In the experiment, the users were asked to browse freely. In addition, they also browsed on a large scale and a dense hypertext. The hypertext included about twenty thousand nodes, each node with about four hundred links to other nodes (each node has sixty-eight indexes and each index is shared by seven nodes on the average). Furthermore, the hypertext was an encyclopedia, so the content of each node had high independency. These conditions allowed the users to browse following their changeable interests. When these conditions aren't satisfied, OM-1 may be not useful. The context-sensitive browsing, or surfing, however, becomes one of the most important behaviors of information gathering. Hypertexts are becoming larger and denser rapidly. Diffusion of search engines in WWW also enables a user to browse following his/her changeable interests. The browsing behavior, which OM-1 supports effectively, can steadily becomes widespread.

4. Related Works

Many researchers are developing support facilities (or agents) for browsing. Several promising results have been reported [5, 10]. The browsing task in these investigations is limited, though, for two reasons: (1) the purpose should be specified before a user begins to browse, (for example, looking for a particular software module [7] or technical papers [1]), and (2) the user's interests should be consistent during the browsing. Under these limitations, the browsing task has many repeated behaviors done by users. Assuming that these repeated behaviors include many recurrent patterns of browsing, machine learning is a promising method to predict user's behaviors [11]. Most research has adopted the machine learning approach, where the systems monitor the user's behaviors and find regularities and recurrent patterns.

In the context-sensitive browsing, however, a user begins to browse with a wide variety of purposes. When this occurs, the interests often change. Such browsing is often called "surfing." Balabanovic and Shoham reported that the machine learning approach is often useless to support surfing [2]. Lieberman suggested that even when a user states her/his interests before browsing, the interests decay over time [8]. In the context-sensitive browsing, a user browses information depending upon the local context. Our method which uses the local context for filtering is suitable to deal with the context-sensitive browsing. Besides, our method was able to be evaluated by real users. Few other investigations were evaluated by real users. The reason for this may be that the context-sensitive browsing is natural browsing for them.

5. Conclusion Remarks

In this paper, we have introduced a context-sensitive filtering method for context-sensitive browsing. In the context-sensitive browsing, user's interests gradually shift depending on the browsing context. The main characteristic of context-sensitive filtering is the model of user's shifting interests. Our filtering method can order candidate nodes according to the model. We have implemented a browser with this filtering method as an encyclopedia in CD-ROM format. The effectiveness of this method was confirmed through an experiment where real users browse nodes freely, following their interests.

References

[1] Armstrong, R., Freitag, D., Joachims, T., Mitchell, T.: 1995, 'WebWatcher: A Learning Apprentice for the World Wide Web'. *On-line Working Notes of AAAI Symposium on Information Gathering from Distributed, Heterogeneous Environments* (available at http://WWW.isi.edu/sims/knoblock/sss95/info-gathering.html).

[2] Balabanovic, M., Shoham, Y., : 1995, 'Learning Information Retrieval Agents: Experiments with Automated Web Browsing'. *On-line Working Notes of AAAI Spring Symposium on Information Gathering from Distributed, Heterogeneous Environments,* (available at http: //WWW.isi.edu/sims/knoblock/sss95/info-gathering.html).

[3] Beaumont, I., Brusilovsky, P.: 1995, 'Adaptive Educational Hypermedia: From Ideas to Real Systems'. *Proc. of ED-MEDIA'95 - World Conference on Educational Multimedia and Hypermedia,* pp.93-98.

[4] Belkin, N.J., Croft, W.B.: 1992, 'Information Filtering and Information Retrieval: Two Sides of the Same Coin?'. *CACM,* Vol.35, No.12, pp.29-38.

[5] Brusilovsky, P.:1996, 'Methods and Techniques of Adaptive Hypermedia'. User Modeling and User-Adaptive Interaction, Vol.6, pp.87-129.

[6] Hirashima, T., K.Hachiya, A.Kashihara, J.Toyoda:(accepted), 'Information Filterng Using User's Context on Browsing in Hypertext', *User Modeling and User-Adapted Interaction.*

[7] Holte, R.C. & Drummond, C.: 1994, 'A Learning Apprentice for Browsing'. *Proc. of AAAI Spring Symposium on Software Agents.*

[8] Lieberman, H.: 1995, 'Letizia: An Agent That Assists Web Browsing'. *Proc. of IJCAI95,* pp.924-929.

[9] Kaplan, C., Fenwick, J., Chen, J.: 1993, 'Adaptive Hypertext Navigation Based on User Goals and Context'. *User Modeling and User-Adapted Interaction,* Vol.3, No.3, pp.193-220.

[10] Knoblock, C. & Levy, A.(Eds.): 1995, *'On-line Working Notes of the AAAI Spring Symposium Series on Information Gathering from Distributed, Heterogeneous Environments'.* (http://www.isi.edu/sims/knoblock/sss95 /proceedings.html).

[11] Maes, P.: 1994, 'Agents that Reduce Work and Information Overload'. *CACM,* Vol.37, No.7, pp.31-40.

[12] Schneiderman, B.: 1993, *'Designing the User Interface'.* Addison-Wesley Publishing.

The T-SOM (Tree-SOM)

Vincent Sauvage

LLAIC ,Université d'Auvergne, Clermont Ferrand I,
IUT d'AUBIERE   Département Informatique   BP86 63172 Aubière, France
email: sauvage@llaic.univ-bpclermont.fr

Abstract. I introduce the T-SOM, an unsupervised neural network model based on well-known Kohonen Self-Organizing Maps. This model adds to SOM-properties the next new characteristics : a multiresolution knowledge representation, a low complexity algorithm and a simplified learning parameters tuning. A T-SOM network is a data analysis tool specially efficient in large volume data processing. The real purpose of this article is not to present one more neural network model but to show all advantages of such a hierarchical structure, both in learning and results exploitation.

1 Introduction

Kohonen self organizing maps have proved their efficiency in lot of domains (data analysis, classification, compression, ..). However, in real word applications, a problem concerns the number of neurons needed to reach an expected accuracy or threshold of error tolerance. First, it is difficult to determine the optimal number of neurons. Secondly, maps could be very large and then problems occur with parameters tuning and computation time in learning. Neural network solutions are computationally expensive methods. This is especially true for SOM which need much more neurons.

Here, I present a model based on Kohonen maps : the Tree Self Organizing Maps (T-SOM). It is composed of one entry layer and a set of output layers making a tree. This neural network structure provides some interesting properties. a) The projection is made on several output spaces. Each of them has a different dimension and then offers a different exactitude. b) The number of activity computations and updating of weight is very much inferior to those of any SOM. c) Thanks to level computing algorithm, bad learning parameters choice is soon detected. With T-SOM, one can get results as good as those of SOM with a lower computing cost, a multiresolution projection and an easier tuning of parameters, namely learning rate, neighborhood function and stopping condition.

First of all, I emphasize on the advantages of a tree structure both in learning and results exploitation. The accent is first put on computational complexity and parameters tuning. Secondly, multiresolution mapping is illustrated.

2   Some variants of SOM

(For an exhaustive list, please report to [1])

Both neighborhood of an output space unit (i.e. a neuron of the map) and the matching between an input space element and weight vectors can be defined in many ways, depending on the application, and then are not observed here. Models not related with this article topics will neither be taken into account. I restrict myself to variants presenting characteristics close to T-SOM, that is to say I consider only evolutive and multilayer SOM models.

In [2] and [12], the authors propose evolutive architectures. In these models, the number of neurons is changing during the learning. Neurons adding has to respect the inner inital structure of the map (respectively hypercube and hyper-tetraedron). Stopping condition heavily depends on an expected final number of neurons. Computational complexity grows with map size. In [8], a decomposition method is proposed. Neurons are grouped into disjoint clusters. This partition decrease computational complexity and is suited to parallel implemention. In a different way, number of multilayer models are one application oriented (cf. [4], [3] and [7] for respectively OCR, image segmentation and pattern recognition). Others algorithms propose dynamically defined topology or conscience factor. Topological alterations go against continuity of the map but allow better approximation of input data distribution. At the opposite, with conscience factor, one can't get anymore probability density function projection but reach more accurate vector quantization. Finally, hierarchical models are proposed in [10] and [11]. They mainly aim to reduce the winner neuron search time. Here we point out the main purpose of this paper : Using such hierarchical architectures, namely here tree structures applied to SOM, provides some more advantages than the use of a unique fast search of winner.

3   The T-SOM

I introduce the Tree Self-Organizing Map. For notation and results clarity, neurons are arranged in a two dimensional square array. This can be done without loss of generality. Learning examples are two dimensionnal data and several structured distributions are used. When it is sole, the exponent indicate a level, say C^k. When it is preceeded by ^, the exponent indicate a power, say $M^{\wedge(p-1)}$.

3.1   Architecture

I note e the entry layer and C^k one of the p output maps structured in a p levels tree. Each of the n^k neurons c^k of layer C^k is connected to e. I note Ω_j^k the weight vector between c_j^k and e(cf. figure 1).

3.2   Heritage and Learning

Learning is done step by step, from first to last level. The learning of level k depends on the learning of the previous level $k-1$. Classic SOM learning

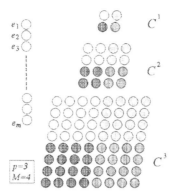

Fig. 1. A T-SOM architecture

Each neuron c^{k-1} has M children c^k. This relation is neither a neighborhood relation nor a connexion but it is widly used in learning. One simple rule on the structure is : $n^k = n^{k-1} * M$ with $1 < k \leq p$ and $M > 1$. I note F_j^k the set of M children c^{k+1} of the neuron c_j^k.

algorithm with weights random initialization is used for first level. When it finishes, C^1 has to be correctly organized before learning next levels. If not, the whole learning process ends and a better parameters tuning should be found(cf. figure 5). For next levels C^k, learning depends on previous level learning. We distinguish two stages : the *heritage* and the *learning*.

In the heritage phase, the algorithm exploits the tree structure. In a semantic way, heritage allows to speed up a learning by taking advantage of previous generation experience. Level C^k inherits topology conservation and weight vectors from lowest level C^{k-1}. It is realized by the weight vectors transfert from each c_j^{k-1} to their M children $(c^k \in F_j^{k-1})$.

In the learning phase, weight vectors are no more randomly initialized but inherited from father neuron. So, they are already ordered and learning just consists in converging. Initial low values can be fixed for learning rate and neighborhood functions.

A method is proposed to illustrate the heritage phase. (Other policies are obviously possible but they must guarantee the organization heritage. In other words, once heritage is done, topological preservation has to be observed both in father and child levels.). The inherited weight vector is the result of linear interpolation between several reference neurons of the previous level. Children are then locally organized and learning can start with even lower learning rate (about 0.2) and neighborhood equal to 1 whatever values of the number of neurons in the level can be(cf. table 1). One can see heritage as an alternative of linear initialization habitually used.

For instance, this heritage can be expressed by

$$\omega_j^k = \frac{\sum\limits_{s=1}^{t} Coeff_s \cdot \omega_{j_s}^{k-1}}{\sum\limits_{s=1}^{t} Coeff_s} \tag{1}$$

where j is the index of one C^k neuron, j_s is one of the t nearest reference neurons, $Coeff_s$ is the interpolation coefficient of reference neuron.

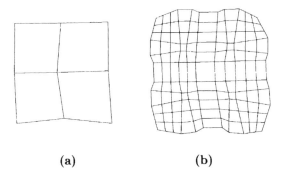

(a)   (b)

Fig. 2. Heritage ($M = 16$ children)

Maps are 2-dimensional and samples issued from uniform distribution in $[0..1]^2$. **(a)** $k-1$ level map at the end of its learning **(b)** k-th level map which weights are inherited from $k-1$ level map.

3.3 Activity computation

The k-th level activity computation exploits the advantages of the structure. First level activity is computed and a winner neuron v^1 is elected. For the other levels, in the order C^2 to C^k, just the neurons of F_v^{k-1} are concerned by activity computation. Figure 3 illustrates 4th level computation when learning of levels 1 to 3 are already done. The neurons whose the activity has to be computed to elect the last level winner neuron, are colored. Black neurons indicate the winner of a level. For a classical 24*24 neurons SOM, the cost for electing the winner is of 576 activity computations. With this T-SOM, the cost is reduced to 21.

Effect of quantization error: The feature space represented by a neuron does not exactly overlap with those represented by its children. In other words, an input space element could by represented by c_j^k and $c_{j'}^{k+1}$ respectively in C^k and

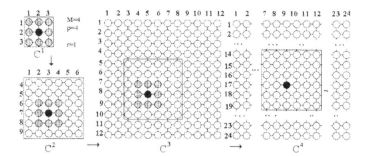

Fig. 3. Last level activity computation

Each neuron c^{k-1} has four chidren c^k. The activity of colored neurons is computed and a winner neuron(in black) is elected for each level.

C^{k+1} levels with $c_{j'}^{k+1} \notin F_j^k$. The reason is that the heritage is achieved only one time, once learning of parent level is done, while children neurons weights are modified during their learning. So, deviations between initial inherited weights of children neurons and its final learned values imply that input space represented by a parent is less or more than the sum of those represented by its chidren.

To obtain an expected accuracy, a paramter r is added to the definition of the model. Not only one but r neurons are elected, those whose activity is minimum(if Euclidean distance is use to compute distorsion error between weights and entry neurons). They form the set $R = \{v_1^k, v_2^k, .., v_r^k\}$. Next level neurons concerned by activity computation are then designed by $\cup_{i=1...r} F_{v_i}^k$. Note that the search of the r neurons is quite inexpensive since they belong to the closely neighborhood of the winner neuron. In the above example, the cost is of 69 activity computations with parameter r fixed to 5.

Finaly, in some applications(e.g. classification), the importance is put on the conservation of input space topology on map. Neurons neighborhood has to closely follow the input distribution and then minimum error is no more the main criterion. The parameter r can be fixed to a low value.

(For clarity, we assume below that $r = 0$.)

3.4 Complexity

T-SOM and SOM complexities are investigated. For an objective comparison, T-SOM last level and Kohonen map must have the same number of neurons, so that they can theoretically reach same results.

$$n_{SOM} = n^p = n^1.M^{(p-1)} \qquad (2)$$

Spatial complexity :

$$SC_{SOM} = m + (m+1).n_{SOM} \tag{3}$$

$$SC_{T-SOM} = SC_{SOM} + (m+1).\sum_{k=1}^{p-1} n^k \tag{4}$$

Note that spatial complexity isn't anymore a decision criterion, due to technical progress and low hardware cost.

Computational complexity : The numbers of learning algorithm iterations are different from one application to another according to some external criteria like data type and dimension, number of learning patterns, etc. So, model complexity can not be expressed independently of the environment.

Algorithm complexity described above concerns one algorithmic step. It is estimated by AC, the number of activity computations needed for the election of the winner, and WM the number of weight vector modifications occured during learning.

At one learning step:

$$AC_{SOM} = n \tag{5}$$

$$AC_{T-SOM} = n^1 + M.(p-1) \tag{6}$$

$$WM_{SOM} = 1 + \sum_{d=1}^{\beta(t)} 8 * d \tag{7}$$

$$WM_{T-SOM} = 1 + \sum_{d=1}^{\beta^k(t)} 8 * d \tag{8}$$

To emphasize on the complexity differences, remind that T-SOM neighborhood is very low (1 or 2) from the learning start when initial neighborhood of SOM is equal to $n-1$ to ensure global organization (cf. table 1).

M and p values tuning for an optimal learning cost: Making the hypothesis that fisrt level is composed of a single neuron, the complexity (6) can be expressed by :

$$AC_{T-SOM} = M.\log_M(n) \tag{9}$$

It can be demonstrated that

$$AC' > AC \qquad \forall M' > M, \ \forall M \neq 2 \tag{10}$$

This imply one should take smallest m value, and consequently large value for number p of levels, to decrease computation time.

3.5 Experimental results

Learning is realized on architectures and with parameters described below. Parameters α and β respectively decrease by $\Delta\alpha$ and 1 at $T\Delta\alpha$ and $T\Delta\beta$ periods. The folowing tables show architectures, parameters tuning and experimental results.

In order to test the learning, I choose two usual methods. The first one, noted Q, measures map organization quality while Err makes a quantitative analysis providing the mean distance between the entry and the weight vector of the winner. (For other measures, see [5], [6] , [9]). For T-SOM, the measures are applied to last level.

Note that both results could be optimized, e.g. by applying some heuristics like conscience factor or better initial weight vector values. Anyway, the purpose of this paper is to compare complexity but not to optimize results So, simplest versions of the two models were used.

Table 1. Learning parameters

	n	β $t=0$	$T\Delta B$	α $t=0$	$\Delta\alpha$	$T\Delta\alpha$
SOM	576	15	100	0.80	0.80	600
T−SOM k=1	9	2	200	0.85	0.80	150
$p=4$ k=2	36	1	400	0.25	0.95	100
$M=4$ k=3	144	1	400	0.20	0.95	100
k=4	576	1	400	0.20	0.95	200

Table 2. Performance comparison

		Q	Err	Pattern Pres.	WM	AC	Time
SOM		0,979	13,85	13 800	321 938	7 951 104	21,57
T-SOM	$r=1$	0,992	15,15	32 900	158 462	560 360	07,56
Rapport				**238,41%**	**49,22%**	**7,05%**	**35,05%**
T-SOM	$r=9$	0,990	13,83	32 900	160 392	1 946 352	11,89
Rapport				**238,41%**	**49,82%**	**24,48%**	**55,12%**

3.6 Properties

Lower complexity : T-SOM decreases the learning cost in several ways : lower number of activity computations, lower number of updating of the weights and elimination of the ordering phase. Despite an important number of patterns presentations, final complexity of T-SOM is lower. That results in an half-time execution. Final experimental results support the theoretical lower complexity at one iteration. Note that lower number of activity computations is still effective in the exploitation phase and contributes too to reduce its cost. On an other hand, time saving is also possible thanks to multiresolution, which can prevent from computing all levels, and to an easier parameters tuning, concerning both learning parameters and neural network size(see below).

Multiresolution knowledge : Each level is a projection whose the precision depends on number of neurons (cf. figure 4). Then, each level can either be independly run, or use previous levels to speed up its activity computation.

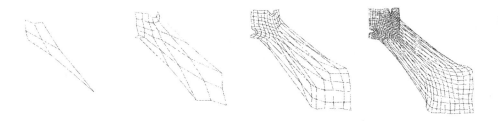

Fig. 4. T-SOM : Density function approximation and neighborhood conservation

The number of levels, whose activity has to be computed, depends on needed accuracy . To illustrate this, let us see the use of T-SOM in some classification problem. To know whether two input space elements belong to the same class, one can compare their last level image(as with a classical SOM) but computation could stop from the coarse representation of first level if their images are distant enough to make the decision.

Stopping condition and parameters tuning are simplified : Figure 5 shows the consequences of bad learning of first level: the bad organization of initial level is transmited by heritage to next levels that are unable to handle with this problem. In this case, bad parameters tuning is soon detected (at level 1) and learning can be early stopped.

For the T-SOM model, parameters tuning only concerns initial level. For next levels, learning only consists in fitting with accuracy weight vectors and then starts with minimal parameters (β and α) values (see table 1). Moreover, the number of neurons has not to be defined before learning. A growth process(by addition of new levels) is achieved until a performance criterion is met.

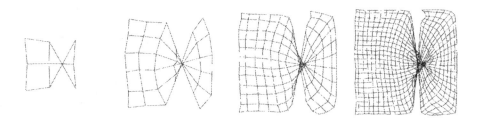

Fig. 5. Heritage and parameters tuning

Maps which level is greater than 1 inherit from bad organization of first level. Learning should be stopped from the end of first level learning.

4 Conclusion

Tree-SOM are an adaptation of Kohonen topological maps. Applications are data analysis and visualization. My motivations are not founded on biological or mathematical considerations. I used practical criteria to define its specifications. For industrial applications, T-SOM add to SOM interesting properties, namely knowledge multiresolution mapping, low computation complexity and an easier parameters tunning. We get an alternative for SOM with time or results accuracy gain.

With regard to experiments, the T-SOM has shown many interesting qualities besides a fast winner election. Research remain to be done essentialy on the expression of the theoretical complexity on the whole learning process(not only at one learning step) to confirm the promising experimental results. Others extensions could be investigated such as conscience factor in heritage or a non-fixed number of children to get several resolutions on one map.

References

1. Kohonen, T. : Self-organizing Maps. Springer Eds (1995) 143–173
2. Fritzke, B.: Growing cell structures : a self organizing net for unsupervised and supervised learning. Int. Comp. Sc.Inst. California, Berkeley. (1993)
3. Koh, J., Suk, M., Bhandarkar, S.M.: A multilayer self-organizing feature map for range image segmentation. Neural Networks 8 (1995) 67–86
4. Sabourin, M., Mitiche, A.: Modeling and classification of shape using a KAM with selective multiresolution. Neural Networks 6 (1993) 275–283
5. Bauer, H.U., Pawelzik, K.R.: Quantifying the neighborhood preservation of self-organizing feature maps. IEEE Trans. on Neural Networks. 3 (1992) 570–578
6. Zhao, Z.: Weight distance display of Kohonen maps. NeuroNîmes. (1992) 611–620
7. Lampinen, J., Oja, E.: Distortion tolerant pattern recognition based on self organizing feature extraction. IEEE Trans. on Neural Networks. 6 (1995).
8. Smagt, P.V.D., Krose, B.: Using many particle decomposition to get a parallel self-organizing map. Joint Nat. Conf. in Computer Science (1995)
9. Zbrehen, S.,Blayo, F.: A geometric organization measure for Kohonen's maps. NeuroNîmes (1992) 603–610
10. Li, K.P.: A Learning algoritm with multiple criteria for self-organizing feature map. Artificial Neural Networks (1991) 1353–1356.
11. Koikkalainen, P., Oja, E.: Self organizing hierarchical feature maps. Int. Join. Conf. on Neural Networks II 279–284.
12. Bauer, H.U., Villman, Th.: Growing a hypercubical output space in a self-organizing feature map. Int. Comp. Sc.Inst. California, Berkeley. (1995)

Extending and Benchmarking the CasPer Algorithm

N.K. Treadgold and T.D. Gedeon
Department of Information Engineering
School of Computer Science & Engineering
The University of New South Wales
Sydney N.S.W. 2052 AUSTRALIA
{ nickt I tom }@cse.unsw.edu.au
http://www.cse.unsw.edu.au/{~nickt I ~tom}

Abstract - The CasPer algorithm is a constructive neural network algorithm. CasPer creates cascade network architectures in a similar manner to Cascade Correlation. CasPer, however, uses a modified form of the RPROP algorithm, termed Progressive RPROP, to train the whole network after the addition of each new hidden neuron. Previous work with CasPer has shown that it builds networks which generalise better than CasCor, often using less hidden neurons. This work adds two extensions to CasPer. First, an enhancement to the RPROP algorithm, SARPROP, is used to train newly installed hidden neurons. The second extension involves the use of a pool of hidden neurons, each trained using SARPROP, with the best performing selected for insertion into the network. These extensions are shown to result in CasPer producing more compact networks which often generalise better than those produced by the original CasPer algorithm.

Keywords - Neural, Network, Constructive, Cascade, RPROP.

1 INTRODUCTION

The CasPer [1] algorithm has been shown to be a powerful method for training neural networks. CasPer is a constructive algorithm which inserts hidden neurons one at a time to form a cascade architecture, similar to Cascade Correlation (CasCor) [2]. CasPer has been shown to produce networks with fewer hidden neurons than CasCor, while also improving the resulting network generalisation, especially with regression tasks [1]. The reasons for CasPer's improved performance is that it does not use either Cascor's correlation measure, which can cause poor generalisation performance [3], or weight freezing, which can lead to oversize networks [4].

A difficult problem faced by both CasPer and CasCor is that the newly created hidden neuron may have difficulty in converging to a good solution on the error surface. One main cause for this poor convergence may be the presence of local minima. CasCor addresses this problem by creating a pool of hidden neurons, each with a different set of starting weights, thus enabling a wider search of the error surface and reducing the chance of convergence to a poor local minimum.

In order to improve the convergence ability of CasPer, two extensions are proposed. The first is to employ the SARPROP algorithm [5] to train the newly inserted hidden neuron. SARPROP is based on the RPROP algorithm [6], and uses Simulated Annealing to enhance the convergence properties of RPROP. SARPROP has been shown to be successful in escaping local minima [5], a property which will enable a better search of the error surface by the new hidden neuron. The second extension involves CasPer training a pool of hidden neurons, as is done in CasCor. Each hidden neuron in the pool is trained using SARPROP, as in the first extension.

2 THE CASPER ALGORITHM

CasPer uses a modified version of the RPROP algorithm for network training. RPROP is a gradient descent algorithm which uses separate adaptive learning rates for each weight. Each weight begins with an initial learning rate, which is then adapted depending on the sign of the error gradient seen by the weight as it traverses the error surface. This results in the update value for each weight adaptively growing or shrinking as a result of the sign of the gradient seen by that weight.

The CasPer algorithm constructs cascade networks in a similar manner to CasCor: CasPer starts with a single hidden neuron and successively inserts hidden neurons. RPROP is used to train the whole network each time a hidden neuron is added. The use of RPROP is modified, however, such that when a new neuron is inserted, the initial learning rates for the weights in the network are reset to values which depend on the position of the weight in the network (hence the name Progressive RPROP). The network is divided into three separate groups, each with its own initial learning rate: $L1$, $L2$ and $L3$ (Figure 1). The first group is made up of all weights connecting to the new neuron from previous hidden and input neurons. The second group consists of all weights connecting the output of the new neuron to the output neurons. The third group is made up of the remaining weights, which consist of all weights connected to, and coming from, the old hidden and input neurons.

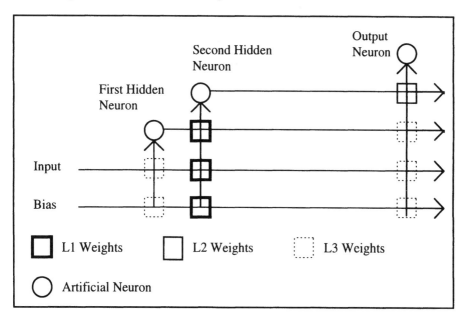

Fig. 1. The CasPer architecture - a second hidden neuron has just been added. The vertical lines sum all incoming inputs.

The values of *L1*, *L2* and *L3* are set such that *L1* >> *L2* > *L3*. The reason for these settings is similar to the reason that CasCor uses the correlation measure: the high value of *L1* as compared to *L2* and *L3* allows the new hidden neuron to learn the remaining network error. Similarly, having *L2* larger than *L3* allows the new neuron to reduce the network error, without too much interference from other weights. Importantly, however, no weights are frozen, and hence if benefit can be gained by the network by modifying an old weight, this occurs, albeit at an initially slower rate than the weights connected to the new neuron.

CasPer also makes use of weight decay as a means to improve the generalisation properties of the constructed network. After some experimentation it was found that the addition of a Simulated Annealing (SA) term applied to the weight decay, as used in the SARPROP algorithm [5], often improved convergence and generalisation. Each time a new hidden neuron is inserted, the weight decay begins with a large magnitude, which is then reduced by the SA term. The amount of weight decay is proportional to the square of the weight magnitude. This results in larger weights decaying more rapidly. The error gradient used in CasPer thus becomes:

$$\delta E/\delta w_{ij}^{CasPer} = \delta E/\delta w_{ij} - D^* \, sign(w_{ij})^* w_{ij}^2 * 2^{-0.01*HEpoch}$$

HEpoch refers to the number of epochs elapsed since the addition of the last hidden neuron, *sign* returns the sign (positive/negative) of its operand, and *D* is a user defined parameter which effects the magnitude of weight decay used.

In CasPer a new neuron is inserted when the RMS Error falls by less than 1% of its previous value. The time period in epochs over which this measure is taken is given by the heuristic formula: $15 + L*N$, which was found experimentally to give good results (*N* is the number of currently inserted neurons, and *L* is the training length parameter which is set prior to training). The result of this training method is that CasPer increases the period over which the network is trained as the network grows in size.

3 EXTENSIONS TO THE CASPER ALGORITHM

The first extension to the CasPer algorithm involves the use of the SARPROP algorithm to train all the incoming weights of the newly inserted hidden neuron (that is, all weights in group L1). All remaining weights are still trained by RPROP.

The SARPROP algorithm is based on RPROP, but uses a noise factor to enhance the ability of the network to escape from local minima. Noise is added to the update value of a weight when both the error gradient changes sign in successive epochs (indicating the presence of a minimum), and the magnitude of the update value is less than a threshold value. The amount of noise added falls as training continues via a Simulated Annealing term. This combination of techniques has been shown to improve RPROP's ability to escape local minima [5]. The equation used to modify the update value, Δ_{ij}, whenever a change in error gradient sign is encountered is:

$$\Delta_{ij}(t+1) = \Delta_{ij}(t) \, \eta^- + k_1 rS \quad \text{if } \Delta_{ij}(t) < k_2 *S$$
$$= \Delta_{ij}(t) \, \eta^- \quad \text{otherwise}$$

where r is a random number between 0 and 1, η^- is the standard RPROP update constant, k_1 and k_2 are constants, and S is the SA term which is set to $2^{-0.03*HEpoch}$. The version of CasPer employing this extension will be termed S_CasPer.

The second extension involves the use of a pool of hidden neurons, each with different initial random starting weights, as in CasCor. Each hidden neuron in the pool is trained using SARPROP, as in the first extension. The network giving the smallest RMS Error value is selected once all hidden neurons complete training. In the case where one or more hidden neurons manage to learn the problem to satisfaction, the hidden neuron with best performance on the test set is chosen. It should be noted that in CasPer the whole network must be trained for each hidden neuron in the pool, so this extension will be computationally expensive. This extension will be term SP_CasPer.

Two minor modifications were also made to the original CasPer algorithm. First, training was started with no hidden neurons. The reason for this change is that many problems can be satisfactorily solved with no hidden neurons. Second, the time period over which hidden neuron training is performed was simplified from 15+L*N to L. This was done to allow the SA term to act over a longer period (a larger L value is used than in the original CasPer). These modifications were used by both S_CasPer and SP_CasPer.

4 COMPARITIVE SIMULATIONS

To test the effectiveness of S_CasPer and SP_CasPer, their performance was compared against that of CasPer and CasCor on a number of benchmark problems. CasPer, S_CasPer, and SP_CasPer share a number of parameters which were set as follows. The following (standard) RPROP values were used: $\eta^+ = 1.2$, $\eta^- = 0.5$, $\Delta_{max} = 50$, $\Delta_{min} = 1x10^{-6}$. A constant value of 0.0001 was added to the derivative of the sigmoid in order to overcome the 'flat spot' problem, and the hyperbolic arctan error function was used [7]. Weights in the initial network were initialised to evenly distributed random values in the range -0.7 to 0.7. All weights associated with newly inserted hidden neurons were initialised in the range -0.1 to 0.1.

Training of the initial network used the initial update value $\Delta_0 = 0.2$. The values of L1, L2, and L3 were set to 0.2, 0.005, and 0.001 respectively. All of the above parameter values were found to be essentially problem independent, and hence are treated as constants. The remaining parameter values D (the weight decay value) and L (the training length), were set depending on the problem. CasPer halts training when network outputs for all patterns are within 0.2 of the required training outputs, in which case the training set was considered completely learnt. This more restricted value (0.4 being the more traditional value [7]) was chosen since it was found that it improved CasPer's performance on the test set, although it did result in additional training time, and sometimes in larger networks. S_CasPer and SP_CasPer use the same criterion. For judging success on the test set for classification problems the traditional criterion [7] was used: a pattern was considered correct if all its outputs were within 0.4 of the required outputs.

For S_CasPer and SP_CasPer, the SARPROP parameters used were: $k_1 = 1$, and $k_2 = 0.4$. SP_CasPer used a pool of eight hidden neurons. The CasCor algorithm used for benchmarking was obtained from the public domain Carnegie Mellon University (CMU) AI Repository. For all comparisons, a pool of eight candidate neurons were used and a maximum learning iteration of 100 was set for both the hidden and output neurons, as used by Fahlman [2] for the two spirals data set. All other CasCor parameters were kept at the default values.

4.1 TWO SPIRALS DATA SET

The first data set in the comparison was the two spirals problem, consisting of two interlocked spirals, each made up of 97 points, which the network must learn to distinguish. Each training pattern consists of two inputs (the x,y coordinates) and a single output (the spiral classification). This problem was used by Fahlman [2] to demonstrate the effectiveness of the CasCor algorithm on a problem known to be very difficult for traditional Back Propagation to solve. In order to compare CasPer and CasCor on this problem, 100 independent runs were performed using each algorithm. The standard test set for the two spirals data set (as supplied with the CasCor algorithm) was used to measure the resulting generalisation ability of the networks. This test set consists of two spirals each made up of 96 points, slightly rotated relative to the original spirals.

The parameter values used for the CasPer algorithm were $L = 5$ and $D = 5 \times 10^{-3}$. S_CasPer and SP_CasPer used $L = 100$ and $D = 1 \times 10^{-2}$. The standard symmetric sigmoid non linearity (-0.5, 0.5) was used. Since the two spirals problem is an artificial data set without the presence of noise, training was continued until the training set was learnt completely. At this point the mean, standard deviation and median for the following characteristics were measured: epochs trained, hidden neurons inserted, number of connection crossings and percentage correct on the test set. Fahlman [2] defines the term connection crossings as "the number of multiply-accumulate steps to propagate activation values forward through the network and error values backward". This term is a more valid way to compare learning times than number of epochs trained, since CasCor makes use of weight freezing and caching which greatly improves the algorithm's efficiency. It should be noted that in CasCor an epoch is defined as single pass of all training patterns through all the candidate neurons, and is not calculated on a per candidate basis, as it is for SP_CasPer. For this reason also, connection crossings give a much better indication of computational cost.

The results for CasPer, S_CasPer, SP_CasPer and CasCor on the two spirals problem are shown in Table 1. S_CasPer was able to produce networks with two less hidden neurons in the median case than CasPer, which equates to 31 less weights being used because of the cascade architecture. S_CasPer also gave improved test set results. One reason for this improvement may be due to the smaller networks created by S_CasPer. In terms of connection crossings S_CasPer and CasPer were approximately equal.

SP_CasPer showed moderately improved performance over that of S_CasPer, with SP_CasPer producing networks with 10 hidden neurons in the median case. SP_CasPer is thus producing networks in the median case which use less than half the number of weights than those of CasCor (88 weights compared to 187). SP_CasPer also produced a slight improvement in the test set results compared to S_CasPer. As expected, SP_CasPer was more computationally expensive, with it performing approximately six times as many connection crossings as S_CasPer.

	Epochs	Hidden Neurons	Conn. Crossings	Test Set %
CasPer				
Average	2437	13.49	9.57×10^7	97.80
Median	2307	13.00	8.56×10^7	98.44
Std. Dev.	627	2.41	5.37×10^7	2.22
S_CasPer				
Average	4392	11.64	1.12×10^8	98.38
Median	4294	11.00	1.03×10^8	98.96
Std. Dev.	755	2.34	4.38×10^7	1.73
SP_CasPer				
Average	27445	10.35	6.07×10^8	98.81
Median	26593	10.00	5.42×10^8	98.96
Std. Dev.	5797	2.29	3.17×10^8	1.38
CasCor				
Average	1686	15.96	2.02×10^7	96.13
Median	1689	16.00	1.99×10^7	96.35
Std. Dev.	209	2.17	4.47×10^6	2.11

Table 1. Results on the Two Spiral data set.

Fig. 2. CasCor.   **Fig. 3.** CasPer.   **Fig. 4.** S_CasPer.

For the two spirals data set, CasCor produced 3 networks which gave 100% correct on the test set. CasPer, S_CasPer and SP_CasPer produced 30, 34 and 41 of these networks respectively. Of those networks producing 100% on the test set, Figures 2, 3 and 4 are plots produced from CasCor, CasPer and S_CasPer runs, which illustrate qualitatively both CasPer and S_CasPer's better generalisation compared to CasCor even in cases where a 100% correct result was achieved on the test set.

4.2 IRIS DATA SET

Fisher's classic Iris data, which classifies irises into three classes, was used for the next comparison. The Iris data set was obtained from the UCI database [8], and consists of 150 patterns, of which 120 were randomly selected as training patterns, leaving 30 as test patterns. Each Iris pattern consists of 4 input and 3 output values. The parameter values used for the CasPer algorithm were $L = 5$ and $D = 1 \times 10^{-5}$, while S_CasPer and SP_CasPer used $L = 100$ and $D = 1 \times 10^{-3}$. The asymmetric sigmoid (0, 1) non linearity was used, since the output values of this data set are in the range 0 to 1. One hundred separate training runs with different initial weight values were performed for the Iris data set, and the results are shown in Table 2.

	Epochs	Hidden Neurons	Conn. Crossings	Test Set %
CasPer				
Average	326	4.01	2.89×10^6	88.87
Median	316	4.00	2.62×10^6	90.00
Std. Dev.	72	1.02	1.07×10^6	3.75
S_CasPer				
Average	1227	3.46	8.73×10^6	88.97
Median	1194	3.00	7.81×10^6	90.00
Std. Dev.	283	1.44	3.99×10^6	3.94
SP_CasPer				
Average	4462	1.82	2.64×10^7	87.43
Median	4567	2.00	2.70×10^7	86.67
Std. Dev.	799	0.54	6.22×10^6	3.09
CasCor				
Average	431	2.60	1.47×10^6	72.22
Median	430	3.00	1.40×10^6	73.33
Std. Dev.	95	0.69	4.74×10^5	7.10

Table 2. Results on the Iris data set.

The performance of each network on the test set after the addition of each new hidden neuron was measured. A plot of the median values obtained is shown in Figure 5. S_CasPer was again able to reduce the average network size produced compared to CasPer. In addition, Figure 5 shows that S_CasPer's initial performance on the test set was significantly better than CasPer, although the two became approximately the same as additional neurons were inserted. SP_CasPer was able to produce further decreases in network size, although a slight drop in generalisation was produced. It seems likely that this is due to overfitting, since in SP_CasPer the hidden neuron selected is the one which gives the largest decrease in error, resulting in networks which may overfit the data set. The maximum number of hidden neurons inserted by SP_CasPer was 3, hence its cutoff in Figure 5.

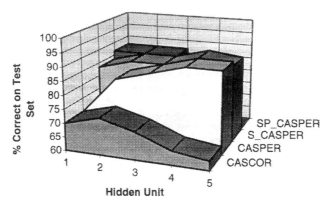

Fig. 5. Performance on the Iris test set after the insertion of each hidden neuron.

The reason for S_CasPer's increased computational cost compared to CasPer in this problem is that the training period for CasPer is initially very small, and only increases as the network grows in size. Since only small networks were produced for this data set, CasPer is less expensive than S_CasPer, as S_CasPer uses a constant value as the training period (100 in this case). Again, SP_CasPer is computationally more expensive than S_CasPer: SP_CasPer performs approximately 3 times as many connection crossings as S_CasPer.

5 DISCUSSION

In both comparisons S_CasPer is shown to produce decreases in network size compared to CasPer. This can attributed in the main to the new hidden neuron being trained by SARPROP, which allows this neuron to perform a better search of the error surface. S_CasPer is generally able to maintain, and sometimes improve the good generalisation ability of CasPer.

Similar improvements are made by the SP_CasPer algorithm. The amount of improvement in hidden neurons inserted by SP_CasPer over S_CasPer, while significant, is not in proportion to the amount of extra computational cost involved in performing the additional search provided by using a pool of hidden neurons. One reason for this may be that the search performed by S_CasPer is very successful at finding a good solution, and this is not much improved even when additional searches are performed. An advantage of SP_CasPer, however, is that it is ideally suited for parallel implementation, with each network in the pool trained on a separate processor. This largely overcomes the additional time required to train a pool of neurons.

The ability to create cascade networks with smaller numbers of hidden neurons is especially relevant to the area of VLSI implementation of these networks. Cascade networks result in deep networks with large fan-in and propagation delays [2]. Smaller networks reduce these difficulties. One problem not addressed by these improvements to CasPer is that the size of the constructed network is difficult to estimate prior to training. A VLSI implementation, however, will need to set an upper bound on both fan in and network depth. Future work with CasPer is aimed at addressing this problem.

6 CONCLUSION

The S_CasPer extension of the CasPer algorithm, which uses SARPROP as the training method for the newly inserted hidden neurons, results in smaller networks, often with better generalisation. The SP_CasPer extension, which uses of a pool of hidden neurons trained by SARPROP, results in further improvements in network size, although there is an increased computational cost. Additional comparisons between CasPer, S_CasPer and SP_CasPer using regression benchmarks [9] support the conclusions drawn here.

REFERENCES

[1]   Treadgold, N.K. and Gedeon, T.D. "A Cascade Network Employing Progressive RPROP", *Int. Work Conf. on Artificial and Natural Neural Networks*, pp. 733-742, 1997.

[2]   Fahlman, S.E. and Lebiere, C. "The cascade-correlation learning architecture," *Advances in Neural Information Processing*, vol. 2, D.S. Touretzky, (Ed.) San Mateo, CA: Morgan Kauffman, pp. 524-532, 1990.

[3]   J. Hwang, S. You, S. Lay, and I. Jou, "The Cascade-Correlation Learning: A Projection Pursuit Learning Perspective", *IEEE Trans. Neural Networks* 7(2), pp. 278-289, 1996.

[4]   T. Kwok and D. Yeung, "Experimental Analysis of Input Weight Freezing in Constructive Neural Networks", *Proc IEEE Int. Conf. On Neural Networks*, pp. 511-516, 1993.

[5]   Treadgold, N.K. and Gedeon, T.D. "A Simulated Annealing Enhancement to Resilient Backpropagation," *Proc. Int. Panel Conf. Soft and Intelligent Computing*, Budapest, pp. 293-298, 1996.

[6]   Riedmiller, M. and Braun, H. "A Direct Adaptive Method for Faster Backpropagation Learning: The RPROP Algorithm," *Proc IEEE Int. Conf. on Neural Networks*, pp. 586-591, 1993.

[7]   Fahlman, S.E. "An empirical study of learning speed in back-propagation networks," Technical Report CMU-CS-88-162, Carnegie Mellon University, Pittsburgh, PA, 1988.

[8]   Murphy, P.M. and Aha, D.W. "UCI Repository of machine learning databases," [http://www.ics.uci.edu/~mlearn/MLRepository.html], Irvine, CA: University of California, Department of Information and Computer Science, 1994.

[9]   Treadgold, N.K. and Gedeon, T.D. "Extending CasPer: A Regression Survey", *Int. Conf. On Neural Information Processing,* to appear, 1997.

Disconcepts and Fuzzy Cognitive Maps

Thapa R.B. and Sadananda R.
Computer Science and Information Management Program
Asian Institute of Technology,
G.P.O. 4, Klong Luang, Pathumthani 12120
E-mail: {ramesh,sada}@cs.ait.ac.th

Abstract: *Formal reasoning involves establishment of causal relationships between concepts and a process of chaining through them. Cognitive maps and Fuzzy Cognitive Maps have been proposed as formalisms. In this paper we examine Fuzzy Cognitive Maps with Concepts as nodes and bivalent outputs, and point out inadequacies of such formalism. We propose the introduction of Disconcepts to meet this situation. We demonstrate the strength of resulting formalism by examples.*

Keywords: Temporal associative memory, concept, disconcept, neural networks.

1. Introduction

Most knowledge for decision making is expressed using causal reasoning. Concepts used in causal reasoning are usually fuzzy [1]. Various systems such as political, social, social-economic and other systems are dynamic containing feedback loops. Similarly, in such systems we may have to consider expertise of not only one expert but many. Traditional artificial intelligence approach relies on first order logic and symbol manipulation. This makes it inappropriate to deal with fuzzy knowledge. Similarly, traditional expert systems that rely on tree structured knowledge representations are inefficient in handling feedback loops and knowledge of multiple experts. Furthermore, in such knowledge representation scheme, search time increases with tree size [2]. Fuzzy Cognitive Maps (FCMs) may be one of the solutions to these problems.

FCMs introduced by Kosko [1] are the extension of Axelrod's [3] Cognitive Maps (CMs). Since then, FCMs have been applied in many fields. Such as, Taber [4], [5] has used them to model popular political and social system. Styblinski and Meyer [6] have applied them to analyze electrical circuits. Zhang [7] has used them to analyze the extended graph-theoretic behavior. Lee et al. [8] have used them to analyze the stock market.

FCMs have been viewed as temporal associative memory (TAM) that quickly settles [2] down to some limit cycles indicating the inference. Output of FCMs, in most cases, is thresholded in $\{0,1\}$ which turns on or off each node of FCMs [2], [9]. However, such approach may produce spurious result and hinders the automating the inference mechanism.

2. Fuzzy Cognitive Maps

A FCM is a fuzzy signed digraph with feedback [2]. A *simple* FCM has causal edge weights in $\{-1, 0, 1\}$. In general, FCM causal weights can be in $[-1, 1]$ [2]. We will call this continuous FCMs. The fuzzy edge function value e_{ij} represents a degree of causality from node C_i to C_j. In the case of continuos FCMs, $e_{ij} = 0$ indicates no causality, $e_{ij} > 0$ indicates positive causality, $e_{ij} < 0$ indicates negative causality. The edge value can also be linguistic fuzzy quantifier such as very low, low, very high, more or less, a little, etc. In literature, FCMs have also been classified by the state vector. According to this, there are bivalent-state FCM, trivalent-state FCMs and continuous-state FCMs corresponding to the range of values of state vectors [5]. FCM methodology broadly consists of knowledge acquisition, FCM combining and inference extractions.

Simple FCMs rather than continuous FCMs are easier to derive from experts. We can also extract simple FCM from articles, editorials, or survey [2]. However, in the case of continuous FCMs, we may have to use interview and questionnaire with the expert extensively and interact intensively. However, they may provide more information than simple FCMs.

Various methods have been proposed for combining FCM from experts [8], [11]. Here, a method described by Kosko [2], [9] has been described. Arbitrary FCM connection matrices $E_1,..., E_k$ can be combined by adding augmented FCM matrices $F_1,..., F_k$. Each augmented matrix F_i has n rows and n columns. n equals the total number of distinct concepts used by the experts. Then F_i is added pointwise to yield the combined FCM matrix F:

$$F = \sum_i F_i \qquad (1)$$

Credibility value, w_i, can be assigned to each ith expert. Where w_i is from the range [0,1], with $w_i = 1$ as the default weight.

$$F_w = \sum_i w_i F_i \qquad (2)$$

Combined FCM is produced by,

$$F = (1/k) \sum_{i=1}^{k} F_i \qquad (3)$$

($1/k$) normalizes the edge value. For weighted experts one can also use the normalization factor $1/w$, where w is the sum of credibility weights, $w = \sum w_i$. Other way of combining FCM, in case of continuous FCM, is using t-norm and t-conorm operator pointwise.

2.1 Inference Mechanism

Each node C_i may represent a nonlinear function like sigmoid function. Its input value is edge function value [2]. In case of bivalent C_i, we may write

$$C_i(t+1) = \begin{cases} 1 \text{ if } C(t)E^i > T \\ 0 \text{ if } C(t)E^i \le T \end{cases} \qquad (4)$$

Where $C(t) = [C_1(t), \cdots, C_n(t)]$ is the state vector of causal activation at discrete time t, and E^i is the ith column of the FCM connection matrix E. T is thresholding value. Let us represent for convenience state vector $C(0)$ as C^0, $C(1)$ as C^1, etc. Let $C^0 = [C_1^0, \cdots, C_n^0]$ be the initial state vector. To find out the sustained effect of a concept C_i on other concepts we assign $C_i^0 = 1$ and 0 to all other concepts. This process is also known as policy enforcement [5]. Now, we propagate effect of concept C_i with vector matrix operations and thresholding.

$$C^1 = [C_1^1,\ldots,C_n^1], C_j^1 = \Theta(C^0 E^j) \text{ and set } C_i^1 = 1, \text{ where } j = 1,2,\ldots,n$$
$$C^2 = [C_1^2,\ldots,C_n^2], C_j^2 = \Theta(C^1 E^j) \text{ and set } C_i^2 = 1, \text{ where } j = 1,2,\ldots,n$$
$$\vdots$$

Here Θ represents thresholding function. After thresholding, node C_i at each step is activated. For simple FCMs and many continuous FCMs, the causal flow immediately stabilizes on a C^k for a particular k or oscillates between repeating sequence of vector $C^l,\cdots,C^{l+n},C^l$. The former case is known as fixed point. In rest of the paper we are considering FCMs in which output value is thresholded in $\{0,1\}$.

Let us consider C_k^2 before thresholding.

$$C^1 E^k = C_1^1.e_{1k} + C_2^1.e_{2k} + \cdots + C_n^1.e_{nk} = \sum_{j=1}^{n} C_j^1.e_{jk} \tag{5}$$

Intuitively value of C_k^2 before thresholding represents *total effect* on it at discrete time 2. More generally, $C^J E^k$ for j>0, before thresholding represents the total effect exerted on it at discrete time j. This total effect may be positive, negative or zero. Subsequent thresholding yields node's value in the range $\{0,1\}$. In this way negative value is suppressed to zero, which may cause undesirable effect, since it may turn off the subsequent node. It is illustrated, in the following section.

Thresholded value of $C^J E^k$ may represent the direction of total effect, that is one represents positive causality zero represents absence or negative causality. On the other hand, since, threshold represents node value another representation may be the absence (deactivation) or presence (activation) of the node according to one or zero value of the node.

For example if C_1 is the sustained node and $C^k = [1\ 0\ 1\ 1]$ as some intermediate or final state vector, then we may infer that C_1 has positive effect on C_3 and C_4, and absence or negative effect on C_2. Another way of representing inference may be that sustained effect of C_1 lead to presence (activation) of nodes C_3 and C_4, and deactivation (absence) of node C_2.

3. Inference Inadequacy

Now let us consider examples that show that thresholding negative causalities to zero may give inadequate inference. Here we assign value 0.5 to T in equation 4.

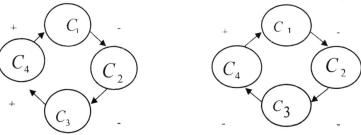

Fig. 1.   **Fig. 2.**

For the first figure, we have,

$$E = \begin{bmatrix} 0 & -1 & 0 & 0 \\ 0 & 0 & -1 & 0 \\ 0 & 0 & 0 & 1 \\ 1 & 0 & 0 & 0 \end{bmatrix} \quad (6)$$

$$C^0 = \begin{bmatrix} 1 & 0 & 0 & 0 \end{bmatrix}$$
$$C^0 \times E = \begin{bmatrix} 0 & -1 & 0 & 0 \end{bmatrix}$$
$$C^1 = \begin{bmatrix} 1 & 0 & 0 & 0 \end{bmatrix}$$
$$C^1 \times E = \begin{bmatrix} 0 & -1 & 0 & 0 \end{bmatrix}$$
$$C^2 = \begin{bmatrix} 1 & 0 & 0 & 0 \end{bmatrix} = C^1$$

Similarly, for the second figure we have,

$$E = \begin{bmatrix} 0 & -1 & 0 & 0 \\ 0 & 0 & -1 & 0 \\ 0 & 0 & 0 & -1 \\ 1 & 0 & 0 & 0 \end{bmatrix} \quad (7)$$

$$C^0 = \begin{bmatrix} 1 & 0 & 0 & 0 \end{bmatrix}$$
$$C^0 \times E = \begin{bmatrix} 0 & -1 & 0 & 0 \end{bmatrix}$$
$$C^1 = \begin{bmatrix} 1 & 0 & 0 & 0 \end{bmatrix}$$
$$C^1 \times E = \begin{bmatrix} 0 & -1 & 0 & 0 \end{bmatrix}$$
$$C^2 = \begin{bmatrix} 1 & 0 & 0 & 0 \end{bmatrix} = C^1$$

As we see for both FCM corresponding to figure 1 and 2, in response to our question "what if" C_1, we have identical answers. Although In figure 1 we have two negative effects in the path, from C_1 to C_2 and C_2 to C_3, and in figure 2 there are three negatives in the path from C_1 to C_4. From simple causal algebra rules [1], and other cognitive map literature [3], [12] it follows that even number of negative in a path should produce positive effect, and odd number of negative in a path should produce negative effect. Simple intuition also coincides with the cognitive map theory. Following these rules, we should have in figure 1 C_3 and C_4 positive. Similarly in figure 2 we should have C_4 as positive. Figure 1 and Figure 2 are example of deviation amplifying and deviation counteracting loop. Such loops play important roles in an organization [13]. Such kind of inadequate inference is obtained not only in the feed back loops but also in the cases such as C_1, C_3, C_4 and C_2 connected in a sequence, and we have different signs corresponding to different connections in between them. Such type of inference may be obtained because thresholding negative effect to zero may turn off the subsequent node value to zero. Second problem with such inference is dual interpretation of value zero, which may be interpreted as absence of effect or presence of negative effect. This may create problems while we try to automate the inference mechanism. This is illustrated in figure 3.

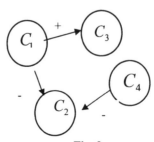

Fig. 3.

$$E = \begin{bmatrix} 0 & -1 & 1 & 0 \\ 0 & 0 & 0 & 0 \\ 0 & 0 & 0 & 0 \\ 0 & -1 & 0 & 0 \end{bmatrix} \quad (8)$$

$$C^0 = \begin{bmatrix} 1 & 0 & 0 & 0 \end{bmatrix}$$
$$C^0 \times E = \begin{bmatrix} 0 & -1 & 1 & 0 \end{bmatrix}$$
$$C^1 = \begin{bmatrix} 1 & 0 & 1 & 0 \end{bmatrix}$$
$$C^1 \times E = \begin{bmatrix} 0 & -1 & 1 & 0 \end{bmatrix}$$
$$C^2 = \begin{bmatrix} 1 & 0 & 1 & 0 \end{bmatrix} = C^1$$

Here as we find for both C_2 and C_4 we have similar inference. However, in figure 3 it is obvious that C_1 has negative effect on C_2 and no effect on C_4. So, for question "what if" C_1, we have misleading inference, as zero may be no effect or negative effect.

4. A Solution to the Problem

To solve this problem, this paper suggests using disconcpets along with concepts. Representation of concept node as concept and disconcept has been suggested by [1], [2]. This was suggested for converting negative weightage in a link to positive causalities that allow the use of standard fuzzy method. However, we extend this idea to obtain inference from FCMs with disconcepts using temporal associative memory recall process.

In this scheme we represent each node $\hat{C}_i$ obtained in knowledge acquisition with two nodes: concept C_i and disconcept $\sim C_i$. Carrot on top of concept represents original node. Thus for n original nodes, we will have 2xn nodes representing concepts and disconcepts and corresponding connection matrix enlarged to 2nx2n.

To distribute the causalities in the connection matrix, in case of simple FCM, if we have positive effect from $\hat{C}_i$ to $\hat{C}_j$ than in the connection matrix for proposed scheme we fill edge value C_i to C_j as 1 and $\sim C_i$ to $\sim C_j$ as 1, similarly if we have negative effect from $\hat{C}_i$ to $\hat{C}_j$, then in the connection matrix we fill cell value C_i to $\sim C_j$ as 1 and $\sim C_i$ to C_j as 1. Same procedure is carried out for continuous FCMs, only difference is we are dealing with real value. In this way we fill up all 2nx2n connection matrix. Here, we are assuming that the edge value between transformed disconcepts is the same as between the untransformed concepts. In general cases, the weights may be different. Now, we have only positive links in the FCMs. This is illustrated in (13) and (14). As in previous case, we have initial state vector as,

$$C^0 = [C_1^0, \sim C_1^0 \cdots, C_n^0, \sim C_n^0] \quad (9)$$

Here an interesting property has emerged. Due to the presence of concept and dis-concept, we can activate any one of it, and see its effect. For example, if we have stability as an issue in a society, we can observe effect of this phenomenon and the effect instability (dis-stability) in the society. This has increased the power of FCMs.

To find the sustained effect of a concept or disconcept, we assign the corresponding $C_i^0 = 1$ or $\sim C_i^0 = 1$ as the case may be, and assign 0 to all the other concepts and disconcpets. For a sustained concept C_i the effect of propagation can be seen as follows

$$C^1 = [C_1^1, \sim C_1^1 \cdots, C_n^1, \sim C_n^1] \tag{10}$$

$$C^2 = [C_1^2, \sim C_2^2 \ldots, C_n^2, \sim C_n^2], \tag{11}$$

$$\vdots$$

$$C^k = [C_1^k, \sim C_2^k \ldots, C_n^k, \sim C_n^k], \tag{12}$$

$$\vdots$$

Now to propagate the causalities we follow a procedure as in TAM recall. Here in every new cycle we may have values both in C_i and $\sim C_i$. In such cases, we calculate the resultant effect and update the value accordingly. There may arise three cases: 1) equal value in C_i and $\sim C_i$, 2) value in C_i greater than $\sim C_i$ or 3) value in C_i less than $\sim C_i$. In the first case we assign both C_i and $\sim C_i$, with zero value, which may be interpreted that both nodes are neutralized and cannot propagate effect forward. In the second case we assign positive value to C_i and negative value to $\sim C_i$, and in the third case we assign negative value to C_i and positive value to $\sim C_i$. Here in every new cycle we may have values both in C_i and $\sim C_i$. In such cases, we calculate the resultant effect and update the value accordingly. There may arise three cases: 1) equal value in C_i and $\sim C_i$, 2) value in C_i greater than $\sim C_i$ or 3) value in C_i less than $\sim C_i$. In the first case we assign both C_i and $\sim C_i$, with zero value, which may be interpreted that both nodes are neutralized and cannot propagate effect forward. In the second case we assign positive value to C_i and negative value to $\sim C_i$, and in the third case we assign negative value to C_i and positive value to $\sim C_i$. Subsequent thresholding turns off the negative value.

Inference mechanism continues in the similar manner until limit cycles are found. We can make inference of the intermediate state vector or final limit cycles as describe below. If we represent concept as C_k and disconcept as $\sim C_k$ for node $\hat{C}_k$ then node $\hat{C}_k$ experience,

$$\begin{cases} \text{positive effect, or activation of } C_k \text{, if concept } C_k = 1 \text{ and } \sim C_k = 0 \\ \text{no effect if both concept } C_k = 0 \text{ and } \sim C_k = 0 \\ \text{negative effect, or activation of } \sim C_k \text{, if concept } C_k = 0 \text{ and } \sim C_k = 1 \end{cases}$$

This kind of representation may facilitate automation of inference obtained through FCMs. This will also circumvent the difficulty of expressing final results in terms of disconcept. Since, sometimes it is hard to express and understand disconcepts of a concept.

As in TAM recall, in this scheme, for many simple FCMs and continuous FCMs, the causal flow stabilizes on a limit cycle. Figure 4 and Figure 5 are the transformed form of figure 1 and 2.

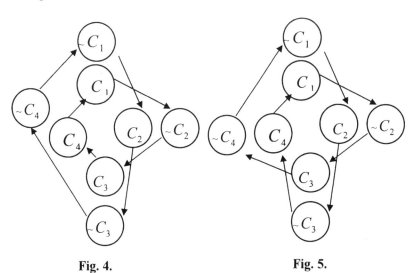

Fig. 4.   Fig. 5.

In case of figure 4 we have ,

$$E = \begin{array}{c} \\ C_1 \\ \sim C_1 \\ C_2 \\ \sim C_2 \\ C_3 \\ \sim C_3 \\ C_4 \\ \sim C_4 \end{array} \begin{bmatrix} \begin{array}{cccccccc} C_1 \sim C_1 & C_2 \sim C_2 & C_3 \sim C_3 & C_4 \sim C_4 \\ 0 & 0 & 0 & 1 & 0 & 0 & 0 & 0 \\ 0 & 0 & 1 & 0 & 0 & 0 & 0 & 0 \\ 0 & 0 & 0 & 0 & 0 & 1 & 0 & 0 \\ 0 & 0 & 0 & 0 & 1 & 0 & 0 & 0 \\ 0 & 0 & 0 & 0 & 0 & 0 & 1 & 0 \\ 0 & 0 & 0 & 0 & 0 & 0 & 0 & 1 \\ 1 & 0 & 0 & 0 & 0 & 0 & 0 & 0 \\ 0 & 1 & 0 & 0 & 0 & 0 & 0 & 0 \end{array} \end{bmatrix} \quad (13)$$

$$C^0 = \begin{bmatrix} 1 & 0 & 0 & 0 & 0 & 0 & 0 & 0 \end{bmatrix}$$
$$C^0 \times E = \begin{bmatrix} 0 & 0 & 0 & 1 & 0 & 0 & 0 & 0 \end{bmatrix}$$
$$C^1 = \begin{bmatrix} 1 & 0 & 0 & 1 & 0 & 0 & 0 & 0 \end{bmatrix}$$
$$C^1 \times E = \begin{bmatrix} 0 & 0 & 0 & 1 & 1 & 0 & 0 & 0 \end{bmatrix}$$
$$C^2 = \begin{bmatrix} 1 & 0 & 0 & 1 & 1 & 0 & 0 & 0 \end{bmatrix}$$
$$C^2 \times E = \begin{bmatrix} 0 & 0 & 0 & 1 & 1 & 0 & 1 & 0 \end{bmatrix}$$
$$C^3 = \begin{bmatrix} 1 & 0 & 0 & 1 & 1 & 0 & 1 & 0 \end{bmatrix}$$
$$C^3 \times E = \begin{bmatrix} 1 & 0 & 0 & 1 & 1 & 0 & 1 & 0 \end{bmatrix}$$
$$C^4 = \begin{bmatrix} 1 & 0 & 0 & 1 & 1 & 0 & 1 & 0 \end{bmatrix} = C^3$$

This inference could be interpreted as sustained effect of concept C_1 having negative effect on $\hat{C}_2$ and positive effect on $\hat{C}_3$ and $\hat{C}_4$. Same inference can be interpreted as the activities of $\sim C_2$ C_3 and C_4 are due to sustained effect of the concept C_1. Moreover, value of C_1 in $C^3 \times E$ shows the presence of positive feedback loop.

Again, consider figure 5 that is obtained from figure 2.

$$
\begin{array}{c}
\quad\quad C_1 \sim C_1 \;\; C_2 \sim C_2 \;\; C_3 \sim C_3 \;\; C_4 \sim C_4 \\
E = \begin{array}{c} C_1 \\ \sim C_1 \\ C_2 \\ \sim C_2 \\ C_3 \\ \sim C_3 \\ C_4 \\ \sim C_4 \end{array}
\begin{bmatrix}
0 & 0 & 0 & 1 & 0 & 0 & 0 & 0 \\
0 & 0 & 1 & 0 & 0 & 0 & 0 & 0 \\
0 & 0 & 0 & 0 & 0 & 1 & 0 & 0 \\
0 & 0 & 0 & 0 & 1 & 0 & 0 & 0 \\
0 & 0 & 0 & 0 & 0 & 0 & 0 & 1 \\
0 & 0 & 0 & 0 & 0 & 0 & 1 & 0 \\
1 & 0 & 0 & 0 & 0 & 0 & 0 & 0 \\
0 & 1 & 0 & 0 & 0 & 0 & 0 & 0
\end{bmatrix}
\end{array} \quad (14)
$$

$$C^0 = \begin{bmatrix} 1 & 0 & 0 & 0 & 0 & 0 & 0 & 0 \end{bmatrix}$$
$$C^0 \times E = \begin{bmatrix} 0 & 0 & 0 & 1 & 0 & 0 & 0 & 0 \end{bmatrix}$$
$$C^1 = \begin{bmatrix} 1 & 0 & 0 & 1 & 0 & 0 & 0 & 0 \end{bmatrix}$$
$$C^1 \times E = \begin{bmatrix} 0 & 0 & 0 & 1 & 1 & 0 & 0 & 0 \end{bmatrix}$$
$$C^2 = \begin{bmatrix} 1 & 0 & 0 & 1 & 1 & 0 & 0 & 0 \end{bmatrix}$$
$$C^2 \times E = \begin{bmatrix} 0 & 0 & 0 & 1 & 1 & 0 & 0 & 1 \end{bmatrix}$$
$$C^3 = \begin{bmatrix} 1 & 0 & 0 & 1 & 1 & 0 & 0 & 1 \end{bmatrix}$$
$$C^3 \times E = \begin{bmatrix} 0 & 1 & 0 & 1 & 1 & 0 & 0 & 1 \end{bmatrix}$$
$$C^4 = \begin{bmatrix} 1 & 0 & 0 & 1 & 1 & 0 & 0 & 1 \end{bmatrix} = C^3$$

This inference could be interpreted as sustained effect of concept C_1 has negative effect on $\hat{C}_2$ and $\hat{C}_4$ and positive effect on $\hat{C}_3$. Same inferences can be interpreted as activities of $\sim C_2$, $\sim C_4$ and C_3 are due to sustained effect of concept C_1. Moreover, value of $\sim C_1$ in $C^3 \times E$ shows the presence of negative feedback loop. In case of figure 3 performing the similar procedure as for figure 1 and figure 2, we obtain

$$C^3 = \begin{bmatrix} 1 & 0 & 0 & 1 & 1 & 0 & 0 & 0 \end{bmatrix} = C^2$$

This inference could be interpreted as sustained effect of concept C_1 has negative effect on $\hat{C}_2$ positive effect on $\hat{C}_3$ and no effect on $\hat{C}_4$. Due to sustained effect of concept C_1; $\sim C_2$ and C_3 are activated whereas C_4 and $\sim C_4$ experience no effect.

5. Implentation

The approach described here has been tested on examples available in the literature [13], [9], [2] and computer simulated cognitive maps. For instance Hall [13] deals with the policy decision of Curtis Publishing Company, where policy *variables* for the cognitive map are subscription rate, advertising rate, and circulation promotional expenditure. The computer simulations show that the proposed method has more elaborate inference than FCMs without disconcpets.

C={ C_1, C_2, C_3, C_4, C_5, C_6, A_1, A_3, A_5, E_3, P_3, B_6, B_7, B_4, E_2, A_4, B_5, B_8}, where

C_1 -Subscription Rate
C_2 -Circulation Promotion Budget
C_3 -Trial Readers
C_4, -Circulation Revenue
C_6 -Circulation Promotion expenses
P_3 -Amount of printing
B_7 -Total Revenue
A_3 -Advertising Rate per thousand Readers
E_2 -Editorial Pages

B_4 -Production Expenses
A_4 -Advertising Revenue
B_5 -Costs
C_5 -Readers
E_3 -Magazine Volume Pages
B_6 -Revenue
A_1 -Advertising Rate
A_5 -Advertising Pages Sold

For an example, we enforce the policy of increasing circulation promotion budget (C_2) using only concepts.

```
C1={  0 1 0 0 0 0 0 0 0 0 0 0 0 0 0 0 0 0}
C1 X E ={  0 0 0 0 0 1 0 0 0 0 0 0 0 0 0 0 0 0}
---->C2={  0 1 0 0 0 1 0 0 0 0 0 0 0 0 0 0 0 0}
                    ⋮
C7 X E ={  0 0 1 1 1 1 0 -1 0 0 1 1 1 1 0 0 2 0}
---->C7={  0 1 1 1 1 1 0 0 0 0 1 1 1 1 0 0 1 0}
```

Thus, an increase in circulation promotion budget leads to increase in trial readers, circulation revenue, readers, circulation promotion expenses, amount of printing, revenue, total revenue, production expenses and costs.

Now we enforce the same policy of increasing circulation promotion budget with the proposed method.

```
 C1={  0 0 1 0 0 0 0 0 0 0 0 0 0 0 0 0 0 0 0 0 0 0 0 0 0 0 0 0 0 0 0 0 0 0 0 0 0 0}
C1 X E ={  0 0 0 0 0 0 0 0 0 0 1 0 0 0 0 0 0 0 0 0 0 0 0 0 0 0 0 0 0 0 0 0 0 0 0 0 0 0}
---->C2={  0 0 1 0 0 0 0 0 0 0 1 0 0 0 0 0 0 0 0 0 0 0 0 0 0 0 0 0 0 0 0 0 0 0 0 0 0 0}
                    ⋮
---->C7={  0 0 1 0 1 0 1 0 1 0 1 0 0 0 0 1 1 0 1 0 1 0 1 0 1 0 1 0 1 0 1 0 1 0 0 1}
C7 X E ={  0 0 0 0 1 0 1 0 2 0 1 0 0 0 0 1 1 0 2 0 2 0 2 0 1 0 1 0 1 0 1 0 2 0 1 1}
---->C8={  0 0 1 0 1 0 1 0 1 0 1 0 0 0 0 1 1 0 1 0 1 0 1 0 1 0 1 0 1 0 1 0 1 0 0 0}
C8 X E ={  0 0 0 0 1 0 1 0 2 0 1 0 0 0 0 1 1 0 2 0 2 0 2 0 1 0 1 0 1 0 1 0 2 0 1 1}
---->C8={  0 0 1 0 1 0 1 0 1 0 1 0 0 0 0 1 1 0 1 0 1 0 1 0 1 0 1 0 1 0 1 0 1 0 0 0}
```

Thus also, increase in circulation promotion budget leads to increase in trial readers, circulation revenue, readers, circulation promotion expenses, amount of printing, revenue, total revenue, production expenses and costs. However, with this approach we note that there is a decrease in advertising rate per thousand readers, which has resulted in increase in advertising pages sold magazine volume pages, advertising revenue and editorial pages.

6. Conclusions

FCMs with only concepts as nodes and bivalent outputs, provide a precise formalism for propagating casual relations in complex inter-related dynamic situations. However, there are inadequacies in the inference process that are intuitively unacceptable. We have proposed the introduction of "Disconcepts" in the FCMs. The resulting FCMs with both concepts and disconcepts satisfy the intuitive requirements. Further we can represent the situation in which we may have different edge values between transformed disconcepts. The need to express every concept along with its disconcept may bring in semantic difficulties, but at the same time compels accuracy at the initial stage of design of the map which has clear advantages. The improved accuracy of design, clearer user perception and the intuitive acceptability of FCMs with disconcepts bring in the need to face the increased complexity due to the addition of nodes. Further research is needed especially for FCMs representing large number of Concepts and Disconcepts. The domain dependent investigations of FCMs are promising.

References

[1] B. Kosko. Fuzzy Cognitive Maps, *International Journal of Man Machine Studies*, vol. 24, pp. 65-75, 1986.

[2] B. Kosko. Hidden Patterns in Combined and Adaptive Knowledge networks. *International Journal of Approximate Reasoning*, Vol. 2, pp. 337-393, 1988.

[3] R. Axelrod. *Structure of Decision*, Princeton Uiversity Press, USA, 1976.

[4] R. Taber. Knowledge Processing with Fuzzy Cognitive Maps, *Expert Systems with Applications*, vol. 2, No. 1, pp. 83-87, 1991.

[5] R. Taber. Fuzzy Cognitive Maps Model Social Systems, *AI Expert*, vol. 9, No. 7, pp. 18-23, 1994.

[6] M. A. Styblinski and B. D. Meyer. Fuzzy Cognitive Maps, Signal Flow Graphs and Qualatitive Circuit Analysis, *Proceedings of the 2nd IEEE International Conference on Neural Networks(ICNN-87)*, Vol. II, pp. 549-556, 1988.

[7] W. Zhang and S. Chen. An Architecture for Cognitive Maps, *Proc. IEEE Second Int. Conference on Neural Networks (San Diego)*, Vol II, CA, July 24-27, pp. 231-238, 1988.

[8] K. C. Lee, S. C. Chu, and H.S. Kim. Fuzzy Cognitive Map-Based Knowledge Acquisition Algorithm: Application to Stock Investment Analysis, *Proceeding of the 1st International Conference on POM/MIS*, 1993.

[9] J. A. Dickerson and B. Kosko. Virtual Worlds as Fuzzy Cognitive Maps, *Presence*, vol. 3, No. 2, MIT Press, pp. 173-189, 1994.

[10] B. Kosko. *Neural Networks and Fuzzy Systems: A Dynamical System Approach to Machine Intelligence*, Prentice-Hall, 1992.

[11] Zhang W., Chen S., Wang W., and King, R. S. A Cognitive-Map-Based Approach to the Coordination of Distributed Cooperative Agents, *IEEE Transaction on System, Man, And Cybernetics*, Vol 22,No. 1,pp. 31-39, 1992.

[12] M. Bougon, K. Weick, D. Binkhorst. Cognition in Organisation: An Analysis of the Utrecht Jazz Orchestra, *Administrative Science Quarterly*, vol. 22, pp. 606-639, 1977.

[13] R. I. Hall. The Natural Logic of Management Policy Making: Its Implication for the Survival of an Organisation. *Management Science*, vol. 30, pp. 905-937, 1984.

Weight Sensitive Boolean Extraction Produces Compact Expressions

Lawrence Peh and C. P. Tsang

Logic and Artificial Intelligence Group
Department of Computer Science
The University of Western Australia
Crawley, Western Australia 6907
Phone: (618) 93802716
Fax: (618) 93801089
peh@cs.uwa.edu.au tsang@cs.uwa.edu.au

Abstract. Artificial neural networks are universal function approximators. The function actually implemented by a network is fully defined by its weights, but the representation in terms of weights is difficult for humans to understand or reason with. It is helpful to efficiently express the network's function in a symbolic form. Golea argues that extracting the minimum disjunctive normal form (DNF) of a network's function is difficult, but near–minimum DNF expressions may be extractable.

In an earlier work, we presented a technique for extracting a Boolean function from a single neuron efficiently. The computational complexity is linear in the size of the extracted expression. Our algorithm exploits the relative sizes of a neuron's weights to produce a natural and compact Boolean expression. We call this algorithm *weight sensitive extraction*. Tsukimoto and Morita recently presented an alternate technique using multilinear functions to extract Boolean functions in a disjunctive form. We show that the computational complexity of their algorithm is exponential in the length of each disjunct.

The two algorithms are compared in a series of experiments, and weight sensitive extraction is found to produce shorter expressions. We also examine our choice of weight ordering experimentally by using simulated annealing to find an order which produces a near–global minimum–length expression. We find that the order used in our earlier paper produces near–minimal expressions. Even in the cases where simulated annealing produces a better order, the difference in the length of the extracted expressions is only about one tenth of the expressions' length. This indicates that weight sensitivity is an important consideration in designing extraction algorithms to produce compact expressions.

Keywords: neural network, rule extraction, boolean expression, weight sensitivity, disjunctive normal form

1 Introduction

Artificial neural networks are universal function approximators, and they have been successfully used in many artificial intelligence applications such as pattern recognition and machine learning [1–3].

The weights of a neural network fully define the function it implements. These weights are usually refined by applying a training algorithm to a given set of training vectors; the training algorithm minimises a chosen criterion function defined over the network.

While these neural network approximators have useful applications, the functions they implement are not easy to decipher. It is also difficult to vary the training vectors after training, to resume training using different training sets, to form a new network by combining trained networks, and to reason with a trained network. In practice, it is difficult to make symbolic deductions from trained networks. These problems stem from an inability to easily extract symbolic meaning from a neural network.

The network is a good representation for storing and evaluating Boolean functions, but it is a very bad representation for understanding the function as a Boolean object. Even if the original training set is known, it may be incomplete or inconsistent. In addition, training may terminate with some residual training errors. We still would not have a symbolic representation of the function implemented by the trained network.

There are many other motivations supporting the extraction of symbolic information from a neural network. For example, if a neural network is trained to implement a Boolean function, it would be interesting to see at what stage a correct (or nearly correct) Boolean function begins to develop. It is also useful to investigate the issue of symbolic generalisation with reference to training and neural representations.

In an earlier work [4], we presented an algorithm that expresses a given neuron's Boolean function in symbolic form. This paper verifies that the algorithm produces compact expressions efficiently.

Section 2 summarises our earlier work on weight sensitive extraction (WSX). Recently, Tsukimoto and Morita [5] presented an algorithm that extracts a neuron's Boolean function in a minimal disjunctive form. Our understanding of their algorithm is outlined in Sect.3.

The complexity of each algorithm is discussed briefly in Sect.4. Section 5 contains some experimental results that compare the lengths of expressions generated by the two algorithms. The weight ordering used in standard WSX is also examined by comparing the results with those of orderings determined by simulated annealing..

We conclude that when the weights are considered in decreasing order of magnitude, weight sensitive extraction produces compact Boolean expressions with linear complexity in the length of the expression.

1.1 Classification

The review paper by Andrews, Diederich and Tickle [6] summarises the main approaches currently used to extract rules from neural networks. Some extraction methods change the network under consideration [7], and some make assumptions regarding the semantics of individual neurons [8]. Most of the methods do not extract the complete function implemented by a network. *Pedagogical* algorithms, by definition, treat a network as a black box, and hence cannot extract the complete function of a network efficiently. The two methods discussed in this paper overcome these problems. They fit into the taxonomy of Andrews, et al. as follows.

Peh and Tsang [4] developed a weight sensitive extraction algorithm (WSX) that expresses the Boolean function implemented by an arbitrary neuron in a compact form. The compact form has the same *expressiveness* as Boolean functions that can be implemented by a single neuron.

Tsukimoto and Morita [5] use multilinear functions to extract Boolean functions from arbitrary neurons in a minimal disjunctive form. The disjunctive form has the *expressiveness* of a general Boolean function. We call their algorithm MFX in this paper.

Both WSX and MFX take a *decompositional* approach to function extraction. The algorithms extract the given neuron's function exactly (maximal *fidelity*). As such, the extracted expressions have the same *accuracy* (correct classification of previously unseen examples) as the given neuron, and both algorithms have the same *consistency* (classification of previously unseen examples by rules extracted from neurons which have been trained in different training sessions) as the training algorithm. The *comprehensibility* of the extracted expressions is high in both cases since they produce optimised expressions. The algorithms do not depend on specialised *training regimes*. The *computational complexity* of WSX is linear in the length of the extracted expression; the complexity of MFX is exponential in the number of literals in each term of the expression it extracts, and hence more than linear in the length of the extracted expression. The results in this paper indicate that WSX expressions are often smaller than MFX expressions.

1.2 Extracting Compact Forms

A Boolean function can be expressed in many forms, such as DNF and CNF (disjunctive and conjunctive normal forms). Boolean functions can also be expressed in terms of a neuron's activation function. The convenience of one form over another depends on the context in which the function is used. For example, the disjunction of DNF expressions is easy to produce, but if an approximation to the disjunction of a set of inconsistent data is desired, a neuron representation may be favoured for its other properties.

Function extraction is the conversion of a function from one form to another. Clearly, it is inefficient to extract the function in a non-compact form and minimise it later. Golea [9] argues that "extracting the minimum DNF expression equivalent to a trained feed-forward neural net is hard..." even for decompositional rule extraction techniques, but "the result does not imply that near-minimum DNF expressions are not extractable."

The objective of weight sensitive extraction is to produce near-minimum Boolean, though not necessarily DNF, expressions directly.

2   Weight Sensitive Extraction (WSX)

Peh and Tsang [4] presented a weight sensitive extraction algorithm which directly constructs a compact form for the Boolean function of a neuron. We call the algorithm *WSX* in this paper.

Consider the output o for a given input pattern $\mathbf{x}$. Now invert x_k. The probability that o changes depends on the size of the weight w_k associated with x_k, relative to the other weights in the neuron. The output is more sensitive to larger weights, so it is natural for an extraction algorithm to consider larger weights first. If w_k is too small, x_k has no effect on o. WSX uses this property to terminate the algorithm quickly.

The form of the extracted expression is also optimised. Boolean functions that can be expressed as a single neuron are less expressive than general Boolean functions [10]. By constraining the form in which expressions are extracted, compact Boolean expressions can be produced directly.

2.1   WSX Algorithm

Let $f(\mathbf{x})$ be the Boolean function implemented by a neuron with Boolean inputs $\mathbf{x} = (x, y, ...)$, respective weights $\mathbf{w} = (w_x, w_y, ...)$ and bias b, where $w_i, b \in \mathbb{R}$.

If we identify *False* (F) with 0 and *True* (T) with 1, then any instantiation of the inputs that satisfies f also activates the neuron. The neuron's activation function is defined as

$$f(\mathbf{x}) = \begin{cases} True, & \mathbf{x} \cdot \mathbf{w} \geq b \\ False, & \mathbf{x} \cdot \mathbf{w} < b \end{cases} . \tag{1}$$

In our earlier work [4], the case $\mathbf{x} \cdot \mathbf{w} = b$ was mapped to *False*. It is mapped to *True* in this paper to allow a direct comparison between WSX and MFX (defined in the next section).

Let $\mathbf{w}^+$ and $\mathbf{w}^-$ contain all the positive and negative weights in $\mathbf{w}$, respectively. The sum $\mathbf{x} \cdot \mathbf{w}$ is bounded by $[\sum \mathbf{w}^-, \sum \mathbf{w}^+]$.

The algorithm terminates immediately if f is constant. Now, $f(\mathbf{x}) \equiv True$ iff $\sum \mathbf{w}^- \geq b$, and $f(\mathbf{x}) \equiv False$ iff $\sum \mathbf{w}^+ < b$. If f is not constant, we proceed as follows.

Since f is a Boolean function, it can be rewritten as

$$f(x, y, ...) = x f(True, y, ...) \vee \overline{x} f(False, y, ...) . \tag{2}$$

Suppose $w_x > 0$. Then, by inspecting (1),

$$f(T, y, ...) = F \Rightarrow f(F, y, ...) = F$$

i.e.
$$f(T, y, ...) = f(T, y, ...) \vee f(F, y, ...)$$

∴ from (2),
$$f(x, y, ...) = x(f(T, y, ...) \vee f(F, y, ...)) \vee \overline{x} f(F, y, ...)$$
$$= x f(T, y, ...) \vee f(F, y, ...) .$$

Likewise, when $w_x < 0$, $f(x, y, ...) = f(T, y, ...) \vee \overline{x} f(F, y, ...)$.

If $w_x = 0$, the input x is disconnected from the neuron, and so

$$w_x = 0 \Rightarrow f(x, y, ...) = f(True, y, ...) = f(F, y, ...) \ .$$

WSX uses variable ordering explicitly. Now, different variable orders can produce different expressions of the same function. For example, a neuron with inputs (x, y), weights $(1, 3)$ and bias 2 is extracted as $xy \vee y$ if x is considered first, and as y if y is considered first. Since the weight with the largest magnitude has the most effect on the activation function, we have chosen to order the weights in decreasing order of magnitude.

Let w_1^+ be the largest weight in $\mathbf{w}^+$ and let x_1^+ be the corresponding input. Also, let $\mathbf{w}_T^+ = \mathbf{w}^+ - \{w_1^+\}$. The symbols w_1^-, x_1^-, and $\mathbf{w}_T^-$ are similarly defined. Then $WSX(\mathbf{w}^+, \mathbf{w}^-, b)$ is the Boolean function of the neuron, where

$$WSX(\mathbf{w}^+, \mathbf{w}^-, b)$$

$$= \begin{cases} True, & \sum \mathbf{w}^- \geq b \\ False, & \sum \mathbf{w}^+ < b \\ x_1^+ WSX(\mathbf{w}_T^+, \mathbf{w}^-, b - w_1^+) \vee WSX(\mathbf{w}_T^+, \mathbf{w}^-, b), & |w_1^+| \geq |w_1^-| \\ x_1^- WSX(\mathbf{w}^+, \mathbf{w}_T^-, b) \vee WSX(\mathbf{w}^+, \mathbf{w}_T^-, b - w_1^-), & |w_1^+| < |w_1^-| \end{cases} \quad (3)$$

3 Using Multilinear Functions to Extract Boolean Functions

Tsukimoto and Morita [5] recently presented an algorithm which uses multilinear functions to extract Boolean[1] functions from a neuron. For ease of reference, we call this algorithm *MFX*. MFX produces expressions in a minimal disjunctive form, and is independent of the training regime.

Given a neuron with inputs $\mathbf{x} \in \{0, 1\}^n$, weights $\mathbf{w} \in \mathbb{R}^n$, bias $b \in \mathbb{R}$, and activation function $f(\mathbf{x}) = (\mathbf{x} \cdot \mathbf{w} \geq b)$ as before, let MIN be the sum of all the negative weights in the neuron.

MFX constructs $f(\mathbf{x})$ in disjunctive form (disjunction of conjunctions of literals) by testing whether particular terms (conjunction of an arbitrary number of literals) appear in the expression. A minimal disjunctive form is obtained by considering terms with fewer literals before considering terms with more literals. At any stage, if a term X satisfies $f(\mathbf{x})$, then terms of the form XY are not tested. This is valid since $X \vee XY = X$.

Let $\mathbf{x}_P$ and $\mathbf{x}_N$ be the sets of positive and negative literals of $\mathbf{x}$, respectively. Then, given $\mathbf{x}_p \subseteq \mathbf{x}_P$ and $\mathbf{x}_n \subseteq \mathbf{x}_N$ and respective weight sets $\mathbf{w}_p$ and $\mathbf{w}_n$, the term $(\bigwedge \mathbf{x}_p)(\bigwedge \mathbf{x}_n)$ appears in $f(\mathbf{x})$ iff $\sum \mathbf{w}_p + (MIN - \sum \mathbf{w}_n) \geq b$.

Example 1. Consider a neuron with inputs (x, y, z) and weights $(10, -8, 4)$.

If the bias is 5, WSX extracts the expression $x(\bar{y} \vee z)$ in 7 calls, 4 of which terminate immediately. MFX produces $x\bar{y} \vee xz$ with 7 comparisons.

However, if the bias is 12, WSX produces $x\bar{y}z$ in 7 calls, 4 of which terminate immediately. MFX produces the same expression in 8 comparisons.

---

[1] Tsukimoto and Morita claimed that the approach also works for inputs in $[0, 1]$, but the corresponding algorithm was not presented in the paper.

4 Computational Complexity

The computational complexity of WSX or MFX refers to the time taken to generate a Boolean representation of the function implemented by a given neuron. Since the expressions are restricted to recursive conjunctions and disjunctions of literals, the complexity of displaying an expression of n variables is already $O(2^n)$. However, we contend that extraction algorithms should produce small expressions quickly. It is thus appropriate to measure the complexity of an extraction algorithm in terms of the size of extracted expressions.

The complexity of WSX is linear in the total number of literals in the extracted expression, where each occurrence is counted.

Proof. In (3), each literal, say, l, is generated in the context $l \wedge WSX(\ldots) \vee WSX(\ldots)$.

Since WSX has not terminated, the function is not constant. In particular, it is not $False$, hence $\sum \mathbf{w}^+ > b$. The first recursive call to WSX keeps $\sum \mathbf{w}^+ - b$ constant, and hence can never return $False$. If it returns $True$, it does so immediately. Similarly, the second recursive call never returns $True$, and if it returns $False$, it does so immediately.

Therefore every literal that WSX generates is also present in the extracted expression. As the complexity of generating each literal is $O(1)$, the complexity of WSX follows.

The computational complexity of the MFX algorithm is $O(\sum 2^{e_i})$, where e_i is the length of the ith term in the extracted expression.

Proof. Let L be a set containing e literals of the input variables $\mathbf{x}$. If the term $\bigwedge L$ appears in the expression extracted by MFX, then for each $M \subseteq L$, MFX would have first considered and then discarded all the terms $\bigwedge M$. As L has 2^e subsets, the complexity of MFX follows.

The length of an MFX expression varies linearly with the number of occurences of literals in the expression. Hence the complexity of MFX is greater than linear in the length of its extracted expression. Furthermore, the empirical results below indicate that MFX expressions tend to be larger than WSX expressions. The complexity analysis thus indicates that WSX is more efficient than MFX.

5 Results

The following experiments compare the length of WSX expressions with the length of MFX expressions. The experiments also compare the weight ordering chosen for WSX with sampled weight orderings, and orderings produced by simulated annealing.

We trained 100 neurons by standard backpropagation with momentum using *trainbpx* from the commercial package *Matlab*. Each neuron was trained from a random start with a learning rate of 0.01 and a sum squared error–goal of

0.02. A training set with 9 random patterns of 16 inputs and one output was generated for each neuron. If *trainbpx* did not converge within 1000 epochs, the training set was discarded and a new set generated.

WSX and MFX were used to extract Boolean expressions from each neuron; the lengths of the expressions were then compared.

The standard variable ordering used in WSX was also examined by using variable orderings determined in two other ways. A near–optimal order was found by simulated annealing [11]. We label this variant of WSX as WSX(SA). The energy function was defined as $log_2(length)$, and the schedule was $T(t) = 1000 - 0.1t$, from $t = 0$ to $t = 9999$. A neighbour was defined as a variable order differing by a single swap of a pair of adjacent variables.

Sampled variable orderings were also considered in the experiments. The 16! possible variable orders were hashed to the interval $[0, 16! - 1]$, and 10^4 samples were taken evenly from the interval. The mean length for the 10^4 samples was used for comparisons. This procedure was labelled as WSX(Mean).

5.1 Length of WSX and MFX expressions

There are several ways of displaying a WSX or MFX expression without changing its form or the algorithm's complexity. In particular, expressions may be displayed in prefix, infix, or postfix notation (e.g. $\lor ab, a \lor b, ab\lor$). Given the form and notation of an expression, certain classes of symbols may be redundant. To be fair to both algorithms, the lengths of the expressions were based on an optimal *Boolean* representation of each type of formula.

Since MFX produces expressions in a disjunctive form, brackets and conjunction symbols are redundant in infix MFX expressions. WSX expressions have a more complex, recursive form. This form is optimally expressed in prefix or postfix notation, where brackets are redundant, but all other symbols are retained.

The length of an expression is defined as the number of non–redundant symbols it contains. Table 1 records the mean lengths, together with their standard deviations, of WSX and MFX expressions extracted from the neurons in the experiment.

The lengths of standard WSX expressions relative to MFX, WSX(SA), and sampled WSX are summarised in Fig.1.

Table 1. Mean and Standard deviation for lengths of MFX and WSX expressions

Algorithm	Mean	Standard Deviation
WSX	6457	3499
MFX	10372	6133

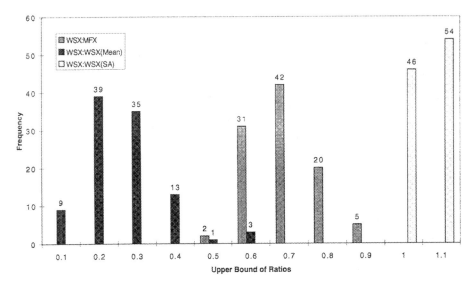

Fig. 1. Ratios of lengths of expressions extracted from 100 neurons — WSX:MFX, WSX:WSX(mean), WSX:WSX(SA)

5.2 Discussion

WSX was designed to extract compact Boolean expressions from trained neurons directly. In these experiments, WSX consistently produced shorter expressions than MFX. Since MFX expresses functions in the shortest possible disjunctive form, the results verify that WSX produces compact Boolean expressions.

WSX uses variable ordering explicitly, so it is interesting to see whether other variable orderings can produce better results.

Consider the ratios in Fig.1 that compare standard WSX with its variants. The mean lengths from sampled WSX were usually longer than MFX lengths, and often more than three times that of standard WSX. It appears that the WSX form alone is unable to account for the algorithm's efficiency. Hence, properties related to variable orderings are significant. Weight sensitivity is thus an important consideration in designing extraction algorithms that produce short expressions.

When we compare the standard WSX order with variable orderings produced by simulated annealing, it appears that standard WSX is close to optimal. WSX uses implicit optimisations such as $Z \wedge (x \vee xY) = Z \wedge x$ and $Z \wedge (x \vee \overline{x}Y) = Z \wedge (x \vee Y)$, where x is restricted to a single variable. The restriction explains why the standard ordering sometimes produced worse results than orders determined by simulated annealing. However, even in such situations, the lengths of the expressions were within one tenth of each other.

The results also give an insight into the way back propagation 'generalises' from a training set. As the training sets were largely unconstrained, one could form a crude generalisation of the set by mapping all unspecified input patterns to *False*. The disjunctive normal form of this function has 6 disjuncts of 16 literals; hence its length is bounded above by $6*(16*2)+5 = 197$ when negation and disjunction symbols are counted. It may be possible to do better if the unconstrained data points were mapped more appropriately. However, table 1 shows that expressing the functions actually learned by the trained neurons required several thousand symbols. The training regime had not 'generalised' the training set in a natural way for Boolean functions, but simply produced a function convenient to itself. Such generalisations are not necessarily desirable.

6 Conclusions

We have demonstrated via complexity analysis and empirical results that the weight sensitive extraction algorithm (WSX) usually constructs a neuron's Boolean function more quickly and more compactly than MFX. A natural compact form for the extracted expression arose by considering the inputs in a specified order. A good order is achieved by choosing the input whose weight has the largest effect on the neuron's output at each stage.

The forms of expressions extracted by WSX and MFX are different. MFX uses an optimal disjunctive form, while WSX uses a recursive Boolean form which has the same expressiveness as Boolean functions that can be implemented on a single neuron. To be fair to both algorithms, a different representation was used to calculate the length of each type of expression. Although MFX can sometimes produce shorter expressions than WSX due to asymmetric counting, it did not do so in our experiments.

A limitation of neural representations is that trained neurons cannot be combined easily. Both WSX and MFX convert a neural representation to a Boolean representation, thus removing the limitation. The expressiveness of WSX expressions is restricted to that of neurons, so some Boolean operations do not preserve the WSX form. However, the results of equivalent operations using a neural representation also cannot be expressed as single neurons. Nevertheless, once a neuron's function is extracted as a Boolean expression, it can participate in any Boolean operation. WSX extracts compact Boolean expressions in time that varies linearly with the length of the expression. Hence it is feasible to make use of the non–Boolean properties of neural representations, such as learning from noisy or incomplete data sets, without losing the benefits of symbolic representations.

Both the MFX and WSX algorithms can be modified for early termination. In MFX, the search for terms is stopped once the number of literals in the terms is large enough. The disadvantage of this approach is that minterms are discarded arbitrarily. In the extreme case of a function with only one minterm, that term is never found by early termination. Early termination is implemented in WSX by generalising the bias from a single value to an interval. The extraction algorithm is modified so that minterms falling within the bias interval are treated as *don't care* terms, and are assigned whatever Boolean value minimises the extracted expression. See our earlier work [4] for a more detailed treatment. The result is that minterms which produce unstable outputs (that is, the neuron's output may change if the weights are slightly perturbed) can be remapped to shorten the expression while the values of stable minterms are retained. This helps to maintain the *consistency* of the extracted expression over neurons from multiple training runs.

In conclusion, when the weights of a neuron are considered in decreasing order of magnitude, weight sensitive extraction extracts compact Boolean expressions from arbitrary neurons in an efficient manner. We are investigating the extraction of compact Boolean expressions from arbitrary neural networks.

References

1. A. Frosini, M. Gori, and P. Priami, "A neural network-based model for paper currency recognition and verification," *IEEE transactions on neural networks*, vol. 7, pp. 1482–1490, 1996.

2. S. Lawrence, C. Giles, A. Tsoi, and A. Back, "Face recognition: A convolutional neural-network approach," *IEEE transactions on neural networks*, vol. 8, pp. 98–113, 1997.

3. S. Amari, "A universal theorem on learning curves," *Neural Networks*, vol. 6, pp. 161–166, 1993.

4. L. Peh and C. P. Tsang, "Information measure of knowledge extracted from neurons as a tool for analyzing boolean learning in artificial neural networks," in *International Conference on Neural Networks*, vol. 1, pp. 95–100, 1995.

5. H. Tsukimoto and C. Morita, "An algorithm for extracting propositions from trained neural networks using multilinear functions," in *Rules and networks* (R. Andrews and J. Diederich, eds.), pp. 103–114, Queensland University of Technology Neurocomputing Research Centre, Queensland University of Technology, April 1996.

6. R. Andrews, J. Diederich, and A. B. Tickle, "A survey and critique of techniques for extracting rules from trained artificial neural networks," *Knowledge-Based Systems*, vol. 8, no. 6, pp. 373–389, 1995.

7. R. Kane, L. Tchoumatchenko, and M. Milgram, "Extraction of knowledge from data using constrained neural networks," in *Machine Learning: European conference on machhine learning proceedings* (P. B. Brazdil, ed.), vol. 667 of *Lecture Notes in Artificial Intelligence*, pp. 420–425, Springer-Verlag, 1993.

8. G. Towell and J. W. Shavlik, "Interpretation of artificial neural networks: mapping knowledge-based neural networks into rules," in *Advances in neural information processing systems*, vol. 4, pp. 977–984, 1992.

9. M. Golea, "On the complexity of rule-extraction from neural networks and network querying," in *Rules and networks* (R. Andrews and J. Diederich, eds.), pp. 51–59, Queensland University of Technology Neurocomputing Research Centre, Queensland University of Technology, April 1996.

10. M. L. Minski and S. A. Papert, *Perceptrons: An introduction to computational geometry.* Cambridge, MA: MIT press, 1988. Expanded version.

11. M. H. Hassoun, *Fundamentals of Artificial Neural Networks*, pp. 424–428. The MIT Press, 1995.

Learning Temporal Sequences in Recurrent Self-Organising Neural Nets

Garry Briscoe and Terry Caelli

School of Computing, Curtin University,
G.P.O. Box U 1987, Perth 6001, W.A., Australia.

Abstract. The learning of temporal sequences is an extremely important component of human and animal behaviour. As well as the motor control involved in routine behaviour such as walking, running, talking, tool use and so on, humans have an apparently remarkable capacity for learning (and subsequently reproducing) temporal sequences. A new connectionist model of temporal sequence learning is described which is based on recurrent self-organising maps. The model is shown to be both powerful and robust, and to exhibit a strong generalisation effect not found in simple recurrent networks (SRN). The model combines two important developments in artificial neural networks; recursion and self-organising maps (SOM). Both are found in the primate cortex; topological maps appear to be ubiquitous in the cerebral cortex of higher animals, especially in the primary sensory areas, and the neuroanatomy of the cortex also reveals numerous and consistent recurrent linkages between regions.

1 Introduction

Much of human behaviour requires the learning of temporal sequences. A classical pianist is able to learn and reproduce long and complicated sequences of hand movements; gymnasts and ballet dancers are able to display fine muscle control for extended periods; poets and musicians can reproduce at will sequences of many thousands of words or intonations.

Repetition and practice—learning—is certainly an important element in these endeavours. Unless one takes the view that these behaviours are innate and only need to be activated in some manner, then the learning, and in some cases the subsequent re-generation of temporal sequences, is seen as an important component of cognition.

There have been a number of previous studies on the learning of temporal sequences using neural networks, many in connection with speech recognition and language. Various approaches have been used to incorporate the temporal component, both explicitly and implicitly. One approach is to incorporate time explicitly by a transformation into a spatial dimension [8, 9].

Recurrent neural connections were introduced by Jordan [5, 7, 6] who was concerned with the parallelism of speech production, and the relationship between these parallel properties and the overarching sequential nature of speech.

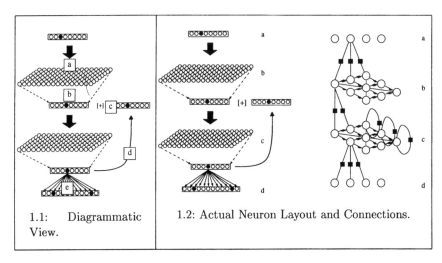

1.1: Diagrammatic View.

1.2: Actual Neuron Layout and Connections.

Fig. 1. Temporal Learning Components

Elman [3,4] conducted a series of important experiments in temporal learning. The network used by Elman consisted of a recurrent feed-forward network, with the hidden layer units copied back to the input layer on a one-for-one basis. The input layer thus consisted of two components; the external inputs that contained the elements of the sequence, and the recurrent copies of the hidden units as a contextual input.

2 Temporal Learning Model

The model we propose brings together two important developments in artificial neural networks; recursion and self-organising maps. Although some have tentatively combined these two elements before (e.g., Scholtes [10]), their combination has not been given sufficient attention in our opinion, and the research has tended to concentrate on simple recurrent networks (SRN) using the back-propagation update rule.

To learn a temporal sequence, we first consider the arrangement as shown in Figure 1.1. Here two self-organising maps (we use the Kohonen mapping algorithm) are combined together, with the second having a recurrent connection back to itself. This arrangement is similar in principle to that used by Elman, but uses self-organised maps and Hebbian learning rather than a feed-forward net with backpropagation. This arrangement[1] is first described in some detail.

The first component (a) is a standard self-organising mapping from an input vector onto the SOM surface. The mapping is indicated by the solid arrow. Rather than being considered as separate entities, the input vectors are to be regarded as a sequence of vectors $v_t, t = 0, \ldots, n$. The aim of the learning al-

---

[1] This network is referred to as SOMA (self-organised motor action).

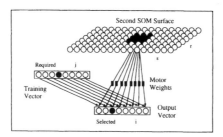

Fig. 2. Hebbian Update of Motor Control Weights.

gorithm is to find some temporal relationship between the v_t vectors such that $v_t = v_t(v_{t-1}, v_{t-2}, v_{t-3}, \ldots, v_{t-p})$ where $p \leq n$.

The output from the initial SOM is 'vectorised' as indicated in Figure 1.1 (b). The process of 'vectorisation' is merely a method of obtaining a vector from an array by some process of linearising the matrix. The rows (or columns) of the array may be simply stacked end-on-end to produce a vector. The order of the vectorisation process is not relevant as the algorithm is order independent.

The vector that is mapped to the second SOM surface is made by forming a vector concatenation of two other vectors—the 'vectorised' output from the first map, and the 'vectorised' output from the second map on the previous epoch (c). That is, if we assume time-locking of steps in the process, and the input to SOM 1 is given by t_q, then the relevant output from the first SOM surface will have been formed at t_{q-1}, and the recurrent output vector from the second map will have been formed at t_{q-2}. The new total vector forms the input to the next stage—mapping to the second SOM surface.

The 'vectorised' output of second SOM surface is recurrently linked back to its inputs via the connection shown in Figure 1.1 (d).

The final component of this initial temporal configuration is a weighted, fully-connected layer that is updated via Hebbian learning (e). This component learns each output vector that is to be associated with the corresponding input vectors.

The proposed system is based on 'matrix' or 'array' transformations—essentially transforming one SOM surface into the next. However, it is sometimes easier to conceptualise the model if, at times, we think of these arrays as vectors. This enables us to better fit the ideas expressed about the model into the current literature on artificial neural networks. The vectorisation steps as shown in Figure 1.1 are only for diagrammatic convenience in that it makes it easier to understand the overall processes. In fact, the vectors as shown in Figure 1.1 are not really necessary, and in a biological system, the outputs of the first SOM would connect directly to those of the second, without the intermediate vector of neurons. This is indicated in Figure 1.2 which shows the actual neuron connections between the various layers.

The output motor weights are modified via Hebbian learning to reproduce the required output vectors. The Hebbian update of the motor weights is illustrated in Figure 2. This figure shows the actual output vector connected directly to the SOM surface and not via an intermediate vector as in Figure 1.1 (e). The connections from the training vector to the output vector are not weighted, and the updating of the weights is supervised.

The algorithm uses an extension to standard Hebbian learning in that, as well as the weights being increased for temporally synchronised pre- and post-synaptic activity, the weights are also *decreased* when the pre- and post-synaptic neurons are not temporally correlated [12].

The learning of a mapping onto each SOM surface requires that an appropriate learning rate and neighbourhood radius be altered over a number of epochs. To ensure stability of the algorithm, different periods of learning are used in updating the weights of each Kohonen map, and for the motor action weights. For example, the learning on the first map (SOM1) may extend for 100 epochs, after which time no further learning takes place for these weights (learning rate = 0, learning radius = 0). This means that the input vectors for this map must have been separated and distributed over the surface neurons within this period. The second map (SOM2) will need to learn for a longer period, say for 200 epochs. The stability of the output from SOM1 after epoch 100 ensures that SOM2 is able to learn to separate and distribute the combined vectors over the surface neurons at least from epoch 100 on. The motor action weights in turn may need to be trained over say 300 epochs, as the stability of the output from SOM2 is not found until say epoch 150 onwards. Typically we found that the learning regime: SOM1 100, SOM2 200, and motor action weights 300 epochs, was required for successful learning. Increasing the number of epochs usually did not alter the final learned result.

3 Temporal Learning—Experimental Results

We have conducted a number of computational experiments in order to duplicate some of the temporal learning results in the literature, and to determine the learning abilities of the network. These results are not covered in any detail here (see [1] for further details). However, we briefly mention some of the results obtained in this section.

For the 'symbolic' temporal sequence learning experiments described below, random vectors were assigned to each symbol. The network was trained by supplying a continuous stream of inputs—at the end of a finite string the first element is wrapped around to begin a new sequence. In most of these experiments the system is trained to predict the next value in the sequence.

Temporal XOR The temporal XOR, as described by Elman [3], is a standard test for both historical and practical reasons. Inputs consist of binary triplets, the first two of which are random and the third the result of the XOR rule applied to the first two. The binary values are supplied to the network one at a time and the system attempts to learn a temporal relationship between these inputs. As each third input value does follow some rule (the XOR), the SOMA network is able to learn to correctly predict every third value.

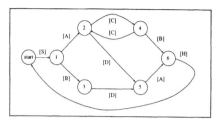

Fig. 3. Bidirectional Link.

Elman's Consonant/Vowel Sequences In this case, the input is in the form of a random sequence of characters (**b, d, g**), with each of these consonants being followed by a particular vowel. Every **b** is followed by exactly one **a** character; every **d** is followed by two **i** characters, and each **g** is followed by three **u** characters. An input string in this scheme might be, for example, **diibaguuubadiidiiguuu ...** [3].

The consonants, being randomly distributed, are obviously not able to be predicted, but whereas Elman's system could only give a statistical indication of the learning of the vowel sequences, we were able to obtain 100% accuracy in the vowels at the end of the training epochs.

Bidirectional Link The task here is to learn the sequences generated by the finite-state transition network (FSTN) shown in Figure 3. The importance of this network is that it can generate a variable number of embedded **C** characters. Various studies attempting to learn this (or similar) sequences with SRNs have shown that the SRN is unable to generalise the loop between states **2** and **4**, but rather learns specific path information [11, 2].

Sharkey and Sharkey [11] found that an SRN could not learn the FSTN of Figure 3 at all. They concluded that this was a problem that could not be avoided with SRNs when trying to learn a bidirectional link. If the system does not generalise but records specific paths only, then no matter how many embedded **C**s the network is trained on, the final **C** must predict a **B** only. Thus a test using more embedded **C**s than the training set will fail.

Sharkey and Sharkey could only get an SRN to learn the FSTN by explicit restriction and training of the hidden units. In this way, they showed that the network architecture was capable of learning the required generalised transitions, but the backpropagation algorithm could not do so.

The SOMA network was able to learn the FSTN as shown in Figure 4. This description was obtained by examining the allowed transitions from the output of the network and the winning nodes of each SOM surface. The one difference between this network and the original is that the network was unable to determine if an even or odd number of **C**s was significant. Examination of the winning nodes did show however that the network had been able to generalise as opposed to the SRN network.

The use of winning nodes and lateral inhibition associated with the Kohonen self-organising mapping process allows for a more 'symbolic-like' behaviour

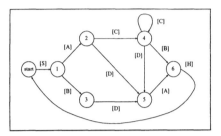

Fig. 4. Actual FSTN Learned By System—Extended Learning.

in the learning of sequences, and provides a strong generalisation effect, thus producing a significant increase in the systematicity of the network.

In order to learn the original FSTN it is necessary that the two **CC** transitions are separated, and that the second match up with and generalise with the **SA** winning node. One method of ensuring that this could occur has been explored. If each node has some form of *refractory period*, that is, a period following firing during which it is unable to fire again, then the successive **C**s would be forced to take alternate winning nodes. This was in fact tried and did succeed in splitting two successive **C** characters into separate nodes.

Counting & Memory Given that the SOMA network is capable of retaining information about past inputs and using this information to learn temporal sequences, it is appropriate to ask how far back this 'memory' extends. In order to test this, the SOMA network was trained on the continuous sequence

$$7\ a\ a\ a\ a\ a\ a\ 7\ a\ a\ a\ a\ a\ a\ \ldots$$

Without the refractory period (RP) extension, the network was only able to learn up to 6 characters. However with the RP extension installed, the network was able to learn the above sequence to 100% accuracy. It would correctly predict a **7** after 6 **a** characters, then another 6 **a** characters in sequence, and so on. Despite considerable effort, we were not able to get the system to 'count' to eight.

Other counting exercises with strings such as **01a2bb3ccc4dddd5eeeee** and the context sensitive **01a2ba3cba** were able to be learned to 100% accuracy.

The description of the results is necessarily brief. Further details may be found in [1].

4 Learning the Alphabet

We move on now to a simple example of sequence learning, but one that demonstrates the working of the system quite nicely. Figure 5 shows a typical 'pixel'

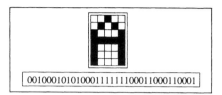

Fig. 5. "Visual" Representation Of Characters.

representation of the letter **A** and an equivalent 'linearised' vector representation.

The task was to teach the network to reproduce the alphabetic sequence by training it to predict the next letter in the sequence, given a particular letter; for example, given D predict E, given P predict Q, and so on. The training data consisted of a single string of characters

A B C D E F G H I J K L M N O P Q R S T U V W X Y Z

which was repeated end-on-end so that A followed Z to start another cycle. The input vectors were binary values as described above, and the system output was a 26 bit vector in which the appropriate positional bit was reinforced to indicate the next letter in the sequence.

The network was able to learn the alphabet to 100% accuracy in the training phase. Testing of the learned sequence used a separate program to read in the calculated weights for the two SOM surfaces and the motor weights. The test program fed in characters as input and checked the resultant output vectors. The output vectors matched the required (next character) vectors in 100% of the test cases.

It is instructive to examine the locations of the winning nodes associated with each letter. On the first SOM surface, shown in Figure 6 (a), letters which *look* similar (and hence have similar input vectors) will be located near each other on the mapping surface. For example, P and R, Q and O, E and F (as well as others) are neighbours on the surface.

Figure 6 (b) shows the winning nodes on the second SOM surface for each transition. The first character of each pair is the character from the previous iteration whose outputs are taking part in the mapping via the recurrent loop. The second character (after the slash) is the current character. Thus A/B is the winning node for the transition A → B, which is expected to produce a vector corresponding to the letter C as output.

5 Discussion Of Temporal Learning Results

What we have found is a very powerful temporal learning mechanism. The generalisation achieved on the SOM surfaces means that the temporal learning is able to generalise much more than for SRNs to the effect that much more 'symbolic'-like behaviour is found.

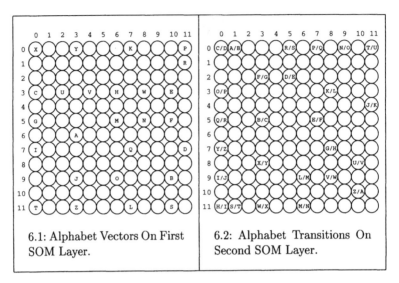

6.1: Alphabet Vectors On First SOM Layer.

6.2: Alphabet Transitions On Second SOM Layer.

Fig. 6. Mapping Of Alphabet On SOM Surfaces.

References

1. Garry J. Briscoe. *Adaptive Behavioural Cognition.* PhD thesis, School of Computing, Curtin University of Technology, Perth, Western Australia, 1997.

2. Axel Cleeremans. *Mechanisms of Implicit Learning: Connectionist Models of Sequence Processing.* The MIT Press, A Bradford Book; Cambridge, MA, 1993.

3. Jeffrey L. Elman. Finding Structure in Time. *Cognitive Science,* 14:179–211, 1990.

4. Jeffrey L. Elman. Learning and development in neural networks: the importance of starting small. *Cognition,* 48:71–99, 1993.

5. Michael I. Jordan. Attractor Dynamics and Parallelism in a Connectionist Sequential Machine. In *Proceedings of the Eighth Annual Conference of the Cognitive Science Society,* pages 112–127, 1986.

6. Michael I. Jordan. Serial order: A parallel, distributed processing approach. In J.L. Elman and D.E. Rumelhart, editors, *Advances in Connectionist Theory: Speech.* Hillsdale, NJ: Erlbaum, 1989.

7. Michael I. Jordan and David A. Rosenbaum. Action. In Michael I. Posner, editor, *Foundations of Cognitive Science,* chapter 18, pages 727–767. The MIT Press: A Bradford Book: Cambridge, MA, 1989.

8. Jari Kangas. Time-Delayed Self-Organizing Maps. *Proc. IJCNN'89 Int. Joint Conf. on Neural Networks,* II:331–336, 1989.

9. K.J. Lang, A.H. Waibel, and G.E. Hinton. A Time-Delay Neural Network Architecture for Isolated Word Recognition. *Neural Networks,* 3:33–43, 1990. Reproduced in *Readings in Machine Learning* Shavlik and Dietterich (eds), Morgan Kaufmann, 1990, pages 150–170.

10. J.C. Scholtes. Recurrent Kohonen Self-Organization in Natural Language Processing. In T. Kohonen, K. Mäkisara, O. Simula, and J. Kangas, editors, *Artificial Neural Networks - Volume 2 (Proceedings of the 1991 International Conference on Artificial Neural Networks (ICANN-91), Espoo, Finland, (June 1991),* pages 1751–1754. North-Holland, 1991.

11. Noel E. Sharkey and Amanda J.C. Sharkey. Separating Learning and Representation. In Stefan Wermter, Ellen Riloff, and Gabriele Scheler, editors, *Connectionist, Statistical and Symbolic Approaches to Learning for Natural Language Processing*, pages 17–32. Springer, 1996.
12. Harel Z. Shouval and Michael P. Perrone. Post-hebbian learning rules. In Michael A. Arbib, editor, *The Handbook of Brain Theory and Neural Networks*, pages 745–748. The MIT Press: A Bradford Book: Cambridge, MA, 1995.

Three-Dimensional Scene Analysis Using Multiple Range Finders – Data Capture, Coordinate Transformations and Initial Segmentation

Irving Hofman and Ray Jarvis

Intelligent Robotics Research Centre
Department of Electrical and Computer Systems Engineering
Monash Univeristy
Clayton, VIC, Australia 3168

Abstract

A system for acquiring a complete three-dimensional surface description of a complex scene using multiple rangefinders is described. These scenes may contain multiple free-form objects with both convex and concave surface elements. A unique approach for registering each of the views is also proposed. A diamond shaped model with known geometric properties is used to register each of the six views. Range data acquired from each of the views is transformed to match the model using affine transforms that are calculated using a least squares minimisation approach. Once the transformation is known, it can be used for all successive range data acquisition. This method is accurate, requires very little computation time, and is invariant to initial conditions. An efficient method for calculating surface normals at each data point is also described. It makes use of the rectangular grid of points in the image from which each three-dimensional data set is extracted. Low level processing of the registered data using the shared nearest neighbour clustering technique is also described. This provides a very rich set of semantic free partitions upon which to base higher level processing. This will ultimately lead to complete scene descriptions, including object identity, pose and juxtaposition, suitable for supporting intelligent robotic manipulation.

1. Introduction

Machine vision involves the acquisition, processing and interpretation of data extracted from a scene using cameras and rangefinders to provide a meaningful three-dimensional description of the environment, including the position/orientation, identity and juxtaposition geometry of the objects within it. There are many application domains for this capability, including robotic hand/eye coordination, mobile robot navigation, product inspection in manufacturing industry and medical diagnosis. This paper describes the initial stages of the development of a three-dimensional machine vision system in the Intelligent Robotics Research Centre, within the Department of Electrical and Computer Systems Engineering, Monash University. Data from six stripe-light rangefinders are combined to produce a single, registered three-dimensional scene representation.

Many different approaches to providing range data for machine vision systems have been explored [1]. Both passive and active methodologies have been successful in limited application domains. Generally speaking, where active methods can be conveniently applied, more reliable, dense and accurate results have been provided in this way. Time-of-flight and triangulation based active methods have both been reasonably successful in this regard. Striped light triangulation has met with favour in relatively small and ambient lighting controlled environments, despite its intrinsic 'hidden parts' disadvantage. We have chosen to use active coded stereopsis rangefinders for our system [2]. These provide accurate, dense and reasonably fast data sets for subsequent analysis.

No matter what type of rangefinder is used, a particular viewpoint can, at best, only provide range data to approximately half of the surfaces of a given scene, since, on average half the surfaces face away from the instrument. For complex scenes even two viewpoints cannot provide a complete three-dimensional data set since surface shape concavities and object visual juxtaposition frustrate this hope. In our system six rangefinders are used in an effort to extract a very complete three-dimensional surface description of objects in the scene to be analysed.

The use of multiple rangefinders introduces the complexity of combining their data into one consistent coordinate system. This fusion of multiple data sets into one requires transformations from many local coordinate systems to a global one. This is one essential methodology focused upon in this paper. The other is the semantic-free process of initial scene segmentation.

Besl and McKay [3] developed an algorithm known as iterative closest point (ICP) for determining the transformation that registers two data sets. It minimises a mean square distance metric between points in the first view and the corresponding closest points in the second view. No point-to-point correspondence is required. Unfortunately, the algorithm will only converge to the nearest local minimum so a good initial transformation must be specified. Zhang [4] extends the basic ICP approach. A maximum tolerance for the distance between points as well as an orientation consistency is specified. Point pairs that fail to meet these criteria are excluded. Furthermore, statistics of all the point-to-point distances at each iteration are analysed and used to discard additional points. These enhancements make the method robust to statistical outliers and occlusion.

Chen and Medioni [5] also improved the ICP technique by using a better distance metric between surfaces. They minimise the distance between points from the first view and tangent planes at intersected points in the second view. This requires the calculation of surface normals at each point. In addition, rather than using all points in the first view they select only a subset of control points from smooth regions on the surface. Bergevin et al. [6] extended the method even further by registering multiple views simultaneously rather than sequentially. This results in an equal distribution of registration errors.

A completely different and interesting approach is that of the extended Gaussian image (EGI) developed by Horn [7]. The surface normals of all points on an object are mapped onto a Gaussian sphere. This approach is translation invariant and the registration of two views only involves determining the rotation between two EGI's. This only works for convex objects, and cannot accommodate scaling or occlusion. In Delingette et al. [8] a variation to the EGI called simplex angle image (SAI) is used where curvature measures rather than normals are used. In addition, the adjacency relationships between points on the object are maintained. It is capable of accommodating concave objects and occlusion.

Various hardware configurations have been used to accomplish the multiple view requirement. Higuchi et al. [9] utilised an indexing table to rotate the scene relative to a stationary range finder. Unfortunately, this fails to completely represent a scene. Chen and Medioni [5] also use an indexing table but obtained top and bottom views of the scene by requiring the user to manually change the orientation of the object. Unfortunately, this approach cannot be used for scenes consisting of multiple objects and the user is required to estimate three rotation angles for the manual orientation change. An obvious solution is to use multiple range finders positioned at suitable viewpoints so that all parts of the scene are visible.

Once a complete set of raw data has been acquired, higher level processing can be used to analyse the scene. Analysis may include object recognition, determining the juxtaposition between objects in a scene, grip site determination, and manipulator path planning. This involves using some sort of higher level description that is derived from the raw data.

2. System Layout

The range finders used in this research were developed in the Department of Electrical and Computer Systems Engineering at Monash University almost a decade ago. They consist of a monochrome CCD camera and a projector capable of illuminating the scene with a series of stripes. The maximum resolution of the range finder is 8192 sample points, although typically the number of points obtained is less than half of this.

Range finders are mounted onto a custom built chassis in six different (fixed) viewing positions as shown in Figure 1. There are four side views, a top view, and a bottom view. This results in a very complete scene representation, unlike those obtained in most other experiments. A video cross bar is used to multiplex the six video signals into a single frame grabber. Only a single range finder is used at any one time. All other projector lenses are covered to avoid interference from the emitted light. This is under complete computer control via a set of servo motors.

Objects in the scene are placed onto a metallic mesh located at the centre of the rig. Surprisingly the mesh does not interfere with the operation of the bottom range finder. The rig is completely shielded from external light sources when in operation.

An attempt at obtaining colour information for each sampled point is also being undertaken by mounting a colour wheel to the top of each camera. The wheels are controlled by servo motors. Three separate images are obtained using a red, green and blue filter, which are later combined to form a full colour image. Since range data is extracted from image data anyway it is trivially easy to register the colour and range information. Colour information is useful for scene segmentation.

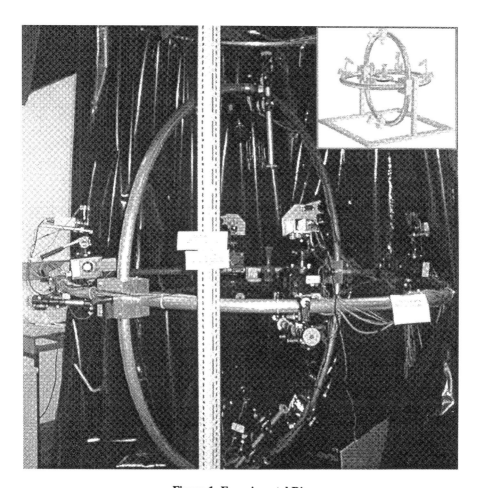

Figure 1: Experimental Rig

Software for acquiring the range data has been already developed by the department [2] and resides on a 486 based PC. Software for automating the acquisition of multiple data sets, registration and processing of the raw data is being written in Borland Delphi on a Pentium based PC. The two computers communicate with each other via an Ethernet network link.

3. View Registration

Each of the six sensor views describing the scene consists of a set of points expressed in the coordinate frame of the sensor. Each data set is completely independent. By combining the six sets of data together a substantially more complete surface representation is attained. This is accomplished by determining the affine transformations that transform the points in each data set into a new set of points. By combining these new sets together a representation containing all six sensor views in one common frame of reference is obtained.

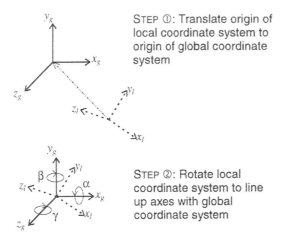

STEP ①: Translate origin of local coordinate system to origin of global coordinate system

STEP ②: Rotate local coordinate system to line up axes with global coordinate system

Figure 2: Transforming from local to global coordinate system

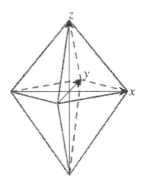

Figure 3: Diamond Model

The affine transformations can be divided up into two independent components – translation followed by rotation. Translation aligns the origins of the two coordinate systems. It consists of three parameters t_x, t_y and t_z, which represent translation along the x-, y- and z-axes respectively. Rotation aligns the principal axes of the two coordinate systems. It consists of three parameters α, β and γ, which represent rotation about the x-, y- and z-axes respectively. In total, six degrees of freedom must be rigidly determined. This is illustrated in Figure 2.

The approach taken in this research was to use a symmetrical diamond shaped registration frame of known geometric properties (Figure 3). The diamond consists of eight faces and is positioned such that each sensor views exactly four faces. The centre of the diamond is designated as the origin of the global coordinate system. The range data from each view is then segmented into four data sets, each representing one face. A plane is fitted to each face using the method of total least squares regression. The normal vector of each face can be easily determined from the equation of the plane. The calculation of normal vectors is extremely accurate due to the large number of points used in the plane fitting. The intersection of the planes in each view yields the position of a vertex. Since the dimensions of the diamond are known, the position of its centre can also be determined.

A least squares minimisation approach is used to align the four sensed normal vectors with those of the model after the translation component has been determined. Powell's method is used which does not require derivatives to be calculated. Brent's method is incorporated as the one-dimensional minimisation sub-algorithm. Storage is of order N^2. Convergence to the minimum typically takes around six iterations. Although it has not been formally proven, experiments have shown that the nature of the problem to be solved is not susceptible to local minima. Consequently, the initial conditions used are not important. Computational efficiency arises from the fact that only four features are used in the minimisation as opposed to hundreds or even thousands in ICP based approaches.

4. Low Level Processing

Once the raw data has been acquired, processing can begin. The raw data in its most basic form is a set of triplets (x, y, z) in three-dimensional Cartesian space, one set for each viewpoint. Each data point has an additional attribute of colour (r, g, b). Firstly, statistical outliers are removed. A point is denoted an outlier if its position in three-dimensional Cartesian space is greater than some threshold distance from the origin. Statistical outliers are typically caused by background objects (e.g. chassis).

The surface normals (n_x, n_y, n_z) at each point are then computed. This step makes use of the regular grid of sampled points in the two-dimensional images acquired with the camera. For each point, vectors are formed with its neighbouring points. A neighbouring point is defined as edge-adjacent and corner-adjacent points. The cross products of these vectors are used to compute the normals of each triangular polygonal region. The median of these sets of normals is then designated as the normal for the point. This method is very computationally efficient, however, at object edges the technique breaks down. Points belonging to another face cannot be used in the normal calculations. Consequently, a method for deciding if a neighbouring point should be included in a normal calculation based on normal vector prediction has been used.

Each point is effectively represented by a nine component vector $(x, y, z, r, g, b, n_x, n_y, n_z)$. Clustering in this nine dimensional space can produce meaningful segmentations. This provides a very rich set of semantic free partitions upon which to base scene segmentation components. If semantic binding is delayed until the above type of generalised information is nicely structured, the whole scene analysis task may well be more robust and simpler as well.

The clustering method used is shared nearest neighbour clustering. It is a simple but effective approach. The Euclidean distance from each data point to every other data point is first computed. Lists of neighbouring data points ordered by distance are then assigned to each data point. Two points are considered to belong to the same cluster if they share at least some threshold number of neighbouring points. This method is capable of handling clusters of varying density, although this does not really occur in the raw data. Parameters can be adjusted to generate various grouping perspectives. The reader is referred to the paper by Jarvis [10] for a detailed description of this algorithm. A data structure based on K-D trees has been used for computing the k-nearest neighbours, resulting in a computational efficiency of order $N\log N$.

In any case, models of objects must be used at some stage in the analysis if object recognition is to take place. When this a priori information is introduced, however, is what sets different approaches apart. There are two different approaches. The top-down approach is model driven. The bottom-up approach is data driven. Higher level semantic-free descriptions are used and matching against known models takes place very late in the recognition process. The philosophy behind this research is to acquire a very rich set of raw data without using any a priori knowledge and to delay using model information until it is absolutely necessary. This strategy is expected to provide partially general and highly robust results. This idea was already suggested by Jarvis [11].

5. Preliminary Results

Current results were obtained using a cardboard version of the diamond registration frame (Figure 4). Typical registration error is approximately 2-3mm. A high quality precision-made aluminium version of the registration frame will be constructed in the future, which should yield significantly better results.

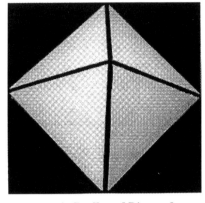

Figures 5 and 6 show some sample registrations between two views obtained so far. Figure 7 shows a different object to which clustering has been applied to segment the points into surfaces. In Figure 7c different symbols have been used to distinguish

Figure 4: Cardboard Diamond

between the various clusters found. The points on the four faces of the object have clearly been grouped together.

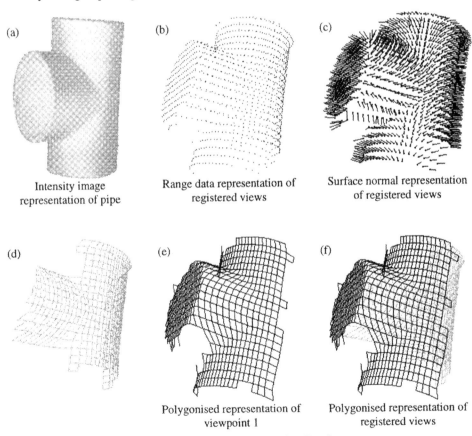

Figure 5: Preliminary Registration Results

(a)

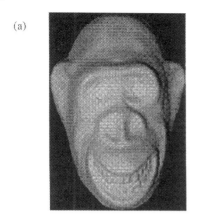

(b)

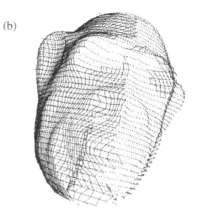

Intensity image representation of a mask

Two registered views of mask

(c)

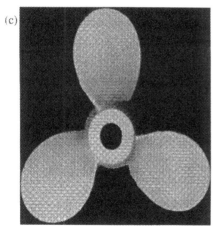

(d)

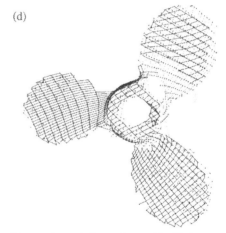

Intensity image representation
of a propeller blade

Two registered views of propeller blade

Figure 6: More Sample Merged Views

(a)

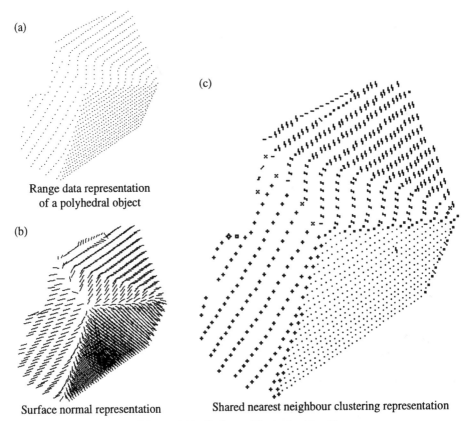

Range data representation
of a polyhedral object

(b)

(c)

Surface normal representation   Shared nearest neighbour clustering representation

Figure 7: Preliminary Clustering Results

6. Conclusions

The use of multiple range finders for acquiring a complete three-dimensional representation of a scene combined with colour data yields a very rich of set of raw data. The low level processing techniques implemented are completely non-domain specific. The more that can be done without domain specific knowledge, the more general the methodology. Moreover, the approach taken is an excellent basis for further higher level processing, although it's implementation will be far from trivial.

This approach is deliberately the antithesis of the trendier 'active' vision approach which seeks to combine intelligent selective exploration with data acquisition. Active vision uses a repeated cycle of analysis followed by action to arrive at conclusions. Unless significant care is taken, a single error in the chain of decisions of the 'active' approach can lead to an irrecoverable breakdown of correct analysis, thus rendering this procedure fragile outside strictly defined domains. Our approach, we expect, will avoid fragility by delaying the binding of domain specific information and providing very rich semantic-free structural descriptions before that binding is activated.

The registration method described for fusing the different views has certain beneficial advantages. It is extremely computationally efficient and does not require an initial transformation to be specified. Registering two views takes less than one second. Using a precision made registration frame should result in even better accuracy. Unlike some other systems, once the transformations between views have been determined, they need not be recomputed as the scene changes. Scenes containing multiple free-form objects can later be used. This approach could easily be adapted to other range finder configurations. Any geometric object which allows each range finder to sense at least three non-parallel faces is all that's required.

The procedure for determining a normal vector at each data point is also extremely efficient. The use of Delaunay triangulations may result in more accurate results but due to the large number of points possible from fusing six views together it is not computationally viable. Methods of further improving the current approach are being investigated. Surface curvatures have not been calculated because the noise inherent in the range data would produce erroneous results.

References

[1] R. A. Jarvis, "Range sensing for computer vision," in *Three-Dimensional Object Recognition Systems*, Elsevier Science, 1993, pp. 17-56

[2] B. Alexander, "High accuracy non-contact three dimensional shape measurement," PhD Thesis, Monash Univeristy Department of Electrical and Computer Systems Engineering, 1989

[3] P. J. Besel and N. D. McKay, "A method for registration of 3-D shapes," *IEEE Transactions on Pattern Analysis and Machine Intelligence*, vol. 14, no. 2, 1992, pp. 239-25

[4] Z. Zhang, "Iterative point matching for registration of free-form curves and surfaces," *International Journal of Computer Vision*, Vol. 13, no. 2, 1994, pp. 119-152

[5] Y. Chen and G. Medioni, "Object modelling by registration of multiple range images," *Image and Vision Computing*, vol. 10, no. 3, 1992, pp. 145-155

[6] R. Bergevin, M. Soucy, and H. Gagnon, "Towards a general multi-view registration technique," *IEEE Transactions on Pattern Analysis and Machine Intelligence*, vol. 18, no. 5, 1996, pp. 540-547

[7] B. K. P. Horn, "Extended Gaussian Images," *Proceedings of the IEEE*, vol. 72, no. 12, 1984, pp. 1671-1686

[8] H. Delingette, M. Hebert, and K. Ikeuchi, "A spherical representation for the recognition of curved objects," *Proceedings Fourth International Conference on Computer Vision*, 1993, pp. 102-112

[9] K. Higuchi, M. Hebert, and K. Ikeuchi, "Building 3-D models from unregistered range images," *Graphical Models and Image Processing*, vol. 57, no. 4, 1995, pp. 315-333

[10] R. A. Jarvis and E. A. Patrick, "Clustering using a similarity measure based on shared near neighbours," *IEEE Transactions on Computers*, vol. 22, no. 11, 1973, pp. 1025-1034

[11] R. A. Jarvis, "3D shape and surface colour sensor fusion for robot vision," *Robotica*, vol. 10, 1992, pp. 389-396

Sensor-Based Robotic Automation of Mushroom Farming - Preliminary Considerations

Ray Jarvis
Intelligent Robotics Research centre
Monash University
Wellington Road, Clayton, Victoria 3168 Australia
e-mail: Ray.Jarvis@eng.monash.edu.au

0. Abstract

This paper explores an approach to robotic automation of mushroom farming, particularly the harvesting process, which involves the application of image processing, 3D range finding and robotic manipulation to realise a system which could make a major contribution to a rapidly growing Australian industry. The main emphasis is on the application of Hough Transform methodology to the selection of appropriate mushrooms to harvest at any one inspection of the crop and the combination of this analysis and that involving range finding and robotic manipulation in actualising the selective harvesting process. Other aspects of automation of the whole mushroom farming process are also described.

1. Introduction

In recent times there has been increasing interest in realising the potential of sensor, computer, artificial intelligence and robotic technology in automating tasks in environments which, of their nature, are much less structured than those in which traditional manufacturing takes place. As an example, many of the basic machine vision methodologies developed over the last two decades have reached maturity and can provide robust solutions to segmentation, recognition and robotic grip site determinations under conditions of variable lighting, position, orientation and clutter. Combined with robotics technology, such capabilities can readily be applied to many automation tasks where the accommodation of variability is critical.

One such unstructured or semi-structured domain is that of horticulture, particularly the automation of hot-house production, grafting and spraying. By combining manipulation and mobility an autonomous robot system could relieve the tedium of repetitive operations, leaving exceptions and higher level management tasks to humans. The essential capabilities of such robotic systems are reliable navigation, dextrous manipulation and customisation to accommodate the particular application domain.

These capabilities are particularly relevant in supporting the automation of mushroom growing and harvesting. By applying methods which are already well understood through extensive experimentation involving the design, construction and testing of working robotic systems, reasonable success in extensively automating mushroom farming could be demonstrated within three years with reasonable funding. Working under the close supervision of accomplished researchers at Monash University, a small number of appropriate technical assistants could bring such a plan to reality. What is being proposed here is not just academic research but the practical application of research know-how accumulated over a considerable number of years.

To put this project in its industrial context [1], the following points are worth noting:

(a) Mushrooms are currently Australia's third most valuable vegetable crop after potatoes and tomatoes.

(b) Most local production is consumed in the domestic market as fresh mushrooms, only a small proportion of the total yield being processed.

(c) Imported mushrooms have reduced significantly in percentage of the domestic market over recent years to approximately 20%.

(d) Domestic mushroom production has increased at an annual rate of 10% for the last twenty years.

(e) Mushrooms are farmed commercially in enclosed, atmosphere controlled environments with conditions tuned to various stages of the growth cycle. All year production is thus possible with farm location of irrelevance except for physical proximity to the market and sources of peat moss, labour etc.

(f) Mushroom crop cycles of approximately 40 days are the norm, with actual picking taking up about 10 days of this cycle.

(g) Harvesting is currently carried out manually by teams of trained pickers. Picking is done with a small twist of the mushroom before lifting it out of its bed, preferably with the stem intact and removal of the minimal amount of soil.

(h) Wastes from other primary industries make up the compost material in which mushrooms are grown and the wastes from mushroom production are ideal as potting mix and garden mulch.

(i) Hygiene is critical with harvest workers wearing gloves, hairnets and clean clothing.

(j) A mushroom should be picked just before it opens under the cap since after this stage spore which drop can be picked up by a draft and can be the mechanism by which disease spreads.

(k) The stem is cut with the stubs collected (not left in bed); these can be used for animal food.

(l) In addition to temperature and humidity controlled stages, mushroom beds also require a strict watering regime.

(m) The commercial shelf life of mushrooms is approximately 4 days at room temperature.

(n) Crop yield by weight of the mulch material is usually between 25 to 30%.

Not all the above observations have equal impact on designing a system to automate the whole mushroom farming process.

The following sections will deal with the overall transport through stages of the mushroom farming cycle, the automation of picking requirements and the Hough Transform/range finding aspects. Then follows a preliminary attempt to define an overall automation strategy, discussion and concluding remarks.

2. Transport through Stages of Farming

Whilst there are variations of detail, the current practice used in commercial mushroom farming consists of multiple stages defined in terms of environmental conditions which in turn are associated with transportation to different locations where those conditions are controlled. This staging structure can be thought of as an assembly line in which considerable human resources are used at every stage, including transport, watering, picking etc. It would appear that many of these stages could be made more efficient through the costly redesign of the whole farming environment. For example, growing trays could be carried on trolleys through a linear sequence of appropriately controlled environments in various sheds on rails instead of using fork-lift trucks to keep moving stacks of growing trays to various locations as required. Also, watering could be carried out with distributed sprinkler systems or a mobile robotic watering station. Whilst it may be difficult to justify the expense of redesigning sheds and transport systems it seems less difficult to justify the automation of the actual harvesting phase which last for approximately 25% of the 40 days production cycle, since this is the most human resource intensive stage and one which is especially tedious and exacting to carry out.

3. Hough Transform Based Mushroom Selection for Harvesting

The most popular variety of mushroom used domestically in an unprocessed form is usually firm, smooth and uniformly shaped at picking. This means that viewed from above as a creamy white against the conventional dark mulch they are grown in, one observes a set of circulerly shaped buttons of various sizes, with some partially obscured by others, well contrasted against the background.

The Hough Transform [2], initially applied to the discovery of colinearity in images and easily extended to other geometric forms and further generalised to non-geometric forms [3], is an almost ideal methodology for the discovery of mushrooms ready to pick within size limit specifications, their centres being fairly precisely located. Partial obscurence does not frustrate this approach although some distortions of perceived size and location result.

In the original slope/intercept formulation of the Hough Transform for colinearity detection, the unboundedness of the infinite slope of a vertical line renders this form impractical. In the polar form [4] this ill-posedness is neatly side stepped.

The Hough Transform formulation for circle detection is straightforward. However, for both line and circle structure detection, if only the location of contributing image points are available, the computational cost of accumulating evidence for deciding relevant outcomes is very high and is proportional to the resolution raised to the power of the number of parameters being extracted times the number of points in the image being analysed. For example, if a one in one hundred resolution is required for circle detection with respect to radius and centre location, some 1,000,000 accumulation cells are required; if 10,000 points in an image are being processed, some 10^{10} vote allocations are required. Further processing is, of course, required to scan the evidence once it has been accumulated and to decide upon its adequacy in indicating the presence and parameters of the forms being sought.

A circle can be parametized by:

$$(x-a)^2 + (y-b)^2 = r^2, \text{ with centre at a,b and of radius, r.}$$

For each (x,y) point in the image a conic surface defined by treating the individual (x,y) values as constants in the above equation needs be sampled at a set of quantised a,b,r values in three space. High accumulations of samples in specified cells in quantised a x b x r space indicate the occurrence of a circle with corresponding centre location and radius.

Fortunately, if the local gradient of elements of the sought for form can be extracted from the image, the processing requirements can be significantly reduced [5].

If the gradient angle $\emptyset$ is known, the following form can be analysed instead:

$a = x - r \operatorname{Sin} \emptyset$
$b = y + r \operatorname{Cos} \emptyset$
where $dy/dx = \tan \emptyset$

For high contrast figures against a background, the required gradient can be extracted using local image mask operators.

A more intuitively simple way of considering the search for the centre of a circle is to think of each fragment of its outline providing a tangent line. A line perpendicular to this tangent line would go through the centre of the potential circle that edge fragment might belong to. A high number of intersections of these perpendicular lines at a given point provides evidence of a circle centre at that point but does not distinguish between contributions from fragments of different concentric circles. Thus, in constructing the traces of these perpendicular lines through quantised centre location space, the distance from the contributing fragment must also be kept (in quantised form). In other words, perpendicular line traces leave accumulative votes in quantised a,b and r space.

In the case of looking for mushrooms of a specified range of sizes (ready for picking) one need only generate the tangent perpendicular line traces for the corresponding range of distances away from the edge fragments they represent.

The generation of the edge gradient information can be easily extracted using simple edge finding masks when he contrast is high and the circle edge smooth. In our work, a Sobel operator [6] was used to provide both edge gradient magnitude and direction. The gradient magnitude was thresholded interactively to remove edge fragment noise. However, once a particular threshold is selected, the same value works quite well over other images obtained with the same lighting conditions.

The mushroom detector system we have developed allows for interactively adjusting parameters such as Sobel gradient magnitude threshold, image sampling quantisation and radius range as well as Hough accumulator evidence thresholds. We have been pleased to find that, within a few minutes, an operation can select an appropriate set of settings to produce very reliable results for whatever range of sizes of mushrooms are to be selected for harvesting.

Figure 1(a) shows a box of mushrooms at various stages of growth. Figure 1(b) shows the Sobel/Hough/Gradient selection of large and medium sized mushrooms as may be suitable for picking. The degree of obscurance is very high in this example but the system has, nevertheless, done a reasonable job of extraction, although some flaws may be observed.

However, for robotically automating the picking process, the centre locations of appropriate sized mushrooms are not enough to provide the necessary details for manipulation in all situations.

4. Range Finding from Above

It may be the case that, in addition to the centre location of selected mushrooms, as provided by the calculations described in Section 3, above, the obscurance relationship must be resolved using other sensors. A moments consideration of the growing situation of live mushrooms provides an easy solution to most of the uncertainties which may arise in this regard. In nearly every case the larger mushrooms spread their caps over the smaller ones since they are at a more mature stage of growth, having usually started earlier. Thus, if the largest mushrooms are harvested first, they are not likely to disturb the small ones when they are being pulled out, provided that the end effector of the robot manipulator can vacuum pick on the surface of the cap of each mushroom. A twist and a smooth, slow pull may be all that is required to meet the requirements of (g) in Section 1.

There could be some exceptions however. There is also the problem of knowing how much to lower the 'hand' of a robot to attach a vacuum end effector. One approach would be to continuously measure the vacuum and to stop the lowering process once contact is made as indicated by a sudden change of vacuum pressure. Another approach is to use a range finder pointing down on the growing bed to provide the height information directly, but this may be an overkill approach. Nevertheless, we have experimented with this idea in mind to test its feasibility.

The overall experimental set-up is shown in Figure 2. with both the camera used for image capture and an active binary coded stereopsis stripe light range finder pointing down on a bed of mushrooms. Figure 3 shows a side view of range data collected from above where mushroom height is clearly indicated.

It is thus fairly clear that the combination of Hough Transform based location detection and range finder height detection could provide all the necessary information for robotic mushroom harvesting.

5. Overall Mushroom Farming Automation Strategy

In this section a first try at suggesting an overall strategy for automating mushroom forming is described. This strategy, of course, includes the detection and picking methods given in the previous section. Figure 4 shows the overall scheme. Trays of mulch move on a closed track which passes through the various necessary stages of processing, including mulch packing, spore 'seeding', various humidity/temperature/watering stages and harvesting. Sheds are each sealed off from the others. The timing requirements for each stage must be carefully included in the batch transport strategy. For any one batch, a ten day period for harvesting must be included. In the harvesting shed a robot arm with a vacuum picking end effector moves up and down on its own tracks pulling two containers, one for the mushrooms and one for the stubs. The range finder/video camera is hung over the tray being harvested and moves with the robot station. For each location of the robot harvesting station the Hough Transform based selection plus the range finder height detection procedure is carried out and mushrooms are picked, each having its stub cut off when the robot delivers it to a stub cutter; the remaining mushroom cap and stem are gently packed in the second container. The robot mushroom harvesting station moves up and down the rows of growing mushrooms during the entire ten day harvesting periods. Full containers of stubs and mushrooms are removed at appropriate intervals. The notional two or three passes over the batch during the 10 day harvesting period can be abandoned since the robot system can be vigilant night and day over its crop and collect 'ready' mushrooms in multiple sweeps over the batch. Even the idea of a 'batch' can be relaxed to some extent since a more continuous flow of processing may have advantages.

Of course, there are many other practical considerations to deal with and these are best addressed over detailed consultation with commercial mushroom growers. Aspects other than harvesting, for example, watering, could also be easily automated robotically.

6. Discussion and Conclusions

The cost of reconfiguring an assembly line based production site for mushroom farming may be justified if on-going production costs can be considerably reduced by the introduction of the appropriate level of robotic automation. If the higher quality of disease control is possible with the use of a robotic harvester system is also included in the assessment of feasibility, it may be that a commercially viable system could be developed along the lines suggested in this paper.

It would be naive not to expect that there are many more factors to be considered than are covered here, but this paper represents only a first look at automating mushroom farming. Subsequent refinements will certainly be required. An early commitment to combine automation with the scaling up of production could put Australia in an excellent marketting position in relation to export potential, since we currently enjoy an internationally recognised reputation as a supplier of clean, uncontaminated and healthy foods.

In conclusion, this paper has presented a first look at the robotic automation of mushroom farming, having concentrated particularly on the harvesting process and the application of computer vision methodology to support it. Initial experimental results have been very encouraging. A fuller investigation is almost certainly justified.

7. Bibliography

1. Australian Mushroom Growers Association, The Mushroom Industry in Australia, July 1994 (7 pages).

2. Hough, P.V.C. Method and means for recognising complex patterns. U.S. Patent 3, 069, 654, Dec. 18, 1962.

3. Ballard, D.H. and Brown, C.M., Computer Vision, Prentice Hall Inc. 1982, page 128.

4. Duda, R.O. and Hart, P.E., Use of the Hough Transform To Detect Lines and Curves in Pictures, Comms. of the A.C.M., Jan 1972, Vol.15, No.1, pp. 11-15.

5. Ballard, D.H. and Brown, C.M., Computer Vision, Prentice Hall Inc. 1982, page 124.

6. Pratt, W.K., Digital Image Processing, John Wiley and Sons, 1978, page 487.

Figure 1(a)   Box of Mushrooms

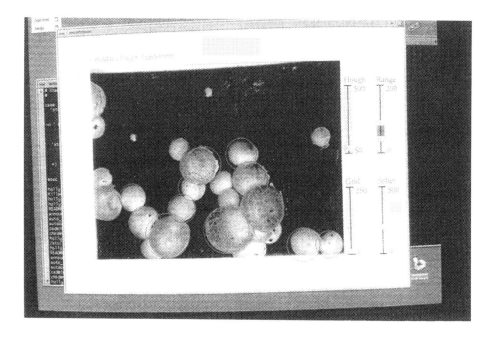

Figure 1(b)   Selected Large and Medium Sized Mushrooms

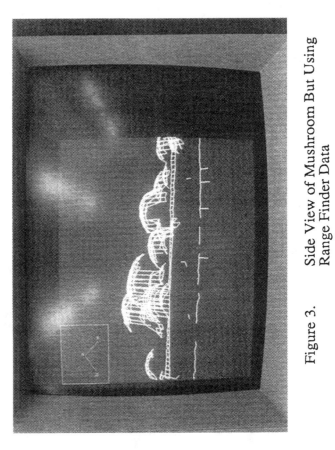

Figure 3. Side View of Mushroom But Using Range Finder Data

Figure 2 Mushroom Analysis Experimental Set-up

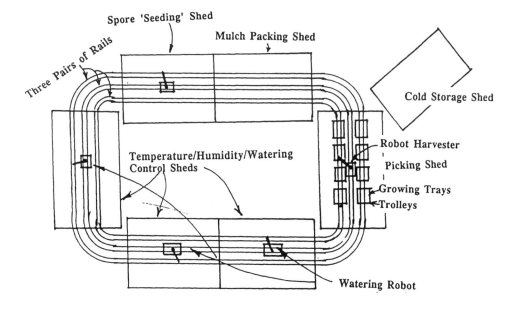

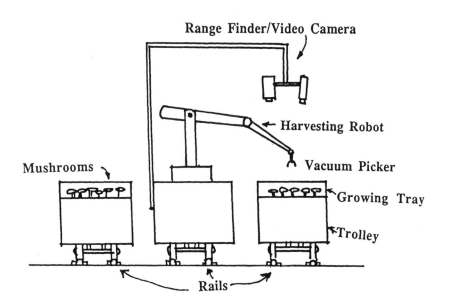

Figure 4   Mushroom Farming Automation Plan

Creating Adroit Mechanisms by Using Large Numbers of Simple Homogeneous Structures

R. Andrew Russell
Intelligent Robotics Research Centre
Department of Electrical and Computer Systems Engineering
Monash University, Clayton, VIC 3168
AUSTRALIA

Abstract. The project described in this paper investigates the idea that, in some circumstances, the functions of a complex mechanism can be performed by a large number of simpler units. There are example in nature that support this approach. In the case of locomotion this is seen in the starfish that walks on a large number of tube feet. The structure and control of starfish feet are both simpler than would be the case if the starfish had a small number of more complex legs. There are similar examples in the case of manipulation. Cilia, which line the bronchial passages, work together to transport foreign particles out of the lungs. Individual cilia are simple and their great numbers provide reliability through redundancy. In this paper the idea of creating a versatile system from many elementary units is developed in the context of a multi fingered gripper. The prototype gripper has eight simple, one degree-of-freedom fingers. It is found that this gripper provides excellent grasp stability for a wide range of object shapes and is able to translate, rotate and measure the surface profile of gripped objects. This paper outlines the gripper design together with algorithms for performing grasping, repositioning and object recognition. Experimental results are also presented which illustrate the performance of the gripper.

1 Introduction

There are many examples in nature where an organism performs a relatively complicated task using a large number of simple appendages. In the case of locomotion this is often seen in relatively primitive creatures. Starfish are equipped with many simple tube-like feet. These allow the starfish to creep in any direction, cling to steep surfaces and force open molluscs so that they can be eaten [1]. The outer surface of microscopic protozoa are covered with motile hairs or cilia. By beating the cilia in a coordinated manner a protozoa can swim towards food and swim away from obstacles or other undesirable stimuli [2]. On land, centipedes and millipedes employ many pairs of quite rudimentary legs to carry their long thin bodies [1].

Manipulation is also possible based on the same principle of employing large numbers of elementary units. Vast numbers of cilia move sheets of mucus to remove particles that have found their way into the lungs [3].

In this paper the idea of creating a versatile system from many simple units is developed in the context of a robotic gripper. A number of advanced robotic grippers have been developed and tested. Notable examples are the Stanford/JPL [4], Utah/MIT [5] and Hitachi [6] dexterous robot hands. These and many other examples of robotic gripper design are very anthropomorphic in form, incorporating complex 3 and 4 degrees-of-freedom serial link fingers. By contrast the prototype gripper developed in this project has eight simple 1 degree-of-freedom fingers. It has been found that this gripper provides good grasp stability for a wide range of object shapes and is able to translate, rotate and measure the surface profile of gripped objects. By further increasing the number of fingers it is hoped to extend this essentially planar gripper to function in three dimensions.

An important area of application for this idea is considered to be in the design of micromechanisms. Using photolithography microscopic mechanical devices can be produced in large numbers. However, because of the size of the mechanisms locating faults and executing repairs will prove to be very difficult. The easy fabrication of simple parts and natural redundancy of multiple units makes this approach ideal for the development of micromechanical systems.

2 OctoGripper construction

Gripper construction is based around a 1 degree-of-freedom finger unit. Each unit consists of a finger positioned by a single rotary actuator. The fingertip is located on a curved arm 42mm from the centre of rotation of the actuator. In the prototype gripper the finger has a range of movement from a radius of 6mm to a radius of 26mm from the centre of the gripper. The fingertips are cylindrical with a diameter of 4mm and length of 7mm. Fingers can move from fully open to fully closed in less than 0.1 second and exert a maximum gripping force of 13.5 Newtons. As a starting point it was decided to build a prototype gripper incorporating eight finger units. Figure 1 illustrates the layout of the finger units in this 'OctoGripper'.

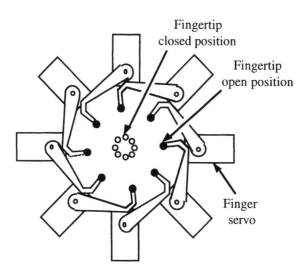

Figure 1 The structure of the OctoGripper.

A microcontroller sets the required fingertip position for each finger unit and measures the actual finger positions. Low level commands are transferred to the microcontroller from a supervisory computer (a Macintosh IIci personal computer) over an RS232 serial link. These commands move all fingers to their fully open position, move all fingers to their fully closed position, disable the servo motors, enable servo motors, read current finger positions and move each finger to an individually specified position.

3 Manipulation

All manipulation operations are coordinated by the supervisory computer. In its present form this computer provides a user interface for monitoring the operation of the gripper and formulates sequences of commands for the gripper system to undertake the higher level tasks of gripping, translating, rotating and recognising a grasped object. The user interface includes the gripper status display shown in figure 2.

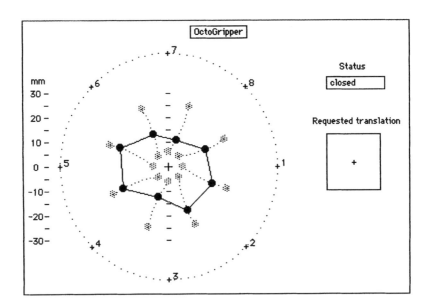

Figure 2   OctoGripper status while grasping a rectangular block.

4 Grasping

The servos actuating the gripper fingers are position controlled with a proportional control law. If the fingers are forced away form their target position the servos act like a spring generating a restoring force proportional to distance from the target. In order to grasp an object the target positions of the fingertips are positioned inside the grasped object.

To perform a 'gentle' grasp of an unknown object the finger target positions are stepped in towards the centre of the gripper. Stepping continues until each finger makes contact with the object and the desired error (equivalent to grasping force) has been established or the servos reach the limit of their travel. The alternative fast grasp commands the fingers to their centre position. This may generate large gripping forces and, depending on the object shape and position, tend to displace the object. As more fingers hold an object the grasp becomes more resistant to forces tending to dislodge the object. Experimental results supporting this conclusion are shown in figure 3. Starting with an eight fingered grasp, fingers were removed in the order shown on the accompanying diagram. In each case a torque was applied to the grasped object until it rotated by one degree. Removing the first two fingers had relatively little effect because they lay on the axis of rotation. Fingers 3 to 6 were located away form the axis of rotation and contributed a similar amount to the stability of the grasp. These results indicate that increasing the number of fingers in contact with a grasped object will reduce the effect of external forces tending to displace the object.

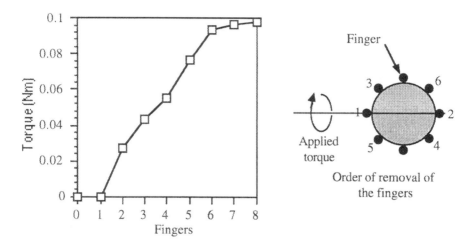

Figure 3   **The torque required to rotate a grasped 25mm diameter cylinder 1° as the number of fingers is reduced.**

5   Translation

The fingers of the OctoGripper have only one degree of freedom. Therefore, in general, the fingertips must slide over the surface of a grasped object in order for the object to move relative to the gripper. Translation is achieved by moving the fingers to the position they would have to adopt to grasp the object in its new location. Effectively the fingers form a cavity the same shape as the object . This cavity is moved to a new location and the grasped object follows. The process of translation is illustrated in figure 4. A desired translation is specified in polar coordinates with origin at the centre of the gripper. Thus the magnitude of the translation r in millimetres and the angle θ in degrees are specified. To perform a translation the grasped object is assumed to be polygonal with eight vertices located at each finger tip as shown in figure 5. With reference to the fingertip at point $p1$ (figure 6), as the grasped object is repositioned the fingertip will either slide onto face l_{01} or face l_{12}.

> if $\phi p1 < \theta$ then the fingertip will slide on face l_{12},
> if $\phi p1 > \theta$ then the fingertip will slide on face l_{01}, and
> if $\phi p1 = \theta$ then the fingertip will not slide at all.

Having decided which edge or point will define the new position of the fingertip, that edge or point is translated distance r in direction θ to give the new location of the fingertip. For fingertip 1 the resulting incremental movement of the fingertip Δ_1 is given by:

$$\Delta_1 = r \frac{\sin(\psi_{12} - \theta)}{\sin(180 + \phi_1 - \psi_{12})} \tag{1}$$

New positions are calculated for each fingertip and these are then adjusted to give the required gripping force. In this analysis the circular motion of the fingertip has been approximated by a straight line segment.

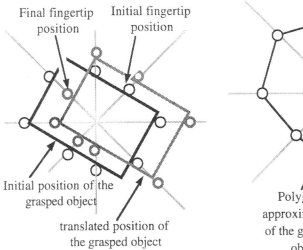

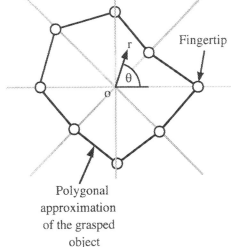

Figure 4   Fingertip movements used to translate a grasped object.

Figure 5   Polygonal approximation to a grasped object.

When the fingers are commanded to their new positions the object does not move precisely to its required location. The error is the result of friction between the fingertips and grasped object and the approximate object model used in the calculations. Translational accuracy is greatly improved by a process of releasing and regrasping with each finger in turn. This procedure is repeated several times and helps to reduce tangential forces acting on the fingertips due to sliding in the presence of friction.

Figure 7 shows movement of the centre of a rectangular block as the gripper is commanded to translate the block from 0mm to 6mm in steps of one millimetre in the x-direction. At a requested translation of 6mm the position error increases rapidly due to the limitations of the polygonal model of the grasped object. This increase in the position error could be alleviated by increasing the number of fingers and hence obtaining a more precise model of the grasped object. Alternatively the model of the grasped object could be updated after a translation of 4mm.

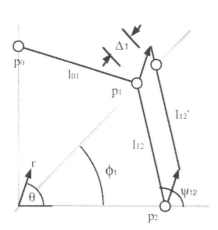

Figure 6   Adjusting the grasp during translation.

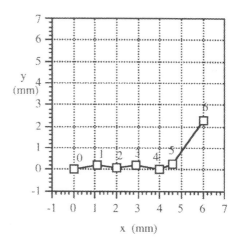

Figure 7   Translation of a rectangular block.

6   Rotation

In general the gripper is not able to rotate a grasped object particularly an object that has close to a circular cross-section. However, for many objects a variation on the translation procedure can be effective. Finger positions are calculated to grasp the object in its new orientation. To calculate the new finger positions it is convenient to assume that the fingers are rotated $-r$ and calculate where they fall on the object faces. For finger 1 the change in finger position d_1 to produce a rotation r is:

$$\delta_1 = r + \frac{r\sin(\phi_1 - \psi_{12})}{\sin(180 + \phi_1 - \psi_{12} - \rho)} \qquad (2)$$

Table 2 shows the actual rotations achieved for a range of requested rotations. In theory a pure rotation would not cause any translation of the block. In practice the centre of the block 'drifted' from its theoretical position and table 2 also shows the unintended translation of the block. As might be expected the undesired translation increases rapidly above a certain magnitude of requested rotation. Converting a large rotation into a number of smaller rotations might be effective in reducing undesirable translations.

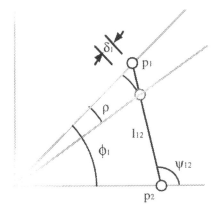

Requested rotation degrees	Actual rotation degrees	Object translation	
		x mm	y mm
0	0	0	0
5	4.4	0	1.0
7.5	6.5	0	1.0
10	8.0	0.3	1.5
12.5	9.0	0.1	2.1
15	10.0	0.3	2.0

Figure 8 Adjusting the grasp during rotation.

Table 2 Rotation of a rectangular block.

7 Object recognition

The OctoGripper measures the location of eight points on the surface of a gripped object. This information is sufficient to distinguish between objects that differ in their coarse features. With an increased number of fingers it would be possible to resolve finer detail.

An experiment was conducted to investigate the possibility of using the OctoGripper to recognise the shape of grasped objects. For this experiment a simple form of template matching was implemented. The five objects shown in figure 9 were chosen for their distinct cross-sections

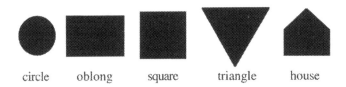

circle   oblong   square   triangle   house

Figure 9 The five shapes used in the object recognition experiment.

Templates were obtained by grasping each of the n objects $(n = 1..5)$ in turn and recording the distance t_{mn} from the centre of the gripper to each of the m fingertips $(m = 1..8)$. When an object is grasped by the gripper one point on the object cross-section will coincide with the centre of the gripper. In theory this point will be independent of angle of rotation between gripper and object. As the number of fingers in the gripper is increased so any variation due to rotation will decrease. A second set of data readings d_{mn} was taken with each object rotated to present a distinct cross-section to the gripper.

To find the correspondence between template readings and data readings a simple template matching procedure was implemented [7]. For the ith set of eight template readings t_{il} and the jth data readings dj_l (l = 1..7) an measure of how well they agree can be determined by calculating their mismatch s_{ij}. This is the sum of the absolute values of the difference between template and data value:

$$\sigma_{ij} = \sum_{l=0}^{7} \left| t_{il} - d_{jl} \right| \tag{3}$$

To allow for relative rotation of the gripped object between the template and data readings all eight relative rotations are considered and the lowest mismatch selected:

$$\sigma_{ij} = \mathbf{Min}_{k=0..7} \sum_{l=0}^{7} \left| t_{il} - d_{j((k+1)\bmod 8)} \right| \tag{4}$$

where

s_{mn}	= the mismatch between template m and data set n,
t_{mn}	= the mth element of template n, and
d_{mn}	= the mth element of data set n.

There are five sets of values in the library of templates and so each data set is compared with each template. The results of comparing all of the templates with all of the data sets is shown in table 3.

			second data set				
			circle	oblong	square	triangle	house
		circle	6.5	41.8	34.8	39.4	41.5
		oblong	39.3	17.4	24.8	25.0	23.4
first data set		square	34.5	21.9	13.2	17.3	14.6
		triangle	35.9	22.7	11.8	14.7	16.7
		house	29.4	21.8	9.9	16.9	14.4

Table 3   The mismatch between sets of finger positions recorded for the OctoGripper.

The results show that there is a relatively low mismatch when the two sets of data correspond to the same object. Therefore, recognition involves finding the template which has the lowest mismatch when compared with the unknown data. However, in one case the square has been identified as the house shape and the triangle also had a lower mismatch than the correct square shape. With the relatively coarse sampling of only eight points it is possible for this technique to provide an incorrect match.

The technique could be improved by rotating the template in smaller increments either by interpolating the template readings or by using a geometric model of the object. Adding more fingers to the gripper would provide more data points and reduce the possibility of confusion.

8   Conclusions

An eight fingered gripper has been constructed to investigate the idea that adroit mechanisms can be produced by using a large number of simple units. A photograph of the prototype gripper is shown in figure 10. In this photograph the OctoGripper is being used as a versatile fixturing device.

Figure 10   A photograph of the OctoGripper acting as a fixturing device during a disassembly operation.

A number of interesting mobile robots have been developed made up of many relatively simple identical segments [8]. These also seem to support the idea of creating complex devices using large numbers of simple homogeneous units.

Practical experiments have shown that the prototype eight fingered gripper can provide a stable grasp for a wide range of object shapes. The gripper can also translate grasped objects in an arbitrary direction and for certain objects impart a rotation as well. It seems that the grasping and manipulation capabilities of the gripper will all improve as the number of fingers increases.

A simple template matching technique has been implemented which shows promising results for object recognition. The current implementation did incorrectly classify one of the data readings. This is inevitable with such a small number of data points. However, there are opportunities for improving the performance by refining the template matching technique and by increasing the number of gripper fingers.

The OctoGripper has shown that a versatile gripping mechanism can be constructed using a number of simple finger units. This device can be used to provide a stable grasp of a wide range of object shapes, translate and rotate grasped objects and provide information to aid object recognition. These abilities of the gripper seem to improve with the number of fingers. This is seen to support the idea that versatile mechanisms can be created using a multiplicity of identical simple mechanisms.

In the future it is hoped to increase the number of fingers in the circle and to extend the current planar gripper to three dimensions by adding further circles of fingers.

Acknowledgments

The project presented in this paper was supported by grants from the Australian Research Council and the Harold Armstrong Memorial Fund.

References

1. Russell-Hunter, W,D., *A Life of Invertebrates*, Macmillan Publishing Co. Inc., New York, 1979.
2. *Cilia and Flagella*, M.A. Sleigh (Ed.), Academic Press, London, 1974.
3. Satir, P., 'How cilia move', *Scientific American,* Vol. 231, No. 4, October 1974, pp. 44-52.
4. Salisbury, J. K., and Craig, J. J. Articulated Hands: Force Control and Kinematic Issues, *The International Journal of Robotics Research,* **1**, 1 , 4-17, (1982).
5. Jacobsen, S. C., et al. Design of The Utah/MIT Dextrous Hand, *IEEE International Conference on Robotics and Automation,* San Francisco, California, 1520-32, (1986).
6. Nakano, Y., Fujie, M., and Hosada, Y., 'Hitachi's Robot Hand', *Robotics Age,* Vol.6, No.7, July 1984, pp. 18-20.
7. Jain, A.I. *Fundamentals of Digital Image Processing*, Prentice Hall, Eaglewood Cliffs, NJ, 1989.
8. Hirose, S., *Biologically Inspired Robots (Snake-like Locomotor and Manipulator)*, Oxford University Press, 1993.

A Nephelometric Tactile Sensor

R. Andrew Russell
Intelligent Robotics Research Centre
Department of Electrical and Computer Systems Engineering
Monash University, Clayton, VIC 3168
AUSTRALIA

Abstract. This paper describes the design and construction of a novel robot tactile sensor array. The sensory principle employed is the measurement of diffuse reflected light emanating from a turbid liquid when the liquid is illuminated by a collimated light source. External objects pressed against the sensor vary the thickness of a layer of turbid liquid. Light entering this liquid is back-scattered in proportion to the liquid thickness. If the light passes through more liquid then more light is back-scattered. Operation of the sensor does not rely on light being reflected by the outer flexible membrane which contains the liquid. This is seen as an advantage of this sensor design. Being optical the transduction mechanism is immune to electric and magnetic interference. Compliance of the sensor surface would accommodate a degree of inaccuracy in positioning, aid stable grasping and resist damage in robotic applications. Results obtained using a prototype version of the sensor are also presented.

1. Introduction

We must all be aware that tactile sensation is vitally important to our ability to hold and manipulate objects. When our sense of touch is diminished by cold or by temporary loss of blood circulation then manipulation tasks such as buttoning a shirt become much more difficult. The task is performed slower and requires close visual monitoring. It is assumed that tactile sensing from skin-like sensors will also be necessary for competent robotic grasping and manipulation. Currently there are no tactile sensor equipped robotic grippers that can in any way approach the dexterity of the human hand. There are many reasons for this situation. However, the lack of suitable tactile sensors is one contributing factor.

Many different designs and operating principles have been proposed for skin-like tactile sensors [1, 2, 3]. Unfortunately, none of the currently proposed designs is ideal. The majority of these sensors are relatively stiff 'force' sensors which provide little information about surface contours [4]. Compliant tactile sensors have a number of potential advantages including:

- increased area of contact and therefore the ability to provide more information about the object surface,
- more kinematic coupling which ensures a more stable grasp, and
- compliance to accommodate positioning and manipulation errors.

A number of tactile sensor designs contain a capsule of fluid and use different methods to determine the fluid depth at an array of closely spaced points [5, 6, 7, 8, 9]. Of the available depth sensing techniques optical methods are immune to outside interference and do not have the corrosion problems associated with electrical resistance based methods. Depth measuring using optical attenuation caused by varying depths of a semi-transparent medium depends upon light being reflected from an outer membrane. For accurate depth measurements reflection must be independent of the profile of the outer membrane (the angle between the incident light and the membrane surface). In the sensor described here light is back-scattered from a cloudy fluid and the outer membrane is non-reflecting. The light absorbing properties are largely independent of the shape taken up by the membrane.

This paper describes the construction, calibration and operation of the sensor and presents some experimental results obtained using the prototype sensor.

2 Sensor Design

When light passes through a medium containing small particles the light is scattered [10]. Raleigh scattering occurs when the radius of the scatterer is 1/20 or less of the wavelength of the incident radiation. The intensity of scattering is proportional to the fourth power of frequency. Thus higher frequency blue light tends to be scattered by the oxygen and nitrogen molecules in the atmosphere giving the blue sky we see. Red light is transmitted to give the red of the setting sun. When the radius is not so small scattering is practically independent of frequency and therefore the scattered light is white. If a beam of light is projected into a turbid medium then a proportion of the light will be back-scattered towards the light source. The thicker the turbid layer the greater is the back-scattering. This is the principle that the tactile sensor uses. A similar technique is used in nephelometric analysis; a method of chemical analysis based on measuring the cloudiness of solutions

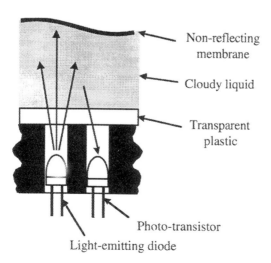

Non-reflecting
membrane

Cloudy liquid

Transparent
plastic

Photo-transistor

Light-emitting diode

Figure 1 A cross-section view of the sensor.

In the tactile sensor light is emitted by a light emitting diode (LED). The in-built lens of the LED and collimating tube ensure that the light beam entering the cloudy liquid is reasonably collimated. As the light travels through the liquid scattering occurs and a portion of the light is diffusely reflected to an adjacent phototransistor (see figure 1). The further the light beam travels through the fluid the more light is reflected back and this gives a measure of the thickness of the fluid layer. The membrane containing the liquid is non-reflecting and absorbs light which travels the full thickness of the fluid layer. The response of this sensor is highly non-linear and in these initial experiments a calibration table is used to recover the correct depth reading. Later it is hoped to produce a mathematical model of the back scattering process to provide an alternative method of correcting the sensor readings.

3 The Sensor Construction

In order to measure the surface profile of the outer membrane of the sensor on a grid of closely spaced points an array of alternating LEDs and phototransistors was constructed. The pattern of emitters and detectors is shown in figure 2. Every emitter/detector is adjacent to four detectors/emitters (except around the edge of the sensor). The region between each adjacent emitter and detector is a sensor point at which the membrane height is measured (indicated by the grey circles in figure 2). Both the emitters and detectors are housed in 3mm diameter packages and they are spaced on a 4mm grid in the sensor array. However, because the sensitive points lie between emitters and detectors the separation between sensitive points is approximately 2.8mm.

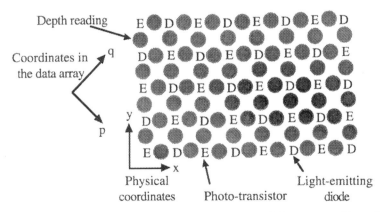

Figure 2   Light-emitting diodes and photo-transistors are alternated across the sensor and a height reading is taken between every adjacent emitter and detector.

Scanning of the sensor array and transmission of the sensor data via an RS232 serial link is performed by a 68HC11E2 microcontroller. Electrically the LEDs are arranged in a 4 by 5 array. One specific LED is illuminated by setting a high voltage on the corresponding port B row line (all others are low) and setting a low voltage on the corresponding port A column line (all others are high). Other diodes in the same row and column have zero voltage across them and the remaining diodes are reverse biased. Therefore only the selected diode is illuminated.

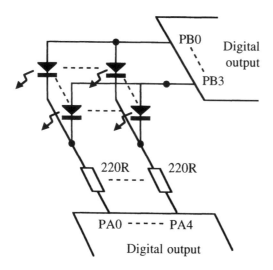

Figure 3a Light-emitting diode array

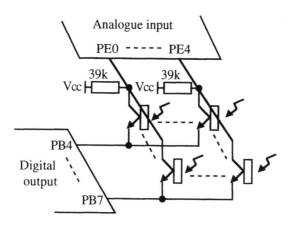

Figure 3b Photo-transistor array

Figure 3 The circuits used to selectively illuminate one light-emitting diode and to read the current through one photo-transistor.

The phototransistors are also arranged in a 4 by 5 array. Photo-current in each transistor must be measured individually and this function is performed by the circuit shown in figure 3b. One specific phototransistor is selected by pulling the associated row line (connected to port B) to ground. Non-selected rows are held high. Current from the selected transistors flows through the associated 39k resistor and the resulting voltage drop constitutes the sensor output. This voltage is measured by one of the port E analogue inputs. Non-selected transistors have zero or slightly negative collector-emitter voltage and so little or no current flows through them.

The nephelometric tactile sensor was filled with Shell soluble oil (cutting fluid) Dromus B dissolved 14 parts water to 1 part oil. This mixture was used as the turbid measuring medium and forms a thick white emulsion. Black neoprene rubber was used as the non-reflecting membrane material which absorbs any light transmitted through the turbid liquid. The membrane also contains the liquid and conforms to the shape of any indented object. Major components of the prototype sensor are show below in figure 4.

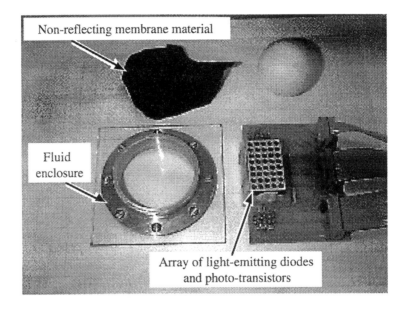

Non-reflecting membrane material

Fluid enclosure

Array of light-emitting diodes and photo-transistors

Figure 4   The parts of the prototype sensor

4   Experimental Results

The arrays of light emitting diodes and photo transistors are made from discrete components and the characteristics of individual devices vary over a considerable range. In order to equalise the response of each emitter/detector pair a set of calibration readings is taken for constant fluid depth (the undeflected case). New sensor readings are then divided by the recorded initial values to give sensor output relative to the undeflected condition.

Plots of compensated sensor output are shown in figures 5, 6 and 7. The indenting objects were the circular end of a 6mm diameter cylinder, a ping pong ball and the edge of a nut (a wedge shape with 120° between faces). These surface plots are indicative of the shape of the indenting object. However, the surface shape is distorted. The sensor response is non-linear and this can be seen in figure 7 where flat surfaces of the indenting object appear curved. In order to recover a true representation of the indenting surface it is necessary to incorporate a compensation for the sensor response.

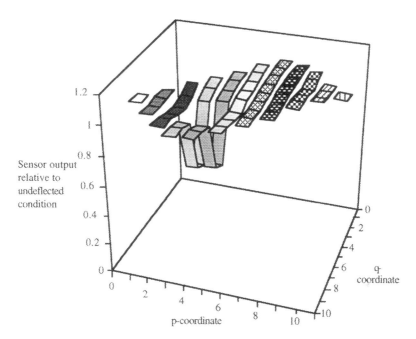

Figure 5 **The sensor response when indented by a 6mm diameter cylinder.**

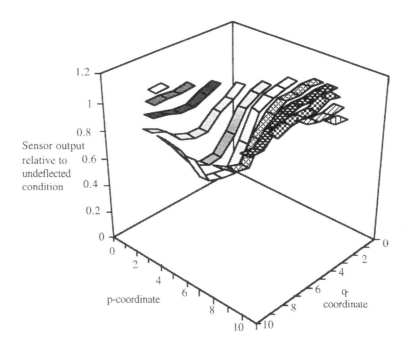

Figure 6 **The sensor response when indented by a ping pong ball.**

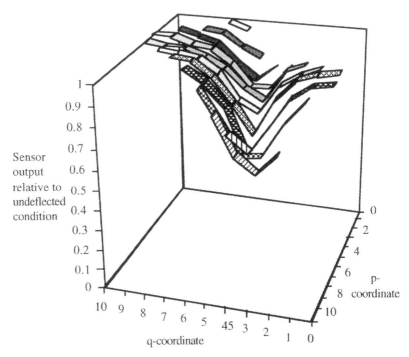

Figure 7   The sensor response when indented by the edge of a nut.

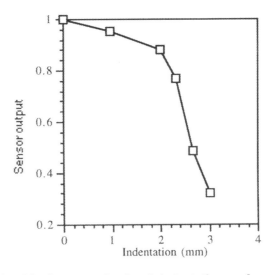

Figure 8   Relationship between depth of indentation and sensor output.

The collimated light source used in the nephelometric tactile sensor can be modelled as a cylindrical light source whose intensity falls exponentially as the light penetrates the cloudy medium. Back-scattering towards the photodetector could be modelled by a diffusion model (11). The resulting equations do not have an analytical solution and can only be solved numerically. At this stage in the project it was decided to calibrate the sensor by direct measurement. A micrometer was used to indent into the sensor a known distance. Figure 8 shows the relationship between depth of indentation and sensor output. Using this graph the data displayed in figure 7 was converted to indicate depth of indentation (figure 9).

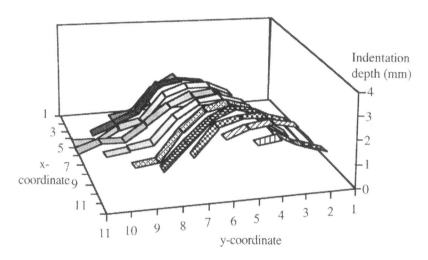

Figure 9   Depth of indentation produced by the edge of a nut.

5   Conclusions

A novel compliant tactile sensor array has been designed and constructed. The sensitive element of the sensor consists of a circular capsule of cloudy fluid 50mm in diameter and 3.5mm deep. An interleaved array of light-emitting diodes and phototransistors sense the thickness of the fluid at 67 closely spaced points.

The sensor surface is compliant and allows the surface profile to be measured. High levels of compliance allow the sensor to conform to the surface profile of touched objects which improves the sensing of object shape and increases stability of grip. Apart from the general advantage of optically-base tactile sensors that they are resistant to electromagnetic interference, the sensor does not rely on reflection from the outer membrane. Reflection is usually dependent on the angle of incidence of light and this would change depending upon the shape of the indenting object. By varying the density of emulsion particles, the amount of light emitted by the LED and the phototransistor series resistor (39k) different depths of fluid can be accommodated. The scanning rate of the sensor has not been accurately assessed. However, in the current design scanning rate is limited by the conversion time of the analogue to digital converter which converts 30,000 sample per second.

The nephelometric sensor requires further refinement in physical construction and data processing algorithms to improve the quality of the tactile image. However, the prototype sensor produces encouraging results.

6 Acknowledgments

I would like to thank Paul Beeley for constructing the prototype sensor and for gathering experimental results. This work has been supported by grants from the Australian Research Council.

References

1. *Tactile Sensors for Robotics and Medicine*, (John G. Webster, ed.), John Wiley & Sons, N.Y., 1988.
2. Nicholls, H.R. and Lee, M.H. 'A survey of robot tactile sensing technology', *The International Journal of Robotics Research*, Vol. 8, No. 3, June, 1989, pp. 3-30.
3. Russell, R.A. *Robot tactile Sensing*, Prentice Hall, Australia, 1990.
4. Brady, M., 'Forward', *The International Journal of Robotics Research*, Vol. 7, No. 6, 1988, pp. 2-4.
5. Helsel, M. et al 'An impedance tomographic tactile sensor', *Sensors and Actuators*, Vol.14, 1988, pp93-98.
6. Russell, R.A. and Parkinson, S. 'Sensing surface shape by touch', *Proceedings of the IEEE International Conference on Robotics and Automation*, May 2-7, 1993, Atlanta, pp. 423-428.
7. Brockett, R.W. 'Robotic hands with rheological surfaces', *Proceedings of the IEEE International Conference on Robotics and Automation*, St. Louis, March, 1985, pp942-946.
8. Nowlin, W.C., 'Experimental results of baysian algorithms for interpreting compliant tactile sensing data', *Proceedings of the IEEE International Conference on Robotics and Automation*, Sacramento, April 9-11, 1991, pp. 378-383.
9. Tsikos, C. Two-dimensional pressure sensor using retro-reflective tape and semi-transparent medium, US Patent 4,547,668, October 15th 1985.
10. Kolthoff, I.M., Sandell, E.B., Meehan, E.J. and Bruckenstein, S., Quantitive Chemical Analysis, Fourth Edition, The Macmillan Company, London.
11. Eason, G., Veitch, A.R., Nisbet, R.M. and Turnbull, F.W., 'The theory of the back-scattering of light by blood', *Journal of Applied Physics D: Applied Physics*, Vol. 11, pp. 1463-1479, 1978.

Finger Track - A Robust and Real-Time Gesture Interface

Rochelle O'Hagan
Department of Computer Science
Faculty of Engineering & Information Technology
The Australian National University
CANBERRA ACT 0200
rohagan@syseng.anu.edu.au
Tel. (02) 6216 7092   Fax. (02) 6279 8688

Alexander Zelinsky
Department of Systems Engineering
Research School of Information Sciences & Engineering
The Australian National University
CANBERRA ACT 0200
alex@syseng.anu.edu.au
Tel. (02) 6279 8840   Fax. (02) 6279 8688

Abstract

Real-time computer vision combined with robust gesture recognition provides a natural alternative to traditional computer interfaces. Human users have plenty of experience with actions and the manipulation of objects requiring finger movement. In place of a mouse, users could use their hands to select and manipulate data. This paper presents a first step in this approach using a finger as a pointing and selection device.

A major feature of a successful tracking system is robustness. The system must be able to acquire tracked features upon startup, and reacquire them if lost during tracking. Re-acquisition should be fast and accurate (i.e. it should pick up the correct feature). Intelligent search algorithms are needed for speedy, accurate acquisition of lost features with the frame. The prototype interface presented in this paper is based on finger tracking as a means of input to applications. The focus of the discussion is how the system can be made to perform robustly in real-time. Dynamically distributed search windows are defined for searching within the frame. The location and number of search windows are dependent on the confidence in the tracking of features. Experimental results showing the effectiveness of these techniques are presented.

Introduction

Gesture forms a major part of human communication. In fact one definition of gesture is "body movements which are used to convey some information from one person to another" [Vaananen & Bohm]. The form of gestures may vary, but most cultures use gesture to convey information in addition to speech. Humans are also very familiar with direct manipulation of objects. People use their hands to move and shape objects and to learn about their environment. Direct manipulation gesture-based interfaces to computers should, therefore, be intuitive and familiar to users.

Gesture is either spontaneous or conscious. Spontaneous gestures are usually associated with speech and are the primary form of gesture. Conscious gestures provide other information - they can be used as a means of learning the environment through tactile experience, and as a manipulation device. In order to avoid pre-defined interaction techniques and use gesture as an alternative to the mouse for object positioning and manipulation, conscious gestures must be recognised and understood [Cassell]. To determine an appropriate subset of gestures, it is important to understand different types of gesture and the purpose for which various gestures are used.

Two methods of classifying gestures are by type and by function. Cassell classifies conscious gesture by type into groups such as *emblematic* or *propositional* gestures. Examples of emblematic gestures include the "V-for-victory" gesture and "thumbs up" or "okay" ring. Propositional gestures are also associated with speech, and consist of gestures such as using the hands to indicate size while saying "it was this big". Conscious gestures have three functional roles: *semiotic, ergotic* and *epistemic* [Cadoz 94]. Gesture in interaction with computers has traditionally focused on the ergotic function - for example typing on a keyboard, moving a mouse and clicking buttons. Both tie the user to the computer by wired hardware. Neither is a natural interface, merely a means of transferring information to the computer.

Computer vision allows body parts and gestures to be an effective and non-intrusive means of input into the computer. The camera can be located as an unobtrusive sensor of human movement. No wired components or markers need to be introduced into the system allowing greater flexibility of action. Various work has been carried out using computer vision with gesture recognition. Crowley *et al* have shown a system using a finger or other object such as a pencil as an input interface to a simple painting program. The system starts tracking when an object is moved into a trigger region. If tracking of the object is lost, the system waits until another object enters the trigger area and then continues tracking the new object. We believe that automatic recovery is necessary in a tracking system. If the target moves out of the workspace and then reenters, it shouldn't have to move to a specific area for tracking to continue, but should be automatically reacquired by the system.

A system developed by Pavlovic *et al* uses two cameras and special lighting to track the motion of the hand and recognise gestures at approximately 10 frames per second. This is slower than the NTSC video rate (30Hz) and doesn't allow for real-time performance of rapid motion gesture. The development of real-time hardware vision systems [Inoue *et. al.*] allows successful tracking at video rate. These systems have been used for robot vision and head tracking. Zelinsky *et. al.*, using the Fujitsu vision system, have produced a system capable of tracking and recognising facial gestures at frame rate. The head-tracking system uses Kalman filters and a relative feature location network to provide robustness. It relies on located features to help determine the position of other features. This works well with the head and face, but is not appropriate for single feature tracking.

The fundamental requirements of such systems are speed, robustness and adaptability. Tracking of features and processing of gestures must be accomplished in real-time (30 Hz for NTSC video). The system must be able to initially acquire, and when lost automatically reacquire, features quickly and accurately. The system must also not rely on special lighting, marks or stickers on the hands, specific "trigger" locations or any other artificial means of aiding tracking.

Finger Track

As a first step toward full hand tracking in three dimensions, we developed the two-dimensional finger tracking interface. The main purpose of the interface was to support investigation into ways of improving the reacquisition of lost features, and hence the robustness of the tracking system. Exhaustive systematic searching of the entire video frame takes too long to be a viable option. Also, as the system is dynamic, there are no guarantees that the object (hand) will stop moving just because tracking has been lost, so a systematic search could fail to find the object completely. Intelligent search algorithms are needed. The tracking system gives two basic pieces of information - the location where the feature was last detected, and the vector of movement at that time. Our system implements a dynamic search pattern focusing initially on areas where the feature is most likely to be found, and widening the search area over time as the feature remains undetected.

The system used a single video camera and dedicated image processing hardware to track the motion of the user's finger. Image correlation was used to determine the location of the finger in the video frame. Positional information and point or click status was sent to a server program which generated events similar to mouse events for the application programs. Search algorithms were implemented to produce a robust tracking system.

Advances in computer vision have led to achievable real-time performance in tracking features. Dedicated hardware allows processing of video images at frame-rate giving rise to the possibility of performing real-time tracking and recognition of gestures. In any vision based tracking system, tracked features will be lost at some stage. Indeed the system will be in a "lost" state at startup and will have to find the required features within the whole frame. In order to accomplish this reacquisition as quickly as possible, given a limited amount of processing power available, intelligent search methods are needed. A systematic search of the whole image is time-consuming and, with features that are probably moving, quite likely to fail to find the features. A search process that distributes search windows based on the last known location of the feature and the direction of movement is likely to find the feature more quickly than an exhaustive search. The searched area of the frame is initially constrained to the probable location of the feature, and then gradually increased as the feature remains undetected.

The Vision System Used in this Prototype

The Fujitsu MEP tracking vision system was used to track the finger pointer for the gesture interface. This system is designed to track multiple templates in the frames of a NTSC video stream in real time. The vision system consists of two VME-bus cards - a video module and a tracking module which can track up to 100 templates simultaneously at video frame rate (30 Hz for NTSC). The vision system is controlled by a MC68040 processor card running VxWorks (see Figure 1).

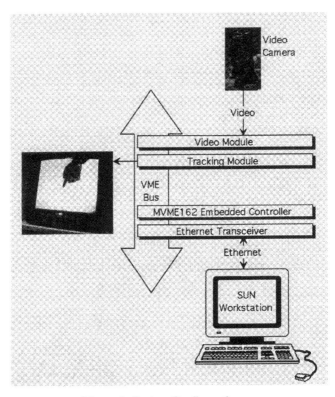

Figure 1. System Configuration

Object tracking is based on comparison of templates within a defined search window. Templates can be either 8x8 or 16x16 pixels in size, with a magnification of up to 4 times a template. The video module digitises the video input stream and stores the digital images in dedicated video memory (VRAM) which is also accessed by the tracking module. The tracking module performs a comparison between the stored templates and the live video at a given location within the frame. The comparison is done using a cross correlation which sums the absolute difference between corresponding pixels in the template and frame. The resulting value is called the distortion, and measures the similarity between the two images. The formula for distortion is shown in Equation 1 where *Size* is the size of the template (8 or 16),

$$D = \sum_{x=0}^{Size} \sum_{y=0}^{Size} \left| g_t\left(x_t : y_t\right) - g_f\left(x_f : y_f\right)\right|$$

where $x_t = x \times m_x$

$$y_t = y \times m_y$$

$$x_f = x \times m_x + o_x$$

$$y_f = y \times m_y + o_y$$

Equation 1

High distortions indicate a poor match while low distortions result when two very similar images are compared. The distortion provides a measure of confidence in the tracking of features. A threshold value of 4000 was determined for the fingertip beyond which tracking seemed to fail. Confidence in tracking was high for distortion values much less than 4000, but dropped off markedly for values above 4000. The linear relationship between distortion and confidence was used in the calculation of search window locations where raw distortion values were too large.

For successful feature tracking it is necessary to calculate the distortion at a number of points within the search window. The tracking system performs up to 256 cross correlations per feature within the search window and finds the position in the image frame where the feature matches with the lowest distortion. Motion is represented by a vector to the origin of the lowest distortion. The search window can be moved along the axis of the motion vector to track an object. For objects that do not change their appearance or shade and are never occluded by other objects, the tracking system works perfectly.

Tracking the Finger

Problems occur when trying to track finger and hand movements as the fingers (in a 16x16 template) do not differ significantly from each other. Also, the shape of the finger is altered by rotation which often occurs when moving the finger over the workspace. Fortunately, the hand's rotation is physically limited in the plane and does not pose difficulty in tracking.

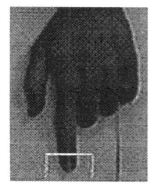

Figure 2. Point Gesture

Figure 3. Click Gesture

The vision system was used to track the fore-finger of the hand. Templates were defined of the finger in the "point" position (see Figure 2), and in the "click" position, with the second finger brought alongside the first as shown in Figure 3.

To fully exploit the capability of the vision system, templates were compared not only with the expected position of the finger in the frame, but with surrounding areas as well. The location and number of the surrounding search windows is dependent on the confidence in the current position estimate. When confidence that the finger is being accurately tracked is high, search windows are distributed closely around the expected position. When the feature's position is less certain, the area search windows spread out to cover a wider area of the frame. Fewer search windows are used when the feature is tracking well. If the object is determined to have been lost completely, a search is performed to find it again.

The tracking program allowed the user to define the workspace, move the "mouse" around within the workspace and have the corresponding movement echoed within the application program, and to select screen objects by "clicking" on them. The user's workspace needed to be defined so that accurate relative positions could be mapped to the screen. The user set up the workspace at the beginning of the session by moving the forefinger to the upper-left and lower-right hand corners of the workspace, and performing the clicking action (see Figure 4). This provided the reference coordinates for the workspace area. After setting up the workspace, the user could move the

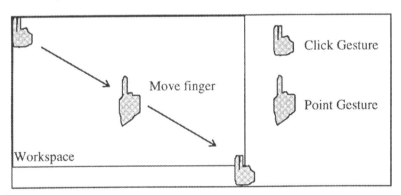

Figure 4. Defining the workspace

mouse cursor around the application program by moving their finger within the defined workspace, and select objects by performing the click action. Double-clicking was achieved by repeating the click action within a short time. The tracking system was set up as a server on VxWorks and passed event calls to application programs as they occurred. This is similar to the way a mouse works. Changes in the position of the finger were sent by the server using Xevents to the application programs. When "clicks" and "double-clicks" were detected, the change in state was also passed to the application. The Finger Tracker interface was trialed with programs such as xv and xfig. This showed that the finger could be tracked in real-time with cursor movement on the screen providing feedback to the user. This was sufficient to test the robustness of the tracking system.

Building Robustness

To initially acquire the finger and start tracking it, it was necessary to find the feature within the frame. The number and location of search windows was determined by the distortion values obtained from the vision system. The program always knows the expected location of the feature and eight surrounding search areas to search in each frame. As the distortion values increased, the certainty that the feature is tracking declines and so more search windows are introduced. It was also important to know that the system was tracking the correct feature. To ensure this, a malus factor was defined, and when the distortion of the new object in relation to the current feature went below the malus factor, tracking switched to the new feature.

Search windows were distributed at a distance, d, from the last known position of the feature, and at an angle θ, from the feature's direction of movement. The distribution

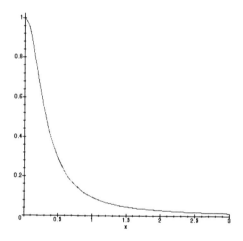

**Figure 5. Search window distribution
function f(d).**

function (Figure 5 & Equation 2) was determined experimentally. The distance d was calculated in (Equation 3), where a, P are dependent on the confidence of the last known position, and y is a random value between 0 - 511 (the maximum size of the frame). This distribution meant that when the confidence in the previous location of the feature was high, the search windows were mostly distributed close to the previous location. When confidence decreased, the windows were more widely spread away from the last location.

$$f(d) = \frac{1}{1 + a|d|^P} \qquad \text{\textbf{Equation 2}}$$

$$|d| = \frac{1}{a}\left(\left(\frac{1}{y}\right)^{\frac{1}{P}} - 1\right) \qquad \text{\textbf{Equation 3}}$$

The vision system calculates a movement vector for each template in every frame. This vector gives the direction of motion of the feature when tracking was lost or became uncertain. This movement vector can be used to limit the area of the frame that is initially searched as it is likely that the feature will be somewhere in the direction it was last moving. The confidence in the tracking is used to specify an angle, α (between 15° and 180°), which constrains the search window placement directions. Search windows are placed within $\pm \alpha$° of the movement vector direction at a randomly generated angle. When the feature was completely lost, for example at startup, α was set to 180, giving a full 360° of search area. As the time that the feature has been lost increased, α was increased to search a wider area of the frame. Figure 6a shows the system when it is tracking the finger. Search windows for a feature that was lost with no reliable movement vector is shown in Figure 6b. The windows are distributed in the full 360° around the centre of the frame. Figure 6c shows the search windows generated for a feature with the movement vector headed straight down the workspace.

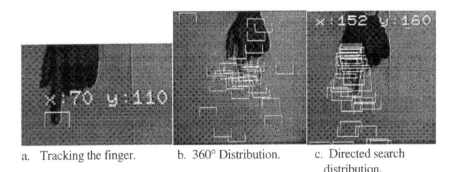

a. Tracking the finger. b. 360° Distribution. c. Directed search
distribution.

Figure 6. Search Window Distribution

The vision system can track ~100 templates at frame rate. However, there is limited computation time (33ms) between frame grabs. If the system isn't released in time for the next frame grab it waits for the following time slot and so tracking slows down. The computation time is used to calculate the best template match from the distortion values and to calculate the locations of all the search windows. It is important therefore, to only process as many search windows as are necessary to find the feature. The number of search windows was varied according to the confidence of tracking.

When the feature was completely lost, the maximum number of search windows were allocated to maximise the chance of finding the feature in the frame.

Conclusions & Further Work

An un-obtrusive, prototype gesture interface allowed investigation of techniques for robust, real-time feature tracking. Fingers of the hand were tracked and events generated and passed through a server to the application program in the same manner as mouse events. When the system lost the finger or confidence in the tracking decreased, more search windows were allocated to recover the feature. A dynamic distribution of the search windows concentrating on the last known location and direction of movement of the object improved the ability of the system to recover the feature and resume tracking.

The long-term goal of the work reported in this paper is to develop a robust, real-time gesture interface for three-dimensional virtual environments. Two-dimensional pointing devices are inadequate for three-dimensional environments such as the Virtual Workbench [Poston et. al.]. Currently available interfaces such as data-gloves and the Polhemus FastTrak stylus and switch can be awkward to use in rotation and manipulation of objects in virtual space. These devices are also intrusive, physically connecting the user to the hardware and thus limiting freedom of movement. A vision-based gesture interface could provide an unobtrusive, flexible interface to the virtual world and allow natural manipulation of virtual objects.

The current work forms a good base for tracking the hand and recognising other gestures in three dimensions. The techniques used for feature recovery and acquisition can be transferred to a full hand tracking system, thus providing robustness.

Acknowledgements

This research is supported by The Australian National University and the Co-operative Research Centre for Advanced Computational Systems. The presentation of this report was greatly improved by the assistance of Duncan Stevenson. Technical assistance was gratefully received from Jochen Heinzmann, Gordon Cheng and David Jung.

Bibliography

[Cadoz] C. Cadoz, "Les realites virtuelles", Dominos, Flammarion, 1994.

[Cassell] J. Cassell. "What You Need to Know about Spontaneous Gesture, and Why You Need to Know It". 2nd International Conference on Automatic Face and Gesture Recognition, Vermont, October 1996.

[Crowley] J. Crowley and J. Coutaz, "Vision for Man Machine Interaction", EHCI, Grand Targhee, August 1995.

[Crowley *et. al.*] J. Crowley, F. Berard, and J. Coutaz, "Finger Tracking as an Input Device for Augmented Reality", International Workshop on Gesture and Face Recognition, Zurich, June 1995.

[Inoue *et. al.*] H. Inoue, T. Tachikawa and M. Inaba, "Robot Vision System with a Correlation Chip for Real-time Tracking, Optical Flow and Depth Map Generation", Proceedings 1992 IEEE International Conference on Robotics and Automation, pp.1621 - 1626, 1992.

[Pavlovic *et. al.*] V. Pavlovic, R. Sharma and T. Huang, "Gestural Interface to a Visual Computing Environment for Molecular Biologists", Proceedings of the 2d International Conference on Automatic Face and Gesture Recognition, pp. 30-35, 1996.

[Poston *et. al.*] T. Poston and L. Serra, "The Virtual Workbench: Dextrous VR", Proceedings ACM VRST'94 - Virtual Reality Software and Technology, pp. 111-122, 1994.

[Vaananen & Bohm] Gesture-driven interaction as a human factor in virtual environments-an approach with neural networks. In R.A. Earnshaw, M.A. Gigante & H. Jones (Eds.), *Virtual Reality Systems*. London: Academic Press Ltd.

[Zelinsky *et. al.*] A. Zelinsky and J. Heinzmann, "Real-Time Visual Recognition of Facial Gestures for Human-Computer Interaction", Proceedings of the 2nd International Conference on Automatic Face and Gesture Recognition, pp. 351-356, 1996.

A Constraint Mechanism for Knowledge Specification of Simulation Systems Based on Temporal Logic

Chuchang Liu and Mehmet A. Orgun

Department of Computing, Macquarie University, NSW 2109, Australia
E-mail: {cliu, mehmet}@krakatoa.mpce.mq.edu.au

Abstract. Knowledge specification can be used as a basis for developing and maintaining simulation systems. This paper presents a knowledge specification methodology based on the temporal logic TLC for solving simulation problems. In this methodology, we build a specific constraint mechanism as a standard prototype for a class of simulation problems which may have some common properties. Such a standard prototype can be used to test and improve the knowledge specification of the target system of any problem belonging to this class. When we obtain a satisfactory knowledge specification, a simulation program in Chronolog(MC), a logic programming language based on TLC, can be produced.

Keywords: temporal logic, logic programming, simulation, knowledge specification.

1 Introduction

Recently, there has been a growing interest in knowledge-based simulation methods [4, 10]. Several approaches based on temporal logic languages have been proposed for specifying simulation systems. The notion of time is implicitly built into temporal logic languages, which is essential in simulation, and the logical formalisation of these languages can be especially applied to knowledge representation. They are also directly executable. Therefore, temporal languages, such as Tempura [5], Templog [1], SimTL [10] and Chronolog [2, 6], are particularly suitable for knowledge-based simulation applications.

To improve the quality and reliability of a knowledge-based system, it is helpful to make a knowledge specification during the design stage. A good knowledge specification can help developers to eliminate design failures and reduce production costs. There have been a number of methods proposed for specifying AI systems [7, 11]. In order to obtain a stable and satisfactory specification in building a knowledge-based system, Slagle et. al. [7] proposed using prototypes to test and improve knowledge specification generated from the knowledge acquisition process. The specification is then served as the solution specification for the design and implementation of the target system.

Knowledge specifications can also be used as a basis for developing and maintaining simulation systems. In [4], Liu and Orgun proposed a knowledge-based simulation methodology. In the methodology, a knowledge specification is made based on TLC [3], a linear temporal logic with multiple granularity of time. Such kind of specifications have a clear semantics, so that they are easy for experts to read and understand for verification or validation. Also, representing knowledge in TLC ensures that the specification is intuitive and natural, which simplifies communication with nontechnical users. In this paper, based on Slagle's method, we present a knowledge specification technique for simulation problems, called constraint mechanism technique (CMT). This technique involves building a specific constraint set as a standard prototype for a class of simulation problems which have some common properties. Such a prototype can be applied to all problems of the class. Therefore, once we obtain a standard prototype for a class of simulation problems, we may use it to test and improve the knowledge specification for any particular simulation problem belonging to that class.

CMT is a powerful means for helping the user to capture knowledge and verify it in the knowledge acquisition process. Also, because the specific constraint mechanism can easily be modified and it can be reused, we may spend less time and costs for the development of knowledge-based simulation systems.

This paper is organized as follows. A brief introduction to the temporal logic TLC is provided in next section. In section 3, a summary of knowledge specification for simulation systems is presented. Section 4 presents a constraint mechanism for a particular class of simulation problems – simulating concurrent systems. Section 5 discusses how to use the CMT technique to verify a knowledge system. Finally, we summarise our methodology and outline future work.

2 Temporal Logic TLC

TLC is an extension of temporal logic, in which each predicate is defined over a clock, a subsequence of the discrete global timeline. In this section, we briefly introduce TLC, including its syntax and semantics. For more details, we refer the reader to Liu and Orgun [3].

2.1 Syntax In TLC, there are two temporal operators: first and next, which refer to the initial moment and the next moment in time, respectively. TLC formulas are constructed by the following rules: (1) any formula of first-order logic is a formula of TLC; (2) if A is a formula, so are first A and next A. We also use the notation next(k) A to represent the formula formed by k applications of next to the formula A.

We define that the global clock is the increasing sequence of all natural numbers: $< 0, 1, 2, \ldots >$. A local clock is a subsequence of the global clock, i.e., a local clock is a strictly increasing sequence of natural numbers, either infinite or finite: $< t_0, t_1, t_2, \ldots >$. Let $\mathcal{CK}$ be the set of all clocks and $\sqsubseteq$ be an ordering relation on the elements of $\mathcal{CK}$ defined as follows: for any $ck_1, ck_2 \in \mathcal{CK}$, $ck_1 \sqsubseteq ck_2$ iff for all $t \in ck_1$, $t \in ck_2$, where $t \in ck_i$ denotes the fact that t is a moment in time on the clock ck_i. It is easy to show that $(\mathcal{CK}, \sqsubseteq)$ is a complete lattice.

We use a clock assignment to assign a local clock for each predicate symbol.

A clock assignment ck is a map from the set of predicate symbols to the set of all clocks. The clock associated with a predicate symbol p is denoted by $ck(p)$. For any formula, its local clock is defined based on the structure of the formula.

Let A be a formula and ck a clock assignment. The local clock associated with A, denoted as ck_A, is defined inductively as follows:

- If A is an atomic formula $p(x_1, \ldots, x_n)$, then $ck_A = ck(p)$.
- If $A = \neg B$, first B, $(\forall x)B$ or $(\exists x)B$ then $ck_A = ck_B$.
- If $A = B \wedge C$, $B \vee C$, $B \to C$ or $B \leftrightarrow C$, then $ck_A = ck_B \sqcap ck_C$, where $\sqcap$ is the "greatest lower bound" operator with the relation $\sqsubseteq$ on $\mathcal{CK}$.
- If $A = $ next B, then (1) $ck_A = <t_0, t_1, \ldots, t_{n-1}>$ when $ck_B = <t_0, t_1, \ldots, t_n>$ is non-empty and finite; (2) $ck_A = ck_B$ when ck_B is infinite or empty.

This definition actually indicates that every TLC formula can be clocked. Note that the difference between $ck_{\text{next}A}$ and ck_A is only that ck_A has one more element than $ck_{\text{next}A}$ does when ck_A is finite. Actually, in this case, $ck_{\text{next}A}$ is generated by just deleting the last element t_n in ck_A because t_n does not have a next moment defined for it.

In the following, we use $ck_0, ck_1, \ldots$ or $ck_A, ck_B, \ldots$ to represent local clocks, in particular, we denote the global clock as gck. Given a local clock $ck_i = <t_0, t_1, t_2, \ldots>$, we define the rank of t_n on ck_i to be n, written as $rank(t_n, ck_i) = n$. Inversely, we write $t_n = ck_i^{(n)}$, which means that t_n is the moment in time on ck_i whose rank is n. Obviously, for any given formula A, if $t \in ck_{\text{next}A}$, then we have that $rank(t, ck_A) = rank(t, ck_{\text{next}A})$.

2.2 Semantics In TLC, the semantics of formulas with logical connectives are defined in the usual way, but with respect to local clocks [3]. Here we only give the meaning of temporal operators:

- For any $t \in ck_A$, first A is true at t if and only if A is true at $ck_A^{(0)}$.
- For any $t \in ck_{\text{next}A}$, next A is true at t if and only if A is true at $ck_A^{(i+1)}$, where $i = rank(t, ck_A)$.

The axioms and rules of inference of TLC can be found in [3].

3 Knowledge Specification for Simulation Problems

Usually, there are three types of work which are involved in a simulation problem:

- Understanding the problem and providing a specification for a solution;
- Translating the specification into a program as the simulation system;
- Running the system to obtain simulation results which are used for analysing and designing a real system.

Knowledge specification corresponds to the first type of work. In order to obtain an effective simulation system for a given problem, it is helpful to make a satisfactory knowledge specification first. To do this, we need to recognize the existence of different forms of knowledge to capture necessary knowledge, and also need to analyse the protocol about the problem for eliciting certain kinds of knowledge. An appropriate knowledge representation would be helpful for capturing and eliciting knowledge as well as making a knowledge specification to be easily transformed into a program. Recently, some researchers proposed that the knowledge used to solve a problem is hierarchically organized and can be conceptually decomposed [7]. In particular, conceptual structures [8, 9] has been widely used as knowledge specification languages.

A simulated system can be thought of as composed of a finite set of interacting components. Each component is partially independent from the others and the only dependencies between components are given by interactions. Each component has its local behavior and its activities are modeled by a sequence of events. An event may be either internal to a component and cause only local dynamic changes, or may involve interactions with other components. These concepts lead us to consider each component as having its own local clock, but the global clock is still needed when we consider interactions which may cause global dynamic changes. Thus, a formal specification of such a simulation system is a knowledge base of the form $< \mathcal{V}, \mathcal{P}, \mathcal{C}, ck, \mathcal{R}, \mathcal{I} >$, where

- $\mathcal{V}$ – a variable declaration set, in which each element has the form of [X:S], where X is a variable identifier and S the type of X,
- $\mathcal{P}$ – a set of predicate definitions, in which the definition of a predicate is represented as a pair of the form (P:I), where P is a predicate identifier and I the definition of P,
- $\mathcal{C}$ – a set of (local) clock definitions involved in the system,
- ck – a map from the set of predicate symbols to $\mathcal{C}$,
- $\mathcal{R}$ – a set of rules which describe the behavior of each component and interactions between components, and
- $\mathcal{I}$ – a set of initial conditions represented as facts which are all true at the initial time when the system starts.

In a system composed of interacting components, such as concurrent systems, there may exist several processes running concurrently, and each process can therefore be viewed as an independent component. In order to construct a knowledge specification for a simulation system, we have to:

(1) Identify the components of the system and, for each component,
  - Identify variables, including state variables and action variables.
  - Define predicates used for describing the behavior of the component and its interactions with other components.
  - Define local clocks, which are usually specified as Chronolog programs.
  - Assign clocks to predicates. In knowledge specification, a fact "$ck(p)$ is ck_i" is simply represented as a program clause is_ck(p,cki).
  - Identify rules based on the analysis of the behavior of the component.

(2) Identify rules which are involved in the interactions between components.
(3) Identify facts as the initial conditions.

In our methodology, the rules may be specified as a group of Chronolog(MC) program clauses. Chronolog(MC) is a temporal logic programming language based on TLC. For instance,

```
next state(Y) <- state(X), action(U).
next action(V) <- state(X), action(U).
```

denote that the next state will be Y and the next action will be V if, at the current moment in time, the state is X and the action U is executed. An initial condition can be represented as a fact in the knowledge specification. For example, we may have the facts:

```
first action(wait).
first next state(tom,ready).
```

As an example, a knowledge specification for a Petrol-station-Filling System (PFS) is given in the appendix.

4 Building a Constraint Mechanism

Knowledge acquisition process usually includes the following activities: *Knowledge gathering, Knowledge classification and structuring, Verification and consistency checking,* and *Updating the knowledge base.* The first two activities, depending on the protocol analysis and the experts' knowledge, give the primary form of a knowledge specification. The last two activities lead to a stable and satisfactory knowledge specification. For a class of simulation problems which have some common properties, we want to build a specific constraint mechanism. Such a constraint mechanism is used in the process of knowledge acquisition to elicit knowledge for completing a knowledge specification through testing and verifying its consistency.

We now present a constraint mechanism for knowledge specification of simulation problems based on the structural representation discussed above. The mechanism consists of a set of constraints, which includes: variable constraints, $\mathcal{P}$-generation constraints, clock-definition constraints, clock-assignment constraints, and time-dependent relation constraints.

Variable constraints impose restrictions on types of variables. Such kind of constrains may require that each variable has a unique type, and they may also require that the set of values of a variable satisfies a given condition, and so on.

$\mathcal{P}$-generation constraints impose restrictions on the type of predicates and the use of predicate symbols. Defining predicates is based on experts' key concepts and the relations among concepts. The set of predicates includes: the predicates modeling the local behavior (such as states, control and so on) of individual components and the predicates describing the global behavior (such as the global states, interactive relationships and so on) of the system. $\mathcal{P}$-generation constraints help developers to generate a consistent predicate set.

The clock-definition constraints impose restriction on the clock definition. The definition of local clocks depends on "local time" associated with individual components of the system, and it might come from experts' knowledge or from documentation. To guarantee that a clock specification, usually written in ordinary Chronolog [6], represent a "real" clock, we stipulate that the specification satisfy the clock-definition constraints.

The clock-assignment constraints impose restriction on ck, the map from the set of predicate symbols to $\mathcal{C}$. The clock-assignment constraints help developers to make a real and reliable map, so that each predicate symbol appearing in $\mathcal{P}$ has a local clock assigned to it and there are no predicates associated with two or more different clocks.

The time-dependent constraints provide a partial order relation between events with respect to time. Rules and facts are acquired from experts' knowledge about the behavior and timing properties of the system. We collect the rules and initial conditions by identifying facts, relations among concepts and time, constraint mechanisms on concepts and events and so on. The time-dependent constraints help developers to obtain "correct" rules and initial conditions. For example, assume that the action U is the execution of the statement $x := x + 1$, then the change of the state of the variable x should satisfy the following constraint: For any pair of the state values X and Y of x, if X<Y, then the event "first next(k) state(Y)" happens after the the event "first next(r) state(X)". Therefore, if some rule can not satisfy the constraint, there must be an error. The following are some examples of constraints.

Constraint 1 *Any variable has a unique type, that is, if* [X:S]$\in \mathcal{V}$*, then* S *is the unique type of the variable* X*.*

Constraint 2 *Let S_1 and S_2 be two sets of predicates, which describe the behavior local to any two different components of the simulated system respectively. Then $S_1 \cap S_2 = \emptyset$, i.e. the empty set.*

Constraint 3 *For any* p$\in \mathcal{P}$ *and the query* <- is-ck(p,X) *with respect to* ck*, there exists a solution, and if both* cki *and* ckj *are solutions to the query, then* cki =ckj*.*

Constraint 4 *Let $p, q \in \mathcal{P}$, $ck(p) = ck(q)$, e_r =first next(k1) $p(a_1, \ldots, a_r)$ and e_s =first next(k2) $q(b_1, \ldots, b_s)$. If $e_r \prec e_s$, where $\prec$ is a partial relation over the set of events (read $\prec$ as "happen-after"), then* k1<k2*.*

Constraint 5 *Let e_r =first next(k1) produce(M) and e_s =first next(k2) consume(M). Then we have $e_r \prec e_s$. That is, the event that a message M is produced must appear before the event that the message is consumed.*

To obtain a powerful constraint mechanism for a given class of simulation problem, the developer needs to consult experts and carefully study the protocols. The constraint mechanism can usually be obtained by analysing the functions, roles representation form of each part in the knowledge specification and finding the common properties and requirements of the class of simulation problems we are trying to solve.

5 Verifying Knowledge Specification by CMT

If a constraint set, denoted as $\mho$, is sound with respect to the meaning of the formal specification of a simulation system, then the verification technique of knowledge specification will be based on the following principle:

- A consistent knowledge specification $< \mathcal{P}, \mathcal{C}, ck, \mathcal{R}, \mathcal{I} >$ must satisfy the constraint set $\mho$.

Therefore, to obtain a consistent knowledge specification for a simulation system, a necessary condition is to check if any knowledge acquired from any resource satisfies the constraint set. Usually, some syntactic and semantics verification can be done by checking whether the structure of the knowledge specification meets the constraint mechanism.

In our technique, a constraint mechanism is usually represented as logical formulas. The formal representation of constraint mechanisms is more useful in verifying knowledge specifications. For example, we have the following constraints:

($[X:S1] \in \mathcal{V}) \wedge ([X:S2] \in \mathcal{V}) \rightarrow (S1=S2)$.
($(P:I1) \in \mathcal{P}) \wedge ((P:I2) \in \mathcal{P}) \rightarrow (I1=I2)$.

The first formula can be used to check whether a variable has a unique type; the second one can be used to check whether a predicate is well-defined. For example, suppose one wants to know whether the type of the variable X is unique. Then what he needs to do is to make a query [X:?] to the sub-knowledge base $\mathcal{V}$ of the knowledge specification and look at the answer. If more than one answer are obtained, there must be an error.

For a further discussion, we now consider the PFS System, whose specification is given in the appendix. PFS consists of three components – the queue management process qm and pump service processes $ps1$ and $ps2$.

In the following, we show how to use a constraint mechanism to check the consistency of the knowledge acquired in the knowledge acquisition process. Suppose that at some stage of the knowledge acquisition process, we have defined the following predicates for ps1:

(state_1(X,Flag) : at $ps1$, the customer X is served at the status Flag).
(action_1(W) : an action W is executed at $ps1$).

and we also have predicates for ps2 as follows:

(state_1(X,Flag) : at ps2, the customer X is served at the status Flag).
(action_2(X,W) : an action W is executed on $ps2$).

Then, we find that errors have occurred. The first error is that the predicate state_1(X,Flag) has two different meanings, i.e., it has two different definitions. To avoid such an error, when defining a new predicate P, we only need to make query (P:?) to $\mathcal{P}$ which have been obtained. If there is an answer, we should choose another symbol for the new predicate. The second error is that the predicate `action_2(X,W)` does not match its definition. It is more difficult to detect such errors. So a smarter constraint for removing such an error is needed. For instance, we may adopt the following constraint to deal with such an error:

$(P(...,X,...):I) \in \mathcal{P} \rightarrow$ X occurs in I.

The following constraints can be used for proving the consistency of the clock definition: Any clock `cki` should satisfy

```
first next(m) cki(X)→m ≤ X.
first next(m) cki(X)∧first next(m) cki(Y)→X = Y.
first next(m) cki(X)∧first next(n) cki(Y)∧m < n→X<Y.
```

These constraints guarantee that the defined clock is linear. That is, if a definition of a clock satisfies these constraints, then the clock is sound. By checking whether the constraints are satisfied, we can show that the definitions of the clock `ck1` and `ck2` in the knowledge specification of PFS are consistent. An inconsistent clock definition can be found by running the definition. For example, when running the following definition:

```
first ck2(0).
next ck2(N) <- ck2(M), N is M+1.
next ck2(N) <- ck2(M), N is M+3.
```

we can easily find that the definition of `ck2` does not satisfy the second and the third constraints.

To check the consistency of ck, we can use the following formal constraints which correspond to the constraint 4 given in the previous section:

```
(p(...):I)∈ 𝒫 → (∃cki)is_ck(p,cki).
(is_ck(p,cki) ∧ is_ck(p,ckj)) → cki = ckj.
```

To check the consistency of $\mathcal{R}$ and $\mathcal{I}$, we need to run the program consisting of $\mathcal{R}$ and $\mathcal{I}$ in the specification. For example, for any customer X, if we have that

```
first next(m) customer_f(X).
first next(n) state_1(X,occupied).
```

we then must have an event ordering that

```
first next(m) customer_f(X) ≺ first next(n) state_1(X,occupied).
```

where `customer_f(X)` means that X is the first customer in the queue waiting for service. Such an event ordering can be used for checking the consistency of rules and initial conditions. For example, if we add a new rule into the knowledge specification of PFS as follows:

```
next customer_f(X) <- state_1(X,occupied), action_1(wait).
```

then, when running the specification, we can easily find an inconsistency with the event ordering. Therefore, there must be an error with the new rule if we have checked the consistency of other rules in the specification and no errors have been found. Because of space limitations, more details of verification techniques of the knowledge specification will not be given.

6 Concluding Remarks

In this paper, we have proposed an approach to construct a powerful constraint mechanism based on the formal structure of the knowledge specification for simulation systems, and have also presented a verification technique by CMT for the knowledge specification. Such a constraint mechanism can be applied for building a stable and satisfactory knowledge specification for a class of simulation problems having some common properties.

When we obtain a satisfactory knowledge specification $< \mathcal{V}, \mathcal{P}, \mathcal{C}, ck, \mathcal{R}, \mathcal{I} >$, a simulation program written in Chronolog(MC) can be directly obtained from the specification. The program consists of the following components: a declaration (about variables and predicates) which is formed by $\mathcal{V}$ and $\mathcal{P}$, clock definition $\mathcal{C}$, clock assignment ck and the program body which is the combination of $\mathcal{R}$ and $\mathcal{I}$. Then, by running the program, we may obtain some simulation results.

CMT technique can serve as an efficient means for communication between experts and the developers of simulation systems. Future work includes investigating the formal representation of constraint mechanisms for a variety of problems and providing approaches for automated production of constraint sets.

Acknowledgements

The work presented in this article has been supported in part by an Australian Research Council (ARC) Grant. C. Liu has been supported by an Australian Postgraduate Award (APA) and an MPCE Postgraduate Research Scholarship at Macquarie University.

References

1. M. Abadi and Z. Manna. Temporal logic programming. *Journal of Symbolic Computation*, 8:277–295, 1989.
2. C. Liu and M. A. Orgun. Chronolog as a simulation language. In Michael Fisher, editor, *Proceedings of IJCAI-95 Workshop on Executable Temporal Logics*, pages 109–119, Montreal, Canada, August 19-21 1995.
3. C. Liu and M. A. Orgun. Dealing with multiple granularity of time in temporal logic programming. *Journal of Symbolic Computation*, 22:699–720, 1996.
4. C. Liu and M. A. Orgun. Towards a knowledge-based simulation methodology based on Chronolog(MC). In Jan Žižka, editor, *Artificial Intelligence Techniques - AIT'96*, pages 83–91. PC-DIR Ltd., 1996.
5. B. Moszkowski. *Executing Temporal Logic Programs*. Cambridge University Press, 1986.

6. M. A. Orgun and W. W. Wadge. Theory and practice of temporal logic programming. In L. Fariñas del Cerro and M. Penttonen, editors, *Intensional Logics for Programming*, pages 23–50. Oxford University Press, 1992.

7. J. R. Slagle, D. A. Gardiner, and K. Han. Knowledge specification of an expert system. *IEEE Expert*, 4(5):29–38, 1990.

8. J.F. Sowa. *Conceptual Structures: Information Processing in Mind and Machine*. Addison-Wesley, Reading, Mass., 1984.

9. J.F. Sowa, N.Y. Foo, and A. Rao. *Conceptual Graphs for Knowledge Systems*. Addison-Wesley, Reading, Mass., 1990.

10. A. Tuzhilin. Simtl: A simulation language based on temporal logic. *Transactions of the Society of Computer Simulation*, 9(2):86–99, 1992.

11. J. Yen and J. Lee. A task-based methodology for specifying expert systems. *IEEE Expert*, 1(8):8–15, 1993.

Appendix: A Knowledge Specification for PFS System

The PFS system (Petrol-station-Filling System) consists of two petrol-pumps and a queue of customers waiting for service. Customers in the queue can be served by any petrol-pump, but, at any time, only one customer can be served at each pump. In short, PFS can be viewed as consisting of three processes–the queue management process, denoted as qm, and two pump service processes, denoted by $ps1$ and $ps2$ respectively. Thus, we may represent the system as: PFS $=ps1 \parallel ps2 \parallel qm$, where $\parallel$ means parallel composition, that is, these components in the system can be executed in parallel.

To keep PFS simple, we assume that the queue is never empty. Furthermore, we assume that the pump service for each customer involves the following steps: service started, money deposited, petrol filling, service ended. At $ps1$ the time units for performing these steps are 1, 1, 4 and 1 respectively, and at $ps2$ the time units for performing these steps are 2, 2, 2 and 2 respectively. Thus, apart from the global clock, we may use the local clocks $ck_1 =< 0, 1, 2, 6, 7, 8, \ldots >$ and $ck_2 =< 0, 2, 4, 6, 8, \ldots >$ as the local clocks of $ps1$ and $ps2$, respectively. The actions involved in qm are: get a message from $ps1$, get a message from $ps2$ and pop a customer from the queue. The local clock involved in the process qm is gck. Thus, we have a knowledge specification for PFS as follows:

Declaration of variables: $\mathcal{V}$

```
[X:{nobody,tom,peter,...}].
[Flag:{ready,occupied}].
[W:{start, wait, money_deposit, petrol-fill}].
[V:{get_message1, get_message2, pop_customer}]
[L:{...}].
```

Here L is a list of customers that range over the set of all lists and X ranges over the set of customers, which contains a special customer called nobody. nobody does not represent any realistic customer.

Declaration of Predicates: $\mathcal{P}$

```
(state_1(X,Flag): at ps1, the customer X is served at the status Flag).
(action_1(W): an action W is executed on ps1).
(state_2(X,Flag): at ps2, the customer X is served at the status Flag).
(action_2(W): an action W is executed on ps2).
(queue(L): L is the queue of customers waiting for service).
```

(customer_f(X) : X is the first customer in the queue L).
(action_qm(V) : an action V is executed on qm).

Clock Definition: $\mathcal{C}$

```
first ck1(0).
first add(0).
next add(1) <- add(0).
next add(2) <- add(1).
next add(0) <- add(2).
next ck1(N) <- ck1(M), add(0), N is M+1.
next ck1(N) <- ck1(M), add(1), N is M+1.
next ck1(N) <- ck1(M), add(2), N is M+4.

first ck2(0).
next ck2(N) <- ck2(M), N is M+2.
```

The clock definition is written in ordinary Chronolog, in which each predicate symbol is defined on the global clock. Note that the global clock is not included in $\mathcal{C}$; it is accessible using the symbol gck.

Clock Assignment: ck

```
is_ck(state_1,gck).
is_ck(action_1,ck1).
is_ck(state_2,gck).
is_ck(action_2,ck2).
is_ck(customer_f,gck).
is_ck(queue,gck).
is_ck(action_qm,gck).
```

The set of rules: $\mathcal{R}$

We do not list all the rules. As examples, we provide the following rules which describe the behavior of $ps1$ and its interaction with the process qm.

```
next action_1(money-deposit) <- state_1(X,occupied), action_1(start).
next state_1(X,occupied) <- state_1(X,occupied), action_1(start).
next action_1(petrol_fill) <- state_1(X,occupied),
                              action_1(money_deposit).
next state_1(X,occupied) <- state_1(X,occupied),
                            action_1(money_deposit).
next action_1(wait) <- state_1(X,occupied), action_1(petrol_fill).
next state_1(nobody,ready) <- state_1(X,occupied),
                              action_1(petrol_fill).
next action_1(start) <- state_1(nobody,ready),
                        action_1(wait),customer_f(X).
next state_1(X,occupied) <- state_1(nobody,ready),
                            action_1(wait),customer_f(X).
```

Initial Conditions: $\mathcal{I}$

```
first action_1(wait).
first state_1(nobody,ready).
first customer_f(tom).
```

Controlling Engineering Problem Solving

Yusuf Pisan

Northwestern University

1890 Maple Ave

Evanston, IL, USA

Email: y-pisan@nwu.edu

Abstract

Engineering problem solving requires both domain knowledge and an understanding of how to apply that knowledge. While much of the recent work in qualitative physics has focused on building reusable domain theories, there has been little attention paid to representing the control knowledge necessary for applying these models. This paper shows how qualitative representations and compositional modeling can be used to create control knowledge for solving engineering problems. This control knowledge includes modeling assumptions, plans and preferences. We describe an implemented system, called TPS (Thermodynamics Problem Solver) that illustrates the utility of these ideas in the domain of engineering thermodynamics. To date, TPS has solved over 30 problems, and its solutions are similar to those of experts. We argue that our control vocabulary can be extended to most engineering problem solving domains and employed in a variety of problem solving architectures.

1. Introduction

Engineering problem solving requires both domain knowledge and an understanding of how to apply that knowledge. Recent work in qualitative physics has focused on building reusable domain theories, concentrating on the fundamental physical laws of various domains. However, there has been little research on representing the control knowledge necessary for applying these models. Qualitative representations have been successfully used for designing binary distillation plants (Sgouros, 1993) and for designing controllers (Kuipers & Shults, 1994).

However, since de Kleer's (de Kleer, 1975) original work highlighting how qualitative reasoning was needed to solve physics problems, the task of engineering analysis, as exemplified by textbook engineering problems, has been mostly ignored. An exception was a foray into problem solving in thermodynamics (Skorstad & Forbus, 1990), in a system called SCHISM. While SCHISM pioneered some useful ideas (e.g., heuristics for choosing good control volumes), both its domain knowledge and control knowledge were too limited to solve more than a handful of examples. CyclePad (Forbus & Whalley, 1994) contains enough qualitative and quantitative domain knowledge to carry out numerical steady-state analyses of continuous-flow systems. However, it also is excessive in its computations, sometimes solving hundreds of equations that it doesn't need to. A computational account of engineering problem solving must explain the efficiency of expert solutions by showing how to achieve similar efficiencies in software.

We claim that qualitative representations and compositional modeling can be used to create control knowledge for solving engineering problems efficiently. In this paper we describe an implemented system, called TPS (Thermodynamics Problem Solver) that has been developed to explore the use of qualitative representations in controlling engineering problem solving. TPS represents domain knowledge via compositional modeling techniques. TPS' control knowledge includes modeling assumptions, plans and preferences that are used in constraining search. Currently, TPS is able to solve 30 representative thermodynamics problems from various chapters of an introductory thermodynamics book and produce expert-like solutions.

Section 2 describes expert problem solving. Section 3 analyzes the global structure of the thermodynamics domain. Section 4 presents the primitives of our modeling language. Section 5 describes TPS' architecture and presents an example of TPS solving a problem. Section 6 discusses related work and proposes possible extensions to TPS.

2. Expert Problem Solving

Control knowledge can be encoded by a domain expert as a part of domain knowledge or learned through solving problems by identifying paths that lead to failure or success. Strategies for automatically generating control knowledge through solving problems (Laird, Rosenbloom, & Newell, 1986) (Dejong, 1986) have not scaled up to complex systems due to their limitations in re-representing their domain knowledge. Fundamental concepts of the domain that are not initially identified cannot be learned. For complex domains, such as thermodynamics, where the problem space is large and not uniform, control knowledge needs to be identified and encoded by a domain expert. The incremental improvements that are provided by today's speedup learning algorithms are insufficient to automatically construct such knowledge.

Looking at expert and novice differences in problem solving is one way of understanding the control knowledge of the expert. There have been contradictory findings about what differentiates expert and novice problem solving behavior which suggests a finer analysis is needed (Larkin, McDermott, Simon, & Simon, 1980; Priest & Lindsay, 1992). We conjecture that the expert-novice difference is due to the difference in control knowledge. Control knowledge, which determines whether and when an equation should be used, is expressed to a large degree using qualitative knowledge. To adequately express control knowledge the domain knowledge must make fundamentals of the domain explicit. In TPS we achieve this goal by representing thermodynamics knowledge using qualitative representations and compositional modeling. TPS' problem solving involves abstract plans, minimal search of the problem space and a combination of backward and forward inferences to produce expert-like efficient problem solving behavior. Although TPS includes weak methods (such as backward chaining, forward chaining, and loop detection) as part of its control knowledge, its expert-like behavior is the result of domain and task specific knowledge.

3. Analysis of the Thermodynamics Domain

Thermodynamics is the study of how energy can be transferred from one form to another. Engineering thermodynamics provides the theoretical underpinnings for power plants, engines of all types, refrigerators, and heat pumps. What makes thermodynamics difficult for students is not the complexity of equations, which are no more complex than those found in, say, dynamics. The challenge lies in the fact that the properties being modeled are subtle, meaning that there are more equations and that the range of their applicability is more limited. Engineering thermodynamics requires more explicit reasoning about modeling assumptions in order to derive a consistent set of equations than many domains. In many engineering domains modeling assumptions are givens, i.e., ignoring air friction in most elementary dynamics, or ignoring tolerances of components in DC circuit analysis. In thermodynamics, assumptions are resolved by deriving or comparing values for particular parameters, which in turn opens up the possibility of making further modeling assumptions. Discussions with domain experts (P. B. Whalley, personal communication) suggest that textbook problems are reasonable approximations for engineering analyses performed in industry.

We have used compositional modeling (Falkenhainer & Forbus, 1991) for representing the thermodynamics knowledge in TPS. Our thermodynamics domain model is based on the model used in CyclePad (Forbus & Whalley, 1994). It is organized around processes and pure substances that are transformed by processes. A *process* is an instantiation of a physical process, such as heating or cooling, or a combination of basic processes, where energy is transformed form one form to another. A pure *substance* is a homogeneous collection and has associated parameters such as mass, volume, temperature and specific volume that are constant throughout the substance.

4. Primitives of our Modeling Language

TPS integrates the "physics" of the domain with control knowledge for problem solving. This makes it possible to represent and reason about control knowledge explicitly. Control decisions, suggestions and plans for guiding problem solving are part of the model for the domain, just like equations of the domain. This has required creating a compositional modeling language that includes control knowledge in an integrated fashion. We believe the set of modeling primitives we use are applicable across a variety of engineering domains. They are:

defEntity, define-Process: These statements are used to define conceptual entities and physical processes. Each entity and each process has a set of parameters that are instantiated when it exists. Constraints and relations of entities and processes are expressed using define-relation and equations.

defAssumptionClass: An assumption class provides a taxonomy of modeling assumptions. During problem solving, finding the right modeling assumption is necessary before equations and tables can be used.

```
(defAssumptionClass (decide (phase-of ?stuff))
    :triggers ((thermodynamic-stuff ?stuff))
    :choices ((gas ?stuff) (saturated ?stuff) (liquid ?stuff)))
```

Figure 1: An assumption class, specifying the three phases of a substance

For example, the phase of substance is the primary modeling assumption about a substance. Fixing the phase of a substance is necessary because it provides the most information for finding the set of applicable equations and tables. The three phases a thermodynamic stuff can be in is represented as an assumption class (Figure 1). When there is a *thermodynamic-stuff* the possible phases of the stuff are instantiated. When a control decision is made to decide the phase of the stuff, the choices for phase are examined further.

defBackground-fact: Background facts are instantiated when their triggers are satisfied. Common assumptions can be modeling assumptions that are specific to a process or a numerical value such as molar-mass of water. (See Figure 2 for an example)

define-Relation: Define-relation is used to define logical relations among modeling assumptions and numerical values. One possible method to determine if a modeling assumption is true is to calculate the relation between the numerical values implicated by the modeling assumption.

defEquation: There are over 100 equations in TPS. Equations are instantiated and become *available* when the trigger conditions are satisfied. When the assumptions of an equation are satisfied the equation becomes *applicable* and can be used for finding the values of parameters. As described above, each equation can also have control knowledge that guide TPS in using it appropriately.

TPS uses *preferences*, common assumptions and plans for choosing among equations. Preferences are local control decisions that reflect how an equation is typically used in problem solving by indicating which parameter the equation is often solved for. Preferences do not eliminate decisions, so TPS can still solve a problem that does not fit its plans through backtracking. We have found preferences to be more robust than global control knowledge about equations.

define-Plan: A plan is instantiated when its triggers are satisfied and provides a list of steps to achieve its goals. The triggers of the plan determine when the plan becomes applicable. A simple plan is shown in Figure 4. The steps of the plan are an ordered set of statements that needs to be achieved. If the goals of the plan were found while executing the plan or while solving for another goal, TPS would declare the plan dead and not use it. One of the functions of plans is to interleave forward and backward chaining by directing the problem solver towards resolving modeling assumptions. The plan given in Figure 4 directs the problem solver to fix the phase of the substance, which is needed in order to figure out which equations may be appropriate.

Control knowledge for a domain needs to be part of how the domain is modeled. In TPS, we use plans, preferences and common assumptions to guide the problem solving. Plans provide a framework for the problem, preferences are used to decide among choices and common assumptions are used for making assumptions when there is not contradictory information.

```
(defbackground-fact ((turbine ?name ?from ?to))
   (common-assumption (NOT (consider-ke (turbine ?name))))))
```

Figure 2: A background fact

Modeling assumptions determine the level of granularity of the model we instantiate for a specific problem. Common modeling assumptions are assumptions that are made frequently to simplify problems. Knowing what common assumptions are applicable is an important piece of control knowledge since assumptions are necessary for finding applicable equations and simplifying them. For example, change in kinetic energy is usually ignored for turbines, so when applying the first law to a turbine, TPS makes an attempt to see if a kinetic energy difference can be derived. The common-assumption about turbines is given as a background fact (Figure 2) and is instantiated when TPS is working with a turbine.

5. TPS architecture and an Extended Example

TPS uses the *suggestion architecture* (Forbus & de Kleer, 1993) to solve problems. A problem is provided in the form of some initial assertions and a goal. A logic-based truth maintenance system (Forbus & de Kleer, 1993; McAllester, 1978) is used to keep track of all data and control dependencies, such as the relationships between goals and the relevance of plans and equations.

A central controller selects what goal to work on next. Working on a goal consists of (1) asking for *suggestions* as to how to achieve that goal and (2) selecting one of the suggestions to act upon. In TPS, the modeling language primitives are automatically compiled into pattern-directed rules that make suggestions and carry them out when the appropriate control assertions are made by the central controller. Carrying out a suggestion can either directly solve the problem, or introduce new problems that must be solved in order to use the proposed method. This process continues until either the original problem is solved or the system runs out of things to try or until resource bounds are exceeded.

TPS' control knowledge is not dependent on the architecture of the problem solver. The problem solver needs to be able to execute plans suggested by plans, subgoal on resolving modeling assumptions when necessary and use equation preferences for choosing between equations. Although the control knowledge can be used with other problem solvers, the representation of the domain model needs to make fundamental concepts of the domain explicit to allow integration and use of control knowledge.

A problem description is given in Figure 3 and the plan chosen for this problem is given in Figure 4. Temperatures are given in Kelvins and the pressures are given in Pascals.

```
(add-problem
  :name 'Wylen&Sonntag-Ex5.10
  :givens '((turbine TUR s1 s2)
            (thermodynamic-stuff s1)   (thermodynamic-stuff s2)
            (substance-of s1 water)
            ((mass-flow (turbine TUR)) NVALUE 1.5)
            ((Q (turbine TUR)) NVALUE 8500)
            ((P s1) NVALUE 2000000)   ((T s1) NVALUE 623.15)
            ((velocity s1) NVALUE 50)   ((height s1) NVALUE 6)
            ((P s2) NVALUE 100000)      ((dryness s2) NVALUE 1)
            ((velocity s2) NVALUE 200)  ((height s2) NVALUE 3)
            ((gravity-on s1) NVALUE 9.8066))
  :goal '(find-numerical-value (work-done (turbine TUR)))))
```

Figure 3: TPS' representation of problem 5.10 from Van Wylen & Sonntag (1985)

The plan given in Figure 4 is one of the most general plans TPS uses. This plan applies to all processes and tries to apply the first law. The first two steps of the plan are for fixing the initial and the final state of the substance. The modeling assumptions about the process are determined next and finally the first law is applied.

When there are multiple suggestions and there is no explicit control knowledge to choose among suggestions, suggestions are evaluated and scored. TPS' scoring mechanism is domain independent, giving priority to shorter plans and showing assumptions. Suggestions with low scores are not eliminated, which ensures that even when a problem has to be solved in an obscure manner (i.e., using equations differently than normal), finding a solution is still possible.

```
(define-plan analyze-process-with-first-law
    :triggers ((process ?process ?from ?to)
               (thermodynamic-stuff ?from)
               (thermodynamic-stuff ?to))
    :goals ((or (find-numerical-value (work-done ?process))
                (find-numerical-value (Q ?process))))
    :steps ((show (fixed-phase ?from))
            (show (fixed-phase ?to))
            (show (resolve-modeling-assumptions ?process))
            (show (apply-first-law ?process))))
```

Figure 4: Plan chosen by TPS to solve the problem given in Figure 3

Plans are used to interleave backward and forward chaining. An equation, which is a simple plan, requires finding the values of variables and showing necessary assumptions to solve for the current goal. Since each step required by the equation is necessary, equation plans cause the problem solver to perform backward chaining through subgoaling. Other plans, such as the one given in Figure 4 propose subgoals that may not be essential to the current goal. Subgoals that are not essential to the current goal cause the problem solver to forward chain. Although forward chaining could potentially cause exploring part of the problem space that was not needed for the current problem, it is necessary for solving complex problems and reflects experts' pattern of problem solving. In TPS, plans force the assumptions of equations to be resolved before a commitment is made to using an equation. Once the relevant assumptions are resolved, the number of choices is reduced and heuristics are used.

```
Control Volume:  Turbine
Inlet State: Fixed
Exit State: Fixed
Process:  SSSF
Model:  Steam tables
Analysis:  First Law:
    Q_cv + m(H_i + V_i^2/2 + gZ_i) = m(H_e + V_e^2/2 + gZ_e) + W_cv
    Q_cv = -8.5kW
Solution:
    h_i = 3137.0 (from the steam tables)
    V_i^2/2 = (50 x 50) / (2 x 1000) = 1.25 kJ/kg
    gZ_i = (6 x 9.8066) / 1000 = 0.059 kJ/kg
    Similarly, h_e, V_e^2/2 and gZ_e are calculated
    Substituting all into first law gives:  W_cv = 655.7 kW
```

Figure 5: The expert solution to problem given in Figure 3 as given in Van Wylen & Sonntag (1985).

The expert solution to the problem given in Figure 3 is shown in Figure 5. An expert solution uses the minimal number of equations with no backtracking. The solution in Figure 5 uses five equations (kinetic energy and potential energy equations are used twice) and two table-lookups to solve the problem. TPS' solution for the problem involves 3 table lookups, and solving 12 equations. CyclePad (Forbus & Whalley, 1994) which uses the same domain knowledge, instantiates 42 equations and calculates the values for 67 parameters in solving a simpler version of the same problem.

TPS is not able to solve all textbook thermodynamics problems for several reasons. TPS' domain model covers steady-state steady flow problems and processes acting on contained substances. Uniform state uniform flow problems, such as a filling a container, are not covered in TPS' domain model. We are currently extending TPS' domain model to cover this class of problems. The equation solver used in TPS performs limited symbolic algebra, so TPS cannot currently solve problems requiring an equation as an answer. We will be remedying this problem by building one ourselves. We believe that TPS will be able to solve all of the problems found in an introductory thermodynamics textbook with these extensions.

```
TPS starts the problem by looking for an appropriate plan
The plan given in Figure 4 is chosen
Executing the plan:
Step 1: Fixing the state at the inlet.
Assume (gas s1) and verify it using saturation temperature.
Step 2: Fixing the state at the exit
Infer that exit is saturated since dryness is given.
Step 3: Resolving modeling assumptions about the Turbine
        Reject no-KE assumption because velocity is given
        Reject no-PE assumption because height is given(
        Reject no-Heat assumption, the value for heat is given
        Not consider Isentropic assumption since it is not
adiabatic
Step 4: Applying first law:
        Q = ΔH + ΔKE + ΔPE + W
        Q = 8.5Kw     Given in problem statement
        (spec-h s1) is marked known using tables
Propagating known information:
        (H s1) is marked known using equation
            (H s1) = (mass-flow s1)*(spec-h s1)
        Information about known parameters get propagated.
Equation solving begins after work is marked as known.
Calculating the answer:
        Calculating (change-in-enthalpy (turbine TUR))
        (H S1) = (mass-flow S1)*(spec-h s1) =4705.5
            (2 equations, 1 table lookup)
        (H S2) = (mass-flow S2)*(spec-h s2) = 4012.5
            (2 equations solved, 1 table lookup)
        (change-in-enthalpy (turbine TUR)) = (H S2) - (H S1)
            (1 equation solved)
        change-in-ke is calculated by finding KE of S1 and S2
            (3 equations solved)
        change-in-pe is calculated by finding PE of S1 and S2
            (3 equations solved)
        W = 655.7kW is found by solving the first law.
            (1 equation solved)
```

Figure 6: TPS' solution to problem given in Figure 3

6. Related Work and Discussion

In SCHISM Skorstad and Forbus (Skorstad & Forbus, 1990) use molecular collection ontology to determine the control volume for analysis. Compared to SCHISM that constructs a control volume by following a *piece-of-stuff* around the cycle, TPS uses initial state, the process and the final state of the substance to form control volumes.

Kuipers (Kuipers & Shults, 1994) uses qualitative simulation to predict the set of possible behaviors for the system, which can then be used by a controller. When solving textbook problems, we are interested in finding what the current behavior is rather than controlling the behavior. TPS' control knowledge is useful for finding the behavior of the system without considering all the possible alternative behaviors.

Previous work on engineering problem solving has concentrated on building problem solvers with general strategies and automatically generated control knowledge from examples. Since our theories of learning and re-representation are not adequate, these programs have had little success. Research in qualitative physics has focused on constructing domain theories, but has not focused sufficiently on how these domain theories can be used for problem solving.

TPS demonstrates how domain specific control knowledge can be created using qualitative representations and compositional modeling principles. TPS has solved over 30 problems and its solutions are similar to those of experts. We expect that TPS' coverage can be extended to the majority of textbook thermodynamics problems. To completely cover such problems two additional extensions are needed. TPS currently cannot read or produce graphs when solving problems. We are planning on integrating TPS with SKETCHY (Pisan, 1995) to enable TPS to solve problems that require interpreting graphs and diagrams. Another avenue of research is incorporating qualitative simulation as one of TPS' plans. Qualitative simulation can be used to explore possible scenarios for problems where device behavior is ambiguous. We also plan to test our ideas in other engineering domains to determine their generality.

7. Bibliography

de Kleer, J. (1975). *Qualitative and quantitative knowledge in classical mechanics* (Technical Report 352.). Cambridge, MA.: MIT AI Lab.

Dejong, G. F. (1986). Explanation based Learning, *Machine Learning: An Artificial Intelligence Approach, Vol. II* . Los Altos, CA: Morgan Kaufman.

Falkenhainer, B., & Forbus, K. (1991). Compositional modeling: Finding the right model for the job. *Artificial Intelligence, 51*, 95-143.

Forbus, K., & de Kleer, J. (1993). *Building Problem Solvers*: MIT Press.

Forbus, K., & Whalley, P. B. (1994). Using qualitative physics to build articulate software for thermodynamics education. *In Proceedings of the International Joint Conference on Artificial Intelligence.*

Kuipers, B. J., & Shults, B. (1994). Reasoning in logic about continuous systems. *In Proceedings of the 8th International Workshop on Qualitative Reasoning about Physical Systems*, Nara, Japan.

Laird, J., Rosenbloom, P., & Newell, A. (1986). *Universal Subgoaling and Chunking*: Kluwer Academic Publishers.

Larkin, J., McDermott, J., Simon, D. P., & Simon, H. A. (1980). Models of competence in solving physics problems. *Cognitive Science, 4*(4), 317-345.

McAllester, D. (1978). *A three-valued truth maintenance system.* Ph.D Thesis, Department of Electrical Engineering, MIT, Cambridge, MA.

Pisan, Y. (1995). A Visual Routines Based Model of Graph Understanding. *In Proceeding of the Seventeenth Annual Conference of the Cognitive Science Society*, Hillsdale, NJ.

Priest, A., & Lindsay, R. (1992). New light on novice-expert differences in physics problem solving. *British journal of Psychology*(83), 389-405.

Sgouros, N. M. (1993). *Representing physical and design knowledge in innovative engineering design.* Ph.D Thesis, Department of Computer Science, Northwestern University, Evanston, IL.

Skorstad, G., & Forbus, K. (1990). Qualitative and quantitative reasoning about thermodynamics. *In Proceedings of the 10th Annual Conference of the Cognitive Science Society.*

Evaluating a Qualitative Reasoner

Sam Waugh[1], Tim Menzies[2], and Simon Goss[1]

[1] Air Operations Division, Defence Science and Technology Organisation, Melbourne,
Australia; {sam.waugh,simon.goss}@dsto.defence.gov.au
[2] Artificial Intelligence Department, School of Computer Science & Engineering,
University of NSW, Sydney, Australia; timm@cse.unsw.edu.au

Abstract. In order to support verification, validation and analysis of
dynamic Operations Research (OR) models a method of testing models
against data is required. In the case of the QCM qualitative reasoning
system (QRS) this requires an extension to accommodate temporal data
streams. This paper examines a number of temporal reasoning methods
for QCM. On the basis of this a general methodology for evaluating QRSs
and a statement of success criteria have been developed, and will be used
in future work.

1 Introduction

This paper examines a number of methods for extending an existing qualitative
reasoning system (QRS), the QCM algorithm [11], to handle time-based reasoning.
This system contains a static model compiler, a data compiler, and a hypothesis
tester for the model and data. QCM has been able to detect previously invisible errors in theories published in the international neuroendocrinological literature [4,11]. However, QCM is restricted to *non-temporal* theories with the invariant
that no variable can have two different values. In the case of time-based simulation, this invariant is inappropriate since variables can have different values at
different times. One way to extend QCM to time-based simulation is to rename
variables at each time point in the simulation; e.g. *population* could be renamed
to *population*1, *population*2 ... *population*T where T is some time point. Once
these renamed variables are created, the design issue becomes "how should we
best *link* variables at time i to time j?". In this paper, we assess eight possible
linking policies for TQCM, a QCM variant which allows the processing of time series
data.

Overview articles which contrast different approaches to qualitative reasoning
(QR) (e.g. [2, 3, 5, 7, 11, 12]) have little to say about how to choose between
different systems. There is also a lack of guidelines for developing and testing
new modelling approaches. In the process of testing the different TQCM linking
policies we have developed a more general framework for assessing QRSs. We
identify *critical success metrics* (CSMs) for QR, and develop a test engine to
collect the CSMs for the different variants of TQCM. In order for this testing to
be comprehensive, a wide range of representative models must be examined. A
model mutator is used to generate large numbers of these test models. We argue

that this QR evaluation framework is a process applicable to many domains. However, (i) it is only practical after automating the test engine and (ii) it is only reliable if the model mutator covers a sufficient range.

The following sections detail the CSMs (§2); QCM (§3) and eight linking policies for implementing TQCM (§3.1); the test engine for calculating performance (§4); and present our results (§5), discussion (§6) and conclusions (§7).

2 Critical Success Metrics

This section develops success criteria for a QRS; i.e. an ideal QRS must be *accurate, restrictive* and *practical*. A QRS translates the continuous variables in quantitative models to a small number of discrete values [5]. In order to test if the translation is valid then (success criteria #1) an *accurate* QRS must be able to reproduce the known behaviour of the quantitative system it is modelling. For the purposes of validation, (success criteria #2) a *restrictive* QRS must be able to exclude a significant percentage of impossible behaviours.

The resulting qualitative model is less defined than the original quantitative model, and combinations of poorly-defined influences may be undefined. For example, consider two continuous variables whose qualitative representation is taken from the sign of the first derivative of their values; i.e. up, down or steady. If we add two increasing values, the result must also be increasing; i.e. up + up = up. However, it is unclear what will result from certain other combinations; e.g. up + down = up or down or steady. This is the "chatter" problem. QRSs generate the superset of behaviours possible from a model [6]. The generation of these extra behaviours takes time and can cripple a QRS. Therefore, (success criteria #3) a *practical* QRS must tame the chatter problem. In practice, chatter reduces restrictiveness by the generation of such behaviours.

We can visualise the satisfaction of these criteria in Fig. 1. Consider an human operator trying to express an understanding of a quantitative model in a qualitative approximation. We say that their qualitative model is good if it can explain everything observed in the quantitative model (point A: success criteria of accuracy); and we say their model is poor if it can explain nothing (point B: success criteria of restrictiveness). As the qualitative model degrades from good to poor we would like to see curve1; i.e. we quickly get feedback that we can explain progressively less and less of the behaviour of the quantitative model. However, even curve2 would satisfy the success criteria of restrictiveness. Lastly, we would declare the chatter problem to be manageable if qualitative indeterminacy does not cripple the QRS; i.e. we achieve low runtimes (the dotted line) when we run the system on a poor model (success criteria of practicality).

3 QCM: A Qualitative Reasoning System

QCM takes a graph-theoretic view of QR. Qualitative statements from domain experts are treated like macros that contribute edges to a search space. For example, if the expert says "weight gain encourages heart disease and exercise

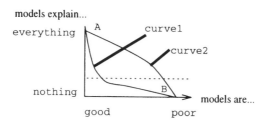

Fig. 1. Visualising success

reduces weight gain" then (i) we would record it as `weightGain ++ heartDisease` and `exercise -- weightGain` and (ii) expand it internally into the search space of Fig. 2. This space is then searched by an abductive inference engine looking for consistent connections between known inputs and known outputs. QR indeterminacy is handled by generating different extensions. For full details, see [11].

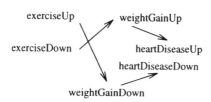

Fig. 2. Weight gain, heart disease, and exercise

QCM is much simpler than other QR approaches (e.g. time averaging [7], consolidation [3], first-order logic qualitative modelling [2], non-linear QR [12], or linear equation QR [5] such as QSIM [6]). Menzies and Compton [10] remark that seemingly naive systems can in fact produce satisfactory competency with far less effort than alternative "more sophisticated" approaches. QCM has detected errors in theories of neuroendocrinology published in the international peer-reviewed journals that were invisible to both the reviewers of those journals and the authors of those theories [4,11]. Hence we say that is if QCM works in our domain (i.e. satisfies the test criteria of §2), then we lack the motivation to explore more complex approaches.

3.1 Linking Options

This section discusses extensions to QCM to handle time-based simulation. QCM cannot validate theories performing time-based simulations since it assumes that it is inconsistent to believe that objects like `heartDisease` have multiple values. While this is a valid assumption for non-time based inferencing, a variable in a simulation run can take multiple values over time, e.g. a sensor maintaining a real-world quantity.

In order to handle the temporal simulations, we extend QCM to TQCM. In TQCM one copy of the model is created for each time step in the simulation, as each model represents the processes occurring at one time step. The question then becomes how can we sensibly link these copies of the search space together? That is, where do we place our links between models? We can identify three types of linking strategies: (1) linking via nodes or via edges; (2) implicit versus explicit time notation; and (3) varying the linking look ahead.

1) Node vs. Edge Linking: In node linking an "appropriate" model node is somehow identified and directly linked to future instances of that node; for example, X is expanded to X(t=i) ++ X(t=i+1)[1]. Alternatively, we could link by picking an edge in the model consistent with a time connection, then creating a new edge with the starting node of the edge in one time step and the end node the subsequent time step; for example, X to Y is expanded to X(t=i) to Y(t=i+1)[2]. This method is called edge linking.

2) Implicit vs. Explicit Linking: "Appropriate" nodes or edges can be manually chosen by the model author to explicitly link models (given a "*" marking). Alternatively, an implicit linking process can decide that every edge or node is "appropriate". Explicit linking requires some domain knowledge as to where linking is sensible, but results in much fewer links between time steps which reflects more semantic knowledge about the domain.

Implicit node linking (TQCM^{inode}) was explored by Menzies & Cohen [8,9]. In TQCM^{inode}, every node at time i is connected to the node of the same name at time i+1. The regularity of this linking policy permits some general statements about the computational complexity of generating proof trees over time-series simulations. TQCM^{inode} has the interesting property that if a proof cannot be generated in 3 copies, it can never be generated at all. This 3-copy-limit may be used to significantly optimise the search strategy.

3) Future Linking: How far ahead should we place time edges? The obvious solution is to just connect ahead one time step. However, without any domain knowledge stating this to be the case, we need to consider the possibility that a node should be connected to all subsequent steps. That is, for times i=1 to N link copy i to f where f is a *future* copy that will take values i+1...N. Alternative combinations of forward linking are possible, but will not be considered here.

Table 1 summarises the eight linking options, including abbreviations.

4   A Test Engine

Our test engine has four sub-routines: (1) representative model selection; (2) data generation; (3) model mutation; and (4) option exploration.

1) Representative model selection: The "fisheries simulation model" (Fig. 3) is similar to models developed for pursuit and surveillance in the military domain.

---

[1] X(t=i) represents a value X at time i.
[2] Let "to" denote an edge annotated as either ++ or --.

Table 1. Summary of linking policies. f denotes some time from i+1...N where N is the last time copy.

Linking style	Abbreviation	Theory feature	New time links
implicit edge	TQCM^iedge	X to Y	X(t=i) to Y(t=i+1)
implicit edge forward	TQCM^iedgef	X to Y	X(t=i) to Y(t=f)
implicit node	TQCM^inode	X	X(t=i) ++ X(t=i+1)
implicit node forward	TQCM^inodef	X	X(t=i) ++ X(t=f)
explicit edge	TQCM^xedge	X to* Y	X(t=i) to Y(t=i+1)
explicit edge forward	TQCM^xedge	X to* Y	X(t=i) to Y(t=f)
explicit node	TQCM^xnode	X*	X(t=i) ++ X(t=i+1)
explicit node forward	TQCM^xnodef	X*	X(t=i) ++ X(t=f)

It includes feedback loops; qualitative states; and measurable entities. A precise mathematical expression of this model is available [1, pp135-141].

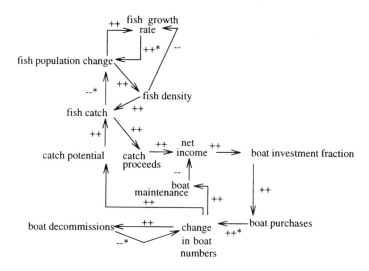

Fig. 3. The fisheries model showing explicit time edges. Adapted from [1, pp135-141].

2) Data generation: The selected qualitative model was run 15 times over five time steps to generate numeric test data using different input parameters to create an array of quantitative observations measure[1..15]. From each comparison of measure[i] with measure[j] (i < j ≤ 15), 105 entries were written to an array of qualitative observations changes[1..105]. For example, if in comparison change[33], the fish density h was increased and the fish catch b was always seen to decrease at all time steps, then change[33].in is h=up and change[33].out is b(t=1)=down, b(t=2)=down, b(t=3)=down, b(t=4)=down, b(t=5)=down.

3) *Model mutation*: This process must be repeated for a large number of representative models from a domain. As these are hard to find in practice, we generate them using a *mutation strategy*, in which a random sample of X statements in the qualitative form of the known representative model are corrupted. Given a model with E edges, then as we vary X from 0 to E, we are moving from a good model to a poor model; i.e. the x-axis of Fig. 1. We corrupted the model by flipping the annotation on an edge (e.g. ++ to -- or visa versa). The corruption-model-mutator picks its edges to corrupt at random, and we repeat the corruption a statistically significant number of times (20 repeats). The only exceptions are when X=0 or E, where there is only a single possible model. Fisheries has 17 edges which allows us to generate 2^{17} possible theories (including the original).

4) *Option exploration*: We created six model copies copy[0..5]. Copy[i] was connected to copy[i+1] (and latter copies for forward linking) according to each of the eight linking policies. Change inputs were mapped into copy[0]. Change outputs were mapped into some copy[1..5]. The success of each run was assessed using the generated data, by recording the percentage of the *explicable outputs* i.e. those outputs that the model could connect back to inputs. Returning to Fig. 1, everything=100% explicable and nothing=0% explicable. Proofs for outputs at time $T = 5$ must be consistent with proofs from $T = 1...4$. Hence, all the proofs must be built together (see runQualitativeModel in Fig. 4). For this study, we only collected percentage explicable figures for outputs at time $T = 5$. The final experimental design is shown in Fig. 4.

5 Results

Figure 5 shows the results of applying the test engine to the fisheries model. The success of each linking policy was assessed via comparing its plot against the goal plot of curve1 in Fig. 1.

TQCM^{xnode} was the clear winner showing accuracy and restrictiveness closest to the ideal of curve1. However these linking policies could still offer explanations for about 20% of data, even for very poor models. We attribute these *residual explanations* to the indeterminacy of qualitative models.

TQCM^{iedge} was nearly as accurate as explicit node linking, but could never explain 100% of the behaviour of uncorrupted models (maximum explicable=85%). TQCM^{redge} proved to be not accurate as, even on good models, it could not explain most outputs. TQCM^{inode} was not sufficiently restrictive as, even on poor models, it could explain most outputs.

Forward linking provided no advantages for the fisheries model. TQCM^{inode} and TQCM^{inodef}, and TQCM^{xnode} and TQCM^{xnodef} behaved in virtually the same way. TQCM^{iedgef} was inferior to TQCM^{iedge} since it was far less restrictive than TQCM^{iedge}. TQCM^{xedgef} was more permissive than TQCM^{xedge}, but its maximum explicable rate was too low to be useful (62%). We speculate that forward linking was not useful was due to the nature of the fisheries model. The equations of fisheries all assumed a "one-year-lookahead" as its time step increments. We speculate

```
Inputs:  1) the quantitative fisheries model M0
         2) the qualitative fisheries model M1 with E := 17 edges
         3) T                := 5 maximum time steps
         4) linkingPolicies := [iedge,iedgef,xedge,xedgef,
                                 inode,inodef,xnode,xnodef]
Outputs: explicable, runtime

measure[1..15]  := runQuantitativeModel(T,M0)
change[1..105]  := comparisons(measure)
for policy ∈ linkingPolicies do
  for corrupted := 0 to E do
    if corrupted = 0 or E then repeats := 1 else repeats := 20
    for r := 1 to repeats do
      M2 := corruptSomeEdgesChoosenAtRandom(corrupted,M1)
      for t := 0 to T   do copy[t]:= M2 done
      for t := 0 to T-1 do timeConnect(copy[t],copy[t+1],policy) done
      for i := 1 to |change| do
        <in,out[1..T]>   := change[i]
        startTime        := timeNow()
        explained[1..T]  := runQualitativeModel(copy,in,out)
        runtime[policy,r,corrupted,i]    := timeNow() - startTime
        explicable[policy,r,corrupted,i] := |explained[T]|*100/|out[T]|
done done done done
```

Fig. 4. Experimental design for fisheries model

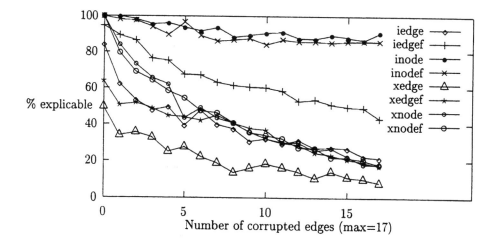

Fig. 5. CSM results for fisheries model

that models with time links of variable delays may benefit more from forward linking.

For the satisfactory linking policies (TQCM^{xnode}, TQCM^{iedge}), after only a third of the model being mutated, only around half the outputs are inexplicable. This is a nice result: we get clear, early indications if we are straying from a good model.

The average runtimes in seconds for each trial are shown in Fig. 6. Forward linking was always slower than non-forward linking. The satisfactory linking policies had similar runtimes. However, TQCM^{xnode} and TQCM^{xedge} were fastest since these define the smallest number of time links and, hence, the smallest search space to explore. Hence, we are satisfied that the success criteria of practicality is satisfied. One interesting feature of Fig. 6 is that as the models grow more corrupted, it becomes faster to determine what outputs are explicable. This is a another nice result: we can reject nonsense faster.

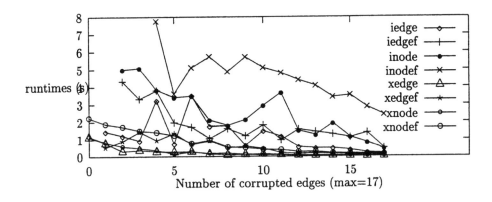

Fig. 6. Runtimes for fisheries model

6 Discussion

In extending QCM to time-based simulations, TQCM^{xnode} was best, with TQCM^{iedge} a close second. Since TQCM^{inode} performed so poorly, this study is pessimistic about the practicality of the Menzies & Cohen 3-copy-limit optimisation. However, in a personal communication, Cohen reports early results indicating that a small variant on the 3-copy-limit proof for TQCM^{inode} may prove that there is only a 2-copy-limit for TQCM^{iedge}. That is, if we are willing to have a small inexplicable rate for correct models (5%), we can run TQCM^{iedge} models for very long periods of time. This is an exciting possibility which is currently being actively explored.

Our approach is practical in domains where practioners can build an automatic test engine: a non-trivial task. Our original work took weeks to generate a single line on Fig. 5. However, once the test engine was operational, the utility of modelling options can be assessed very quickly. For example, whilst writing this article, we detected a small data collection error. Re-running all the linking options took less than three days (the results shown here come from the re-run).

One drawback with the current study is that its conclusions are very dependent on our experiments with a single model (fisheries). Note that this restriction does not invalidate the evaluation method proposed here. Further, our current mutator did not vary the topology of the graph, merely its edge annotations. The next generation of mutators will address this issue.

7 Conclusion

We have offered a general framework for evaluating a QRS. We propose critical success metrics (e.g. Fig. 1) to test the utility of modelling options within a QRS. Three general QRS CSMs are *accuracy, restrictiveness* and *practicality* (§2). A useful tool for this process is a model mutator (§4) that can build test models from representative models. A desirable property of such a mutator is *graded degradation*, e.g Fig. 1; i.e. a method of generating a range of good to poor models.

This framework has been used to test linking policies for qualitative temporal models, and subsequently identifying three useful methods.

This work represents an incremental advance towards our long term research objective of establishing methodologies for OR model validation. Immediate future work includes decreasing the number of measurements made, increasing the number of time steps modelled, and studies with other simulation models.

Acknowledgment

Kingsley Jones (DSTO) initially proposed the model mutator used in this study.

References

1. H. Bossel. *Modeling and Simulations*. A.K. Peters Ltd, 1994. ISBN 1-56881-033-4.
2. I. Bratko, I. Mozetic, and N. Lavrac. *KARDIO: a Study in Deep and Qualitative Knowledge for Expert Systems*. MIT Press, 1989.
3. T. Bylander. A Critique of Qualitative Simulation from a Consolidation Viewpoint. *IEEE Transactions on Systems, Man, and Cybernetics*, 18(2):252–263, March/April 1988.
4. B. Feldman, P. Compton, and G. Smythe. Towards Hypothesis Testing: JUSTIN, Prototype System Using Justification in Context. In *Proceedings of the Joint Australian Conference on Artificial Intelligence, AI '89*, pages 319–331, 1989.
5. Y. Iwasaki. Qualitative Physics. In P.R. Cohen A. Barr and E.A. Feigenbaum, editors, *The Handbook of Artificial Intelligence*, volume 4, pages 323–413. Addison Wesley, 1989.

6. B. Kuipers. Qualitative Simulation. *Artificial Intelligence*, 29:229–338, 1986.
7. R. Levins and C.J. Puccia. *Qualitative Modeling of Complex Systems: An Introduction to Loop Analysis and Time Averaging*. Harvard University Press, Cambridge, Mass., 1985.
8. T.J. Menzies and R.E. Cohen. "And" Can You Validate It? In *Submitted to the Australian AI '97 conference.*, 1997.
9. T.J. Menzies and R.E. Cohen. A Graph-Theoretic Optimisation of Temporal Abductive Validation. In *European Symposium on the Validation and Verification of Knowledge Based Systems, Leuven, Belgium*, 1997.
10. T.J. Menzies and P. Compton. Knowledge Acquisition for Performance Systems; or: When can "tests" replace "tasks"? In *Proceedings of the 8th AAAI-Sponsored Banff Knowledge Acquisition for Knowledge-Based Systems Workshop, Banff, Canada*, 1994.
11. T.J. Menzies and P. Compton. Applications of Abduction: Hypothesis Testing of Neuroendocrinological Qualitative Compartmental Models. *Artificial Intelligence in Medicine*, (10):145–175, 1997.
12. K.M. Yip. Understanding Complex Dynamics by Visual and Symbolic Reasoning. *Artificial Intelligence*, 51:179–221, 1991.

Author Index

Lecture Notes in Artificial Intelligence (LNAI)

Lecture Notes in Computer Science